Handbook of Indian Literature

Editor
Ricarda Whittaker

Scribbles

Year of Publication 2018

ISBN : 9789352979745

Book Published by

Scribbles

(An Imprint of Alpha Editions)

email - alphaedis@gmail.com

Produced by: PediaPress GmbH
Limburg an der Lahn
Germany
http://pediapress.com/

The content within this book was generated collaboratively by volunteers. Please be advised that nothing found here has necessarily been reviewed by people with the expertise required to provide you with complete, accurate or reliable information. Some information in this book may be misleading or simply wrong. Alpha Editions and PediaPress does not guarantee the validity of the information found here. If you need specific advice (for example, medical, legal, financial, or risk management) please seek a professional who is licensed or knowledgeable in that area.

Sources, licenses and contributors of the articles and images are listed in the section entitled "References". Parts of the books may be licensed under the GNU Free Documentation License. A copy of this license is included in the section entitled "GNU Free Documentation License"

The views and characters expressed in the book are those of the contributors and his/her imagination and do not represent the views of the Publisher.

Contents

Articles   1
Introduction   1

Ancient Literature   3
Vedas   3
Indian epic poetry 22
Mahabharata 26
Ramayana 55
Sanskrit literature 90
Pāli Canon 96

In common Indian languages   115
Assamese literature 115
Buranji 124
Assamese poetry 126

Bengali literature   129
Bengali literature 129

Bhojpuri literature   147
Bhojpuri literature 147

Indian English literature   149
Indian English literature 149

Hindi literature   **161**
    Hindi literature 161

Kannada literature   **177**
    Kannada literature 177

Kashmiri literature   **209**
    Literature of Kashmir 209

Malayalam literature   **217**
    Malayalam literature 217

Meitei literature   **235**
    Meitei literature 235

Marathi literature   **239**
    Marathi literature 239

Mizo literature   **249**
    Mizo literature 249

Odia literature   **257**
    Odia literature 257

Punjabi literature   **279**
    Punjabi literature 279

Rajasthani literature   **285**
    Rajasthani literature 285

Sanskrit literature   **287**

Sindhi literature   **289**
    Sindhi literature 289

Tamil literature   **299**

    Tamil literature 299

Telugu literature   **321**

    Telugu literature 321

Tulu literature   **343**

    Tulu language 343

Urdu literature   **361**

    Urdu literature 361

Appendix   **373**

    References 373

    Article Sources and Contributors 396

    Image Sources, Licenses and Contributors 399

Article Licenses   **403**

Index   **405**

Introduction

Indian literature refers to the literature produced on the Indian subcontinent until 1947 and in the Republic of India thereafter. The Republic of India has 22 officially recognized languages. The earliest works of Indian literature were orally transmitted. Sanskrit literature begins with the oral literature of the Rig Veda a collection of sacred hymns dating to the period 1500–1200 BCE. The Sanskrit epics Ramayana and Mahabharata appeared towards the end of the 2nd millennium BCE. Classical Sanskrit literature developed rapidly during the first few centuries of the first millennium BCE, as did the Tamil Sangam literature, and the Pāli Canon. In the medieval period, literature in Kannada and Telugu appeared in the 9th and 11th centuries respectively. Later, literature in Marathi, Odia and Bengali appeared. Thereafter literature in various dialects of Hindi, Persian and Urdu began to appear as well. Early in the 20th century, Bengali poet Rabindranath Tagore became India's first Nobel laureate. In contemporary Indian literature, there are two major literary awards; these are the Sahitya Akademi Fellowship and the Jnanpith Award. Eight Jnanpith Awards each have been awarded in Hindi and Kannada, followed by five in Bengali and Malayalam, four in Odia, three in Gujarati, Marathi, Telugu and Urdu, two each in Assamese and Tamil, and one in Sanskrit.

Ancient Literature

Vedas

<indicator name="pp-default"> 🔒 </indicator>

Part of a series on
Hindu scriptures and texts

- Shruti
- Smriti

Related Hindu texts

- v
- t
- e[1]

The **Vedas** (/ˈveɪdəz, <wbr />ˈviː-/;[2] Sanskrit: वेद *veda*, "knowledge") are a large body of knowledge texts originating in the ancient Indian subcontinent. Composed in Vedic Sanskrit, the texts constitute the oldest layer of Sanskrit literature and the oldest scriptures of Hinduism.[3,4] Hindus consider the Vedas to

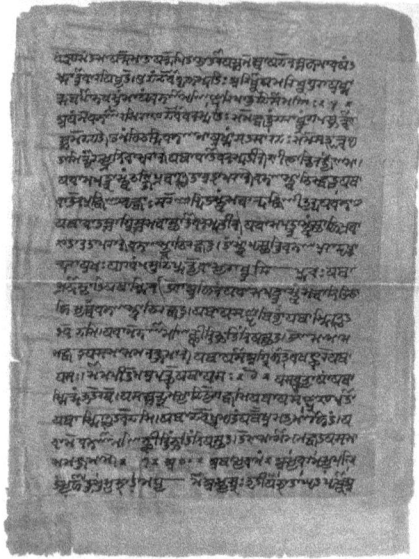

Figure 1: *The Vedas are ancient Sanskrit texts of Hinduism. Above: A page from the Atharvaveda.*

be *apauruṣeya*, which means "not of a man, superhuman"[5] and "impersonal, authorless".[6,7,8]

Vedas are also called *śruti* ("what is heard") literature, distinguishing them from other religious texts, which are called *smṛti* ("what is remembered"). The Veda, for orthodox Indian theologians, are considered revelations seen by ancient sages after intense meditation, and texts that have been more carefully preserved since ancient times.[9,10] In the Hindu Epic the Mahabharata, the creation of Vedas is credited to Brahma.[11] The Vedic hymns themselves assert that they were skillfully created by *Rishis* (sages), after inspired creativity, just as a carpenter builds a chariot.[12]</ref>

There are four Vedas: the Rigveda, the Yajurveda, the Samaveda and the Atharvaveda.[13] Each Veda has been subclassified into four major text types – the Samhitas (mantras and benedictions), the Aranyakas (text on rituals, ceremonies, sacrifices and symbolic-sacrifices), the Brahmanas (commentaries on rituals, ceremonies and sacrifices), and the Upanishads (texts discussing meditation, philosophy and spiritual knowledge).[14,15,16] Some scholars add a fifth category – the Upasanas (worship).[17,18]

The various Indian philosophies and denominations have taken differing positions on the Vedas. Schools of Indian philosophy which cite the Vedas as their scriptural authority are classified as "orthodox" (āstika).[19] (Note: This differentiation between epistemic and deontic authority is true for all Indian religions)</ref> Other śramaṇa traditions, such as Lokayata, Carvaka, Ajivika, Buddhism and Jainism, which did not regard the Vedas as authorities, are referred to as "heterodox" or "non-orthodox" (nāstika) schools.[20] Despite their differences, just like the texts of the śramaṇa traditions, the layers of texts in the Vedas discuss similar ideas and concepts.

Etymology and usage

The Sanskrit word *véda* "knowledge, wisdom" is derived from the root *vid-* "to know". This is reconstructed as being derived from the Proto-Indo-European root **u̯eid-*, meaning "see" or "know".

The noun is from Proto-Indo-European **u̯eidos*, cognate to Greek (ϝ)εῖδος "aspect", "form" . Not to be confused is the homonymous 1st and 3rd person singular perfect tense *véda*, cognate to Greek (ϝ)οῖδα *(w)oida* "I know". Root cognates are Greek ἰδέα, English *wit*, etc., Latin *video* "I see", etc.[21]

The Sanskrit term *veda* as a common noun means "knowledge".[22] The term in some contexts, such as hymn 10.93.11 of the *Rigveda*, means "obtaining or finding wealth, property",[23] while in some others it means "a bunch of grass together" as in a broom or for ritual fire.[24]

A related word *Vedena* appears in hymn 8.19.5 of the *Rigveda*.[25] It was translated by Ralph T. H. Griffith as "ritual lore",[26] as "studying the Veda" by the 14th-century Indian scholar Sayana, as "bundle of grass" by Max Müller, and as "with the Veda" by H.H. Wilson.[27]

Vedas are called *Maṟai* or *Vaymoli* in parts of South India. Marai literally means "hidden, a secret, mystery".[28,29] In some south Indian communities such as Iyengars, the word Veda includes the Tamil writings of the Alvar saints, such as Divya Prabandham, for example Tiruvaymoli.[30]

Chronology

The Vedas are among the oldest sacred texts. The Samhitas date to roughly 1700–1100 BCE, and the "circum-Vedic" texts, as well as the redaction of the Samhitas, date to c. 1000-500 BCE, resulting in a Vedic period, spanning the mid 2nd to mid 1st millennium BCE, or the Late Bronze Age and the Iron Age.[31] The Vedic period reaches its peak only after the composition of the mantra texts, with the establishment of the various shakhas all over Northern India which annotated the mantra samhitas with Brahmana discussions of their meaning, and reaches its end in the age of Buddha and Panini and the rise of the

Mahajanapadas (archaeologically, Northern Black Polished Ware). Michael Witzel gives a time span of c. 1500 to c. 500-400 BCE. Witzel makes special reference to the Near Eastern Mitanni material of the 14th century BCE, the only epigraphic record of Indo-Aryan contemporary to the Rigvedic period. He gives 150 BCE (Patañjali) as a terminus ante quem for all Vedic Sanskrit literature, and 1200 BCE (the early Iron Age) as terminus post quem for the Atharvaveda.[32]

Transmission of texts in the Vedic period was by oral tradition, preserved with precision with the help of elaborate mnemonic techniques. A literary tradition is traceable in post-Vedic times, after the rise of Buddhism in the Maurya period,[33] perhaps earliest in the Kanva recension of the Yajurveda about the 1st century BCE; however oral tradition of transmission remained active. Witzel suggests the possibility of written Vedic texts towards the end of 1st millennium BCE.[34] Some scholars such as Jack Goody state that "the Vedas are not the product of an oral society", basing this view by comparing inconsistencies in the transmitted versions of literature from various oral societies such as the Greek, Serbia and other cultures, then noting that the Vedic literature is too consistent and vast to have been composed and transmitted orally across generations, without being written down. However, adds Goody, the Vedic texts likely involved both a written and oral tradition, calling it a "parallel products of a literate society".

Due to the ephemeral nature of the manuscript material (birch bark or palm leaves), surviving manuscripts rarely surpass an age of a few hundred years. The Sampurnanand Sanskrit University has a Rigveda manuscript from the 14th century; however, there are a number of older Veda manuscripts in Nepal that are dated from the 11th century onwards.

Ancient universities

The Vedas, Vedic rituals and its ancillary sciences called the Vedangas, were part of the curriculum at ancient universities such as at Taxila, Nalanda and Vikramashila.[35,36]

Categories of Vedic texts

The term "Vedic texts" is used in two distinct meanings:

1. Texts composed in Vedic Sanskrit during the Vedic period (Iron Age India)
2. Any text considered as "connected to the Vedas" or a "corollary of the Vedas"[37]

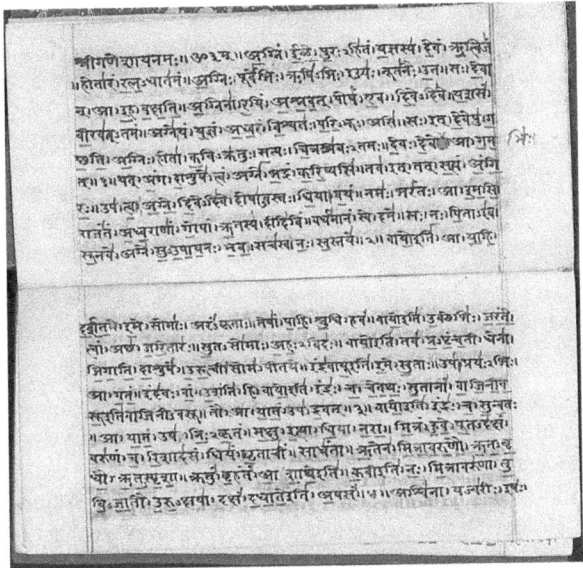

Figure 2: *Rigveda manuscript in Devanagari*

Vedic Sanskrit corpus

The corpus of Vedic Sanskrit texts includes:

- The Samhitas (Sanskrit *saṃhitā*, "collection"), are collections of metric texts ("mantras"). There are four "Vedic" Samhitas: the Rig-Veda, Sama-Veda, Yajur-Veda, and Atharva-Veda, most of which are available in several recensions (*śākhā*). In some contexts, the term *Veda* is used to refer to these Samhitas. This is the oldest layer of Vedic texts, apart from the Rigvedic hymns, which were probably essentially complete by 1200 BCE, dating to c. the 12th to 10th centuries BCE. The complete corpus of Vedic mantras as collected in Bloomfield's *Vedic Concordance* (1907) consists of some 89,000 padas (metrical feet), of which 72,000 occur in the four Samhitas.[38]
- The Brahmanas are prose texts that comment and explain the solemn rituals as well as expound on their meaning and many connected themes. Each of the Brahmanas is associated with one of the Samhitas or its recensions.[39] The Brahmanas may either form separate texts or can be partly integrated into the text of the Samhitas. They may also include the Aranyakas and Upanishads.
- The Aranyakas, "wilderness texts" or "forest treaties", were composed by people who meditated in the woods as recluses and are the third part

of the Vedas. The texts contain discussions and interpretations of ceremonies, from ritualistic to symbolic meta-ritualistic points of view. It is frequently read in secondary literature.
- Older Mukhya Upanishads (*Bṛhadāraṇyaka*, Chandogya, *Kaṭha*, Kena, Aitareya, and others).[40]

The Vedas (sruti) are different from Vedic era texts such as Shrauta Sutras and Gryha Sutras, which are smriti texts. Together, the Vedas and these Sutras form part of the Vedic Sanskrit corpus.[41,42]

While production of Brahmanas and Aranyakas ceased with the end of the Vedic period, additional Upanishads were composed after the end of the Vedic period.

The Brahmanas, Aranyakas, and Upanishads, among other things, interpret and discuss the Samhitas in philosophical and metaphorical ways to explore abstract concepts such as the Absolute (Brahman), and the soul or the self (Atman), introducing Vedanta philosophy, one of the major trends of later Hinduism. In other parts, they show evolution of ideas, such as from actual sacrifice to symbolic sacrifice, and of spirituality in the Upanishads. This has inspired later Hindu scholars such as Adi Shankara to classify each Veda into *karma-kanda* (कर्म खण्ड, action/ritual-related sections) and *jnana-kanda* (ज्ञान खण्ड, knowledge/spirituality-related sections).[43]

Shruti literature

The texts considered "Vedic" in the sense of "corollaries of the Vedas" is less clearly defined, and may include numerous post-Vedic texts such as the later Upanishads and the Sutra literature. Texts not considered to be *shruti* are known as *smriti* (Sanskrit: *smṛti*; "the remembered"), or texts of remembered traditions. This indigenous system of categorization was adopted by Max Müller and, while it is subject to some debate, it is still widely used. As Axel Michaels explains:

> These classifications are often not tenable for linguistic and formal reasons: There is not only one collection at any one time, but rather several handed down in separate Vedic schools; Upaniṣads ... are sometimes not to be distinguished from Āraṇyakas...; Brāhmaṇas contain older strata of language attributed to the Saṃhitās; there are various dialects and locally prominent traditions of the Vedic schools. Nevertheless, it is advisable to stick to the division adopted by Max Müller because it follows the Indian tradition, conveys the historical sequence fairly accurately, and underlies the current editions, translations, and monographs on Vedic literature."

The Upanishads are largely philosophical works, some in dialogue form. They are the foundation of Hindu philosophical thought and its diverse traditions.[44]

Of the Vedic corpus, they alone are widely known, and the central ideas of the Upanishads are at the spiritual core of Hindus.[45,46]

Vedic schools or recensions

The four Vedas were transmitted in various *śākhā*s (branches, schools). Each school likely represented an ancient community of a particular area, or kingdom. Each school followed its own canon. Multiple recensions are known for each of the Vedas. Thus, states Witzel as well as Renou, in the 2nd millennium BCE, there was likely no canon of one broadly accepted Vedic texts, no Vedic "Scripture", but only a canon of various texts accepted by each school. Some of these texts have survived, most lost or yet to be found. Rigveda that survives in modern times, for example, is in only one extremely well preserved school of Śākalya, from a region called Videha, in modern north Bihar, south of Nepal.[47] The Vedic canon in its entirety consists of texts from all the various Vedic schools taken together.

Each of the four Vedas were shared by the numerous schools, but revised, interpolated and adapted locally, in and after the Vedic period, giving rise to various recensions of the text. Some texts were revised into the modern era, raising significant debate on parts of the text which are believed to have been corrupted at a later date.[48,49] The Vedas each have an Index or Anukramani, the principal work of this kind being the general Index or *Sarvānukramaṇī*.[50,51]

Prodigious energy was expended by ancient Indian culture in ensuring that these texts were transmitted from generation to generation with inordinate fidelity. For example, memorization of the sacred *Vedas* included up to eleven forms of recitation of the same text. The texts were subsequently "proof-read" by comparing the different recited versions. Forms of recitation included the *jaṭā-pāṭha* (literally "mesh recitation") in which every two adjacent words in the text were first recited in their original order, then repeated in the reverse order, and finally repeated in the original order. That these methods have been effective, is testified to by the preservation of the most ancient Indian religious text, the *Rigveda*, as redacted into a single text during the *Brahmana* period, without any variant readings within that school.

The Vedas were likely written down for the first time around 500 BCE. However, all printed editions of the Vedas that survive in the modern times are likely the version existing in about the 16th century AD.[52]

Four Vedas

Part of a series on Hindu scriptures
Vedas and their Shakhas

<templatestyles src="Nobold/styles.css"/>Hinduism portal
- v
- t
- e[53]

The canonical division of the Vedas is fourfold (*turīya*) viz.,[54]
1. Rigveda (RV)
2. Yajurveda (YV, with the main division TS vs. VS)
3. Samaveda (SV)
4. Atharvaveda (AV)

Of these, the first three were the principal original division, also called "*trayī vidyā*"; that is, "the triple science" of reciting hymns (Rigveda), performing sacrifices (Yajurveda), and chanting songs (Samaveda).[55] The Rigveda is the oldest work, which Witzel states are probably from the period of 1900 to 1100 BCE. Witzel, also notes that it is the Vedic period itself, where incipient lists divide the Vedic texts into three (trayī) or four branches: Rig, Yajur, Sama and Atharva.

Each Veda has been subclassified into four major text types – the Samhitas (mantras and benedictions), the Aranyakas (text on rituals, ceremonies such as newborn baby's rites of passage, coming of age, marriages, retirement and cremation, sacrifices and symbolic-sacrifices), the Brahmanas (commentaries on rituals, ceremonies and sacrifices), and the Upanishads (text discussing meditation, philosophy and spiritual knowledge). The Upasanas (short ritual worship-related sections) are considered by some scholars as the fifth part. Witzel notes that the rituals, rites and ceremonies described in these ancient texts reconstruct to a large degree the Indo-European marriage rituals observed in a region spanning the Indian subcontinent, Persia and the European area, and some greater details are found in the Vedic era texts such as the Grhya Sūtras.[56]

Only one version of the Rigveda is known to have survived into the modern era. Several different versions of the Sama Veda and the Atharva Veda are known, and many different versions of the Yajur Veda have been found in different parts of South Asia.[57]

Rigveda

<templatestyles src="Template:Quote_box/styles.css" />

Nasadiya Sukta (Hymn of non-Eternity):

Who really knows?
Who can here proclaim it?
Whence, whence this creation sprang?
Gods came later, after the creation of this universe.

Who then knows whence it has arisen?
Whether God's will created it, or whether He was mute;
Only He who is its overseer in highest heaven knows,
He only knows, or perhaps He does not know.

—Rig Veda 10.129.6-7[58]

The Rigveda Samhita is the oldest extant Indic text.[59] It is a collection of 1,028 Vedic Sanskrit hymns and 10,600 verses in all, organized into ten books (Sanskrit: *mandalas*).[60] The hymns are dedicated to Rigvedic deities.[61]

The books were composed by poets from different priestly groups over a period of several centuries from roughly the second half of the 2nd millennium BCE (the early Vedic period), starting with the Punjab (Sapta Sindhu) region of the northwest Indian subcontinent.[62] The Rigveda is structured based on clear principles – the Veda begins with a small book addressed to Agni, Indra, and other gods, all arranged according to decreasing total number of hymns in each deity collection; for each deity series, the hymns progress from longer to shorter ones, but the number of hymns per book increases. Finally, the meter too is systematically arranged from jagati and tristubh to anustubh and gayatri as the text progresses.[63] In terms of substance, the nature of hymns shift from praise of deities in early books to Nasadiya Sukta with questions such as, "what is the origin of the universe?, do even gods know the answer?", the virtue of Dāna (charity) in society,[64] and other metaphysical issues in its hymns.[65]

There are similarities between the mythology, rituals and linguistics in Rigveda and those found in ancient central Asia, Iranian and Hindukush (Afghanistan) regions.[66]

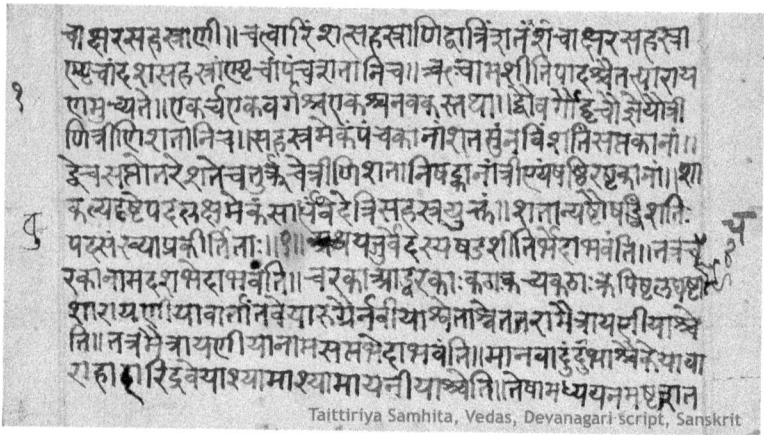

Figure 3: *A page from the Taittiriya Samhita, a layer of text within the Yajurveda*

Samaveda

The Samaveda Samhita[67] consists of 1549 stanzas, taken almost entirely (except for 75 mantras) from the Rigveda.[68] The Samaveda samhita has two major parts. The first part includes four melody collections (gāna, गान) and the second part three verse "books" (ārcika, आर्चिक). A melody in the song books corresponds to a verse in the *arcika* books. Just as in the Rigveda, the early sections of Samaveda typically begin with hymns to Agni and Indra but shift to the abstract. Their meters shift also in a descending order. The songs in the later sections of the Samaveda have the least deviation from the hymns derived from the Rigveda.

In the Samaveda, some of the Rigvedic verses are repeated.[69] Including repetitions, there are a total of 1875 verses numbered in the Samaveda recension translated by Griffith.[70] Two major recensions have survived, the Kauthuma/Ranayaniya and the Jaiminiya. Its purpose was liturgical, and they were the repertoire of the *udgātṛ* or "singer" priests.[71]

Yajurveda

The Yajurveda Samhita consists of prose mantras.[72] It is a compilation of ritual offering formulas that were said by a priest while an individual performed ritual actions such as those before the yajna fire.

The earliest and most ancient layer of Yajurveda samhita includes about 1,875 verses, that are distinct yet borrow and build upon the foundation of verses in Rigveda.[73] Unlike the Samaveda which is almost entirely based on Rigveda mantras and structured as songs, the Yajurveda samhitas are in prose and linguistically, they are different from earlier Vedic texts.[74] The Yajur Veda has been the primary source of information about sacrifices during Vedic times and associated rituals.[75]

There are two major groups of texts in this Veda: the "Black" (*Krishna*) and the "White" (*Shukla*). The term "black" implies "the un-arranged, motley collection" of verses in Yajurveda, in contrast to the "white" (well arranged) Yajurveda.[76] The White Yajurveda separates the Samhita from its Brahmana (the Shatapatha Brahmana), the Black Yajurveda intersperses the Samhita with Brahmana commentary. Of the Black Yajurveda, texts from four major schools have survived (Maitrayani, Katha, Kapisthala-Katha, Taittiriya), while of the White Yajurveda, two (Kanva and Madhyandina).[77] The youngest layer of Yajurveda text is not related to rituals nor sacrifice, it includes the largest collection of primary Upanishads, influential to various schools of Hindu philosophy.[78,79]

Atharvaveda

The Artharvaveda Samhita is the text 'belonging to the Atharvan and Angirasa poets. It has about 760 hymns, and about 160 of the hymns are in common with the Rigveda. Most of the verses are metrical, but some sections are in prose. Two different versions of the text – the *Paippalāda* and the *Śaunakīya* – have survived into the modern times.[80] The Atharvaveda was not considered as a Veda in the Vedic era, and was accepted as a Veda in late 1st millennium BCE.[81,82] It was compiled last,[83] probably around 900 BCE, although some of its material may go back to the time of the Rigveda, or earlier.

The Atharvaveda is sometimes called the "Veda of magical formulas",[84] an epithet declared to be incorrect by other scholars.[85] The Samhita layer of the text likely represents a developing 2nd millennium BCE tradition of magico-religious rites to address superstitious anxiety, spells to remove maladies believed to be caused by demons, and herbs- and nature-derived potions as medicine.[86,87] The text, states Kenneth Zysk, is one of oldest surviving record of the evolutionary practices in religious medicine and reveals the "earliest forms of folk healing of Indo-European antiquity".[88] Many books of the Atharvaveda Samhita are dedicated to rituals without magic, such as to philosophical speculations and to theosophy.

The Atharva veda has been a primary source for information about Vedic culture, the customs and beliefs, the aspirations and frustrations of everyday Vedic life, as well as those associated with kings and governance. The text also includes hymns dealing with the two major rituals of passage – marriage and cremation. The Atharva Veda also dedicates significant portion of the text asking the meaning of a ritual.[89]

Embedded Vedic texts

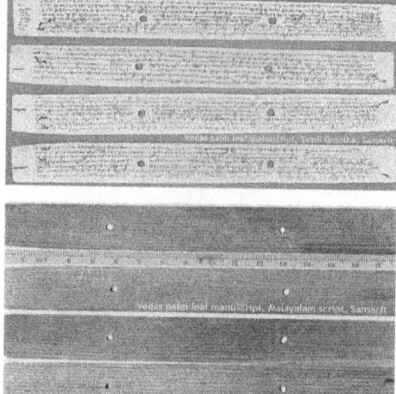

Manuscripts of the Vedas are in the Sanskrit language, but in many regional scripts in addition to the Devanagari. Top: Grantha script (Tamil Nadu), Below: Malayalam script (Kerala).

Brahmanas

The Brahmanas are commentaries, explanation of proper methods and meaning of Vedic Samhita rituals in the four Vedas. They also incorporate myths, legends and in some cases philosophy.[90,91] Each regional Vedic *shakha* (school) has its own operating manual-like Brahmana text, most of which have been lost.[92] A total of 19 Brahmana texts have survived into modern times: two associated with the Rigveda, six with the Yajurveda, ten with the Samaveda and one with the Atharvaveda. The oldest dated to about 900 BCE, while the youngest Brahmanas (such as the Shatapatha Brahmana), were complete by about 700 BCE.[93,94] According to Jan Gonda, the final codification of the Brahmanas took place in pre-Buddhist times (ca. 600 BCE).[95]

The substance of the Brahmana text varies with each Veda. For example, the first chapter of the Chandogya Brahmana, one of the oldest Brahmanas, includes eight ritual *suktas* (hymns) for the ceremony of marriage and rituals at the birth of a child.[96] The first hymn is a recitation that accompanies offering a Yajna oblation to *Agni* (fire) on the occasion of a marriage, and the hymn prays for prosperity of the couple getting married.[97,98] The second hymn wishes for their long life, kind relatives, and a numerous progeny. The third hymn is a mutual marriage pledge, between the bride and groom, by which the two bind themselves to each other. The sixth through last hymns of the first chapter in Chandogya Brahmana are ritual celebrations on the birth of a child and wishes for health, wealth, and prosperity with a profusion of cows and artha. However, these verses are incomplete expositions, and their complete context emerges only with the Samhita layer of text.[99]

Aranyakas and Upanishads

The Aranyakas layer of the Vedas include rituals, discussion of symbolic meta-rituals, as well as philosophical speculations.[100]

Aranyakas, however, neither are homogeneous in content nor in structure. They are a medley of instructions and ideas, and some include chapters of Upanishads within them. Two theories have been proposed on the origin of the word *Aranyakas*. One theory holds that these texts were meant to be studied in a forest, while the other holds that the name came from these being the manuals of allegorical interpretation of sacrifices, for those in Vanaprastha (retired, forest-dwelling) stage of their life, according to the historic age-based Ashrama system of human life.[101]

The Upanishads reflect the last composed layer of texts in the Vedas. They are commonly referred to as *Vedānta*, variously interpreted to mean either the "last chapters, parts of the Vedas" or "the object, the highest purpose of the Veda".[102] The concepts of Brahman (Ultimate Reality) and Ātman (Soul, Self) are central ideas in all the Upanishads,[103,104] and "Know your Ātman" their thematic focus.[105] The Upanishads are the foundation of Hindu philosophical thought and its diverse traditions.[106] Of the Vedic corpus, they alone are widely known, and the central ideas of the Upanishads have influenced the diverse traditions of Hinduism.[107]

Aranyakas are sometimes identified as *karma-kanda* (ritualistic section), while the Upanishads are identified as *jnana-kanda* (spirituality section).[108] In an alternate classification, the early part of Vedas are called Samhitas and the commentary are called the Brahmanas which together are identified as the ceremonial *karma-kanda*, while *Aranyakas* and *Upanishads* are referred to as the *jnana-kanda*.[109]

Post-Vedic literature

Vedanga

The Vedangas developed towards the end of the vedic period, around or after the middle of the 1st millennium BCE. These auxiliary fields of Vedic studies emerged because the language of the Vedas, composed centuries earlier, became too archaic to the people of that time.[110] The Vedangas were sciences that focused on helping understand and interpret the Vedas that had been composed many centuries earlier.[110]

The six subjects of Vedanga are phonetics (*Śikṣā*), poetic meter (*Chandas*), grammar (*Vyākaraṇa*), etymology and linguistics (Nirukta), rituals and rites of passage (*Kalpa*), time keeping and astronomy (*Jyotiṣa*).[111,112,113]

Vedangas developed as ancillary studies for the Vedas, but its insights into meters, structure of sound and language, grammar, linguistic analysis and other subjects influenced post-Vedic studies, arts, culture and various schools of Hindu philosophy.[114,115] The Kalpa Vedanga studies, for example, gave rise to the Dharma-sutras, which later expanded into Dharma-shastras.[110]

Parisista

Pariśiṣṭa "supplement, appendix" is the term applied to various ancillary works of Vedic literature, dealing mainly with details of ritual and elaborations of the texts logically and chronologically prior to them: the Samhitas, Brahmanas, Aranyakas and Sutras. Naturally classified with the Veda to which each pertains, Parisista works exist for each of the four Vedas. However, only the literature associated with the Atharvaveda is extensive.

- The *Āśvalāyana Gṛhya Pariśiṣṭa* is a very late text associated with the Rigveda canon.
- The *Gobhila Gṛhya Pariśiṣṭa* is a short metrical text of two chapters, with 113 and 95 verses respectively.
- The *Kātiya Pariśiṣṭas*, ascribed to *Kātyāyana*, consist of 18 works enumerated self-referentially in the fifth of the series (the *Caraṇavyūha*) and the *Kātyāyana Śrauta Sūtra Pariśiṣṭa*.
- The *Kṛṣṇa Yajurveda has 3 parisistas The Āpastamba Hautra Pariśiṣṭa, which is also found as the second* praśna *of the Satyasāḍha Śrauta Sūtra'*, the *Vārāha Śrauta Sūtra Pariśiṣṭa*
- For the Atharvaveda, there are 79 works, collected as 72 distinctly named parisistas.[116]

Upaveda

The term **upaveda** ("applied knowledge") is used in traditional literature to designate the subjects of certain technical works.[117] Lists of what subjects are included in this class differ among sources. The Charanavyuha mentions four Upavedas:

- Archery (Dhanurveda), associated with the Yajurveda
- Architecture (Sthapatyaveda), associated with the Atharvaveda.
- Music and sacred dance (*Gāndharvaveda*), associated with the Samaveda
- Medicine (*Āyurveda*), associated with either the Rigveda or the Atharvaveda .

"Fifth" and other Vedas

Some post-Vedic texts, including the Mahabharata, the Natyasastra[118] and certain Puranas, refer to themselves as the "fifth Veda". The earliest reference to such a "fifth Veda" is found in the Chandogya Upanishad in hymn 7.1.2.[119]
<templatestyles src="Template:Quote/styles.css"/>

> *Let drama and dance (Nātya, नाट्य) be the fifth vedic scripture. Combined with an epic story, tending to virtue, wealth, joy and spiritual freedom, it must contain the significance of every scripture, and forward every art. Thus, from all the Vedas, Brahma framed the Nātya Veda. From the Rig Veda he drew forth the words, from the Sama Veda the melody, from the Yajur Veda gesture, and from the Atharva Veda the sentiment.*
>
> —First chapter of Nātyaśāstra, Abhinaya Darpana

"Divya Prabandha", for example Tiruvaymoli, is a term for canonical Tamil texts considered as Vernacular Veda by some South Indian Hindus.

Other texts such as the Bhagavad Gita or the Vedanta Sutras are considered *shruti* or "Vedic" by some Hindu denominations but not universally within Hinduism. The Bhakti movement, and Gaudiya Vaishnavism in particular extended the term *veda* to include the Sanskrit Epics and Vaishnavite devotional texts such as the Pancaratra.

Puranas

The *Puranas* is a vast genre of encyclopedic Indian literature about a wide range of topics particularly myths, legends and other traditional lore.[120] Several of these texts are named after major Hindu deities such as Vishnu, Shiva and Devi.[121] There are 18 *Maha Puranas* (Great Puranas) and 18 *Upa Puranas* (Minor Puranas), with over 400,000 verses.

The Puranas have been influential in the Hindu culture.[122,123] They are considered *Vaidika* (congruent with Vedic literature).[124] The Bhagavata Purana has been among the most celebrated and popular text in the Puranic genre, and is of non-dualistic tenor.[125] The Puranic literature wove with the Bhakti movement in India, and both Dvaita and Advaita scholars have commented on the underlying Vedanta themes in the *Maha Puranas*.[126]

Western Indology

The study of Sanskrit in the West began in the 17th century. In the early 19th century, Arthur Schopenhauer drew attention to Vedic texts, specifically the Upanishads. The importance of Vedic Sanskrit for Indo-European studies was also recognized in the early 19th century. English translations of the Samhitas were published in the later 19th century, in the *Sacred Books of the East* series edited by Müller between 1879 and 1910.[127] Ralph T. H. Griffith also presented English translations of the four Samhitas, published 1889 to 1899.

Voltaire regarded Vedas to be exceptional, he remarked that:

<templatestyles src="Template:Quote/styles.css"/>

> The Veda was the most precious gift for which the West had ever been indebted to the East.[128,129]

Rigveda manuscripts were selected for inscription in UNESCO's Memory of the World Register in 2007.

Bibliography

- Apte, Vaman Shivram (1965), *The Practical Sanskrit Dictionary* (4th revised & enlarged ed.), Delhi: Motilal Banarsidass, ISBN 81-208-0567-4<templatestyles src="Module:Citation/CS1/styles.css"></templatestyles>.
- Avari, Burjor (2007), *India: The Ancient Past*, London: Routledge, ISBN 978-0-415-35616-9<templatestyles src="Module:Citation/CS1/styles.css"></templatestyles>
- Harold G. Coward (1990). Karl Potter, ed. *The Philosophy of the Grammarians, in Encyclopedia of Indian Philosophies*[130]. **5**. Princeton University Press. ISBN 978-81-208-0426-5.<templatestyles src="Module:Citation/CS1/styles.css"></templatestyles>
- Filliozat, Pierre-Sylvain (2004), "Ancient Sanskrit Mathematics: An Oral Tradition and a Written Literature"[131], in Chemla, Karine; Cohen, Robert S.; Renn, Jürgen; et al., *History of Science, History of Text (Boston Series in the Philosophy of Science)*, Dordrecht: Springer Netherlands, ISBN 9781402023200<templatestyles src="Module:Citation/CS1/styles.css"></templatestyles>
- Flood, Gavin (1996), *An Introduction to Hinduism*, Cambridge University Press, ISBN 0-521-43878-0<templatestyles src="Module:Citation/CS1/styles.css"></templatestyles>
- Flood, Gavin, ed. (2003), *The Blackwell Companion to Hinduism*, Malden, Massachusetts: Blackwell, ISBN 1-4051-3251-5<templatestyles src="Module:Citation/CS1/styles.css"></templatestyles>

- Holdrege, Barbara A. (1995). *Veda and Torah*. SUNY Press. ISBN 0-7914-1639-9.
- MacDonell, Arthur Anthony (1900), *A History of Sanskrit Literature*, New York: D. Appleton and Co, OCLC 713426994[132] (full text online[133])
- Mahadevan, T. M. P (1952), Sarvepalli Radhakrishnan; Ardeshir Ruttonji Wadia; Dhirendra Mohan Datta, eds., *History of Philosophy, Eastern and Western*, George Allen & Unwin, OCLC 929704391[134]
- Michaels, Axel (2004), *Hinduism: Past and Present*, Princeton University Press, ISBN 0-691-08953-1
- Monier-Williams, Monier, ed. (1851), *Dictionary, English and Sanskrit*[135], London: Honourable East-India Company, OCLC 5333096[136] (reprinted 2006 as ISBN 1-881338-58-4)
- Muir, John (1861). *Original Sanskrit Texts on the Origin and Progress of the Religion and Institutions of India*[137]. Williams and Norgate.
- Müller, Max (1891). *Chips from a German Workshop*[138]. New York: C. Scribner's sons.
- Patrick Olivelle (1999). *Dharmasutras: The Law Codes of Ancient India*[139]. Oxford University Press. ISBN 978-0-19-283882-7.
- Radhakrishnan, Sarvepalli; Moore, Charles A., eds. (1957), *A Sourcebook in Indian Philosophy* (12th Princeton Paperback ed.), Princeton University Press, ISBN 0-691-01958-4
- Staal, Frits (1986), *The Fidelity of Oral Tradition and the Origins of Science*, Mededelingen der Koninklijke Nederlandse Akademie von Wetenschappen, North Holland Publishing Company
- Smith, Brian K. (1992), "Canonical Authority and Social Classification: Veda and 'Varṇa' in Ancient Indian Texts", *History of Religions*, The University of Chicago Press,

pp. 103–125, doi: 10.2307/1062753[140]<templatestyles src="Module:Citation/CS1/styles.css"></templatestyles>
- Sullivan, B. M. (Summer 1994), "The Religious Authority of the Mahabharata: Vyasa and Brahma in the Hindu Scriptural Tradition", *Journal of the American Academy of Religion*, **62** (1): 377–401, doi: 10.1093/jaarel/LXII.2.377[141]<templatestyles src="Module:Citation/CS1/styles.css"></templatestyles>
- Annette Wilke; Oliver Moebus (2011). *Sound and Communication: An Aesthetic Cultural History of Sanskrit Hinduism*[142]. Walter de Gruyter. ISBN 978-3-11-018159-3.<templatestyles src="Module:Citation/CS1/styles.css"></templatestyles>
- Witzel, Michael (ed.) (1997), *Inside the Texts, Beyond the Texts. New Approaches to the Study of the Vedas*, Harvard Oriental Series, Opera Minora vol. 2, Cambridge: Harvard University Press<templatestyles src="Module:Citation/CS1/styles.css"></templatestyles>
- Zaehner, R. C. (1966), *Hindu Scriptures*, London: Everyman's Library<templatestyles src="Module:Citation/CS1/styles.css"></templatestyles>

Further reading

Overviews

- J. Gonda, *Vedic Literature: Saṃhitās and Brāhmaṇas*, A History of Indian literature. Vol. 1, Veda and Upanishads, Wiesnaden: Harrassowitz (1975), <templatestyles src="Module:Citation/CS1/styles.css" />ISBN 978-3-447-01603-2.
- J. A. Santucci, *An Outline of Vedic Literature*, Scholars Press for the American Academy of Religion, (1976).
- S. Shrava, *A Comprehensive History of Vedic Literature — Brahmana and Aranyaka Works*, Pranava Prakashan (1977).

Concordances

- M. Bloomfield, *A Vedic Concordance* (1907)
- Vishva Bandhu, Bhim Dev, S. Bhaskaran Nair (eds.), *Vaidika-Padānukrama-Koṣa: A Vedic Word-Concordance*, Vishveshvaranand Vedic Research Institute, Hoshiarpur, 1963–1965, revised edition 1973-1976.

Conference proceedings

- Griffiths, Arlo and Houben, Jan E. M. (eds.), *The Vedas : texts, language & ritual: proceedings of the Third International Vedic Workshop, Leiden 2002*, Groningen Oriental Studies 20, Groningen : Forsten, (2004), <templatestyles src="Module:Citation/CS1/styles.css" />ISBN 90-6980-149-3.

External links

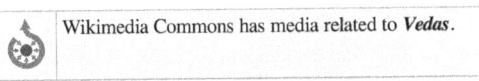
Wikimedia Commons has media related to *Vedas*.

 Look up *Veda* or *Vedic* in Wiktionary, the free dictionary.

Wikiquote has quotations related to: *Vedas*

- Sketch of the Historical Grammar of the Rig and Atharva Vedas[143], Edward Vernon Arnold, Journal of the American Oriental Society
- On the History and the Present State of Vedic Tradition in Nepal[144], Michael Witzel
- GRETIL etexts[145]
- A Vedic Concordance[146], Maurice Bloomfield, Harvard University (an alphabetic index to every line, every stanza of the Vedas published before 1906)
- An Enlarged Electronic Version of Bloomfield's A Vedic Concordance[147], Harvard University
- The Vedas at sacred-texts.com[148]

Indian epic poetry

Indian epic poetry is the epic poetry written in the Indian subcontinent, traditionally called *Kavya* (or *Kāvya*; Sanskrit: काव्य, IAST: *kāvyá*). The *Ramayana* and the *Mahabharata*, which were originally composed in Sanskrit and later translated into many other Indian languages, and The Five Great Epics of Tamil Literature and Sangam literature are some of the oldest surviving epic poems ever written.

Sanskrit epics

The ancient Sanskrit epics the *Ramayana* and *Mahabharata* comprise together the Itihāsa ("History") or Mahākāvya ("Great Compositions"), a canon of Hindu scripture. Indeed, the epic form prevailed and verse remained until very recently the preferred form of Hindu literary works. Hero-worship is a central aspect of Indian culture, and thus readily lent itself to a literary tradition that abounded in epic poetry and literature. The Puranas, a massive collection of verse-form histories of India's many Hindu gods and goddesses, followed in this tradition. Itihāsas and Purāṇas are mentioned in the Atharva Veda[150] and referred to as the *fourth Veda*.[151]

The language of these texts, termed **Epic Sanskrit**, constitutes the earliest phase of Classical Sanskrit, following the latest stage of Vedic Sanskrit found in the Shrauta Sutras.

The Buddhist kavi Aśvaghoṣa wrote two epics and one drama. He lived in the 1st-2nd century. He wrote a biography of the Buddha, titled Buddhacarita. His second epic is called Saundarananda and tells the story of the conversion of Nanda, the younger brother of the Buddha. The play he wrote is called Śariputraprakaraṇa, but of this play only a few fragments remained.

The famous poet and playwright Kālidāsa also wrote two epics: *Raghuvamsha* (*The Dynasty of Raghu*) and *Kumarasambhava* (*The Birth of Kumar Kartikeya*). Other Classical Sanskrit epics are the "Slaying of Śiśupāla" Śiśupālavadha of Māgha, "Arjuna and the Mountain Man" Kirātārjunīya of Bhāravi, the "Adventures of the Prince of Nishadha" Naiṣadhacarita of Śrīharṣa and "Bhaṭṭi's Poem" Bhaṭṭikāvya of Bhaṭṭi.

Kannada epic poetry

Kannada epic poetry mainly consists of Jain religious literature and Lingayat literature. Asaga wrote *Vardhaman Charitra*, an epic which runs in 18 cantos, in 853 CE, the first Sanskrit biography of the 24th and last tirthankara of Jainism, Mahavira, though his Kannada language version of Kalidasa's epic poem, *Kumārasambhava, Karnataka Kumarasambhava Kavya* is lost. The most famous poet from this period is Pampa (902-975 CE), one of the most famous writers in the Kannada language. His *Vikramarjuna Vijaya* (also called the *Pampabharatha*) is hailed as a classic even to this day. With this and his other important work Ādi purāṇa he set a trend of poetic excellence for the Kannada poets of the future. The former work is an adaptation of the celebrated Mahabharata, and is the first such adaptation in Kannada. Noted for the strong human bent and the dignified style in his writing, Pampa has been one of the most influential writers in Kannada. He is identified as *Adikavi* "first poet". It is only in Kannada that we have a Ramayana and a Mahabharata based on the Jain tradition in addition to those based on Brahmanical tradition.

Shivakotiacharya was the first writer in prose style. His work Vaddaradhane is dated to 900 CE. Sri Ponna (939-966 CE) is also an important writer from the same period, with Shanti Purana as his magnum opus. Another major writer of the period is *Ranna* (949-? CE). His most famous works are the Jain religious work *Ajita Tirthankara Purana* and the Gada Yuddha, a birds' eye view of the *Mahabharata* set in the last day of the battle of Kurukshetra and relating the story of the Mahabharata through a series of flashbacks. Structurally, the poetry in this period is in the *Champu* style, essentially poetry interspersed with lyrical prose.

The Siribhoovalaya is a unique work of multilingual Kannada literature written by Kumudendu Muni, a Jain monk. The work is unique in that it does not employ letters, but is composed entirely in Kannada numerals. The *Saangathya* metre of Kannada poetry is employed in the work. It uses numerals 1 through 64 and employs various patterns or *bandhas* in a frame of 729 (27×27) squares to represent letters in nearly 18 scripts and over 700 languages. Some of the patterns used include the *Chakrabandha, Hamsabandha, Varapadmabandha, Sagarabandha, Sarasabandha, Kruanchabandha, Mayurabandha, Ramapadabandha, Nakhabandha*, etc. As each of these patterns are identified and decoded, the contents can be read. The work is said to have around 600,000 verses, nearly six times as big as the ancient Indian epic Mahabharata.

The Prabhulingaleele, Basava purana, Channabasavapurana and Basavarajavijaya are a few of the Lingayat epics.

Tamil epics

The post-sangam period (2nd century-6th century) saw many great Tamil epics being written, including *Cilappatikaram* (or *Silappadhikaram*), *Manimegalai, Civaka Cintamani, Valayapathi* and *Kundalakesi*. Later, during the Chola period, Kamban (12th century) wrote what is considered one of the greatest Tamil epics — the *Kamba Ramayanam* of Kamban, based on the Valmiki Ramayana. The Thiruthondat Puranam (or Periya Puranam) of Chekkizhar is the great Tamil epic of the Shaiva Bhakti saints and is part of the religious scripture of Tamil Nadu's majority Shaivites.

Out of the five, *Manimegalai* and *Kundalakesi* are Buddhist religious works, *Civaka Cintamani* and *Valayapathi* are Tamil Jain works and *Silappatikaram* has a neutral religious view. They were written over a period of 1st century CE to 10th century CE and act as the historical evidence of social, religious, cultural and academic life of people during the era they were created. *Civaka Cintamani* introduced long verses called *virutha pa* in Tamil literature.,[152] while *Silappatikaram* used *akaval* meter (monologue), a style adopted from Sangam literature.

Tamil epics such as Silappathikaram and Periya Puranam are unique in Indian literature as they employ characters and stories associated with the people and language of the poets (Tamil) and take place within the Tamil country. This is in contrast to other Indian languages which are based on Sanskrit works and deal with Sanskrit mythology based on North Indian works.

Hindi epics

The first epic to appear in Hindi was Tulsidas' (1543–1623) *Ramacharitamanas*, also based on the *Ramayana*. It is considered a great classic of Hindi epic poetry and literature, and shows the author Tulsidas in complete command over all the important styles of composition — narrative, epic, lyrical and dialectic. He has given a divine character to Rama, the Hindu Avatar of Vishnu, portraying him as an ideal son, husband, brother and king.

In modern Hindi literature, *Kamayani* by Jaishankar Prasad has attained the status of an epic. The narrative of Kamayani is based on a popular mythological story, first mentioned in Satapatha Brahmana. It is a story of the great flood and the central characters of the epic poem are Manu (a male) and Shraddha (a female). Manu is representative of the human psyche and Shradha represents love. Another female character is Ida, who represents rationality. Some critics surmise that the three lead characters of Kamayani symbolize a synthesis of knowledge, action and desires in human life.

Apart from Kamayani; *Kurukshetra (Epic Poetry)* (1946), *Rashmirathi* (1952) and *Urvashi* (1961) by Ramdhari Singh 'Dinkar' have attained the status of epic poetry.

Likewise *Lalita Ke Aansoo*[153] by Krant M. L. Verma (1978)[154] narrates the tragic story about the death of Lal Bahadur Shastri through his wife Lalita Shastri.[155]

References

- Arthur Anthony Macdonell (1900). "The epics". *A History of Sanskrit Literature*. New York: D. Appleton and company.<templatestyles src="Module:Citation/CS1/styles.css"></templatestyles>
- Oliver Fallon (2009). "Introduction". *Bhatti's Poem: The Death of Rávana (Bhaṭṭikāvya)*. New York: New York University Press, Clay Sanskrit Library.<templatestyles src="Module:Citation/CS1/styles.css"></templatestyles>

Mahabharata

<indicator name="pp-default">  </indicator>

Mahabharata	

Manuscript illustration of the Battle of Kurukshetra	
Information	
Religion	Hinduism, Jainism, Indonesian philosophy
Author	Vyasa
Language	Sanskrit
Verses	200,000

Part of a series on
Hinduism

• Hindu • History
• Glossary of Hinduism terms • 🕉 *Hinduism portal*

Mahabharata

- v
- t
- e[156]

The *Mahābhārata* (US: /məhɑːˈbɑːrətə/,[157] UK: /ˌmɑːhəˈbɑːrətə/;[158] Sanskrit: महाभारतम्, *Mahābhāratam*, pronounced [məhɑːˈbʰɑːrət̪əm]) is one of the two major Sanskrit epics of ancient India, the other being the *Rāmāyaṇa*. The title may be translated as "the great tale of the Bhārata dynasty".

The *Mahābhārata* is an epic legendary narrative of the Kurukṣetra War and the fates of the Kaurava and the Pāṇḍava princes. It also contains philosophical and devotional material, such as a discussion of the four "goals of life" or *puruṣārtha* (12.161). Among the principal works and stories in the *Mahābhārata* are the *Bhagavad Gita*, the story of Damayanti, an abbreviated version of the *Rāmāyaṇa*, and the story of Ṛṣyasringa, often considered as works in their own right.

Traditionally, the authorship of the *Mahābhārata* is attributed to Vyāsa. There have been many attempts to unravel its historical growth and compositional layers. The oldest preserved parts of the text are thought to be not much older than around 400 BCE, though the origins of the epic probably fall between the 8th and 9th centuries BCE.[159] The text probably reached its final form by the early Gupta period (c. 4th century CE).[160] According to the *Mahābhārata* itself, the tale is extended from a shorter version of 24,000 verses called simply *Bhārata*.[161]

The *Mahābhārata* is the longest epic poem known and has been described as "the longest poem ever written". Its longest version consists of over 100,000 *śloka* or over 200,000 individual verse lines (each shloka is a couplet), and long prose passages. At about 1.8 million words in total, the *Mahābhārata* is roughly ten times the length of the *Iliad* and the *Odyssey* combined, or about four times the length of the *Rāmāyaṇa*.[162,163] W. J. Johnson has compared the importance of the *Mahābhārata* in the context of world civilization to that of the Bible, the works of William Shakespeare, the works of Homer, Greek drama, or the Quran. Within the Indian tradition it is sometimes called the Fifth Veda.

Textual history and structure

The epic is traditionally ascribed to the sage Vyāsa, who is also a major character in the epic. Vyāsa described it as being *itihāsa* (history). He also describes the Guru-shishya parampara, which traces all great teachers and their students of the Vedic times.

Figure 4: *Krishna and Arjuna at Kurukshetra, 18th–19th-century painting*

Figure 5: *Modern depiction of Vyasa narrating the Mahābhārata to Ganesha at the Murudeshwara temple, Karnataka.*

Figure 6: *Sauti recites the slokas of the Mahabharata.*

The first section of the Mahābhārata states that it was Gaṇeśa who wrote down the text to Vyasa's dictation.

The epic employs the story within a story structure, otherwise known as frametales, popular in many Indian religious and non-religious works. It is first recited at *Takshashila* by the sage Vaiśampāyana, a disciple of Vyāsa, to the King Janamejaya who is the great-grandson of the Pāṇḍava prince Arjuna. The story is then recited again by a professional storyteller named Ugraśrava Sauti, many years later, to an assemblage of sages performing the 12-year sacrifice for the king Saunaka Kulapati in the Naimiśa Forest.

The text was described by some early 20th-century western Indologists as unstructured and chaotic. Hermann Oldenberg supposed that the original poem must once have carried an immense "tragic force" but dismissed the full text as a "horrible chaos."[164] Moritz Winternitz (*Geschichte der indischen Literatur* 1909) considered that "only unpoetical theologians and clumsy scribes" could have lumped the parts of disparate origin into an unordered whole.[165]

Accretion and redaction

Research on the Mahābhārata has put an enormous effort into recognizing and dating layers within the text. Some elements of the present Mahābhārata can be traced back to Vedic times.[166] The background to the Mahābhārata suggests the origin of the epic occurs "after the very early Vedic period" and before "the first Indian 'empire' was to rise in the third century B.C." That this is "a date not too far removed from the 8th or 9th century B.C."[167] is likely. Mahābhārata started as an orally-transmitted tale of the charioteer bards. It is generally agreed that "Unlike the Vedas, which have to be preserved letter-perfect, the epic was a popular work whose reciters would inevitably conform to changes in language and style," so the earliest 'surviving' components of this dynamic text are believed to be no older than the earliest 'external' references we have to the epic, which may include an allusion in Panini's 4th century BCE grammar Aṣṭādhyāyī 4:2:56. It is estimated that the Sanskrit text probably reached something of a "final form" by the early Gupta period (about the 4th century CE). Vishnu Sukthankar, editor of the first great critical edition of the *Mahābhārata*, commented: "It is useless to think of reconstructing a fluid text in a literally original shape, on the basis of an archetype and a *stemma codicum*. What then is possible? Our objective can only be to reconstruct *the oldest form of the text which it is possible to reach* on the basis of the manuscript material available."[168] That manuscript evidence is somewhat late, given its material composition and the climate of India, but it is very extensive.

The Mahābhārata itself (1.1.61) distinguishes a core portion of 24,000 verses: the *Bhārata* proper, as opposed to additional secondary material, while the *Aśvalāyana Gṛhyasūtra* (3.4.4) makes a similar distinction. At least three redactions of the text are commonly recognized: *Jaya* (Victory) with 8,800 verses attributed to Vyāsa, *Bhārata* with 24,000 verses as recited by Vaiśampāyana, and finally the Mahābhārata as recited by Ugraśrava Sauti with over 100,000 verses.[169,170] However, some scholars, such as John Brockington, argue that *Jaya* and *Bharata* refer to the same text, and ascribe the theory of *Jaya* with 8,800 verses to a misreading of a verse in *Ādiparvan* (1.1.81). The redaction of this large body of text was carried out after formal principles, emphasizing the numbers 18[171] and 12. The addition of the latest parts may be dated by the absence of the *Anuśāsana-parva* and the *Virāta parva* from the "Spitzer manuscript".[172] The oldest surviving Sanskrit text dates to the Kushan Period (200 CE).

According to what one character says at Mbh. 1.1.50, there were three versions of the epic, beginning with *Manu* (1.1.27), *Astika* (1.3, sub-parva 5) or *Vasu* (1.57), respectively. These versions would correspond to the addition of one and then another 'frame' settings of dialogues. The *Vasu* version would omit the frame settings and begin with the account of the birth of Vyasa. The

Figure 7: *The snake sacrifice of Janamejaya*

astika version would add the *sarpasattra* and *aśvamedha* material from Brahmanical literature, introduce the name *Mahābhārata*, and identify Vyāsa as the work's author. The redactors of these additions were probably Pāñcarātrin scholars who according to Oberlies (1998) likely retained control over the text until its final redaction. Mention of the Huna in the *Bhīṣma-parva* however appears to imply that this parva may have been edited around the 4th century-Wikipedia:Citation needed.

The Ādi-parva includes the snake sacrifice (*sarpasattra*) of Janamejaya, explaining its motivation, detailing why all snakes in existence were intended to be destroyed, and why in spite of this, there are still snakes in existence. This *sarpasattra* material was often considered an independent tale added to a version of the Mahābhārata by "thematic attraction" (Minkowski 1991), and considered to have a particularly close connection to Vedic (Brahmana) literature. The Pañcaviṁśa Brahmana (at 25.15.3) enumerates the officiant priests of a *sarpasattra* among whom the names Dhṛtarāṣtra and Janamejaya, two main characters of the *Mahābhārata*'s *sarpasattra*, as well as Takṣaka, the name of a snake in the *Mahābhārata*, occur.[173]

Historical references

The earliest known references to the Mahābhārata and its core *Bhārata* date to the *Aṣṭādhyāyī* (sutra 6.2.38) of Pāṇini (*fl.* 4th century BCE) and in the *Aśvalāyana Gṛhyasūtra* (3.4.4). This may mean the core 24,000 verses, known as the *Bhārata*, as well as an early version of the extended *Mahābhārata*, were composed by the 4th century BCE. A report by the Greek writer Dio Chrysostom (c. 40 - c. 120 CE) about Homer's poetry being sung even in India[174] seems to imply that the *Iliad* had been translated into Sanskrit. However, Indian scholars have, in general, taken this as evidence for the existence of a Mahābhārata at this date, whose episodes Dio or his sources identify with the story of the *Iliad*.[175]

Several stories within the Mahābhārata took on separate identities of their own in Classical Sanskrit literature. For instance, Abhijñānaśākuntala by the renowned Sanskrit poet Kālidāsa (c. 400 CE), believed to have lived in the era of the Gupta dynasty, is based on a story that is the precursor to the *Mahābhārata*. Urubhaṅga, a Sanskrit play written by Bhāsa who is believed to have lived before Kālidāsa, is based on the slaying of Duryodhana by the splitting of his thighs by Bhīma.

The copper-plate inscription of the Maharaja Sharvanatha (533–534 CE) from Khoh (Satna District, Madhya Pradesh) describes the Mahābhārata as a "collection of 100,000 verses" (*śata-sahasri saṃhitā*).

The 18 parvas or books

The division into 18 parvas is as follows:

Parva	Title	Sub-parvas	Contents
1	Adi Parva *(The Book of the Beginning)*	1–19	How the Mahābhārata came to be narrated by Sauti to the assembled rishis at Naimisharanya, after having been recited at the *sarpasattra* of Janamejaya by Vaishampayana at *Takṣaśilā*, modern-day Taxila, Pakistan. The history and genealogy of the Bharata and Bhrigu races is recalled, as is the birth and early life of the Kuru princes (*adi* means first).
2	Sabha Parva (The Book of the Assembly Hall)	20–28	Maya Danava erects the palace and court (*sabha*), at Indraprastha. Life at the court, Yudhishthira's Rajasuya Yajna, the game of dice, the disrobing of Pandava wife Draupadi and eventual exile of the Pandavas.
3	Vana Parva *also* Aranyaka-parva, Aranya-parva (The Book of the Forest)	29–44	The twelve years of exile in the forest (*aranya*).

4	Virata Parva (The Book of Virata)	45–48	The year spent incognito at the court of Virata.
5	Udyoga Parva (The Book of the Effort)	49–59	Preparations for war and efforts to bring about peace between the Kaurava and the Pandava sides which eventually fail (*udyoga* means effort or work).
6	Bhishma Parva (The Book of Bhishma)	60–64	The first part of the great battle, with Bhishma as commander for the Kaurava and his fall on the bed of arrows. (Includes the *Bhagavad Gita* in chapters 25-42.)
7	Drona Parva (The Book of Drona)	65–72	The battle continues, with Drona as commander. This is the major book of the war. Most of the great warriors on both sides are dead by the end of this book.
8	Karna Parva (The Book of Karna)	73	The continuation of the battle with Karna as commander of the Kaurava forces.
9	Shalya Parva (The Book of Shalya)	74–77	The last day of the battle, with Shalya as commander. Also told in detail, is the pilgrimage of Balarama to the fords of the river Saraswati and the mace fight between Bhima and Duryodhana which ends the war, since Bhima kills Duryodhana by smashing him on the thighs with a mace.
10	Sauptika Parva (The Book of the Sleeping Warriors)	78–80	Ashvattama, Kripa and Kritavarma kill the remaining Pandava army in their sleep. Only 7 warriors remain on the Pandava side and 3 on the Kaurava side.
11	Stri Parva (The Book of the Women)	81–85	Gandhari and the women (*stri*) of the Kauravas and Pandavas lament the dead and Gandhari cursing Krishna for the massive destruction and the extermination of the Kaurava.
12	Shanti Parva (The Book of Peace)	86–88	The crowning of Yudhishthira as king of Hastinapura, and instructions from Bhishma for the newly anointed king on society, economics and politics. This is the longest book of the Mahabharata. Kisari Mohan Ganguli considers this Parva as a later interpolation.'
13	Anushasana Parva (The Book of the Instructions)	89–90	The final instructions (*anushasana*) from Bhishma.
14	Ashvamedhika Parva (The Book of the Horse Sacrifice)[176]	91–92	The royal ceremony of the Ashvamedha (Horse sacrifice) conducted by Yudhishthira. The world conquest by Arjuna. The Anugita is told by Krishna to Arjuna.
15	Ashramavasika Parva (The Book of the Hermitage)	93–95	The eventual deaths of Dhritarashtra, Gandhari and Kunti in a forest fire when they are living in a hermitage in the Himalayas. Vidura predeceases them and Sanjaya on Dhritarashtra's bidding goes to live in the higher Himalayas.
16	Mausala Parva (The Book of the Clubs)	96	The materialisation of Gandhari's curse, i.e., the infighting between the Yadavas with maces (*mausala*) and the eventual destruction of the Yadavas.
17	Mahaprasthanika Parva (The Book of the Great Journey)	97	The great journey of Yudhishthira, his brothers and his wife Draupadi across the whole country and finally their ascent of the great Himalayas where each Pandava falls except for Yudhishthira.

18	Svargarohana Parva (The Book of the Ascent to Heaven)	98	Yudhishthira's final test and the return of the Pandavas to the spiritual world (*svarga*).
khila	Harivamsa Parva (The Book of the Genealogy of Hari)	99–100	This is an addendum to the 18 books, and covers those parts of the life of Krishna which is not covered in the 18 parvas of the *Mahabharata*.

Historical context

The historicity of the Kurukshetra War is unclear. Many historians estimate the date of the Kurukshetra war to Iron Age India of the 10th century BCE.[177] The setting of the epic has a historical precedent in Iron Age (Vedic) India, where the Kuru kingdom was the center of political power during roughly 1200 to 800 BCE.[178] A dynastic conflict of the period could have been the inspiration for the *Jaya*, the foundation on which the Mahābhārata corpus was built, with a climactic battle eventually coming to be viewed as an epochal event.

Puranic literature presents genealogical lists associated with the Mahābhārata narrative. The evidence of the Puranas is of two kinds. Of the first kind, there is the direct statement that there were 1015 (or 1050) years between the birth of Parikshit (Arjuna's grandson) and the accession of Mahapadma Nanda (400-329 BCE), which would yield an estimate of about 1400 BCE for the Bharata battle.[179] However, this would imply improbably long reigns on average for the kings listed in the genealogies.[180] Of the second kind are analyses of parallel genealogies in the Puranas between the times of Adhisimakrishna (Parikshit's great-grandson) and Mahapadma Nanda. Pargiter accordingly estimated 26 generations by averaging 10 different dynastic lists and, assuming 18 years for the average duration of a reign, arrived at an estimate of 850 BCE for Adhisimakrishna, and thus approximately 950 BCE for the Bharata battle.[181]

B. B. Lal used the same approach with a more conservative assumption of the average reign to estimate a date of 836 BCE, and correlated this with archaeological evidence from Painted Grey Ware (PGW) sites, the association being strong between PGW artifacts and places mentioned in the epic.[182] John Keay confirm this and also gives 950 BCE for the Bharata battle.

Attempts to date the events using methods of archaeoastronomy have produced, depending on which passages are chosen and how they are interpreted, estimates ranging from the late 4th to the mid-2nd millennium BCE.[183] The late 4th-millennium date has a precedent in the calculation of the Kaliyuga epoch, based on planetary conjunctions, by Aryabhata (6th century). Aryabhata's date of 18 February 3102 BCE for Mahābhārata war has become widespread in Indian tradition. Some sources mark this as the disappearance of Krishna from earth. The Aihole inscription of Pulikeshi II, dated to

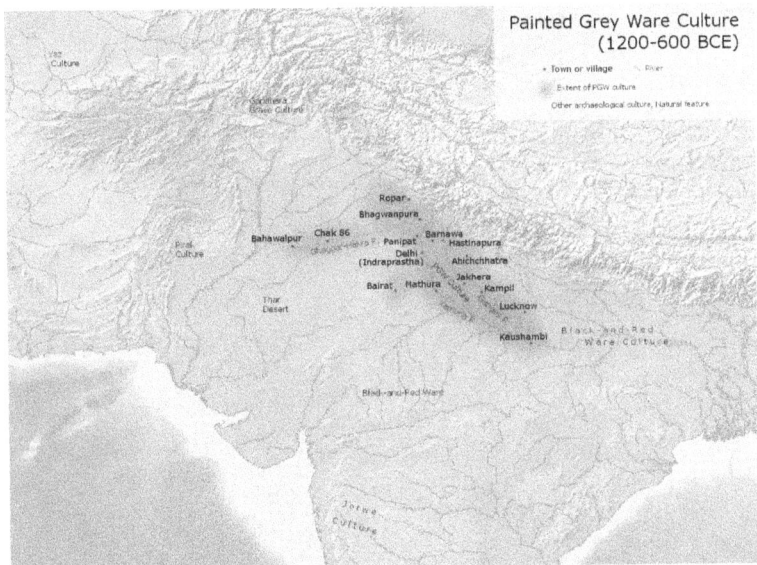

Figure 8: *Map of some Painted Grey Ware (PGW) sites.*

Saka 556 = 634 CE, claims that 3735 years have elapsed since the Bharata battle, putting the date of Mahābhārata war at 3137 BCE.[184] Another traditional school of astronomers and historians, represented by Vriddha-Garga, Varahamihira (author of the *Brhatsamhita*) and Kalhana (author of the *Rajatarangini*), place the Bharata war 653 years after the Kaliyuga epoch, corresponding to 2449 BCE.[185]

Synopsis

The core story of the work is that of a dynastic struggle for the throne of Hastinapura, the kingdom ruled by the Kuru clan. The two collateral branches of the family that participate in the struggle are the Kaurava and the Pandava. Although the Kaurava is the senior branch of the family, Duryodhana, the eldest Kaurava, is younger than Yudhishthira, the eldest Pandava. Both Duryodhana and Yudhishthira claim to be first in line to inherit the throne.

The struggle culminates in the great battle of Kurukshetra, in which the Pandavas are ultimately victorious. The battle produces complex conflicts of kinship and friendship, instances of family loyalty and duty taking precedence over what is right, as well as the converse.

The Mahābhārata itself ends with the death of Krishna, and the subsequent end of his dynasty and ascent of the Pandava brothers to heaven. It also marks

Figure 9: *Ganesha writing the Mahabharata*

the beginning of the Hindu age of Kali Yuga, the fourth and final age of humankind, in which great values and noble ideas have crumbled, and people are heading towards the complete dissolution of right action, morality and virtue.

The older generations

King Janamejaya's ancestor Shantanu, the king of Hastinapura, has a short-lived marriage with the goddess Ganga and has a son, Devavrata (later to be called Bhishma, a great warrior), who becomes the heir apparent. Many years later, when King Shantanu goes hunting, he sees Satyavati, the daughter of the chief of fisherman, and asks her father for her hand. Her father refuses to consent to the marriage unless Shantanu promises to make any future son of Satyavati the king upon his death. To resolve his father's dilemma, Devavrata agrees to relinquish his right to the throne. As the fisherman is not sure about the prince's children honouring the promise, Devavrata also takes a vow of lifelong celibacy to guarantee his father's promise.

Shantanu has two sons by Satyavati, Chitrāngada and Vichitravirya. Upon Shantanu's death, Chitrangada becomes king. He lives a very short uneventful life and dies. Vichitravirya, the younger son, rules Hastinapura. Meanwhile, the King of Kāśī arranges a swayamvara for his three daughters, neglecting to invite the royal family of Hastinapur. In order to arrange the marriage of young

Figure 10: *Shantanu woos Satyavati, the fisherwoman. Painting by Raja Ravi Varma.*

Vichitravirya, Bhishma attends the swayamvara of the three princesses Amba, Ambika and Ambalika, uninvited, and proceeds to abduct them. Ambika and Ambalika consent to be married to Vichitravirya.

The oldest princess Amba, however, informs Bhishma that she wishes to marry king of Shalva whom Bhishma defeated at their swayamvara. Bhishma lets her leave to marry king of Shalva, but Shalva refuses to marry her, still smarting at his humiliation at the hands of Bhishma. Amba then returns to marry Bhishma but he refuses due to his vow of celibacy. Amba becomes enraged and becomes Bhishma's bitter enemy, holding him responsible for her plight. Later she is reborn to King Drupada as Shikhandi (or Shikhandini) and causes Bhishma's fall, with the help of Arjuna, in the battle of Kurukshetra.

The Pandava and Kaurava princes

When Vichitravirya dies young without any heirs, Satyavati asks her first son Vyasa to father children with the widows. The eldest, Ambika, shuts her eyes when she sees him, and so her son Dhritarashtra is born blind. Ambalika turns pale and bloodless upon seeing him, and thus her son Pandu is born pale and unhealthy (the term Pandu may also mean 'jaundiced'). Due to the physical challenges of the first two children, Satyavati asks Vyasa to try once again.

Figure 11: *Draupadi with her five husbands - the Pandavas. The central figure is Yudhishthira; the two on the bottom are Bhima and Arjuna. Nakula and Sahadeva, the twins, are standing. Painting by Raja Ravi Varma, c. 1900.*

However, Ambika and Ambalika send their maid instead, to Vyasa's room. Vyasa fathers a third son, Vidura, by the maid. He is born healthy and grows up to be one of the wisest characters in the *Mahabharata*. He serves as Prime Minister (Mahamantri or Mahatma) to King Pandu and King Dhritarashtra.

When the princes grow up, Dhritarashtra is about to be crowned king by Bhishma when Vidura intervenes and uses his knowledge of politics to assert that a blind person cannot be king. This is because a blind man cannot control and protect his subjects. The throne is then given to Pandu because of Dhritarashtra's blindness. Pandu marries twice, to Kunti and Madri. Dhritarashtra marries Gandhari, a princess from Gandhara, who blindfolds herself so that she may feel the pain that her husband feels. Her brother Shakuni is enraged by this and vows to take revenge on the Kuru family. One day, when Pandu is relaxing in the forest, he hears the sound of a wild animal. He shoots an arrow in the direction of the sound. However the arrow hits the sage Kindama, who curses him that if he engages in a sexual act, he will die. Pandu then retires to the forest along with his two wives, and his brother Dhritarashtra rules thereafter, despite his blindness.

Pandu's older queen Kunti, however, had been given a boon by Sage Durvasa that she could invoke any god using a special mantra. Kunti uses this boon to ask Dharma the God of justice, Vayu the god of the wind, and Indra the lord of the heavens for sons. She gives birth to three sons, Yudhishthira, Bhima, and Arjuna, through these gods. Kunti shares her mantra with the younger queen Madri, who bears the twins Nakula and Sahadeva through the Ashwini twins. However, Pandu and Madri indulge in sex, and Pandu dies. Madri Commits Sati out of remorse. Kunti raises the five brothers, who are from then on usually referred to as the Pandava brothers.

Dhritarashtra has a hundred sons through Gandhari, all born after the birth of Yudhishthira. These are the Kaurava brothers, the eldest being Duryodhana, and the second Dushasana. Other Kaurava brothers were Vikarna and Sukarna. The rivalry and enmity between them and the Pandava brothers, from their youth and into manhood, leads to the Kurukshetra war.

Lakshagraha (the house of lac)

After the deaths of their mother (Madri) and father (Pandu), the Pandavas and their mother Kunti return to the palace of Hastinapur. Yudhishthira is made Crown Prince by Dhritarashtra, under considerable pressure from his courtiers. Dhritarashtra wanted his own son Duryodhana to become king and lets his ambition get in the way of preserving justice.

Shakuni, Duryodhana and Dusasana plot to get rid of the Pandavas. Shakuni calls the architect Purochana to build a palace out of flammable materials like lac and ghee. He then arranges for the Pandavas and the Queen Mother Kunti to stay there, with the intention of setting it alight. However, the Pandavas are warned by their wise uncle, Vidura, who sends them a miner to dig a tunnel. They are able to escape to safety and go into hiding. Back at Hastinapur, the Pandavas and Kunti are presumed dead.

Marriage to Draupadi

Whilst they were in hiding the Pandavas learn of a swayamvara which is taking place for the hand of the Pāñcāla princess Draupadī. The Pandavas enter the competition in disguise as Brahmins. The task is to string a mighty steel bow and shoot a target on the ceiling, which is the eye of a moving artificial fish, while looking at its reflection in oil below. Most of the princes fail, many being unable to lift the bow. Arjuna succeeds however. The Pandavas return home and inform their mother that Arjuna has won a competition and to look at what they have brought back. Without looking, Kunti asks them to share whatever it is Arjuna has won among themselves. On explaining the previous life of Draupadi, she ends up being the wife of all five brothers.

Figure 12: *Arjuna piercing the eye of the fish as depicted in Chennakesava Temple built by Hoysala Empire*

Indraprastha

After the wedding, the Pandava brothers are invited back to Hastinapura. The Kuru family elders and relatives negotiate and broker a split of the kingdom, with the Pandavas obtaining a new territory. Yudhishthira has a new capital built for this territory at Indraprastha. Neither the Pandava nor Kaurava sides are happy with the arrangement however.

Shortly after this, Arjuna elopes with and then marries Krishna's sister, Subhadra. Yudhisthra wishes to establish his position as king; he seeks Krishna's advice. Krishna advises him, and after due preparation and the elimination of some opposition, Yudhishthira carries out the *rājasūya yagna* ceremony; he is thus recognised as pre-eminent among kings.

The Pandavas have a new palace built for them, by Maya the Danava. They invite their Kaurava cousins to Indraprastha. Duryodhana walks round the palace, and mistakes a glossy floor for water, and will not step in. After being told of his error, he then sees a pond, and assumes it is not water and falls in. Bhima, Arjun, the twins and the servants laugh at him. In popular adaptations, this insult is wrongly attributed to Draupadi, even though in the Sanskrit epic, it was the Pandavas (except Yudhisthira) who had insulted Duryodhana. Enraged

Figure 13: *Draupadi humiliated*

by the insult, and jealous at seeing the wealth of the Pandavas, Duryodhana decides to host a dice-game at Shakuni's suggestion.

The dice game

Shakuni, Duryodhana's uncle, now arranges a dice game, playing against Yudhishthira with loaded dice. Yudhishthira loses all his wealth, then his kingdom. He then even gambles his brothers, himself, and finally his wife into servitude. The jubilant Kauravas insult the Pandavas in their helpless state and even try to disrobe Draupadi in front of the entire court, but her honour is saved by Krishna who miraculously creates lengths of cloth to replace the ones being removed.

Dhritarashtra, Bhishma, and the other elders are aghast at the situation, but Duryodhana is adamant that there is no place for two crown princes in Hastinapura. Against his wishes Dhritarashtra orders for another dice game. The Pandavas are required to go into exile for 12 years, and in the 13th year must remain hidden. If discovered by the Kauravas, they will be forced into exile for another 12 years.

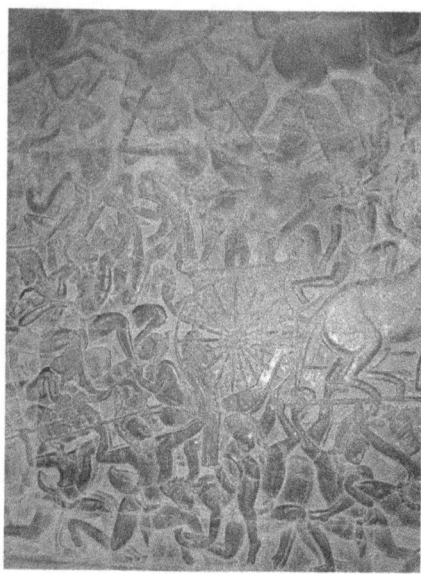

Figure 14: *A scene from the Mahābhārata war, Angkor Wat: A black stone relief depicting a number of men wearing a crown and a dhoti, fighting with spears, swords and bows. A chariot with half the horse out of the frame is seen in the middle.*

Exile and return

The Pandavas spend thirteen years in exile; many adventures occur during this time. They also prepare alliances for a possible future conflict. They spend their final year in disguise in the court of Virata, and are discovered just after the end of the year.

At the end of their exile, they try to negotiate a return to Indraprastha with Krishna as their emissary. However, this fails, as Duryodhana objects that they were discovered while in hiding, and that no return of their kingdom was agreed. War becomes inevitable.

The battle at Kurukshetra

The two sides summon vast armies to their help and line up at Kurukshetra for a war. The kingdoms of Panchala, Dwaraka, Kasi, Kekaya, Magadha, Matsya, Chedi, Pandyas, Telinga, and the Yadus of Mathura and some other clans like the Parama Kambojas were allied with the Pandavas. The allies of the Kauravas included the kings of Pragjyotisha, Anga, Kekaya, Sindhudesa (including Sindhus, Sauviras and Sivis), Mahishmati, Avanti in Madhyadesa, Madra,

Figure 15: *Gandhari, blindfolded, supporting Dhrtarashtra and following Kunti when Dhrtarashtra became old and infirm and retired to the forest. A miniature painting from a 16th-century manuscript of part of the Razmnama, a Persian translation of the Mahabharata*

Gandhara, Bahlika people, Kambojas and many others. Before war being declared, Balarama had expressed his unhappiness at the developing conflict and leaves to go on pilgrimage; thus he does not take part in the battle itself. Krishna takes part in a non-combatant role, as charioteer for Arjuna.

Before the battle, Arjuna noticing that the opposing army includes his own kith and kin, including his great grandfather Bhishma and his teacher Drona, has grave doubts about the fight and falls into despair.At this time,Krishna reminds him of duty as a Kshatriya to fight for his just cause in the famous Bhagavad Gita section of the epic.

Though initially sticking to chivalrous notions of warfare, both sides soon adopt dishonourable tactics. At the end of the 18-day battle, only the Pandavas, Satyaki, Kripa, Ashwatthama, Kritavarma, Yuyutsu and Krishna survive.

The end of the Pandavas

After "seeing" the carnage, Gandhari, who had lost all her sons, curses Krishna to be a witness to a similar annihilation of his family, for though divine and capable of stopping the war, he had not done so. Krishna accepts the curse, which bears fruit 36 years later.

The Pandavas, who had ruled their kingdom meanwhile, decide to renounce everything. Clad in skins and rags they retire to the Himalaya and climb towards heaven in their bodily form. A stray dog travels with them. One by one the brothers and Draupadi fall on their way. As each one stumbles, Yudhishthira gives the rest the reason for their fall (Draupadi was partial to Arjuna, Nakula and Sahadeva were vain and proud of their looks, and Bhima and Arjuna were proud of their strength and archery skills, respectively). Only the virtuous Yudhishthira, who had tried everything to prevent the carnage, and the dog remain. The dog reveals himself to be the god Yama (also known as Yama Dharmaraja), and then takes him to the underworld where he sees his siblings and wife. After explaining the nature of the test, Yama takes Yudhishthira back to heaven and explains that it was necessary to expose him to the underworld because (Rajyante narakam dhruvam) any ruler has to visit the underworld at least once. Yama then assures him that his siblings and wife would join him in heaven after they had been exposed to the underworld for measures of time according to their vices.

Arjuna's grandson Parikshit rules after them and dies bitten by a snake. His furious son, Janamejaya, decides to perform a snake sacrifice (*sarpasattra*) in order to destroy the snakes. It is at this sacrifice that the tale of his ancestors is narrated to him.

The reunion

The Mahābhārata mentions that Karna, the Pandavas, Draupadi and Dhritarashtra's sons eventually ascended to svarga and "attained the state of the gods" and banded together — "serene and free from anger."

Themes

Just war

The *Mahābhārata* offers one of the first instances of theorizing about *dharmayuddha*, "just war", illustrating many of the standards that would be debated later across the world. In the story, one of five brothers asks if the suffering caused by war can ever be justified. A long discussion ensues between the siblings, establishing criteria like *proportionality* (chariots cannot attack cavalry, only other chariots; no attacking people in distress), *just means* (no poisoned or barbed arrows), *just cause* (no attacking out of rage), and fair treatment of captives and the wounded.

Figure 16: *The Pandavas and Krishna in an act of the Javanese wayang wong performance*

Versions, translations, and derivative works

Critical Edition

Between 1919 and 1966, scholars at the Bhandarkar Oriental Research Institute, Pune, compared the various manuscripts of the epic from India and abroad and produced the *Critical Edition* of the *Mahabharata*, on 13,000 pages in 19 volumes, followed by the *Harivamsha* in another two volumes and six index volumes. This is the text that is usually used in current Mahābhārata studies for reference.[186] This work is sometimes called the "Pune" or "Poona" edition of the *Mahabharata*.

Regional versions

Many regional versions of the work developed over time, mostly differing only in minor details, or with verses or subsidiary stories being added. These include the Tamil street theatre, terukkuttu and kattaikkuttu, the plays of which use themes from the Tamil language versions of *Mahabharata*, focusing on Draupadi.

Outside the Indian subcontinent, in Indonesia, a version was developed in ancient Java as Kakawin Bhāratayuddha in the 11th century under the patronage of King Dharmawangsa (990–1016) and later it spread to the neighboring island of Bali, which remains a Hindu majority island today. It has become the fertile source for Javanese literature, dance drama (wayang wong), and wayang shadow puppet performances. This Javanese version of the Mahābhārata differs slightly from the original Indian version. For example, Draupadi is only wed to Yudhishthira, not to all the Pandava brothers; this might demonstrate ancient Javanese opposition to polyandry.Wikipedia:Citation needed The author later added some female characters to be wed to the Pandavas, for example, Arjuna is described as having many wives and consorts next to Subhadra. Another difference is that Shikhandini does not change her sex and remains a woman, to be wed to Arjuna, and takes the role of a warrior princess during the war.Wikipedia:Citation needed Another twist is that Gandhari is described as antagonistic character who hates the Pandavas: her hate is out of jealousy because during Gandhari's swayamvara, she was in love with Pandu but was later wed to his blind elder brother instead, whom she did not love, so she blindfolded herself as protest.Wikipedia:Citation needed Another notable difference is the inclusion of the Punakawans, the clown servants of the main characters in the storyline. These characters include Semar, Petruk, Gareng and Bagong, who are much-loved by Indonesian audiences.Wikipedia:Citation needed There are also some spin-off episodes developed in ancient Java, such as Arjunawiwaha composed in 11th century.

A Kawi version of the *Mahabharata*, of which eight of the eighteen *parvas* survive, is found on the Indonesian island of Bali. It has been translated into English by Dr. I. Gusti Putu Phalgunadi.Wikipedia:Citation needed

Translations

A Persian translation of *Mahabharta*, titled *Razmnameh*, was produced at Akbar's orders, by Faizi and 'Abd al-Qadir Bada'uni in the 18th century.

The first complete English translation was the Victorian prose version by Kisari Mohan Ganguli,[187] published between 1883 and 1896 (Munshiram Manoharlal Publishers) and by M. N. Dutt (Motilal Banarsidass Publishers). Most critics consider the translation by Ganguli to be faithful to the original text. The complete text of Ganguli's translation is in the public domain and is available online.[188]

Another English prose translation of the full epic, based on the *Critical Edition*, is in progress, published by University Of Chicago Press. It was initiated by Indologist J. A. B. van Buitenen (books 1–5) and, following a 20-year hiatus caused by the death of van Buitenen, is being continued by D. Gitomer of DePaul University (book 6), J. L. Fitzgerald of Brown University (books 11–13) and Wendy Doniger of the University of Chicago (books 14–18).

An early poetry translation by Romesh Chunder Dutt and published in 1898 condenses the main themes of the Mahābhārata into English verse.[189] A later poetic "transcreation" (author's own description) of the full epic into English,

Figure 17: *Bhishma on his death-bed of arrows with the Pandavas and Krishna. Folio from the Razmnama (1761–1763), Persian translation of the Mahabharata, commissioned by Mughal emperor Akbar. The Pandavas are dressed in Persian armour and robes.*

done by the poet P. Lal, is complete, and in 2005 began being published by Writers Workshop, Calcutta. The P. Lal translation is a non-rhyming verse-by-verse rendering, and is the only edition in any language to include all slokas in all recensions of the work (not just those in the *Critical Edition*). The completion of the publishing project is scheduled for 2010.Wikipedia:Manual of Style/Dates and numbers#Chronological items Sixteen of the eighteen volumes are now available.

A project to translate the full epic into English prose, translated by various hands, began to appear in 2005 from the Clay Sanskrit Library, published by New York University Press. The translation is based not on the *Critical Edition* but on the version known to the commentator Nīlakaṇṭha. Currently available are 15 volumes of the projected 32-volume edition.

Indian economist Bibek Debroy has also begun an unabridged English translation in ten volumes. Volume 1: Adi Parva[190] was published in March 2010.

Many condensed versions, abridgements and novelistic prose retellings of the complete epic have been published in English, including works by Ramesh

Menon, William Buck, R. K. Narayan, C. Rajagopalachari, K. M. Munshi, Krishna Dharma, Romesh C. Dutt, Bharadvaja Sarma, John D. Smith and Sharon Maas.

Derivative literature

Bhasa, the 2nd- or 3rd-century CE Sanskrit playwright, wrote two plays on episodes in the Marabharata, *Urubhanga* (Broken Thigh), about the fight between Duryodhana and Bhima, while *Madhyamavyayoga* (The Middle One) set around Bhima and his son, Ghatotkacha. The first important play of 20th century was *Andha Yug* (*The Blind Epoch*), by Dharamvir Bharati, which came in 1955, found in *Mahabharat*, both an ideal source and expression of modern predicaments and discontent. Starting with Ebrahim Alkazi it was staged by numerous directors. V. S. Khandekar's Marathi novel, *Yayati* (1960) and Girish Karnad's debut play *Yayati* (1961) are based on the story of King Yayati found in the *Mahabharat*. Bengali writer and playwright, Buddhadeva Bose wrote three plays set in Mahabharat, *Anamni Angana*, *Pratham Partha* and *Kalsandhya*.[191] Pratibha Ray wrote an award winning novel entitled Yajnaseni from Draupadi's perspective in 1984. Later, Chitra Banerjee Divakaruni wrote a similar novel entitled *The Palace of Illusions: A Novel* in 2008. Gujarati poet Chinu Modi has written long narrative poetry *Bahuk* based on character Bahuka. Krishna Udayasankar, a Singapore-based Indian author has written several novels which are modern-day retellings of the epic, most notably the Aryavarta Chronicles Series. Suman Pokhrel wrote a solo play based on Ray's novel by personalizing and taking Draupadi alone in the scene.

Amar Chitra Katha published a 1,260 page comic book version of the *Mahabharata*.

In film and television

In Indian cinema, several film versions of the epic have been made, dating back to 1920.[192] In Telugu film Daana Veera Soora Karna (1977) directed by and starring N. T. Rama Rao depicts Karna as the lead character. The Mahābhārata was also reinterpreted by Shyam Benegal in Kalyug. Prakash Jha directed 2010 film Raajneeti was partially inspired by the *Mahabharata*. A 2013 animated adaptation holds the record for India's most expensive animated film.

In the late 1980s, the *Mahabharat* TV series, directed by Ravi Chopra,[193] was televised on India's national television (Doordarshan). The same year as *Mahabharat* was being shown on Doordarshan, that same company's other television show, *Bharat Ek Khoj*, also directed by Shyam Benegal, showed a 2-episode abbreviation of the *Mahabharata*, drawing from various interpretations of the work, be they sung, danced, or staged. In the Western world,

Figure 18: *Krishna as portrayed in Yakshagana from Karnataka which is based largely on stories of Mahabharata*

a well-known presentation of the epic is Peter Brook's nine-hour play, which premiered in Avignon in 1985, and its five-hour movie version *The Mahābhārata* (1989).[194] In the late 2013 Mahabharat was televised on STAR Plus. It was produced by Swastik Productions Pvt.

Uncompleted projects on the Mahābhārata include a ones by Rajkumar Santoshi, and a theaterical adaptation planned by Satyajit Ray.

Jain version

Jain versions of Mahābhārata can be found in the various Jain texts like *Harivamsapurana* (the story of Harivamsa) *Trisastisalakapurusa Caritra* (Hagiography of 63 Illustrious persons), *Pandavacaritra* (lives of Pandavas) and *Pandavapurana* (stories of Pandavas).[195] From the earlier canonical literature, *Antakrddaaśāh* (8th cannon) and *Vrisnidasa* (*upangagama* or secondary canon) contain the stories of Neminatha (22nd Tirthankara), Krishna and Balarama.[196] Prof. Padmanabh Jaini notes that, unlike in the Hindu Puranas, the names Baladeva and Vasudeva are not restricted to Balarama and Krishna in Jain puranas. Instead they serve as names of two distinct class of mighty brothers, who appear nine times in each half of time cycles of the Jain cosmology and rule the half the earth as half-chakravartins. Jaini traces the origin

Figure 19: *Depiction of wedding procession of Lord Neminatha. The enclosure shows the animals that are to be slaughtered for food for weddings. Overcome with Compassion for animals, Neminatha refused to marry and renounced his kingdom to become a Shramana*

of this list of brothers to the Jinacharitra by Bhadrabahu swami (4th–3rd century BCE).[197] According to Jain cosmology Balarama, Krishna and Jarasandha are the ninth and the last set of Baladeva, Vasudeva, and Partivasudeva.[198] The main battle is not the Mahabharata, but the fight between Krishna and Jarasandha (who is killed by Krishna). Ultimately, the Pandavas and Balarama take renunciation as Jain monks and are reborn in heavens, while on the other hand Krishna and Jarasandha are reborn in hell.[199] In keeping with the law of karma, Krishna is reborn in hell for his exploits (sexual and violent) while Jarasandha for his evil ways. Prof. Jaini admits a possibility that perhaps because of his popularity, the Jain authors were keen to rehabilitate Krishna. The Jain texts predict that after his karmic term in hell is over sometime during the next half time-cycle, Krishna will be reborn as a Jain Tirthankara and attain liberation. Krishna and Balrama are shown as contemporaries and cousins of 22nd Tirthankara, Neminatha. According to this story, Krishna arranged young Neminath's marriage with Rajamati, the daughter of Ugrasena, but Neminatha, empathizing with the animals which were to be slaughtered for the marriage feast, left the procession suddenly and renounced the world.[200]

Kuru family tree

This shows the line of royal and family succession, not necessarily the parentage. See the notes below for detail.

Key to Symbols

- Male: *blue border*
- Female: *red border*
- Pandavas: *green box*
- Kauravas: *yellow box*

Notes

- **a**: Shantanu was a king of the Kuru dynasty or kingdom, and was some generations removed from any ancestor called Kuru. His marriage to Ganga preceded his marriage to Satyavati.
- **b**: Pandu and Dhritarashtra were fathered by Vyasa in the *niyoga* tradition after Vichitravirya's death. Dhritarashtra, Pandu and Vidura were the sons of Vyasa with Ambika, Ambalika and a maid servant respectively.
- **c**: Karna was born to Kunti through her invocation of Surya, before her marriage to Pandu.
- **d**: Yudhishthira, Bhima, Arjuna, Nakula and Sahadeva were acknowledged sons of Pandu but were begotten by the invocation by Kunti and Madri of various deities. They all married Draupadi (not shown in tree).
- **e**: Duryodhana and his siblings were born at the same time, and they were of the same generation as their Pandava cousins.
- **f** : Although the succession after the Pandavas was through the descendants of Arjuna and Subhadra, it was Yudhishthira and Draupadi who occupied the throne of Hastinapura after the great battle.

The birth order of siblings is correctly shown in the family tree (from left to right), except for Vyasa and Bhishma whose birth order is not described, and Vichitravirya and Chitrangada who were born after them. The fact that Ambika and Ambalika are sisters is not shown in the family tree. The birth of Duryodhana took place after the birth of Karna, Yudhishthira and Bhima, but before the birth of the remaining Pandava brothers.

Some siblings of the characters shown here have been left out for clarity; these include Chitrāngada, the eldest brother of Vichitravirya. Vidura, half-brother to Dhritarashtra and Pandu.

Cultural influence

In the *Bhagavad Gita*, Krishna explains to Arjuna his duties as a warrior and prince and elaborates on different Yogic and Vedantic philosophies, with examples and analogies. This has led to the Gita often being described as a concise guide to Hindu philosophy and a practical, self-contained guide to life.[201] In more modern times, Swami Vivekananda, Bal Gangadhar Tilak, Mahatma Gandhi and many others used the text to help inspire the Indian independence movement.[202,203]

Various modern day television shows and novels have taken inspiration from the Mahabharata.

Editions

- *The Mahabharata: Complete and Unabridged* (set of 10 volumes) by Bibek Debroy, Penguin Books India.
- *The Mahābhārata of Vyasa* (18 volumes), transcreated from Sanskrit by P. Lal, Writers Workshop.

Sources

- Badrinath, Chaturvedi. *The Mahābhārata : An Inquiry in the Human Condition*, New Delhi, Orient Longman (2006)
- Bandyopadhyaya, Jayantanuja (2008). *Class and Religion in Ancient India*[204]. Anthem Press.
- Basham, A. L. (1954). *The Wonder That Was India: A Survey of the Culture of the Indian Sub-Continent Before The Coming of the Muslims*. New York: Grove Press.<templatestyles src="Module:Citation/CS1/styles.css"></templatestyles>
- Bhasin, R.V. *"Mahabharata"* published by National Publications, India, 2007.
- J. Brockington. *The Sanskrit Epics*[205], Leiden (1998).
- Buitenen, Johannes Adrianus Bernardus (1978). *The Mahābhārata*[206]. 3 volumes (translation / publication incomplete due to his death). University of Chicago Press.
- Chaitanya, Krishna (K.K. Nair). *The Mahabharata, A Literary Study*, Clarion Books, New Delhi 1985.
- Gupta, S.P. and Ramachandran, K.S. (ed.). *Mahabharata: myth and reality*. Agam Prakashan, New Delhi 1976.
- Hiltebeitel, Alf. *The Ritual of Battle, Krishna in the Mahabharata*, SUNY Press, New York 1990.
- Hopkins, E. W. *The Great Epic of India*[207], New York (1901).

- Jyotirmayananda, Swami. *Mysticism of the Mahabharata*, Yoga Research Foundation, Miami 1993.
- Katz, Ruth Cecily *Arjuna in the Mahabharata*, University of South Carolina Press, Columbia 1989.
- Keay, John (2000). *India: A History*[208]. Grove Press. ISBN 978-0-8021-3797-5.<templatestyles src="Module:Citation/CS1/styles.css"></templatestyles>
- Majumdar, R. C. (general editor) (1951). *The History and Culture of the Indian People: (Volume 1) The Vedic Age*. London: George Allen & Unwin Ltd.<templatestyles src="Module:Citation/CS1/styles.css"></templatestyles>
- Lerner, Paule. *Astrological Key in Mahabharata*, David White (trans.) Motilal Banarsidass, New Delhi 1988.
- Mallory, J. P (2005). *In Search of the Indo-Europeans*. Thames & Hudson. <templatestyles src="Module:Citation/CS1/styles.css" />ISBN 0-500-27616-1
- Mehta, M. *The problem of the double introduction to the Mahabharata*, JAOS 93 (1973), 547–550.
- Minkowski, C.Z. *Janamehayas Sattra and Ritual Structure*, JAOS 109 (1989), 410–420.
- Minkowski, C.Z. 'Snakes, *Sattras* and the Mahabharata', in: *Essays on the Mahabharata*, ed. A. Sharma, Leiden (1991), 384–400.
- Oldenberg, Hermann. *Zur Geschichte der Altindischen Prosa*, Berlin (1917)
- Oberlies, Th. 'The Counsels of the Seer Narada: Ritual on and under the Surface of the Mahabharata', in: *New methods in the research of epic*[209] (ed. H. L. C. Tristram), Freiburg (1998).
- Oldenberg, H. *Das Mahabharata*, Göttingen (1922).
- Pāṇini. *Ashtādhyāyī*. Book 4[210]. Translated by Chandra Vasu. Benares, 1896. (in Sanskrit)(in English)
- Pargiter, F.E. *Ancient Indian Historical Tradition*, London 1922. Repr. Motilal Banarsidass 1997.
- Sattar, Arshia (transl.) (1996). *The Rāmāyaṇa by Vālmīki*. Viking. p. 696. ISBN 978-0-14-029866-6.<templatestyles src="Module:Citation/CS1/styles.css"></templatestyles>
- Sukthankar, Vishnu S. and Shrimant Balasaheb Pant Pratinidhi (1933). *The Mahabharata: for the first time critically edited*. Bhandarkar Oriental Research Institute.
- Sullivan, Bruce M. *Seer of the Fifth Veda, Krsna Dvaipayana Vyasa in the Mahabharata*, Motilal Banarsidass, New Delhi 1999.
- Sutton, Nicholas. *Religious Doctrines in the Mahabharata*[211], Motilal Banarsidass, New Delhi 2000.

- Utgikar, N. B. *The mention of the Mahābhārata in the Ashvalayana Grhya Sutra*, Proceedings and Transactions of the All-India Oriental Conference, Poona (1919), vol. 2, Poona (1922), 46–61.
- Vaidya, R.V. *A Study of Mahabharat; A Research*, Poona, A.V.G. Prakashan, 1967
- Witzel, Michael, *Epics, Khilas and Puranas: Continuities and Ruptures*, Proceedings of the Third Dubrovnik International Conference on the Sanskrit Epics and Puranas, ed. P. Koskiallio, Zagreb (2005), 21–80.

External links

 Sanskrit Wikisourcehas original text related to this article: *Mahabharata*

 Wikiquote has quotations related to: *Mahabharata*

 Wikisourcehas original text related to this article: **The Mahabharat**

 Wikimedia Commons has media related to *Mahabharata*.

- Mahābhārata online[212]
- All volumes in 12 PDF-files[213] (Holybooks.com, 181 MB in total)
- Reading Suggestions, J. L. Fitzgerald, Das Professor of Sanskrit, Department of Classics, Brown University[214]

Ramayana

Ramayana	
 Rama with his wife Sita and brother Lakshmana during exile in forest, manuscript, ca. 1780	
Information	
Religion	Hinduism
Author	Valmiki
Language	Sanskrit
Verses	24,000

Part of a series on
Hinduism
ॐ
• Hindu • History

- Glossary of Hinduism terms
- ॐ Hinduism portal
- v
- t
- e[215]

Ramayana (/rɑːˈmɑːjənə/;[216] Sanskrit: रामायणम्, *Rāmāyaṇam* [rɑːˈmɑːjəɳəm]) is an ancient Indian epic poem which narrates the struggle of the divine prince Rama to rescue his wife Sita from the demon king Ravana. Along with the *Mahabharata*, it forms the Hindu Itihasa.

The epic, traditionally ascribed to the Hindu sage Valmiki, narrates the life of Rama, the legendary prince of the Kosala Kingdom. It follows his fourteen-year exile to the forest from the kingdom, by his father King Dasharatha, on request of his second wife Kaikeyi. His travels across forests in India with his wife Sita and brother Lakshmana, the kidnapping of his wife by Ravana, the demon king of Lanka, resulting in a war with him, and Rama's eventual return to Ayodhya to be crowned king.

There have been many attempts to unravel the epic's historical growth and compositional layers; various recent scholars' estimates for the earliest stage of the text range from the 7th to 4th centuries BCE, with later stages extending up to the 3rd century CE.

The *Ramayana* is one of the largest ancient epics in world literature. It consists of nearly 24,000 verses (mostly set in the Shloka meter), divided into seven Kandas and about 500 sargas (chapters). In Hindu tradition, it is considered to be the *adi-kavya* (first poem). It depicts the duties of relationships, portraying ideal characters like the ideal father, the ideal servant, the ideal brother, the ideal husband and the ideal king. *Ramayana* was an important influence on later Sanskrit poetry and Hindu life and culture. Like *Mahabharata*, *Ramayana* is not just a story: it presents the teachings of ancient Hindu sages in narrative allegory, interspersing philosophical and ethical elements. The characters Rama, Sita, Lakshmana, Bharata, Hanuman, Shatrughna, and Ravana are all fundamental to the cultural consciousness of India, Nepal, Sri Lanka and south-east Asian countries such as Thailand, Cambodia, Malaysia and Indonesia.

There are many versions of *Ramayana* in Indian languages, besides Buddhist, Sikh and Jain adaptations. There are also Cambodian, Indonesian, Filipino, Thai, Lao, Burmese and Malaysian versions of the tale.

Figure 20: *An artist's impression of Valmiki Muni composing the Ramayana*

Etymology

The name *Ramayana* is a tatpuruṣa compound of the name *Rāma*.

Textual History & Structure

According to Hindu tradition, and the *Ramayana* itself, the epic belongs to the genre of *itihasa* like *Mahabharata*. The definition of *itihāsa* is a narrative of past events (*purāvṛtta*) which includes teachings on the goals of human life. According to Hindu tradition, *Ramayana* takes place during a period of time known as Treta Yuga.[217]

In its extant form, Valmiki's *Ramayana* is an epic poem of some 24,000 verses. The text survives in several thousand partial and complete manuscripts, the oldest of which is a palm-leaf manuscript found in Nepal and dated to the 11th century CE. A Times of India report dated 18 December 2015 informs about the discovery of a 6th-century manuscript of the *Ramayana* at the Asiatic Society library, Kolkata. The *Ramayana* text has several regional renderings, recensions and sub recensions. Textual scholar Robert P. Goldman differentiates two major regional revisions: the northern (n) and the southern (s). Scholar Romesh Chunder Dutt writes that "the *Ramayana*, like the *Mahabharata*, is a growth of centuries, but the main story is more distinctly the creation of one mind."

There has been discussion as to whether the first and the last volumes (bala kandam and uttara kandam) of Valmiki's *Ramayana* were composed by the original author. Most Hindus still believe they are integral parts of the book, in spite of some style differences and narrative contradictions between these two volumes and the rest of the book.

Retellings include Kamban's *Ramavataram* in Tamil (c. 11th–12th century), Gona Budda Reddy's *Ramayanam* in Telugu (c. 13th century), Madhava Kandali's Saptakanda Ramayana in Assamese (c. 14th century), Krittibas Ojha's Krittivasi Ramayan (also known as *Shri Rama Panchali*) in Bengali (c. 15th century), Sarala Das' Vilanka Ramayana (c. 15th century) and Balaram Das' *Dandi Ramayana* (also known as the *Jagamohan Ramayana*) (c. 16th century) both in Odia, sant Eknath's Bhavarth Ramayan (c. 16th century) in Marathi, Tulsidas' Ramcharitamanas (c. 16th century) in Awadhi (which is an eastern form of Hindi) and Thunchaththu Ezhuthachan's Adhyathmaramayanam in Malayalam.

Period

Ramayana predates Mahabharata. However, the general cultural background of Ramayana is one of the post-urbanization periods of the eastern part of north India and Nepal, while Mahabharata reflects the Kuru areas west of this, from the Rigvedic to the late Vedic period.

By tradition, the text belongs to the Treta Yuga, second of the four eons (yuga) of Hindu chronology. Rama is said to have been born in the Treta yuga to king Dasharatha in the Ikshvaku dynasty.

The names of the characters (Rama, Sita, Dasharatha, Janaka, Vashista, Vishwamitra) are all known in late Vedic literature. However, nowhere in the surviving Vedic poetry is there a story similar to the Ramayana of Valmiki. According to the modern academic view, Vishnu, who, according to Bala Kanda, was incarnated as Rama, first came into prominence with the epics themselves and further, during the puranic period of the later 1st millennium CE. Also, in the epic Mahabharata, there is a version of Ramayana known as Ramopakhyana. This version is depicted as a narration to Yudhishthira.

Books two to six form the oldest portion of the epic, while the first and last books (Bala Kanda and Uttara Kanda, respectively) are later additions, as some style differences and narrative contradictions between these two volumes and the rest of the book. The author or authors of Bala Kanda and Ayodhya Kanda appear to be familiar with the eastern Gangetic basin region of northern India

Figure 21: *Rama (left third from top) depicted in the Dashavatara, the ten avatars of Vishnu. Painting from Jaipur, now at the Victoria and Albert Museum*

and with the Kosala, Mithila and Magadha regions during the period of the sixteen Mahajanapadas, based on the fact that the geographical and geopolitical data accords with what is known about the region.

Characters

Ikshvaku dynasty

- **Dasharatha** is king of Ayodhya and father of Rama. He has three queens, Kausalya, Kaikeyi and Sumitra, and three other sons: Bharata, and twins Lakshmana and Shatrughna. Kaikeyi, Dasharatha's favourite queen, forces him to make their son Bharata crown prince and send Rama into exile. Dasharatha dies heartbroken after Rama goes into exile.
- **Rama** is the main character of the tale. Portrayed as the seventh avatar of god Vishnu, he is the eldest and favourite son of Dasharatha, the king of Ayodhya and his Chief Queen, Kausalya. He is portrayed as the epitome of virtue. Dasharatha is forced by Kaikeyi to command Rama to relinquish his right to the throne for fourteen years and go into exile. Rama kills the evil demon Ravana, who abducted his wife Sita, and later returns to Ayodhya to form an ideal state.

Figure 22: *Rama seated with Sita, fanned by Lakshmana, while Hanuman pays his respects*

Figure 23: *Rama and the monkey chiefs*

- **Sita** is another of the tale's protagonists. She is a daughter of Mother Earth, adopted by King Janaka, and Rama's beloved wife. Rama went to Mithila and got a chance to marry her by breaking the Shiv Dhanush (bow) while trying to tie a knot to it in a competition organized by King Janaka of Mithila in Dhanusa. The competition was to find the most suitable husband for Sita and many princes from different states competed to win her. Sita is the avatara of goddess Lakshmi, the consort of Vishnu. Sita is portrayed as the epitome of female purity and virtue. She follows her husband into exile and is abducted by the demon king Ravana. She is imprisoned on the island of Lanka, until Rama rescues her by defeating Ravana. Later, she gives birth to twin boys Luv and Kusha.
- **Bharata** is the son of Dasharatha and Queen Kaikeyi. When he learns that his mother Kaikeyi has forced Rama into exile and caused Dasharatha to die brokenhearted, he storms out of the palace and goes in search of Rama in the forest. When Rama refuses to return from his exile to assume the throne, Bharata obtains Rama's sandals and places them on the throne as a gesture that Rama is the true king. Bharata then rules Ayodhya as the regent of Rama for the next fourteen years, staying outside the city of Ayodhya. He was married to Mandavi.
- **Lakshmana** is a younger brother of Rama, who chose to go into exile with him. He is the son of King Dasharatha and Queen Sumitra and twin of Shatrughna. Lakshmana is portrayed as an avatar of Shesha, the nāga associated with the god Vishnu. He spends his time protecting Sita and Rama, during which time he fights the demoness Surpanakha. He is forced to leave Sita, who was deceived by the demon Maricha into believing that Rama was in trouble. Sita is abducted by Ravana upon his leaving her. He was married to Sita's younger sister Urmila.
- **Shatrughna** is a son of Dasharatha and his third wife Queen Sumitra. He is the youngest brother of Rama and also the twin brother of Lakshmana. He was married to Shrutakirti.

Allies of Rama

Vanara

- **Hanuman** is a vanara belonging to the kingdom of Kishkindha. He is an ideal bhakta of Rama. He is born as son of Kesari, a Vanara king in Sumeru region and the goddess Añjanā. He plays an important part in locating Sita and in the ensuing battle. He is believed to live until our modern world.
- **Sugriva**, a vanara king who helped Rama regain Sita from Ravana. He had an agreement with Rama through which Vali – Sugriva's brother and king of Kishkindha – would be killed by Rama in exchange for Sugriva's

Figure 24: *The vanaras constructing the Rama Setu Bridge to Lanka, makaras and fish also aid the construction. A 9th century Prambanan bas-relief, Central Java, Indonesia.*

help in finding Sita. Sugriva ultimately ascends the throne of Kishkindha after the slaying of Vali and fulfills his promise by putting the Vanara forces at Rama's disposal.
- **Angada** is a vanara who helped Rama find his wife Sita and fight her abductor, Ravana, in Ramayana. He was son of Vali and Tara and nephew of Sugriva. Angada and Tara are instrumental in reconciling Rama and his brother, Lakshmana, with Sugriva after Sugriva fails to fulfill his promise to help Rama find and rescue his wife. Together they are able to convince Sugriva to honour his pledge to Rama instead of spending his time carousing and drinking.

Riksha

- **Jambavan/Jamvanta** is known as Riksharaj (King of the Rikshas). Rikshas are bears. In the epic Ramayana, Jambavantha helped Rama find his wife Sita and fight her abductor, Ravana. It is he who makes Hanuman realize his immense capabilities and encourages him to fly across the ocean to search for Sita in Lanka.

Griddha

- **Jatayu**, son of Aruṇa and nephew of Garuda. A demi-god who has the form of a vulture that tries to rescue Sita from Ravana. Jatayu fought valiantly with Ravana, but as Jatayu was very old, Ravana soon got the better of him. As Rama and Lakshmana chanced upon the stricken and dying Jatayu in their search for Sita, he informs them of the direction in which Ravana had gone.
- **Sampati**, son of Aruna, brother of Jatayu. Sampati's role proved to be instrumental in the search for Sita.

Rakshasa

- **Vibhishana**, youngest brother of Ravana. He was against the abduction of Sita and joined the forces of Rama when Ravana refused to return her. His intricate knowledge of Lanka was vital in the war and he was crowned king after the fall of Ravana.

Foes Of Rama

Rakshasas

- **Ravana**, a rakshasa, is the king of Lanka. He was son of a sage named Vishrava and daitya princess Kaikesi. After performing severe penance for ten thousand years he received a boon from the creator-god Brahma: he could henceforth not be killed by gods, demons, or spirits. He is portrayed as a powerful demon king who disturbs the penances of rishis. Vishnu incarnates as the human Rama to defeat him, thus circumventing the boon given by Brahma.
- **Indrajit** or **Meghnadha**, the eldest son of Ravana who twice defeated Rama and Lakshmana in battle, before succumbing to Lakshmana. An adept of the magical arts, he coupled his supreme fighting skills with various stratagems to inflict heavy losses on Vanara army before his death.
- **Kumbhakarna**, brother of Ravana, famous for his eating and sleeping. He would sleep for months at a time and would be extremely ravenous upon waking up, consuming anything set before him. His monstrous size and loyalty made him an important part of Ravana's army. During the war he decimated the Vanara army before Rama cut off his limbs and head.
- **Surpanakha**, Ravana's demoness sister who fell in love with Rama and had the magical power to take any form she wanted.

Vanara

- **Vali**, was king of Kishkindha, husband of Tara, a son of Indra, elder brother of Sugriva and father of Angada. Vali was famous for the boon that he had received, according to which anyone who fought him in single-combat lost half his strength to Vali, thereby making Vali invulnerable to any enemy. He was killed by Lord Rama, an Avatar of Vishnu.

Figure 25: *The marriage of the four sons of Dasharatha with the four daughters of Siradhvaja and Kushadhvaja Janakas. Rama and Sita, Lakshmana and Urmila, Bharata and Mandavi and Shatrughna with Shrutakirti.*

Synopsis

Bala Kanda

Dasharatha was the king of Ayodhya. He had three wives: Kaushalya, Kaikeyi and Sumitra. He was childless for a long time and anxious to produce an heir, so he performs a fire sacrifice known as *putra-kameshti yagya*. As a consequence, Rama is first born to Kaushalya, Bharata is born to Kaikeyi, Lakshmana and Shatrughna are born to Sumitra. These sons are endowed, to various degrees, with the essence of the Supreme Trinity Entity Vishnu; Vishnu had opted to be born into mortality to combat the demon Ravana, who was oppressing the gods, and who could only be destroyed by a mortal. The boys are reared as the princes of the realm, receiving instructions from the scriptures and in warfare from Vashistha. When Rama is 16 years old, sage Vishwamitra comes to the court of Dasharatha in search of help against demons who were disturbing sacrificial rites. He chooses Rama, who is followed by Lakshmana, his constant companion throughout the story. Rama and Lakshmana receive instructions and supernatural weapons from Vishwamitra and proceed to destroy the demons.

Janaka was the king of Mithila. One day, a female child was found in the field by the king in the deep furrow dug by his plough. Overwhelmed with joy, the

Figure 26: *Rama leaving for fourteen years of exile from Ayodhya*

king regarded the child as a "miraculous gift of god". The child was named Sita, the Sanskrit word for furrow. Sita grew up to be a girl of unparalleled beauty and charm. The king had decided that who ever could lift and wield the heavy bow, presented to his ancestors by Shiva, could marry Sita. Sage Vishwamitra takes Rama and Lakshmana to Mithila to show the bow. Then Rama desires to lift it and goes on to wield the bow and when he draws the string, it breaks. Marriages are arranged between the sons of Dasharatha and daughters of Janaka. Rama gets married to Sita, Lakshmana to Urmila, Bharata to Mandavi and Shatrughna to Shrutakirti. The weddings are celebrated with great festivity in Mithila and the marriage party returns to Ayodhya.

Ayodhya Kanda

After Rama and Sita have been married for twelve years, an elderly Dasharatha expresses his desire to crown Rama, to which the Kosala assembly and his subjects express their support. On the eve of the great event, Kaikeyi – her jealousy aroused by Manthara, a wicked maidservant – claims two boons that Dasharatha had long ago granted her. Kaikeyi demands Rama to be exiled into the wilderness for fourteen years, while the succession passes to her son Bharata. The heartbroken king, constrained by his rigid devotion to his given word, accedes to Kaikeyi's demands. Rama accepts his father's reluctant decree with absolute submission and calm self-control which characterises him throughout the story. He is joined by Sita and Lakshmana. When he asks Sita not to follow him, she says, "the forest where you dwell is Ayodhya for me and Ayodhya without you is a veritable hell for me." After Rama's departure, King Dasharatha, unable to bear the grief, passes away. Meanwhile, Bharata

Figure 27: *Ravana fights Jatayu as he carries off the kidnapped Sita. Painting by Raja Ravi Varma*

who was on a visit to his maternal uncle, learns about the events in Ayodhya. Bharata refuses to profit from his mother's wicked scheming and visits Rama in the forest. He requests Rama to return and rule. But Rama, determined to carry out his father's orders to the letter, refuses to return before the period of exile. However, Bharata carries Rama's sandals and keeps them on the throne, while he rules as Rama's regent.Wikipedia:Citation needed

Aranya Kanda

After thirteen years of exile, Rama, Sita and Lakshmana journey southward along the banks of river Godavari, where they build cottages and live off the land. At the Panchavati forest they are visited by a rakshasi named Surpanakha, sister of Ravana. She tries to seduce the brothers and, after failing, attempts to kill Sita. Lakshmana stops her by cutting off her nose and ears. Hearing of this, her brother Khara organises an attack against the princes. Rama defeats Khara and his raskshasas.

When the news of these events reach Ravana, he resolves to destroy Rama by capturing Sita with the aid of the *rakshasa* Maricha. Maricha, assuming the form of a golden deer, captivates Sita's attention. Entranced by the beauty of the deer, Sita pleads with Rama to capture it. Rama, aware that this is the ploy of the demons, cannot dissuade Sita from her desire and chases the deer into the forest, leaving Sita under Lakshmana's guard. After some time, Sita hears Rama calling out to her; afraid for his life, she insists that Lakshmana rush to his aid. Lakshmana tries to assure her that Rama is invincible and that it is best if he continues to follow Rama's orders to protect her. On the verge of hysterics, Sita insists that it is not she but Rama who needs Lakshmana's help. He obeys her wish but stipulates that she is not to leave the cottage or entertain any stranger. He draws a chalk outline, the Lakshmana rekha, around the cottage and casts a spell on it that prevents anyone from entering the boundary but allows people to exit. With the coast finally clear, Ravana appears in the guise of an ascetic requesting Sita's hospitality. Unaware of her guest's plan, Sita is tricked into leaving the rekha and is then forcibly carried away by Ravana.[218]

Jatayu, a vulture, tries to rescue Sita, but is mortally wounded. At Lanka, Sita is kept under the guard of *rakshasis*. Ravana asks Sita to marry him, but she refuses, being eternally devoted to Rama. Meanwhile, Rama and Lakshmana learn about Sita's abduction from Jatayu and immediately set out to save her. During their search, they meet Kabandha and the ascetic Shabari, who direct them towards Sugriva and Hanuman.

Kishkindha Kanda

Kishkindha Kanda is set in the ape (*Vanara*) citadel Kishkindha. Rama and Lakshmana meet Hanuman, the biggest devotee of Rama, greatest of ape heroes and an adherent of Sugriva, the banished pretender to the throne of Kishkindha. Rama befriends Sugriva and helps him by killing his elder brother Vali thus regaining the kingdom of Kishkindha, in exchange for helping Rama to recover Sita. However Sugriva soon forgets his promise and spends his time in enjoying his powers. The clever former ape queen Tara (wife of Vali) calmly intervenes to prevent an enraged Lakshmana from destroying the ape citadel. She then eloquently convinces Sugriva to honour his pledge. Sugriva then sends search parties to the four corners of the earth, only to return without success from north, east and west. The southern search party under the leadership of Angada and Hanuman learns from a vulture named Sampati (elder brother of Jatayu), that Sita was taken to Lanka.

Sundara Kanda

Sundara Kanda forms the heart of Valmiki's Ramayana and consists of a detailed, vivid account of Hanuman's adventures. After learning about Sita, Hanuman assumes a gargantuan form and makes a colossal leap across the sea to Lanka. On the way he meets with many challenges like facing a Gandharva kanya who comes in the form of a demon to test his abilities. He encounters

Figure 28: *A stone bas-relief at Banteay Srei in Cambodia depicts the combat between Vali and Sugriva (middle). To the right, Rama fires his bow. To the left, Vali lies dying.*

Figure 29: *Ravana is meeting Sita at Ashokavana. Hanuman is seen on the tree.*

a mountain named Mainakudu who offers Lord Hanuman assistance and offers him rest. Lord Hanuman refuses because there is little time remaining to complete the search for Sita.

After entering into Lanka, he finds a demon, Lankini, who protects all of Lanka. Hanuman fights with her and subjugates her in order to get into Lanka. In the process Lankini, who had an earlier vision/warning from the gods that the end of Lanka nears if someone defeats Lankini. Here, Hanuman explores the demons' kingdom and spies on Ravana. He locates Sita in Ashoka grove, where she is being wooed and threatened by Ravana and his rakshasis to marry Ravana. Hanuman reassures Sita, giving Rama's signet ring as a sign of good faith. He offers to carry Sita back to Rama; however, she refuses and says that it is not the dharma, stating that Ramayana will not have significance if Hanuman carries her to Rama – "When Rama is not there Ravana carried Sita forcibly and when Ravana was not there, Hanuman carried Sita back to Rama". She says that Rama himself must come and avenge the insult of her abduction.

Hanuman then wreaks havoc in Lanka by destroying trees and buildings and killing Ravana's warriors. He allows himself to be captured and delivered to Ravana. He gives a bold lecture to Ravana to release Sita. He is condemned and his tail is set on fire, but he escapes his bonds and leaping from roof to roof, sets fire to Ravana's citadel and makes the giant leap back from the island. The joyous search party returns to Kishkindha with the news.

Yuddha Kanda

Also known as *Lanka Kanda*, this book describes the Ramayana War between the army of Rama and the army of Ravana. Having received Hanuman's report on Sita, Rama and Lakshmana proceed with their allies towards the shore of the southern sea. There they are joined by Ravana's renegade brother Vibhishana. The apes named Nala and Nila construct a floating bridge (known as Rama Setu)[219] across the sea, using stones that floated on water because they had Rama's name written on them. The princes and their army cross over to Lanka. A lengthy war ensues. During a battle, Ravana's son Indrajit hurls a powerful weapon at Lakshmana, who is badly wounded and is nearly killed.Wikipedia:Citation needed So Hanuman assumes a gigantic form and flies from Lanka to the Himalayas. Upon reaching Mount Sumeru, Hanuman was unable to identify the herb that could cure Lakshmana and so decided to bring the entire mountain back to Lanka. Eventually, the war ends when Rama kills Ravana. Rama then installs Vibhishana on the throne of Lanka.

On meeting Sita, Rama asks her to undergo an Agni Pariksha (test of fire) to prove her chastity, as he wants to get rid of the rumors surrounding her purity.

Figure 30: *The Battle at Lanka, Ramayana by Sahibdin.* It depicts the monkey army of the protagonist Rama (top left, blue figure) fighting Ravana—the demon-king of the Lanka—to save Rama's kidnapped wife, Sita. The painting depicts multiple events in the battle against the three-headed demon general Trisiras, in bottom left. Trisiras is beheaded by Hanuman, the monkey-companion of Rama.

When Sita plunges into the sacrificial fire, Agni, lord of fire raises Sita, unharmed, to the throne, attesting to her innocence. The episode of *Agni Pariksha* varies in the versions of Ramayana by Valmiki and Tulsidas. In Tulsidas's Ramacharitamanas, Sita was under the protection of Agni (see Maya Sita) so it was necessary to bring her out before reuniting with Rama. At the expiration of his term of exile, Rama returns to Ayodhya with Sita and Lakshmana, where the coronation is performed. This is the beginning of Ram Rajya, which implies an ideal state with good morals. Ramayan is not only the story about how truth defeats the evil, it also teaches us to forget all the evil and arrogance that resides inside ourselves.

Uttara Kanda

Uttara Kanda concerns the final years of Rama, Sita and Rama's brothers. After being crowned king, Rama passes time pleasantly with Sita. After some time, Sita gets pregnant with twin children. However, despite *Agni Pariksha* ("fire ordeal") of Sita, rumours about her "purity" are spreading among the populace of Ayodhya. Rama yields to public opinion and reluctantly banishes Sita to the forest, where the sage Valmiki provides shelter in his *ashrama* ("hermitage"). Here, she gives birth to twin boys, Lava and Kusha, who become pupils of Valmiki and are brought up in ignorance of their identity.

Figure 31: *Sita in the hermitage of Valmiki*

Valmiki composes the *Ramayana* and teaches Lava and Kusha to sing it. Later, Rama holds a ceremony during the *Ashwamedha yagna*, which sage Valmiki, with Lava and Kusha, attends. Lava and Kusha sing the *Ramayana* in the presence of Rama and his vast audience. When Lava and Kusha recite about Sita's exile, Rama becomes grief-stricken and Valmiki produces Sita. Sita calls upon the Earth, her mother, to receive her and as the ground opens, she vanishes into it. Rama then learns that Lava and Kusha are his children. Many years later, a messenger from the Gods appears and informs Rama that the mission of his incarnation is over. Rama returns to his celestial abode along with his brothers. It was dramatised as *Uttararamacarita* by the Sanskrit poet Bhavabhuti.

Versions

As in many oral epics, multiple versions of the *Ramayana* survive. In particular, the *Ramayana* related in north India differs in important respects from that preserved in south India and the rest of southeast Asia. There is an extensive tradition of oral storytelling based on *Ramayana* in Indonesia, Cambodia, Philippines, Thailand, Malaysia, Laos, Vietnam and Maldives. Father Kamil Bulke, author of *Ramakatha*, has identified over 300 variants of the *Ramayana*.

Figure 32: *The epic story of Ramayana was adopted by several cultures across Asia. Shown here is a Thai historic artwork depicting the battle which took place between Rama and Ravana.*

Figure 33: *Relief with part of the Ramayana epic, shows Rama killed the golden deer that turn out to be the demon Maricha in disguise. Prambanan Trimurti temple near Yogyakarta, Java, Indonesia.*

India

There are diverse regional versions of the *Ramayana* written by various authors in India. Some of them differ significantly from each other. During the 12th century, Kamban wrote Ramavataram, known popularly as Kambaramayanam in Tamil. A Telugu version, Ranganatha Ramayanam, was written by Gona Budda Reddy in the 14th century. The earliest translation to a regional Indo-Aryan language is the early 14th century Saptakanda Ramayana in Assamese by Madhava Kandali. Valmiki's *Ramayana* inspired Sri Ramacharit Manas by Tulsidas in 1576, an epic Awadhi (a dialect of Hindi) version with a slant more grounded in a different realm of Hindu literature, that of bhakti; it is an acknowledged masterpiece of India, popularly known as *Tulsi-krita Ramayana*. Gujarati poet Premanand wrote a version of the *Ramayana* in the 17th century. Other versions include Krittivasi Ramayan, a Bengali version by Krittibas Ojha in the 15th century; Vilanka Ramayana by 15th century poet Sarala Dasa and *Dandi Ramayana* (also known as *Jagamohana Ramayana*) by 16th century poet Balarama Dasa, both in Odia; a Torave Ramayana in Kannada by 16th-century poet Narahari; Adhyathmaramayanam, a Malayalam version by Thunchaththu Ramanujan Ezhuthachan in the 16th century; in Marathi by Sridhara in the 18th century; in Maithili by Chanda Jha in the 19th century; and in the 20th century, Rashtrakavi Kuvempu's Sri Ramayana Darshanam in Kannada.

There is a sub-plot to the *Ramayana*, prevalent in some parts of India, relating the adventures of Ahiravan and Mahi Ravana, evil brother of Ravana, which enhances the role of Hanuman in the story. Hanuman rescues Rama and Lakshmana after they are kidnapped by the Ahi-Mahi Ravana at the behest of Ravana and held prisoner in a subterranean cave, to be sacrificed to the goddess Kali. Adbhuta Ramayana is a version that is obscure but also attributed to Valmiki – intended as a supplementary to the original Valmiki Ramayana. In this variant of the narrative, Sita is accorded far more prominence, such as elaboration of the events surrounding her birth – in this case to Ravana's wife, Mandodari as well as her conquest of Ravana's older brother in her Mahakali form.

Mappillapattu – a genre of song popular among the Muslims belonging to Kerala and Lakshadweep – has incorporated some episodes from the *Ramayana* into its songs. These songs, known as *mappila ramayana*, have been handed down from one generation to the next orally. In *mappila ramayana*, the story of *Ramayana* has been changed into that of a sultan and there are no major changes in the names of characters except for that of Rama which is *Laman* in many places. The language and the imagery projected in the Mappilapattu are in accordance with the social fabric of the earlier Muslim community.

Buddhist Version

In the Buddhist variant of the *Ramayana* (*Dasarathajātaka*, #467), Dasharatha was king of Benares and not Ayodhya. Rama (called Rāmapaṇḍita in this version) was the son of Kaushalya, first wife of Dasharatha. Lakṣmaṇa (Lakkhaṇa) was a sibling of Rama and son of Sumitra, the second wife of Dasharatha. Sita was the wife of Rama. To protect his children from his wife Kaikeyi, who wished to promote her son Bharata, Dasharatha sent the three to a hermitage in the Himalayas for a twelve-year exile. After nine years, Dasharatha died and Lakkhaṇa and Sita returned; Rāmapaṇḍita, in deference to his father's wishes, remained in exile for a further two years. This version does not include the abduction of Sītā. There is no Ravan in this version i.e. no Ram-ravan war.

In the explanatory commentary on Jātaka, Rāmapaṇḍita is said to have been a previous incarnation of the Buddha, and Sita an incarnation of Yasodharā.

But, Ravana appears in other Buddhist literature, the Lankavatara Sutra.

Jain Version

Jain versions of the *Ramayana* can be found in the various Jain agamas like Ravisena's Padmapurana (story of Padmaja and Rama, Padmaja being the name of Sita), Hemacandra's Trisastisalakapurusa charitra (hagiography of 63 illustrious persons), Sanghadasa's *Vasudevahindi* and *Uttarapurana* by Gunabhadara. According to Jain cosmology, every half time cycle has nine sets of Balarama, Vasudeva and prativasudeva. Rama, Lakshmana and Ravana are the eighth baladeva, vasudeva and prativasudeva respectively. Padmanabh Jaini notes that, unlike in the Hindu puranas, the names Baladeva and Vasudeva are not restricted to Balarama and Krishna in Jain Puranas. Instead they serve as names of two distinct classes of mighty brothers, who appear nine times in each half time cycle and jointly rule half the earth as half-chakravartins. Jaini traces the origin of this list of brothers to the *jinacharitra* (lives of jinas) by Acharya Bhadrabahu (3d-4th century BCE).

In the Jain epic of *Ramayana*, it is not Rama who kills Ravana as told in the Hindu version. Perhaps this is because Rama, a liberated Jain Soul in his last life, is unwilling to kill. Instead, it is Lakshmana who kills Ravana. In the end, Rama, who led an upright life, renounces his kingdom, becomes a Jain monk and attains moksha. On the other hand, Lakshmana and Ravana go to Hell. However, it is predicted that ultimately they both will be reborn as upright persons and attain liberation in their future births. According to Jain texts, Ravana will be the future Tirthankara (omniscient teacher) of Jainism.

The Jain versions have some variations from Valmiki's *Ramayana*. Dasharatha, the king of Saketa had four queens: Aparajita, Sumitra, Suprabha and Kaikeyi. These four queens had four sons. Aparajita's son was Padma and he became known by the name of Rama. Sumitra's son was Narayana: he came to be known by another name, Lakshmana. Kaikeyi's son was Bharata and Suprabha's son was Shatrughna. Furthermore, not much was thought of Rama's fidelity to Sita. According to the Jain version, Rama had four chief queens: Maithili, Prabhavati, Ratinibha, and Sridama. Furthermore, Sita takes renunciation as a Jain ascetic after Rama abandons her and is reborn in heaven. Rama, after Lakshmana's death, also renounces his kingdom and becomes a Jain monk. Ultimately, he attains Kevala Jnana omniscience and finally liberation. Rama predicts that Ravana and Lakshmana, who were in the fourth hell, will attain liberation in their future births. Accordingly, Ravana is the future tirthankara of the next half ascending time cycle and Sita will be his Ganadhara.

Sikh Version

In Guru Granth Sahib, there is a description of two types of *Ramayana*. One is a spiritual *Ramayana* which is the actual subject of Guru Granth Sahib, in which Ravana is ego, Sita is *budhi* (intellect), Rama is inner soul and Laxman is *mann* (attention, mind). Guru Granth Sahib also believes in the existence of Dashavatara who were kings of their times which tried their best to restore order to the world. King Rama (Ramchandra) was one of those who is not covered in Guru Granth Sahib. Guru Granth Sahib states:

ਹੁਕਮਿ ਉਪਾਏ ਦਸ ਅਉਤਾਰਾ ॥

हुकमि उपाए दस अउतारा ॥

By hukam (supreme command), he created his ten incarnations

This version of the *Ramayana* was written by Guru Gobind Singh, which is part of Dasam Granth.

He also said that the almighty, invisible, all prevailing God created great numbers of Indras, Moons and Suns, Deities, Demons and sages, and also numerous saints and Brahmanas (enlightened people). But they too were caught in the noose of death (Kaal) (transmigration of the soul). This is similar to the explanation in Bhagavad Gita which is part of the *Mahabharata*.Wikipedia:Citation needed

Figure 34: *Cambodian classical dancers as Sita and Ravana, the Royal Palace in Phnom Penh (c. 1920s)*

Nepal

Besides being the site of discovery of the oldest surviving manuscript of the *Ramayana*, Nepal gave rise to two regional variants in mid 19th – early 20th century. One, written by Bhanubhakta Acharya, is considered the first epic of Nepali language, while the other, written by Siddhidas Mahaju in Nepal Bhasa was a foundational influence in the Nepal Bhasa renaissance.

Ramayana written by Bhanubhakta Acharya is one of the most popular verses in Nepal. The popularization of the *Ramayana* and its tale, originally written in Sanskrit Language was greatly enhanced by the work of Bhanubhakta. Mainly because of his writing of Nepali Ramayana, Bhanubhakta is also called *Aadi Kavi* or *The Pioneering Poet*.

Southeast Asian

Cambodia

The Cambodian version of the *Ramayana*, Reamker (Khmer: ░░░░░░░░░ - *Glory of Rama*), is the most famous story of Khmer literature since the Kingdom of Funan era. It adapts the Hindu concepts to Buddhist themes and shows the balance of good and evil in the world. The Reamker has several differences

Figure 35: *Lakshmana, Rama and Sita during their exile in Dandaka Forest depicted in Javanese dance*

from the original *Ramayana*, including scenes not included in the original and emphasis on Hanuman and Sovanna Maccha, a retelling which influences the Thai and Lao versions. Reamker in Cambodia is not confined to the realm of literature but extends to all Cambodian art forms, such as sculpture, Khmer classical dance, theatre known as *lakhorn luang* (the foundation of the royal ballet), poetry and the mural and bas-reliefs seen at the Silver Pagoda and Angkor Wat.

Indonesia

Indonesia has some adaptations of Ramayana, including *Kakawin Ramayana* of Java, and *Ramakavaca* of Bali (Indonesia). Javanese version of Ramayana has some differences if compared with the original Hindu version. The first half of *Kakawin Ramayana* is similar to the original Sanskrit version, while the latter half is very different from the original Ramayana. One of the recognizable modification in Javanese version of Ramayana is the inclusion of the indigenous Javanese guardian god, Semar, and his misshapen sons, Gareng, Petruk, and Bagong who make up the numerically significant four Punokawan or "clown servants". *Kakawin Ramayana* is believed to have been written in Central Java circa 870 AD during the reign of Mpu Sindok in Medang Kingdom.:[128] The Javanese *Kakawin Ramayana* is not based on Valmiki's epic, which was then the most famous version of Rama's story, but based on *Ravanavadha* or the "Ravana massacre", which is the sixth or seventh century poetry by Indian poets Bhattikavya.

Kakawin Ramayana has also become the reference of Ramayana in the neighboring island of Bali which developed the Balinese *Ramakavaca*. The bas reliefs of Ramayana and Krishnayana scenes are carved on balustrades wall of 9th century Prambanan temples in Yogyakarta, as well as in East Java 14th century bas-relief of Penataran temple. In Indonesia, Ramayana has been integrated into local culture especially those of Javanese, Balinese and Sundanese people, and has become the source of moral and spiritual guidance as well as aesthetic expression and also for entertainment, like in wayang and traditional dances.[220] The Balinese *kecak* dance drama for example, represent the story taken from Ramayana episodes, where dancers that play as Rama, Sita, Lakshmana, Jatayu, Hanuman, Ravana, Kumbhakarna and Indrajit, performed and surrounded by a troupe of over 50 bare-chested men who serve as the chorus chanting "cak" chant. The performance also include a fire show to describe the burning of Lanka by Hanuman. In Yogyakarta, the *Wayang Wong* Javanese dance drama also performed a Javanese rendering of Ramayana episodes. The most spectacular Ramayana performance in Java would be the Ramayana Ballet performed on the Trimurti Prambanan open air stage, with backdrop view of the three main prasad spires of Prambanan Hindu temple.

Laos

Phra Lak Phra Lam is a Lao language version, whose title comes from Lakshmana and Rama. The story of Lakshmana and Rama is told as the previous life of Gautama buddha.

Malaysia

The Hikayat Seri Rama of Malaysia incorporated element of both Hindu and Islamic mythology.

Myanmar

Yama Zatdaw is the Burmese version of Ramayana. It is also considered the unofficial national epic of Myanmar. There are nine known pieces of the Yama Zatdaw in Myanmar. The Burmese name for the story itself is Yamayana, while zatdaw refers to the acted play or being part of the jataka tales of Theravada Buddhism. This Burmese version is also heavily influenced by Ramakien (Thai version of Ramayana) which resulted from various invasions by Konbaung Dynasty kings toward the Ayutthaya Kingdom.

Figure 36: *Rama (Yama) and Sita (Me Thida) in Yama Zatdaw, the Burmese version of Ramayana*

Philippines

The *Maharadia Lawana*, an epic poem of the Maranao people of the Philippines, has been regarded as an indigenized version of the Ramayana since it was documented and translated into English by Professor Juan R. Francisco and Nagasura Madale in 1968.(p"264") The poem, which had not been written down before Francisco and Madale's translation,(p"264") narrates the adventures of the monkey-king, Maharadia Lawana, whom the Gods have gifted with immortality.

Francisco, an indologist from the University of the Philippines Manila, believed that the Ramayana narrative arrived in the Philippines some time between the 17th to 19th centuries, via interactions with Javanese and Malaysian cultures which traded extensively with India.(p101)

By the time it was documented in the 1960s, the character names, place names, and the precise episodes and events in Maharadia Lawana's narrative already had some notable differences from those of the Ramayana. Francisco believed that this was a sign of "indigenization", and suggested that some changes had already been introduced in Malaysia and Java even before the story was heard by the Maranao, and that upon reaching the Maranao homeland, the story

Figure 37: *The Thai retelling of the tale—Ramakien—is popularly expressed in traditional regional dance theatre*

was *"further indigenized to suit Philippine cultural perspectives and orientations."*(p"103")

Thailand

Thailand's popular national epic Ramakien (Thai:รามเกียรติ์, from Sanskrit *rāmakīrti*, *glory of Rama*) is derived from the Hindu epic. In Ramakien, Sita is the daughter of Ravana and Mandodari (*thotsakan* and *montho*). Vibhishana (*phiphek*), the astrologer brother of Ravana, predicts the death of Ravana from the horoscope of Sita. Ravana has thrown her into the water, but she is later rescued by Janaka (*chanok*).:[149] While the main story is identical to that of *Ramayana*, many other aspects were transposed into a Thai context, such as the clothes, weapons, topography and elements of nature, which are described as being Thai in style. It has an expanded role for Hanuman and he is portrayed as a lascivious character. Ramakien can be seen in an elaborate illustration at Wat Phra Kaew in Bangkok.

Critical Edition

A critical edition of the text was compiled in India in the 1960s and 1970s, by the Oriental Institute at Maharaja Sayajirao University of Baroda, India, utilizing dozens of manuscripts collected from across India and the surrounding region. An English language translation of the critical edition was completed in November 2016 by Sanskrit scholar Robert P. Goldman of the University of California, Berkeley.

Figure 38: *A Ramlila actor wears the traditional attire of Ravana.*

Influence On Culture & Art

One of the most important literary works of ancient India, the *Ramayana* has had a profound impact on art and culture in the Indian subcontinent and southeast Asia with the lone exception of Vietnam. The story ushered in the tradition of the next thousand years of massive-scale works in the rich diction of regal courts and Hindu temples. It has also inspired much secondary literature in various languages, notably Kambaramayanam by Tamil poet Kambar of the 12th century, Telugu language *Molla Ramayanam* by poet Molla and Ranganatha Ramayanam by poet Gona Budda Reddy, 14th century Kannada poet Narahari's Torave Ramayana and 15th century Bengali poet Krittibas Ojha's Krittivasi Ramayan, as well as the 16th century Awadhi version, Ramacharitamanas, written by Tulsidas.

Ramayanic scenes have also been depicted through terracottas, stone sculptures, bronzes and paintings. These include the stone panel at Nagarjunakonda in Andhra Pradesh depicting Bharata's meeting with Rama at Chitrakuta (3rd century CE).

The *Ramayana* became popular in Southeast Asia during 8th century and was represented in literature, temple architecture, dance and theatre. Today, dramatic enactments of the story of the *Ramayana*, known as Ramlila, take place all across India and in many places across the globe within the Indian diaspora.

Figure 39: *Hanuman discovers Sita in her captivity in Lanka, as depicted in Balinese kecak dance.*

In Indonesia, especially Java and Bali, Ramayana has become a popular source of artistic expression for dance drama and shadow puppet performance in the region. Sendratari Ramayana is Javanese traditional ballet of wayang orang genre, routinely performed in Prambanan Trimurti temple and in cultural center of Yogyakarta. Balinese dance drama of Ramayana is also performed routinely in Balinese Hindu temples, especially in temples such as Ubud and Uluwatu, where scenes from Ramayana is integrap part of kecak dance performance. Javanese wayang kulit purwa also draws its episodes from Ramayana or Mahabharata.

Ramayana has also been depicted in many paintings, most notably by the Malaysian artist Syed Thajudeen in 1972. The epic tale was picturized on canvas in epic proportions measuring 152 x 823 cm in 9 panels. The painting depicts three prolific parts of the epic, namely The Abduction of Sita, Hanuman visits Sita and Hanuman Burns Lanka. The painting is currently in the permanent collection of the Malaysian National Visual Arts Gallery.

Ramayana

Figure 40: *Deities Sita (far right), Rama (center), Lakshmana (far left) and Hanuman (below, seated) at Bhaktivedanta Manor, Watford, England*

Religious Significance

Rama, the hero of the *Ramayana*, is one of the most popular deities worshipped in the Hindu religion. Each year, many devout pilgrims trace their journey through India and Nepal, halting at each of the holy sites along the way. The poem is not seen as just a literary monument, but serves as an integral part of Hinduism and is held in such reverence that the mere reading or hearing of it or certain passages of it, is believed by Hindus to free them from sin and bless the reader or listener.

According to Hindu tradition, Rama is an incarnation (Avatar) of god Vishnu. The main purpose of this incarnation is to demonstrate the righteous path (dharma) for all living creatures on earth.

Ramayana In Popular Culture

Multiple modern, English-language adaptations of the epic exist, namely Ram Chandra Series by Amish Tripathi, Ramayana Series by Ashok Banker and a mythopoetic novel, *Asura: Tale of the Vanquished* by Anand Neelakantan. Another Indian author, Devdutt Pattanaik, has published three different retellings and commentaries of Ramayana titled *Sita*, *The Book Of Ram* and

Hanuman's Ramayan. A number of plays, movies and television serials have also been produced based upon the *Ramayana*.

In Indonesia, "Ramayana" department store is named after the epic. The company which owns it is known as *PT Ramayana Lestari Sentosa* founded in 1978 with its main office located in Jakarta.

Stage

Starting in 1978 and under the supervision of Baba Hari Dass, Ramayana has been performed every year by Mount Madonna School in Watsonville, California. Currently, it is the largest yearly, Western version of the epic being performed. It takes the form of a colorful musical with custom costumes, sung and spoken dialog, jazz-rock orchestration and dance. This performance takes place in a large audience theater setting usually in June, in San Jose, CA. Baba Hari Dass has taught acting arts, costume-attire design, mask making and choreography to bring alive characters of Sri Ram, Sita, Hanuman, Lakshmana, Shiva, Parvati, Vibhishan, Jatayu, Sugriva, Surpanakha, Ravana and his rakshasa court, Meghnadha, Kumbhakarna and the army of monkeys and demons.

Movies

- *Sampoorna Ramayanam* – a Telugu/Tamil bilingual film starring N. T. Rama Rao (1958)
- *Sampoorna Ramayana* – a Hindi film directed by Babubhai Mistry (1961)
- *Lava Kusha* – a Uttara Kanda-based bilingual Telugu movie and Tamil movie starring N. T. Rama Rao (1963)
- *Sampoorna Ramayanamu* – a Telugu film directed by Bapu, starring Sobhan Babu, Chandrakala, S V Ranga Rao (1971)
- *Kanchana Sita* – a Malayalam film by G. Aravindan (1977)
- *Ramayana: The Legend of Prince Rama* – a Indo-Japanese traditional animation feature film (1992)
- *A Little Princess* (1995) – an American film chronicling the time of an orphaned child during WWI in an all-girl's boarding school. The story of Rama and Sita is told by the main character to the other girls and is constantly referenced throughout the plot.
- *Opera Jawa* – an Indonesian-Austrian film in the Indonesian language; inspired by the story of the abduction of Sita (2008)
- *Sita Sings the Blues* – an independent animated film (2008).
- *Lava Kusa: The Warrior Twins* – animated film based on *Uttara Kanda* (2010)
- *Ramayana: The Epic* – a Warner Bros. Indian animated film (2010)

- *Sri Rama Rajyam* – based on *Uttara Kanda*, a Telugu film starring Nandamuri Balakrishna (2011).
- *Yak: The Giant King* – a re-interpretation of Ramayana, the Thai animation film tells the story of a giant robot, Na Kiew, who is left wandering in a barren wasteland after a great war. Na Kiew meets Jao Phuek, a puny tin robot who has lost his memory and is now stuck with his new big friend. Together they set out across the desert populated by metal scavengers, to look for Ram, the creator of all robots. (2012).
- *Mumbai Musical* – DreamWorks Animation (2016)

Plays

- *Kanchana Sita, Saketham* and *Lankalakshmi* – award-winning trilogy by Malayalam playwright C. N. Sreekantan Nair
- *Lankeswaran* – a play by the award-winning Tamil cinema actor R. S. Manohar
- Kecak - a Balinese traditional folk dance which plays and tells the story of Ramayana

Exihibitions

- Gallery Nucleus:Ramayana Exhibition -Part of the art of the book Ramayana:Divine Loophole by Sanjay Patel.
- The Rama epic:Hero.Heroine,Ally,Foe by The Asian Art Museum.

Books

- "*The Song of Rama*" by Vanamali
- "*Ramayana*" by William Buck and S Triest
- "*Ramayana:Divine Loophole*" by Sanjay Patel
- "*Sita: An Illustrate Retelling of the Ramayana*" By Devdutt Pattanaik

TV Series

- *Ramayan* – originally broadcast on Doordarshan, produced by Ramanand Sagar in 1987
- *Jai Hanuman* – originally broadcast on Doordarshan, produced and directed by Sanjay Khan
- *Ramayan* (2002) – originally broadcast on Zee TV, produced by BR Films
- *Ramayan* (2008) – originally broadcast on Imagine TV, produced by Ramanand Sagar
- *Ramayan* (2012) – a remake of the 1987 series and aired on Zee TV
- *Antariksh* (2004) – a sci-fi version of *Ramayan*. Originally broadcast on Star Plus

- *Raavan* – series on life of Ravana based on Ramayana. Originally broadcast on Zee TV
- *Sankatmochan Mahabali Hanuman* – 2015 series based on the life of Hanuman presently broadcasting on Sony TV
- *Siya Ke Ram* – a series on Star Plus, originally broadcast from November 16, 2015 to November 4, 2016

References

<templatestyles src="Refbegin/styles.css" />

- Arya, Ravi Prakash (ed.).*Ramayana of Valmiki: Sanskrit Text and English Translation*. (English translation according to M. N. Dutt, introduction by Dr. Ramashraya Sharma, 4-volume set) Parimal Publications: Delhi, 1998, <templatestyles src="Module:Citation/CS1/styles.css" />ISBN 81-7110-156-9
- Bhattacharji, Sukumari (1998). *Legends of Devi*[221]. Orient Blackswan. p. 111. ISBN 978-81-250-1438-6.<templatestyles src="Module:Citation/CS1/styles.css"></templatestyles>
- Brockington, John (2003). "The Sanskrit Epics". In Flood, Gavin. *Blackwell companion to Hinduism*[222]. Blackwell Publishing. pp. 116–128. ISBN 0-631-21535-2.<templatestyles src="Module:Citation/CS1/styles.css"></templatestyles>
- Buck, William; van Nooten, B. A. (2000). *Ramayana*[223]. University of California Press. p. 432. ISBN 978-0-520-22703-3.<templatestyles src="Module:Citation/CS1/styles.css"></templatestyles>
- Dutt, Romesh C. (2004). *Ramayana*[224]. Kessinger Publishing. p. 208. ISBN 978-1-4191-4387-8.<templatestyles src="Module:Citation/CS1/styles.css"></templatestyles>
- Dutt, Romesh Chunder (2002). *The Ramayana and Mahabharata condensed into English verse*[225]. Courier Dover Publications. p. 352. ISBN 978-0-486-42506-1.<templatestyles src="Module:Citation/CS1/styles.css"></templatestyles>
- Fallon, Oliver (2009). *Bhatti's Poem: The Death of Rávana (Bhaṭṭikāvya)*[226]. New York: New York University Press, Clay Sanskrit Library. ISBN 978-0-8147-2778-2.<templatestyles src="Module:Citation/CS1/styles.css"></templatestyles>
- Keshavadas, Sadguru Sant (1988). *Ramayana at a Glance*[227]. Motilal Banarsidass Publ.,. p. 211. ISBN 978-81-208-0545-3.<templatestyles src="Module:Citation/CS1/styles.css"></templatestyles>

- Goldman, Robert P. (1990). *The Ramayana of Valmiki: An Epic of Ancient India: Balakanda*[228]. Princeton University Press. ISBN 978-0-691-01485-2.<templatestyles src="Module:Citation/CS1/styles.css"></templatestyles>
- Goldman, Robert P. (1994). *The Ramayana of Valmiki: An Epic of Ancient India: Kiskindhakanda*[229]. Princeton University Press. ISBN 978-0-691-06661-5.<templatestyles src="Module:Citation/CS1/styles.css"></templatestyles>
- Goldman, Robert P. (1996). *The Ramayana of Valmiki: Sundarakanda*[230]. Princeton University Press. ISBN 978-0-691-06662-2.<templatestyles src="Module:Citation/CS1/styles.css"></templatestyles>
- B. B. Lal (2008). *Rāma, His Historicity, Mandir, and Setu: Evidence of Literature, Archaeology, and Other Sciences*[231]. Aryan Books. ISBN 978-81-7305-345-0.<templatestyles src="Module:Citation/CS1/styles.css"></templatestyles>
- Mahulikar, Dr. Gauri. *Effect Of Ramayana On Various Cultures And Civilisations*, Ramayan Institute
- Rabb, Kate Milner, *National Epics*, 1896 – see eText[232] in Project Gutenburg
- Murthy, S. S. N. (November 2003). "A note on the Ramayana"[233] (PDF). *Electronic Journal of Vedic Studies*. New Delhi. **10** (6): 1–18. ISSN 1084-7561[234]. Archived from the original[235] (PDF) on 8 August 2012.<templatestyles src="Module:Citation/CS1/styles.css"></templatestyles>
- Prabhavananda, Swami (1979). *The Spiritual Heritage of India*[236]. Vedanta Press. p. 374. ISBN 978-0-87481-035-6.<templatestyles src="Module:Citation/CS1/styles.css"></templatestyles> (see also Wikipedia article on book)
- Raghunathan, N. (transl.), *Srimad Valmiki Ramayanam*, Vighneswara Publishing House, Madras (1981)
- Rohman, Todd (2009). "The Classical Period". In Watling, Gabrielle; Quay, Sara. *Cultural History of Reading: World literature*[237]. Greenwood. ISBN 978-0-313-33744-4.<templatestyles src="Module:Citation/CS1/styles.css"></templatestyles>
- Sattar, Arshia (transl.) (1996). *The Rāmāyaṇa by Vālmīki*[238]. Viking. p. 696. ISBN 978-0-14-029866-6.<templatestyles src="Module:Citation/CS1/styles.css"></templatestyles>
- Sundararajan, K.R. (1989). "The Ideal of Perfect Life : The Ramayana". In Krishna Sivaraman; Bithika Mukerji. *Hindu spirituality: Vedas through Vedanta*[239]. The Crossroad Publishing Co. pp. 106–126. ISBN 978-0-8245-0755-8.<templatestyles

src="Module:Citation/CS1/styles.css"></templatestyles>
- *A different Song* – Article from "The Hindu" 12 August 2005 – "The Hindu : Entertainment Thiruvananthapuram / Music : A different song"[240]. Hinduonnet.com. 12 August 2005. Archived from the original[241] on 27 October 2010. Retrieved 1 September 2010.<templatestyles src="Module:Citation/CS1/styles.css"></templatestyles>
- *Valmiki's Ramayana illustrated with Indian miniatures from the 16th to the 19th century*[242], 2012, Editions Diane de Selliers, <templatestyles src="Module:Citation/CS1/styles.css" />ISBN 9782903656768

Further reading

Sanskrit text

- Electronic version of the Sanskrit text[243], input by Muneo Tokunaga
- Sanskrit text[244] on GRETIL

Translations

- *Jain Ramayana of Hemchandra*[245] English translation; seventh book of the Trishashti Shalaka Purusha Caritra; 1931
- *Valmiki Ramayana*[246] verse translation by Desiraju Hanumanta Rao, K. M. K. Murthy et al.
- *Summary of The Ramayana*[247] Summary of Maurice Winternitz, A History of Indian Literature, trans. by S. Ketkar.
- *Valmiki Ramayana*[248] translated by Ralph T. H. Griffith (1870–1874) (Project Gutenberg)
- *The Ramayana condensed into English verse*[249] by R. C. Dutt (1899) at archive.org[250]
- Prose translation of the complete *Ramayana* by M. N. Dutt (1891–1894): Balakandam[251], Ayodhya Kandam[252], Aranya Kandam[253], Kishkindha Kandam[254], Sundara Kandam[253], Yuddha Kandam[255], Uttara Kandam[256]
- *Rāma the Steadfast: an early form of the Rāmāyaṇa*[257] translated by J. L. Brockington and Mary Brockington. Penguin, 2006. <templatestyles src="Module:Citation/CS1/styles.css" />ISBN 0-14-044744-X.

Secondary sources

- Jain, Meenakshi. (2013). *Rama and Ayodhya*. Aryan Books International, 2013.

External Links

 Wikiquote has quotations related to: *Ramayan*

 Sanskrit Wikisourcehas original text related to this article:
Ramayana

 Wikisourcehas original text related to this article:
Ramayana

 Wikimedia Commonshas media related to:
Ramayana(category)

- A condensed verse translation[258] by Romesh Chunder Dutt sponsored by the Liberty Fund
- The *Ramayana* as a Monomyth[259] from UC Berkeley (archived)

Sanskrit literature

History of literature
<templatestyles src="Nobold/styles.css"/>by era

Bronze Age

- Ancient Egyptian
- Akkadian
- Sumerian

Classical

- Avestan
- Chinese
- Greek
- Hebrew
- Latin
- Pali
- Prakrit
- Sanskrit
- Syriac
- Tamil

Early Medieval

- Matter of Rome
- Matter of France
- Matter of Britain
- Armenian
- Byzantine
- Georgian
- Japanese
- Kannada
- Middle Persian

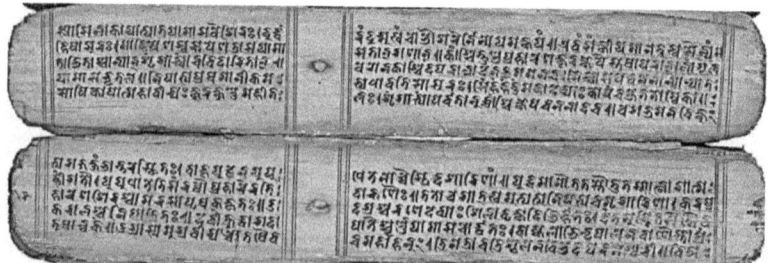

Figure 41: *The 11th-century Sanskrit manuscript of the Devi Māhātmya on palm-leaf, Bihar or Nepal.*

Sanskrit literature

• Turkish
Medieval
• Old Bulgarian • Old English • Middle English • Arabic • Persian • Armenian • Byzantine • Castilian • Catalan • Dutch • French • Georgian • German • Bengali • Indian • Old Irish • Italian • Korean • Nepal Bhasa • Norse • Russian • Telugu • Serbian • Turkish • Welsh
Early Modern
• Renaissance • Baroque
Modern by century
• 18th • 19th • 20th • 21st
📖 **Literature portal**
• v • t • e[260]

Sanskrit literature refers to texts composed in Sanskrit language since the 2nd-millennium BCE. Many of the prominent texts are associated with Indian religions, i.e., Hinduism, Buddhism, and Jainism, and were composed in ancient India. However, others were composed central, East or Southeast Asia and the canon includes works covering secular sciences and the arts. Early works of Sanskrit literature were transmitted through an oral tradition for centuries before they were written down in manuscript form.

Hindu texts

Part of a series on Hindu scriptures
Vedas and their Shakhas

<templatestyles src="Nobold/styles.css"/>Hinduism portal
- v
- t
- e[261]

Hindu Sanskrit texts are manuscripts and historical literature related to any of the diverse traditions within Hinduism. A few texts are shared resources across these traditions and broadly considered as Hindu scriptures.[262] These include the *Shruti*, namely the Vedas and the early Upanishads. Many scholars include the Bhagavad Gita and Agamas as Hindu scriptures,[263,264,265] while Dominic Goodall includes Bhagavata Purana and Yajnavalkya Smriti to the list of Hindu scriptures.

The *Smriti* Sanskrit texts are a specific body of Hindu texts attributed to an author,[266] as a derivative work they are considered less authoritative than *Sruti* in Hinduism.[267] The Smrti literature is a vast corpus of diverse texts, and includes but is not limited to Vedāngas, the Hindu epics, the Sutras and Shastras, the texts of Hindu philosophies, the Puranas, the Kāvya or poetical literature, the *Bhasyas*, and numerous *Nibandhas* (digests) covering politics, ethics, culture, arts and society.[268,269]

Many ancient and medieval Hindu texts were composed in Sanskrit, many others in regional Indian languages. In modern times, most ancient texts have been translated into other Indian languages and some in Western languages. Prior to the start of the common era, the Hindu texts were composed orally, then memorized and transmitted orally, from one generation to next, for more than a millennia before they were written down into manuscripts.[270] This verbal tradition of preserving and transmitting Hindu texts, from one generation to next, continued into the modern era.[271]

Jaina texts

Tattvartha Sutra is a Jain text written in the Sanskrit language.[272] It is regarded as one of the earliest, most authoritative books on Jainism, and the only text authoritative in both the *Digambara* and *Śvētāmbara* sects.[273]

Modern Sanskrit literature

Literature in Sanskrit continues to be produced. These works, however, have a very small readership. In the introduction to *Ṣoḍaśī: An Anthology of Contemporary Sanskrit Poets* (1992), Radhavallabh Tripathi writes: <templatestyles src="Template:Quote/styles.css"/>

> Sanskrit is known for its classical literature, even though the creative activity in this language has continued without pause from the medieval age till today. [...] Consequently, contemporary Sanskrit writing suffers from a prevailing negligence.

Most current Sanskrit poets are employed as teachers, either pandits in *pāṭhaśāla*s or university professors. However, Tripathi also points out the abundance of contemporary Sanskrit literature: <templatestyles src="Template:Quote/styles.css"/>

> On the other hand, the number of authors who appear to be very enthusiastic about writing in Sanskrit during these days is not negligible. [...] Dr. Ramji Upadhyaya in his treatise on modern Sanskrit drama has discussed more than 400 Sanskrit plays written and published during the nineteenth and twentieth centuries. In a thesis dealing with Sanskrit mahākāvyas written in a single decade, 1961–1970, the researcher has noted 52 Sanskrit mahākāvyas (epic poems) produced in that very decade.

Similarly, Prajapati (2005), in *Post-Independence Sanskrit Literature: A Critical Survey*, estimates that more than 3000 Sanskrit works were composed in the period after Indian Independence (i.e., since 1947) alone. Further, much of this work is judged as being of high quality, both in comparison to classical Sanskrit literature, and to modern literature in other Indian languages.

Since 1967, the Sahitya Akademi, India's national academy of letters, has had an award for the best creative work written that year in Sanskrit. In 2009, Satyavrat Shastri became the first Sanskrit author to win the Jnanpith Award, India's highest literary award. Vidyadhar Shastri wrote two epic poems (*Mahakavya*), seven shorter poems, three plays and three songs of praise (*stavana kavya*), he received the *Vidyavachaspati* award in 1962. Some other modern Sanskrit composers include Abhiraj Rajendra Mishra (known as *Triveṇī Kavi*, composer of short stories and several other genres of Sanskrit literature), Jagadguru Rambhadracharya (known as *Kavikularatna*, composer of two epics, several minor works and commentaries on *Prasthānatrayī*).

References

5. ^ Bhattacharji Sukumari, History of Classical Sanskrit Literature, Sangam Books, London, 1993, <templatestyles src="Module:Citation/CS1/styles.css" />ISBN 0-86311-242-0, p. 148.

Further reading

- Jain, Vijay K. (2011), *Acharya Umasvami's Tattvarthsutra*[274] (1st ed.), Uttarakhand: Vikalp Printers, ISBN 81-903639-2-1, <q> ⓔ *This article incorporates text from this source, which is in the public domain.*</q><templatestyles src="Module:Citation/CS1/styles.css"></templatestyles>
- Jaini, Padmanabh S. (1998) [1979], *The Jaina Path of Purification*[275], Delhi: Motilal Banarsidass, ISBN 81-208-1578-5<templatestyles src="Module:Citation/CS1/styles.css"></templatestyles>
- Arthur Anthony Macdonell, A History of Sanskrit Literature, New York 1900
- Winternitz, M. A History of Indian Literature. Oriental books, New Delhi, 1927 (1907)
- J. Gonda (ed.) *A History of Indian Literature*, Otto Harrasowitz, Wiesbaden.
- Prajapati, Manibhai K. (2005), *Post-Independence Sanskrit Literature: A Critical Survey*, Standard Publishers (India)<templatestyles src="Module:Citation/CS1/styles.css"></templatestyles>
- S. Ranganath, *Modern Sanskrit Writings in Karnataka*[276], Rashtriya Sanskrit Sansthan, 2009.

External links

Sanskrit edition of Wikipedia, the free encyclopedia

Wikibooks has a book on the topic of: *Sanskrit*

- GRETIL: Göttingen Register of Electronic Texts in Indian Languages[277] a cumulative register of the numerous download sites for electronic texts in Indian languages.
- Sanskrit Wikibooks[278]
- TITUS Indica[279]
- Vedabase.net[280]: Vaishnava literatures with word for word translations from Sanskrit to English.
- Official page[281] of the Clay Sanskrit Library, publisher of classical Indian literature with facing-page texts and translations. Also offers numerous downloadable materials.
- Sanskrit Documents Collection[282]: Documents in ITX format of Upanishads, Stotras etc., and a metasite with links to translations, dictionaries, tutorials, tools and other Sanskrit resources.

Pāli Canon

Part of *a series* on
Theravāda Buddhism

- v
- t
- e[283]

Part of a series on
Buddhism

- Outline
- Buddhism portal
- v
- t
- e[284]

Pāli Canon

Figure 42: *Standard edition of the Thai Pali Canon*

Pāli Canon

Vinaya Pitaka

- Suttavibhanga
- Khandhaka
- Parivara

Sutta Pitaka

- Digha Nikaya
- Majjhima Nikaya
- Samyutta Nikaya
- Anguttara Nikaya
- Khuddaka Nikaya

Abhidhamma Pitaka

- Dhammasangani
- Vibhanga
- Dhatukatha and Puggalapannatti
- Kathavatthu
- Yamaka
- Patthana

- $\underline{v}$
- $\underline{t}$
- $\underline{e}^{285}$

The **Pāli Canon** is the standard collection of scriptures in the Theravada Buddhist tradition, as preserved in the Pāli language.[286] It is the most complete extant early Buddhist canon.[287,288]

During the First Buddhist Council, Ananda recited the Sutta Pitaka, Upali the Vinaya Pitaka thirty years after the parinibbana of Gautama Buddha in Rajgir. The Arhats present accepted the recitations and henceforth the teachings were preserved orally by the Sangha. The Tipitaka that was transmitted to Sri Lanka during the reign of King Asoka were initially preserved orally and were later written down during the Fourth Buddhist Council in 29 BCE, approximately 454 years after the death of Gautama Buddha.[289]</ref> Textual fragment of similar teachings have been found in the agama of other major Buddhist schools in India. They were however written down in various Prakrits other than Pali as well as Sanskrit. Some of those were later translated into Chinese (earliest dating to the late 4th century CE). The surviving Sri Lankan version is the most complete, but one that was extensively redacted about 1,000 years after Buddha's death, in the 5th or 6th century CE.[290] The earliest textual fragments of canonical Pali were found in the Pyu city-states in Burma dating only to the mid 5th to mid 6th century CE.[291]

The Pāli Canon falls into three general categories, called *pitaka* (from Pali *piṭaka*, meaning "basket", referring to the receptacles in which the palm-leaf manuscripts were kept).[292] Because of this, the canon is traditionally known as the ***Tipiṭaka*** ("three baskets"). The three pitakas are as follows:

1. Vinaya Pitaka ("Discipline Basket"), dealing with rules or discipline of the sangha;[292]
2. Sutta Pitaka (Sutra/Sayings Basket), discourses and sermons of Buddha, some religious poetry and is the largest basket;[292]
3. Abhidhamma Pitaka, treatises that elaborate Buddhist doctrines, particularly about mind, also called the "systematic philosophy" basket, likely composed starting about and after 300 BCE.[292]

The Vinaya Pitaka and the Sutta Pitaka are remarkably similar to the works of the early Buddhist schools, often termed Early Buddhist Texts. The Abhidhamma Pitaka, however, is a strictly Theravada collection and has little in common with the Abhidhamma works recognized by other Buddhist schools.[293]

The Canon in the tradition

The Canon is traditionally described by the Theravada as the Word of the Buddha (*buddhavacana*), though this is not intended in a literal sense, since it includes teachings by disciples.[294]

Pāli Canon

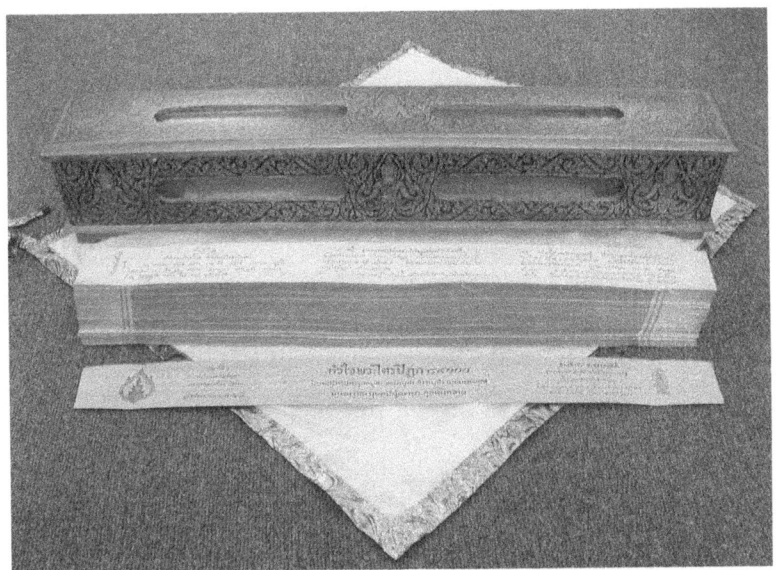

Figure 43: *In pre-modern times the Pali Canon was not published in book form, but written on thin slices of wood (Palm-leaf manuscript or Bamboo). The leaves are kept on top of each other by thin sticks and the scripture is covered in cloth and kept in a box.*

The traditional Theravādin (Mahavihārin) interpretation of the Pali Canon is given in a series of commentaries covering nearly the whole Canon, compiled by Buddhaghosa (fl. 4th–5th century CE) and later monks, mainly on the basis of earlier materials now lost. Subcommentaries have been written afterward, commenting further on the Canon and its commentaries. The traditional Theravādin interpretation is summarized in Buddhaghosa's Visuddhimagga.[295]

An official view is given by a spokesman for the Buddha Sasana Council of Burma:[296] the Canon contains everything needed to show the path to nirvāna; the commentaries and subcommentaries sometimes include much speculative matter, but are faithful to its teachings and often give very illuminating illustrations. In Sri Lanka and Thailand, "official" Buddhism has in large part adopted the interpretations of Western scholars.[297]

Although the Canon has existed in written form for two millennia, its earlier oral nature has not been forgotten in actual Buddhist practice within the tradition: memorization and recitation remain common. Among frequently recited texts are the Paritta. Even lay people usually know at least a few short texts by heart and recite them regularly; this is considered a form of meditation, at least if one understands the meaning. Monks are of course expected to know quite a bit more (see Dhammapada below for an example). A Burmese monk named Vicittasara even learned the entire Canon by heart for the Sixth Council (again according to the usual Theravada numbering).[298,299]

The relation of the scriptures to Buddhism as it actually exists among ordinary monks and lay people is, as with other major religious traditions, problematic: the evidence suggests that only parts of the Canon ever enjoyed wide currency, and that non-canonical works were sometimes very much more widely used; the details varied from place to place.[300] Rupert Gethin suggests that the whole of Buddhist history may be regarded as a working out of the implications of the early scriptures.[301]

Origins

According to a late part of the Pali Canon, the Buddha taught the three pitakas.[302] It is traditionally believed by Theravadins that most of the Pali Canon originated from the Buddha and his immediate disciples. According to the scriptures, a council was held shortly after the Buddha's passing to collect and preserve his teachings. The Theravada tradition states that it was recited orally from the 5th century BCE to the first century BCE, when it was written down.[303] The memorization was enforced by regular communal recitations. The tradition holds that only a few later additions were made. The Theravādin pitakas were first written down in Sri Lanka in the Alu Viharaya Temple no earlier than 29-17 B.C.E.

Much of the material in the Canon is not specifically Theravādin, but is instead the collection of teachings that this school preserved from the early, non-sectarian body of teachings. According to Peter Harvey, it contains material which is at odds with later Theravādin orthodoxy. He states that "the Theravādins, then, may have *added* texts to the Canon for some time, but they do not appear to have tampered with what they already had from an earlier period."[304] A variety of factors suggest that the early Sri Lankan Buddhists regarded canonical literature as such and transmitted it conservatively.[305]

Authorship

Authorship according to Theravadins

Prayudh Payutto argues that the Pali Canon represents the teachings of the Buddha essentially unchanged apart from minor modifications. He argues that it also incorporates teachings that precede the Buddha, and that the later teachings were memorized by the Buddha's followers while he was still alive. His thesis is based on study of the processes of the first great council, and the methods for memorization used by the monks, which started during the Buddha's lifetime. It's also based on the capability of a few monks, to this day, to memorize the entire canon.

Bhikkhu Sujato and Bhikkhu Brahmali argue that it is likely that much of the Pali Canon dates back to the time period of the Buddha. They base this on many lines of evidence including the technology described in the canon (apart from the obviously later texts), which matches the technology of his day which was in rapid development, that it doesn't include back written prophecies of the great Buddhist ruler King Ashoka (which Mahayana texts often do) suggesting that it predates his time, that in its descriptions of the political geography it presents India at the time of Buddha, which changed soon after his death, that it has no mention of places in South India, which would have been well known to Indians not long after Buddha's death and various other lines of evidence dating the material back to his time.

Authorship according to academic scholars

The views of scholars concerning the authorship of the Pali Canon can be grouped into three categories:Wikipedia:Citation needed

1. Attribution to the Buddha himself and his early followers
2. Attribution to the period of pre-sectarian Buddhism
3. Agnosticism

Scholars have both supported and opposed the various existing views.

Views concerning authorship of the Buddha himself

Several scholars of early Buddhism argue that the nucleus of the Buddhist teachings in the Pali Canon may derive from Gautama Buddha himself, but that part of it also was developed after the Buddha by his early followers. Richard Gombrich says that the main preachings of the Buddha (as in the Vinaya and Sutta Pitaka) are coherent and cogent, and must be the work of a single person: the Buddha himself, not a committee of followers after his death.[306]</ref>[307]

Other scholars are more cautious, and attribute part of the Pali canon to the Buddha's early followers. Peter Harvey[308] also states that "much" of the Pali

Canon must derive from the Buddha's teaching, but also states that "parts of the Pali Canon clearly originated after the time of the Buddha."[309]</ref> A.K. Warder has stated that there is no evidence to suggest that the shared teaching of the early schools was formulated by anyone else than the Buddha and his immediate followers.[310]</ref> J.W. de Jong has said it would be "hypocritical" to assert that we can say nothing about the teachings of earliest Buddhism, arguing that "the basic ideas of Buddhism found in the canonical writings could very well have been proclaimed by him [the Buddha], transmitted and developed by his disciples and, finally, codified in fixed formulas."[311] Alex Wynne has said that some texts in the Pali Canon may go back to the very beginning of Buddhism, which perhaps include the substance of the Buddha's teaching, and in some cases, maybe even his words.[312]</ref>. He suggests that the canon was composed early on soon after Buddha's paranirvana, but after a period of free improvisation, and then the core teachings were preserved nearly verbatim by memory. Hajime Nakamura writes that while nothing can be definitively attributed to Gautama as a historical figure, some sayings or phrases must derive from him.[313]

Views concerning authorship in the period of pre-sectarian Buddhism

Most scholars do agree that there was a rough body of sacred literature that a relatively early community maintained and transmitted.[314,315]</ref>

Much of the Pali Canon is found also in the scriptures of other early schools of Buddhism, parts of whose versions are preserved, mainly in Chinese. Many scholars have argued that this shared material can be attributed to the period of Pre-sectarian Buddhism.Wikipedia:Citation needed This is the period before the early schools separated in about the fourth or third century BCE.

Views concerning agnosticism

Some scholars see the Pali Canon as expanding and changing from an unknown nucleus.[316] Arguments given for an agnostic attitude include that the evidence for the Buddha's teachings dates from (long) after his death.

Some scholars of later Indian Buddhism and Tibetan Buddhism say that little or nothing goes back to the Buddha. Ronald Davidson[317] has little confidence that much, if any, of surviving Buddhist scripture is actually the word of the historical Buddha.[314] Geoffrey Samuel[318] says the Pali Canon largely derives from the work of Buddhaghosa and his colleagues in the 5th century AD.[319] Gregory Schopen argues[320] that it is not until the 5th to 6th centuries CE that we can know anything definite about the contents of the Canon. This position was criticized by A. Wynne.[321]

The earliest books of the Pali Canon

Different positions have been taken on what are the earliest books of the Canon. The majority of Western scholars consider the earliest identifiable stratum to be mainly prose works,[322] the Vinaya (excluding the Parivāra)[323] and the first four nikāyas of the Sutta Pitaka,[324,325] and perhaps also some short verse works[326] such as the Suttanipata.[323] However, some scholars, particularly in Japan, maintain that the Suttanipāta is the earliest of all Buddhist scriptures, followed by the Itivuttaka and Udāna.[327] However, some of the developments in teachings may only reflect changes in teaching that the Buddha himself adopted, during the 45 years that the Buddha was teaching.[328]</ref>

Scholars generally agree that the early books include some later additions.[329] Aspects of these late additions are or may be from a much earlier period.[330,331,332] Other aspects of the Pali Canon, such as the information about society and South Asian history, are in doubt because the Pali Canon was extensively redacted in the 5th- or 6th-century CE, nearly a thousand years after the death of the Buddha. Further, this redacted Pali Canon of Sri Lanka itself mentions that the compilation had previously been redacted towards the end of 1st-century BCE. According to the Early Buddhism scholar Lars Fogelin, the Pali Canon of Sri Lanka is a modified Canon and "there is no good reason to assume that Sri Lankan Buddhism resembles Early Buddhism in the mainland, and there are numerous reasons to argue that it does not."

One of the edicts of Ashoka, the 'Calcutta-Bairat edict', lists several works from the canon which he considers advantageous. According to Alexander Wynne:

> The general consensus seems to be that what Asoka calls Munigatha correspond to the Munisutta (Sn 207-21), Moneyasute is probably the second half of the Nalakasutta (Sn 699-723), and Upatisapasine may correspond to the Sariputtasutta (Sn 955-975). The identification of most of the other titles is less certain, but Schmithausen, following Oldenberg before him, identifies what Asoka calls the Laghulovada with part of a prose text in the Majjhima Nikaya, the Ambalatthika-Rahulovada Sutta (M no.61).[333]

This seems to be evidence which indicates that some of these texts were already fixed by the time of the reign of Ashoka (304–232 BCE), which means that some of the texts carried by the Buddhist missionaries at this time might also have been fixed.[333]

According to the Sri Lankan Mahavamsa, the Pali Canon was written down in the reign of King Vattagāmini (*Vaṭṭagāmiṇi*) (1st century BCE) in Sri Lanka, at the Fourth Buddhist council. Most scholars hold that little if anything was added to the Canon after this,[334,335,336] though Schopen questions this.

Figure 44: *Burmese-Pali manuscript copy of the Buddhist text Mahaniddesa, showing three different types of Burmese script, (top) medium square, (centre) round and (bottom) outline round in red lacquer from the inside of one of the gilded covers*

Texts

Manuscripts

The climate of Theravāda countries is not conducive to the survival of manuscripts. Apart from brief quotations in inscriptions and a two-page fragment from the eighth or ninth century found in Nepal, the oldest manuscripts known are from late in the fifteenth century,[337] and there is not very much from before the eighteenth.

Printed editions and digitized editions

The first complete printed edition of the Canon was published in Burma in 1900, in 38 volumes.[338] The following editions of the Pali text of the Canon are readily available in the West:

- Pali Text Society edition, 1877–1927 (a few volumes subsequently replaced by new editions), 57 volumes including indexes.

- The Pali scriptures and some Pali commentaries were digitized as an MS-DOS/extended ASCII compatible database through cooperation between the Dhammakaya Foundation and the Pali Text Society in 1996 as *PALITEXT version 1.0: CD-ROM Database of the Entire Buddhist Pali Canon* <templatestyles src="Module:Citation/CS1/styles.css" />ISBN 978-974-8235-87-5.[339]
- Thai edition, 1925–28, 45 volumes; more accurate than the PTS edition, but with fewer variant readings;[340]
  - BUDSIR on Internet free with login; and electronic transcript by BUDSIR: Buddhist scriptures information retrieval, CD-ROM and on-line, both requiring payment.
- Sixth Council edition, Rangoon, 1954–56, 40 volumes; more accurate than the Thai edition, but with fewer variant readings;[341]
  - electronic transcript by Vipāssana Research Institute available online in searchable database free of charge, or on CD-ROM (p&p only) from the institute.
  - Another transcript of this edition, produced under the patronage of the Supreme Patriarch of Thailand, World Tipitaka Edition, 2005, 40 volumes, published by the Dhamma Society Fund, claims to include the full extent of changes made at the Sixth Council, and therefore reflect the results of the council more accurately than some existing Sixth Council editions. Available for viewing online (registration required) at Tipiṭaka Quotation WebService.[342]
- Sinhalese (Buddha Jayanti) edition, 1957–?1993, 58 volumes including parallel Sinhalese translations, searchable, free of charge (not yet fully proofread.) Available at Journal of Buddhist Ethics.[343]
- Sinhalese (Buddha Jayanti). Image files in Sinhala script. The only accurate version of the Sri Lankan text available, in individual page images. Cannot be searched though.
  - Transcript in BudhgayaNews Pali Canon. In this version it is easy to search for individual words across all 16,000+ pages at once and view the contexts in which they appear.

No one edition has all the best readings, and scholars must compare different editions.[344]

- The Complete Collection of Chinese Pattra Scripture as preserved by the Dai people.

Translations

Pali Canon in English Translation, 1895-, in progress, 43 volumes so far, Pali Text Society, Bristol; for details of these and other translations of individual books see the separate articles. In 1994, the then President of the Pali Text Society stated that most of these translations were unsatisfactory.[345] Another former President said in 2003 that most of the translations were done very badly.[346] The style of many translations from the Canon has been criticized[347] as "Buddhist Hybrid English", a term invented by Paul Griffiths for translations from Sanskrit. He describes it as "deplorable", "comprehensible only to the initiate, written by and for Buddhologists".[348]

Selections: see List of Pali Canon anthologies.

A translation by Bhikkhu Nanamoli and Bhikkhu Bodhi of the Majjhima Nikaya was published by Wisdom Publications in 1995.

Translations by Bhikkhu Bodhi of the Samyutta Nikaya and the Anguttara Nikaya were published by Wisdom Publications in 2003 and 2012, respectively.

In 2018, new translations of the entirety of the five Nikayas were made freely available on the website suttacentral[349] by the Australian Bhikkhu Sujato, the translations were also released into the Public Domain.

A Japanese translation of the Canon, edited by Takakusu Junjiro, was published in 65 volumes from 1935 to 1941 as The Mahātripiṭaka of the Southern Tradition (南伝大□□ *Nanden daizōkyō*).

A Chinese translation of the above-mentioned Japanese translation was undertaken between 1990-1998 and thereafter printed under the patronage of Kaoshiung's Yuan Heng Temple.

Contents of the Canon

As noted above, the Canon consists of three pitakas.

- Vinaya Pitaka (*vinayapiṭaka*)
- Sutta Pitaka or Suttanta Pitaka
- Abhidhamma Pitaka

Details are given below. For more complete information, see standard references on Pali literature.[350,351]

Vinaya Pitaka

The first category, the *Vinaya Pitaka*, is mostly concerned with the rules of the *sangha*, both monks and nuns. The rules are preceded by stories telling how the Buddha came to lay them down, and followed by explanations and analysis. According to the stories, the rules were devised on an ad hoc basis as the Buddha encountered various behavioral problems or disputes among his followers. This pitaka can be divided into three parts:

- Suttavibhanga (*-vibhaṅga*) Commentary on the Patimokkha, a basic code of rules for monks and nuns that is not as such included in the Canon. The monks' rules are dealt with first, followed by those of the nuns' rules not already covered.
- Khandhaka Other rules grouped by topic in 22 chapters.
- Parivara (parivāra) Analysis of the rules from various points of view.

Sutta Pitaka

The second category is the *Sutta Pitaka* (literally "basket of threads", or of "the well spoken"; Sanskrit: *Sutra Pitaka*, following the former meaning) which consists primarily of accounts of the Buddha's teachings. The Sutta Pitaka has five subdivisions, or nikayas:

- Digha Nikaya (dīghanikāya) 34 long discourses.[352] Joy Manné argues[353] that this book was particularly intended to make converts, with its high proportion of debates and devotional material.
- Majjhima Nikaya 152 medium-length discourses.[352] Manné argues[353] that this book was particularly intended to give a solid grounding in the teaching to converts, with a high proportion of sermons and consultations.
- Samyutta Nikaya (*saṃyutta-*) Thousands of short discourses in fifty-odd groups by subject, person etc. Bhikkhu Bodhi, in his translation, says this nikaya has the most detailed explanations of doctrine.
- Anguttara Nikaya (*aṅguttara-*) Thousands of short discourses arranged numerically from ones to elevens. It contains more elementary teaching for ordinary people than the preceding three.
- Khuddaka Nikaya A miscellaneous collection of works in prose or verse.

Abhidhamma Pitaka

The third category, the *Abhidhamma Pitaka* (literally "beyond the dhamma", "higher dhamma" or "special dhamma", Sanskrit: *Abhidharma Pitaka*), is a collection of texts which give a scholastic explanation of Buddhist doctrines particularly about mind, and sometimes referred to as the "systematic philosophy" basket.[292] There are seven books in the Abhidhamma Pitaka:

- Dhammasangani (-saṅgaṇi or -saṅgaṇī) Enumeration, definition and classification of dhammas
- Vibhanga (vibhaṅga) Analysis of 18 topics by various methods, including those of the Dhammasangani
- Dhatukatha (dhātukathā) Deals with interrelations between ideas from the previous two books
- Puggalapannatti (-paññatti) Explanations of types of person, arranged numerically in lists from ones to tens
- Kathavatthu (kathā-) Over 200 debates on points of doctrine
- Yamaka Applies to 10 topics a procedure involving converse questions (e.g. Is X Y? Is Y X?)
- Patthana (paṭṭhāna) Analysis of 24 types of condition[354]

The traditional position is that *abhidhamma* refers to the absolute teaching, while the suttas are adapted to the hearer. Most scholars describe the abhidhamma as an attempt to systematize the teachings of the suttas:[354,355] Cousins says that where the suttas think in terms of sequences or processes the abhidhamma thinks in terms of specific events or occasions.[356]

Use of Brahmanical devices

The Pali Canon uses many Brahmanical terminology and concepts. For example, in Samyutta Nikaya 111, Majjhima Nikaya 92 and Vinaya i 246 of the Pali Canon, the Buddha praises the Agnihotra as the foremost sacrifice and the Gayatri mantra as the foremost meter:

<templatestyles src="Template:Quote/styles.css"/>

> *aggihuttamukhā yaññā sāvittī chandaso mukham. Sacrifices have the agnihotra as foremost; of meter the foremost is the Sāvitrī.*

Comparison with other Buddhist canons

The other two main Buddhist canons in use in the present day are the Chinese Buddhist Canon and the Tibetan Kangyur.

The standard modern edition of the Chinese Buddhist Canon is the Taishō Revised Tripiṭaka, with a hundred major divisions, totaling over 80,000 pages. This includes Vinayas for the Dharmaguptaka, Sarvāstivāda, Mahīśāsaka, and Mahāsaṃghika schools. It also includes the four major Āgamas, which are analogous to the Nikayas of the Pali Canon. Namely, they are the Saṃyukta Āgama, Madhyama Āgama, Dīrgha Āgama, and Ekottara Āgama. Also included are the Dhammapada, the Udāna, the Itivuttaka, and Milindapanha. There are also additional texts, including early histories, that are preserved from the early Buddhist schools but not found in Pali. The canon contains voluminous works of Abhidharma, especially from the Sarvāstivāda school. The Indian works preserved in the Chinese Canon were translated mostly from Buddhist Hybrid Sanskrit, Classical Sanskrit, or from regional Prakrits. The Chinese generally referred to these simply as "Sanskrit" (Ch. 梵語, Fànyǔ). The first woodblock printing of the entire Chinese Buddhist Canon was done during the Song dynasty by imperial order in China in CE 971; the earliest dated printed Buddhist sutra was the Diamond Sutra printed in CE 868 (printed by an upasaka for free distribution);although printing of individual Buddhist sutras and related materials may have started as early as the 7th century CE.

The Tibetan Kangyur comprises about a hundred volumes and includes versions of the Vinaya Pitaka, the Dhammapada (under the title *Udanavarga*) and parts of some other books. Due to the later compilation, it contains comparatively fewer early Buddhist texts than the Pali and Chinese canons.

The Chinese and Tibetan canons are not translations of the Pali and differ from it to varying extents, but contain some recognizably similar early works. However, the Abhidharma books are fundamentally different works from the Pali Abhidhamma Pitaka. The Chinese and Tibetan canons also consist of Mahāyāna sūtras and Vajrayāna tantras, which have few parallels in the Pali Canon.[357]</ref>

Sources

<templatestyles src="Refbegin/styles.css" />

- "《中国贝叶经全集》新闻发布会暨出版座谈会_华人佛教_凤凰网"[358], *Fo.ifeng.com*, retrieved 2012-10-14<templatestyles src="Module:Citation/CS1/styles.css"></templatestyles>
- Allon, Mark (1997), "An Assessment of the Dhammakaya CD-ROM: Palitext Version 1.0", *Buddhist Studies (Bukkyō Kenkyū)*, **26**: 109–29<templatestyles src="Module:Citation/CS1/styles.css"></templatestyles>
- Bechert, Heinz; Gombrich, Richard F. (1984), *The world of buddhism : buddhist monks and nuns in society and culture*, London: Thames and Hudson<templatestyles src="Module:Citation/CS1/styles.css"></templatestyles>
- Brown, E K; Anderson, Anne (2006), *Encyclopedia of language &linguistics*, Boston: Elsevier<templatestyles src="Module:Citation/CS1/styles.css"></templatestyles>
- *BUDSIR (Buddhist scriptures information retrieval) for Thai Translation*[359], retrieved 2012-10-14<templatestyles src="Module:Citation/CS1/styles.css"></templatestyles>

- Buswell, Robert E (2004), *Encyclopedia of Buddhism*, USA: Macmillan Reference<templatestyles src="Module:Citation/CS1/styles.css"></templatestyles>
- Cone, Margaret (2001), *Dictionary of Pali, vol. I*, Oxford: Pali Text Society<templatestyles src="Module:Citation/CS1/styles.css"></templatestyles>
- Cousins, L. S. (1984), *In Richard Gombrich and K. R. Norman (ed.): Dhammapala, Buddhist studies in honour of Hammalava Saddhatissa*, Nugegoda, Sri Lanka: University of Sri Jayawardenapura, p. 56<templatestyles src="Module:Citation/CS1/styles.css"></templatestyles>
- Cousins, L. S. (1982), *Pali oral literature. In Denwood and Piatigorski, eds.: Buddhist Studies, ancient and modern*, London: Curzon Press, pp. 1–11<templatestyles src="Module:Citation/CS1/styles.css"></templatestyles>
- Davidson, Ronald M. (2003), *Indian Esoteric Buddhism*, New York: Indian Esoteric BuddhismColumbia University Press, ISBN 0231126182<templatestyles src="Module:Citation/CS1/styles.css"></templatestyles>
- De Jong, J.W. (1993), "The Beginnings of Buddhism", *The Eastern Buddhist*, **26** (2): 25<templatestyles src="Module:Citation/CS1/styles.css"></templatestyles>
- Encyclopædia Britannica: ultimate reference suite (2008), *Buddhism*, Encyclopædia Britannica<templatestyles src="Module:Citation/CS1/styles.css"></templatestyles>
- Gethin, Rupert (1998), *Foundations of Buddhism*, Oxford ; New York: Oxford University Press<templatestyles src="Module:Citation/CS1/styles.css"></templatestyles>
- Gethin, Rupert (1992), *The Buddha's Path to Awakening*, Leiden: E. J. Brill<templatestyles src="Module:Citation/CS1/styles.css"></templatestyles>
- Gombrich (b), Richard, *Interview by Kathleen Gregory*[360], archived from the original[361] on January 24, 2016, retrieved 2011 Check date values in: | accessdate= (help)<templatestyles src="Module:Citation/CS1/styles.css"></templatestyles>
- Gombrich, Richard F (2006), *Theravada Buddhism* (2nd ed.), London: Routledge<templatestyles src="Module:Citation/CS1/styles.css"></templatestyles>
- Griffiths, Paul J. (1981), "Buddhist Hybrid English: Some Notes on Philology and Hermeneutics for Buddhologists"[362], *Journal of the International Association of Buddhist Studies*, **4** (2): 17–32<templatestyles src="Module:Citation/CS1/styles.css"></templatestyles>

- Grönbold, Günter (1984), *Der buddhistische Kanon: eine Bibliographie*, Wiesbaden: Otto Harrassowitz<templatestyles src="Module:Citation/CS1/styles.css"></templatestyles>
- Hamm (1973), In: *Cultural Department of the German Embassy in India*, ed., Varanasi: Chowkhamba Sanskrit Series Office, German Scholars on India, volume I<templatestyles src="Module:Citation/CS1/styles.css"></templatestyles>
- Harvey, Peter (1995), *The Selfless Mind.*, Surrey: Curzon Press<templatestyles src="Module:Citation/CS1/styles.css"></templatestyles>
- Harvey, Peter (1990), *Introduction to Buddhism*, New York: Cambridge University Press<templatestyles src="Module:Citation/CS1/styles.css"></templatestyles>
- Jones, Lindsay (2005), *Councils, Buddhist*. In: *Encyclopedia of religion*, Detroit: Macmillan Reference<templatestyles src="Module:Citation/CS1/styles.css"></templatestyles>
- Maguire, Jack (2001), *Essential Buddhism: A Complete Guide to Beliefs and Practices*[363], Simon and Schuster, ISBN 978-0-671-04188-5<templatestyles src="Module:Citation/CS1/styles.css"></templatestyles>
- Manné, Joy (1990), "Categories of sutta in the Pali Nikayas"[364] (PDF), *Journal of the Pali Text Society*, **XV**: 29–88, archived from the original[365] (PDF) on September 1, 2014<templatestyles src="Module:Citation/CS1/styles.css"></templatestyles>
- McDaniel, Justin T. (2005), "The art of reading and teaching Dhammapadas: reform, texts, contexts in Thai Buddhist history"[366], *Journal of the International Association of Buddhist Studies*, **28** (2): 299–336<templatestyles src="Module:Citation/CS1/styles.css"></templatestyles>
- Mendelson, E. Michael (1975), *Sangha and State in Burma*, Ithaca, New York: Cornell University Press<templatestyles src="Module:Citation/CS1/styles.css"></templatestyles>
- Morgan, Kenneth W. (1956), *Path of the Buddha*, New York: Ronald Press<templatestyles src="Module:Citation/CS1/styles.css"></templatestyles>
- Nakamura, Hajime (1999), *Indian Buddhism: A Survey with Bibliographical Notes*, Delhi: Motilal Banarsidass<templatestyles src="Module:Citation/CS1/styles.css"></templatestyles>
- Ñāṇamoli, Bhikkhu;; Warder, Anthony Kennedy (1982), *Introduction to Path of Discrimination*, London: Pali Text Society: Distributed by Routledge and Kegan Paul<templatestyles src="Module:Citation/CS1/styles.css"></templatestyles>
- Norman, K.R. (1983), *Pali Literature*, Wiesbaden: Otto Harrassowitz<templatestyles src="Module:Citation/CS1/styles.css"></templatestyles>

templatestyles>
- Norman, K.R. (1996), *Collected Papers, volume VI*, Bristol: Pali Text Society<templatestyles src="Module:Citation/CS1/styles.css"></templatestyles>
- Norman, K. R. (2005). *Buddhist Forum Volume V: Philological Approach to Buddhism*[367]. Routledge. pp. 75–76. ISBN 978-1-135-75154-8.<templatestyles src="Module:Citation/CS1/styles.css"></templatestyles>
- *Pali Canon Online Database*[368], Bodhgaya News, retrieved 2012-10-14<templatestyles src="Module:Citation/CS1/styles.css"></templatestyles>
- Samuel, Geoffrey (2012), *Introducing Tibetan Buddhism*, New York: Routledge<templatestyles src="Module:Citation/CS1/styles.css"></templatestyles>
- Schopen, Gregory (1997), *Bones, Stones, and Buddhist Monks*, Honolulu: University of Hawai'i Press<templatestyles src="Module:Citation/CS1/styles.css"></templatestyles>
- Skilling, P.; ed. (1997). *Mahasutras, volume I, Parts I & II*. Oxford: Pali Text Society.<templatestyles src="Module:Citation/CS1/styles.css"></templatestyles>
- *Sri Lankan Pāḷi Texts*[369], retrieved 2013-01-15<templatestyles src="Module:Citation/CS1/styles.css"></templatestyles>
- "The Pali Tipitaka"[370], *Tipitaka.org*, retrieved 2012-10-14<templatestyles src="Module:Citation/CS1/styles.css"></templatestyles>
- "Vipassana Research Institute"[371], *Vri.dhamma.org*, VRI Publications, retrieved 2012-10-14<templatestyles src="Module:Citation/CS1/styles.css"></templatestyles>
- von Hinüber, Oskar (2000), *A Handbook of Pāli Literature*[372], Berlin; New York: Walter de Gruyter, ISBN 978-3-11-016738-2<templatestyles src="Module:Citation/CS1/styles.css"></templatestyles>
- Warder, A. K. (1963), *Introduction to Pali*, London: Published for the Pali Text Society by Luzac<templatestyles src="Module:Citation/CS1/styles.css"></templatestyles>
- Warder, Anthony Kennedy (2000), *Indian Buddhism* (3rd ed.), Delhi: Motilal Banarsidass<templatestyles src="Module:Citation/CS1/styles.css"></templatestyles>
- Wynne, Alexander (2003), *How old is the Suttapiṭaka? The relative value of textual and epigraphical sources for the study of early Indian Buddhism*[373] (PDF), St John's College, archived from the original[374] (PDF) on March 9, 2015<templatestyles src="Module:Citation/CS1/styles.css"></templatestyles>

- Wynne, Alexander (2004). "The Oral Transmission of the Early Buddhist Literature"[375]. *Journal of the International Association of Buddhist Studies*. **27** (1): 97–128.<templatestyles src="Module:Citation/CS1/styles.css"></templatestyles>
- Wynne, Alexander (2007), *The origin of Buddhist meditation*, New York: Routledge<templatestyles src="Module:Citation/CS1/styles.css"></templatestyles>

Further reading

- Hinüber, Oskar von (2000). *A Handbook of Pāli Literature*. Berlin: Walter de Gruyter. <templatestyles src="Module:Citation/CS1/styles.css" />ISBN 3-11-016738-7.
- B. C. Law, *History of Pali Literature*[376], volume I, Trubner, London 1931
- Russell Webb (ed.), *Analysis of the Pali Canon*[377], The Wheel Publication No 217, Buddhist Publication Society, Kandy, Sri Lanka, 3rd ed. 2008.
- Ko Lay, U. (2003), *Guide to Tipiṭaka*[378], Selangor, Malaysia: Burma Piṭaka Association. Editorial Committee, Archived from the original on July 24, 2008<templatestyles src="Module:Citation/CS1/styles.css"></templatestyles>

External links

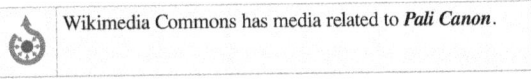

Wikimedia Commons has media related to *Pali Canon*.

- Sayadaw U Vicittasara Mingun Sayadaw: A Fabulous Memory[379]
- Beginnings: The Pali Suttas by [[Samanera Bodhesako[380]]]

English translations

- Access to Insight[381] has many suttas translated into English
- Tipitaka Online[382] of Nibbana.com. Burma (Myanmar)
- English translations by Bhikkhu Bodhi of selected suttas of the Majjhima Nikaya are made available by the Foundation for the Preservation of the Mahayana Tradition at Wisdom Publications[383]
- English translations by Bhikkhu Bodhi of selected suttas from the Anguttara Nikaya at Wisdom Publications[384]

Pali Canon online

- Vipassana Research Institute[370] (Based on 6th Council – Burmese version) (this site also offers a downloadable program which installs the entire Pali Tipitaka on your desktop for offline viewing)
- Sutta Central[385] Early Buddhist texts, translations, and parallels (Multiple Languages)
- Thai Tripitaka[386] (Thai version)
- Sinhala Tipitaka[387] (Translated into Sinhala by a Government of Sri Lanka initiative)

Pali dictionary

- Online Pali-English Dictionary[388]

In common Indian languages

Assamese literature

Indian literature
• Assamese
• Bengali
• Bhojpuri
• English
• Gujarati
• Hindi
• Kannada
• Kashmiri
• Konkani
• Malayalam
• Meitei
• Marathi
• Mizo
• Nepali
• Odia
• Punjabi
• Rajasthani
• Sanskrit
• Sindhi
• Tamil
• Telugu
• Urdu
• v • t • e[389]

Part of a series on the
Culture of Assam
Religion
• Assam portal
• v • t • e[390]

Assamese literature
Asamiya literature (By category) Asamiya
Asamiya literary history
History of Asamiya literature
Asamiya language authors
List of Asamiya writers
Asamiya Writers
Writers • Dramatists & Playwrights • Poets
Forms
Books – Buranjis – Poetry
Institution & Awards

Assamese literature

Assam Sahitya Sabha Assam Ratna Assam Valley Literary Award Kamal Kumari National Award
Related Portals Literature Portal Assam Portal

- v
- t
- e[391]

History of literature <templatestyles src="Nobold/-styles.css"/>by region or country

General topics
- Basic topics - Literary terms - Criticism - Theory
Types
- Epic - Novel - Poetry - Prose - Romance
Lists
- Books - Authors
Middle Eastern

- Ancient
- Sumerian
- Babylonian
- Egyptian
  - Ancient Egyptian
- Hebrew
- Pahlavi
- Persian
- Arabic
- Israeli

European

- Greek
- Latin
- Early Medieval
  - Matter of Rome
  - Matter of France
  - Matter of Britain
- Medieval
- Renaissance

Modern

- Structuralism
- Poststructuralism
- Deconstruction
- Modernism
- Postmodernism
- Post-colonialism
- Hypertexts

North and South American

- American
- Canadian
- Mexican
- Jamaican

Latin American

- Argentine
- Brazilian
- Colombian
- Cuban
- Peruvian

Australasian

- Australian
- New Zealand

Asian

East / Southeast

- Chinese
- Japanese
- Korean
- Vietnamese
- Thai

South

- Sanskrit
- Indian
- Pakistani
- Assamese
- Bengali
- Gujurati
- Hindi
- Kannada
- Kashmiri
- Malayalam
- Marathi
- Nepali
- Rajasthani
- Sindhi
- Tamil
- Telugu
- Urdu
- Indian writing in English

African

• Moroccan • Nigerian • South African • Swahili
Related topics
• History of science fiction • List of years in literature • Literature by country • History of theatre • History of ideas • Intellectual history
📚 **Literature portal**
• v • t • e[392]

Assamese literature (Assamese: অসমীয়া সাহিত্য, translit. *Ôxômiya xahittô*) is the entire corpus of poetry, novels, short stories, documents and other writings in the Assamese language. It also includes popular ballads in the older forms of the language during its evolution to the contemporary form. The literary heritage of the Assamese language can be traced back to the c. 9-10th century in the *Charyapada*, where the earliest elements of the language can be discerned.

History

The history of the Assamese literature may be broadly divided into three periods:

Early Assamese (6th to 15th century)

Even though systematic errors in the Sanskrit of Kamarupa inscriptions betray an underlying Pakrit in the pre-12th century period, scarce examples of the language exist. The *Charyapada*s, the Buddhist ballads of 8th-10th century some of whose composers were from Kamarupa and the language of which bear strong affinities with Assamese (beside Bengali, Maithili and Oriya), are considered the first examples of Assamese literature. The spirit of the *Charyapadas* are found in later-day *Deh-Bicaror Geet* and other aphorisms; and some of the ragas found their way to the 15th-16th century *Borgeets*. In the 12th-14th century period the works of Ramai Pundit (*Sunya Puran*), Boru Chandidas (*Krishna Kirtan*), Sukur Mamud (*Gopichandrar Gan*), Durllava Mullik (*Gobindachandrar Git*) and Bhavani Das (*Mainamatir Gan*) bear strong grammatical relationship to Assamese; and their expressions and their use of *adi-rasa* are found in the later Panchali works of Mankar and Pitambar. These works too are claimed as examples of Bengali literature. After this period of shared legacy a fully differentiated Assamese literature finally emerged in the 14th century.

Pre-Sankardeva period

This period saw the flourishing of two kinds of literary activity: translations and adaptations, and choral songs.

Translations and Adaptations

Harivara Vipra, a court poet of Durlabhnarayana (1330–1350) of Kamata, with his work *Vavruvahanar Yuddha* (based on the Mahabharata)[393] and *Lava-Kuxar Yuddha* (based on the Ramayana) provides the first date-able examples of Assamese literature. Though translated works, they contain local descriptions and embellishments, a feature that describes all translated work of this period. His Vavruvahanar Yuddha, for instance makes references to articles of the Ahom kingdom,[394] which at that time was a small kingdom in the east, and describes the undivided Lakhimpur region, and in *Lava-Kushar Yuddha* he departs from the original and describes local customs for Rama and Sita's *pumsavana* ceremony. Other works in this class and period are Hema Saraswati's *Prahlada-caritra* and *Hara-Gauri-Samvada*; Kaviratna Saravati's *Jayadratha-vadha*; Rudra Kandali's *Satyaki-pravesa*. All these works are associated with Durlabhanarayan of Kamata and his immediate successors.

The major work from this period that left a lasting impression is *Saptakanda Ramayana*, composed by Madhava Kandali, and recited[395] in the court of a 14th-century Barahi-Kachari king Mahamanikya (Mahamanikpha) who ruled either in the Nagaon or the Golaghat region. In chronology, among vernacular translations of the original Sanskrit, Kandali's Ramayana comes after Kamban's (Tamil), and ahead of Kirttivas' (Bengali, 15th century), Tulsidas' (Awadhi, 16th century), Balaram Das' (Oriya) etc. The literary language (as opposed to the colloquial Assamese) this work adopted became the standard literary language for much of the following periods, till the rise of new literature in the 19th century. That his work was a major influence can be inferred from Sankardeva's tribute to the "unerring predecessor poet".[396] The *pada* form of metrical verse (14 syllables in each verse with identical two syllables at the end of each foot in a couplet) became a standard in Assamese *kavya* works, something that continued till the modern times. Though a translated work, it is infused with local color, and instead of the heroic, Kandali instead emphasized the homely issues of relationships etc. Among the two kinds of *alamkara's*, *arthalankaras* were used extensively, with similes and metaphors taken from the local milieu even though the original works are set in foreign lands; whereas the *shabdalankara* (alliteration etc.) were rarely used.

Choral songs

Choral songs composed for a popular form of narration-performances called *Oja-pali*, a precursor to theater and theatrical performances, came to be known as *Panchali* works. Though some of these works are contemporaneous to Sankardeva's, they hark back to older forms free of Sankardeva's influences and so are considered pre-Sankardeva literature. The *Oja-palis* follow two different traditions: *biyah-gowa* which tells stories from the Mahabharata and *Maroi*, which tells stories on the snake goddess *Manaxa*. The poets—Pitambar, Durgabar, Mankar and Sukavi Narayan—are well known for the compositions. The *Oja-palis* follow two different traditions: *biyah-gowa* which tells stories from the Mahabharata and *Maroi*, which tells stories on the snake goddess *Manaxa*.

Middle Assamese (17th to 19th century)

This is a period of the prose chronicles (*Buranji*) of the Ahom court. The Ahoms had brought with them an instinct for historical writings. In the Ahom court, historical chronicles were at first composed in their original Tibetan-Chinese language, but when the Ahom rulers adopted Assamese as the court language, historical chronicles began to be written in Assamese. From the beginning of the 17th century onwards, court chronicles were written in large numbers. These chronicles or buranjis, as they were called by the Ahoms, broke away from the style of the religious writers. The language is essentially modern except for slight alterations in grammar and spelling.

Modern Assamese

Effect of British rule

The British imposed Bengali in 1836 in Assam after the state was occupied in 1826. Due to a sustained campaign, Assamese was reinstated in 1873 as the state language. Since the initial printing and literary activity occurred in eastern Assam, the Eastern dialect was introduced in schools, courts and offices and soon came to be formally recognized as the Standard Assamese. In recent times, with the growth of Guwahati as the political and commercial center of Assam, the Standard Assamese has moved away from its roots in the Eastern dialect.

Influence of Missionaries

The modern Assamese period began with the publication of the Bible in Assamese proseWikipedia:Citation needed by the American Baptist missionaries in 1819. The currently prevalent standard Asamiya has its roots in the Sibsagar dialect of Eastern Assam. As mentioned in Bani Kanta Kakati's "Assamese, its Formation and Development" (1941, Published by Sree Khagendra Narayan Dutta Baruah, LBS Publications, G.N. Bordoloi Road, Gauhati-1, Assam, India) – " The Missionaries made Sibsagar in Eastern Assam the centre of their activities and used the dialect of Sibsagar for their literary purposes". The American Baptist Missionaries were the first to use this dialect in translating the Bible in 1813.

The Missionaries established the first printing press in Sibsagar in 1836 and started using the local Asamiya dialect for writing purposes. In 1846 they started a monthly periodical called *Arunodoi*, and in 1848, Nathan Brown published the first book on Assamese grammar. The Missionaries published the first Assamese-English Dictionary compiled by M. Bronson in 1867. One of the major contributions of the American Baptist missionaries to the Assamese language is the reintroduction of Assamese as the official language in Assam. In 1848 missionary Nathan Brown published a treatise on the Assamese language.[397] This treatise gave a strong impetus towards reintroducing Assamese the official language in Assam. In his 1853 official report on the province of Assam, British official Moffat Mills wrote:

> "
> ...the people complain, and in my opinion with much reason, of the substitution of Bengalee for the Vernacular Assamese. Bengalee is the language of the court, not of their popular books and shashtras, and there is a strong prejudice to its general use. ...Assamese is described by Mr. Brown, the best scholar in the province, as a beautiful, simple language, differing in more respects from, than agreeing with, Bengalee, and I think we made a great mistake in directing that all business should be transacted in Bengalee, and that the Assamese must acquire it. It is too late now to retrace our steps, but I would strongly recommend Anandaram Phukan's proposition to the favourable consideration of the Council of Education, viz., the substitution of the vernacular language in lieu of Bengalee, and completion of the course of the Vernacular education in Bengalee. I feel persuaded that a youth will, under this system of tuition, learn more in two than he now acquires in four years. An English youth is not taught in Latin until he is well grounded in English, and in the same manner, an Assamese should not be taught in a foreign language until he knows his own.
> "

398

Beginning of Modern Literature

"ব্যাকৰণ,অভিধান নাথাকিলে ভাষা আৰু সাহিত্য হেদাওঁতি মেলা খৰচ দৰে হ'ব আৰু সেই সাহিত্যৰ, সেই ভাষাৰ উপযুক্ত টাঁটী-চেকাৰা এখনো নাথাকিব!"

--লক্ষ্মীনাথ বেজবৰুৱা

The period of modern literature began with the publication the Assamese journal *Jonaki* (জোনাকী) (1889), which introduced the short story form first by

Lakshminath Bezbaroa. Thus began the Jonaki period of Assamese literature. In 1894 Rajanikanta Bordoloi published the first Assamese novel *Mirijiyori*Wikipedia:Citation needed.

The modern Assamese literature has been enriched by the works of Jyoti Prasad Agarwalla, Birinchi Kumar Barua, Hem Barua, Atul Chandra Hazarika, Nalini Bala Devi, Navakanta Barua, Mamoni Raisom Goswami, Bhabendra Nath Saikia, Homen Borgohain, Nirupama Borgohain, Kanchan Baruah, Saurabh Kumar Chaliha and others. Moreover, as regards the spreading of Assamese literature outside Assam, the complete work of Jyoti Prasad Agarwala has been translated into Hindi to reach a wider audience by Devi Prasad Bagrodia. Bagrodia has also translated Shrimanta Shankardev's 'Gunamala' into Hindi.

In 1917 the Asam Sahitya Sabha was formed as a guardian of the Assamese society and the forum for the development of Assamese language and literature. Padmanath Gohain Baruah was the first president of the society.

Contemporary literature

Contemporary writers include Arupa Patangia Kalita,Monikuntala Bhattacharya,Mousumi Kondoli, Monalisa Saikia.

References

<templatestyles src="Refbegin/styles.css" />

- Kakati, Banikanta, ed. (1953), *Aspects of Early Assamese Literature*, Gauhati: Gauhati University<templatestyles src="Module:Citation/CS1/styles.css"></templatestyles>
- Barpujari, H K, ed. (1990). "Language and Literature". *The Comprehensive History of Assam*. **1**. Guwahati: Publication Board.<templatestyles src="Module:Citation/CS1/styles.css"></templatestyles>
- Neog, Maheshwar (1953), "Assamese Literature before Sankaradeva", in Kakati, Banikanta, *Aspects of Early Assamese Literature*, Gauhati: Gauhati University<templatestyles src="Module:Citation/CS1/styles.css"></templatestyles>
- Sastry, Biswanarayan (1988). "Influence: Sanskrit (Assamese)". In Datta, Amaresh. *Encyclopedia of Indian Literature*[399]. **2**. New Delhi: Sahitya Akademi. pp. 1692–1694.<templatestyles src="Module:Citation/CS1/styles.css"></templatestyles>
- Saikia, Nagen (1997). "Medieval Assamese Literature". In Ayyappa Panicker, K. *Medieval Indian Literature: Assamese, Bengali and Dogri*[400]. **1**. New Delhi: Sahitya Akademi. pp. 3–20.<templatestyles src="Module:Citation/CS1/styles.css"></templatestyles>

- Sharma, Mukunda Madhava (1978). *Inscriptions of Ancient Assam*[401]. Guwahati, Assam: Gauhati University.<templatestyles src="Module:Citation/CS1/styles.css"></templatestyles>

External links

- Life and Works of Bhattadeva, the Father of Assamese Prose[402]
- Assamese proverbs, published 1896[403]

Buranji

Buranjis are a class of historical chronicles, written initially in the Ahom and afterwards in Assamese language.[404,405] The first such Buranji was written on the instructions of the first Ahom king Sukaphaa who established the Ahom kingdom in 1228. There were two kinds of Buranjis: one maintained by the state (official) and the other maintained by families.[406] Many such manuscripts were written by scribes under the office of the *Likhakar Barua*, which were based on state papers, diplomatic correspondences, judicial proceedings, etc. Others were written by nobles or by people under their supervision, sometimes anonymously. These documents reveal chronology of events, language, culture, society and the inner workings of the state machinery of the kingdom. They were written in "simple, lucid and unambiguous but expressive language with utmost brevity and least exaggeration." The tradition of writing Buranjis survived more than six hundred years well into the British period, till a few decades after the demise of the Ahom kingdom.

Literally, Buranji means "a store that teaches the ignorant" (in the Ahom language: *bu* ignorant person; *ran* teach; *ji* store). The Buranjis not only describe the Ahom kingdom, but also the neighbours (*Chutiya*, *Kachari* and *Tripura* Buranjis) and those with whom the Ahom kingdom had diplomatic and military contacts (*Padshah* Buranji). They were written on the barks of the *Sanchi* tree or aloe wood. Though many such Buranjis have been collected, compiled and published, an unknown number of Buranjis are still in private hands.Wikipedia:Citation needed

During the reign of Rajeswar Singha, Kirti Chandra Borbarua had many Buranjis destroyed because he suspected they contained information on his lowly birth.[407]

Language

Western Assamese was the dominant literary language and the "sole medium of all ancient Asamiya literature including the Burañjīs written in the Ahom courts". The Eastern Assamese dialect became the standard literary language of the region in around the early-19th century.[408] Gargaya, a style of Assamese writing that developed between the 17th and 19th centuries, was notably used in eastern Assam for writing Buranjis.[409]

List of well-known Buranjis

No.	Name	Author
1	Assam Buranji	Harakanta Baruah
2	Assam Buranji	Kasinath Tamuli Phukan
3	Asamar Padya Buranji	(Buranji of Assam in verse)
4	Ahom Buranji	Golap Chandra Barua
5	Changrung Phukanar Buranji	
6	Deodhai Asam Buranji	
7	Chutiya Buranji	
8	Padshah Buranji	
9	Purani Assam Buranji	Hemchandra Goswami
10	Satasari Assam Buranji	
11	Tungkhungia Buranji	Surya Kumar Bhuyan
12	Tripura Buranji	Ratna Kandali and Arjun Das, 1724

References

<templatestyles src="Refbegin/styles.css" />

- Barua, B K (1953). "Early Assamese Prose". In Kakati, Banikanta. *Aspects of Early Assamese Literature*[410]. Guwahati: Gauhati University, Assam. pp. 124–147. Retrieved 2018-02-12.<templatestyles src="Module:Citation/CS1/styles.css"></templatestyles>
- Goswami, G. C.; Tamuli, Jyotiprakash (2007), "Asamiya", in Cordona, George; Jain, Dhanesh, *The Indo-Aryan Languages*[411], Routledge, pp. 429–484<templatestyles src="Module:Citation/CS1/styles.css"></templatestyles>

- Saikia, Yasmin (2004). *Fragmented Memories: Struggling to be Tai-Ahom in India*[412]. Duke University Press. ISBN 082238616X.<templatestyles src="Module:Citation/CS1/styles.css"></templatestyles>
- Hartmann, John F. (7 April 2011). "Phongsawadan Tai-Ahom: Ahom Buranji [Tai-Ahom Chronicles], 2 Vols. Transcribed and translated by Renu Wichasin. Bangkok: Amarin Printing and Publishing Ltd. Pp. xxiv, 993 [Continuous Pagination]. Map, Photos, Tables, Glossary. [In Thai]". *Journal of Southeast Asian Studies*. **28** (01): 227–229. doi: 10.1017/S002246340001554X[413].<templatestyles src="Module:Citation/CS1/styles.css"></templatestyles>
- Saikia, Arupjyoti (2008). "History, buranjis and nation: Suryya Kumar Bhuyan's histories in twentieth-century Assam". *The Indian Economic and Social History Review*. **45** (4): 473–507. doi: 10.1177/001946460804500401[414].<templatestyles src="Module:Citation/CS1/styles.css"></templatestyles>
- Sarkar, J. N. (1992) *The Buranjis: Ahom and Assamese* in The Comprehensive History of Assam Vol II (ed H K Barpujari), Publication Board, Assam

Assamese poetry

Assamese poetry is poetry in Assamese language. It borrows many themes from Sanskrit literature, and is mainly devotional in tone. The origins of Assamese poetry are considered to have taken place in the early 13th century, the *Bhagavat Purana* being one of the most notable examples

History

Sanskrit literature, the fountain head of most of the Indian literature, supplied not only the themes of medieval Assamese literature, but also has inspired many a writer of modern Assamese literature to undertake creative writings in context of modern literary trends and styles. Literature starting with poetry in Sanskrit was mainly devotional in tone and tenor, and so does the Assamese version. Since all the adaptations are being rooted in Sanskrit, making no contrary to this Assamese literature (poetry) was at the devotional tone and tenor. The starting of Assamese Poetry is marked with the adaptation from Sanskrit *puranas* into Assamese by the poet-scholar *Hema Saravswati* in the early 13th century. His first adaptation was *Prahlad-Charita* adapted from *Vamana Purana*.

Starting with a very few adaptations, Assamese Poetry were of devotional type in the very beginning. Later the adaptations got divided into two types – religious and secular. During the period of Vaishnavite revivalism, the secularism trend got into much demand. The Bhagavat Purana was considered to be the most important among all the puranas. Sankardev (1449–1568), the initiator of the Bhakti movement, started the process of translating and adapting different books and episodes of Bhagavat-Purana by rendering more than seven books (SKANDHA) and composed a few kabyas basing on that. He was the introducer of *BORGEET*, the most initial form of Assamese poems. (There is still confusion to call them poems since they were sung with musical instruments like KHOL and TAAL).[415]

Sources

- *Modern Assamese poetry*, by Hem Barua. Pub. Kavita, 1960.
- *History of Assamese literature*, Birinchi Kumar Barua. East-West Center Press, 1965. Chapter VII: Poetry
- Sailen Bharali (1992). "Modern Assamese Literature". *Modern Indian literature, an anthology, Volume 2*[416]. Sahitya Akademi. ISBN 81-7201-324-8.<templatestyles src="Module:Citation/CS1/styles.css"></templatestyles>
- *Mysticism in Indian poetry: a critical study of the Assamese mystic poets of the romantic age*, by Kamal Narayan Choudhury. Punthi-Pustak, 1996. <templatestyles src="Module:Citation/CS1/styles.css" />ISBN 81-85094-95-0.

Bengali literature

Bengali literature

Bengali literature বাংলা সাহিত্য
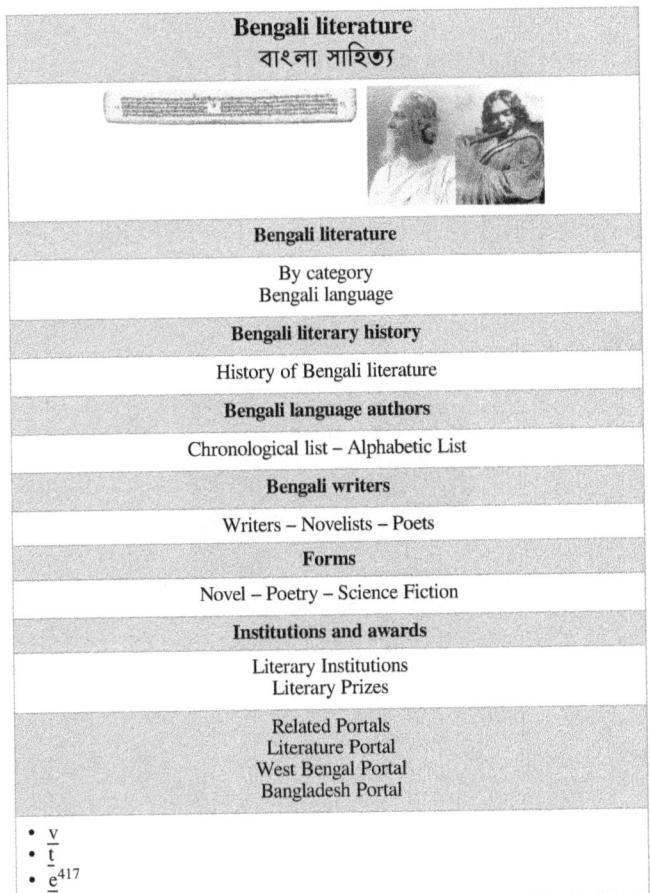
Bengali literature
By category Bengali language
Bengali literary history
History of Bengali literature
Bengali language authors
Chronological list – Alphabetic List
Bengali writers
Writers – Novelists – Poets
Forms
Novel – Poetry – Science Fiction
Institutions and awards
Literary Institutions Literary Prizes
Related Portals Literature Portal West Bengal Portal Bangladesh Portal

- v
- t
- e[417]

Medieval and Renaissance literature
Early medieval
• Matter of Rome • Matter of France • Matter of Britain • Byzantine • Kannada
Medieval
• Hebrew • Persian • Arabic • Bengali • Telugu
By century
• 10th • 11th • 12th • 13th • 14th
European Renaissance
• 15th century
📚 Literature portal
• v • t • e[418]

Part of a series on
Bengalis
• v • t • e[419]

Bengali literature (Bengali: বাংলা সাহিত্য, *Bangla Sahityô*) denotes the body of writings in the Bengali language. The earliest extant work in Bengali liter-

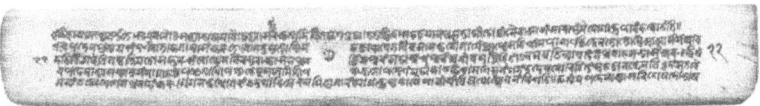

Figure 45: *Charyapada manuscript*

ature is the *Charyapada*, a collection of Buddhist mystic songs dating back to the 10th and 11th centuries. Thereafter, the timeline of Bengali literature is divided into two periods – medieval (1360-1800) and modern (after 1800).

Medieval Bengali literature consists of various poetic genres, including Hindu religious scriptures (e.g. Mangalkavya), Islamic epics (e.g. works of Syed Sultan and Abdul Hakim), translations of Sanskrit, Arabic and Persian texts, Vaishnava texts (e.g. biographies of Chaitanya Mahaprabhu), and secular texts by Muslim poets (e.g. works of Alaol).

Novels were introduced to Bengali literature in the mid-19th century. Rabindranath Tagore, poet, playwright, novelist, painter, essayist, musician, and social reformer, is the best known figure of Bengali literature to the world. He won the Nobel Prize for Literature in 1913. After the post-partition era, Bengali literature comprises literature of erstwhile East Pakistan (modern-day Bangladesh) and of West Bengal.

Old Bengali literature

The first works in Bengali, written in new Bengali, appeared between 10th and 12th centuries C.E. It is generally known as the *Charyapada*. These are mystic songs composed by various Buddhist seer-poets: Luipada, Kanhapada, Kukkuripada, Chatilpada, Bhusukupada, Kamlipada, Dhendhanpada, Shantipada, Shabarapada etc. The famous Bengali linguist Haraprasad Shastri discovered the palm leaf *Charyapada* manuscript in the Nepal Royal Court Library in 1907.

Figure 46: *Nabanarikunjara, one of the themes of Mediaeval Vishnava lyrics, engraved on a temple pillar at Bishnupur, Bankura.*

Middle Bengali literature

Pre-Chaitanya Vaishnava literature

Pre-Chaitanya or Early Vaishnava literature denotes the literature of the time preceding the time of Chaitanya Mahaprabhu, the founder of Gaudiya Vaishnavism. These include: *Sri Krishna Kritana* by Boru Chandidas; lyrical poems, known as the *Vaishnava Padavali* of Vidyapati and Chandidas; *Sri Krishna Vijaya*, the partial translation of *Bhagavata Purana* by Maladhar Basu and *Krittivasi Ramayana* by Krittivas Ojha.

Shrikrishna Kirtana

Basanta Ranjan Roy Bidyatvallava discovered the torn manuscript of the *Sri Krishna Kirtana* from the cowshed of Debendranath Chatterjee's house at Kakinlya village, Bankura district in modern-day Paschimbanga (West Bengal). *Sri Krishna Kirtana* was written by Boru Chandidas in the later half of 14th century CE. It is considered as the second oldest work of Bengali literature after *Charyapada*.

Figure 47: *Krittibas Memorial at Phulia, Nadia.*

Vaishnava lyrics by Vidyapati and Chandidas

The 15th century is marked by the emergence of Vaishnava lyrical poetry or the *padavali* in Bengal. The poetry of Vidyapati, the great Maithili poet, though not written in Bengali, influenced the literature of the time so greatly that it makes him a vital part of Middle Bengali literature. He flourished in the modern-day Darbhanga district of Bihar, India in the 14th century. His Vaishnava lyrics became very popular among the masses of Bengal. The first major Bengali poet to write Vaishnava lyrics was Chandidas, who belonged to the modern-day Birbhum district (or, according to another opinion, Bankura district), Paschimbanga in the 15th century. Chandidas is also known for his humanist proclamation—"*Sabar upare manush satya, tahar upare nai*" ("সবার উপরে মানুষ সত্য তাহার উপরে নাই ।")—"The supreme truth is man, there is nothing more important than he is.".

Maladhar Basu and Krittibas Ojha

The Bengali translations of two great Sanskrit texts the *Bhagavata Purana* and the *Ramayana* played a crucial role in the development of Middle Bengali literature. Maladhar Basu's *Sri Krishna Vijaya* (শ্রীকৃষ্ণবিজয়, *Triumph of Lord Krishna*), which is chiefly a translation of the 10th and 11th cantos of the *Bhagavata Purana*, is the earliest Bengali narrative poem that can be assigned

Figure 48: *A scene from Manasa Mangal.*

to a definite date. Maladhar Basu flourished in the modern-day Bardhaman district of Paschimbanga in the 15th century. Composed between 1473 and 1480 C.E., *Sri Krishna Vijaya* is also the oldest Bengali narrative poem of the Krishna legend.

The *Ramayana*, under the title of *Sri Rama Panchali*, more popularly known as the *Krittibasi Ramayana*, was translated by Krittibas Ojha who belonged to the modern-day Nadia district, Paschimbanga. He also, like Maladhar Basu, flourished in the 15th century.[420]

Post–Chaitanya Vaishnava literature

Post-Chaitanya or Late Vaishnava literature denotes the literature of the time succeeding the time of Chaitanya Mahaprabhu. These include: biographies of Chaitanya by Gaudiya Vaishnava scholar-poets and later Vaishnava *Padavali* with a special subgenre based on the life of Chaitanya. Major figures of the Late Vaishnava literature are Krishnadasa Kaviraja, Vrindavana Dasa Thakura, Jayananda, Govindadasa, Jnandada, Balaram Dasa etc.

Mangalkavya

Mangal-Kāvya (মঙ্গলকাব্য, "Poems of Benediction"), a group of Hindu narrative poetry, composed more or less between 13th Century and 18th Century, eulogise the indigenous deities of rural Bengal in the social scenario of the Middle Ages. *Mansa Mangal, Chandi Mangal* and *Dhormo Mangal,* the three major genus of *Mangal-Kāvya* tradition include the portrayal of the magnitude of Manasā, Chandī and Dharmathakur, who are considered the greatest among all the native divinities in Bengal, respectively. There are also minor *Mongolkabbosomogro* known as *Shivāyon, Kālikā Mangal, Rāy Mangal, Shashthi Mangal, Shitol Mangal* and *Komolā Mangal* etc. Major poets of Mangalkavya tradition are Mukundram Chakrabarty, Bijay Gupta, Rupram Chakrabarty etc.

19th century

In the middle of 19th century, Bengali literature gained momentum. During this period, the Bengali *Pandits* of Fort William College did the tedious work of translating the text books in Bengali to help teach the British some Indian languages including Bengali. This work played a role in the background in the evolution of Bengali prose. In 1814, Raja Ram Mohan Roy arrived in Calcutta and engaged in literary pursuits. Translating from Sanskrit to Bengali, writing essays on religious topics and publishing magazines were some the areas he focussed on. He established a cultural group in the name of 'Atmiya Sabha' (Club of Kins) in 1815. Another significant contributor of Bengali literature in its early stage was Ishwar Chandra Bandyopadhyaya.

In 1857, the famous 'Sipahi Bidroha' (Sepoy Mutiny) took place. With the wind of it, 'Nil Bidroho' (Indigo Revolt) scattered all over then Bengal region. This Nil Bidroha lasted for more than a year (In 1859-1860). The literature world was shaken with this revolt. In the light of this revolt, a great drama was published from Dhaka in the name of 'Nil Darpan' (The Indigo Mirror). Dinabandhu Mitra was the writer of this play.

Michael Madhusudan Dutt

Michael Madhusudan Dutt (1824–1873) introduced blank verse (*Amitrakshar Chhanda*), literary epics and sonnets in Bengali language. Dutt's first epic *Tilottama Sambhab Kabya* (তিলোত্তমাসম্ভব কাব্য, *Birth of Tilottama*) was published in 1860. This was the first Bengali poem written in blank verse. The story of *Tilottama Sambhab Kabya* is taken from Hindu Puranas. Dutt's greatest work *Meghnad Badh Kabya* (মেঘনাদবধ কাব্য, *Slaying of Meghnad*) was published in two parts in 1861. The story of *Meghnad Badh Kabya*

Figure 49: *Michael Madhusudan Dutt*

was borrowed from Hindu epic the *Ramayana* and deals chiefly the final battle, death and funeral of Meghnad, son of Ravana during the Lanka War. Dutt also wrote a lyrical poem–*Brajangana Kavya* (ব্রজাঙ্গনা কাব্য, *Women from Braj*, 1861)–and an epistolary poem *Birangana Kavya* (বীরাঙ্গনা কাব্য, *Valiant Ladies*, 1861–62). Dutt's last book of poems, *Chaturdashpadi Kabitabali* (চতুর্দশপদী কবিতাবলী, *Sonnets*), is a collection of 102 sonnets written at Versailles, France in 1865. Dutt also wrote four plays–*Sharmishtha* (শর্মিষ্ঠা, 1859), *Padmavati* (পদ্মাবতী, 1860), *Krishnakumari* (কৃষ্ণকুমারী, 1861) and *Maya-Kanan* (মায়া-কানন, *The Magical Forest*, 1874)–and two farces–*Ekei Ki Bole Sabhyata?* (একেই কি বলে সভ্যতা, *Is That What You Call Good Manners?*, 1860) and *Buro Shalikher Ghare Ro* (বুড়ো শালিখের ঘাড়ে রো, *Old Man Rejuvenated*, 1860)

In this time, Michael Madhusudan Dutt emerged as the first epic-poet of modern Bengali literature. Dutt, a Christian by conversion, is best known for his Ramayana-based masterpiece, "The Slaying of Meghnadh," (in Bengali "*Meghnadh Bodh Kabyo*" (মেঘনাদ বধ কাব্য)), which essentially follows in the poetic tradition of Milton's *Paradise Lost*. Those who have read it consider this work a world-class epic poem of the modern era. Michael Madhusudan Dutta is also credited with the introduction of sonnets to Bengali literature. He ruled the Bengali literature world for more than a decade (1858–1863). Dutt

Figure 50: *Bankim Chandra Chattopadhyay*

can also be credited to be a pioneer of the blank verse in Bengali literature. His style was deemed as "Amitrakshar Chhanda".

Bankim Chandra Chattopadhyay

Bankim Chandra Chattopadhyay (1838–1894) is considered one of the leading Bengali novelist and essayist of the 19th century. His first novel *Durgeshnandini*, considered a benchmark in the history of Bengali literature, was published in 1865. He also wrote "Vande Mātāram", the national song of India, which appears in his novel *Anandamath* (1882). His other novels include: *Kapalkundala, Bishabriksha, Krishnakanter Will, Rajsingha, Devi Chaudhurani* etc. Bankim Chandra has critically analysed the *Bhagavat Gita* and the problems of Krishnaism from a historical perspective in his *Dharmatattva* (1888) and *Krishna Charitra* (1882). *Kamalakanter Daptar* (1875) is one of his best known humorous sketches.

Others

Bengali literature has also produced many other notable talents. For example, famous and popular Bengali poets include Ishwar Chandra Gupta, Biharilal

Chakraborty, and Kaykobad. Romesh Chunder Dutt and Mir Mosharraf Hossain are notable for their works of fiction. Girish Chandra Ghosh and Dwijendralal Ray were prominent playwrights of the time, whereas Akshay Kumar Boral and Ramendra Sundar Tribedi are famous for their influential essays. Rassundari Devi authored the first full-fledged autobiography in modern Bengali literature in 1876.

This era also saw a rise in new literary publications, magazines and newspapers. A number of educational institutes also appeared all over the region. Both these developments helped to nurture and advance the modern Bengali literary movement.

The Pre-Tagore era also saw an undercurrent of popular literature which was focused on daily life in contemporary Bengal. The prose style, as well as the humour in these works, were often crass, blunt and accessible. A masterpiece in this regard was "Hutom Pechar Naksha" (The Sketch of the Owl) written by Kaliprasanna Singha, and satirically depicts "Babu" culture in 19th century Kolkata. Other notable works in this regard are "Alaler Ghorer Dulal" (The Spoilt Brat) by Peary Chand Mitra, "Ramtanu Lahiri o tatkalin Banga shamaj" (Ramtanu Lahiri & contemporary Bengali society) by Nyaymohan Tarkalankar, and "Naba Babu Bilas" & "Naba Bibi Bilas" by Bhabanicharan Bandopadhyay. These books arguably portrayed contemporary Bengali dialect and popular society effectively, and also incorporated now-extinct music genres such as Khisti, Kheur and Kabiyal gaan by stalwarts like Rupchand Pakhi and Bhola Moyra. Books like these have become rarer since the emergence of Tagore culture, and the burgeoning preference for literary elegance and refinement in Bengali society.

Influence of Rabindranath Tagore

Possibly the most prolific writer in Bengali is Nobel laureate Rabindranath Tagore. Tagore dominated both the Bengali and Indian philosophical and literary scene for decades. His 2,000 *Rabindrasangeets* play a pivotal part in defining Bengali culture, both in West Bengal and Bangladesh. He is the author of the national anthems of both India and Bangladesh, both composed in Bengali. Other notable Bengali works of his are *Gitanjali*, a book of poems for which he was awarded the Nobel Prize for Literature in 1913, and many short stories and a few novels. It is widely accepted that Bengali Literature accomplished its contemporary look by the writings and influence of Rabindranath.

In the fields of Drama and Satire, he influenced and created a very worthy posterity of him in Natyaguru Nurul Momen. Nurul Momen was an educationist, playwright, director, humorist, lawyer, broadcaster, philanthropist and

Figure 51: *Rabindranath Tagore, Asia's first Nobel laureate*

essayist of Bangladesh. He is recognized as the pioneer of modern Bengali drama,"acting as a bridge between earlier and later playwrights in terms of content and style", and even referred to as the "Father of Bangladeshi theater".

Kazi Nazrul Islam

In the similar category is Kazi Nazrul Islam, who was invited to post-partition Bangladesh as the National Poet (he had been suffering from dementia and aphasia since 1942) and whose work transcends sectarian boundaries. Adored by Bengalis both in Bangladesh and West Bengal, his work includes 3,000 songs, known as both as *nazrul geeti* and "nazrul sangeet". He is frequently called the "rebel poet" mainly because of his most famous and electrifying poem "Bidrohi" or "The Rebel", and also because of his strong sympathy and support for revolutionary activities leading to India's independence from British Rule. His songs and poems were frequently used during the Bangladesh Liberation War as well. Though he is acknowledged as the rebel poet, Nazrul very effectively contributed in all branches of literature. He wrote poems that light the fire against inequality or injustice and at the same time is known for his poignant romantic poems as well. He wrote a lot of Islami Ghazals and in the same time wrote a number of *Shyama Sangeet* (songs for the Hindu Mother Goddess, Kali). Nazrul was not only a poet, he was writer, musician,

Figure 52: *Nazrul playing a flute, Chittagong, 1926*

journalist and philosopher. He was sent to jail for his literary works against the then prevailing British rule.

Other notable names

Playwrights

After Rabindranath Tagore, two dramatists radically brought about a major change in Bengali theatre. One was Nurul Momen and the other was Bijon Bhattacharya. Nurul Momen created the first modern and experimental plays from East Bengal, which later became East Pakistan and subsequently, Bangladesh. Nurul Momen (1908–1990), also known as Natyaguru, was an educationist, playwright, director, humorist, lawyer, broadcaster, philanthropist and essayist of Bangladesh. He is recognized as the pioneer of modern Bengali drama, "acting as a bridge between earlier and later playwrights in terms of content and style", and even referred to as the "Father of Bangladeshi theatre".

Bengali literature 141

Novelists

Sarat Chandra Chattopadhyay was one of the most popular novelists of early 20th century whose speciality was exploring the life and suffering of women in contemporary rural Bengal. His sympathy towards the common rural folks in "pallisamaj" and a trademark simplified Bengali as a writing style made him one of the most popular writers in his time. Even long after his death many Bengali and Bollywood blockbusters were based on his novels. After him Tarashankar Bandopadhyay, Bibhutibhushan Bandopadhyay and Manik Bandopadhyay were the three Bandopadhyays who broke out into a new era of realistic writing style. Where Bibhutibhusan and Manik had long standing influence on the two of the most brilliant film directors from Bengal, Satyajit Ray and Ritwik Ghatak respectively. Other famous Bengali novelists include Humayun Ahmed, Jagadish Gupta, Satinath Bhaduri, Balai Chand Mukhopadhyay (Banophool), Shawkat Osman, Saradindu Bandopadhyay, Kamal Kumar Majumdar, Sunil Gangopadhyay, Syed Shamsul Haque, Akhteruzzaman Elias, Sandipan Chattopadhyay, Bimal Mitra, Bimal Kar, Samaresh Basu, Mani Shankar Mukherjee (Shankar), Shyamal Gangapadhyay and Amar Mitra. Humayun Ahmed is one of the most popular Bengali writers of fiction and drama. Seeds of Bengali science fiction are evident in the writings of Jagadish Chandra Bose, which was later put into a definite genre by writers such as Jagadananda Roy, Begum Roquia Sakhawat Hussain, and Premendra Mitra, Satyajit Ray. Professor Muhammed Zafar Iqbal, Humayun Ahmed and Abdullah-Al-Muti are also very popular in this genre.

Short story writers

Bengali literature is also famous for short stories. Some famous short story writers are Rabindranath Tagore, Manik Bandopadhyay, Jagadish Gupta, Tarashankar Bandopadhyay, Bibhutibhushan Bandopadhyay, Rajshekhar Basu (Parasuram), Syed Mujtaba Ali, Premendra Mitra, Kamal Kumar Majumdar, Shibram Chakrabarti, Saradindu Bandopadhyay, Subodh Ghosh, Narendranath Mitra, Narayan Gangopadhyay, Satyajit Ray, Leela Majumdar, Shirshendu Mukhopadhyay, Ratan Lal Basu, Sandipan Chattopadhyay, Samir Roychoudhury, Subimal Basak, Basudeb Dasgupta, Subimal Mishra, Syed Waliullah, Amar Mitra, Shawkat Osman, Akhtaruzzaman Ilias, Hasan Azizul Huq, Shahidul Zahir, etc.

Poets

Rajanikanta Sen, Atulprasad Sen, Dwijendralal Ray, Jatindramohan Bagchi, Kumud Ranjan Mullick, Kazi Nazrul Islam, Jibanananda Das, along with Buddhadeva Bose, marks the beginning of the major move to transcend the Tagore

Figure 53: *Poetry seminars at Nandan*

legacy . Commonly called "polli-kobi" (*pastoral poet*) Jasimuddin, Shamsur Rahman, widely known for his 'playing with words' are also notable. Others are Al Mahmud, [[Sayeed Abubakar]], Abul Hasan and Abdul Mannan Syed.

Musicians

Seminal Hindu religious works in Bengali include the many songs of Ramprasad Sen. His works (still sung today) from the 17th century cover an astonishing range of emotional responses to the goddess Kali, detailing complex philosophical statements based on Vedanta teachings and more visceral pronouncements of his love of the goddess. They are known as *Shyama Sangeet* and were the literary inspiration for Kazi Nazrul Islam's later, famed Shyama Sangeet. There are also the laudatory accounts of the lives and teachings of the Vaishnava saint Chaitanya Mahaprabhu (the *Choitanyo Choritāmrit*) and Shri Ramakrishna (the *Ramakrishna Kathamrita*, translated roughly as Gospel of Ramakrishna). There is also a large body of Islamic literature, that can be traced back at least to *Noornama* by Abdul Hakim. *Bishad Sindhu* depicting the death of Hussain in Karbala is very popular novel written by Mir Mosharraf Hossain. Later works influenced by Islam include devotional songs written by Nazrul, and popularized by Abbas Uddin, among others.

Figure 54: *Baul singers at Vasantotsav, Shantiniketan.*

Bauls and traditional singers

The mystic Bauls of the Bengal countryside who preached the boundless spiritual truth of *Sôhoj Pôth* (the Simple, Natural Path) and *Moner Mānush* (A person of The Heart) drew on Vedantic philosophy to propound transcendental truths in song format, traveling from village to village proclaiming that there was no such thing as Hindu, Muslim or Christian, only *moner mānush*.

The literature discussed so far can be more or less regarded as the common heritage of both Bangladesh and West Bengal. Since the partition of Bengal in 1947, the east and west parts of Bengal have also developed their own distinctive literatures. For example, the Naxalite movement has influenced much of West Bengal's literature, whereas the Liberation War has had a similarly profound impact on Bangladeshi literature.

Major literary figures in (East Bengal) Bangladesh

Nurul Momen, Syed Waliullah, Shahidullah Kaisar, Shawkat Osman, Ahsan Habib, Farrukh Ahmed, Syed Ali Ahsan, Syed Shamsul Haque, Abu Zafar Obaidullah, Sufia Kamal, Al Mahmud, Abubakar Siddique, Ghulam Murshid, Hasan Azizul Huq, Selina Hossain, Arunabh Sarkar, Shawkat Ali, Akhtaruzzaman Ilias, Rafiq Azad, Nirmalendu Goon, Taslima Nasrin, Abul Hasan, Abid

Figure 55: *Shaheed Minar, Dhaka as displayed on the annual anniversary of Bengali Language Movement.*

Azad, Humayun Ahmed, Muhammed Zafar Iqbal, Hasan Hafizur Rahman, Shaheed Quaderi, Khondakar Ashraf Hossain, and Helal Hafiz to name a few.

West Bengal literature

Nihar Ranjan Gupta, Ashutosh Mukhopadhyay, Kamal Kumar Majumdar, Sunil Gangopadhyay, Nabaneeta Dev Sen, Syed Mustafa Siraj, Shirshendu Mukhopadhyay, Samaresh Basu, Atin Bandyopadhyay, Sandipan Chattopadhyay, Shakti Chattopadhyay, Mahasweta Devi, Moti Nandi, Bimal Kar, Narayan Gangopadhyay, Shankar, Suchitra Bhattacharya, Bani Basu, Buddhadeb Guha, Abdul Jabbar, Amar Mitra, Satyajit Ray and others.

1947-1965

Rajshekhar Basu (1880–1960) was the best-known writer of satiric short story in Bengali literature. He mocked the charlatanism and vileness of various classes of the Bengali society in his stories written under the pseudonym "Parashuram". His major works include: *Gaddalika* (1924), *Kajjwali* (1927), *Hanumaner Swapna* (1937), *Gamanush Jatir Katha* (1945), *Dhusturimaya Ityadi Galpa* (1952), *Krishnakali Ittadi Galpa* (1953), *Niltara Ittadi Galpa* (1956), *Anandibai Ittadi Galpa* (1958) and *Chamatkumari Ittadi Galpa* (1959). He received the Rabindra Puraskar, the highest literary award of Paschimbanga in 1955 for *Krishnakali Ityadi Galpa*. Rajsheshkar was also

Figure 56: *Bhasha Smritistambha, Kolkata.*

a noted lexicographer, translator and essayist. His *Chalantika* (1937) is one of the most popular concise Bengali dictionaries, while his Bengali-language translations of *Meghaduta* (1943), the *Ramayana* (1946), the *Mahabharata* (1949) and the *Bhagavat Gita* (1961) are also acclaimed. His major essays are included in *Laghuguru* (1939) and *Bichinta* (1955).

Important novelists and short story writers of post-independence West Bengal are Jagadish Gupta (1886–1957), Tarasankar Bandyopadhyay (1889–1971), Bibhutibhushan Bandyopadhyay (1894–1950), Premendra Mitra (1904–1988), Manik Bandyopadhyay (1908–1956), Bibhutibhushan Mukhopadhyay (1894–1987), Sharadindu Bandyopadhyay (1899–1970), Achintya Kumar Sengupta (1903–1986), Annadashankar Roy (1904–2002), Buddhadeb Basu (1908–1974), Satinath Bhaduri (1906–1965), Narayan Gangopadhyay (1918–1970), and Subodh Ghosh (1900–1980). Noted poets of this age are Jibanananda Das (1899–1954), Sudhindranath Dutta (1901–1960), Bishnu Dey (1909–1982), Amiya Chakrabarty (1901–1986), Samar Sen (1916–1987), Subhas Mukhopadhyay (1919–2003) and Sukanta Bhattacharya (1926–1947). Major dramatists include: Sachin Sengupta (1892–1961) and Bidhayak Bhattacharya (1907–1986). Prominent prose-writers of this age are Suniti Kumar Chattopadhyay (1890–1977), Sukumar Sen (1900–1992), and Pramathanath Bishi (1901–1985).

Hungryalism

One of the path-breaking literary movements in West Bengal is known as The Hungry generation or HungryalismWikipedia:Citation needed. The famous poets of this movement are Malay Roy Choudhury, Shakti Chattopadhyay, Binoy Majumdar, Utpalkumar Basu Samir Roychoudhury, Falguni Roy, and Tridib Mitra. The fiction writers are Sandipan Chattopadhyay, Basudeb Dasgupta, Subimal Basak, Malay Roy Choudhury and Samir Roychoudhury. The painters are Anil Karanjai and Karunanidhan Mukhopadhyay. In 2011 director Srijit Mukherji incorporated the Hungry generation movement into mainstream cinema when he directed Baishe Srabon wherein famous film director Gautam Ghose portrayed the role of an anti-establishment Hungryalist poet. Mrigankashekhar Ganguly directed and produced a short film based on Malay Roy Choudhurys poem Stark Electric Jesus.

Prakalpana Movement

Prakalpana Movement, branded by Steve LeBlanc, the noted US critic, as 'a tiny literary revolution', 'nurtured' by Kolkata, has been fostering its new genres of Prakalpana fiction, Sarbangin poetry and Chetanavyasism for over four decades, spearheaded by Vattacharja Chandan, beginning in 1969. It is probably the only bilingual (Bengali -English) literary movement in India mothered by Bengali literature, that has spread its wings worldwide through the participation of well known international avant-garde writers and mail artists such as Richard Kostelanetz, John M. Bennett, Sheila Murphy, Don Webb, with notable Bengali poets, writers and artists like Vattacharja Chandan.[421]

External links

 Wikimedia Commons has media related to *Bengali literature*.

- Library of Congress - Bengali Section[422]
- Bengali Literature Archive[423]
- Influence of Baudelaire on Bengali Poetry baudelaireetbengale.blogspot.com[424]
- An English Magazine on Bengali literature edited by Sayeed Abubakar[425]

Bhojpuri literature

Bhojpuri literature

Bhojpuri literature includes literature written in Bhojpuri language, a language spoken primarily in Eastern parts of the Indian state of Uttar Pradesh and adjoining districts of Bihar state as well as some other parts of the world. Until recently there was little written in the language other than poetry and songs.

Distinct literary traditions in Bhojpuri language date back to medieval periods when saints and *bhakts* of the region adapted a mixed language for their works.

Lorikayan, or the story of *Veer Lorik*, is a famous Bhojpuri folklore of Eastern Uttar Pradesh. Bhikhari Thakur's *Bidesiya* is another famous book.

The first Bhojpuri novel *Bindiā* was written in 1956 by Ram Nath Pandey. It was published by Bhojpuri Sansad, Jagatganj, Varanasi.[426,427]

Notable Bhojpuri novelists are Ram Nath Pandey, Viveki Rai, Pandey Kapil , Ramesh Chandra Jha and Pradhyapak Achal who has written the famous bhojpuri novel *Sunnar kaka*[428]

Periods

Initial period (1947 to 1961): First Bhojpuri short story *Jehali ke Sanad* was published in this period. The first Bhojpuri novel *Bindiā* by Ram Nath Pandey also published in 1956.

Between 1961 and 1975:- Nearly ten novels were published. Notable are *Tharuhat ke babua aur bahuriya* (1965), *Jeevan Saah* (1964), *Semar ke phool* (1966), *Rahanidaar beti* (1966), *Ego subah ego saanjh* (1967), *Sunnar kaka* (1976). Most of these are social drama while the first one is called a regional novel which elaborates life of Tharu tribal people.

Modern Period (After 1975): More than 30 novels have been written. Some notable of these are - *Phulsunghi* (1977), *Bhor musukaail* (1978), *Ghar-tola-gaon* (1979), *Jinigi ke raah* (1982), *Darad ke dahar* (1983), *Achhoot* (1986), mahendar Misisr (1994), Imiritiya Kaki (1997), *Amangal hari* (1998), *Awa lavati chalin ja* (2000), *Adhe aadh* (2000) etc. of which *Phulsunghi* by Pandey kapil is one of the best novels written in Bhojpuri. *Amangal hari* (1998) was written by Viveki Rai, a critic himself. *Surma Sagun Bichare Na* is a notable novel written by Ramesh Chandra Jha.

Purvi Ke Dhah, written by Jauhar Safiavadi, is the first Bhojpuri novel to be published by National Book Trust. It was launched by prominent Hindi critic Namvar Singh at Chhapra.[429]

Bhojpuri Poet Manoj Bhawuk has written many books and been honored with the Bhartiya Bhasha Parishad Award in 2006 for his Ghazal collection *Tasveer zindagi ke*. He has also written a history of Bhojpuri cinema.

External links

- Fictions: Literary Realism and the Crisis of Caste[430]

Indian English literature

Indian English literature

History of
modern literature By decade

- List of years in literature

Early modern by century

- 16th
- 17th

Mid-modern by century

- 18th
- 19th

20th–21st century

- Modernism
- Structuralism
- Deconstruction
- Poststructuralism
- Postmodernism
- Post-colonialism
- Hypertexts

By region

Africa
• Nigerian • South African
Americas
• American
• Argentine
• Brazilian
• Canadian
• Colombian
• Cuban
• Jamaican
• Mexican
• Peruvian
Asia
• Bengali
• Bangladeshi English
• Chinese
• Gujarati
• Hindi
• Indian   • Indian English
• Japanese
• Kannada
• Kashmiri
• Korean
• Malayalam
• Marathi
• Pakistani   • Pakistani English
• Pashto
• Punjabi
• Sindhi
• Tamil
• Telugu
• Urdu
• Vietnamese
Australasia
• Australian • New Zealand
Europe

Related topics

- History of science fiction

- Literature by country
- History of theater
- History of ideas
- Intellectual history

📚 Literature portal

- v
- t
- e[431]

Indian English literature (**IEL**) refers to the body of work by writers in India who write in the English language and whose native or co-native language could be one of the numerous languages of India. Its early history began with the works of Michael Madhusudan Dutt followed by R. K. Narayan, Mulk Raj Anand and Raja Rao who contributed to Indian fiction in the 1930s. It is also associated with the works of members of the Indian diaspora, such as V. S. Naipaul, Kiran Desai, Jhumpa Lahiri, Kovid Gupta, Agha Shahid Ali, Rohinton Mistry and Salman Rushdie, who are of Indian descent.

It is frequently referred to as **Indo-Anglian** literature. (*Indo-Anglian* is a specific term in the sole context of writing that should not be confused with *Anglo-Indian*). As a category, this production comes in the broader realm of postcolonial literature—the production from previously colonised countries such as India.

History

IEL has a relatively recent history, being only one and a half centuries old. The first book written by an Indian in English was *Travels of Dean Mahomet*, a travel narrative by Sake Dean Mahomet published in England in 1793. In its early stages, IEL was influenced by the Western novel. Early Indian writers used English unadulterated by Indian words to convey an experience which was essentially Indian. Bankim Chandra Chattopadhyay (1838–1894) wrote *Rajmohan's Wife* and published it in 1864; it is the first Indian novel written in English. Raja Rao (1908–2006), Indian philosopher and writer, authored *Kanthapura* and *The Serpent and the Rope*, which are Indian in terms of their storytelling qualities. Kisari Mohan Ganguli translated the Mahabharata into English, the only time the epic has ever been translated in its entirety into a European language. Rabindranath Tagore (1861–1941) wrote in Bengali and English and was responsible for the translations of his own work into English. Dhan Gopal Mukerji (1890–1936) was the first Indian author to win a literary award in the United States. Nirad C. Chaudhuri (1897–1999), a writer of nonfiction, is best known for his *The Autobiography of an Unknown Indian* (1951), in which he relates his life experiences and influences. P. Lal (1929–2010), a poet, translator, publisher and essayist, founded a press in the 1950s for Indian English writing, Writers Workshop. Ram Nath Kak (1917–1993), a Kashmiri veterinarian, wrote his autobiography *Autumn Leaves*, which is one of the most vivid portraits of life in 20th century Kashmir and has become a sort of a classic.Wikipedia:Manual of Style/Words to watch#Unsupported attributions

R. K. Narayan (1906–2001) contributed over many decades and continued to write till his death. He was discovered by Graham Greene in the sense that the latter helped him find a publisher in England. Greene and Narayan remained close friends till the end. Similar to the way Thomas Hardy used Wessex, Narayan created the fictitious town of Malgudi where he set his novels. Some criticise Narayan for the parochial, detached and closed world that he created in the face of the changing conditions in India at the times in which the stories are set. Others, such as Greene, however, feel that through Malgudi they could vividly understand the Indian experience. Narayan's evocation of small town life and its experiences through the eyes of the endearing child protagonist Swaminathan in *Swami and Friends* is a good sample of his writing style. Simultaneous with Narayan's pastoral idylls, a very different writer, Mulk Raj Anand (1905–2004), was similarly gaining recognition for his writing set in rural India, but his stories were harsher, and engaged, sometimes brutally, with divisions of caste, class and religion. According to writer Lakshmi Holmström, "The writers of the 1930s were fortunate because after many years of use, English had become an Indian language used widely and at different levels of society, and therefore they could experiment more boldly and from a more secure position." Kamala Markandeya is an early writer in IEL who has often grouped with the trinity of R.K. Narayan, Mulk Raj Anand and Raja Rao. The contributions of Manoj Das and Manohar Malgoankar to growth of IEL largely remains unacknowledged.

Later history

Among the later writers, the most notable is Salman Rushdie, born in India, now living in the USA. Rushdie with his famous work *Midnight's Children* (Booker Prize 1981, Booker of Bookers 1992, and Best of the Bookers 2008) ushered in a new trend of writing. He used a hybrid language – English generously peppered with Indian terms – to convey a theme that could be seen as representing the vast canvas of India. He is usually categorised under the magic realism mode of writing most famously associated with Gabriel García Márquez. Nayantara Sehgal was one of the first female Indian writers in English to receive wide recognition. Her fiction deals with India's elite responding to the crises engendered by political change. She was awarded the 1986 Sahitya Akademi Award for English, for her novel, *Rich Like Us* (1985), by

Figure 57: *Arundhati Roy*

the Sahitya Akademi, India's National Academy of Letters. Anita Desai, who was shortlisted for the Booker Prize three times, received a Sahitya Akademi Award in 1978 for her novel *Fire on the Mountain* and a British Guardian Prize for *The Village by the Sea*. Her daughter Kiran Desai won the 2006 Man Booker Prize for her second novel, The Inheritance of Loss. Ruskin Bond received Sahitya Akademy Award for his collection of short stories *Our Trees Still Grow in Dehra* in 1992. He is also the author of a historical novel *A Flight of Pigeons*, which is based on an episode during the Indian Rebellion of 1857.

Vikram Seth, author of *The Golden Gate* (1986) and *A Suitable Boy* (1994) is a writer who uses a purer English and more realistic themes. Being a self-confessed fan of Jane Austen, his attention is on the story, its details and its twists and turns. Vikram Seth is notable both as an accomplished novelist and poet. Vikram Seth's outstanding achievement as a versatile and prolific poet remains largely and unfairly neglected.

Another writer who has contributed immensely to the Indian English Literature is Amitav Ghosh who is the author of *The Circle of Reason* (his 1986 debut novel), *The Shadow Lines* (1988), *The Calcutta Chromosome* (1995), *The Glass Palace* (2000), *The Hungry Tide* (2004), and *Sea of Poppies* (2008), the first volume of *The Ibis* trilogy, set in the 1830s, just before the Opium

Figure 58: *Salman Rushdie*

War, which encapsulates the colonial history of the East. Ghosh's latest work of fiction is *River of Smoke* (2011), the second volume of *The Ibis* trilogy.

Rohinton Mistry is an India born Canadian author who is a Neustadt International Prize for Literature laureate (2012). His first book Tales from Firozsha Baag (1987) published by Penguin Books Canada is a collection of 11 short stories. His novels Such a Long Journey (1991) and A Fine Balance (1995)earned him great acclaim.

Shashi Tharoor, in his *The Great Indian Novel* (1989), follows a story-telling (though in a satirical) mode as in the Mahabharata drawing his ideas by going back and forth in time. His work as UN official living outside India has given him a vantage point that helps construct an objective Indianness. Vikram Chandra is another author who shuffles between India and the United States and has received critical acclaim for his first novel *Red Earth and Pouring Rain* (1995) and collection of short stories *Love and Longing in Bombay* (1997). His namesake Vikram A. Chandra is a renowned journalist and the author of *The Srinagar Conspiracy* (2000). Suketu Mehta is another writer currently based in the United States who authored Maximum City (2004), an autobiographical account of his experiences in the city of Mumbai. In 2008, Arvind Adiga received the Man Booker Prize for his debut novel The White Tiger.

Recent writers in India such as Arundhati Roy and David Davidar show a direction towards contextuality and rootedness in their works. Arundhati Roy, a trained architect and the 1997 Booker prize winner for her *The God of Small Things*, calls herself a "home grown" writer. Her award winning book is set in the immensely physical landscape of Kerala. Davidar sets his *The House of Blue Mangoes* in Southern Tamil Nadu. In both the books, geography and politics are integral to the narrative. In his novel Lament of Mohini (2000), Shreekumar Varma touches upon the unique matriarchal system and the *sammandham* system of marriage as he writes about the Namboodiris and the aristocrats of Kerala. Similarly, Arnab Jan Deka, a trained engineer and jurist, writes about both physical and ethereal existentialism on the banks of the mighty river Brahmaputra, and his co-authored book of poetry with British poet-novelist Tess Joyce appropriately titled *A Stanza of Sunlight on the Banks of Brahmaputra*(1983) published from both India and Britain(2009) which is set under this backdrop evokes the spirit of flowing nature of life. His most recent book *Brahmaputra and Beyond : Linking Assam to the World*(2015) made a conscious effort to connect to a world divided by racial, geographic, linguistic, cultural and political prejudices. His highly acclaimed short story collection *The Mexican Sweetheart & other stories*(2002) was another landmark book of this genre. Jahnavi Barua, a Bangalore based author from Assam has set her critically acclaimed collection of short stories *Next Door* on the social scenario in Assam with insurgency as the background.

The stories and novels of Ratan Lal Basu reflect the conditions of tribal people and hill people of West Bengal and the adjacent states of Sikkim, Bhutan and Nepal. Many of his short stories reflect the political turmoil of West Bengal since the Naxalite movement of the 1970s. Many of his stories like 'Blue Are the Far Off Mountains', 'The First Rain' and 'the Magic Marble' glorify purity of love. His novel 'Oraon and the Divine Tree' is the story of a tribal and his love for an age old tree. In Hemingway style language the author takes the reader into the dreamland of nature and people who are inexorably associated with nature.

Debates

One of the key issues raised in this context is the superiority/inferiority of IWE (Indian Writing in English) as opposed to the literary production in the various languages of India. Key polar concepts bandied in this context are superficial/authentic, imitative/creative, shallow/deep, critical/uncritical, elitist/parochial and so on.

The views of Salman Rushdie and Amit Chaudhuri expressed through their books *The Vintage Book of Indian Writing* and *The Picador Book of Modern Indian Literature* respectively essentialise this battle.

Rushdie's statement in his book – "the ironic proposition that India's best writing since independence may have been done in the language of the departed imperialists is simply too much for some folks to bear" – created a lot of resentment among many writers, including writers in English. In his book, Amit Chaudhuri questions – "Can it be true that Indian writing, that endlessly rich, complex and problematic entity, is to be represented by a handful of writers who write in English, who live in England or America and whom one might have met at a party?"

Chaudhuri feels that after Rushdie, IWE started employing magical realism, bagginess, non-linear narrative and hybrid language to sustain themes seen as microcosms of India and supposedly reflecting Indian conditions. He contrasts this with the works of earlier writers such as Narayan where the use of English is pure, but the deciphering of meaning needs cultural familiarity. He also feels that Indianness is a theme constructed only in IWE and does not articulate itself in the vernacular literatures. He further adds "the post-colonial novel, becomes a trope for an ideal hybridity by which the West celebrates not so much Indianness, whatever that infinitely complex thing is, but its own historical quest, its reinterpretation of itself".

Some of these arguments form an integral part of what is called postcolonial theory. The very categorisation of IWE – as IWE or under post-colonial literature – is seen by some as limiting. Amitav Ghosh made his views on this very clear by refusing to accept the Eurasian Commonwealth Writers Prize for his book *The Glass Palace* in 2001 and withdrawing it from the subsequent stage.

The renowned writer V. S. Naipaul, a third generation Indian from Trinidad and Tobago and a Nobel prize laureate, is a person who belongs to the world and usually not classified under IWE. Naipaul evokes ideas of homeland, rootlessness and his own personal feelings towards India in many of his books.

Jhumpa Lahiri, a Pulitzer prize winner from the U.S., is a writer uncomfortable under the label of IWE.

Poetry

An overlooked category of Indian writing in English is poetry. Rabindranath Tagore wrote in Bengali and English and was responsible for the translations of his own work into English. Other early notable poets in English include Derozio, Michael Madhusudan Dutt, Toru Dutt, Romesh Chunder Dutt, Sri Aurobindo, Sarojini Naidu, and her brother Harindranath Chattopadhyay. "Sarojini Naidu and her art of poetry" is one of the finest efforts made by Dr. Deobrata Prasad in order to bring forth the real psyche of Sarojini Naidu through her poetry.This book was published by Delhi-based Capital Publishing House in 1988 in the field of 'women and Anglo-Indian literature'.Dr Deobrata Prasad has very carefully taken into account all the nuances of Sarojini Naidu's poetry.The significance of this work towards Indian English Literature was first brought into perspective by University of Michigan. Such a systematic work is rare to single out in today's era. Notable 20th Century authors of English poetry in India include Dilip Chitre, Kamala Das, Eunice De Souza, Nissim Ezekiel, Kersy Katrak, Shiv K. Kumar, Arun Kolatkar, P. Lal, Jayanta Mahapatra, Dom Moraes, Gieve Patel, and A. K. Ramanujan, and Madan Gopal Gandhi,Dr Avdhesh Yadav, among several others.

The younger generation of poets writing in English include Abhay K, Arundhathi Subramaniam, Anju Makhija, Arnab Jan Deka, Bibhu Padhi, Ranjit Hoskote, Sudeep Sen, Smita Agarwal, Makarand Paranjape, Jeet Thayil, Mani Rao, Jerry Pinto, K. V. Dominic[432], Meena Kandasamy, Nalini Priyadarshni, Gopi Kottoor, Tapan Kumar Pradhan, Rukmini Bhaya Nair, Robin Ngangom, Vihang A. Naik,Dr Avdhesh Yadav and K Srilata.

Modern expatriate Indian poets writing in English include Agha Shahid Ali, Sujata Bhatt, Richard Crasta, Yuyutsu Sharma, Tabish Khair and Vikram Seth.

Alternative writing

India's experimental and avant garde counterculture is symbolized in the Prakalpana Movement. During the last four decades this bilingual literary movement has included Richard Kostelanetz, John M. Bennett, Don Webb, Sheila Murphy and many others worldwide and their Indian counterparts. Vattacharja Chandan is a central figure who contrived the movement.[433] Prakalpana fiction is a fusion of prose, poetry, play, essay, and pictures. An example of a Prakalpana work is Chandan's bilingual *Cosmosphere 1* (2011).

Some bilingual writers have also made significant contributions, such as Paigham Afaqui with his novel *Makaan* in 1989.

References

<templatestyles src="Refbegin/styles.css" />

- Haq, Kaiser (ed.). *Contemporary Indian Poetry*. Columbus: Ohio State University Press, 1990.
- Haq, Rubana (ed.). *The Golden Treasury of Writers Workshop Poetry*. Kolkata: Writers Workshop, 2008.
- Hoskote, Ranjit (ed.). *Reasons for Belonging: Fourteen Contemporary Indian Poets*. Viking/Penguin Books India, New Delhi, 2002.

- Singh, Bijender. "Indian Writing in English: Critical Insights." New Delhi, Authorspress, 2014.
- Indian Writing in English[434] | Men and Dreams in the Dhauladhar by Novels by Indian Authors - Kochery C Shibu[435]
- Joseph, Margaret Paul. "Jasmine on a String: a Survey of Women Writing English Fiction in India." Oxford University Press, 2014.
- King, Bruce Alvin. *Modern Indian Poetry in English: Revised Edition*. New Delhi: Oxford University Press, 1987, rev. 2001. ("the standard work on the subject and unlikely to be surpassed" — Mehrotra, 2003).
- King, Bruce Alvin. *Three Indian Poets: Nissim Ezekiel, A K Ramanujan, Dom Moraes*. Madras: Oxford University Press, 1991.
- Mehrotra, Arvind Krishna (ed.). *The Oxford India Anthology of Twelve Modern Indian Poets*. Calcutta: Oxford University Press, 1992.
- Mehrotra, Arvind Krishna (ed.). *A History of Indian Literature in English*. New York: Columbia University Press, 2003. Distributed in India by Doaba Books Shanti Mohan House 16, Ansari Road, New Delhi.
- Parthasarathy, R. (ed.). *Ten Twentieth-Century Indian Poets (New Poetry in India)*. New Delhi: Oxford University Press, 1976.
- Prem, PCK. *English Poetry in India: A Comprehensive Survey of Trends and Thought Patterns* New Delhi: Authorspress, 2011.ASIN 8172736029[436]
- Reddy, T. Vasudeva. *A Critical Survey of Indo-English Poetry* New Delhi: Authorspress, 2016.ASIN 9352072499[437]
- Roy, Pinaki. "*Encountering the West*: A Very Brief Overview of the Indian Diasporic Novelists". *Journal of Higher Education and Research Society* (ISSN 2321-9432) 1(1), October 2013: http://herso.org/vol-1-issue-1-oct-2013/
- Roy, Pinaki. "*Dramatic Chronicle*: A Very Brief Review of the Growth of Indian English Plays". *Indian Drama in English: Some Perspectives*. Ed. Kaushik, A.S. New Delhi: Atlantic Publishers and Distributors Pvt. Ltd., 2013 (<templatestyles src="Module:Citation/CS1/styles.css" />ISBN 978-81-269-1772-3). pp. 272–87.
- Sadana, Rashmi. "Writing in English," in *The Cambridge Companion to Modern Indian Culture*. Cambridge: Cambridge University Press, 2012.
- Sadana, Rashmi. *English Heart, Hindi Heartland: the Political Life of Literature in India*. Berkeley: University of California Press, 2012.
- Shivdasani, Menka (ed.). *Anthology of Contemporary Indian Poetry* : USA, BigBridge.Org, Michael Rothenberg, 2004.
- Souza, Eunice de. "Nine Indian Women Poets", Delhi, Oxford University Press, 1997.
- Souza, Eunice de. *Talking Poems: Conversations With Poets*. New Delhi: Oxford University Press, 1999.

- Souza, Eunice de. *Early Indian Poetry in English: An Anthology : 1829-1947.* New Delhi: Oxford University Press, 2005.
- Srikanth, Rajini. *The World Next Door: South Asian American Literature and the Idea of America'.* Asian American History and Culture. Philadelphia: Temple UP, 2004.
- Mahapatra, Jayanta & Sharma, Yuyutsu (ed.). *Ten: The New Indian Poets.* New Delhi: Nirala Publications, 1993. http://niralapublications.com/new-release-ten-the-new-indian-poets/
- Jha, Vivekananad. (ed) *The Dance of the Peacock.* Canada: Hidden Brook Press, 2014.

Hindi literature

Hindi literature

Indian literature
• Assamese
• Bengali
• Bhojpuri
• English
• Gujarati
• Hindi
• Kannada
• Kashmiri
• Konkani
• Malayalam
• Meitei
• Marathi
• Mizo
• Nepali
• Odia
• Punjabi
• Rajasthani
• Sanskrit
• Sindhi
• Tamil
• Telugu
• Urdu
• v • t • e[438]

Hindi literature (Hindi: हिन्दी साहित्य, Hindi Sahitya) includes literature in the various Central Zone Indo-Aryan languages which have writing systems. It is broadly classified into four prominent forms (styles) based on the date of production. They are:

- Vir-Gatha kal (poems extolling brave warriors) – 11th–14th century
- Bhakti kal poems (devotional poems) – 14th–18th century
- Riti or Srngar kal poems (poems of romance) – 18th–20th century
- Adhunik kal (modern literature) – 20th century onwards

The literature was produced in dialects such as Braj, Bundeli, Awadhi, Kannauji, Khariboli, Marwari, Magahi, Bhojpuri and Chhattisgarhi.[439] From the 20th century, works produced in Standard Hindi, a register of Hindustani written in the Devanagari script, are sometimes regarded as the only basis of modern literature in Hindi.[440]

History

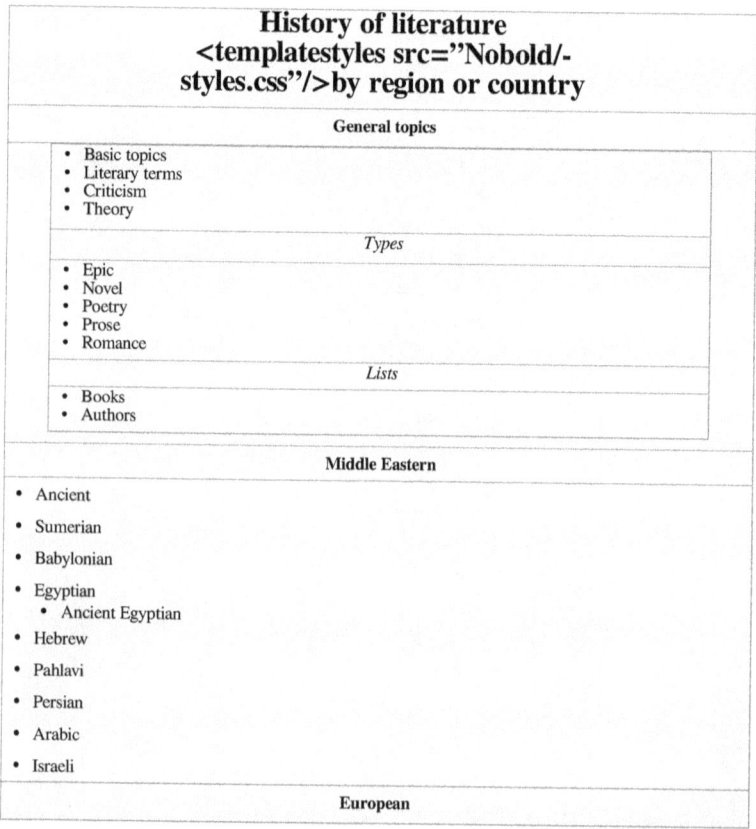

History of literature <templatestyles src="Nobold/-styles.css"/>by region or country
General topics
• Basic topics • Literary terms • Criticism • Theory
Types
• Epic • Novel • Poetry • Prose • Romance
Lists
• Books • Authors
Middle Eastern
• Ancient
• Sumerian
• Babylonian
• Egyptian   • Ancient Egyptian
• Hebrew
• Pahlavi
• Persian
• Arabic
• Israeli
European

Hindi literature 163

- Greek
- Latin
- Early Medieval
  - Matter of Rome
  - Matter of France
  - Matter of Britain
- Medieval
- Renaissance

Modern

- Structuralism
- Poststructuralism
- Deconstruction
- Modernism
- Postmodernism
- Post-colonialism
- Hypertexts

North and South American

- American
- Canadian
- Mexican
- Jamaican

Latin American

- Argentine
- Brazilian
- Colombian
- Cuban
- Peruvian

Australasian

- Australian
- New Zealand

Asian

East / Southeast

- Chinese
- Japanese
- Korean
- Vietnamese
- Thai

South

- Sanskrit
- Indian
- Pakistani
- Assamese
- Bengali
- Gujurati
- Hindi
- Kannada
- Kashmiri
- Malayalam
- Marathi
- Nepali
- Rajasthani
- Sindhi
- Tamil
- Telugu
- Urdu
- Indian writing in English

African

- Moroccan
- Nigerian
- South African
- Swahili

Related topics

- History of science fiction
- List of years in literature
- Literature by country
- History of theatre
- History of ideas
- Intellectual history

Literature portal

- v
- t
- e[441]

Adi kal or Vir-Gatha kal (c. 1050 to 1375)

Literature of *Adi kal* (c. before the 15th century CE) was developed in the regions of Kannauj, Delhi, Ajmer stretching up to central India.[442] *Prithviraj Raso*, an epic poem written by Chand Bardai (1149 – c. 1200), is considered as one of the first works in the history of Hindi literature. Chand Bardai was a court poet of Prithviraj Chauhan, the famous ruler of Delhi and Ajmer during the invasion of Muhammad of Ghor.

Jayachand, the last ruler of Kannauj belonging to the Rathore Rajput clan, gave more patronage to Sanskrit rather than local dialects. Harsha, the author of *Naishdhiya Charitra*, was his court poet. Jagnayak (sometimes Jagnik), the royal poet in Mahoba, and Nalha, the royal poet in Ajmer, were the other prominent literary figures in this period. However, after Prithviraj Chauhan's defeat in the Second Battle of Tarain, most literary works belonging to this period were destroyed by the army of Muhammad of Ghor. Very few scriptures and manuscripts from this period are available and their genuineness is also doubted.

Some Siddha and Nathpanthi poetical works belonging to this period are also found, but their genuineness is again, doubted. The Siddhas belonged to the Vajrayana, a later Buddhist sect. Some scholars argue that the language of Siddha poetry is not an earlier form of Hindi, but Magadhi Prakrit. Nathpanthis were yogis who practised the Hatha yoga. Some Jain and *Rasau* (heroic poets) poetry works are also available from this period.

In the Deccan region in South India, Dakkhini or Hindavi was used. It flourished under the Delhi Sultanate and later under the Nizams of Hyderabad. It was written in the Persian script. Nevertheless, the Hindavi literature can be considered as proto-Hindi literature. Many Deccani experts like Sheikh Ashraf or Mulla Vajahi used the word *Hindavi* to describe this dialect. Others such as Roustami, Nishati etc. preferred to call it Deccani. Shah Buharnuddin Janam Bijapuri used to call it Hindi. The first Deccani author was Khwaja Bandanawaz Gesudaraz Muhammad Hasan. He wrote three prose works – Mirazul Aashkini, Hidayatnama and Risala Sehwara. His grandson Abdulla Hussaini wrote *Nishatul Ishq*. The first Deccani poet was Nizami.

During the later part of this period and early Bhakti Kala, many saint-poets like Ramanand and Gorakhnath became famous. The earliest form of Hindi can also be seen in some of Vidyapati's Maithili works.

Bhakti kaal (c. 1375 to 1700)

The medieval Hindi literature is marked by the influence of Bhakti movement and composition of long, epic poems.

[Avadhi] and [Brij Bhasha] were the dialects in which literature was developed. The main works in Avadhi are Malik Muhammad Jayasi's *Padmavat* and Tulsidas's *Ramacharitamanas*. The major works in Braj dialect are Tulsidas's *Vinaya Patrika* and Surdas's *Sur Sagar*. Sadhukaddi was also a language commonly used, especially by Kabir in his poetry and dohas.[443]

The Bhakti period also marked great theoretical development in poetry forms chiefly from a mixture of older forms of poetry. These included Verse Patterns like *Doha* (two-liners), *Sortha*, *Chaupaya* (four-liners) etc. This was also the age when Poetry was characterised under the various Rasas. Unlike the Adi Kaal (also called the Vir Gatha Kaal) which was characterised by an overdose of Poetry in the *Vir Rasa* (Heroic Poetry), the Bhakti Yug marked a much more diverse and vibrant form of poetry which spanned the whole gamut of rasas[444] from *Shringara rasa* (love), *Vir Rasa* (Heroism).

Bhakti poetry had two schools – the *Nirguna* school (the believers of a formless God or an abstract name) and the *Saguna* school (the believers of a God with attributes and worshippers of Vishnu's incarnations). Kabir and Guru Nanak belong to the Nirguna school, and their philosophy was greatly influenced by the Advaita Vedanta philosophy of Adi Sankaracharya. They believed in the concept of Nirgun Nirakaar Bramh or the Shapeless Formless One. The Saguna school was represented by mainly Vaishnava poets like Surdas, Tulsidas and others and was a logical extension of the Dvaita and Vishishta Advaita Philosophy propounded by the likes of Madhavacharya etc. This school was chiefly Vaishnava in orientation as in seen in the main compositions like Ramacharitamanas, Sur Saravali, Sur Sagar extoling Rama and Krishna.

This was also the age of tremendous integration between the Hindu and the Islamic elements in the Arts with the advent of many Muslim Bhakti poets like

Abdul Rahim Khan-I-Khana who was a court poet to Mughal emperor Akbar and was a great devotee of Krishna. The Nirgun School of Bhakti Poetry was also tremendously secular in nature and its propounders like Kabir and Guru Nanak had a large number of followers irrespective of caste or religion.

Riti-kavya kal (c. 1700 to 1900)

In the *Ritikavya* or *Ritismagra Kavya* period, the erotic element became predominant in the Hindi literature. This era is called Riti (meaning 'procedure') because it was the age when poetic figures and theory were developed to the fullest. But this emphasis on poetry theory greatly reduced the emotional aspects of poetry—the main characteristic of the Bhakti movement—and the actual content of the poetry became less important. The Saguna School of the Bhakti Yug split into two schools (Rama bhakti and Krishna bhakti) somewhere in the interregnum of the Bhakti and the Reeti Eras. Although most Reeti works were outwordly related to Krishna Bhakti, their emphasis had changed from total devotion to the supreme being to the Shringar or erotic aspects of Krishna's life—his Leela, his pranks with the Gopis in Braj, and the description of the physical beauty of Krishna and Radha,(Krishna's Consort). The poetry of Bihari, and Ghananand Das fit this bill. The most well known book from this age is the Bihari Satsai of Bihari, a collection of Dohas (couplets), dealing with *Bhakti* (devotion), *Neeti* (Moral policies) and *Shringar* (love).

The first Hindi books, using the Devanagari script or Nāgarī script were one Heera Lal's treatise on Ain-i-Akbari, called Ain e Akbari ki Bhasha Vachanika, and Rewa Mharaja's treatise on Kabir. Both books came out in 1795. Munshi Lallu Lal's Hindi translation of Sanskrit Hitopadesha was published in 1809. Lala Srinivas Das published a novel in Hindi Pariksha guru in the Nāgarī script in 1886. Shardha Ram Phillauri wrote a Hindi novel Bhagyawati which was published in 1888.

Chandrakanta, written by Devaki Nandan Khatri in 1888, is considered the first authentic work of prose in modern Hindi. The person who brought realism in the Hindi prose literature was Munshi Premchand, who is considered as the most revered figure in the world of Hindi fiction and progressive movement.

Adhunik kal (c. 1900 onwards)

In 1800, the British East India Company established Fort William College at Calcutta. The College president J. B. Gilchrist hired professors to write books in Hindustani. Some of these books were *Prem Sagar* by Lallu Lal, *Naasiketopaakhyan* by Sadal Mishra, *Sukhsagar* by Sadasukhlal of Delhi and *Rani Ketaki ki kahani* by Munshi Inshallah Khan.

Hindi literature

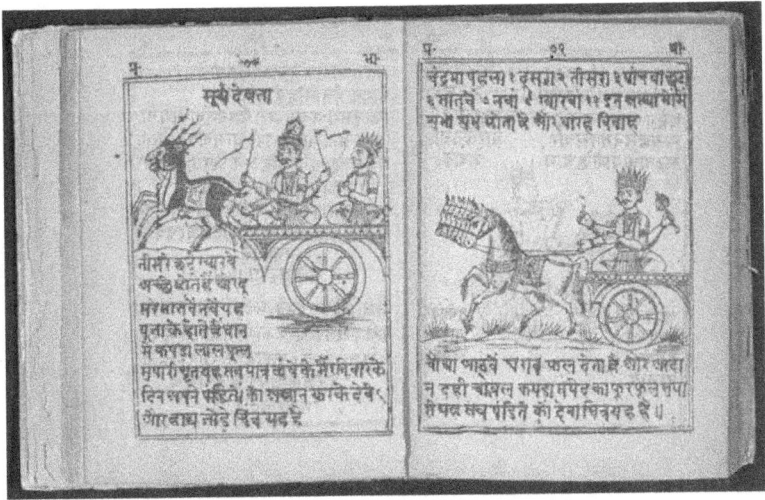

Figure 59: *A depiction of Surya in an 1884 book, Indrajalakala (The Art of Magic); Jwala Prakash Press, Meerut*

The person who brought realism in the Hindi prose literature was Munshi Premchand, who is considered as the most revered figure in the world of Hindi fiction and progressive movement. Before Premchand, the Hindi literature revolved around fairy or magical tales, entertaining stories and religious themes. Premchand's novels have been translated into many other languages.

Gocharya ji authored Krishna Cahrit Manas in the poetic form describing about the full life of Lord Krishna (from birth to Nirvana).

Dwivedi Yug

The *Dwivedi Yug* ("Age of Dwivedi") in Hindi literature lasted from 1900 to 1918. It is named after Mahavir Prasad Dwivedi, who played a major role in establishing the modern Hindi language in poetry and broadening the acceptable subjects of the Hindi poetry from the traditional ones of religion and romantic love. He encouraged poetry in Hindi dedicated to nationalism and social reform.[445]

Dwivedi became the editor of *Saraswati* in 1903, the first Hindi monthly magazine of India, which was established in 1900. He used it to crusade for reforms in the Hindi literature. One of the most prominent poems of the period was Maithili Sharan Gupt's *Bharat-bharati*, which evokes the past glory of India. Shridhar Prathak's *Bharatgit* is another renowned poem of the period.

Some scholars have labelled much of the poetry of this period as "versified propaganda". According to Lucy Rosenstein: "It is verse of public statement; its language is functional but aesthetically unappealing. Earnestly concerned with social issues and moral values, it is puritanical poetry in which aesthetic considerations are secondary. Imagination, originality, poetic sensibility and expression are wanting, the metre is restrictive, the idiom clumsy." She adds, however, that the period was important for laying the foundations to

the modern Hindi poetry and that it did reflect sensitivity to social issues of the time. However, she also adds that the inelegance is a typical feature of a "young" poetry, as she concludes Modern Hindi.

Without a poetic tradition in modern Hindi, poets often modeled their forms on Braj, and later on Sanskrit, Urdu, Bengali and English forms, often ill-suited to Hindi. The subjects of the poems tended to be communal rather than personal. Characters were often presented not as individuals but as social types.

Chhayavaadi Yug

In the 20th century, Hindi literature saw a romantic upsurge. This is known as *Chhayavaad* (*shadowism*) and the literary figures belonging to this school are known as *Chhayavaadi*. Jaishankar Prasad, Suryakant Tripathi 'Nirala', Mahadevi Varma and Sumitranandan Pant, are the four major *Chhayavaadi* poets. Poet Ramdhari Singh 'Dinkar' was another great poet with some Chayavaadi element in his poetry although he wrote in other genres as well.

This period of Neo-romanticism, represents the adolescence of Hindi Poetry. It is marked by beauty of expression and flow of intense emotion. The four representative poets of this era represent the best in Hindi Poetry. A unique feature of this period is the emotional (and sometimes active) attachment of poets with national freedom struggle, their effort to understand and imbibe the vast spirit of a magnificent ancient culture and their towering genius which grossly overshadowed all the literary 'talked abouts' of next seven decades.

Other important genres of *Adhunik Sahitya* (Modernism) are: **Prayogvad** (Experimentalism) of Ajneya and the *Tar Saptak* poets, also known as *Nayi Kavita* (New Poetry) and *Nayi Kahani* (New Story) of Nirmal Verma and others; followed by **Pragativad** (Progressivism) of Gajanan Madhav Muktibodh and other authors.[446]

Nakenwad

Among the numerous schools of poetry which sprang up in the fifties of this century was *Nakenwad*, a school deriving its nomenclature from the first letters of the names of its three pioneers – Nalin Vilochan Sharma, Kesari Kumar, and Naresh Mehta all poets of note in their own right. Apart from being poets,

Nalin Vilochan and Kesari Kumar were also brilliant critics, with a wide perspective on literary history. Their critical attitude is marked by a synthesis or coordination of various disciplines of human knowledge – philosophy, history, art and culture, all pressed into the service of literary appraisal and analysis.

Hindi Kavita (Poetry)

Hindi has a rich legacy of poetry. There are several genres of Kavita based on Ras, Chhand and Alankar e.g. Shringar, Karun, Veer, Hāsya etc. *Hasya Kavita* is humorous comic poetry in Hindi. It is particularly famous due to Hindi kavi sammelans. Bal Kavita is children's rhymes in Hindi.

Many attempts have been made to document Hindi poetry. Some of the most comprehensive online collections for Hindi poetry are Kavitakosh[447] and Geeta-Kavita[448]. The most classy content that has created new audiences who were not looking for Hindi poetry or Hindi content is Hindi Kavita[449]. This movement started in 2014 by Manish Gupta[450] has generated an entirely new market and brought many projects to the fore. Many award-winning poets, scholars, journalists and celebrities from Film, Television and Theatre have come forward to support the cause and take it further. Wikipedia:NOT#SOAPBOX

Vyangya (Hindi Satire)

The rhetoric of satire is called Vyangya in Hindi. Vyangya writings includes the essence of sarcasm and humour. Some of the better known writers in this genre are, Harishankar Parsai(Hindi: हरिशंकर परसाई) (August 22, 1924 – 1995) was a Hindi writer. He was a noted satirist and humorist of modern Hindi literature and is known for his simple and direct style., Sri Lal Sukla, Suryakumar Pandey etc.[451]

Hindi travel literature

Rahul Sankrityayan, Bhadant Anand Kausalyayan, Sachchidananda Hirananda Vatsyayan 'Ajneya' and Baba Nagarjun were some of the great Indian writers who dedicated themselves entirely to the Hindi Travel Literature (*Yatra Vritanta*). Rahul Sankrityayan was one of the greatest travelled scholars of India, spending forty-five years of his life on travels away from his home. He is known as the (*"Father of Hindi Travel literature"*). Baba Nagarjun was a major Hindi and Maithili poet who has also penned a number of novels, short stories, literary biographies and travelogues, and was known as ("*Janakavi- the People's Poet*").

Hindi playwriting

The pioneer of Hindi theatre as well as playwrighting, Bhartendu Harishchandra wrote *Satya Harishchandra* (1875), *Bharat Durdasha* (1876) and *Andher Nagari* (1878), in the late 19th century, Jaishankar Prasad became the next big figure in Hindi playwriting with plays like *Skanda Gupta* (1928), *Chandragupta* (1931) and *Dhruvswamini* (1933).[452,453]

As the Independence struggle was gathering steam playwrights broaching issues of nationalism and subversive ideas against the British, yet to dodge censorship they adapted themes from mythology, history and legend and used them as vehicle for political messages, a trend that continues to date, though now it was employed to bring out social, personal and psychological issues rather than clearly political, though street theatre broke this trend in coming decades in post-independence era, like IPTA-inspired, Naya Theatre of Habib Tanvir did in the 1950s–90s, Jana Natya Manch of Safdar Hashmi did in the 1970s–80s. Post-independence the emerging republic threw up new issues for playwrights to tackle and express, and Hindi playwriting showed greater brevity and symbolism, but it was not as prolific as in case with Hindi poetry or fiction.[454] Yet we have playwrights like Jagdish Chandra Mathur (*Konark*) and Upendranath Ashk (*Anjo Didi*), who displayed a steadily evolving understanding of stagecraft. These were followed another generation of pioneers in Hindi playwrighting, Mohan Rakesh, who started with *Ashadh Ka Ek Din* (1958), *Adhe Adhure* and *Lehron Ke Rajhans*, Dharamvir Bharati, who wrote *Andha Yug*, and other playwrights like Surendra Verma, and Bhisham Sahni.

Hindi essay-writing

Kuber Nath Rai is one of the writers who dedicated themselves entirely to the form of essay-writing. His collections of essays *Gandha Madan, Priya neel-kanti, Ras Aakhetak, Vishad Yog, Nishad Bansuri, Parna mukut* have enormously enriched the form of essay. A scholar of Indian culture and western literature, he was proud of Indian heritage. His love for natural beauty and Indian folk literatures and preference for agricultural society over the age of machines, his romantic outlook, aesthetic sensibility, his keen eye on contemporary reality and classical style place him very high among contemporary essayists in Hindi.

Prominent figures

- Chand Bardai (1148–1191), author of *Prithviraj Raso* first to write in khari boli.
- Amir Khusro (1253–1325 AD), author of pahelis and mukris in the "Hindavi" dialect.

Hindi literature

Figure 60: *Devaki Nandan Khatri*

Figure 61: *Camille Bulcke*

- Vidyapati (1352–1448), a prominent poet of Eastern dialects.
- Kabir (1398–1518), a major figure of the bhakti (devotional) movement.
- Surdas (1467–1583) author of Sahitya lahri, Sur Sarawali, *Sur Sagar* etc.
- Malik Muhammad Jayasi (1477–1542) author of the *Padmavat* (1540) etc.
- Mirabai (1504–1560) author of *Mira Padavali* etc.
- Tulsidas (1532–1623) author of *Ramacharitamanas Vinay Patrika*
- Keshavdas (1555–1617) author of *Rasikpriya* etc.
- Bihari (1595–1664) became famous by writing *Satasai* (Seven Hundred Verses).
- Guru Gobind Singh (1669–1708) author of *Bichitra Natak* etc.
- Ganga Das(1823–1913) was a revered saint of udasi sect and known for piety and Hindi poetry, who composed about 50 kavya-granthas and thousands of padas, who is known as Bhismpita of the Hindi poetry.[455]
- Bharatendu Harishchandra (1850–1885), whose works are compiled in *Bharatendu Granthavali*
- Devaki Nandan Khatri (1861–1913) author of *Chandrakanta* etc.
- Munshi Premchand (1880–1936), considered one of the greatest Hindi novelists of all time
- Maithili Sharan Gupt (1886–1964), pioneer of Khadiboli poetry
- Babu Gulabrai (1888–1963): an eminent critic, philosopher and essay writer, known for his biography *Meri Asafaltaein*
- Jaishankar Prasad (1889–1937), stalwart of the literary movement called Chhayavaad.
- Sahajanand Saraswati (1889–1950), books on peasant movement and the nationalist struggle, autobiography(mera jeevan sangharsh) and many others.
- Rahul Sankrityayan (1893–1963), widely travelled scholars of India
- Guru Bhakt Singh 'Bhakt' (1893–1983)
- Suryakant Tripathi 'Nirala' (1899–1961)
- Sumitranandan Pant, (1900–1977) eminent Hindi poet who wrote mainly on nature
- Suryakumar Pandey (b. 1954), Poet, Writer
- Yashpal (1903–1976), author of *Jhutha Sach*
- Jainendra Kumar (1905–1988), An extremely influential figure in 20th-century Hindi literature.
- Hazariprasad Dwivedi (1907–1979)
- Mahadevi Varma (1907–1987), one of the "four pillars" of the *Chhayavada* movement
- Ramdhari Singh Dinkar (1908–1974), hailed as a Rashtrakavi.
- Ram Ratan Bhatnagar (1914–1992) writer and critic of Hindi literature and poetry.

- Phanishwar Nath 'Renu' (1921–1977) freedom fighter, socialist, his best work considered to be Maila Anchal
- Ramesh Chandra Jha (1925–1994) freedom fighter, journalist, eminent poet and novelist.
- Harishankar Parsai (1922–1995), known for satirical works
- Naresh Mehta (1922–2000), Poet
- Bhupendra nath Kaushik"fikr" (1925–2007), Urdu, Hindi writer "Koltar main aks"
- Dharmavir Bharati (1926–1997), a renowned Hindi writer and editor
- Viveki Rai (b. 1927)
- Rajkamal Chaudhary (1929–1967) poet, short story writer, novelist, critic
- Raghuvir Sahay (1929–1990) was a versatile Hindi poet, translator, short-story writer and journalist.
- Nirmal Verma (1929–2005), one of the founders of the *Nai Kahani* (new short story) school
- Badri Narain Sinha (1930–1979), poet, critic, journalist and an Indian Police Service officer of Bihar
- Narendra Kohli (b. 1940) known for his plays, satires, short stories and novels
- Vibhuti Narain Rai (b. 1951), a renowned modern Hindi writer and Police Superintendent.
- Hrishikesh Sulabh (b. 1955) short story writer, playwright, drama critic. Pioneer of modern Hindi theatre in Bihar.
- Mohan Rana (b. 1964), Hindi poet, currently based in Britain
- Mehrunnisa Parvez (b. 1944), Hindi novelist, short story writer and Padma Shri awardee
- Darchhawna (b. 1936), Hindi writer and Padma Shri awardee
- Kamleshwar (1932-2007) author of Kitne Pakistan, Sahitya Akademi and Padma Bhushan awardee

Eminent Hindi journalists

Durgaprasad Mishra

Born in Kashmir, he came to Calcutta and started Bharat Mitra in 1878. In 1879, he began another weekly magazine- Saar Sudhanidhi but it closed down in that same year. On 17 August 1880, he started a 3rd weekly- Ucchit Vakta- meaning Right or Best Time. Ucchit Vakta focused on spreading the truth (about the British Raj) and fighting for justice. It became very popular for many years.

Mishra underwent a lot of difficulties trying to bring out a critical publication at the time of the British Raj. At times he was the editor, writer and also sold the paper himself. He was an inspiration for many journalists, particularly Bal Mukund Gupta.

Dharmvir Bharati

Born on 25 December 1926, Dharamvir Bharati graduated in BA (first class) in 1945 and in 1947 completed his MA in Hindi literature (first class) and finally did his PhD from Allahabad University. For some time he was principal of Allahabad University.

He began his journalist career in Abhyudaya, a journal by Padmakant Malviya. He then joined Sangam, edited by Ilachand Joshi and then became editor of Dharmayug. Thanks to Bharati, this journal became very popular.

During the 1971 war, Bharati reported from the frontlines of the battle. He covered all the horrors of the war. His series of reports, the finest in Hindi war journalism, were published under the title of 'Yudh Yatra'. As an honest and dedicated reporter, Bharati was unrivaled. After the war, he became editor of 2 more journals- Aalochana and Nikarshak.

Bharati was also famous as a short story writer, poet, essayist and novelist. The best known of his works are 'Band Galli ka Aakhiri Makaan', 'Andha Yug', 'Kunpriya'.

Bharatendu Harishchandra

Bharatendu Harishchandra began his career as a journalist at the age of 17. Published Kavi Vachan Sudha (1867) a monthly dedicated to ancient and medieval poetry. Published Harishchandra Magazine in 1873 – a general interest magazine. Published Bala Bodhini from 1874 – for women and young girls.

KVS was acknowledged to be the finest literary journal in any Indian language of that time, and was on par with the best of English journals. Bharatendu kept the journal up until his death 1885. Because of his extraordinary achievements, he is considered the most prolific Hindi journalist.

Madan Mohan Malaviya

Madan Mohan Malaviya was born in 1861 in Allahabad to a Brahmin family. From 1885 to 1887 was the editor of Indian Opinion. He was a strong supporter of the Congress. He helped launch the newspaper Dainik Hindustan and was its editor from 1887 to 1889. He was a close friend of many eminent Hindi writers like Gopalram Gehmari, Amrutlal Chakravarty and Pandit Pratap Narayan Mishra.

Along with Bal Mukund Gupta, he launched an Urdu journal 'Kohinoor' from Lahore. In those days, Gupta was not a facile Hindi scholar, but under Malviya's training, Gupta became editor of Bharat Mitra. In 1908, Malviya founded a new revolutionary journal Abhyudaya from Prayag. The renowned writer Purushottam Das Tandon was a frequent contributor to it.

After Abhyudaya, Malviya founded a monthly magazine 'Maryada', in 1909 he founded a daily 'Leader' and later on another daily – 'Bharat'.

Malviya was a great patriot and his love for his country was seen in all of his writings. He also contributed to Aaj, and helped to found the Hindustan Times in 1933, along with its Hindi counterpart Hindustan. Babu Gulabrai (17 January 1888 – 13 April 1963) (pen name: Gulabrai MA) was one of the greatest literary figures of modern Hindi literature.

Bibliography

- Dr. Nagendra (1988). *Indian Literature*[456]. Prabhat Prakashan.<templatestyles src="Module:Citation/CS1/styles.css"></templatestyles>
- Diana Dimitrova (2004). *Western tradition and naturalistic Hindi theatre*[457]. Peter Lang. ISBN 0-8204-6822-3.<templatestyles src="Module:Citation/CS1/styles.css"></templatestyles>
- Amaresh Datta (2006). *The Encyclopaedia of Indian Literature (Volume Two) (Devraj To Jyoti), Volume 2*[458]. Sahitya Akademi. ISBN 81-260-1194-7.<templatestyles src="Module:Citation/CS1/styles.css"></templatestyles>

Further reading

- *Hindi Literature*, by Ram Awadh Dwivedi. Published by Hindi Pracharak Pustakalaya, 1953.
- *A History of Hindi literature*, by K. B. Jindal. Published by Kitab Mahal, 1955.
- *Hindi Literature from Its Beginnings to the Nineteenth Century*, by Ronald Stuart McGregor. Published by Harrassowitz, 1984. <templatestyles src="Module:Citation/CS1/styles.css" />ISBN 3-447-02413-5.
- *Hindi Literature of the Nineteenth and Early Twentieth Centuries*, by Ronald Stuart McGregor. Published by Harrassowitz, 1974. <templatestyles src="Module:Citation/CS1/styles.css" />ISBN 3-447-01607-8.
- *A New Voice for New Times: The Development of Modern Hindi Literature*, by Ronald Stuart McGregor. Faculty of Asian Studies, Australian National University, 1981. <templatestyles src="Module:Citation/CS1/styles.css" />ISBN 0-909879-13-3.
- *An Encyclopaedia of World Hindi Literature*, by Ganga Ram Garg. Published by Concept Pub. Co., 1986.

External links

Wikisource has the text of the 1911 *Encyclopædia Britannica* article *Hindōstānī Literature*.

- Hindi Language and Literature[459]

Kannada literature

Kannada literature

History of literature <templatestyles src="Nobold/styles.css"/>by era
Bronze Age
- Ancient Egyptian - Akkadian - Sumerian
Classical
- Avestan - Chinese - Greek - Hebrew - Latin - Pali - Prakrit - Sanskrit - Syriac - Tamil
Early Medieval
- Matter of Rome - Matter of France - Matter of Britain - Armenian - Byzantine - Georgian - Japanese - Kannada - Middle Persian - Turkish

Medieval
- Old Bulgarian
- Old English
- Middle English
- Arabic
- Persian
- Armenian
- Byzantine
- Castilian
- Catalan
- Dutch
- French
- Georgian
- German
- Bengali
- Indian
- Old Irish
- Italian
- Korean
- Nepal Bhasa
- Norse
- Russian
- Telugu
- Serbian
- Turkish
- Welsh
Early Modern
- Renaissance
- Baroque
Modern by century
- 18th
- 19th
- 20th
- 21st
📖 Literature portal
- v
- t
- e[460]

Kannada literature (ಕನ್ನಡ ಸಾಹಿತ್ಯ) is the corpus of written forms of the Kannada language, a member of the Dravidian family spoken mainly in the Indian state of Karnataka and written in the Kannada script.[461]

Figure 62: *Old-Kannada inscription dated 578 CE (Badami Chalukya dynasty) outside Badami cave temple no.3*

Attestations in literature span something like one and a half millennia,[462,463,464,465,466] with some specific literary works surviving in rich manuscript traditions, extending from the 9th century to the present.[467] The Kannada language is usually divided into three linguistic phases: Old (450–1200 CE), Middle (1200–1700 CE) and Modern (1700–present);[468] and its literary characteristics are categorised as Jain, Veerashaiva and Vaishnava—recognising the prominence of these three faiths in giving form to, and fostering, classical expression of the language, until the advent of the modern era.[469,470,471] Although much of the literature prior to the 18th century was religious, some secular works were also committed to writing.[472,473]

Starting with the *Kavirajamarga* (c. 850), and until the middle of the 12th century, literature in Kannada was almost exclusively composed by the Jains, who found eager patrons in the Chalukya, Ganga, Rashtrakuta, Hoysala[474,475] and the Yadava kings.[476] Although the *Kavirajamarga*, authored during the reign of King Amoghavarsha, is the oldest extant literary work in the language, it has been generally accepted by modern scholars that prose, verse and grammatical traditions must have existed earlier.[477,478,479]

The Veerashaiva movement of the 12th century created new literature which flourished alongside the Jain works. With the waning of Jain influence during the 14th-century Vijayanagara empire, a new Vaishnava literature grew rapidly in the 15th century; the devotional movement of the itinerant Haridasa saints marked the high point of this era.

After the decline of the Vijayanagara empire in the 16th century, Kannada literature was supported by the various rulers, including the Wodeyars of the

Figure 63: *The Halmidi inscription, usually dated to the fifth century, is the earliest example of written Kannada.*[481]

Kingdom of Mysore and the Nayakas of Keladi. In the 19th century, some literary forms, such as the prose narrative, the novel, and the short story, were borrowed from English literature. Modern Kannada literature is now widely known and recognised: during the last half century, Kannada language authors have received eight Jnanpith awards, 60 Sahitya Akademi awards and 9 Sahitya Akademi Fellowships in India.[480]

Content and genre

Native Kannada prosody from 7th century CE	
Tripadi	7th century
Chattana	pre 9th century
Bedandegabbam	pre 9th century
Melvadu	pre 9th century
Bajanegabbam	pre 9th century
Gadyakatha	pre 9th century
Akkara	pre 9th century

Kannada literature

Ragale	10th century
Vachana	11th century
Shara Shatpadi	11th century
Kusuma Shatpadi	11th century
Bhoga Shatpadi	11th century
Bhamini Shatpadi	11th century
Parivardhini Shatpadi	11th century
Vardhaka Shatpadi	11th century
Bedagu	1160
Hadugabba	1160
Sangatya	1232
Suladi	16th century
Ugabhoga	16th century
Mundige	16th century

In the early period and beginning of the medieval period, between the 9th and 13th centuries, writers were predominantly Jains and Lingayats. Jains were the earliest known cultivators of Kannada literature, which they dominated until the 12th century, although a few works by Lingayats from that period have survived. Jain authors wrote about Tirthankaras and other aspects of religion. The Veerashaiva authors wrote about Shiva, his 25 forms, and the expositions of Shaivism. Lingayat poets belonging to the vachana sahitya tradition advanced the philosophy of Basava from the 12th century.

During the period between the 13th and 15th centuries, there was decline in Jain writings and an increase in the number of works from the Lingayat tradition; there were also contributions from Vaishnava writers. Thereafter, Lingayat and Vaishnava writers dominated Kannada literature. Vaishnava writers focused on the Hindu epics – the Ramayana, the Mahabharata and the Bhagavata – as well as Vedanta and other subjects from the Puranic traditions.[482] The devotional songs of the Haridasa poets, performed to music, were first noted in the 15th century. Writings on secular subjects remained popular throughout this period.

An important change during the Bhakti "devotion" period starting in the 12th century was the decline of court literature and the rise in popularity of shorter genres such as the *vachana* and *kirthane*, forms that were more accessible to the common man.[483] Writings eulogising kings, commanders and spiritual heroes waned, with a proportional increase in the use of local genres. Kannada literature moved closer to the spoken and sung folk traditions, with musicality

Figure 64: *Kannada poetry on stone–7th century Kappe Arabhatta inscription*

being its hallmark, although some poets continued to use the ancient *champu* form of writing as late as the 17th century.[484]

The *champu* Sanskritic metre (poems in verses of various metres interspersed with paragraphs of prose, also known as *champu-kavya*) was the most popular written form from the 9th century onwards, although it started to fall into disuse in the 12th century. Other Sanskritic metres used were the *saptapadi* (seven line verse), the *ashtaka* (eight line verse) and the *shataka* (hundred-line verse).[485,486] There were numerous translations and adaptations of Sanskrit writings into Kannada and, to a lesser extent, from Kannada into Sanskrit. The medieval period saw the development of literary metres indigenous to the Kannada language. These included the *tripadi* (three-line verse, in use from the 7th century), one of the oldest native metres; the *shatpadi* (six-line verse, first mentioned by Nagavarma I in *Chhandombudhi* of c. 984 and in use from 1165), of which six types exist; the *ragale* (lyrical narrative compositions, in use from 1160); the *sangatya* (compositions meant to be sung with a musical instrument, in use from 1232) and the *akkara* which came to be adopted in some Telugu writings.[487,488,489,490] There were rare interactions with Tamil literature, as well.[491]

Though religious literature was prominent, literary genres including romance, fiction, erotica, satire, folk songs, fables and parables, musical treatises and musical compositions were popular. The topics of Kannada literature included grammar, philosophy, prosody, rhetoric, chronicles, biography, history, drama and cuisine, as well as dictionaries and encyclopedias.[492,493] According to critic Joseph T. Shipley, over fifty works on scientific subjects including medicine, mathematics and astrology have been written in the Kannada language.[494]

Kannada literature of this period was mainly written on palm leaves. However, more than 30,000 more durable inscriptions on stone (known as *shilashasana*) and copper plates (known as *tamrashasana*) have survived to inform modern students of the historical development of Kannada literature.[495] The Shravanabelagola inscription of Nandisena (7th century), Kappe Arabhatta inscription (c. 700), and the Hummacha and Soraba inscriptions (c. 800) are good examples of poetry in *tripadi* metre,[496] and the Jura (Jabalpur) inscription of King Krishna III (964) is regarded as an epigraphical landmark of classical Kannada composition, containing poetic diction in *kanda* metre, a form consisting of a group of stanzas or chapters.[497]

Elegiac poetry on hundreds of *veeragallu* and *maastigallu* (hero stones) written by unknown poets in the *kanda* and the *vritta* (commentary) metre mourn the death of heroes who sacrificed their lives and the bravery of women who performed *sati*.[498] According to the scholar T. V. Venkatachala Sastry, the book *Karnataka Kavicharitre* compiled by Kannada scholar R. Narasimhachar lists over one thousand anonymous pieces of Kannada literature that cover an array of topics under religious and secular categories. Some fifty *Vachana* poets are known only by the pen names (*ankita*) used in their poems. Most Jain writings included in the list are from the period 1200–1450 CE, while Veerashaiva and Vaishnava writings are from later periods. Secular topics include mathematics, medicine, science of horses and elephants, architecture, geography and hydrology.[499]

The pace of change towards more modern literary styles gained momentum in the early 19th century. Kannada writers were initially influenced by the modern literature of other languages, especially English.[500] Modern English education and liberal democratic values inspired social changes, intertwined with the desire to retain the best of traditional ways.[501] New genres including short stories, novels, literary criticism, and essays, were embraced as Kannada prose moved toward modernisation.[502]

ಪದನಱಿದು ನುಡಿಯಲುಂ ನುಡಿದುದ
ನಱಿಯಲುಮಾರ್ಪರಾ ನಾಡವರ್ಗಳ್
ಚದುರರ್ ನಿಜದಿಂ ಕುರಿತೋದದೆಯುಂ
ಕಾವ್ಯಪ್ರಯೋಗ ಪರಿಣತಮತಿಗಳ್

Figure 65: *A stanza from Kavirajamarga (c. 850) in Kannada praising the people for their literary skills*

Classical period

Rashtrakuta court

The reign of the imperial Rashtrakutas and their powerful feudatory, the Gangas, marks the beginning of the classical period of writings in the Kannada language under royal patronage, and the end of the age of Sanskrit epics.[503]

There was an emphasis on the adoption of Sanskritic models while retaining elements of local literary traditions, a style that prevailed in Kannada literature throughout the classical period.[504] *Kavirajamarga*, written during this period, is a treatise on the Kannada speaking people, their poetry and their language.[505] A portion of the writing qualifies as a practical grammar. It describes defective and corrective examples (the "do's and don't's") of versification and native composition styles recognised by earlier poets (*puratana kavis*). These composition meters are the *bedande*, the *chattana* and the *gadyakatha* – compositions written in various interspersed metres. In some contexts, the term *puravcharyar*, which may refer to previous grammarians or rhetoricians, have also been mentioned.[506] Some historians attribute *Kavirajamarga* to the Rashtrakuta king Amoghavarsha I, but others believe that the book may have been inspired by the king and co-authored or authored in full by Srivijaya, a Kannada language theorist and court poet.[507,508,509]

The earliest existing prose piece in old Kannada is *Vaddaradhane* ("Worship of Elders", 9th century) by Shivakotiacharya.[510] It contains 19 lengthy stories, some in the form of fables and parables, such as "The Sage and the Monkey". Inspired by the earlier Sanskrit writing *Brihatkatha Kosha*, it is about Jain tenets and describes issues of rebirth, karma, the plight of humans on earth, and social issues of the time such as education, trade and commerce, magic, superstition, and the condition of women in society.[511]

Kannada literature

Figure 66: *Inscribed handwriting of 10th-century poet Ranna reads Kavi Ratna (gem among poets) in Shravanabelagola*

The works of Jain writers Adikavi Pampa, Sri Ponna and Ranna, collectively called the "three gems of Kannada literature", heralded the age of classical Kannada in the 10th century. Pampa, who wrote *Adipurana* in 941, is regarded as one of the greatest Kannada writers.[512] Written in *champu* style, *Adipurana* narrates the life history of the first Jain Thirtankar, Rishabhadeva. In this spiritual saga, Rishabhadeva's soul moves through a series of births before attaining emancipation in a quest for the liberation of his soul from the cycle of life and death.[513] Pampa's other classic, *Vikramarjuna Vijaya* (or *Pampa Bharata*, 941), is loosely based on the Hindu epic the Mahabharata.[514]

Sri Ponna, patronised by King Krishna III, wrote *Santipurana* (950), a biography of the 16th Jain Tirthankar Shantinatha. He earned the title *Ubhaya Kavichakravathi* ("supreme poet in two languages") for his command of both Kannada and Sanskrit.[515,516,517] Although Sri Ponna borrowed significantly from Kalidasa's earlier works, his *Santipurana* is considered an important Jain purana.

Chalukya court

From the late 10th century, Kannada literature made considerable progress under the patronage of the new overlords of the Deccan, the Western Chalukyas and their feudatories: the Hoysalas, the southern Kalachuris of Kalyanis, the Seuna Yadavas of Devagiri and Silharas of Karad.[518] The skill of Kannada poets was appreciated in distant lands. King Bhoja of Malwa in central India presented Nagavarma I, a writer of prosody and romance classics, with horses as a mark of his admiration.[519]

Ranna was the court poet of the Western Chalukya kings Tailapa II and Satyashraya. He was also patronised by Attimabbe, a devout Jain woman. Ranna's poetic writings reached their zenith with *Sahasa Bhima Vijaya* ("Victory of the bold Bhima", also called *Gada Yudda* or "Battle of Clubs", 982), which describes the conflict between Bhima and Duryodhana in his version of the Mahabharata epic, one of the earliest poetic elegies in the Kannada language.[520,521,522] Unlike Pampa, who glorified Arjuna and Karna in his writing, Ranna eulogised his patron King Satyashraya and favourably compared him to Bhima, whom he crowned at the end of the Mahabharata war. His other well-known writing is the *Ajitha purana* (993), which recounts the life of the second Jain Tirthankar Ajitanatha.[523] Ranna was bestowed the title *Kavi Chakravathi* ("Emperor among poets") by his patron king.

Among grammarians, Nagavarma-II, *Katakacharya* (poet laureate) of the Chalukya king Jagadhekamalla II made significant contributions with his works in grammar, poetry, prosody, and vocabulary; these are standard authorities and their importance to the study of Kannada language is well acknowledged.[524,525] Among his other writings, the *Kavyavalokana* on grammar and rhetoric and the *Karnataka Bhashabhushana* (1145) on grammar are historically significant.[526] However, the discovery of *Vardhamana Puranam* (1042), which has been ascribed by some scholars to Nagavarma II, has created uncertainty about his actual lifetime since it suggests that he may have lived a century earlier and been patronised by Jayasimha II.[527]

Hoysala period

In the late 12th century, the Hoysalas, a powerful hill tribe from the Malnad region in modern southern Karnataka, exploited the political uncertainty in the Deccan to gain dominance in the region south of the Krishna River in southern India.[528] A new chronological era was adopted, imperial titles were claimed and Kannada literature flourished with such noted scholars as Janna, Harihara, Rudrabhatta, Raghavanka, Keshiraja and others.[529] An important achievement during this period was the establishment of native metres in literature (the *ragale*, the *tripadi*, the *sangatya* and the *shatpadi*).

Two renowned philosophers who lived during this time, Ramanujacharya and Madhvacharya, influenced the culture of the region.[530] The conversion of the Hoysala King Vishnuvardhana in the early 12th century from Jainism to Vaishnavism was to later prove a setback to Jain literature. In the decades to follow, Jain writers faced competition from the Veerashaivas, to which they responded with rebuttals,[531] and from the 15th century, from the writers of the Vaishnava cadre. These events changed the literary landscape of the Kannada-speaking region forever.[532,533]

Kannada literature

Figure 67: *Hero stone (virgal) with old Kannada elegiac inscription (1220) at the Ishwara temple in Arasikere, Karnataka*

One of the earliest Veerashaiva writers who was not part of the *Vachana* literary tradition, poet Harihara (or Harisvara) came from a family of *karnikas* (accountants), and worked under the patronage of King Narasimha I. He wrote *Girijakalyana* in ten sections following the Kalidasa tradition, employing the old Jain *champu* style, with the story leading to the marriage of Shiva and Parvati.[534] In a deviation from the norm, Harihara avoided glorifying saintly mortals. He is credited with more than 100 poems in *ragale* metre, called the *Nambiyanana ragale* (or *Shivaganada ragale*, 1160) praising the saint Nambiyana and Virupaksha (a form of Hindu god Shiva).[535] For his poetic talent, he has earned the honorific *utsava kavi* ("poet of exuberance").

Harihara's nephew, Raghavanka, was the first to introduce the *shatpadi* metre into Kannada literature in his epic *Harishchandra Kavya* (1200), considered a classic despite occasionally violating strict rules of Kannada grammar.[536] Drawing on his skill as a dramatist, Raghavanka's story of King Harishchandra vividly describes the clash of personalities between sage Vishvamitra and sage Vashisht and between Harishchandra and Vishvamitra. It is believed that this interpretation of the story of Harishchandra is unique to Indian literature. The writing is an original and does not follow any established epic traditions.[537] In addition to Hoysala patronage, Raghavanka was honoured by Kakatiya king Prataparudra I.

Figure 68: *King Krishnadevaraya, patron of Vaishnava literature*

Rudrabhatta, a Smartha Brahmin (believer of monistic philosophy), was the earliest well-known Brahminical writer, under the patronage of Chandramouli, a minister of King Veera Ballala II. Based on the earlier work of *Vishnu Purana*, he wrote *Jagannatha Vijaya* (1180) in the *champu* style, relating the life of Lord Krishna leading up to his fight with the demon Banasura.[538]

In 1209, the Jain scholar and army commander Janna wrote *Yashodhara Charite*, a unique set of stories dealing with perversion. In one of the stories, a king intended to perform a ritual sacrifice of two young boys to Mariamma, a local deity. After hearing the boys' tale, the king is moved to release them and renounce the practice of human sacrifice.[539,540] In honour of this work, Janna received the title *Kavichakravarthi* ("Emperor among poets") from King Veera Ballala II.[541] His other classic, *Anathanatha Purana* (1230), deals with the life of the 14th Tirthankar Ananthanatha.

Vijayanagara period

The 14th century saw major upheavals in geo-politics of southern India with Muslim empires invading from the north. The Vijayanagara Empire stood as a bulwark against these invasions and created an atmosphere conducive to the development of the fine arts.[542] In a golden age of Kannada literature, competition between Vaishnava and Veerashaiva writers was fierce and literary disputations between the two sects were common, especially in the court of King Deva Raya II. Acute rivalry led to "organised processions" in honour of the classics written by poets of the respective sects.[543] The king himself was no less a writer, the romantic stories *Sobagina Sone* (*lit* "The Drizzle of Beauty") and *Amaruka* are assigned to him.[544]

To this period belonged Kumara Vyasa (the pen name of Naranappa), a doyen of medieval epic poets and one of the most influential Vaishnava poets of the time. He was particularly known for his sophisticated use of metaphors and had even earned the title *Rupaka Samrajya Chakravarti* ("Emperor of the land of Metaphors"). In 1430, he wrote the *Gadugina Bharata*, popularly known as *Karnata Bharata Kathamanjari* or *Kumaravyasa Bharata* in the Vyasa tradition. The work is a translation of the first ten chapters of the epic *Mahabharata* and emphasises the divinity and grace of the Lord Krishna, portraying all characters with the exception of Krishna to suffer from human foibles.[545] An interesting aspect of the work is the sense of humour exhibited by the poet and his hero, Krishna. This work marked a transition of Kannada literature to a more modern genre and heralded a new age combining poetic perfection with religious inspiration. The remaining *parvas* (chapters) of *Mahabharata* were translated by Timmanna Kavi (1510) in the court of King Krishnadevaraya. The poet named his work *Krishnaraya Bharata* after his patron king.

Kumara Valmiki (1500) wrote the first complete brahminical adaptation of the epic Ramayana, called *Torave Ramayana*. According to the author, the epic he wrote merely narrated God Shiva's conversation with his consort Parvati. This writing has remained popular for centuries and inspired folk theatre such as the *Yakshagana*, which has made use of its verses as a script for enacting episodes from the great epic. In Valmiki's version of the epic, King Ravana is depicted as one of the suitors at Sita's *Swayamvara* (*lit*. a ceremony of "choice of a husband"). His failure to win the bride's hand results in jealousy towards Rama, the eventual bridegroom. As the story progresses, Hanuman, for all his services to Rama, is exalted to the status of "the next creator". Towards the end of the story, during the war with Rama, Ravana realises that his adversary is none other than the God Vishnu and hastens to die at his hands to achieve salvation.[546]

Chamarasa, a Veerashaiva poet, was a rival of Kumara Vyasa in the court of Devaraya II. His eulogy of the saint Allama Prabhu, titled *Prabhulinga Lile* (1430), was later translated into Telugu and Tamil at the behest of his patron king. In the story, the saint was considered an incarnation of Hindu God Ganapathi while Parvati took the form of a princess of Banavasi.

Interaction between Kannada and Telugu literatures, a trend which had begun in the Hoysala period, increased. Translations of classics from Kannada to Telugu and vice versa became popular. Well-known bilingual poets of this

Figure 69: *Palm leaf with 11th–12th century Vachana poems in old Kannada*

Figure 70: *Akka Mahadevi, 12th century female poet*

period were Bhima Kavi, Piduparti Somanatha and Nilakanthacharya. In fact, so well versed in Kannada were some Telugu poets, including Dhurjati, that they freely used many Kannada terms in their Telugu writings. It was because of this "familiarity" with Kannada, that the notable writer Srinatha even called his Telugu, "Kannada". This process of interaction between the two languages continued into the 19th century in the form of translations by bilingual writers.[547]

Mystic literature

Veerashaiva

In the late 12th century, the Kalachuris successfully rebelled against their overlords, the Western Chalukyas, and annexed the capital Kalyani. During this turbulent period, a new religious faith called Veerashaivism (or Lingayatism) developed as a revolt against the existing social order of Hindu society. Some of the followers of this faith wrote literature called *Vachana Sahitya* ("Vachana literature") or *Sharana Sahitya* ("literature of the devotees") consisting of a unique and native form of poetry in free verse called *Vachana*.[548,549] Basavanna (or Basava, 1134–1196), the prime minister of Kalachuri King Bijjala

Kannada literature

Figure 71: *The bust of Basaveswara, unveiled in London in 2015, facing the UK Parliament*

II, is generally regarded as the inspiration for this movement.[550] Devotees gathered to discuss their mystic experiences at a centre for religious discussion called Anubhava Mantapa ("hall of experience") in Kalyani. Here, they expressed their devotion to God Shiva in simple *vachana* poems. These poems were spontaneous utterances of rhythmic, epigrammatical, satirical prose emphasising the worthlessness of riches, rituals and book learning, displaying a dramatic quality reminiscent of the dialogues of Plato.[551,552]

Basavanna, Allama Prabhu, Devara Dasimayya, Channabasava, Siddharama (1150), and Kondaguli Kesiraja are the best known among numerous poets (called *Vachanakaras*) who wrote in this genre. Akka Mahadevi was prominent among the several women poets; in addition to her poetry, she is credited with two short writings, *Mantrogopya* and *Yogangatrividhi*. Siddharama is credited with writings in *tripadi* metre and 1,379 extant poems (though he has claimed authorship of 68,000 poems).[553,554,555]

The Veerashaiva movement experienced a setback with the assassination of King Bijjala and eviction of the *sharanas* (devotees) from Kalyani; further growth of *Vachana* poetry was curtailed until the 15th century when another wave of writings began under the patronage of the rulers of Vijayanagara.[556] Chieftain Nijaguna Shivayogi originated a new philosophy called *Kaivalya*, founded on the advaitha (monistic) philosophy of Adi Shankara, synthesised with an offshoot of the Veerashaiva faith. A prolific writer, Shivayogi composed devotional songs collectively known as the *Kaivalya sahitya* (or *Tattva Padagalu*, literally "songs of the pathway to emancipation"). His songs were

Figure 72: *Kanaka Dasa (c. 1509–1609)*

reflective, philosophical and concerned with Yoga. Shivayogi also wrote a highly respected scientific encyclopaedia called the *Vivekachintamani*; it was translated into Marathi language in 1604 and Sanskrit language in 1652 and again in the 18th century. The encyclopaedia includes entries on 1,500 topics and covers a wide range of subjects including poetics, dance and drama, musicology and erotics.[557]

Other well-known poet saints of the Veerashaiva tradition include Muppina Sadakshari, a contemporary of Shivayogi, whose collection of songs are called the *Subodhasara*, Chidananda Avadhuta of the 17th century and Sarpabhushana Shivayogi of the 18th century. So vast is this body of literature that much of it still needs to be studied.

Vaishnava

The Vaishnava Bhakti (devotional) movement involving well-known Haridasas (devotee saints) of that time made an indelible imprint on Kannada literature starting in the 15th century, inspiring a body of work called *Haridasa Sahitya* ("Haridasa literature"). Influenced by the Veerashaivism of the 12th century, this movement touched the lives of millions with its strong current of devotion. The Haridasas conveyed the message of Vedantic philosopher Madhvacharya to the common man through simple Kannada language in the form of *devaranamas* and *kirthanas* (devotional songs in praise of god).[558,559] The philosophy of Madhvacharya was spread by eminent disciples including Naraharitirtha, Jayatirtha, Vyasatirtha, Sripadaraya, Vadirajatirtha, Purandara Dasa, and Kanaka Dasa.[560] Chaitanya Mahaprabhu, a prominent saint from distant Bengal, visited the region in 1510, further stimulating the devotional movement.

Purandara Dasa (1484–1564), a wandering bard, is believed to have composed 475,000 songs in the Kannada and Sanskrit languages, though only about 1,000 songs are known today. Composed in various *ragas*, and often ending with a salutation to the Hindu deity Vittala, his compositions presented the essence of the *Upanishads* and the *Puranas* in simple yet expressive language. He also devised a system by which the common man could learn Carnatic music, and codified the musical composition forms *svaravalis*, *alankaras* ("figure of speech") and *geethams*. Owing to such contributions, Purandara Dasa earned the honorific *Karnataka Sangeeta Pitamaha* ("Father of Carnatic Music").[561,562,563]

Kanaka Dasa (whose birth name was Thimmappa Nayaka, 1509–1609) of Kaginele (in modern Haveri district) was an ascetic and spiritual seeker who authored important writings such as *Mohanatarangini* ("River of Delight"), the story of the Hindu god Krishna in *sangatya* metre; *Nrisimhastava*, a work dealing with glory of god Narasimha; *Nalacharita*, the story of Nala, noted for its narration; and *Hari Bhaktisara*, a spontaneous writing on devotion in *shatpadi* metre. The latter writing, which deals with *niti* (morals), *bhakti* (devotion) and *vairagya* (renunciation) has become popular as a standard book of learning for children.[564] Kanaka Dasa authored a unique allegorical poem titled *Ramadhanya Charitre* ("Story of Rama's Chosen Grain"), which exalts ragi over rice. Apart from these classics, about 240 songs written by the Kanaka Dasa are available today.[565]

The Haridasa movement returned to prominence from the 17th through 19th centuries, producing as many as 300 poets in this genre; well-known among them are Vijaya Dasa (1682–1755), Gopala Dasa (1721–1769), Jagannatha Dasa (1728–1809), Mahipathi Dasa (1750), Helavanakatte Giriamma and others.[566] Over time, the movement's devotional songs inspired a form of religious and didactic performing art of the Vaishnava people called the Harikatha ("Stories of Hari"). Similar developments were seen among the followers of the Veerashaiva faith who popularised the *Shivakatha* ("Stories of Shiva").[567]

Figure 73: *King Chikka Devaraja Wodeyar (1673–1704), writer and patron of Kannada literature*

Mysore and Keladi period

With the decline of the Vijayanagara Empire, the Kingdom of Mysore (ಮೈಸೂರು ಸಾಮ್ರಾಜ್ಯ) (1565–1947) and the kingdom of the Keladi Nayakas (1565–1763) rose to power in the southern and western regions of modern Karnataka respectively. Production of literary texts covering various themes flourished in these courts.[568] The Mysore court was adorned by eminent writers who authored encyclopaedias, epics, and religious commentaries, and composers and musicians. The Keladi court is better known for writings on Veerashaiva doctrine.[569] The Mysore kings themselves were accomplished in the fine arts and made important contributions.[570,571,572] A unique and native form of poetic literature with dramatic representation called *Yakshagana* gained popularity in the 18th century.[573]

Geetha Gopala, a well-known treatise on music, is ascribed to King Chikka Devaraja Wodeyar (1673–1704), the earliest composer of the dynasty, who went by the honorific *Sahitya Vidyanikasha Prastharam* ("Expert in literature").[574] Inspired by Jayadeva's *Geetha Govinda* in Sanskrit, it was written in *saptapadi* metre. This is the first writing to propagate the Vaishnava faith in the Kannada language.[575]

Also writing in this period[576,577] was Sarvajna (*lit.* "The all knowing")—a mendicant and drifter Veerashaiva poet who left a deep imprint on Kannada speaking region and its people. His didactic *Vachanas*, penned in the *tripadi* metre, constitute some of Kannada's most celebrated works. With the exception of some early poems, his works focus on his spiritual quest as a drifter.[578] The pithy *Vachanas* contain his observations on the art of living, the purpose of life and the ways of the world.[579] He was not patronised by royalty, nor did he write for fame; his main aim was to instruct people about morality.[580]

The writing of Brahmin author Lakshmisa (or Lakshmisha), a well-known story-teller and a dramatist, is dated to the mid-16th or late 17th century.[581] The *Jaimini Bharata*, his version of the epic Mahabharata written in *shatpadi* metre, is one of the most popular poems of the late medieval period. A collection of stories, the poem includes the tale of the *Sita Parityaga* ("Repudiation of Sita"). The author successfully converted a religious story into a very human tale; it remains popular even in modern times.[582]

The period also saw advances in dramatic works. Though there is evidence that theatre was known from the 12th century or earlier, modern Kannada theatre is traced to the rise of *Yakshagana* (a type of field play), which appeared in the 16th century.[583] The golden age of *Yakshagana* compositions was tied to the rule of King Kanteerava Narasaraja Wodeyar II (1704–1714). A polyglot, he authored 14 *Yakshaganas* in various languages, although all are written in the Kannada script.[584] He is credited with the earliest *Yakshaganas* that included *sangeeta* (music), *nataka* (drama) and *natya* (dance).[585]

Mummadi Krishnaraja Wodeyar (1794–1868), the ruler of the princely state of Mysore, was another prolific writer of the era.[586] More than 40 writings are attributed to him, including a poetic romance called *Saugandika Parinaya* written in two versions, *sangatya* and a drama.[587] His reign signalled the shift from classical genres to modern literature which was to be complemented by the influence of colonial period of India.

Modern period

The development of modern Kannada literature can be traced to the early 19th century when Maharaja Krishnaraja Wodeyar III and his court poets moved away from the ancient *champu* form of prose toward prose renderings of Sanskrit epics and plays. Kempu Narayana's *Mudramanjusha* ("Seal Casket", 1823) is the first modern novel written in Kannada.

Modern Kannada literature was cross-fertilized by the colonial period in India as well.,[588] with translations of Kannada works and dictionaries into European languages as well as other Indian languages, and vice versa, and the

Figure 74: *Maharaja and writer, Jayachamaraja Wodeyar Bahadur (1940–1947) with Queen Elizabeth II*

establishment of European style newspapers and periodicals in Kannada. In addition, in the 19th century, interaction with European technology, including new printing techniques accelerated the development of modern literature.

The first Kannada newspaper called *Mangalore Samachara* was published by Hermann Mögling in 1843; and the first Kannada periodical, *Mysuru Vrittanta Bodhini* was published by Bhashyam Bhashyacharya in Mysore around the same time. Hermann Mögling translated Kannada classics into a series called *Bibliotheca Carnataca* during 1848–1853.,[589] while British officers Benjamin L. Rice and J. H. Fleet edited and published critical editions of literary classics, contemporary folk ballads and inscriptions. Following the rich tradition of dictionaries in Kannada since the 11th century, the first dictionaries expressing meanings of Kannada words in European languages were published in the 19th century, the most prominent of them being Ferdinand Kittel's Kannada-English dictionary in 1894.[590]

There was a push towards original works in prose narratives and a standardisation of prose during the late 19th century.[591] Translations of works from English, Sanskrit and other Indian languages like Marathi and Bengali continued and accelerated. Lakshman Gadagkar's *Suryakantha* (1892) and Gulvadi Venkata Rao's *Indira Bai* (1899) signalled the move away from the highly stylised mores and aesthetics of prior Kannada works to modern prose, establishing the modern novel genre and fundamentally influencing the essay, literary criticism and drama genres.

Figure 75: *Ferdinand Kittel (1832–1903), Christian missionary and writer of Kannada-English dictionary*

Navodaya – A period of modern literature

At the dawn of the 20th century, B. M. Srikantaiah ('B. M. Sri'), regarded as the "Father of modern Kannada literature",[592] called for a new era of writing original works in modern Kannada while moving away from archaic Kannada forms. This paradigmatic shift spawned an age of prolificacy in Kannada literature and came to be dubbed the *Navodaya* (*lit.* 'A new rise') period—a period of awakening. B. M. Sri led the way with his *English Geethagalu* ("English Songs")—a collection of poems translated from English set the tone for more translations using a standardisation of a modern written idiom.[593] Original and seminal works which drew greatly from native and folk traditions also emerged alongside the translations. Stalwarts like S. G. Narasimhachar, Panje Mangesha Rao and Hattiangadi Narayana Rao also contributed with celebrated efforts. Literary subjects now veered from discussing kings and gods to more humanistic and secular pursuits. Kannada writers experimented with several forms of western literature, the novel and the short story in particular. The novel found an early champion in Shivaram Karanth while another prominent writer, Masti Venkatesh Iyengar ('Masti'), laid the foundation for generations of story tellers to follow with his *Kelavu Sanna Kathegalu* ("A few Short Stories", 1920) and *Sanna Kathegalu* ("Short Stories", 1924).[594]

Figure 76: *D. V. Gundappa statue in Bugle Rock Park, Basavanagudi area of Bangalore*

The consolidation of modern drama was pioneered by T. P. Kailasam, with his *Tollu Gatti* ("The Hollow and the Solid", 1918). Kailasam followed this with *Tali Kattoke Cooline* ("Wages for tying the Mangalsutra"), a critique on the dowry system in marriage. His plays mainly focused on problems affecting middle class Brahmin families: the dowry system, religious persecution, woes in the extended family system and exploitation of women. Novels of the early 20th century promoted a nationalist consciousness in keeping with the political developments of the time. While Venkatachar and Galaganath translated Bankim Chandra and Harinarayana Apte respectively, Gulvadi Venkata Rao, Kerur Vasudevachar and M. S. Puttanna initiated the movement toward realistic novels with their works. Aluru Venkatarao's *Karnataka Gatha Vaibhava* had a profound influence on the movement for Karnataka's unification.

1925–50 – The Golden harvest

While the first quarter of the 20th century was a period of experiment and innovation, the succeeding quarter was one of creative achievement. This period saw the rise of acclaimed lyricists whose works combined native folk songs and the mystic poetry of the medieval *vachanas* and *kirthanas* with influences from modern English romantics.[595] D. R. Bendre, with his collection of 27 poems including such masterpieces as *Gari* ("Wing", 1932), *Nadaleele* (1938) and *Sakhigeetha* (1940), was perhaps the most outstanding Kannada lyricist of the period.[596] His poems covered a wide range of themes including patriotism, love of nature, conjugal love, transcendental experiences and sympathy for the poor.[597] Govinda Pai narrated the story of Christ's crucifixion in his work *Golgotha* (1931). The success of this work encouraged Pai to follow with three panegyrics in 1947; *Vaishakhi, Prabhasa* and *Dehali*, narrated the last days of the Buddha, God Krishna and Gandhi respectively.[598] His *Hebberalu* ("Thumb", 1946) dramatises the story of Drona and Ekalavya, characters from the epic Mahabharata.

K.V. Puttappa ('Kuvempu'), who would subsequently become Kannada's first Jnanpith awardee, demonstrated great talent in writing blank verse with his *magnum opus Sri Ramayana Darshanam* (1949).[599] This work marks the beginning of modern Kannada epic poetry. The work, through the use of metaphors and similes, focuses on the concept that all living creatures will eventually evolve into perfect beings.[600] Other important works of the period are Masti's *Navaratri* and P. T. Narasimhachar's *Hanathe*. D. V. Gundappa's *Mankuthimmana Kagga* ("Dull Thimma's Rigmarole", 1943) harkened back to the wisdom poems of the late medieval poet Sarvajna.[601] A celebrated writer of conjugal love poems, K. S. Narasimhaswamy won critical acclaim for *Mysore Mallige* ("Mysore Jasmine", 1942), a description of the bliss of everyday marital life.[602]

Growth in poetic drama was inspired by B.M. Sri's *Gadayuddha Natakam* (1925), an adaptation of Ranna's medieval epic. While Kuvempu and B.M. Sri were inspired by old Kannada, Masti and later P. T. Narasimhachar ('Pu. Ti. Na') explored modern sensibilities in their *Yashodhara* (1938) and *Ahalye* (1940). The 1930s saw the emergence of Sriranga, who joined forces with Samsa and Kailasam to pen some of the most successful plays in Kannada.[603] Samsa completed his trilogy about Ranadhira Kantirava, a Mysore king of yore, with his *Vijayanarasimha* (1936) and *Mantrashakti* (1938). Kailasam's mastery over wit and stage rhetoric come to the fore in his *Home Rule* (1930) and *Vaidyana Vyadi* ("A Doctors Ailment", 1940) while he explores his serious side in *Bhahishkara* (1929); with *Soole* ("Prostitute", 1945), he unleashed his contempt for outdated quasi-religious mores. Societal ills were also examined in Bendre's *Nageya Hoge* ("Fumes of Laughter", 1936), and in Karanth's *Garbhagudi* ("Sanctum", 1932), which decried the exploitation of society in the name of religion.[604]

The novel came of age during this period, with Karanth (*Chomana Dudi*, 1933), Masti (*Subbanna*, 1928) and Kuvempu ("Subbamma Heggadathi of Kanur", 1936) leading the charge.[605] Significantly, writers chose to carry on from where Puttanna, Gulvadi and Kerur had left off around the start of the 20th century rather than continue with popular translations in the style of

Venkatachar and Galaganath. Aesthetic concerns replaced the didactic and a sense of form developed. Devudu Narasimha Shastri distinguished himself with his *Antaranga* (1931) and *Mayura* (1928); the former was a much acclaimed work which delved into the psychology of the protagonist, while the latter was a historical novel tracing the emergence of the Kadamba dynasty. Another high point of this period is Karanth's *Marali Mannige* (1942), the saga of three generations of a family, reflecting the social, cultural and economic developments of over a hundred years.[606]

Literary criticism, which had its beginnings in the first quarter-century, also made significant progress. B.M. Sri's *Kannada Sahitya Charitre* (1947), Gundappa's *Sahitya Shakti* (1950), Masti's *Adikavi Valmiki* (1935), Bendre's *Sahitya Hagu Vimarshe* ("Literature and Criticism", 1932) and Krishna Shastry's *Samskrita Nataka* (1937) are particularly notable. The essay, another form adopted from western literature, was richly served by A N Murthy Rao (*Hagaluganasugalu*, 1937), Gorur Ramaswamy Iyengar's ('Gorur') humorous *Halliya Chitragalu* (1930) and Karanth's *Hucchu manassina Hattu mukhagalu* (1948).[607]

Late Navodaya and the rise of the progressives

As the *Navodaya* period waxed, the *Pragatishila* (progressives) movement led by novelist A. N. Krishna Rao ('Anakru') gained momentum in the early 1940s.[608] This left-leaning school contended that literature must be an instrument of social revolution and considered the *Navodaya* to be the product of aesthetes, too puritanical to be of any social relevance. This movement drew both established and young writers into its fold and, while it produced no poetry or drama of special merit, its contributions to short story and novel forms were appreciable. *Pragatishila* was credited with broadening readers' horizons; works produced during this period dealt extensively with subjects of everyday life, rural themes and the common man. The language was less inhibited and made generous use of colloquialism and slang. Anakru himself was a prolific writer of novels but the best works of this school are attributed to T. R. Subba Rao ('Ta Ra Su'), Basavaraju Kattimani and Niranjana.[609] T. R. Subba Rao initially wrote short stories, although he later turned his talents to novels, which were popular. His early novels, *Purushavatara* and *Munjavininda Munjavu*, told the stories of the underprivileged, the downtrodden and the outcast.[610] Best known among his novels—some of whose plots are centred on his native Chitradurga—are *Masanada Hoovu* ("Flower from a cemetery"), a story about the plight of prostitutes, and historical novel *Hamsa Gite* ("Swan Song"), a story about a dedicated musician of the late 18th century during annexation of Chitradurga by Tipu sultan.

Marked as its influence had been, the *Pragatishila* wave was already in decline by the close of the 1950s. Legendary writers of the previous era continued to produce notable works in the *Navodaya* style. In poetry, Bendre's *Naku Tanti* ("Four Strings", 1964) and Kuvempu's *Aniketana* (1964) stand out. V.K. Gokak brought out the innate insufficiencies of the more advanced western cultures in *Indilla Nale* (1965).[611] *Navodaya*-style novels continued to be successful with such noteworthy works as Karanth's *Mookajjiya Kanasugalu* ("Mookajji's visions", 1968), where Karanth explored the origins of man's faith in the mother goddess and the stages of evolution of civilisation. Kuvempu's *Malegallali Madumagalu* ("The Bride of the Hills", 1967) is about loving relationships that exist in every level of society.[612]

Masti's two classic novels of this era were *Channabasavanayaka* (1950), which describe the defeat of Bidanur's chief Channabasava Nayaka (on Karnataka's coast) by Haider Ali in the late 18th century, and *Chickavirarajendra* (1950), which describes the fall of the tiny kingdom of Coorg (ruled by Chikka Virarajendra) to the British East India Company.[613] The common theme in both works is the despotism and tyranny of the incumbent native rulers resulting in the intervention of a foreign power appearing on the scene to restore order, but with its own imperialistic intentions.[614]

S. L. Bhyrappa, a charismatic young writer, first came to attention in the 1960s with his first novel *Dharmasri*, although it was his *Vamsavriksha* ("Family Tree", 1966) that put him in the spotlight as one of Kannada's most popular novelists. It is a story of a respected scholar, Srinivasa Srotri, his family and their long-held values. The protagonist's young and widowed daughter-in-law wishes to remarry, putting his family tradition at risk.[615] Bhyrappa's best novel of the period was *Grihabhanga* ("Breaking of a Home", 1970), a story of a woman surviving under tragic circumstances. The characters in the story are rustic and often use vulgar language.[616] His other important novel is *Parva*, a major work in Kannada fiction acclaimed as an admirable attempt at recreating life on the sub-continent during the time of the epic Mahabharata.[617]

Navya

In the 1950s, even as the *Pragatishila* merged back into the *Navodaya* mainstream, a new modernist school of writing called *Navya* emerged. Though formally inaugurated by V. K. Gokak with his *Navya Kavitegalu* ("Modern Poems", 1950), it was Gopalakrishna Adiga who best exemplified the ethos of the movement. Poetry and, later, the short story became the most effective vehicles of the movement. With the passing of the Gandhian era and its influences, a new era in which to express modern sensibilities had arrived. The

Figure 77: *Seated L to R: Masti Venkatesh Iyengar, D. V. Gundappa, Kuvempu, M. V. Seetharamiah, K. Shivaram Karanth, A.N. Krishna Rao (Anakru) and G.P. Rajarathnam*

Navya writers questioned the time-honoured standards of plot of the *Navodaya*; life was seen not as a pursuit of already existing values, but as an introspective search for them, occasionally narrated in stream of consciousness technique. Events and details were increasingly treated metaphorically and the short story grew closer to poetry.[618,619] Gopalakrishna Adiga is considered the father of this form of expression with his *Nadedu Banda Dari* ("The Path Traversed", 1952) where he sought inspiration from T. S. Eliot and W. H. Auden. His other well-known poems include *Gondalapura* ("Pandemonium", 1954) and *Bhoota* (1959).[620]

G. S. Shivarudrappa made his mark in the Navya period with *Mumbai Jataka* ("A Horoscope of Bombay", 1966), which takes a closer look at urbanised society in Mumbai. A protégé of Kuvempu, Shivarudrappa's fame came the peak of popularity of romantic poems with his *Samagma* ("Songs of Equanimity", 1951), poems distinguished by an idealistic bent. He continued to write poems in the same vein, although in his later poems there is a gradual shift to social issues with a streak of admiration for god's creation.[621] His critical essay, *Anuranana* (1980), is about the Vachana poets of the 12th century, their tradition, style and influence on later poets.

K. S. Narasimhaswamy remained prominent through this era, writing such landmark poems as *Silalate* ("The Sculptured Creeper", 1958) and *Gadiyaradangadiya Munde* ("Before the Clock Shop").[622] Chandrashekhara Kambar, Chandrashekar Patil, P. Lankesh, and K. S. Nissar Ahmed are among the best-known later generation Navya poets.[623]

Outstanding playwrights from this period are Girish Karnad, P. Lankesh, Chandrashekhara Kambara and Chandrashekar Patil. Karnad's *Tughlaq* (1964) portrays violence caused by idealism gone astray. Considered an important creation in Kannada theatre, the play depicts the 14th-century Sultan of Delhi, Mohammad Tughlaq in contrasting styles, a tyrannical and whimsical ruler and at the same time, an idealist who sought the best for his subjects.[624] Most plays written by Karnad have either history or mythology as their theme, with a focus on their relevance to modern society.

The most acclaimed novel of the era was *Samaskara* by U.R.Anantha Murthy (1965). The novel details the search for new values and identity by the protagonist, a Brahmin, who had sexual intercourse with the untouchable mistress of his heretic adversary.[625] Another notable work is the *Swarupa* (1966) by Poornachandra Tejaswi. Anantha Murthy's *Prasne* (1963) contains his best collection of short stories including *Ghatashraddha*, which describes the tragedy that befell a young pregnant widow, from the point of view of a boy. His collection *Mouni* (1973) includes the stories *Navilugulu* ("Peacocks") and *Clip Joint*.[626]

The Navya movement was not without its critics. The doubt, dilemmas and indecision in every turn of the plot resulted in increasingly sophisticated and complex narrations, which some readers found uninteresting. It was derided as an intellectual exercise of the middle class intelligentsia; in its extreme sophistication, it was thought to have lost its touch with realities of life. This led to a gradual waning of the Navya school as it was supplanted by emerging waves of *Navyottara*, *Bandaya* (protest) and *Dalit* schools.

Post-modern trends

From the early 1970s, a segment of writers including many "Navya" writers started to write novels and stories that were anti-"Navya". This genre was called *Navyottara* and sought to fulfil a more socially responsible role.[627,628] The best-known authors in this form of writing were Poornachandra Tejaswi and Devanur Mahadeva. In his preface to Abachurina Post Office, Tejaswi expressed a path breaking observation towards then prevailing literary movements. Tejaswi won the "most creative novel of the year" for his *Karvalo* in 1980 and *Chidambara Rahasya* in 1985 from the Sahitya Akademi.

Modernisation and westernisation continue to inform sensibilities and spawn new literary techniques and genres.[629] The most striking developments in recent times have been the rise of the prose form to a position of predominance — a position earlier held by poetry — and the prodigious growth in dramatic literature. More recently *Bandaya* (Rebellion) and Dalit literature, in some ways a throwback to the *Pragatishila* (Progressivism) days, have come to the fore. Mahadeva's *Marikondavaru* ("Those who sold themselves") and *Mudala Seemeli Kole Gile Ityadi* ("Murder in the Eastern Region") are examples of this trend.

Kannada writers have been presented with 8 Jnanpith awards, 60 Sahitya Akademi awards and 9 Sahitya Akademi Fellowships in India, and numerous other national and international awards since India's independence.

References

 Wikimedia Commons has media related to *Kannada language literature*.

- Bhat, Thirumaleshwara (1993) [1993]. *Govinda Pai*. Sahitya Akademi. ISBN 81-7201-540-2.<templatestyles src="Module:Citation/CS1/styles.css"></templatestyles>
- Chidananda Murti, M. (1978). "Kannada language and literature during the Chalukyas of Badami (c. 540–750 A.D.)". In M. S. Nagaraja Rao. *The Chalukyas of Badami: Seminar Papers*. Bangalore: Mythic Society.<templatestyles src="Module:Citation/CS1/styles.css"></templatestyles>
- Crystal, David (2001). *A Dictionary of Language*[630]. Chicago and London: University of Chicago Press. Pp. 390. ISBN 0-226-12203-4.<templatestyles src="Module:Citation/CS1/styles.css"></templatestyles>
- Dalby, Andrew (1998). *Dictionary of Languages: The Definitive Reference to More Than 400 Languages*. Columbia University Press. ISBN 0-231-11568-7.<templatestyles src="Module:Citation/CS1/styles.css"></templatestyles>
- Das, Sisir Kumar (1995) [1995]. *A History Of Indian Literature 1911–1956*. Sahitya Akademi. ISBN 81-7201-798-7.<templatestyles src="Module:Citation/CS1/styles.css"></templatestyles>
- Gai, Govind Swamirao (1992). "Studies in Indian History, Epigraphy, and Culture"[631]. Karnataka, India: Shrihari Prakashana. Pp. 346.<templatestyles src="Module:Citation/CS1/styles.css"></templatestyles>
- Gai, Govind Swamirao (1996). *Inscriptions of the early Kadambas*. New Delhi: Indian Council of Historical Research and Pratibha Prakashan. Pp. xv, 170, 88 plates. ISBN 81-85268-47-9.<templatestyles src="Module:Citation/CS1/styles.css"></templatestyles>
- Garg, Ganga Ram (1996) [1987]. *International Encyclopaedia of Indian Literature – vol 4, Kavirajamarga-Kannada*. New Delhi: Mittal Publications. ISBN 81-7099-038-6.<templatestyles src="Module:Citation/CS1/styles.css"></templatestyles>
- Iyer, Panchapakesa A.S. (2006) [2006]. *Karnataka Sangeeta Sastra*. Chennai: Zion Printers.<templatestyles src="Module:Citation/CS1/styles.css"></templatestyles>
- Kamath, Suryanath U. (2001) [1980]. *A concise history of Karnataka : from pre-historic times to the present*. Bangalore: Jupiter books. LCCN 80905179[632]. OCLC 7796041[633].<templatestyles src="Module:Citation/CS1/styles.css"></templatestyles>

- Karmarkar, A.P. (1947) [1947]. *Cultural history of Karnataka : ancient and medieval*. Dharwad: Karnataka Vidyavardhaka Sangha. OCLC 8221605[634].<templatestyles src="Module:Citation/CS1/styles.css"></templatestyles>
- Krishnamurti, Bhadriraju (2003). *The Dravidian Languages (Cambridge Language Surveys)*[635]. Cambridge and London: Cambridge University Press. Pp. 574. ISBN 0-521-77111-0.<templatestyles src="Module:Citation/CS1/styles.css"></templatestyles>
- Masica, Colin P (1993). *The Indo-Aryan Languages*. Cambridge University Press. ISBN 0-521-23420-4.<templatestyles src="Module:Citation/CS1/styles.css"></templatestyles>
- Master, Alfred (1944). "Indo-Aryan and Dravidian". *Bulletin of the School of Oriental and African Studies, University of London*. **11** (2). doi: 10.1017/s0041977x00072487[636].<templatestyles src="Module:Citation/CS1/styles.css"></templatestyles>
- Moorthy, Vijaya (2001) [2001]. *Romance of the Raga*. Abhinav Publications. ISBN 81-7017-382-5.<templatestyles src="Module:Citation/CS1/styles.css"></templatestyles>
- Mugaḷi, Raṃ Śrī (1975) [1975]. *History of Kannada literature*. Sahitya Akademi. OCLC 2492406[637].<templatestyles src="Module:Citation/CS1/styles.css"></templatestyles>
- Mugaḷi, Raṃ Śrī (2006) [1946]. *The Heritage of Karnataka: in relation to India*[638]. Read Books [Bangalore: Satyasodhama]. ISBN 978-1-4067-0232-3.<templatestyles src="Module:Citation/CS1/styles.css"></templatestyles>
- Murthy, K. Narasimha (1992). "Modern Kannada Literature". In George K.M. *Modern Indian Literature:An Anthology – Vol 1*. Sahitya Akademi. ISBN 81-7201-324-8.<templatestyles src="Module:Citation/CS1/styles.css"></templatestyles>
- Nagaraj, D.R. (2003) [2003]. "Critical Tensions in the History of Kannada Literary Culture"[639]. In Sheldon I. Pollock. *Literary Cultures in History: Reconstructions from South Asia*. Berkeley and London: University of California Press. Pp. 1066. pp. 323–383. ISBN 0-520-22821-9.<templatestyles src="Module:Citation/CS1/styles.css"></templatestyles>
- Narasimhacharya, Ramanujapuram (1990) [1934]. *History of Kannada Language*[640]. Mysore: Government Press. Reprinted by Asian Educational Services, New Delhi. ISBN 81-206-0559-4.<templatestyles src="Module:Citation/CS1/styles.css"></templatestyles>
- Narasimhacharya, Ramanujapuram (1988) [1934]. *History of Kannada Literature*[641]. Mysore: Government Press. Reprinted by Asian Educational Services, New Delhi. ISBN 81-206-0303-6.<templatestyles

- Pollock, Sheldon (1998). "The Cosmopolitan Vernacular". *The Journal of Asian Studies*. **57** (1): 6–37. doi: 10.2307/2659022[642]. JSTOR 2659022[643].
- Pollock, Sheldon (2006). *The Language of Gods in the World of Men: Sanskrit, Culture and Power in Pre-modern India*[644]. Berkeley and London: University of California Press. Pp. 703. ISBN 0-520-24500-8.
- Pollock, Sheldon (2007). "Literary Culture and Manuscript Culture in Precolonial India"[645] (PDF). In Simon Elliot et al. (ed.). *Literary Cultures and the Material Book*. London: British Library. pp. 77–94. ISBN 0-7123-0684-6.
- Pranesh, Meera Rajaram (2003) [2003]. *Musical Composers during Wodeyar Dynasty (1638–1947 A.D.)*. Bangalore: Vee Emm.
- Prasad, K.B. Prabhu (1987) [1987]. *Sarvajna*. Sahitya Akademi. ISBN 81-7201-404-X.
- Rice, B.L. (2001) [1897]. *Mysore Gazetteer Compiled for Government-vol 1*. New Delhi, Madras: Asian Educational Services. ISBN 81-206-0977-8.[646]
- Rice, E.P. (1982) [1921]. *A History of Kanarese Literature*. New Delhi: Asian Educational Services. ISBN 81-206-0063-0.
- Ramesh, K. V. (1984). "Indian Epigraphy". Sundeep.
- Rao, Sheshagiri L.S. (1994) [1989]. Amaresh Datta, ed. *Encyclopaedia of Indian literature vol 3, Literature (Kannada)*. Sahitya Akademi. ISBN 81-260-1804-6.
- Sastri, K.A. Nilakanta (2002) [1955]. *A history of South India from prehistoric times to the fall of Vijayanagar*. New Delhi: Indian Branch, Oxford University Press. ISBN 0-19-560686-8.
- Sharma, B.N.K (2000) [1961]. *History of Dvaita school of Vedanta and its Literature* (3rd ed.). Bombay: Motilal Banarsidass. ISBN 81-208-1575-0.

- Shipley, Joseph T. (2007) [2007]. *Encyclopedia of Literature – Vol I.* READ BOOKS. ISBN 1-4067-0135-1.
- Shiva Prakash, H.S. (1997). "Kannada". In Ayyappapanicker. *Medieval Indian Literature:An Anthology.* Sahitya Akademi. ISBN 81-260-0365-0.
- Sinopoli, Carla M. (2003). *The Political Economy of Craft Production: Crafting Empire in South India c. 1350–1650.* Cambridge University. ISBN 0-521-82613-6.
- Sircar, D. C. *Indian Epigraphy.* Motilal Banarsidass Publications. ISBN 81-208-1166-6.
- Steever, S. B. (1998). "Kannada". In Steever, S. B. (ed.). *The Dravidian Languages (Routledge Language Family Descriptions).* London: Routledge. Pp. 436. pp. 129–157. ISBN 0-415-10023-2.
- Thapar, Romila (2004). *Early India: From the origins to AD 1300*[647]. Berkeley: University of California Press. p. 586. ISBN 0-520-24225-4.
- Various (1987) [1987]. Amaresh Datta, ed. *Encyclopaedia of Indian literature – vol 1.* Sahitya Akademi. ISBN 81-260-1803-8.
- Various (1988) [1988]. Amaresh Datta, ed. *Encyclopaedia of Indian literature – vol 2.* Sahitya Akademi. ISBN 81-260-1194-7.
- Various (1992) [1992]. Mohan Lal, ed. *Encyclopaedia of Indian literature – vol 5.* Sahitya Akademi. ISBN 81-260-1221-8.
- T. V. Venkatachala Sastry (1994) [1897]. *Sabdamanidarpanam of Kesiraja.* Bangalore: Kannada Sahitya Parishad.
- Warder, A.K. (1988) [1988]. *Indian Kavya Literature.* Motilal Banarsidass. ISBN 81-208-0450-3.
- Zvelebil, Kamil V. (2008). "Dravidian Languages"[648]. *Encyclopædia Britannica.* Retrieved 2008-04-08.

Kashmiri literature

Literature of Kashmir

Literature of Kashmir has a long history, the oldest texts having been composed in the Sanskrit language. Early names include Patanjali, the author of the *Mahabhashya* commentary on Pāṇini's grammar, suggested by some to have been the same to write the Hindu treatise known as the Yogasutra, and Dridhbala, who revised the Charaka Samhita of Ayurveda.

In medieval times, philosophers of Kashmir Shaivism include Vasugupta (c. 800), Utpala (c. 925), Abhinavagupta, and Kshemaraja as well as Anandavardhana.

Kashmiri language literature

The use of the Kashmiri language began with the work *Mahanayakaprakash* (Light of the Supreme Lord) by Shitikantha (c.1250), and was followed by the poet Lalleshvari or Lal Ded (14th century), who wrote mystical verses in the *vakh* or four-line couplet style. Another mystic of her time equally revered in Kashmir and popularly known as Nund Reshi wrote powerful poetry. Later came Habba Khatun (16th century) with her own style. Other major names are Rupa Bhavani (1621–1721), Arnimal (d. 1800), Mahmud Gami (1765–1855), Rasul Mir (d. 1870), Paramananda (1791–1864), Maqbool Shah Kralawari (1820–1876). Also, the Sufi poets like Shamas Fakir, Wahab Khar, Soch Kral, Samad Mir, and Ahad Zargar. Among modern poets are Ghulam Ahmad Mahjur (1885–1952), Abdul Ahad Azad (1903–1948), and Zinda Kaul (1884–1965).

During the 1950s, a number of well educated youth turned to Kashmiri writing, both poetry and prose, and enriched modern Kashmiri writing by leaps and bounds. Among these writers are Dinanath Nadim (1916–1988), Rahman Rahi, Ghulam Nabi Firaq Amin Kamil (1923-2014), Ali Mohd Lone, Autar

Krishen Rahbar (born 1933), Akhtar Mohiuddin, Sajood Sailani (brn 1933), Som Nath Zutshi, Muzaffar Aazim, and Sarwanand Kaol Premi. Some later day writers are Hari Krishan Kaul, Majrooh Rashid, Rattanlal Shant, Hirdhey Kaul Bharti, Omkar N Koul, Roop Krishen Bhat, Rafiq Raaz, Tariq Shehraz, Shafi Shauq, Showkat Shehri, M H Zaffar, Shenaz Rashid, Shabir Ahmad Shabir, Shabir Magami, and Moti Lal Kemmu.

Contemporary Kashmiri literature appears in such magazines as *Sheeraza* published by the Jammu & Kashmir Academy of Art, Culture and Languages, *Anhar* published by the Kashmirri Department of the Kashmir University, and an independent magazine *Neab International Kashmiri Magazine*[649] published from Boston, *Vaakh* (published by All India Kashmiri Samaj, Delhi) and *Koshur Samachar* (published by Kashmiri Sahayak Sammiti, Delhi).

Ancient writers in Sanskrit

- Lagadha,[650,651,652,653,654,655] between 1400-1200 BC. Wrote Vedanga Jyotisha, the earliest Indian text on astronomy.
- Charaka,[656,657,658,659] c. 300 BC. One of the most important authors in Ayurveda.
- Vishnu Sharma, c. 300 BC. Author of Panchatantra.
- Nagasena,[660,661] c. 2nd century BC. One of the major figures of Buddhism, his answers to questions about the religion posed by Menander I (Pali: Milinda), the Indo-Greek king of northwestern India (now Pakistan), are recorded in the *Milinda Pañha*.
- Tisata, c. 500 AD. A medical writer.[662]
- Jaijjata, 5th century, a medical writer and probably the earliest commentator (known) on the Sushruta Samhita, later quoted by Dalhana.[663]
- Kalidasa,[664,665,666] c. 5th century. Widely regarded as the greatest poet and dramatist in the Sanskrit language.
- Vagbhata,[667,668] c. 7th century. Considered as one of the 'trinity' (with Charaka and Sushruta) of Ayurveda.
- Bhamaha,[669,670,671,672] c. 7th century
- Ravigupta, 700-725. "Ravigupta is, perhaps, the earliest among the Buddhist philosophers of Kashmir..."[673]
- Anandavardhana, 820-890
- Vasugupta, 860-925
- Somananda, 875-925
- Vatesvara,[674,675] b. 880, author of Vaṭeśvara-siddhānta.
- Rudrata, c. 9th century
- Jayanta Bhatta, c. 9th century
- Bhatta Nayaka, c. 9th-10th century, considered by Sheldon Pollock as the greatest author on aesthetics in the pre-modern period

Literature of Kashmir 211

- Medhātithi, c. 9th-10th century, one of the most influential commentators of the Manusmriti
- Utpaladeva, 900-950
- Abhinavagupta, c. 950-1020
- Vallabhadeva,[676,677] c. 10th century. Wrote, amongst other works, *Raghupanchika*, the earliest commentary on the *Raghuvamsa* of Kalidasa.
- Utpala,[678,679,680,681] c. 10th century. An important mathematician.
- Kshemendra, c. 990-1070
- Kshemaraja, c. late 10th century/early 11th century
- Kathasaritsagara, c. 11th century
- Bilhana, c. 11th century
- Kalhana, c. 12th century
- Jalhana,[682] c. 12th century, the author of *Mugdhopadesa* (not to be confused with Jalhana who commissioned the *Suktimuktavali*)
- Sarangadeva, c. 13th century. A musicologist, he wrote Sangita Ratnakara, one of the most important text when it comes to Indian music.
- Kesava Kashmiri Bhattacharya, c. 14th century, a major Vedantic philosopher.
- Mamatta
- Kaihata
- Jaihata
- Ralhana
- Shilhana
- Malhana
- Ruiyaka
- Kuntaka
- Ruchaka
- Udbhatta
- Sankuka
- Gunadhya
- Somvadeva
- Pingala
- Jayadata
- Vamana
- Kshiraswamin
- Mankha
- Pushpadanta
- Jagadhar Bhatta
- Ratnakara
- Manikyacandra

Writers in Persian

After Sanskrit and before the coming Urdu, because of the adoration and patronising policy of foreign culture by the Mughals, Persian became the literary language also of the region. Kashmir was very richly represented in that tradition, as already before the end of the 18th century "Muhammad Aslah's tazkira of the Persian-writing poets of Kashmir, written during the reign of the Mughal emperor Muhammad Shah (1131-61/1719-48), alone lists 303 poets".[683] Late scholar from Pakistan, Pir Hassam-ud-Din Rashidi, edited, translated, and enlarged this work later, and had it published by the Iqbal Academy.

The most famous of them was Muhammad Tahir Ghani (d. 1669), better known as Ghani Kashmiri, whose poetry was recently translated into English, for the first time, by Mufti Mudasir Farooqi and Nusrat Bazaz as 'The Captured Gazelle' in the world-renowned Penguin Classics list. Ghani influenced many generations of Persian-and Urdu writing poets in South Asia including Mir Taqi Mir, Ghalib and most importantly, Iqbal. Ghani's "forte" lies in creating delightful poetic images, usually by stating an abstract idea in the first hemistich and following it up with a concrete exemplification in the other. He also stands out for his multi-layered poems, which exploit the double meaning of words.

Another name is the Sheikh Yaqub Sarfi (1521-1595), a 16th-century Sufi poet-philosopher who was internationally acknowledged and who had for students, amongst others, well-known religious scholar Ahmad Sirhindi (more particularly, he taught him hadith)[684,685] and Persian-language poet Mohsin Fani Kashmiri (d. 1671 or 1672) (himself the teacher of Ghani Kashmiri and author of the pivotal work of comparative religion, the Dabestan-e Mazaheb).

Other of the well-known and influential Persian-language poets of Kashmir would include Habibullah Ghanai (1556-1617), Mirza Dirab Big Juya (d. 1707), Mirza Beg Akmal Kamil (1645-1719), Muhammad Aslam Salim (d. 1718), Mulla Muhammad Taufiq (1765), Muhammed Azam Didamari (d. 1765), Mulla Muhammad Hamid (1848) or Birbal Kachru Varasta (d. 1865), amongst a myriad. Of course, Kashmiri Pandits too played a role in that school, and one exceptional case was Pandit Taba Ram Turki (1776–1847), who was a celebrity as far as Central Asia.

Writers in Urdu

Despite being a numerically reduced community (less than one million), the Kashmiri Pandits are over-represented in their contribution to Urdu literature. One important early example is Daya Shankar Kaul Nasim (1811–1845), a renowned Urdu poet of the 19th century, and hundreds of others followed his path.[686]

Some eminent Urdu literary personalities of Kashmiri origins (from both the Valley and the diaspora) include (in chronological order):

- Mir Tafazzul Hussain Khan Kashmiri (1727-1800), originally from Kashmir,[687,688,689] born in Sialkot[690] where his parents moved and himself based in Lucknow where he served as Prime Minister (or *diwan*) to the Nawab of Oudh Asaf-ud-Daula thanks his erudition. He was called "khan-e-allama" (the Scholarly Khan)[691] due to his deep scholarship on many subjects but is best known today for having translated Sir Isaac Newton's Philosophiæ Naturalis Principia Mathematica from Latin into Arabic.[692]
- Mufti Sadruddin Khan 'Azurda',[693] 1789-1868, apart from being the Grand Mufti of Dehli, he was also a personal friend to Ghalib (whose own mother was from Kashmir)[694] and himself a poet of note in Urdu as well as in Arabic and Persian. He also wrote a *tazkira* (biographical anthology of poets).
- Momin Khan Momin, 1801-1852, considered one of the three pillars of the Delhi school of Urdu poetry, with Ghalib and Zauq.[695] Other fields where he was competent included mathematics, geomancy, astrology, chess or music.[696,697,698]
- Daya Shankar Kaul Nasim, 1811–1845
- Ratan Nath Dhar Sarshar, 1846-1903
- Brij Mohan Datatriya Kaifi, 1866-1955
- Muhammad Iqbal, 1877–1938
- Agha Hashar Kashmiri, 1879–1935 (called "the Shakespeare of Urdu" for his works as playwright)
- Brij Narayan Chakbast, 1882–1926
- Aziz Lucknawi, 1882-1935
- Khalifa Abdul Hakim, 1896-1959 (a philosopher who has the honour of writing the only book on the metaphysics of Persian mystical poet Jalaluddin Rumi)[699]
- Patras Bokhari, 1898–1958
- Ghulam Mustafa Tabassum, 1899–1978
- Justice Anand Narain Mulla, 1901-1997
- Muhammad Din Taseer, 1902-1950 (short-story writer, literary critic and Iqbal scholar. Father of slain Pakistan's Punjab governor Salman Taseer and first individual from the Sub-continent to get a PhD in English Literature from Cambridge University)[700]
- Shaikh Abdullah, 1905–1982
- Bashir Ahmed Dar, 1908-1979 (a philosopher and Iqbal scholar)
- Meeraji, 1912-1949

- Saadat Hasan Manto, 1912–1955
- Aariz Kashmiri, 1916-1965
- Agha Shorish Kashmiri, 1917-1975
- Zaheer Kashmiri, 1919-1996
- Razia Butt, 1924-2012
- Anwar Shemza, 1928-1985
- Hakeem Manzoor, 1937–2006
- Obaidullah Aleem, 1939-2008
- Muhammed Amin Andrabi, 1940-2001, a scholar who belonged to the Traditionalist School of metaphysics, inspired by authors like Ibn Arabi, Muhammad Iqbal, Frithjof Schuon, Seyyed Hossein Nasr and Henry Corbin.[701]
- Allama Mustafa Hussain Ansari, 1945–2006
- Mirza Muhammad Zaman Azurdah, b. 1945, influential contemporary writer from the Valley
- Abid Hassan Minto
- Muhammad Asim Butt
- Muhammad Younis Butt, writer of the most popular political satire show in Pakistan, *Hum Sub Umeed Se Hain*
- Rasheed Amjad
- Shahid Nadeem

Writers in Hindi

- Amar Nath Kak
- Chandrakanta (author)
- Omkar N. Koul
- Rattan Lal Shant
- Hari Krishen Kaul
- Shashi Shekhar Toshkhani
- Bhushan Lal Koul
- Shiban Krishen Raina
- Agnishekher
- Maharaj Krishan Santoshi

Writers in English

- I. K. Taimni
- M. P. Pandit, prolific writer who authored some 150 books and as many articles exposing in English the thought of Sri Aurobindo.
- Chiragh Ali, reformist Islamic scholar

Literature of Kashmir

- Taufiq Rafat, called the 'Ezra Pound of Pakistan' for both his innovative writings and his position as one of - if not the - greatest English-language poets of Pakistan.
- Jawaharlal Nehru
- Vijaya Lakshmi Pandit
- Krishna Hutheesing
- Gopi Krishna
- Gopinath Raina
- Ram Nath Kak
- Subhash Kak
- Nayantara Sahgal
- M.J. Akbar
- Salman Rushdie
- Hari Kunzru
- Kailas Nath Kaul
- Agha Shahid Ali
- Mohammad Tabish
- Basharat Peer
- Hamid Naseem Rafiabadi, contemporary philosopher, affiliated with the University of Kashmir, specialist of Islamic philosophy
- Abdur Rashid Bhat, contemporary philosopher, affiliated with the University of Kashmir, specialist of al Ghazali and Shah Waliullah
- Showkat Ahmad Wani

A srinagar based poet and writer belongs to bandipora dachigam. Well known for blank verse and Urdu nazm.

Malayalam literature

Malayalam literature

Malayalam literature (മലയാള സാഹിത്യം) comprises those literary texts written in Malayalam, a South-Dravidian language spoken in the Indian state of Kerala.

The earliest known extant literary work in Malayalam is *Ramacharitam*, an epic poem written by Cheeraman in 1198 CE. In the subsequent centuries, besides a popular *pattu* ("song") literature, the *manipravalam* poetry also flourished. *Manipravalam* (translates "ruby coral") style mainly consisted of poetry in an admixture of Malayalam and Sanskrit. Then came works such as *champus* and *sandeshakavyas* in which prose and poetry were interspersed. Later, poets like Cherusseri introduced poems on devotional themes. There were also other important works, similar to *manipravalam*, in Arabi Malayalam like Muhyadheen Mala. Ezhuthachan, a strong proponent of Bhakti movement, is known as the father of Malayalam. His poems are classified under the genre of *kilippattu*.

Modern literary movements in Malayalam literature began in the late 19th century with the rise of the famous Modern Triumvirate consisting of Kumaran Asan, Ulloor S. Parameswara Iyer and Vallathol Narayana Menon. Kumaran Asan was temperamentally a pessimist—a disposition reinforced by his metaphysics—yet all his life was active in promoting his downtrodden Hindu-Ezhava community. Ullor wrote in the classical tradition, on the basis of which he appealed for universal love, while Vallathol responded to the human significance of social progress. Contemporary Malayalam poetry records the encounter with problems of social, political, and economic life. The tendency of the modern poetry is often regarded as toward political radicalism. Malayalam spelled backward is still Malayalam.

Early literature

Indian literature
• Assamese
• Bengali
• Bhojpuri
• English
• Gujarati
• Hindi
• Kannada
• Kashmiri
• Konkani
• Malayalam
• Meitei
• Marathi
• Mizo
• Nepali
• Odia
• Punjabi
• Rajasthani
• Sanskrit
• Sindhi
• Tamil
• Telugu
• Urdu
• v • t • e[702]

Pattu

For the first 600 years of the Malayalam calendar, Malayalam literature remained in a preliminary stage. During this time, Malayalam literature consisted mainly of various genres of songs (*Pattu*). The most prominent among these were songs praising the goddesses of the land, ballads of brave warriors, songs related to the work of a particular caste and songs intended just for entertainment. *Bhadrakali pattu, thottam pattu, Mappila pattu, mavaratham pattu, sasthanga pattu, nizhalkoothu pattu, sarpa pattu, sastham pattu, thiyyattu pattu, pulluvar pattu, mannar pattu, panar pattu, krishi pattu, thamburan pattu, pada pattu, villadichan pattu, onappattu, kummi* and lullaby were some of the major subgenres. These names were not used historically, but are used in modern times to describe the song genres of that time.[703]

Ramacharitham

Ramacharitham is a collection of poems written at the end of the preliminary stage in Malayalam literature's evolution. It is the oldest Malayalam book available. The collection has 1,814 poems in it. *Ramacharitham* mainly consists of stories from the Yuddha Kanda of the *Ramayana*. It was written by a poet with the pen name *Cheeramakavi* who, according to poet Ulloor S Parameswara Iyer, was Sree Veerarama Varman, a king of Travancore from AD 1195 to 1208. Other experts, like Dr. K.M. George and P.V. Krishnan Nair, claim that the origins of the book can be found in north Kerala. They cite the use of certain words in the book and also the fact that the manuscript of the book was recovered from Neeleshwaram in north Kerala. Some experts consider it a Tamil literary piece. A. R. Rajaraja Varma, who heavily contributed to the development of Malayalam grammar, is of the opinion that Malayalam originated from ancient Tamil. *Ramacharitham* is considered a book written during the formative years of Malayalam. According to Rev. Dr. Hermann Gundert, who compiled the first dictionary of the Malayalam language, *Ramacharitham* shows the ancient style of the Malayalam language.

Manipravalam

While the *Pattu* school flourished among certain sections of the society, the literature of the elite was composed in the curious mixture of Sanskrit and Malayalam which is referred to as *Manipravalam*, *mani* meaning ruby (Malayalam) and *pravalam* meaning coral (Sanskrit).[704] *Lilathilakam*, a work on grammar and rhetoric, written in the last quarter of the 14th century discusses the relationship between *Manipravalam* and *Pattu* as poetic forms. It lays special emphasis on the types of words that blend harmoniously. It points out that the rules of Sanskrit prosody should be followed in *Manipravalam* poetry. This particular school of poetry was patronised by the upper classes, especially the Nambudiris. Dramatic performances given in *Koothambalams*, known by the names of *Koothu* and *Koodiyottom*, often used Sanskrit and Malayalam. In *Koodiyattom*, the clown (*vidooshaka*) is allowed to use Malayalam while the hero recites *slokas* in Sanskrit. Tholan, a legendary court poet in the period of the Kulasekhara kings, is believed to have started this practice.

The earliest of these works in the *Manipravalam* school is *Vaisika Tantram* written in the 13th century. It contains about 200 quatrains in Sanskrit metres and is in the form of professional advice given to a prostitute or courtesan by her mother. Each quatran is composed with care and due weight is given to the rules of rhetoric. Several quatrains of this type are quoted in *Lilathilakam* by way of illustration for the several rules of grammar and rhetoric.

The most representative of the early *Manipravalam* works are the tales of courtesans (*Achi Charitams*) and the Message Poems (*Sandesa Kavyas*). *Unniyachi Charitam*, *Unnichiruthevi Charitam* and *Unniyadi Charitam* are examples of the former type which is known by the name *champu*. The *Padya* (verse) portion is in Sanskrit metres and the *Gadya* (prose) portion is mostly in Dravidian metres. Authorship of *Unniyachi Charitam* and *Unnichiruthevi Charitam* is not known and only a portion of the works is now available. *Unniyadi Charitam*, which also exists in a fragmented form, is supposed to be written by Damodara Chakkiar. The *Sandesa Kavyas* are an important poetic genre in Sanskrit, and on the model of Kalidasa's *Meghadūta* and Lakshmidasa's *Sukasandesa*, a number of message poems came to be written first in *Manipravalam* and later in pure Malayalam. The best-known among these *sandesas* is perhaps *Unnuneeli Sandesam* written in the 14th century. The poem is written under the pen-name Amruthanilakshi, and some believe that it was written in 1362 CE. The exact identity of the author remains a mystery, but it is widely believed that one of the members of the Travancore Royal Family wrote it.

The next work to be mentioned is *Ramakathapattu*, as it is popularly known, though the author calls it *Ramayanakavyam*. The author is Ayyappilli Asan who lived sometime about 1400 CE at Auvatutura near Kovalam and whom P. K. Narayana Pillai, who discovered the full text of the book in 1965, calls "the Homer of Malayalam." *Ramakathapattu* contains 3163 songs in 279 *Vrittas* or parts.

Niranam poets

While the Manipravala poetry flourished as a diversion from the mainstream, the tradition set up by Cheeraman of *Ramacharitam* and the more enlightened among the anonymous folk poets was resumed and replenished by three writers commonly referred to as Niranam poets, being Madhava Panikkar, Sankara Panikkar and Rama Panikkar. They were influenced by the Bhakti movement. The *Bhakti* school was thus revived, and in the place of the excessive sensuality and eroticism of the *Manipravalam* poets, the seriousness of the poetic vocation was reasserted by them. It is believed that they all belonged to the same Kannassa family and that Madhava Panikkar and Sankara Panikkar were the uncles of Rama Panikkar, the youngest of the three. Their most important work is *Kannasa Ramayanam* which is an important link between *Ramacharitam*, *Ramakathapattu* and Ezhuthachan's *Adhyathmaramayanam*. Ulloor has said that Rama Panikkar holds the same position in Malayalam literature that Edmund Spenser has in English literature.

Later Champus and Krishnagatha

The 15th century CE saw two paralleled movements in Malayalam literature: one spearheaded by the *Manipravalam* works, especially the *Champus*, and the other emanating from the *Pattu* school and adumbrated in Cherusseri's magnum opus, *Krishnagatha* (Song of Krishna). The language of the later *Champus* reads more like modern Malayalam than that of the earlier *Champus* and *Sandesa Kavyas*. *Champus* were mostly works of satire and hyperbole was a regular feature of it. The greatest *Champus* of the 15th century is Punam Nambudiri's *Ramayanam* which uses Puranic themes and episodes unlike the 14th century *Champus* which were tales of the courtesans. Punam also wrote a *Bharatam Champoo*. There are also many others, the authorship of which is ascribed to him. The later *Champus* came to be used for dramatic oral narration by performing artists in their *Koothu* and *Patakam*. Mahishamangalam (or Mazhamangalam) Narayanan Nambudiri who lived in the 16th century is the author of some of the best *Champus* of all time. The most widely known of these is *Naishadham* followed by *Rajaratnavaliyam* and *Kodia Viraham*. *Chandrotsavam*, whose authorship is unknown, is a long narrative poem written in *Manipravalam*.

The elitist *Manipravala Champu* school disappeared by the end of the 16th century. The average readers without much grounding in Sanskrit had their favourite poems and poets in the so-called *Pattu* school. With the writing of *Krishnagatha* by Cherusseri, the validity of the use of spoken Malayalam for literary purposes received its ultimate justification. Unlike the language of *Ramacharitam* and the works of the Niranam poets, the language of *Krishnagatha* marks the culmination of a stage of evolution. There is some dispute about the author's name and his identity. Some scholars are of opinion that he was the same as the Punam Nambudiri of the *Champus*. It is widely believed that Cherusseri lived in the 15th century CE and was the court poet of Udayavarma of Kolathunadu.

Medieval literature: 16th to 19th century

Bhakti era

Malayalam literature passed through a tremendous process of development in the 15th and 16th centuries. Cherusseri's *Krishnagatha* bore witness to the evolution of modern Malayalam language as a proper medium for serious poetic communication. Alongside this, there flourished numerous Sanskrit poets who were very active during this period. The greatest of them was Melpathur Narayana Bhattathiri (1559–1665), the author of *Narayaniyam*. The most significant development of the time took place in the field of Malayalam

Figure 78: *Thunchaththu Ezhuthachan*

poetry. Thunchaththu Ramanujan Ezhuthachan wrote his two great epics *Adhyathmaramayanam* and *Srimahabharatam* and two shorter pieces, *Irupathinalu Vrittam* and *Harinama Kirtanam* and thereby revolutionised Malayalam language and literature at once. Ezhuthachan refined the style of Malayalam language and it was during his period that Malayalam literature attained its individuality and Malayalam became a fully fledged independent language. Today he is known as the father of Malayalam language and its literature. The *Kilippattu* form he adopted in *Ramayanam* and *Bharatam* may be a pointer to his recognition of the importance of sound effect in poetry. Ezhuthachan is perhaps the greatest spokesman of the Bhakti movement in Malayalam but he is more than a writer of devotional hymns. K. Ayyappa Paniker has noted that "the transition from Cherrusseri to Ezhuthachan marks the triumph of modernism over medievalism." Another important poet of this period was Poonthanam Nambudiri (1547–1640). His chief poems are *Jnanappana* (The Song of Divine Wisdom), *Bhasha Karnamritam* and *Kumaraharanam* or *Santanagopalam Pana*.

Performance arts

The 16th century also saw the writing of some dramatic works in *Manipravalam* and pure Malayalam, *Bharatavakyam*, often described as a choral narration, is a work in *Manipravalam* which was used for stage performance. The main development in the cultural field in Kerala in the 17th century was the growth of a new form of visual art called Kathakali, which brought into being a new genre of poetry called Attakkatha consisting of the libretto used for a Kathakali performance. The origins of *aattakatha* literature dates back to the 12th century and it emerged as a literary genre in the 17th century. The earliest of the *aattakathas* is believed to be a cycle of eight *Ramayana* stories (collectively known as *Ramanattam*), composed by Kottarakkara Tampuran and about whose date there is an ongoing controversy. Next in importance are the works of Kottayathu Tampuran whose period is about the middle of the seventeenth century. Since the four *aattakathas* he wrote *Bakavadham, Kalyanasaugandhikam, Kirmeeravadham* and *Kalakeyavadham* punctiliously conform to the strict rules of Kathakali, they are particularly favoured by orthodox artistes and their patrons. Another poet of this category is Irayimman Thampi (1783–1863). Unnayi Variyar's *Nalacharitham Aattakatha* is one of the most famous works in this genre. *Margamkali* was the form of ritual and entertainment among the Syrian Christians corresponding to the *Sanghakali* of the Brahmins. *Margamkalippattu* is the song for this performance depicting the story of Thomas the Apostle. This was one of the numerous pieces of Christian literature that must have gained currency in the 16th and 17th centuries.

In the court of Travancore king Marthanda Varma (1706–1758) and his successor Dharma Raja Kartika Tirunal Rama Varma, there flourished a number of poets distinguished in several ways. Ramapurathu Warrier (1703–1753), the author of *Kuchela Vrittam Vanchippattu*, was one of them. The *Vanchippattu* or Boat song is a poetic form of folk origin composed entirely in the Dravidian metre *nathonnata*. Kunchan Nambiar (1705–1770), the founder of Thullal and its rich literature, is often considered as the master of Malayalam satirist poetry. Born in Killikkurussimangalam, he spent his boyhood at Kudamalur and youth at Ambalappuzha. 1748 he moved to the court of Marthanda Varma and later to the court of his successor Dharma Raja. The word "Thullal" literally means "dance", but under this name Nambiar devised a new style of verse narration with a little background music and dance-like swinging movement to wean the people away from the Chakkiyar Koothu, which was the art form popular till then. He used pure Malayalam as opposed to the stylised and Sanskritised Malayalam language of Chakkiyar Koothu. He also adopted many elements from Padayani and Kolam Thullal and certain other local folk arts. There are three kinds of Tullal distinguished on the

Figure 79: *Kathakali*

basis of the performer's costume and the style of rendering, viz., *Ottan, Sitankan* and *Parayan*. Dravidian metres are used throughout although there is a quatrain in a Sanskrit metre.

Prose literature

There was a great lull in the field of literary creation in Malayalam for nearly a century after the death of Kunchan Nambiar. There was however a consistent and steady development of prose at this time. The evolution of prose literature in the early centuries was a very slow process. In the wake of *Bhashakautaliyam* several translations began to appear in the fifteenth and sixteenth centuries. The prose of *Attaprakarams* was meant to aid the Chakiyars in learning the art of Koodiyattom. *Doothavakyam* (14th century CE) is one of the earliest of these works. 15th century Malayalam prose is represented by *Brahmanda Puranam*, a summary of the original in Sanskrit. A large number of prose works appeared during this period, most of which are either narrative based on *puranas* and religious works in Sanskrit or commentaries on similar works. With the starting of the first printing presses in the 16th century by Christian missionaries, prose literature received a great boost. Several regional versions of *Keralolpathi*, tracing the beginnings of Kerala history, began to appear in the 18th century. Paremmakkal Thoma Kathanar (1737–1799) wrote the first travelogue in Malayalam, *Varthamanapustakam* (Book of News). The works of Christian missionaries like Arnos Patiri (Johann Ernst Hanxleden), 1699–1732) and Paulinose Patiri (John Philip Wesdin, 1748–1806) also led to a widening of the range of topics and themes in Malayalam literature.

Venmani school

The third quarter of the nineteenth century bore witness to the rise of a new school of poets devoted to the observation of life around them and the use of pure Malayalam. The major poets of the Venmani school were Venmani Achhan Nambudiripad (1817–1891), Venmani Mahan Nambudiripad (1844–1893), Poonthottam Achhan Nambudiri (1821–1865), Poonthottam Mahan Nambudiri (1857–1896) and the members of the Kodungallur Kovilakam (Royal Family) such as Kodungallur Kunjikkuttan Thampuran. The style of these poets became quite popular for a while and influenced even others who were not members of the group like Velutheri Kesavan Vaidyar (1839–1897) and Perunlli Krishnan Vaidyan (1863–1894). The Venmani school pioneered a style of poetry that was associated with common day themes, and the use of pure Malayalam rather than Sanskrit. The poetry was therefore easily understood by the common man. The works were known for its humour, wit, and lyrical metre.

Modern prose literature

Nineteenth century was not a very creative period for Malayalam literature (except towards the end) from the point of view of imaginative writing. But the foundations for the great renaissance that began at the end of the century were laid during this period. The establishment of colleges for imparting English education, the translation of the Bible and other religious works, the compilation of dictionaries and grammars, the formation of the text book committee, the growth of printing presses, the starting of newspapers and periodicals, the introduction of science and technology, the beginning of industrialization and the awakening of social and political consciousness: these constitute the giant strides towards modernisation. Like his predecessors Swathi Thirunal and Uthram Thirunal, Ayilyam Thirunal (1832–1880) and Visakham Thirunal (1837–1885) were great patrons of letters and were themselves talented writers. Christian missionaries Benjamin Bailey (1805–1871), Joseph Peet, Richard Collins and George Mathen (1819–1870) were responsible for many works on Malayalam language based on western models. Perhaps the most important of these missionaries was Herman Gundert (1814–1893). Born in Stuttgart in Germany and educated at Tübingen and Switzerland, Gundert came to India in 1836. He wrote over twenty books in Malayalam, the most important of which are *A Malayalam-English Dictionary, A Grammar*

Figure 80: *Herman Gundert*

of *Malayalam, Keralappazhama* and *Pazhamcholmala*. The first authoritative grammar of Malayalam was also Gundert's contribution (1851). This led to the production of a number of grammatical works in Malayalam. Vaikkam Patchu Moothathu (1814–1883) published his *Grammar of Malayalam* in 1876, *Kerala Kaumudi* by Kovunni Nedungadi (1831–1889) came out in 1878. This was soon followed by the first history of the language by P. Govinda Pillai (1849–1897) published in 1881. The first work on rhetoric in Malayalam on the European model was brought out by Father Gerad under the title *Alankara Sastram* in the same year. By the end of the 19th century two different traditions could be clearly distinguished in Malayalam literature: the western school and the oriental or traditionalist school. Writers such as Kerala Varma Valiya Koyithampuran represent the confluence of these two major traditions. His major works include *Mayurasandesam* (Peacock Message) and the translations of Kalidasa's *Abhijñānaśākuntalam* (which got him the title of Kerala Kalidasa), and of Von Limburg Brower's *Akbar*. Meanwhile, many literary magazines were established to encourage all kinds of writers and writings, such as C. P. Achutha Menon's *Vidyavinodini*, Kandathil Varghese Mappillai's *Bhashaposhini* and Appan Thampuran's *Rasikaranjini*.

In the wake of Kerala Varma's translation of *Abhijñānaśākuntalam*, several attempts were made to translate numerous plays from Sanskrit and English into Malayalam. These plays were seldom acted. The stage conditions of

Figure 81: *Kerala Varma Valiya Koyithampuran*

those days were crude and unfit to project a performance. As if irritated by this imitation plays of low quality, P. Rama Kurup wrote *Chakki Chankaram* (1893). Kerala Varma's nephew A. R. Raja Raja Varma went a step further than his uncle in the promotion of a synthesis between the different trends current in the literature of his time. A professor in the His Highness Maharaja's University College, Thiruvananthapuram, he had to modernize the process of teaching Malayalam language and literature; this made him write books on grammar and rhetoric (which earned him the title of Kerala Panini) and eventually prepare the ground for an enlightened renaissance in Malayalam poetry and literary criticism. A close associate of both Kerala Varma and Raja Raja Varma, K. C. Kesava Pillai wrote *Kesaviyam* (a *mahakavya*) and a number of *attakkathas*. Azhakathu Padmanabha Kurup (1869–1932: author of *Ramachandravilasam*), Pandalam Kerala Varma (1879–1919: author of *Rukmangatha Charitam*), Kattakkayam Cherian Mappila (1859 – 1937: author of *Sri Yesu Vijayam*), Ulloor S. Parameswara Iyer (1877–1949 : author of *Umakeralam*) and Vallathol Narayana Menon (1879–1958: author of *Chitrayogam*), all paid their obeisance to this neoclassicist trend.

The developments in prose at this time were very significant, Vengayil Kunhiraman Nayanar (1861–1895), more famous under his pseudonym Kesari, was one of the first to explore the essay form in Malayalam. He was closely associated with periodicals like *Kerala Chandrika* (started in 1879 at Thiruvananthapuram), *Kerala Patrika* (started in 1884 by C. Kunhiraman Menon (1854–1936) and Appu Nedungadi (1866–1934) at Kozhikode), *Kerala Sanchari* (after 1898 under the editorship of Murkoth Kumaran) and the English Journal *Malabar Spectator*. His *Vasanavikriti* is considered by historians and literary experts as the first short story in Malayalam literature. It was published in *Vidyavinodini* in 1891. *Fulmoni Ennum Koruna Ennum Peraya Randu Sthreekalude Katha* (Phulmōni ennuṁ kōruṇa ennuṁ pērāya raṇṭu strīkaḷuṭe katha), a translation of Hana Catherine Mullens's Bengali novel *Fulmoni O Korunar Biboron* by Rev. Joseph Peet, is believed to be the first novel printed and released in Malayalam (1858). *Ghathakawadham* (*Ghātakavadhaṁ*, 1877) by Rev. Richard Collins was the first novel printed and published in Malayalam with a story based in Kerala and around Malayalis.

The first novel conceived and published in Malayalam was Appu Nedungadi's *Kundalatha* (1887). Though *Kundalatha* is not considered a major novel, it gets the pride of place as the first work in the language having the basic characteristics of a novel. O. Chandhu Menon's *Indulekha* was the first major novel in Malayalam language. It was a landmark in the history of Malayalam literature and initiated the novel as a new flourishing genre. The title refers to the main character in this novel, a beautiful, well educated Nair lady of 18 years. C. V. Raman Pillai's *Marthandavarma* (1891) had many distinctions: it was the first historical novel in any South Indian languages, first novel from Travancore, first Malayalam novel to be a part of a trilogy and the first Malayalam novel to have a masculine title. *Marthandavarma* was completed even before *Indulekha* but could not be published until 1891 owing to lack of finance. The novel recounted the history of Venad (Travancore) during the final period of Rajah Rama Varma's reign and subsequently to the accession of Marthanda Varma. The novel had a film adaptation of the same name in 1933 and was the first Malayalam novel to be adapted into film. During the early 20th century, Malayalam received outstanding novels, either as translations or adaptations of Western literature. The post-independence period saw a fresh start in the history of longer fiction in Malayalam as in many other Indian languages, parallel to the evolution of post-world war fiction in other parts of the world. It was both a break and a continuation. P. Kesava Dev, who was a Communist in the thirties and forties turned away from diehard ideologies and wrote a symbolic novel called *Arku Vendi?* (For Whose Sake?) in 1950, challenging the philosophy of Stalinist liquidation of political enemies. It had a special significance in the context of the 'Calcutta thesis'. After portraying the class struggle of farm labourers in *Randidangazhi* (Two Measures) in 1949, Thakazhi Sivasankara Pillai turned away from party politics and produced a moving romance in *Chemmeen* (Shrimps) in 1956. For S. K. Pottekkatt and

Vaikom Muhammad Basheer, who had not dabbled in politics, the continuity is marked in the former's *Vishakanyaka* (Poison Maid, 1948) and the latter's *Ntuppuppakkoranendarnnu* (My Grandpa had an Elephant, 1951). The non-political social or domestic novel was championed by P. C. Kuttikrishnan (Uroob) with his *Ummachu* (1955) and *Sundarikalum Sundaranmarum* (Men and Women of Charm, 1958). In 1957 Basheer's *Pathummayude Aadu* (Pathumma's Goat) brought in a new kind of prose tale, which perhaps only Basheer could handle with dexterity. The fifties thus mark the evolution of a new kind of fiction, which had its impact on the short stories as well. This was the auspicious moment for the entry of M. T. Vasudevan Nair and T. Padmanabhan upon the scene. Front runners in the post-modern trend include Kakkanadan, O. V. Vijayan, M. Mukundan and Anand.

Early prose literature

List of early prose literature in the 19th century.

Allegories

Title	Author	Year	Make	Other notes
Sanchariyude Prayanam (സഞ്ചാരിയുടെ പ്രയാണം – Sancāriyuṭe Prayāṇaṁ)	Rev. C. Muller Rev. P. Chandran	1846	Translation	**More** Translation of *The Pilgrim's Progress* (English, 1674) by John Bunyan
Paradeshi Mokshayathra (പരദേശി മോക്ഷയാത്ര – Paradēśi Mōkṣayātra)	Rev. K. Koshy Rev. Joseph Peet	1844	Translation	**More** Translation of *The Pilgrim's Progress* (English, 1677) by John Bunyan First repeated translation of an English literature to Malayalam
Thirupporattam (തിരുപ്പോരാട്ടം – Tiruppōrāṭṭaṁ)	Archdeacon. K. Koshy	1868	Translation	**More** Translation of *The Holy War* (English, 1682) by John Bunyan

Plays

Title	Author	Year	Make	Other notes
Bashashankunthalam (ഭാഷാശാകന്തളം – Bhaṣāśākuntaḷaṁ)	Ayilyam Thirunal Rama Varma	1850–1860	Translation	**More** Translation of *Abhijnanasakuntalam* (Sanskrit ,1000 B.C-0400) by Kalidasa The first prose translation to Malayalam from Sanskrit literature
Almarattam (ആമ്മാറാട്ടം – Ālmāṟāṭṭaṁ)	Kalloor Umman Philipose	1866	Translation	**More** Translation of *The Comedy of Errors* (1594–1595) by William Shakespeare
Kamakshee Charitham (കാമാക്ഷീചരിതം – Kāmākṣīcaritaṁ)	K. Chidambara Wadhyar	1880–1885	Translation	**More** Translation of *Tales from Shakespeare: As You Like It* by Mary Lamb, (Children's Story Adaptation-English,1807) *As You Like It* (1599–1600) by William Shakespeare
Varshakala Katha (വര്‍ഷകാലകഥ – Varṣakāla Katha)	K. Chidambara Wadhyar	1880–1885	Translation	**More** Translation of *Tales from Shakespeare: The Winter's Tale* by Mary Lamb, (Children's Story Adaptation-English,1807) *The Winter's Tale* (1623) by William Shakespeare

Stories

Title	Author	Year	Make	Other notes
Oru Kuttiyude Maranam (ഒരു കുട്ടിയുടെ മരണം – Oru Kuṭṭiyuṭe Maraṇaṁ)	<Anonymous Writer>	1847	Original	**More** Published in the monthly periodical *Rajyasamacharam* December edition
Vishathinu Marunnu (വിഷത്തിന് മരുന്ന് – Viṣattinŭ Marunnŭ)	<Anonymous Writer>	1848	Original	**More** Published in the monthly periodical *Rajyasamacharam* February edition
Anayum Thunnanum (ആനയും ഉന്നനും – Āṉayuṁ Tunnaṉuṁ)	<Anonymous Writer>	1849	Original	**More** Published in the monthly periodical *Jnananikshepam* August edition
Meenakethanan or Meenakethana Charitham (മീനകേതനം or മീനകേതനചരിതം – Mīṉakētaṉan or Mīṉakētaṉacaritaṁ)	Ayilyam Thirunal Rama Varma	1850–1860	Inspiration	**More** Inspired from 'The Story of the Prince Kamar-Ez-Zeman and the Princess Budoor', *The Thousand And One Nights Vol II* by Edward William Lane (English, 1839) which is a translation of *Kitab Alf Laylah Wa-Laylah* (Arabic, 1100–1200)

Malayalam literature

Title	Author	Year	Make	Other notes
Jathibetham (ജാതിഭേദം – Jātibēdaṁ)	Archdeacon. K. Koshy	1860	Original	**More** Published in the monthly periodical *Jnananikshepam* August, September, November editions
Aayalkarane Konnavante Katha (അയൽക്കാരനെ കൊന്നവന്റെ കഥ – Ayalkārane Konnavaṇṭe Katha)	<Anonymous Writer>	1873	Original	**More**
Kallan (കള്ളൂ – Kallan)	<Anonymous Writer>	1881	Adaptation	**More** Published in the periodical *Vidyavilasini*
Pullelikunchu (പുല്ലേലിക്കുഞ്ചു – Pullēlikkuñcu)	Archdeacon. K. Koshy	1882	Original	**More** Sequel to ജാതിഭേദം *(1860)*, First sequel in Malayalam prose literature Divided into three parts: Part One is a prequel ജാതിഭേദം *(1860)*. Part Two has a plot with same characters of the prequel and some new characters in a new situation. Part Three is presented as a religious tract following incidents of Part Two.
Vasanavikrithi (വാസനാവികൃതി – Vāsanāvikr̥ti)	Vengayil Kunjiraman Nayanar	1891	Original	**More** Regarded as the first short-story of Malayalam literature

Novels

Title	Author	Year	Make	Other notes
Fulmoni Ennum Koruna Ennum Peraya Randu Sthreekalude Katha (ഫുൽമോനി എന്നും കോരുണ എന്നും പേരായ രണ്ടു സ്ത്രീകളുടെ കഥ – Phulmōni ennuṁ kōruṇa ennuṁ pērāya raṇṭu strīkaḷuṭe katha)	Rev. Joseph Peet	1858	Translation	**More** First novel printed and released in Malayalam First novel translated to Malayalam which was originally conceived in an Indian language Translation of *The History of Phulmani and Karuna* (English,1853) by Mrs. (Hana Catherine) Mullens which is a translation of ফুলমনি ও করুণার বিবরণ [*Fulmoni O Korunar Biboron*] (Bengali ,1852) by Mrs. (Hana Catherine) Mullens

Title	Author	Year	Type	More
Ghathakawadham (ഘാതകവധം – Ghātakavadhaṁ)[705]	Rev. Richard Collins	1877	Translation	First novel printed and published in Malayalam with a story based in Kerala and around Malayalees, First novel translated to Malayalam which was originally conceived in English Translation of *The Slayer Slain* (English,1864–1866) by Mrs. (Frances) Richard Collins & Rev. Richard Collins
Pathminiyum Karunayum (പത്മിനിയും കരുണയും – Patminiyuṁ karuṇayuṁ)	<Anonymous Writer>	1884	Translation	First repeated translation of a novel to Malayalam Translation of *The History of Phulmani and Karuna* (English,1853) by Mrs. (Hana Catherine) Mullens which is a translation of ফুলমনি ও করুণার বিবরণ [*Fulmoni O Korunar Biboron*] (Bengali ,1852) by Mrs. (Hana Catherine)
Kundalatha (കുന്ദലത – Kundalata)	Appu Nedungadi	1887	Original	First novel conceived and published in Malayalam, first novel by a Malayalee Keralite, First novel from Malabar First Malayalam novel to have a story outside Kerala and without Malayali characters
Indulekha (ഇന്ദുലേഖ – Indulēkha)	O. Chandumenon	1889	Original	First social novel in Malayalam, first novel made in Malayalam with Malayali characters and a story based in Malabar, Kerala,
Indumathee Swayamvaram (ഇന്ദുമതീസ്വയംവരം – Indumatīsvayaṁvaraṁ)	Padinjare Kovilakathu Ammaman Raja	1890	Original	More
Meenakshi (മീനാക്ഷി – Mīnākṣi)	C. Chathu Nair	1890	Original	More
Marthandavarma (മാർത്താണ്ഡവർമ്മ – Mārttāṇḍavarmma)	C. V. Raman Pillai	1891	Original	First Historical novel in Malayalam, Kerala and South India, First novel from Travancore First Malayalam novel to be a part of a trilogy, First Malayalam novel to have a masculine title

Malayalam literature 233

Saraswatheevijayam (സരസ്വതീവിജയം – Sarasvatīvijayaṁ)	Potheri Kunjanbu	1892	Original	More
Parishkarapathi (പരിഷ്കാരപ്പാതി – Pariṣkārappāti)	Kochuthomman Appothikari	1892	Original	More
Parangodee Parinayam (പറങ്ങോടീപരിണയം – Paraṅṅōṭīpariṇayaṁ)[706]	Kizhakepattu Raman Menon	1892	Original	More First satirical novel in Malayalam
Sarada (ശാരദ – Śārada)	O. Chandumenon	1892	Original	More First novel foretold to have sequels in a trilogy
Lakshmeekeshavam (ലക്ഷ്മീകേശവം – Lakṣmīkēśavaṁ)	Komattil Padu Menon	1892	Original	More
Naluperiloruthan (നാലുപേരിലൊരുത്തൊ – Nālupēriloruttan)	C. Anthapayi	1893	Original	More
Chandrahasan (ചന്ദ്രഹാസം – Candrahāsan)	P. Krishnan Menon T. K. Krishnan Menon C. Govindan Eledam	1893	Translation	More
Akbar (അക്ബം – Akbar)	Kerala Varma Valiya Koi Thampuran	1894	Translation	More First Historical novel translated to Malayalam Translation of *Akbar* (English,1879) by M. M which is a translation of *Akbar* (Dutch ,1872) by Dr. P.A.S van Limburg Brouwer
Kalyani (കല്യാണി – Kalyāṇi)	<Anonymous Writer>	1896	Original	More Published in *Vidyāvinodini* periodical
Sukumari (സൂകമാരി – Sukumāri)	Joseph Mooliyil	1897	Original	More
Saguna (സഗുണ – Saguṇa)	Joseph Mooliyil	1898–1899	Translation	More Translation of *Saguna* (English, 1896) by Kirubai Sathyanathan Ammal
Kamala (കമല – Kamala)	C. Krishnan Nair	1899	Translation	More Translation of *Kamala* (English, 1896) by Kirubai Sathyanathan Ammal

Apologues

Title	Author	Year	Make	Other notes
Rasselas (രാസലസ് – Rāsalas)	Pilo Paul	1895	Translation	**More** Translation of *Rasselas* or *The History of Rasselas, Prince of Abissinia* (English, 1759) by Samuel Johnson
Nandipa Deepika (നന്ദിപദീപിക – Nandipadīpika)	Kunji Kelu Nair	1895	Translation	**More** Translation of *Rasselas* or *The History of Rasselas, Prince of Abissinia* (English, 1759) by Samuel Johnson
Rasalelika (രസലേലിക – Rasalēlika)	Thatha Kanaran	1898	Translation	**More** Translation of *Rasselas* or *The History of Rasselas, Prince of Abissinia* (English, 1759) by Samuel Johnson

Malayalam writers

drbalakrishnankg writer Malayalam-Language articles and poetry major works ente kavithakal vol.1 (2017) ente kavithakal vol.2 (2017) ente kavithakal vol. 3 (2017) published by createspace amazon available worldwide

External links

- Information on Malayalam Literature at Department of Public Relations, Government of Kerala[707]
- Evolution of Malayalam Language[708] on YouTube
- Malayalam Resource Centre[709]

Meitei literature

Meitei literature

Indian literature
• Assamese
• Bengali
• Bhojpuri
• English
• Gujarati
• Hindi
• Kannada
• Kashmiri
• Konkani
• Malayalam
• Meitei
• Marathi
• Mizo
• Nepali
• Odia
• Punjabi
• Rajasthani
• Sanskrit
• Sindhi
• Tamil
• Telugu
• Urdu
• v • t • e[710]

Manipuri literature is the literature written in the Meitei language, including literature composed in Meitei by writers from Manipur, Assam, Tripura,

Myanmar and Bangladesh. The history of Manipur literature dates back to some 1500 BC,[711] when its first articles about Meetei Mayek and about creation theory of Universe is written by the Maichous of Kangla

Early era

The manipuris had a long tradition of writing. It is not completely clear when the archaic Manipuri*puyas* (old scriptures) and the Manipuri script first came into existence. However, the literature of Meitrabak or Manipur includes Loiyamba Shinyen (1110),[712] during the regime of Meidingu Loiyamba (1074–1122), vividly connotes the practice of writing in this era. It has been further confirmed that from the time of Meidingu Thangwai Ningthouba (1467–1508), later as Kiyamba, the Royal Chronicle – *Chitharon Kumpaba* was continued until the end of kingship (Meidingu Bodhchandra, 1941–1955). Wikipedia:Citation needed

The *Numit Kappa* is a common work.[713] The excerpt below in archaic Meitei is from the *Numit Kappa*: *"Haya he Liklaio / Yipungthou nongthourel o lahalnong / Laicha tarang ipakthakta / ... ... "*.Wikipedia:Citation needed

T.C. Hodson was the first English person to attempt to translate this archaic Meetei literary work into English in his book *The Meitheis*.[714]

Ougri

The excerpt in Meitei below is from the beginning part of the *Ougri Sheireng* (i.e. Ougri Poem):

> *"Hoirou haya haya ... ... / He hupe he / Ougri O kollo / Lamlenmada madaimada / Kangleiyonda pungmayonda / Yoimayaibu Taodanbabu / Taoroinaibu Anganbabu /... ... ... "*

Ougri, which was also known as *Leiroi Ngongloi Eshei*, was also an anonymous and undated poetry written in archaic Meitei. But it is believed to have been written in the pre-Christian era.[715]

Medieval era

Puya Meithaba – Burning of the Sanna-mahi Puyas

The Naga boy adopted as son, became King Garibaniwaz, also known as Meidingu Pamheiba and ruled from 1709 to 1748. He was a religious and social reformer, himself a convert from Sanamahi to Chaitanya's school of Vaishnavism (Hinduism). He had led many successful wars, particularly with Burmese kingdoms. In 1729, according to Komo Singha, Meitei Puyas of Sanamahi religion were "burnt completely" at Kangla Uttra under orders of Meidingu Pamheiba. These Puyas contained the holy texts and cultural history of Sanamahi, and were completely devastated.

Discovery of Puya manuscripts

Medieval era Meitei manuscripts have been discovered by scholars and Christian missionaries, particularly the *Puyas*. These are chronicles, and evidence that Hindus arrived from the Indian subcontinent with royal marriages at least by the 14th century, and in centuries thereafter, from what is now modern Assam, Bengal, Uttar Pradesh, Dravidian kingdoms, and other regions. Another manuscript suggests that Muslims arrived in Manipur in the 17th century, from what is now Bangladesh, during the reign of Meidingu Khagemba. Meitei literature documents the persistent and devastating Manipur-Burma wars.

Disagreements

Other scholars provide a different account to that of Komo Singha. The burning year was 1732, and the word *Puya* states Soibam Birajit is not found in Meitei chronicles and archaic inscriptions of Manipur, and it is likely a derivative of the ancient Sanskrit word Puranas. Further, if the manuscripts were completely destroyed, all claims as to what was in them and whether they were scriptures, are speculative and without evidence. The Manipur *Puya* manuscripts that have been discovered, like the Indian Puranas (Hindu, Jain), discuss cosmology, genealogies of gods and goddesses, history of solar (son-based) and lunar (daughter-based) dynasties of kings, and the reign of Manus. While historical evidence suggests Meidingu Pamheiba consigned *Puyas* to flames, the evidence also suggests he did not burn all Puyas, such as *Cheitharol Kumbaba*, *Numit Kappa* and hundreds of classics in his royal library. It is unclear, why the king ordered the burning of a bundle of selected books.

Marathi literature

Marathi literature

Indian literature
• Assamese
• Bengali
• Bhojpuri
• English
• Gujarati
• Hindi
• Kannada
• Kashmiri
• Konkani
• Malayalam
• Meitei
• Marathi
• Mizo
• Nepali
• Odia
• Punjabi
• Rajasthani
• Sanskrit
• Sindhi
• Tamil
• Telugu
• Urdu
• v • t • e[716]

Marathi literature is the body of literature of Marathi, an Indo-Aryan language spoken mainly in the Indian state of Maharashtra and written in the Devanagari script.

History

Yadav period is significant in the history of maharashtra. Marathi literature is the oldest of the Indo-Aryan literatures, dating to about 1000 CE. In the 13th century, two Brahmanical sects arose, the Mahanubhava and the Varakari Panth, that both shaped Marathi literature significantly. The latter sect was perhaps the more productive, for it became associated with bhakti movements, particularly with the popular cult of Vitthoba at Pandharpur. It was out of this tradition that the great names of early Marathi literature came: Jnaneshvara, in the 13th century; Namdev, his younger contemporary, some of whose devotional songs are included in the holy book of the Sikhs, the Adi Granth; and the 16th-century writer Eknath, whose best-known work is a Marathi version of the 11th book of the Bhagavata-purana. Among the bhakti poets of Maharashtra, the most famous is Tukaram, who wrote in the 16th century. A unique contribution of Marathi is the tradition of povadas, heroic stories popular among a martial people. This tradition was particularly vital during the 17th century, when Shivaji, the great Maratha king, led his armies against the might of the Mughal emperor Aurangzeb.

Yadava period

Epigraphic evidence suggests that Marathi was a standard written language by the 12th century. However, the earliest records of actual literature in Marathi appear only in the late 13th century.[717] The early Marathi literature emerged during the Seuna (Yadava) rule, because of which some scholars have theorized that it was produced with support from the Yadava rulers.[718] The Yadavas did regard Marathi as a significant language for connecting with the general public,[719] and Marathi replaced Kannada and Sanskrit as the dominant language of the inscriptions during the last half century of the Yadava rule.[720] However, there is no evidence that the Yadava royal court directly supported the production of Marathi literature with state funds.[721]

The early Marathi literature was mostly religious and philosophical in nature, and was composed by the saint-poets belonging to Mahanubhava and Warkari sects. During the reign of the last three Yadava kings, a great deal of literature in verse and prose, on astrology, medicine, Puranas, Vedanta, kings and courtiers were created. *Nalopakhyan*, *Rukmini Swayamvar* and Shripati's *Jyotishratnamala* (1039) are a few examples.

Figure 82: *Dnyaneshwar as imagined by the Ravi Varma press*

Bhaskarbhatta Borikar of the Mahanubhava sect is the first known poet to have composed hymns in Marathi.

Dnyaneshwar (1275–1296) was the first Marathi literary figure who had wide readership and profound influence. His major works are *Amrutanubhav* and *Bhavarth Deepika* (popularly known as *Dnyaneshwari*). *Bhavarth Deepika* is a 9000-couplets long commentary on the Bhagavad Gita.

Namdev, the Bhakti saint and contemporary of Dnyaneshwar is the other significant literary figure from this era. Namdev composed religious songs in Marathi as well as Hindi; some of his Hindi compositions are included in the Sikh holy book, the Guru Granth Sahib.

Another early Marathi writer was Mukundaraja, who wrote *Vivekasindhu* and *Paramamrita*. Both the works deal with the Advaita philosophy. Some earlier scholars dated him to the 12th century, and considered *Vivekasindhu* as the first literary book in Marathi, dating it to 1188. However, most linguistic historians now date Mukundaraja to 14th century or later: the *Vivekasindhu* was likely written after *Lilacharita* and *Dnyaneshwari*.[722]

Figure 83: *Tukaram*

Sultanate period

There was relatively little activity in Marathi in the early days of the Bahmani Sultanate (1347–1527) and the Bijapur Sultanate (1527–1686). The Warkari saint-poet Eknath (1533–1599), the main successor of Dnyaneshwar, was a major Marathi literary figure during this period. He made available an authentic, edited version of Dnyaneshwari, which had been forgotten after the Islamic invasion of Deccan. He also wrote several abhangs (devotional poems), narratives and minor works that dealt with the Bhagavata Purana He wrote *Eknathi Bhagwat, Bhavarth Ramayan, Rukmini Swayamwar Hastamalak*, and *Bharud*. Dasopant was another minor but notable poet from this era. Mukteshwar (1574-1645), the grandson of Eknath, too, wrote several works in Marathi including a translation of the epic Mahabharata.

Krista Purana, written by the Goa-based Christian missionary Thomas Stephens, was first published in 1616. It is written in a mix of Marathi and Konkani languages, and the first copy was printed in the Roman script, and tells the story of Jesus Christ.

Maratha period

The Marathas, the Marathi-speaking natives, formed their own kingdom in the 17th century. The development of the Marathi literature accelerated dur-

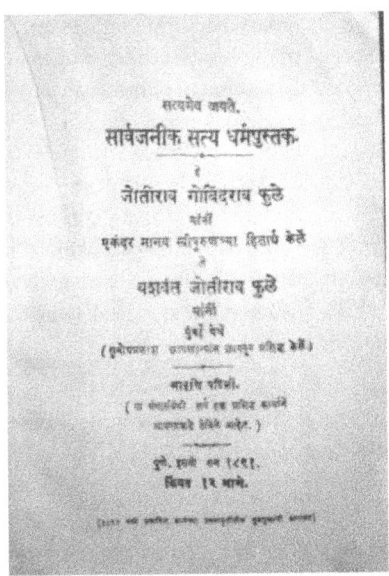

Figure 84: *Front page of the book Sarvajanik Satya Dharma Pustak by Jyotiba Phule.*

ing this period. Although their leader, Shivaji, was formally crowned as the king in 1674, he had been the de facto ruler of a large area in Western Maharashtra for some time.Wikipedia:Citation needed Tukaram and Samarth Ramdas, who were contemporaries of Shivaji, were the well-known poets of the early Maratha period. Tukaram (1608–1650) was the most prominent Marathi Varkari spiritual poet identified with the Bhakti movement, and had a great influence on the later Maratha society. His contemporary, Samarth Ramdas composed *Dasbodh* and *Manache Shlok* in Marathi.

In the 18th century, several well-known works like Yatharthadeepika (by Vaman Pandit), *Naladamayanti Swayamvara* (by Raghunath Pandit), *Pandava Pratap, Harivijay, Ramvijay* (by Shridhar Pandit) and *Mahabharata* (translation by Moropant) were produced. The historical section of the old Marathi literature contained the Bakhars and the *Katavas*. Krishna Dayarnava and Sridhar were other leading poets during the Peshwa rule. Mahipati, the author who wrote the biographies of the Bhakti Saints also belonged to this era.

British Period

The British colonial period (also known as the Modern Period) saw standardisation of Marathi grammar through the efforts of the Christian missionary

William Carey. Carey's dictionary had fewer entries and Marathi words were in Devanagari script instead of the Modi script prevalent at that time.[723] Carey also translated the new and old testament of the bible into Marathi in 1811 and 1820 respectively The most comprehensive Marathi-English dictionaries was compiled by Captain James Thomas Molesworth and Major Thomas Candy in 1831. The book is still in print nearly two centuries after its publication., The colonial authorities also worked on standardizing Marathi under the leadership of Molesworth . They used Brahmins of Pune for this task and adopted the Sanskrit dominated dialect spoken by this caste in the city as the standard dialect for Marathi. The Christian missionaries introduced the Western forms to the Marathi literature.[724]

Marathi at this time was efficiently aided by Marathi Drama. Here, there also was a different genre called 'Sangit Natya' or Musicals. The first play was V.A. Bhave's Sita Swayamvar in 1843 Later Kirloskar (1843–85) and G.B. Deval (1854-1916) brought a romantic aroma and social content. But Krishnaji Prabhakar Khadilkar (1872-1948) with his banned play Kichaka-Vadh (1910) set the trend of political playwriting. These were followed by stalwarts like Ram Ganesh Gadkari and Prahlad Keshav Atre.

The modern poets like Keshavsuta, Balakavi, Govindagraj, and the poets of Ravi Kiran Mandal (such as Madhav Julian) wrote poetry which was influenced by the Romantic and Victorian English poetry. It was largely sentimental and lyrical. Prahlad Keshav Atre, the renowned satirist and a politician wrote a parody of this sort of poetry in his collection *Jhenduchi Phule*.

Sane Guruji (1899–1950) contributed to the children's literature in Marathi. His major works are *Shyamchi Aai,* Astik *and* Gode Shevata. *He translated and simplified many Western Classics and published them in a book of stories titled* Gode Goshti *(Sweet Stories).*

Beginning of journalism

On January 6, 1832, Balshastri Jambhekar of the Elphinstone College began *Darpan*, the first Marathi-English fortnightly magazine.

On 24 October 1841, Govind Vithal Kunte began *Prabhakar*. Kunte was the first professional Marathi journalist. Prabhakar eulogised Indian art and culture. *Jnyanodaya* was begun in 1842 by Christian missionaries in Western India. *Jnyan Prakash* was started on 12 February 1849 in Pune. It was edited by Krishnaraj Trimbak Ranade. It was a weekly till 1904, when it became a daily. It ceased publication in 1951. It was a prestigious journal and supported education and social reform. Hari Narayan Apte, a famous Marathi novelist served as its editor. Some of its contributors included Mahadev Govind Ranade and Gopal Krishna Gokhale.

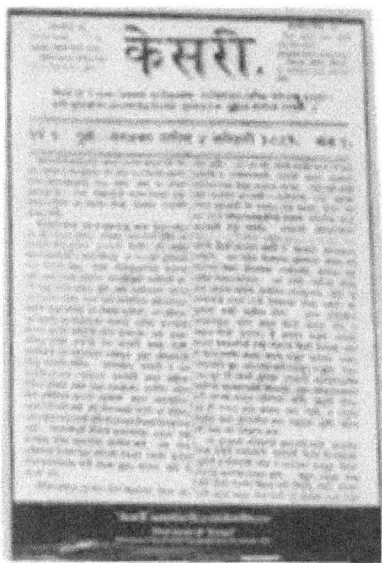

Figure 85: *Kesari*

In the early years of Marathi journalism, most periodicals were concerned with spreading education and knowledge. These include *Jaganmitra* (from Ratnagiri), *Shubh Suchak* (from Satara), *Vartaman Dipika*, *Vartaman Sangrah*. In 1862, *Induprakash* was begun in Bombay (now Mumbai). It was a bilingual journal, edited by M.G. Ranade. It criticised orthodoxy and was the mouthpiece of many social reforms. In 1877, Jyotiba Phule and Krishnarao Bhaskar began *Deenbandhu*, as part of the Dalit upliftment movement. Deenabandhu was the organ of the Satyashodhak Samaj founded by Phule.

On 4 January 1881, Bal Gangadhar Tilak began *Kesari*, along with Gopal Ganesh Agarkar. In 1887, Agarkar left to start *sujeet Sudharak* (bilingual) along with Gopal Krishna Gokhale. After Agarkar's death in 1895, it ceased publication. In 1889, *K. Navalkar* started the weekly Vartahar to highlight atrocities committed by Europeans. In 1890, Hari Narayan Apte began *Karmanuk* as a family entertainment paper. It contained articles on science. Also in 1890, Anandrao Ramachandra Dharandhar started *Bhoot* published every new and full moon day. It was the first Marathi paper to carry cartoons on political and social matters. It was very popular but ceased publication in 1904.

Present times (1947-

Vishnu Sakharam Khandekar (1889–1976)'s *Yayati* won him the Jnanpith Award for 1975. He also wrote many other novels, short stories, essays etc. His major works are *Don Dhruv* (Two Poles), *Ulka* (Meteorite), *Krounchavadh, Jalalela Mohar, Amrutvel*.

Marathi drama flourished in the 1960s and 1970s, with literary figures like Vasant Kanetkar, Kusumagraj and Vijay Tendulkar.

The major paradigm shift Wikipedia:Citation needed in Marathi literature sensibilities began in the forties with the modernist poetry of B.S. Mardhekar. In the mid fifties, the little magazine movement gained momentum. It published writings which were non-conformist, radical and experimental. Dalit literary movement also gained strength due to the little magazine movement. This radical movement was influenced by the philosophy of Babasaheb Ambedkar and challenged the literary establishment which was largely middle class, urban, and upper caste people. The little magazine movement threw up many noted writers. Bhalchandra Nemade is a well-known novelist, critic and poet. Sharad Rane is a well-known child literary figure. The notable poets include Arun Kolatkar, Dilip Chitre, Namdeo Dhasal, Vasant Abaji Dahake and Manohar Oak. Bhau Padhye, Vilas Sarang, Shyam Manohar, Suhas Shirvalkar and Visharm Bedekar are well known fiction writers.

Another major shift sensibility began in the nineties with the poems and criticism of Shridhar Tilve and the poetry of poets associated with Saushthav, Abhidhanantar and Shabadavedh. In the post nineties, this 'new little magazine movement' gained momentum and poets like Shridhar Tilve who stood against postmodernism and nativism and poets like Manya Joshi, Hemant Divate, Sachin Ketkar, Mangesh Narayanrao Kale, Saleel Wagh, Mohan Borse, Nitin Kulkarni, Nitin Arun Kulkarni, Varjesh Solanki, Sandeep Deshpande, Vasant Gurjar who touched the new areas of post-modern life. The poetry collections brought out by Abhidhanantar Prakashan, Time and Space, Popular Prakashan, Navta Prakashan and the regular issues of the magazine Abhidhanantar and IRREGULAR issues of Saushthav, Shabdvedh are taking Marathi poetry to the global standards.Wikipedia:Citation needed Another leading wave in contemporary Marathi poetry is the poetry of new dalit wave poets like Arun Kale, Bhujang Meshram and new deshi wave poets like Pravin Bandekar, Shrikant Deshmukh and Veerdhaval Parab.

Marathi science fiction has a rich heritage and boasts of modern complex stories. The known Marathi science fiction authors are Dr. Jayant Narlikar, Dr Bal Phondke, Subodh Javadekar, Niranjan Ghate, and Laxman Londhe. edh Over the last century or so, a number of producing encyclopedias have been produced in marathi. These include . Shreedhar Venkatesh Ketkar's

'Dnyaankosh', Siddheshwarshastri Chitrao's 'Charitra Kosh', Mahadevshastri Joshi's 'Bharatiy Sanskrutikosh', and Laxmanshastri Joshi's 'Dharmakosh' and 'Marathi Vishwakosh'. The Marathi theatre was complimented by Marathi films which did not enjoy a continuous success. Starting with V. Shantaram and before him the pioneer Dadasaheb Phalke (during the British period), Marathi cinema went on to influence contemporary Hindi cinema. Marathi language as spoken by people here was throughout influenced by drama and cinema along with contemporary literature.Wikipedia:Citation needed

Dalit Literature

It was in 1958, that the term "Dalit literature" was used for the first time, when the first conference of *Maharashtra Dalit Sahitya Sangha* (Maharashtra Dalit Literature Society) was held at Mumbai, a movement inspired by 19th century social reformer, Jyotiba Phule and eminent dalit leader, Dr. Bhimrao Ambedkar.

Baburao Bagul (1930–2008) was a pioneer of Dalit writings in Marathi.[725] His first collection of stories, *Jevha Mi Jat Chorali* (जेव्हा मी जात चोरली) (When I Concealed My Caste), published in 1963, created a stir in Marathi literature with its passionate depiction of a cruel society and thus brought in new momentum to Dalit literature in Marathi.[726,727] Gradually with other writers like, Namdeo Dhasal (who founded Dalit Panther), these Dalit writings paved way for the strengthening of Dalit movement. Notable Dalit authors writing in Marathi include Arun Kamble, Shantabai Kamble, Raja Dhale, Namdev Dhasal, Daya Pawar, Annabhau Sathe, Laxman Mane, Laxman Gaikwad, Sharankumar Limbale, Bhau Panchbhai, Kishor Shantabai Kale, Narendra jadhav, Namdeo Vatkar, Ashok Vatkar, Baliram G. Kamble and Urmila Pawar.

Awards

Four Marathi writers have been honored with the Jnanpith Award:

- Vishnu Sakharam Khandekar
- Vishnu Vaman Shirwadkar (Kusumagraj)
- Vinda Karandikar
- Bhalchandra Nemade

Every year, Sahitya Akademi gives the Sahitya Akademi Award to Marathi writers for their outstanding contribution to Marathi literature. See the List of Sahitya Akademi Award winners for Marathi.

References

Bibliography

- Christian Lee Novetzke (2016). *The Quotidian Revolution: Vernacularization, Religion, and the Premodern Public Sphere in India*[728]. Columbia University Press. ISBN 978-0-231-54241-8.<templatestyles src="Module:Citation/CS1/styles.css"></templatestyles>
- M. K. Nadkarni (1921). *A short history of Marathi literature*[729]. Luhana Mitra Steam Printing Press, Baroda.<templatestyles src="Module:Citation/CS1/styles.css"></templatestyles> (PDF form[730])

External links

 Wikimedia Commons has media related to *Marathi language literature*.

- Marathi Literature in the Twenty-first Century: An Overview[731]
- A Brief Introduction to New Marathi Poetry on Poetry International Web[732]
- Globalization and New Marathi Poetry[733]
- Devotional Aartis of Maharashtra[734]
- Marathi Poetry in the Early Twentieth Century[735]
- Marathi Literature of Maharashtra[736]
- Contemporary Marathi Writers[737]
- Sachin Ketkar's article on Brief History of Marathi poetry in past one hundred years[738]

Mizo literature

Mizo literature

Mizo literature
Mizo language
Mizo literary history
Oral tradition, folklores & folktales Pre-christianisation period (1860-1894) Early period (1894-1920) Middle period (1920-1970) Contemporary Mizo literature (1970-present)
Mizo language authors
James Dokhuma • Vanneihtluanga C. Lalnunchanga C. Laizawna • L.Z. Sailo Lalzuia Colney
Criticism & Awards
Literary theory B. Lalthangliana • Laltluangliana Khiangte R.L. Thanmawia MAL Book of the year
Most visited
James Dokhuma• Vanneihtluanga C. Lalnunchanga C. Laizawna
Mizoram Portal
Literature Portal

Indian literature
• Assamese
• Bengali
• Bhojpuri
• English
• Gujarati
• Hindi
• Kannada
• Kashmiri
• Konkani
• Malayalam
• Meitei
• Marathi
• Mizo
• Nepali
• Odia
• Punjabi
• Rajasthani
• Sanskrit
• Sindhi
• Tamil
• Telugu
• Urdu
• v
• t
• e[739]

Mizo literature is the literature written in Mizo ṭawng, the principal language of the Mizo peoples, which has both written and oral traditions. It has undergone a considerable change in the 20th century. The language developed mainly from the Lushai language, with significant influence from Pawi language, Paite language and Hmar language, especially at the literary level.[740] All Mizo languages such as Pawi language, Paite language etc. remained unwritten until the beginning of the twentieth century. However, there was unwritten secular literature in the form of folktales, war chants etc. passed down from one generation to another. And there was rich religious literature in the form of sacerdotal chants. These are the chants used by the two types of priests, namely *Bawlpu* and *Sadâwt*. This article is about the written literature.

Pre-Christianisation period

This period of Mizo (written) literature usually refers to the period between 1860 and 1894.[741] Although the Mizo alphabet proper was created around May 1894, written Mizo literature can be said to start from the publication of *Progressive Colloquial Exercises in the Lushai Dialect* by Thangliana (which is the Mizo name of Thomas Herbert Lewin) in 1874. In this book he wrote down two Mizo folktales *Chemtatrawta* and *Lalruanga leh Kungawrhi* with their English translations, and included some Mizo words with their English meaning.[742] Along with Sir George Campbell, G.H. Damant, R.G. Woodthorpe etc., other employees of the British East India Company, Thangliana also studied Mizo culture and language, producing important works.

Early period

This is the period between 1894 and 1920, when most of the literary work was produced by the missionaries. Mizo alphabet was created in 1894, and schools were established soon after the creation of Mizo alphabet. On 22 October 1896 the first Mizo language book was published under the title *Mizo Zir Tir Bu* (lit. Mizo primer). This was a book on Christian religion and morality based on Christianity.

The two Christian missionaries J.H. Lorrain (Pu Buanga) and F.W. Savidge (Sap Upa) started translating the book of gospel according to Luke on 21 August 1895. They went on to translate the gospel according to John, and the two books were printed and published in 1898. Other books were also translated soon after. Some of the most well-known books published during this period were:

1. Isua chanchin (1905)
2. Isua hnenah lo kal rawh (1905-6)
3. Thu inchhang (1908)
4. The Lushai Grammar and Dictionary (1898, by J.H. Lorrain)
5. Dictionary of Lushai (J.H. Lorrain)

A number of devotional songs were translated by other missionaries who replaced J.H. Lorrain and F.W. Savidge, such as Edwin Rowlands etc.

Middle period

The middle period of Mizo literature (1920–1970) saw the rise of prominent writers such as Liangkhaia, who published hundreds of articles in the monthly Kristian Tlangau and authored *Mizo chanchin* (in two volumes) which contained, besides a coherent treatment of Mizo history, a number of ancient chants and festive songs which he collected from various sources. Besides this, he and his close friends collected various other ancient Mizo poems, publishing it under a single volume *Zoram kan lo luh hma Pawi rama kan la awm lai leh Zoram luh tirh vela chhuak ṭante*. It contains various *Chai hla, Hlado, Zai* and a number of *Hla*. This collection is one of the most reliable sources of knowledge for ancient Mizo poetry[743]

Authors during this period are usually referred to as *Hranghluite* in Mizo culture.

Poetry

Awithangpa

One of the best known Mizo language poets, Awithangpa (1885–1965) (whose real name is *Hmarlûtvunga*) was active during this period. The beautiful, innovative expressions he used in his poems are now generally thought by most to be part of Mizo poetic language since time immemorial, although he was the first to use them and were in fact mostly his own coinage. Examples include expressions such as *ram loh, chohar di* etc. The great reputation of his *zai* (poems) among Mizo people can be judged from the fact that, although his poems were not initially recorded in writing, when Mizo littérateurs later tried to collect and record his poems, people still remembered most of his poems and could still recite them in full.[744]

Other poets

Various other poets were active during this period of Mizo literature. Some of them were religious poets, writing mainly songs used in various Christian services in the Mizo tradition, which include *Pathianni inkhâwm* (Sunday service), *lènkhâwm* (a get-together for singing), *khawhạr* (condolence service) etc. Although they do not form part of Mizo secular literature, the richness and beauty of Mizo language is manifest in the elegies, worship songs etc. they composed, and their poems have therefore been consistently included in school and university curriculum. Poets of this tradition include Patea (1894–1950) (who composed 55 songs) and Saihnuna (1894–1949)(who composed about 98 songs) and the blind poet Laithangpuia (1885–1935) (who composed about 27 songs) among others.

On the other hand, there were other poets who wrote both religious and secular poems, such as R.L. Kamlala (1902–1980), Damhauhva (1909–1972) etc.

The poet Pu Rokunga is one of the most prolific Mizo poets, composing patriotic songs, festive songs, Christmas songs, idylls, poems about nature etc. He was chosen *Poet of the Century* by the Mizo Millennium Celebration Committee in 2000.

Other best known poets include

1. Capt. L.Z. Sailo
2. Laltanpuia
3. Lalzova Chhangte (usually referred to as *Fam Lalzova*)
4. P. S. Chawngthu
5. Vankhama
6. V. Thangzama

etc.

Play

Mizo language dramatists active during this period include

Dramatist	One work
Ch. Pasena	Fapa tlanbo (1927)
Lalkailuia	Tualvungi leh Zawlpala (1935)
Chawngzika	Pheikhawk siamtu (1952)
Lalthangfala Sailo	Sual man chu thihna
H Lalsiama	Ukil hlawhtling
K. Saibela	Mizo inneihna

Prose

Well-known writers during this period include Nuchhungi Renthlei (1914–2002), and Lalthangfala Sailo, who got Padma Shri award in Literature in 1986 and 2009 respectively. L. Biakliana (1918–1941), who wrote the first Mizo novel *Hawilopari*, Kaphleia (1910–1940), C. Thuamluaia (1922–1959), K.C. Lalvunga, J.F. Laldailova, Siamkima Khawlhring etc.[745]

Modern period

This period of Mizo literature starts in 1970 and continues to the present. The Mizo Academy of Letters started awarding its *Book of the Year* in 1989. The academy also awards lifetime achievement in Mizo literature. Some of the most prominent writers during this period are James Dokhuma (1932–2008), Khawlkungi (1927-2015), B. Lalthangliana (1945-), Siamkima Khawlhring (1938–1992), R.L. Thanmawia (1954-), C. Laizawna (1959-), Laltluangliana Khiangte (1961-), Lalzuahliana (1962-), Vanneihtluanga (1959-), Lalzuia Colney (Padma Shri awardee) etc.

The list of books awarded so far and their authors are tabulated below:[746,747]

Year	Book	Author	Comments on the book
1989	Ka Lungkham	B. Lalthangliana	Literature
1990	Hmangaihzuali	C. Laizawna	Novel
1991	Zoram Khawvel-I	L. Keivom	Contemporary Mizo history
1992	Thangthar Taitesena	Romawia	Novel
1993	Mizo Literature	B. Lalthangliana	Literature
1994	Kum za Kristian Zofate hmabâk	Bangalore Mizo Christian Fellowship	Collection
1995	Ram leh i tan chauh	H. Lallungmuana	Novel
1996	Bible leh Science	P.C. Biaksiama	Creationism
1997	Pasaltha Khuangchera	Laltluangliana Khiangte	Drama
1998	Anita	C. Laizawna	Novel
1999	Tlawm ve lo Lalnu Ropuiliani	Lalsangzuali Sailo	Mizo history
2000	Chawngmawii leh Hrangchhuana	R. Rozika	Novel
2001	Ka khualzin kawng	Robuanga	
2002	Runlum Nuthai	L.Z. Sailo	Eulogy
2003	Kan Bible hi	Zairema	Theology
2004	Zorinpari	H. Lalngurliana	Novel
2005	Damlai thlipui	Lalhriata	Novel
2006	Pasalthate ni hnuhnung	C. Lalnunchanga	Historical adventure novel
2007	Zofate zinkawngah	R. Zamawia	Factual description and idealisation of Mizo uprising
2008	Chun chawi loh	Lalhriata	Novel
2009	Rintei zùnléng	Lalrammawia Ngente	Novel
2010	Beiseina Mittui	Samson Thanruma	Novel

2011	Zodinpuii (posthumously awarded)	Lalchhantluanga	Novel
2012	Sihlipui	Romuanpuii Zadeng	Novel
2013	Thinglubul	Lalpekkima	Novel
2014	Ka Zalenna	B. Lalhriattira	Essay Collection
2015	Kawlkil piah Lamtluang	C. Lalnunchanga	Fantasy Novel
2016	Aizawlah Aizawler	Lalhruaitluanga Chawngte	Contemporary Social Essays

|2017||Savun Kawrfual||Lalhmingchhuanga Zote||Novel|}

References

<templatestyles src="Refbegin/styles.css" />

Others

- Khiangte, Laltluangliana, *Mizo lehkhabu zempui* (A compendium of Mizo bibliography), published by Mizo department of Mizoram University, 2005.
- Khiangte, Laltluangliana, *Lehkhabu Ramtiam*, L.T.L. Publications, Aizawl, 1993.
- Mizo Academy of Letters, *Zo kalsiam*, Aizawl, 1997.
- Vanlawma, R., *Awithangpa*, Aizawl, 1989.
- Lalthangliana, B. (Editor), *Mizo hla leh a phuahtute*, Hrangbana College, Aizawl. First edition 1999.

Further reading

- Khiangte, Laltluangliana, *Mizo drama: origin, development, and themes*. Cosmo Publications, 1993.
- Zoramdinthara, Dr., *Mizo Fiction: Emergence and Development*. Ruby Press & Co[748]. 2013. <templatestyles src="Module:Citation/CS1/styles.css" />ISBN 978-93-82395-16-4

Odia literature

Odia literature

This article is part of a serieson
Odisha
Governance
<ul><li>Governors</li><li>Chief Ministers</li><li>Legislative Assembly</li><li>Political Parties</li><li>High Court</li><li>Police</li></ul>
Topics
<ul><li>Arts</li><li>Cinema</li><li>Cuisine</li><li>Culture<ul><li>Odia Hindu Wedding</li></ul></li><li>Economy</li><li>Education</li><li>Elections</li><li>Festivals</li><li>Flora and Fauna</li><li>Geography</li><li>Highest Point</li><li>History<ul><li>Historic Sites</li><li>Maritime History</li><li>Rulers</li></ul></li></ul>

- Language
  - Alphabet
  - Act
  - Literature
  - Morphology
  - Kosli
- People
  - Tribes
- Odissi
- Politics
- Sports
- Tourism

GI Products

- Berhampur Patta
- Bomkai Sari
- Dhalapathar Parda & Fabrics
- Ganjam Kewda Flower
- Ganjam Kewda Rooh
- Gopalpur Tussar Fabrics
- Habaspuri Saree & Fabrics
- Khandua
- Konark Stone Carving
- Kotpad Handloom fabrics
- Orissa Ikat
- Pattachitra
- Pipili applique work
- Sambalpuri saree

Districts
Divisions

- Angul
- Balangir
- Balasore
- Bargarh
- Bhadrak
- Boudh
- Cuttack
- Deogarh
- Dhenkanal
- Gajapati
- Ganjam
- Jagatsinghpur
- Jharsuguda
- Jajpur
- Kalahandi
- Kandhamal

- Kendrapada
- Kendujhar
- Khordha
- Koraput
- Malkangiri
- Mayurbhanj
- Nabrangpur
- Nayagarh
- Nuapada
- Puri
- Rayagada
- Sambalpur
- Subarnapur
- Sundargarh

Odisha Portal

- v
- t
- e[749]

Indian literature

- Assamese
- Bengali
- Bhojpuri
- English
- Gujarati
- Hindi
- Kannada
- Kashmiri
- Konkani
- Malayalam
- Meitei
- Marathi
- Mizo
- Nepali
- Odia
- Punjabi
- Rajasthani
- Sanskrit
- Sindhi
- Tamil
- Telugu

- Urdu
- v̲
- t̲
- e̲⁷⁵⁰

Odia language literature (Odia: ଓଡ଼ିଆ ସାହିତ୍ୟ)is the predominant literature of the state of Odisha in India. The language is also spoken by minority populations of the neighbouring states of Jharkhand, West Bengal, Chhattisgarh and Andhra Pradesh. The region has been known at different stages of history as Kalinga, Udra, Utkala or Hirakhanda. Odisha was a vast empire in ancient and medieval times, extending from the Ganges in the north to the Godavari in the south. During British rule, however, Odisha lost its political identity and formed parts of the Bengal and Madras Presidencies. The present state of Odisha was formed in 1936. The modern Odia language is formed mostly from Pali words with significant Sanskrit influence. About 28% of modern Odia words have Adivasi origins, and about 2% have Hindustani (Hindi/Urdu), Persian, or Arabic origins. The earliest written texts in the language are about thousand years old. The first Odia newspaper was Utkala Deepika first published on 4 August 1866.

Odia is the only Indo-European language of India other than Sanskrit and the sixth Indian language that has been conferred classical language status and forms the basis of Odissi dance and Odissi music.

Historians have divided the history of the Odia language literature into five main stages: Old Odia (8th century to 1300), Early Middle Odia (1300 to 1500), Middle Odia (1500 to 1700), Late Middle Odia (1700 to 1850) and Modern Odia (1850 to present). Further subdivisions, as seen below, can more accurately chart the language's development.

First Literature of Odisha (4th centuries BC)

The ancientness of the Odia literature is being proved from its soil which says about two types of literature from very beginning. The development of Odia can be seen through its spoken and written forms. The spoken literature are expressed two ways. One preserved through folk forms and the other preserved through inscriptions. The songs sungs at the time of birth, death and work conditions are preserved, stories are painted through cave paintings both represent the creativity of the underlying literature. The inhabitant of this land stated to drown this language at about fifteen thousand years back. The Gudahandi painting of Kalahandi district and the cave art of Khandagiri and Udayagiri are the great achievements of this primitive architecture.

Kharavel's Hatigumpha inscription is the real evidence of past Odia cultural, political, ritual and social status and it is the 1st poetic stake inscription. Though Ashok has created many rock edicts and inscription before Kharavela, yet his instructions for administration have been written in a rude and chocked language. On the other hand, the Hatigumpha inscription show the flexibility of a language in a sweet flow.

Main feature of this inscription was based on principles of Sanskrit poetic structure: such as-

<templatestyles src="Template:Quote/styles.css"/>

Sadvanshah kshyatriya bâ pi dhiirodâttah gunanwitâh I
Ekabanshodva bhupâhâ kulajâ bahabo pi Jâ II
Shrungarabirashantânâmekoangirasa ishyate I
Angâni sarbe<pi rasâha sarbe nâtakasandhyâhâ II
Itihâsodvabam bruttamânânyad bâ sajjanâshrayam I
Chatwarastasya bargahâ syusteshwekam cha phalam bhavet II
Aâdyu namaskriyashribâ bastunirddesha eba bâ I
Kwacinnindâ khalâdinâm satâm cha gunakirttinam II
(Sâhitya darpan- Biswanâth kabirâj)

It means that such creations will be called as poem which Protagonist would be Dhirodatta belonging to an untouchable kshtriya. In Rasa (aesthetics) Srunagâra (Love, Attractiveness), Vîra (Heroic mood), Sânta (Peace or tranquility)among them one would be tha main rasa and others are remain with them as usual. All aspects of drama, historic tales and other legendary folk-lores are present. The description of all the four fold-Dharma, Artha, Kama and Mokshya are still present here, but one should be given priority than other theme. At the beginning it should be written as respective, blissful and subject aware with welfare of people being hatred towards evil and devotional towards sages/saints.

When Hatigumpha Inscription was created by Kharavela, all these principles were traced by him before, which has been followed by Rudradaman (Girinar inscription-150 A.D.), Samudragupta (Prayaga inscription-365 A.D), Kumar-gupta (Mandasore inscription-473A.D.) etc, created their own famous creativities in a decent poetic style on many rocks in Sanskrit language. The trend of writing was not obstructed after Kharavela. From Asanapata inscription in Keonjhar created by Satru Bhanja, (a warrior of Odisha)were engraved in the temple, Laxminarayana of Simhanchalam by Mukunda Deva are such examples. At the beginning, these inscriptions had a dynamic journey from Pali to Sanskrit. They have not lost the sense of Odia. Therefore, Odia language, literature, script and culture are based on the discussions on these inscriptions. The words written in the Hatigumpha Inscription is still used in the present day Odia language.

Age of Charya literature (7th – 8th centuries AD)

The beginnings of Odia poetry coincide with the development of Charyapada or Caryagiti, a literature started by Vajrayana Buddhist poets.[751] This literature was written with a certain metaphor called "Sandhya Bhasha", and some of its poets like Luipa and Kanhupa came from the territory of Odisha. The language of Charya was considered to be Prakrit. In one of his poem, Kanhupa wrote:

<templatestyles src="Template:Quote/styles.css"/>

> *Your hut stands outside the city*
> *Oh, untouchable maid*
> *The bald Brahmin passes sneaking close by*
> *Oh, my maid, I would make you my companion*
> *Kanha is a kapali, a yogi*
> *He is naked and has no disgust*
> *There is a lotus with sixty-four petals*
> *Upon that the maid will climb with this poor self and dance.*

In this poem shakti is replaced by the image of the "untouchable maid". The description of its location outside the city corresponds to being outside the ordinary consciousness. Although she is untouchable the bald Brahmin, or in other words so-called wise man, has a secret hankering for her. But only a *kapali* or an extreme tantric can be a fit companion for her, because he is also an outcast. The kapali is naked because he does not have any social identity or artifice. After the union with the shakti, the shakti and the kapali will climb on the 64-petalled lotus Sahasrara chakra and dance there.

This poet used images and symbols from the existing social milieu or collective psychology so that the idea of a deep realization could be easily grasped by the readers. This kind of poetry, full of the mystery of tantra, spread throughout the northeastern part of India from the 10th to the 14th century, and its style of expression was revived by the Odia poets of the 16th to the 19th century.

Pre-Sarala Age (12th – 14th century AD)

In the pre-Sarala period, Natha and Siddha literature flourished in Odisha. The main works of this period are *Shishu veda* (an anthology of 24 dohas), *Amara Kosha* and *Gorakh Samhita*. *Shishu veda* is mentioned in the works of Sarala Das and the later 16th century poets. It is written in Dandi brutta. Raja Balabhadra Bhanja wrote the love story, *Bhagabati* known for its emotional content.[752] The other important works of this period are the *Kalasha Chautisha* (By Baccha Das), *Somanatha bratakatha, Nagala chauthi, Tapoi* and *Saptanga*.

Rudrasudhanidhi is considered the first work of prose in Odia literature written by Abhadutta Narayan Swami.

Markanda Das composed the first Koili (an ode to cuckoo) in Odia just before the beginning of the age of Sarala Das. His composition *Kesava Koili* describes the pain of separation of Yasoda from her son Krishna. He is also known to compose the epic *Daasagriba badha, Jnaanodaya koili* etc.

Age of Sarala Das

In the 15th century, Sanskrit was the lingua franca for literature in Odisha and Odia was often considered the language of the commoners and shudras (Untouchables), who had no access to Sanskrit education. The first great poet of Odisha with widespread readership is the famous Sarala-Das, who translated the *Mahabharata*. This was not an exact translation from the Sanskrit original, but rather an imitation; for all practical purposes it can be seen as an original piece of work. Sarala Das was given the title Shudramuni, or seer from a backward class. He had no formal education and did not know Sanskrit.

This translation has since provided subsequent poets with the necessary foundation for a national literature, providing a fairly accurate idea of the Odia culture at the time. Sarala-Das, born in the 15th century Odisha of the Gajapati emperor Kapilendra Deva, was acclaimed as the "Adikabi" or first poet. The reign of the Gajapatis is considered the golden period for Odisha's art and literature. Kapilendra Deva patronized Odia language and literature along with Sanskrit unlike his predecessors who used only Sanskrit as their lingua franca. In fact a short Odia poem *Kebana Munikumara* is found in the Sanskrit Drama *Parashurama Vijaya* ascribed to none other than the emperor Kapilendra Deva himself.[753] It is believedWikipedia:Manual of Style/Words to watch#Unsupported attributions that Sarala Das's poetic gift came from the goddess Sarala (Saraswati), and that Sarala-Das wrote the Mahabharata as she dictated it. Though he wrote many poems and epics, he is best remembered for the *Mahabharata*. His other most known works are *Chandi Purana* and the *Vilanka Ramayana*. He also composed the *Lakhsmi-Narayana Bachanika*.

Arjuna Das, a contemporary of Sarala-Das, wrote *Rama-Bibha*, which is a significant long poem in Odia. He is also the author of another kavya called *Kalpalata*.

Age of the Panchasakhas

Five Odia poets emerged during the late 15th and early 16th centuries: Balaram Das, Atibadi Jagannath Das, Achyutananda Das, Ananta Das and Jasobanta Das. Although they wrote over a span of one hundred years they are collectively known as the "Panchasakhas", since they adhered to the same school of thought, Utkaliya Vaishnavism. The word "pancha" means five and the word "sakha", friend.

The Panchasakhas are Vaishnavas by thought. In 1509, Chaitanya came to Odisha with his Vaishnava message of love. Before him, Jaydev had prepared the ground for Vaishnavism through his Gita Govinda. Chaitanya's path of devotion was known as Raganuga Bhakti Marga. He introduced chanting as a way to make spiritual connection & taught the importance of Hare krushna mantra. Unlike Chaitanya, the Panchasakhas believed in Gyana Mishra Bhakti Marga, similar to the Buddhist philosophy of Charya literature stated above.

The Panchasakhas were significant not only because of their poetry but also for their spiritual legacy. In the holy land of Kalinga (Odisha) several saints, mystics, and devotional souls have been born throughout history, fortifying its culture and spiritualism. The area uniquely includes temples of Shakti, Shiva and Jagannâtha Vishnu. Several rituals and traditions have been extensively practised here by various seers - including Buddhist ceremonies, Devi "Tantra" (tantric rituals for Shakti), Shaiva Marg and Vaishnava Marg. There is hardly any "Sadhak" who did not pay a visit to the Shri Jagannâth temple.

There is an interesting description of the origin of the Panchasakhas, in Achyutananda's *Shunya Samhita*. As per his narration, towards the end of Mahabharat when Lord Krishna was leaving his mortal body, Nilakantheswara Mahadeva appeared & revealed to him that the Lord's companions Dama, Sudama, Srivatsa, Subala, and Subahu would reincarnate in the Kali-yuga & be known as Ananta, Acyutananda, Jagannatha, Balarama and Yasovanta, respectively. Thus, believers in the Panchasakha consider them the most intimate friends of Lord Krishna in Dwapara-yuga, who came again in Kali-yuga to serve him. They are also instrumental in performing the crucial & much-awaited Yuga-Karma where they destroy the sinners and save the saints, according to Sanatana-Hindu beliefs.

Balaram Das's *Jagamohan Ramayan* provided one pillar, along with Sarala-Das's *Mahabharata*, upon which subsequent Odia literature was built. His *Laksmi Purana* is considered the first manifesto of women's liberation or feminism in Indian literature. His other major works are *Gita Abakasa, Bhava samudra, Gupta Gita, Vedanta Sara, Mriguni Stuti, Saptanga yogasara tika, Vedanta sara or Brahma tika, Baula gai gita, Kamala lochana chotisa, Kanta koili, Bedha parikrama, Brahma gita, Brahmanda bhugola, Vajra kavacha, Jnana chudamani, Virata gita, Ganesha vibhuti & Amarakosha Gita.*[754]

The most influential work of this period was however Atibadi Jagannath Das's *Bhagabata*, which had a great influence on the Odia people as a day-to-day philosophical guide, as well as a lasting one in Odia culture. His other works include *Gupta Bhagavat, Tula vina, Sola chapadi, Chari chapadi, Tola bena, Daru brahma gita, Diksa samyad, Artha koili, Muguni stuti, Annamaya kundali, Goloka sarodhara, Bhakti chandrika, Kali malika, Indra malika, Niladri vilasa, Nitya gupta chintamani, Sri Krishna bhakti kalpa lata* etc.

Shishu Ananta Das was born in Balipatana near Bhubaneswar in the late 15th century. He wrote *Bhakti mukti daya gita, Sisu Deva gita, Artha tarani, Udebhakara, Tirabhakana*, a *Malika* and several bhajan poetries.

Yashobanta Das was the composer of *Govinda Chandra* (a ballad or Gatha-Sangeeta), *Premabhakti, Brahma Gita, Shiva Swarodaya, Sasti mala, Brahma gita, Atma pariche gita, a Malika* and several bhajans.

Mahapurusha Achyutananda is considered the most prolific writer of the Panchasakhas. He is believed to be born through special divine intervention from Lord Jagannath. The name Achyuta literally means "created from Lord Vishnu". He is also referred to as "Achyuti", i.e. "He who has no fall" in Odia. He was born to Dinabandhu Khuntia & Padma Devi in Tilakona, Nemal around 1485 AD. He established spiritual energetic centers called "gadis" all over east India (in the former states of Anga, Banga, Kalinga, Magadha) and Nepal. Gadis such as Nemal, Kakatpur, Garoi, & Jobra Ghat were places for spiritual actions, discourses and penance. He was learned in Ayurveda, sciences & social regulations. His works are *Harivamsa, Tattva bodhini, Sunya samhita, Jyoti samhita, Gopala Ujjvala, Baranasi Gita, Anakara Brahma Samhita, Abhayada Kavacha, Astagujari, Sarana panjara stotra, Vipra chalaka, Manamahima, Maalika*.

The Panchasakha's individual characteristics are described as follows (in Odia and English):

<templatestyles src="Template:Quote/styles.css"/>

Agamya bhâba jânee Yasovanta
Gâra katâ Yantra jânee Ananta
Âgata Nâgata Achyuta bhane
Balarâma Dâsa tatwa bakhâne
Bhaktira bhâba jâne Jagannâtha
Panchasakhaa e
mora pancha mahanta.

<templatestyles src="Template:Quote/styles.css"/>

Yasovanta knows the things beyond reach
Yantras uses lines and figures known to Ananta
Achyuta speaks the past, present and future
Balarâma Dasa is fluent in tatwa (the ultimate meaning of anything)
Ultimate feelings of devotion are known to Jagannâtha
These five friends are my five mahantas.

During the Panchasakha era another seer Raghu Arakhsita, who was not part of the Panchasakhas but was a revered saint, composed several Padabalis in Odia. The Panchasakha and Arakhshita together are known as the **Sada-Goswami** (six Lords).

Madhavi Pattanayak or Madhavi Dasi is considered as the first Odia woman poet who was a contemporary of Prataprudra Deva and wrote several devotional poetries for Lord Jagannatha.

Imaginative medieval Odia literature (16th – Mid 17th century)

Several Kaalpanika (imaginative) and Pauraanika (Puranic) Kavyas were composed during this period that formed the foundation for Riti Juga. The major works of this era other than those written by the Panchasakhas are *Gopakeli* and *Parimalaa* authored by Narasingha sena, contemporary of Gajapati emperor Prataprudra Deva, *Chataa Ichaamati* and *Rasa* by Banamali Das, *Premalochana, Bada Shakuntala* & *Kalaabati* by Vishnu Das, *Nrushingha purana* and *Nirguna Mahatmya* by Chaitanya Dash (born in Kalahandi), *Lilaabati* by Raghunatha Harichandan, *Usha Bilasa* by Shishu shankar Das, *Sasisena* by Pratap Rai, *Rahashya Manjari* by Devadurlava Das, *Hiraabati* by Ramachandra Chottaray, *Deulatola* by Nilambara Das, *Prema Panchamruta* by Bhupati Pandit, *Rukmini Vivaha* by Kartik Das, *Goparasa* by Danai Das and *Kanchi Kaveri* by Purushotama Das. In the 16th century three major poets translated Jayadeva's Gita Govinda into Odia. They are Dharanidhara Mishra, Brindavan Das(*Rasabaridhi*) and Trilochan Das (*GovindaGita*).[755] Brundabati Dasi, a women poet of great talent wrote *Purnatama Chandrodaya Kavya* towards the end of seventeenth century.

Several Chautishas (a form of Odia poetry where 34 stanzas from "ka" to "Khsya" are placed at the starting of each composition) were composed during this time. The famous ones being *Milana Chautisha, Mandakini Chautisha, Barshabharana Chautisha, Rasakulya Chautisha* etc.

Muslim poet Salabega was one of the foremost devotional poets of this era who composed several poems dedicated to Lord Jagannath during Jahangir's reign in the 17th century.[756]

Riti Yuga/Age of Upendra Bhanja (1650–1850)

After the age of the Panchasakhas, several prominent works were written, including the *Usabhilasa* of Sisu Sankara Das, the *Rahasya-manjari* of Devadurlabha Dasa and the *Rukmini-bibha* of Karttika Das. A new form of novels in verse evolved at the beginning of the 17th century when Ramachandra Pattanayaka wrote *Haravali*. The prominent poets of the period, however, are Dhananjaya Bhanja (born 1611. AD), Dinakrushna Das (born 1650. AD), Kabi Samrat Upendra Bhanja (born 1670. AD) and Abhimanyu Samanta Simhar. Their poetry, especially that of Upendra Bhanja, is characterised by verbal tricks, obscenity and eroticism.

Upendra Bhanja's works like *Baidehisha Bilasa*, *Koti Brahmanda Sundari* and *Labanyabati* are considered landmarks of Odia Literature. He was conferred with the title "Kabi Samrat" of Odia literature for his aesthetic poetic sense and skill with words. He wrote 52 books out of which only 25-26 are available. He alone contributed more than 35000 words to Odia literature and is considered the greatest poet of Riti Juga.

Dhananjaya Bhanja (1611-1701), a poet of repute, king of Ghumusar and grandfather of Upendra Bhanja, wrote several kavyas like *Anangarekha, Ichaavati, Raghunatha Bilasa, Madana Manjari* etc.. Besides Tribikrama Bhanja (author of *Kanakalata*) and Ghana Bhanja (author of *Trailokyamohini, Rasanidhi* and *Govinda Bilasha*) of the Bhanja royal family also enriched Odia Literature. Lokanatha Vidyadhara, a contemporary of Upendra Bhanja wrote *Sarbanga Sundari*.

Dinakrushna Das's *Rasokallola* and Abhimanyu Samanta Simhara's *Bidagdha Chintamani* are also prominent kavyas of this time. *Bidagdha Chintamani* is considered the longest Kavya in Odia literature with 96 cantos exceeding that of Upendra's longest kavya of 52 cantos. Other famous works of Abhimanyu Samanta Simhara are *Sulakhshyana, Prema Chintaamani, Prema Kala, Rasaabati, Premataranginī* etc. These poets significantly influenced modern Odia Literature.

A new form of poetry called *"Bandha kabita"* also started during this time where the poet wrote the poem within the bandha or frame of a picture drawn by him. Upendra Bhanja was the pioneer in this form of pictorial poetry. His Chitrakavya Bandhodaya is the first such creation containing 84 pictorial poems. Poets who wrote in this tradition include Sadananda Kabisurya Bramha (*Lalita Lochana* and *Prema Kalpalata*), Tribikrama Bhanja (*Kanakalata*), Kesabaraja Harichandana (*Rasa Sindhu Sulakhshyana*) etc.

Lyrical Odia Literature towards the end of Riti Juga:

Towards the end of Riti Yuga, four major poets emerged and enriched Odia literature through their highly lyrical creations. These were Kabi Surya Baladeb Rath, Brajanath Badajena, Gopal Krushna Pattanaik and Bhima Bhoi. Kabisurya Baladev Rath wrote his poems in champu (mixture of prose and poetry) and chautisha style of poetry. His greatest work is *Kishore Chandranana Champu* which is a landmark creation extensively used in Odissi Music. Brajanath Badjena started a tradition of prose fiction, though he was not an excellent prose writer. His *Chatur Binoda* (Amusement of Intelligent) seems to be the first work that deals with different kinds of rasas, predominantly the bibhatsa rasa, but often verges on nonsense. The style of *"Chitra Kavya"* (mixture of poetry and paintings) was at its best in the 18th century. Several chitra pothis can be traced to this time.

Bichitra Ramayana of Biswanaath Khuntia is one of the most celebrated works of this period composed in the early 18th century. Pitambar Das wrote the epic *Narasingha Purana* consisting of seven parts called *Ratnakaras* in the 18th century. Maguni Pattanaik composed the *Rama Chandra Vihara*. *Rama Lila* was composed by Vaishya Sadashiva and Ananga Narendra. Bhima Bhoi, the blind poet born in a tribal Khondh family is known for his lucid and humanistic compositions like *Stuthi Chintaamani, Bramha Nirupana Gita, Shrutinishedha Gita* etc.The other major poets towards the end of Riti Yuga are Banamali, Jadumani Mohapatra, Bhaktacharan Das (author of *Manabodha Chautisha* and *Mathura Mangala*), Haribandhu, Gaurahari, Gauracharana, Krishna Simha all of whom enriched Odia lyrical literature.[757]

Age of Radhanath

The first printing of the Odia language was done in 1836 by Christian missionaries, replacing palm leaf inscription and revolutionising Odia literature. After this time books were printed and journals and periodicals became available in Odia. The first Odia magazine, *Bodha Dayini* was published in Balasore in 1861. Its goal was to promote Odia literature and draw attention to lapses in government policy. The first Odia paper *The Utkala Deepika*, was first published in 1866 under editor Gourishankar Ray and Bichitrananda. *The Utkal Deepika* campaigned to bring all Odia-speaking areas together under one administration, to develop the Odia language and literature and to protect Odia interests.

In 1869 Bhagavati Charan Das started another newspaper, *Utkal Subhakari*, to propagate the Brahmo faith. In the last three and a half decades of the 19th century, a number of newspapers were published in Odia. Prominent papers included *Utkal Deepika,Utkal Patra, Utkal Hiteisini* from Cuttack, *Utkal*

Darpan and *Sambada Vahika* from Balasore and *Sambalpur Hiteisini* from Deogarh. The success of these papers indicated the desire and determination of the people of Odisha to uphold their right to freedom of expression and freedom of the press, with the ultimate aim of freedom from British rule. These periodicals performed another vital function, in that they encouraged modern literature and offered a broad reading base for Odia-language writers. Intellectuals who came into contact with Odia literature through the papers were also influenced by their availability.

Radhanath Ray (1849-1908) is the most well-known poet of this period. He wrote with a Western influence, and his kavyas (long poems) included Chandrabhaga, Nandikeshwari, Usha, Mahajatra, Darbar and Chilika.

Fakir Mohan Senapati (1843-1918), the most known Odia fiction writer, was also of this generation. He was considered the Vyasakabi or founding poet of the Odia language. Senapati was born raised in the coastal town of Balasore, and worked as a government administrator. Enraged by the attempts of the Bengalis to marginalize or replace the Odia language, he took to creative writing late in life. Though he also did translations from Sanskrit, wrote poetry and attempted many forms of literature, he is now known primarily as the father of modern Odia prose fiction. His *Rebati* (1898) is widely recognized as the first Odia short story. *Rebati* is the story of a young innocent girl whose desire for education is placed in the context of a conservative society in a backward Odisha village, which is hit by the killer cholera epidemic. His other stories are "Patent Medicine", "Dak Munshi", and "Adharma Bitta". Senapati is also known for his novel Chha Maana Atha Guntha. This was the first Indian novel to deal with the exploitation of landless peasants by a feudal lord. It was written well before the October revolution in Russia and emerging of Marxist ideas in India.

Other eminent Odia writers and poets of the time include Gangadhar Meher (1862-1924), Madhusudan Rao, Chintamani Mohanty, Nanda Kishore Bal and Gaurisankar Ray.

Age of Satyabadi

During the Age of Radhanath the literary world was divided between the classicists, led by the magazine *The Indradhanu*, and the modernists, led by the magazine *The Bijuli*. Gopabandhu Das (1877-1928) was a great balancer and realized that a nation, as well as its literature, lives by its traditions. He believed that a modern national superstructure could only endure if based on solid historical foundations. He wrote a satirical poem in *The Indradhanu*, which led to punishment by the Inspector of Schools, but he refused to apologise.

Gopabandhu joined Ravenshaw College in Cuttack to pursue graduation after this incident. He started the *Kartavya Bodhini Samiti* (Duty Awakening Society) in college to encourage his friends to take on social, economic and political problems and become responsible citizens. While leading a team to serve flood victims, Gopabandhu heard that his son was seriously ill. He preferred, however, to save the "sons of the soil" rather than his son. His mission was to reform society and develop education in the name of a social service vision. He lost his wife at age twenty-eight, and had already lost all three of his sons by this time. He left his two daughters and his property in the village with his elder brother, rejecting worldly life. For this social service mission he is regarded by Odias as the Utkalmani.

As freedom movements began, a new era in literary thought emerged influenced by Gandhi and the trend of nationalism. Gopabandhu was a large part of this idealistic movement, founding a school in Satyabadi and influencing many writers of the period. Other than Gopabandhu himself, other famous writers of the era were Godabarisha Mishra, Nilakantha Dash, Harihara Acharya and Krupasinshu. They are known as 'Panchasakhas' for their similarities with the historical Age of Panchasakhas. Their principle genres were criticism, essays and poetry.

Chintamani Das is particularly renowned. Born in 1903 in Sriramachandrapur village near Sakhigopal, he was bestowed with the Sahitya Akademi Samman in 1970 for his invaluable contribution to Odia literature. Some of his well-known literary works are *Manishi Nilakantha, Bhala Manisa Hua, Usha, Barabati, Byasakabi Fakiramohan* and *Kabi Godabarisha*.

Pragati Yuga

Nabajuga Sahitya Sansad formed in 1935 was one of the first progressive literary organizations in India. It was formed before the National Progressive Writers Association was established in 1936 by Munshi Prem Chand, Sajad Zaheer, Mulk Raj Anand and others. The founders of the Progressive Movement in Orissa were Nabakrushna Choudhury, Bhagabati Panigrahi and Ananta Patnaik. At the inaugural session of Nabajuga Sahitya Sansad, the great freedom fighter Malati Choudhury sang "Nabeena Jugara Taruna Jagare" written by Ananta Patnaik. The mouth piece of Nabajuga Sahity Sansad was Adhunika, the First Progressive Literary Magazine in Oriya. Adhuinka was conceived, initiated, edited, published and nurtured by Bhagabati Charan Panigrahi and Ananta Patnaik. Many writers of that time wrote in Adhunika.

Age of Romanticism or Sabuja Yuga

Influenced by the Romantic thoughts of Rabindranath Tagore during the 1930s when progressive Marxist movements dominated Odia Literature, Kalindi Charan Panigrahi (the brother of Bhagabati Charan Panigrahi who founded Marxism in Odisha) formed a group called "Sabuja Samiti" with two of his writer friends Annada Shankar Ray and Baikuntha Patnaik. This was a very short period in Odia literature, later folded into Gandhian and Marxist work. Kalindi Charan Panigrahi later wrote his famous novel *Matira Manisha*, which was influenced by Gandhism, and Annada Shankar Ray left for Bengali literature. Mayadhar Mansingh was a renowned poet of that time, but though he was considered a Romantic poet he kept his distance from the influence of Rabindranath.

Purnachandra Odia Bhashakosha

The *Purnachandra Odia Bhashakosha* is a monumental 7-volume work of about 9,500 pages published between 1930 and 1940. It was a result of the vision and dedicated work of Gopal Chandra Praharaj (1874–1945) over nearly three decades. Praharaj not only conceived of and compiled the work, he also raised the finances to print it through public donations, grants and subscriptions and supervised the printing and the sales of the published work.

The Purnachandra Odia Bhashakosha is an Odia language dictionary that lists some 185,000 words and their meanings in four languages - Odia, English, Hindi and Bengali. It includes quotations from wide-ranging classical works illustrating the special usage of various words. It also contains specialised information such as botanical names of local plants, information on astronomy and long articles on various topics of local interest. In addition, there are biographies of personalities connected with Odisha's history and culture.

The Purnachandra Odia Bhashakosha is an encyclopaedic work touching on various aspects of the Odia language and Odisha region, as well as many topics of general interest. Its author Praharaj was a lawyer by profession and was ridiculed and reviled by many during production itself. Many printed copies were destroyed unbound and unsold. Many copies sat in libraries of the princes who had patronised the work and most of these copies were sold cheaply when the princes met financial ruin. There are few surviving copies, and those that exist are fragile and worm-damaged. The work is regarded by the older generation, but not well-known among younger Odias.

Post Colonial Age

Poetry

As the successors of Sachi Routray, the father of modern poetry, two poets (Guruprasad Mohanty and Bhanuji Rao) were highly influenced by T.S. Eliot and published a co-authored poetry book *Nutan Kabita*. Ramakanta Rath later modified Eliot's ideas in his own work. According to Rath : "After the publication of Kalapurusha [Guru Prasad's poetry collection influenced by T.S. Eliot's *The Waste Land*] we realized that a sense of alienation is the main ingredient of modern poetry." Before independence Odia poetry was mostly written with Sanskritic or "literary" idiom, but after independence poets freely used of Western concepts, idioms, images and adaptation of Western myths.Ramakanta Rath, Sitakant Mahapatra, Soubhagya Kumar Mishra, Rajendra kishore Panda, Prativa Satpathy, Mamata Dash, Haraprasad Das are the most famous of these poets. The mid 60s and between 70s the prominent poets of Odia were- Radhamohan Gadnayak, Benudhar Rout, Brajanath Rath, Bangali Nanda, Harihar Mishra, Dipak Mishra, Kamalakant Lenka, Banshidhar Sarangi, Durga Charan Parida, Devdas Chhotray, Saroj Ranjan Mohanty, Amaresh Patnaik, Ashutosh Parida, Prasanna Patsani, Hussain Rabi Gandhi, Sadasiba Dash, Goutam Jena, one of the wide circulated odia poet.he is born on 7th.May1959.He is the pioneer of"Groundism", that is"Matimanaskabad".His poem collections are "samaya BISADA nai","Ekaeka Dina", Ranga Siuli", MayaManaska", Panchama Raga", Bahuda Bela", Jibana Veda"and Darsana Yoga. Hrishkesh Mullick, Satrughna Pandab, Prabasini Mahakuda, Aaparna Mohanty, Aswini Mishra, Roninikant Mukherjee, Girija Baliarsingh etc. The early 80s saw in Odia Literature a Group of poets with new thoughts and style who overshadowed the earlier generation. These poets had their root in typical Odia soil. The rich heritage and culture with the feelings of commomen were depicted in their Odia poems. They were somehow more nearer to the readers as there were little ambiguity in their expression These contemporary poems were better than the so-called modern poems. The prominent poets of this time were- Manasi Pradhan, Surya Mishra, Bhagirathi Mishra, Ramakrushna Sahoo, Abani Pradhan, Bijay Mahapatra, Kanhu Charan Panigrahi, Manas Ranjan Mohapatra, Akshaya Behera, Samarendranath Mahapatra, Sunil Prusty, Chittaranjan Misra, Senapati Pradyumna Keshari, Ajay Pradhan, Sucheta Mishra, Manoranjan Panigrahi, Raxak Nayak, Arupananda Panigrahi, Biraja Bala, Khirod Parida, Ranjan Kumar Das, Akhila Nayak, Pabitra Mohan Dash, Kedar Mishra, Basudev Sunani, Lenin Kumar, Dr. Basanta Kishore Sahoo, Dr. suresh Nayak, Bharat Majhi, Preetidhara Samal, Ipsita Sarangi, Swapna Mishra, Kishore Panigrahi, Durga Prasad Panda, Manoj

Nayak, Saroj Bal, Sitanshu Lenka, Gayatribala Panda, Anirudha Behera etc. This generation is the contemporary poet generation as critics say.

Odia Translation of World Classics

Eminent scholar Prof. Ananta Charan Sukla's celebrated Odia Translation (with Commentary, Critical Study and Notes) of Aristotle's Poetics (Aristotle-anka Kabyatatwa) published in the late 1960s is a rare and outstanding work. It is the second translation of the classic work in any Indian language after Bengali. His translation of four classic Greek plays is also a commendable work.

Fiction

Before the 1970s

In the post-independence era Odia fiction took a new direction. The trend Fakir Mohan started developed more after independence, led by Gopinath Mohanty (1914–1991), Surendra Mohanty and Manoj Das (1934-). These authors pioneered the trend of developing or projecting the "individual as protagonist" in Odia fiction. There is some tension between the two Mohantys among critics. Eminent feminist writer and critic Sarojini Sahoo believes that it is not Gopinath's story "Dan", but rather Surendra Mohanty's "Ruti O Chandra" that should be considered the first story of the individualistic approach.[758] The major difference between Surendra and Gopinath is that, where Gopinath is more optimistic, Surendra is nihilistic. This nihilism prepared the ground for the development an existentialist movement in Odia literature.

Surendra Mohanty is a master of language, theme and concept. Some of his famous short story collections and novels are *Krushna Chuda, Mahanagarira Rati, Ruti O Chandra, Maralara Mrutyu, Shesha Kabita, Dura Simanta, Oh Calcutta, Kabi-O- Nartaki, Sabuja Patra-O-Dhusara Golap, Nila Shaila* and *Andha Diganta*.

In his fiction Gopinath Mohanty explores all aspects of Odishan life, both in the plains and in the hills. He uses a unique prose style, lyrical in style, choosing worlds and phrases from the day-to-day speech of ordinary men and women. Gopinath's first novel, *Mana Gahtra Chasa*, was published in 1940, followed by Dadi Budha (1944), Paraja (1945) and Amrutara Santan (1947). He published 24 novels, 10 collections of short stories, three plays, two biographies, two volumes of critical essays and five books on the languages of Kandh, Gadaba and Saora tribes. He also translated Tolstoy's *War and Peace* (*Yuddh O Shanti*) in three volumes (tr. 1985-86) and Togore's *Jogajog* (tr. 1965) into Odia.

The writer Kalpanakumari Devi's sequence of novels, in particular, her *Srushti o pralaya* (1959), documenting the social change in the country have been lauded.

Starting his literary career as a communist and later becoming an Aurobindian philosopher, Manoj Das proved himself as a successful bilingual writer in Odia and English. His major Odia works are: *Shesha Basantara Chithi* (1966), *Manoj Dasanka Katha O Kahani* (1971), *Dhumabha Diganta* (1971), *Manojpancabimsati* (1977) and *Tuma Gam O Anyanya Kabita* (1992). Notable English works include *The crocodile's lady : a collection of stories* (1975), *The submerged valley and other stories*, *Farewell to a ghost : short stories and a novelette* (1994), *Cyclones* (1987) and *A tiger at twilight* (1991).

Renowned writer Ananta Charan Sukla's short story collection, "Sulataku Sesa Chitthi" (Last Letter to Sulata) published in 1965 is also worth mentioning. The ten stories included in this book are "Sulataku Sesa Chitthi", "Kapilas", "Janeika Kulapati-nka Mrutyu", "Tandril Ru Tornoto", "Mystic Realistic", "Prasanta Samudra: Asanta Lahari", "Nalakula Matha, Nepala Babu O Narana", "Daudana Bada Khara", "Duragata" and "Sandipani-ra Symphony". Other significant pre-1970s fiction writers are Chandrasekhar Rath, Shantanu Kumar Acharya, Mohapatra Nilamani Sahoo, Akhil Mohan Patnaik, Gobind Das, Rabi Patnaik and JP Das. Chandra Sekhar Rath's novel *Jantrarudha* is one of the renowned classics of this period. Shantanu Acharya's novel Nara-Kinnara was also influential.

After the 1970s

The trends started by the 1950s and 1960s were challenged by the young writers in the 1970s. This challenge began in the 1960s with a small magazine *Uan Neo Lu* in Cuttack. The title of the magazine was made up of three of the Odia alphabets, which were not in use. Writers associated with the magazines included Annada Prasad Ray, Guru Mohanty (not to be confused with Guru Prasad), Kailash Lenka and Akshyay Mohanty. These writers were not as famous as some contemporaries, but they began a revolution in Odia fiction. They tried to break the monopoly of established writers, introducing sexuality in their work and creating a new prose style. In the late 1960s the Cuttack's in Odia Literature was broken when many "groups" of writers emerged from different parts of Odisha. Anamas from Puri, Abadhutas from Balugaon, Panchamukhi from Balangir, Abujha from Berhampur and Akshara group from Sambalpur created a sensation in Odia literary scene.

The changes that started in the 1960s were confirmed in the next decade. Jagadish Mohanty, Kanheilal Das, Satya Mishra, Ramchandra Behera, Tarun Kanti Mishra, Padmaja Pal, Yashodhara Mishra and Sarojini Sahoo created a new era in Odia fiction. Kanheilal Das and Jagadish Mohanty began creating a new style and language popular among a general audience as well as intellectuals. Kanheilal Das died young and is still considered a great loss for Odia fictions. Jagadish Mohanty introduced existentialism to Odia literature. His renowned works include *Ekaki Ashwarohi, Dakshina Duari Ghara, Album, Dipahara Dekhinathiba Lokotie, Nian O Anyanya Galpo, Mephestophelesera Pruthibi, Nija Nija Panipatha, Kanishka Kanishka, Uttaradhikar* and *Adrushya Sakal.*

Ramchandra Behera is known for short story collections *Dwitiya Shmashana, Abashishta Ayusha, Omkara Dhwani, Bhagnangshara Swapna* and *Achinha Pruthibi*. Padmaj Pal is also known for short story collections including *Eaglera Nakha Danta, Sabuthu Sundar Pakshi, Jibanamaya* and *Uttara Purusha*. Tarun Kanti Mishra emerged during 1970s as a powerful storyteller with an elegant style, full of poise and vigor. His outstanding works include 'Sharadah Shatam' (A Thousand Autumns), - a novel dealing with resettlement and rehabilitation of displaced persons from East Pakistan, now Bangladesh - and anthologies of short stories such as 'Komal Gandhar', 'Bitansa', 'Bhaswati' and 'Akash Setu'.

Sarojini Sahoo, another prominent writer, later famous as a feminist writer, also significantly contributed to Odia fiction. Her novel *Gambhiri Ghara* is not only a landmark Odia novel but has also gained international fame for its feminist and liberal ideas. Her other works include *Amrutara Pratikshare, Chowkatha, Upanibesh, Pratibandi, Paksibasa, Tarlijauthiba Durga, Dukha Apramita, Gambhiri Ghara* and *Mahajatra*. Kanaklata Hati, another women fiction writer in whose writing we will find psychoanalysis of female mind. To date she has published two story collections- 'Nirbak Pahada' & 'Kuhudi Ghara'. She has some translated story collections like 'Galpa Galpantara' and'Praibeshi Galpa'.

Popular fiction writings

A popular Odia literature also emerged in the 1970s, read by rural populace especially women. The best selling writers are Bhagirathi Das, Kanduri Das, Bhagwana Das, Bibhuti Patnaik and Pratibha Ray. Some of their works were made into films in the Odia language. In recent times Rabi Kaunungo, Tarun Kanti Mishra, Ajay Swain, Mrinal Chatterjee, Radhu Mishra, Dr Laxmikant Tripathy, Nisith Bose, Suniti Mund, Anjan Chand and Dr. Kulangara have contributed to popular writing.

Women's writings and feminism

The founding of a women's magazine called *Sucharita* in 1975 by Sakuntala Panda had a significant impact in helping female writers find a voice.Wikipedia:Citation needed Some of those writers are Giribala Mohanty, Jayanti Rath, Susmita Bagchi. Paramita Satpathy, Hiranmayee Mishra, Chirashree Indra Singh, Sairindhree Sahoo, Supriya Panda, Gayatri Saraf, Suniti Mund and Mamatamayi Chowdhry. Giribala Mohanty(1947-) needs a special introduction for her deep sensitiveness for the women issues.her poems depict the emotional binary of social apathy and the self-confidence of women.her collections of Poems 'Streeloka'(Women), 'Kalijhia'(The Dark complexion Girl),'Ma Habara Dukha'(The sorrow of being a mother)and 'Kati Katia Katyayani' expresses her feelings in a lucid and lyrical way.Sarojini Sahoo had a significant influence on these women, paving the way with a feminist approach to fiction and the introduction of sexuality in her work. She is known as the Simone de Beauvoir of India, though theoretically she denies the Hegelian theory of "Other" developed by de Beauvoir in her *The Second Sex*. Unlike de Beauvoir, Sahoo claims that women are an "Other" from the masculine perspective, but that they are entitled to equal human rights according to Plato. Suniti Mund's Story Book 'Anustupa', Poetry Book 'Jhia' And Novel 'Abhisapta', 'Agarbatira Ghara', 'Matrimony dot com','Gigolo' is also feminism voice.

Drama

The traditional Odia theater is the folk opera, or Jatra, which flourishes in the rural areas of Odisha. Modern theater is no longer commercially viable, but in the 1960 experimental theatre made a mark through the works of Manoranjan Das, who pioneered a new theater movement with his brand of experimentalism. Bijay Mishra, Biswajit Das, Kartik Rath, Ramesh Prasad Panigrahi, Ratnakar Chaini, Prasanna Das, Pramod Kumar Tripathy, Sankar Tripathy, Ranjit Patnaik, Dr. Pradip Bhowmic, Hemendra Mahapatra, and Purna Chandra Mallick continued the tradition. Tripathy's contribution to the growth and development of the immensely popular and thought-provoking *lok natakas* is universally recognised and he is often called the Rousseau of lok natakas.Wikipedia:Citation needed Noted writer Ananta Charan Sukla's Odia translation of four classic Greek dramas is a rare contribution to Odia drama literature. His book, "Greek Drama", published in 1974, has translations (with commentary) of Prometheus Bound (by Aeschylus), Oedipus the King (by Sophocles), Medea (by Euripides) and The Frogs (by Aristophanes). Sukla's translations of the plays have been staged in various colleges and universities of Odisha. Besides, his two historical plays on Odia freedom fighters Chakhi Khuntia and Jayee Rajguru have also been widely staged. Though there is no

Odia literature 277

commercially viable modern Odia theater, there are amateur theater groups and drama competitions. Operas, on the other hand, are commercially successful.

Popular science fiction writers from Odisha

Some popular science fiction writers include Prof Prana Krushna Parija, Padmashree Binod Kanungo, Prof Gokulananda Mohapatra, Prof Gadadhar Mishra, Prof Kulamani Samal, Sarat Kumar Mohanty, Prof Amulya Kumar Panda, Dr. Nikhilanand Panigrahy, Dr. Debakanta Mishra, Dr.Ramesh Chandra Parida, Sashibhusan Rath, Dr. Chitta Ranjan Mishra, Dr. Nityananada Swain, Dr. Choudhury Satybrata Nanda, Er. Mayadhar Swain, Kamalakanta Jena, Himansu Sekhar Fatesingh and Bibhuprasad Mohapatra etc.

Dr. Nikhilanand Panigrahy's "Sampratikatara Anuchintare Bigyan O Baigyanik" is a popular book among avid readers. Sashibhusan Rath's *Vigyan Chinta* and Kamalakanta Jena's *Gapare Gapare Bigyan* (Awarded by Odisha Bigyan Academy 2011) are written for children as well as adults.

In the United States

A large initiative, Pratishruti, was started to connect literary minded people in North America with their Indian peers. The goal is to expose Indian-Americans to the best writings of outstanding Odia writers as well as to cultivate new writers in America.

References

- Mansingha, Mayadhar (1962) *History of Oriya literature* Sahitya Akademi, New Delhi
- Sahoo, Krushna Charan (2004) *Oriya Lekhaka Paricaya* Orissa Sahitya Academy, Bhubaneswar, <templatestyles src="Module:Citation/CS1/styles.css" />ISBN 81-7586-097-9, <templatestyles src="Module:Citation/CS1/styles.css" />ISBN 978-81-7586-097-1
- Myers, Carol Fairbanks (1976) *Women in Literature: Criticism of the Seventies* Scarecrow Press, Inc. Metuchen, <templatestyles src="Module:Citation/CS1/styles.css" />ISBN 0-8108-0885-4
- "The History of Orissa: An Introduction"Pages from the history of India and the sub-continent:SOUTH ASIAN HISTORY[759]
- Sahoo, Dr. Basanta Kishore Sahoo (1995) Who's who in Oriya Children's - Literature, Vol. I&II Mayur Publication and RIOCL, <templatestyles src="Module:Citation/CS1/styles.css" />ISBN 8186040447
- Samantray Dr. Natabar (1955) : History of Progressive Oriya Literature

Bibliography

- Neukom, Lukas and Manideepa Patnaik. 2003. *A grammar of Oriya*. (Arbeiten des Seminars für Allgemeine Sprachwissenschaft; 17). Zürich: Seminar für Allgemeine Sprachwissenschaft der Universität Zürich. <templatestyles src="Module:Citation/CS1/styles.css" />ISBN 3-9521010-9-5

Further reading

- Ghosh, A. (2003). *An ethnolinguistic profile of Eastern India: a case of South Orissa*. Burdwan: Dept. of Bengali (D.S.A.), University of Burdwan.
- Masica, Colin (1991). *The Indo-Aryan Languages*. Cambridge Language Surveys. Cambridge: Cambridge University Press. <templatestyles src="Module:Citation/CS1/styles.css" />ISBN 978-0-521-29944-2
- Mohanty, Prasanna Kumar (2007). *The History of: History of Oriya Literature* (Oriya Sahityara Adya Aitihasika Gana).

External links

- Romanised to Unicode Oriya transliterator[760]
- Unicode Entity Codes for the Oriya Script[761]
- Free/Open Source Oriya Computing[762] Rebati project

Punjabi literature

Punjabi literature

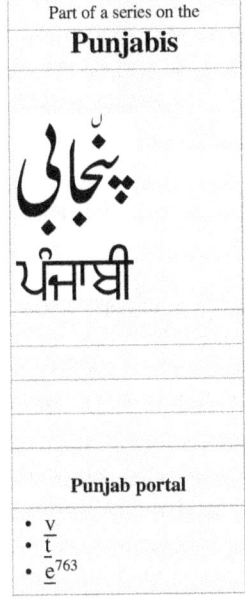

Punjabi literature, specifically literary works written in the Punjabi language, is characteristic of the historical Punjab of India and Pakistan and the Punjabi diaspora. The Punjabi language is written in several scripts, of which the Shahmukhī and Gurmukhī scripts are the most commonly used in Pakistan and India, respectively.

Medieval era

The earliest Punjabi literature is found in the fragments of writings of the 11th Nath yogis Gorakshanath and Charpatnah which is primarily spiritual and mystical in tone.[764] Notwithstanding this early yogic literature, the Punjabi literary tradition is popularly seen to commence with Fariduddin Ganjshakar (1173–1266).[765] whose Sufi poetry was compiled after his death in the *Adi Granth*.

Mughal and Sikh periods

The *Janamsakhis*, stories on the life and legend of Guru Nanak (1469–1539), are early examples of Punjabi prose literature. Nanak himself composed Punjabi verse incorporating vocabulary from Sanskrit, Arabic, Persian, and other South Asian languages as characteristic of the Gurbani tradition. Punjabi Sufi poetry developed under Shah Hussain (1538–1599), Sultan Bahu (1628–1691), Shah Sharaf (1640–1724), Ali Haider (1690–1785), Saleh Muhammad Safoori and Bulleh Shah (1680–1757). In contrast to Persian poets, who had preferred the *ghazal* for poetic expression, Punjabi Sufi poets tended to compose in the *Kafi*.[766]

Punjabi Sufi poetry also influenced other Punjabi literary traditions particularly the Punjabi Qissa, a genre of romantic tragedy which also derived inspiration from Indic, Persian and Quranic sources. The Qissa of *Heer Ranjha* by Waris Shah (1706–1798) is among the most popular of Punjabi qisse. Other popular stories include *Sohni Mahiwal* by Fazal Shah, *Mirza Sahiba* by Hafiz Barkhudar (1658–1707), *Sassi Punnun* by Hashim Shah (1735?–1843?), and *Qissa Puran Bhagat* by Qadaryar (1802–1892).

Heroic ballads known as *Vaar* enjoy a rich oral tradition in Punjabi. Prominent examples of heroic or epic poetry include Guru Gobind Singh's in *Chandi di Var* (1666–1708). The semi-historical *Nadir Shah Di Vaar* by Najabat describes the invasion of India by Nadir Shah in 1739. The Jangnama, or 'War Chronicle,' was introduced into Punjabi literature during the Mughal period; the Punjabi *Jangnama* of Shah Mohammad (1780–1862) recounts the First Anglo-Sikh War of 1845–46.

British Raj era

The Victorian novel, Elizabethan drama, free verse and Modernism entered Punjabi literature through the introduction of British education during the Raj. The first Punjabi printing press (using Gurmukhi font) was established through

Figure 86: *Amrita Pritam*

a Christian mission at Ludhiana in 1835, and the first Punjabi dictionary was published by Reverend J. Newton in 1854.

The Punjabi novel developed through Nanak Singh (1897–1971) and Vir Singh. Starting off as a pamphleteer and as part of the Singh Sabha Movement, Vir Singh wrote historical romance through such novels as Sundari, Satwant Kaur and Baba Naudh Singh, whereas Nanak Singh helped link the novel to the storytelling traditions of Qissa and oral tradition as well as to questions of social reform.

The novels, short stories and poetry of Amrita Pritam (1919–2005) highlighted, among other themes, the experience of women, and the Partition of India. Punjabi poetry during the British Raj moreover began to explore more the experiences of the common man and the poor through the work of Puran Singh (1881–1931). Other poets meanwhile, such as Dhani Ram Chatrik (1876–1957), Diwan Singh (1897–1944) and Ustad Daman (1911–1984), explored and expressed nationalism in their poetry during and after the Indian freedom movement. Chatrik's poetry, steeped in Indian traditions of romance and classical poetry, often celebrated varied moods of nature in his verse as well as feelings of patriotism. Brought up on English and American poetry, Puran Singh was also influenced by Freudian psychology in his oftentimes unabashedly sensuous poetry.

Modernism was also introduced into Punjabi poetry by Prof. Mohan Singh (1905–78) and Shareef Kunjahi. The Punjabi diaspora also began to emerge during the Raj and also produced poetry whose theme was revolt against British rule in *Ghadar di Gunj* (*Echoes of Mutiny*).[767]

Post-Independence

Western Punjab (Pakistan)

Najm Hossein Syed, Fakhar Zaman and Afzal Ahsan Randhawa are some of the more prominent names in West Punjabi literature produced in Pakistan since 1947. Literary criticism in Punjabi has also emerged through the efforts of West Punjabi scholars and poets, Shafqat Tanvir Mirza, Ahmad Salim, and Najm Hosain Syed (b. 1936).

The work of Zaman and Randhawa often treats the rediscovery of Punjabi identity and language in Pakistan since 1947. Ali's short story collection *Kahani Praga* received the Waris Shah Memorial Award in 2005 from the Pakistan Academy of Letters. Mansha Yaad also received the Waris Shah Award for his collection *Wagda Paani* in 1987, and again in 1998 for his novel *Tawan TawaN Tara*, as well as the *Tamgha-e-Imtiaz* (*Pride of Performance*) in 2004. The most critically successful writer in recent times has been Mir Tanha Yousafi who has won the Massod Khaddar Posh Trust Award 4 times, and has had his books transliterated into Gurmukhi for Indian Punjabi readers.

Urdu poets of the Punjab have also written Punjabi poetry including Munir Niazi (1928–2006).

The poet who introduced new trends in Punjabi poetry is Pir Hadi abdul Mannan. Though a Punjabi poet, he also wrote poetry in Urdu.

Eastern Punjab (India)

Amrita Pritam (1919–2005), Jaswant Singh Rahi (1930–1996), Shiv Kumar Batalvi (1936–1973), Surjit Patar (1944–) and Pash (1950–1988) are some of the more prominent poets and writers of East Punjab (India). Pritam's *Sunehe* (*Messages*) received the Sahitya Akademi in 1982. In it, Pritam explores the impact of social morality on women. Kumar's epic *Luna* (a dramatic retelling of the legend of Puran Bhagat) won the Sahitya Akademi Award in 1965. Socialist themes of revolution meanwhile influenced writers like Pash whose work demonstrates the influence of Pablo Neruda and Octavio Paz.

Punjabi fiction in modern times has explored themes in modernist and postmodernist literature. Punjabi culture. Moving from the propagation of Sikh thought and ideology to the themes of the Progressive Movement, the short

Punjabi literature

Figure 87: *Dr. Surjit Patar, a prominent Punjabi writer, poet and lecturer at Guru Nanak Dev University*

story in Punjabi was taken up by Nanak Singh, Charan Singh Shaheed, Joshua Fazal Deen, and Heera Singh Dard. Women writers such as Ajit kaur and Daleep Kaur Tiwana meanwhile have questioned cultural patriarchy and the subordination of women in their work. Hardev Grewal has introduced a new genere to Punjabi fiction called Punjabi Murder Mystery in 2012 with his Punjabi novel "Eh Khudkushi Nahin Janab! Qatl Hai" (published by Lahore Books). Kulwant Singh Virk (1921-1987) won the Sahitya Akedemi award for his collection of short stories "Nave Lok" in 1967. His stories are gripping and provide deep insight into the rural and urban modern Punjab. He has been hailed as the "emperor of Punjabi short stories".

Modern Punjab drama developed through Ishwar Nanda's Ibsen-influenced *Suhag* in 1913, and Gursharan Singh who helped popularize the genre through live theatre in Punjabi villages. Sant Singh Sekhon, Kartar Singh Duggal, and Balwant Gargi have written plays, with Atamjit has also been awarded the Sahitya Akademi Award in 2010 for his play *Tatti Tawi De Vich*.

Diaspora Punjabi literature

Punjabi diaspora literature has developed through writers in the United Kingdom, Canada, Australia, and the United States, as well as writers in Africa such as Ajaib Kamal, born in 1932 in Kenya, and Mazhar Tirmazi, writer of famous song "Umraan Langhiyan Pabhan Bhaar." Themes explored by diaspora writers include the cross-cultural experience of Punjabi migrants, racial discrimination, exclusion, and assimilation, the experience of women in the diaspora, and spirituality in the modern world. Second generation writers of Punjabi ancestry such as Rupinderpal Singh Dhillon (writes under the name Roop Dhillon) have explored the relationship between British Punjabis and their immigrant parents as well as experiment with surrealism, science-fiction and crime-fiction. Bhupinder kaur Sadhaura (1971-)have biography of peer Budhu Shah Ji, book name is Guru Bhagat Peer Budhu Shah (hanoured by Haryana Punjabi Sahitya Academy). Other known writers include Sadhu Binning and Ajmer Rode (Canada), Mazhar Tirmazi, Amarjit Chandan, Avtar Singh Sandhu (Paash) (1950-1988)and Surjit Kalsi. The most successful writer has been Shivcharan Jaggi Kussa.

Genres

Currently Punjabi writing can be split between the following genres

- Punjabi Qissa (Waris Shah)
- Traditional poetry (Surjit Paatar)
- Naxalite poetry (Paash, Amarjit Chandan)
- Lyrical poetry (Rajvinder Singh)
- Punjabi haiku (Amarjit Chandan)
- Yatharthvaad (Realism)
- Pachmi Paryatharvaad (surreal, fantasy, imaginative) Roop Dhillon
- Parvasi (émigré) Sadhu Binning
- Viang (satire) Jagjit Singh Komal
- Punjabi Murder Mystery Hardev Grewal

External links

- Panjab Digital Library[768] - houses digital versions of Punjabi manuscripts covering several centuries.
- Punjabi Literature website[769] - A collection of young and lesser known Panjabi Authors.

Rajasthani literature

Rajasthani literature

Indian literature
• Assamese
• Bengali
• Bhojpuri
• English
• Gujarati
• Hindi
• Kannada
• Kashmiri
• Konkani
• Malayalam
• Meitei
• Marathi
• Mizo
• Nepali
• Odia
• Punjabi
• Rajasthani
• Sanskrit
• Sindhi
• Tamil
• Telugu
• Urdu
• v • t • e[770]

Rajasthani literature written in various genres starting from 1000 AD. But, it is generally agreed that modern **Rajasthani literature** began with the works of

Surajmal Misrana.[771] His most important works are the Vansa Bhaskara and the Vir Satsai. The Vans Bhaskar contains accounts of the Rajput princes who ruled in what was then Rajputana (at present the state of Rajasthan), during the lifetime of the poet (1872–1952). The Vir Satsai is a collection of hundreds of couplets.

Medieval Rajasthani literature is mostly poetry only and it is more about the heroic poetry mentioning of the great kings and fighters of the Rajasthan. as said by Rabindra Nath Tagore once, "The heroic sentiment which is the essence of every song and couplet of a Rajasthani is peculiar emotion of its own of which, however, the whole country may be proud".Wikipedia:Citation needed

Early Rajasthani literature is created by mostly Charans Earlier Rajasthani was known as Charani(or dingal), which was close to Gujarati.

Bibliography

Primary Sources

- Padmanābha, ., & Bhatnagar, V. S. (1991). Kanhadade Prabandha: India's greatest patriotic saga of medieval times : Padmanābha's epic account of Kānhaḍade. New Delhi: Voice of India.

References

- Narrative Traditions of Rajasthan[772]
- Rajasthani[773]

External links

- Centre for Rajasthani Studies[774]
- Ethnologue Report for Rajasthani[775]
- Jain Poets in Rajasthani[776]

Sanskrit literature

Sindhi literature

Sindhi literature

Sindhi literature (Sindhi: سنڌي ادب) writers have contributed extensively in various forms of literature both in poetry and prose. Sindhi language has remained cradle of civilization and confluence of various cultures from the initial times.

Sufi literature and poetry

Modern Asian literature
• Arabic literature
• Bengali literature
• Chinese literature
• Indian literature
• Japanese literature
• Korean literature
• Nepalese literature
• Pakistani literature
• Sindhi literature
• Vietnamese literature
• v • t • e[777]

Sindhi literature

Figure 88: *Sindhi Literature*

Part of a series on
Islamic culture
Architecture

- Azerbaijani
- Indo-Islamic
- Moorish
- Moroccan
- Mughal
- Ottoman
- Pakistani
- Tatar
- Persian
- Somali

Sindhi literature

- Sudano-Sahelian

Art

- Calligraphy
- Miniature
- Oriental rug
- Arab carpet
- Persian carpet
- Turkish carpet

Dress

- Abaya
- Agal
- Boubou
- Burqa
- Chador
- Jellabiya
- Niqāb
- Salwar kameez
- Songkok (Peci)
- Taqiya
- Keffiyeh (Kufiya)
- Thawb
- Jilbab
- Hijab

Holidays

- Ashura
- Arba'een
- al-Ghadeer
- Chaand Raat
- al-Fitr
- al-Adha
- Imamat Day
- New Year
- Isra and Mi'raj
- al-Qadr
- Mawlid
- Ramadan
- Mid-Sha'ban

Literature

- Arabic
- Azerbaijani
- Bengali

- Indonesian
- Javanese
- Kashmiri
- Kurdish
- Malay
- Pashto
- Persian
- Punjabi
- Sindhi
- Somali
- South Asian
- Turkish
- Urdu

Music

- Dastgah
- Ghazal
- Madih nabawi
- Maqam
- Mugam
- Nasheed
- Qawwali
- Sufi

Theatre

- Bangsawan
- Jem
- Karagöz and Hacivat
- Sama
- Ta'zieh

- Islam portal
- v
- t
- e[778]

Indian literature

- Assamese
- Bengali
- Bhojpuri
- English
- Gujarati
- Hindi
- Kannada
- Kashmiri
- Konkani

- Malayalam
- Meitei
- Marathi
- Mizo
- Nepali
- Odia
- Punjabi
- Rajasthani
- Sanskrit
- Sindhi
- Tamil
- Telugu
- Urdu
- v
- t
- e[779]

The earliest reference to Sindhi literature is contained in the writings of Arab historians. It is established that Sindhi was among the earliest languages of the East in which the Quran was translated in the eighth or ninth century AD There is evidence of Sindhi poets reciting their verses before the Muslim Caliphs in Baghdad. It is also recorded that treatises were written in Sindhi on astronomy, medicine and history during the eighth and ninth centuries. Shortly afterwards, Pir Nooruddin, an Ismaili Missionary, wrote Sufistic poetry in Sindhi language. His verses, known as "ginans", can be taken as the specimen of early Sindhi poetry. He came to Sindh during the year 1079 AD. His poetry is an interesting record of the language which was spoken commonly at that time. He was a Sufi and a preacher of Islam. His verses are, therefore, full of mysticism and religion.

After him, Pir Shams Sabzwari Multani, Pir Shahabuddin and Pir Sadardin are recognized as poets of Sindhi language. We even find some verses composed by Baba Farid Ganj Shakar, in Sindhi language. Pir Sadruddin (1290–1409 AD), was a great poet, saint and Sufi of his time. He composed his verses (ginans) in Lari and Katchi dialects of Sindhi. He also composed the "ginans" in the Punjabi, Seraiki, Hindi and Gujarati languages. He modified the old script of Sindhi language, which was commonly used by the lohana catse of Hindus of Sindh who embraced Islam under his teaching and were called by him 'Khuwajas' or 'Khojas'.

During Samma Rule of Sindh(1351 AD-1521 AD) Sindh produced may scholars and poets of high stature.Sammas were original inhabitant of Sindh.This period has been captioned as "Basic period for Sindhi poetry and prose".Mamui Faqirs'(Seven Sages) riddles in versified form are associated with this period.Ishaq Ahingar (Blacksmith) was also a famous poet of this period. The most important person, scholar, Sufi and poet of this period is Qazi Qadan(d-1551 AD).He has composed Doha and Sortha form of poetry and are an important landmark in history of Sindhi literature. Shah Abdul Karim Bulri, Shah lutufullah Qadri, Shah Inayat Rizvi, Makhdoom Nuh of Hala, lakho lutufullah, Mahamati Pirannath and many others are the renowned literary personalities of this period who have enriched Sindhi language with mystic, romantic and epic poetry.

Shah Abdul Latif Bhittai

The age of Shah Abdul Latif(Kalhora period) is most significant in the history of Sindhi literature.It was during this age that Sindhi was standardized.Sindhi classical poetry achieved its full blossom in the poetic work of Shah abdul Latif Bhittai. Dr. Sorely, who compared the poetry of the great poets of all major languages of the world, including Greek, Latin and Arabic, in his book *Musa Pravaganus*, gives first place to Shah Latif for his language and thought. He invented a variant of tanbur, a musical instrument still used when his verses are sung by people who love his literature. He wrote Sassi Punnun, Umar Marvi in his famous book *Shah Jo Risalo*.

Bhittai gave new life, thought and content to the language and literature of Sindh. He traveled to remote corners of Sindh and saw for himself the simple and rustic people of his soil in love with life and its mysteries. He studied the ethos of the people and their deep attachment to the land, the culture, the music, the fine arts and crafts. He described Sindh and its people. Through simple folk tales, Lateef expressed profound ideas about the universal brotherhood of mankind, patriotism, war against injustice and tyranny, and above all the romance of human existence. He was a great musician also and he evolved fifteen new melodies (swaras). The great beauty of his poetry is that his every line or verse is sung till this day with a specific note or melody.

Another notable Sufi poet of Kalhora period is Sultan-al-Aolya Muhammad Zaman whose poetry is published with title *Abyat Sindhi*.

Sachal Sarmast, Saami and Khalifo Nabi Bux Laghari are celebrated poets of the Talpur period in Sindh (1783–1843 AD). Khalifo Nabi Bux is one of the greatest epic poets of Sindh, known for his depictions of patriotic pathos and the art of war. Rohal, Sami, Bedil, Bekas, Misri Shah, Hammal Faqir, Dalpat Sufi, Sabit Ali Shah, Khair Shah, Fateh Faqir and Manthar Faqir Rajar are some of the more noteworthy poets of the pre and early British era.

Early Modern Period

Modern Sindhi literature began with the conquest of Sindh by the British in 1843. The printing press was introduced. Magazines and newspapers brought about a revolution in Sindhi literature. Books were translated from various European languages, especially from English. People were hungry for knowledge and new forms of writing. The accelerated pace of literature production can be judged from the example of Mirza Kalich Beg, who in the last two decades of the nineteenth century and the first two decades of the twentieth wrote more than four hundred books, including poetry, novels, short stories and essays. He also wrote on science, history, economics and politics. Thousands of books were turned out at that time on all forms and facets of literature. Hakim Fateh Mohammad Sewhani, Kauromal Khilnani, Dayaram Gidumal, Parmanand Mewaram, Lalchand Amardinomal, Bheruamal Advani, Dr. Gurbuxani, Jhetmal Parsram, Sayaid Miran Mohammad Shah, Shamsuddin 'Bulbul' and Maulana Din Muhammad Wafai are some of the pioneers of modern literature in Sindhi language.

Modern Sindhi literature

After World War I, the social and economic scene of the world underwent a tremendous change. The aftermath of the war and the socialist revolution of Russia affected the literature of every country. Sindhi literature too was influenced by these trends. Creating new awakening in the minds of the people working in the field of literature, they began to translate the new social consciousness into artistic forms of literature. They were now more objective and less romantic. Progressive thoughts opened the door for new trends in Sindhi literature.

Soon the struggle for freedom from the British also gathered momentum. This gave further momentum to literature. Consciousness about history and cultural heritage of Sindh served as a catalyst for research and intellectual upsurge. Scholars like Allama I. I. Kazi his wife Elsa Kazi, Rasool Bux Palijo, G. M. Syed, Umer Bin Mohammad Daudpota, Pir Ali Muhammad Shah Rashidi, Pir Husamuddin Shah Rashidi, Maulana deen Muhammad Wafai, Chetan Mariwala, Jairamdas Daulatram, Hashoo Kewal Ramani, Bherumal, Mehar Chand Advani, Dr. Abdul Majeed Sindhi (Memon), Badaruddin Dhamraho, Muhammad Ibrahim Joyo, AllahDad Bohyo, Tirath Wasant and many others produced learned treatises on various aspects of history, culture and other social subjects.

Mir Hasan Ali and Mir Abdul Hussain sangi, Khalifo Gul, Fazil Shah, Kasim, Hafiz Hamid, Mohammad Hashim, Mukhlis, Abojho, Surat Singh, Khaki,

Mirza Qalich Baig, Zia and Aziz were the pioneers of poetry in Persian meter.But the modern form and content of Sindhi poetry were given a new impetus by 'Bewas', Hyder Bux Jatoi and Dukhayal. There have been innumerable poets who have composed verses in the same vein.

The novel and short story became the main forms for prose. Hundreds of novel and short stories were translated from the European and modern languages of Pakistan. World War II saw the emergence of novelists and short storywriters like Narain Das Bhambhani, Gobind Malhi, Sushila J. Lalwani, Lokram Dodeja, Sundri Uttamchandani, Popti Hiranandani, Dr. Moti Prakash, Sharma, Kala Sharma, G L Dodeja, Padan Sharma, Ghulam Rabbani Agro, Usman Deplai, Jamal Abro, Shaikh Ayaz, Rasheed Bhatti, Hafeez Akhund, Amar Jaleel, Naseem Kharal, Sirajul Haq Memon, Agha Saleem, Anis Ansari, Tariq Ashraf, Ali Baba, Eshwar Chander, Manak, Asghar Sindhi, Adil Abbasi, Ishtiaq Ansari, Kehar Shaukat, Mushtaq Shoro, Shaukat Shoro, Madad Ali Sindhi, Rasool Memon, Akhlaq Asnari, Reta Shahani, Rehmatullah Manjothi, Badal Jamali, Ishaque Ansari, Jan Khaskheli, Hasan Mansoor, Pervez, Shakoor Nizamani, Tariq Qureshi, Munawwar Siraj, Ismail Mangio, Fayaz Chand Kaleri, Ayaz Ali RindAltaf Malkani and many others. Sindhi dramas have also been flourished during past a few decades. Aziz Kingrani is one of the prominent playwrights who has written scores of Sindhi plays.[780]

For the last several decades, young writers experimented with new forms of prose as well as poetry. Free verses, sonnets and ballads have been written alongside the classical forms of poetry such as Kafi, Vaee, Bait, Geet and Dohira.

A few famous poets of today's Sindh are Makhdoom Muhammad Zaman Talib-ul-Mola, Ustaad Bukhari, Shaikh Ayaz, Darya Khan Rind, Ameen Faheem, and Imdad Hussani. Mubarak Ali Lashari is also a prominent name in literary criticism whose book Kuthyas Kawejan has been published.[781]

In 1952, Noor-ud-din Sarki and Abdul Ghafoor Ansari restructured the literary forum of Sindhi language and called it Sindhi Adabi Sangat. Initially its activities were confined to the city of Karachi. Inspired by the success of its activities in Karachi, interest developed throughout the rest of Sindh, leading to the emergence of branches in other parts of Sindh. It now attracts most of the Sindhi literary figures all over the world; besides branches in Pakistan, there are now chapters overseas as well.

Children's Sindhi Literature

Though Sindhi writers have not given a proper attention towards literature for children yet many writers and institutions have been creating good stuf for the Sindhi children. Gul Phul is one of the most popular children's magazines in Sindhi. Akber Jiskani, a renowned writer has remained its editor for a long time till his death.[782] Laat is another magazine by Mehran Publication which got instant attention of the readers founded by Altaf Malkani and Zulfiqar Ali Bhatti. Sindhi Adabi Board has also taken measures to promote children's literature by publishing books for children.A spy novel, Khofnaak Saazish is also written by Zulfiqar Ali Bhatti which is published by Mehran Publication.[783] Mehran Publication also published another children's magazine Waskaro in Sindhi in 1990.[784] Sindhi Language Authority has also published books for children.

Further reading

- *Sindhi Sahitya Charitre* - Kannaḍa language translation by Sumatheendra Nadig of *History of Sindhi Literature* by L.H. Ajwani. Sahitya Akademi, Rabindra Bhavan, New Delhi 110001. 1981.
- *Indo-Persian Literature in Sindh* in The Rise, Growth And Decline of Indo-Persian Literature by R. M. Chopra, Iran Culture House, New Delhi, 2012.

External links

- The Largest Sindhi Adbi website in Sindhi language[785]
- Sindhi literature magazine of Sindh - Sindhiana[786]
- Shah Jo Risalo - The Selection, translated into English by: Elsa Kazi[787]
- Sindhi Sangat - promoting and preserving the Sindhi heritage, culture and language.[788]

Tamil literature

Tamil literature

Tamil literature (Tamil: தமிழ் இலக்கியம்) refers to the literature in the Tamil language. Tamil literature has a rich and long literary tradition spanning more than two thousand years. The oldest extant works show signs of maturity indicating an even longer period of evolution. Contributors to the Tamil literature are mainly from Tamil people from South India, including the land now comprising Tamil Nadu, Kerala, Sri Lankan Tamils from Sri Lanka, and from Tamil diaspora. The history of Tamil literature follows the history of Tamil Nadu, closely following the social, political and cultural trends of various periods. The early Sangam literature, starting from the period of 2nd century BCE (Akananuru (1, 15, 31, 55, 61, 65, 91, 97, 101, 115, 127, 187, 197, 201, 211, 233, 251, 265, 281, 311, 325, 331, 347, 349, 359, 393, 281, 295), Kurunthogai (11), Natrinai (14, 75) are dated before 300 BCE), contain anthologies of various poets dealing with many aspects of life, including love, war, social values and religion. This was followed by the early epics and moral literature, authored by Hindu, Jain and Buddhist authors, lasting up to the 5th century CE. From the 6th to 12th century CE, the Tamil devotional poems written by Nayanmars (sages of Shaivism) and Azhvars (sages of Vaishnavism), heralded the great Bhakti movement which later engulfed the entire Indian subcontinent. It is during this era that some of the grandest of Tamil literary classics like Kambaramayanam and Periya Puranam were authored and many poets were patronized by the imperial Chola and Pandya empires. The later medieval period saw many assorted minor literary works and also contributions by a few Muslim and European authors.

A revival of Tamil literature took place from the late 19th century when works of religious and philosophical nature were written in a style that made it easier for the common people to enjoy. The modern Tamil literary movement started with Subramania Bharathi, the multifaceted Indian Nationalist poet and author,

Figure 89: *Sage Agastya, Chairman of the first Tamil Sangam, Madurai, Pandiya Kingdom. Statue in Tamil Thai temple, Karaikudi, Tamil Nadu.*

and was quickly followed up by many who began to utilize the power of literature in influencing the masses. With growth of literacy, Tamil prose began to blossom and mature. Short stories and novels began to appear. Modern Tamil literary criticism also evolved. The popularity of Tamil cinema has also interacted with Tamil literature in some mutually enriching ways.

Sangam age

Topics in Sangam literature	
Sangam literature	
Akattiyam	Tholkāppiyam
Patiṉeṇmēlkaṇakku	
Eṭṭuthokai	
Aiṅkurunūru	Akanāṉūru
Puranāṉūru	Kalittokai
Kuruntokai	Natriṇai
Paripāṭal	Patirruppattu

Pattuppattu	
Tirumurukāṟṟuppaṭai	Kuṟiñcippāṭṭu
Malaipaṭukaṭām	Maturaikkāñci
Mullaippāṭṭu	Neṭunalvāṭai
Paṭṭiṉappālai	Perumpāṇāṟṟuppaṭai
Poruṉarāṟṟuppaṭai	Ciṟupāṇāṟṟuppaṭai
Patiṉeṇkīḻkaṇakku	
Nālaṭiyār	Nāṉmaṇikkaṭikai
Iṉṉā Nāṟpatu	Iṉiyavai Nāṟpatu
Kār Nāṟpatu	Kaḷavaḻi Nāṟpatu
Aintiṇai Aimpatu	Tiṇaimoḻi Aimpatu
Aintinai Eḻupatu	Tiṇaimalai Nūṟṟu Aimpatu
Tirukkuṟaḷ	Tirikaṭukam
Ācārakkōvai	Paḻamoḻi Nāṉūṟu
Ciṟupañcamūlam	Mutumoḻikkāñci
Elāti	Kainnilai
Related topics	
Sangam	Sangam landscape
Tamil history from Sangam literature	Ancient Tamil music

[789]

Sangam literature comprises some of the oldest extant Tamil literature, and deals with love, traditions, war, governance, trade and bereavement. Unfortunately much of the Tamil literature belonging to the Sangam period has been lost.[790] The literature currently available from this period is perhaps just a fraction of the wealth of material produced during this golden age of Tamil civilization. The available literature from this period has been broadly divided in antiquity into three categories based roughly on chronology. These are: the Major Eighteen Anthology Series comprising the Eight Anthologies and the Ten Idylls and the Five Great Epics. *Tolkaappiyam*, a commentary on grammar, phonetics, rhetoric and poetics is dated from this period.

Figure 90: *Ilango Adigal (c. 100 CE) wrote Silappathikaaram of Five great epics.*

Figure 91: *Thiruvalluvar wrote Thirukkural (c. 300s BCE), taught in schools today.*

Tamil literature

Tamil	[English Translation][790]
குறிஞ்சி – தலைவன் கூற்று	**Red earth and pouring rain**
யாயும் ஞாயும் யாரா	What could my mother be to yours?
கியரோ	What kin is my father to yours anyway?
எந்தையும் நுந்தையும்	And how
எம்முறைக் கேளிர்	Did you and I meet ever?
யானும் நீயும் எவ்வழி	But in love our hearts have mingled
யறிதும்	like red earth and pouring rain.
செம்புலப் பெயனீர் போல	*(Kuruntokai – 40).* A poem from the *Eight Anthologies*.
அன்புடை நெஞ்சம்	
தாங்கலந் தனவே.	
-செம்புலப் பெயனீரார்.	

Tamil legends hold that these were composed in three successive poetic assemblies *(Sangam)* that were held in ancient times on a now vanished continent far to the south of India.[791] A significant amount of literature could have preceded *Tolkappiyam* as grammar books are usually written after the existence of literature over long periods. Tamil tradition holds the earliest *Sangam* poetry to be over twelve millennia old. Modern linguistic scholarship places the poems between the 1st century BC and the 3rd century AD.[792]

Sangam age is considered by the Tamil people as the golden era of Tamil language. This was the period when the Tamil country was ruled by the three 'crowned kings' the Cheras, Pandyas and the Cholas. The land was at peace with no major external threats. Asoka's conquests did not impact on the Tamil land and the people were able to indulge in literary pursuits. The poets had a much more casual relationship with their rulers than can be imagined in later times. They could chide them when they are perceived to wander from the straight and narrow. The greatness of the Sangam age poetry may be ascribed not so much to its antiquity, but due to the fact that their ancestors were indulging in literary pursuits and logical classification of the habitats and society in a systematic manner with little to draw from precedents domestically or elsewhere. The fact that these classifications were documented at a very early date in the grammatical treatise *Tolkappiyam*, demonstrates the organized manner in which the Tamil language has evolved. *Tolkappiyam* is not merely a textbook on Tamil grammar giving the inflection and syntax of words and sentences but also includes classification of habitats, animals, plants and human beings. The discussion on human emotions and interactions is particularly significant. Tolkappiyam divided into three chapters: orthography, etymology and subject matter *(Porul)*. While the first two chapters of Tolkappiyam help codify the language, the last part, *Porul* refers to the people and their behavior. The grammar helps to convey the literary message on human behavior and conduct, and uniquely merges the language with its people.

The literature was classified into the broad categories of 'subjective' *(akam)* and 'objective' *(puram)* topics to enable the poetic minds to discuss any topic under the sun, from grammar to love, within the framework of well prescribed, socially accepted conventions. Subjective topics refer to the personal or human aspect of emotions that cannot be verbalized adequately or explained fully. It can only be experienced by the individuals and includes love and sexual relationship.

Recognizing that human activities cannot take place in vacuum and are constantly influenced by environmental factors, human experiences, in general, and subjective topics in particular, are assigned to specific habitats. Accordingly, land was classified into five genres (*thinai*): *kurinji* (mountainous regions), *mullai* (forests), *marutham* (agricultural lands), *neithal* (seashore), *paalai* (wasteland). The images associated with these landscapes – birds, beasts, flowers, gods, music, people, weather, seasons – were used to subtly convey a mood, associated with an aspect of life. *Kuruntokai*, a collection of poems belonging to the *Ettuthokai* anthology demonstrates an early treatment of the Sangam landscape. Such treatments are found to be much refined in the later works of *Akananuru* and *Paripaatal*. *Paripaatal* takes its name from the musical *Paripaatal meter* utilised in these poems. This is the first instance of a work set to music. *Akaval* and *kalippa* were the other popular meters used by poets during the Sangam age.

Post-Sangam period

Didactic age

The three centuries after the Sangam age witnessed an increase in the usage of Sanskrit words. This was due to the invasion of Aryans from the North. The invaders replaced number of words and concepts relating to ethics, philosophy and religion of Tamil. As a result, Tamil has around 30% of Sanskrit Parasite in today's use. However, today, the Indo-Aryan Migration theory has been debunked as baseless and without concrete evidence.[793,794] Around 300 CE, the Tamil land was under the influence of a group of people known as the Kalabhras. The Kalabhras were Buddhist and a number of Buddhist authors flourished during this period. Jainism and Buddhism saw rapid growth. These authors, perhaps reflecting the austere nature of their faiths, created works mainly on morality and ethics. A number of Jain and Buddhist poets contributed to the creation of these didactic works as well as grammar and lexicography. The collection the minor eighteen anthology was of this period.

> எப்பொருள் யார்யார்வாய்க் கேட்பினும் அப்பொருள்
> மெய்ப்பொருள் காண்ப தறிவு.
> "The mark of wisdom is to discern the truth

> From whatever source it is heard."
> – (Tirukkural – 423)

The best known of these works on ethics is the *Tirukkural* by Thiruvalluvar. The book is a comprehensive manual of ethics, polity and love, containing 1,330 distichs or *kural* divided into chapters of ten distichs each: the first thirty-eight on ethics, the next seventy on polity and the remainder on love.[795]

Other famous works of this period are *Kaḷavaḻi Nāṟpatu*, *Nalatiyar*, *Inna Narpathu* and *Iniyavai Narpathu*. The Jain texts *Nalatiyar* and *Pazhamozhi Nanuru* each consist of four hundred poems, each of which cites a proverb and then illustrates it with a story.

Hindu devotional period

Tirumurai		
The twelve volumes of Tamil Śaiva hymns of the sixty-three Nayanars		
Parts	Name	Author
1,2,3	Tirukadaikkappu	Sambandar
4,5,6	Tevaram	Tirunavukkarasar
7	Tirupaatu	Sundarar
8	Tiruvacakam & Tirukkovaiyar	Manikkavacakar
9	Tiruvisaippa & Tiruppallaandu	Various
10	Tirumandhiram	Tirumular
11	Various	
12	Periya Puranam	Sekkizhar
Paadal Petra Sthalam		
Paadal Petra Sthalam		
Raja Raja Chola I		
Nambiyandar Nambi		

The fall of the Kalabhras around 500 CE saw a reaction from the thus far suppressed Hindus. The Kalabhras were replaced by the Pandyas in the south and by the Pallavas in the north. Even with the exit of the Kalabhras, the Jain and Buddhist influence still remained in Tamil Nadu. The early Pandya and the

Pallava kings were followers of these faiths. The Hindu reaction to this apparent decline of their religion was growing and reached its peak during the later part of the 7th century. There was a widespread Hindu revival during which a huge body of Saiva and Vaishnava literature was created. Many Saiva Nayanmars and Vaishnava Alvars provided a great stimulus to the growth of popular devotional literature. Karaikkal Ammaiyar who lived in the 6th century CE was the earliest of these Nayanmars. The celebrated Saiva hymnists Sundaramoorthy, Thirugnana Sambanthar and Thirunavukkarasar (also known as *Appar*) were of this period. Of Appar's verses 3066 have survived. Sambandar sang 4,169 verses. Together these form the first six books of the Saiva canon, collected by Nambi Andar Nambi in the 10th century. Sundarar wrote *Tiruttondartokai* which gives the list of sixty-two Nayanmars. This was later elaborated by Sekkilar in his *Periyapuranam*(4,272 verses). Manikkavasagar, who lived around the 8th century CE was a minister in the Pandya court. His *Tiruvasakam* consisting of over 600 verses is noted for its passionate devotion.. These Saivite Hymns collectively called Thirumurai (திருமுறை) is described as SIXTH VEDA next to Bhagavath Geetha in Hindu Tradition.

Along with the Saiva Nayanmars, Vaishnava Alvars were also producing devotional hymns and their songs were collected later into the Four Thousand Sacred Hymns (*Naalayira Divyap Prabhandham*). The three earliest Alvars were Poygai, Pudam and Pey. Each of these wrote one hundred *Venpas*. Tirumalisai Alwar who was a contemporary of the Pallava Mahendravarman I wrote such works as *Naanmugantiruvadiandadi*. Tirumangai Alvar who lived in the 8th century CE was a more prolific writer and his works constitute about a third of the Diyaprabhandam. Periyalvar and his adopted daughter Andal contributed nearly 650 hymns to the Vaishnava canon. Andal symbolised purity and love for the God and wrote her hymns addressing Vishnu as a lover. The hymn of Andal which starts with *Vaaranam Aayiram* (One Thousand Elephants) tells of her dream wedding to Vishnu and is sung even today at Tamil Vaishnava weddings. Nammalvar, who lived in the 9th century, wrote *Tiruvaimoli*. It comprises 1,101 stanzas and is held in great esteem for its elucidation of the Upanishads. This corpus was collected by Nathamuni, around 950 CE and formed the classical and vernacular basis for Sri Vaishnavism. These Hymns 'Naalayira Divya-p-Prabhandham' is respected at par with Vedas by Sri Vaishnavites in sanctity and holiness and hence referred to as 'Dravida Vedam' (திராவிட வேதம்).

Figure 92: *Avvaiyaar (c.1100 CE) wrote Aathichoodi, taught in schools today.*

Narrative epics

Cilappatikaram is one of the outstanding works of general literature of this period. The authorship and exact date of the classic *Cilappatikaram* are not definitely known. Ilango Adigal, who is credited with this work was reputed to be the brother of the Sangam age Chera king Senguttuvan. However we have no information of such a brother in the numerous poems sung on the Chera king. The *Cilappatikaram* is unique in its vivid portrayal of the ancient Tamil land. This is unknown in other works of this period. *Cilappatikaram* and its companion epic *Manimekalai* are Jain in philosophy. *Manimekalai* was written by Sattanar who was a contemporary of Ilango Adigal. Manimekalai contains a long exposition of fallacies of logic which is considered to be based on the 5th century Sanskrit work *Nyayapravesa* by Dinnag.[796] Kongu Velir, a Jain author wrote *Perunkathai* based on the Sanskrit *Brihat-katha*. *Valayapathi* and *Kundalakesi* are the names of two other narrative poems of this period written by a Jain and a Buddhist author respectively. These works have been lost and only a few poems of *Valayapathi* have been found so far.

Medieval literature

The medieval period was the period of the Imperial Cholas when the entire south India was under a single administration. The period between the 11th

Figure 93: *Kambar (c.1100 CE) wrote the Tamil 'Raamaayanam'.*

and the 13th centuries, during which the Chola power was at its peak, there were relatively few foreign incursions and the life for the Tamil people was one of peace and prosperity. It also provided the opportunity for the people to interact with cultures beyond their own, as the Cholas ruled over most of the South India, Sri Lanka and traded with the kingdoms in southeast Asia. The Cholas built numerous temples, mainly for their favourite god Siva, and these were celebrated in numerous hymns. The *Prabhanda* became the dominant form of poetry. The religious canons of Saiva and Vaishnava sects were beginning to be systematically collected and categorised. Nambi Andar Nambi, who was a contemporary of Rajaraja Chola I, collected and arranged the books on Saivism into eleven books called *Tirumurais*. The hagiology of Saivism was standardised in *Periyapuranam* (also known as *Tiruttondar Puranam*) by Sekkilar, who lived during the reign of Kulothunga Chola II (1133–1150 CE). Religious books on the Vaishnava sect were mostly composed in Sanskrit during this period. The great Vaishnava leader Ramanuja lived during the reigns of Athirajendra Chola and Kulothunga Chola I, and had to face religious persecution from the Cholas who belonged to the Saiva sect. One of the best known Tamil works of this period is the *Ramavatharam* by Kamban who flourished during the reign of Kulottunga III. *Ramavatharam* is the greatest epic in Tamil Literature, and although the author states that he followed Valmiki, his work is not a mere translation or even an adaptation of the Sanskrit epic. Kamban imports into his narration the colour and landscape of his own time. A contemporary of Kamban was the famous poet Auvaiyar who found great happiness in writing for young children. Her works, *Athichoodi* and *Konraiventhan* are even now generally read and taught in schools in Tamil Nadu. Her two other works, *Mooturai* and *Nalvali* were written for slightly older children. All the four works are didactic in character. They explain the basic wisdom that should govern mundane life.

Of the books on the Buddhist and the Jain faiths, the most noteworthy is the *Jivaka-chintamani* by the Jain ascetic Thirutakkadevar composed in the 10th century. *Viruttam* style of poetry was used for the first time for the verses in this book. The five Tamil epics *Jivaka-chintamani, Cilappatikaram, Manimekalai, Kundalakesi* and *Valayapathi* are collectively known as The Five Great Epics of Tamil Literature. There were a number of books written on Tamil grammar. *Yapperungalam* and *Yapperungalakkarigai* were two works on prosody by the Jain ascetic Amirtasagara. Buddamitra wrote *Virasoliyam*, another work on Tamil grammar, during the reign of Virarajendra Chola. *Virasoliyam* attempts to find synthesis between Sanskrit and Tamil grammar. Other grammatical works of this period are *Nannul* by Pavanandi, *Vaccanandi Malai* by Neminatha, and the annotations on the puram theme, *Purapporul Venpamalai* by Aiyanaridanar.

There were biographical and political works such as Jayamkondar's Kalingattuparani, a semi-historical account on the two invasion of Kalinga by Kulothunga Chola I. Jayamkondar was a poet-laureate in the Chola court and his work is a fine example of the balance between fact and fiction the poets had to tread. Ottakuttan, a close contemporary of Kambar, wrote three *Ulas* on Vikrama Chola, Kulothunga Chola II and Rajaraja Chola II

Tamil Muslim literature is eight centuries old. The earliest literary works of this coterie could be traced to the 14th century in the form of *Palsanthmalai*, a small work of eight stanzas. In 1572, Seyku Issaku, better known as Vanna Parimala Pulavar, published *Aayira Masala Venru Vazhankum Adisaya Puranam* detailing the Islamic principles and beliefs in a FAQ format. In 1592, Aali Pulavar wrote the *Mikurasu Malai*.

Vijayanagar and Nayak period

The period from 1300 CE to 1650 was a period of constant change in the political situation of Tamil Nadu. The Tamil country was invaded by the armies of the Delhi Sultanate and defeated the Pandya kingdom. The collapse of the Delhi Sultanate triggered the rise of the Bahmani Sultans in the Deccan. Vijayanagar empire rose from the ashes of the kingdoms of Hoysalas and Chalukyas and eventually conquered the entire south India. The Vijayanagar kings appointed regional governors to rule various territories of their kingdom and Tamil Nadu was ruled by the Madurai Nayaks, Thanjavur Nayaks and Gingee Nayaks. This period saw a large output of philosophical works, commentaries, epics and devotional poems. A number of monasteries (*Mathas*) were established by the various Hindu sects and these began to play a prominent role in educating the people. Numerous authors were of either the Saiva or the Vaishnava sects. The Vijayanagar kings and their Nayak governors were ardent Hindus and they patronised these *mathas*. Although the kings and the governors of the Vijayanagar empire spoke Kannada and Telugu they encouraged the growth of Tamil literature as we find no slowing down in the literary output during this period.

There was a large output of works of philosophical and religious in nature, such as the *Sivananabodam* by Meykandar. At the end of the 14th century Svarupananda Desikar wrote two anthologies on the philosophy os *Advaita*, the *Sivaprakasapperundirattu*. Arunagirinathar who lived in Tiruvannamalai in the 14th century wrote *Tiruppugal*. Around 1360 verses of unique lilt and set to unique metres these poems are on the god Muruga. Madai Tiruvengadunathar, an official in the court of the Madurai Nayak, wrote *Meynanavilakkam* on the Advaita Vedanta. Siva prakasar, in the early 17th century wrote a number of works on the Saiva philosophy. Notable among these is the *Nanneri* which deals with moral instructions. A considerable par to the religious and philosophical literature of the age took the form of *Puranas* or narrative epics. A number of these were written on the various deities of the temples in Tamil Nadu and are known as Sthala Puranas, based on legend and folklore. One of the most important of the epics was the Mahabharatam by Villipputturar. He translated Vyasa's epic into Tamil and named it *Villibharatam*. *Kanthapuranam* on the god Murugan was written by Kacchiappa Sivachariyar who lived in the 15th century. This work was based broadly on the Sanskrit *Skandapurana*. Varatungarama Pandya, a Pandya king of the period was a littérateur of merit and wrote *Paditrruppattanthathi*. He also translated into Tamil the erotic book known as *Kokkoha* from Sanskrit.

This period also an age of many commentaries of ancient Tamil works. Adiyarkunallar wrote an annotation on Cilappatikaram. Senavaraiyar wrote a commentary on the Tolkappiyam. Then came the famous Parimelalagar whose commentary on the Tirukkural is still considered one of the best available. Other famous annotators such as Perasiriyar and Naccinarikiniyar wrote commentaries on the various work of Sangam literature. The first Tamil dictionary was attempted by Mandalapurusha who compiled the lexicon *Nigandu Cudamani*. Thayumanavar, who lived in the early 18th century, is famous for a number of short poems of philosophical nature.

Tamil literature

Figure 94: *Subramanya Bharathi (1882-1921)*
Tamil writer, poet, Indian freedom fighter.

The 17th century altruist Syed Khader, known colloquially as Seethakaathi, was a great patron of all Tamil poets. He commissioned Umaruppulavar to pen the first biography of Nabi. The collection of poems was called *Seerapuranam*.[797] The 17th century also saw for the first time literary works by Christian authors. Costanzo Giuseppe Beschi (1680-1746), better known as Veeramamunivar, compiled the first dictionary in Tamil. His *Chathurakarathi* was the first to list the Tamil words in alphabetical order. Veeramamunivar is also remembered for his Christian theological epic *Thembavani* on the life and teaching of Jesus Christ.

Modern era

During the 18th and the 19th century Tamil Nadu witnessed some of the most profound changes in the political scene. The traditional Tamil ruling clans were superseded by European colonists and their sympathisers. The Tamil society underwent a deep cultural shock with the imposition of western cultural influences. The Hindu religious establishments attempted to stem the tide of change and to safeguard the Tamil cultural values. Notable among these were the Saiva monasteries at Tiruvavaduthurai, Dharmapuram, Thiruppananthal and Kundrakudi. Meenakshi Sundaram Pillai(1815-1876) was a Tamil scholar who

Figure 95: *Thani Tamil Iyakkam's Bharathidasan, freedom fighter, Tamil writer, poet.*

taught Tamil at one of these monasteries. He wrote more than eighty books consisting of over 200,000 poems.Wikipedia:Citation needed He is more famous however for encouraging U.V.Swaminatha Iyer to go search for Tamil books that have been lost for centuries. Gopalakrishna Bharathi lived during the early 19th century. He wrote numerous poems and lyrics set to tune in Carnatic music. His most famous work is the *Nandan Charitam* on the life of Nandanar who having been born in a sociologically lower caste, faces and overcomes the social obstacles in achieving his dream of visiting the Chidambaram temple. This work is a revolutionary social commentary considering the period in which it was written, although Gopalakrishna Bharati expanded on the story in *Periyapuranam*. Ramalinga Adigal (Vallalar) (1823–1874) wrote the devotional poem *Tiruvarutpa* is considered to be a work of great beauty and simplicity. Maraimalai Adigal (1876–1950) advocated for the purity of Tamil and wanted to clean it of words with Sanskrit influences. One of the great Tamil poets of this period was Subramanya Bharathi. His works are stimulating in their progressive themes like freedom and feminism. Bharathy introduced a new poetic style into the somewhat rigid style of Tamil poetry writing, which had followed the rules set down in the *Tolkaappiyam*. His *puthukkavithai* (Lit.:new poetry) broke the rules and gave poets the freedom to express themselves. He also wrote Tamil prose in the form of commentaries, editorials, short stories and novels. Some of these were published in the Tamil daily *Swadesamitran* and in his Tamil weekly *India*. Inspired by Bharathi, many poets resorted to poetry as a means of reform. Bharathidasan was one such poet. U.V.Swaminatha Iyer, was instrumental in the revival of interest in the Sangam age literature in Tamil Nadu. He travelled all over the Tamil country, collecting, deciphering and publishing ancient books such as *Cilappatikaram*, *Kuruntokai*, etc. He published over 90 books and wrote *En caritham*, an autobiography.

Tamil novel

The novel as a genre of literature arrived in Tamil in the third quarter of the 19th century, more than a century after it became popular with English writers. Its emergence was perhaps facilitated by the growing population of Tamils with a western education and exposure to popular English fiction. Mayavaram Vedanayagam Pillai wrote the first Tamil novel *Prathapa Mudaliar Charithram* in 1879. This was a romance with an assortment of fables, folk tales and even Greek and Roman stories, written with the entertainment of the reader as the principal motive. It was followed by *Kamalambal Charitram* by B. R. Rajam Iyer in 1893 and *Padmavathi Charitram* by A. Madhaviah in 1898. These two portray the life of Brahmins in 19th century rural Tamil Nadu, capturing their customs and habits, beliefs and rituals. Although it was primarily a powerful narration of the common man's life in a realistic style spiced with natural humour, Rajam Iyer's novel has a spiritual and philosophical undertone. Madhaviah tells the story in a more realistic way with a searching criticism of the upper caste society, particularly the sexual exploitation of girls by older men. **D.Jayakanthan** has enriched the high traditions of literary traditions of Tamil language and contributed towards the shaping of Indian literature. His literature presents a deep and sensitive understanding of complex human nature and is an authentic and vivid index of Indian reality. One famous novel of his is **Sila Nerangalil Sila Manithargal**. Since the 1990s the post modernist writers emerged as a major figures, including Jeyamohan, S.Ramakrishnan, Charu Nivedita. The critically acclaimed works include Vishnupuram by Jeymohan, Ubapandavam by S.Ramakrishnan, Zero degree by Charu Niveditha, Konangi (Paazhi), yumaa vasuki – Ratha vurvu (Blood Relation), Lakshmi Manivannan (appavin Thottathil neer payum idangal ellam ...), nakulan – ninivu-p-padhai., and Konangi, who mixes classical Tamil inflections with experimental sound poets.

There are other less appreciated works involving those translated from other languages, which are often unrecognized by Tamil pundits. The works include "Urumaatram" (translation of Franz Kafka's *The Metamorphosis*), *Siluvayil Thongum Saathaan* (translation of "Devil on the Cross" by Ngũgĩ wa

Thiong'o), *Thoongum azhagigalin Illam* (translation of "House of Sleeping Beauties" by Yasunari Kawabata). Writers like Amarantha, Latha Ramakrishnan are responsible for these works.wikipedia:Citation needed

Periodicals

The increasing demand of the literate public caused a number of journals and periodicals to be published and these in turn provided a platform for authors to publish their work. *Rajavritti Bodhini* and *Dina Varthamani* in 1855 and Salem Pagadala Narasimhalu Naidu's fortnightlies, Salem *Desabhimini* in 1878 and *Coimbatore Kalanidhi* in 1880, were the earliest Tamil journals. In 1882, G. Subramaniya Iyer started the newspaper *Swadesamitran*. It became the first Tamil daily in 1889. This was the start of many journals to follow and many novelists began to serialise their stories in these journal. The humour magazine *Ananda Vikatan* started by S.S. Vasan in 1929 was to help create some of the greatest Tamil novelists. Kalki Krishnamurthy (1899–1954) serialised his short stories and novels in *Ananda Vikatan* and eventually started his own weekly *Kalki* for which he wrote the enduringly popular novels *Parthiban Kanavu*, *Sivagamiyin Sabadham* and *Ponniyin Selvan*. Pudhumaipithan (1906–1948) was a great writer of short stories and provided the inspiration for a number of authors who followed him. The 'new poetry or *pudukkavithai* pioneered by Bharathi in his prose-poetry was further developed by the literary periodicals *manikkodi* and *ezhuttu* (edited by Si Su Chellappa). Poets such as Mu Metha contributed to these periodicals. Tamil Muslim poets like Kavikko Abdul Rahman, Pavalar Inqulab, Manushyaputhiran and Rajathi Salma too have made significant contributions to social reforms. The pioneering fortnightly journal *Samarasam* was established in 1981 to highlight and cater to the ethnic Tamil Muslim community's issues. Another remarkable work was done in Tamil novel field by Mu.Varatharasanar.[Agal vilakku] [Karithundu]. And last but not least Akilan the unique Tamil novelist, short story writer and a social activist is famous for his works like 'Chithirapavai' 'Vengayinmaindan' 'Pavaivilaku'.

Tamil journalism

The first Tamil periodical was published by the Christian Religious Tract Society in 1831 – *The Tamil Magazine*.

The increasing demand of the literate public caused a number of journals and periodicals to be published and these in turn provided a platform for authors to publish their work. Rajavritti Bodhini and Dina Varthamani in 1855 and Salem Pagadala Narasimhalu Naidu's fortnightlies, Salem Desabhimini in 1878 and Coimbatore Kalanidhi in 1880, were the earliest Tamil journals.

The first regular newspaper in Tamil was Swadesamitran in 1882, started by G.Subramaniya Iyer, editor and sponsor of The Hindu and founding member of the Indian National Congress. He created a whole new Tamil political vocabulary. He) was conscious that those with a knowledge of English are a small number and those with a knowledge of Indian languages the vast majority. He felt that unless our people were told about the objectives of British rule and its merits and defects in the Indian languages, our political knowledge would never develop. When Subramania Aiyer quit The Hindu 1898, he made the Swadesamitran his full-time business. In 1899, the first Tamil daily. It was to enjoy this status for 17 years.

Subramania Aiyer's "pugnacious style, never qualifying words to soften the sharp tenor of a sentence," his use of words "dipped in a paste of extra pungent green chillies," made the Swadesamitran sought by Tamils wherever they lived in the world. And the daily became even more popular when Subramania Bharati joined it in 1904. The next year, when Lala Lajpat Rai was arrested and agitation followed in the Punjab, Subramania Aiyer's attitude to the British changed and he became a trenchant political critic of the Raj. His whole political mantra can be summed up in these words: 'Peaceful but tireless and unceasing effort.' Let us sweat ourselves into Swaraj, he would seem to say." Swadesamitran is credited for coining new Tamil words to deal with science, politics and administration. It had the most comprehensive budget of news among all the regional language papers of that time.

In 1917, *Desabhaktan*, another Tamil daily began with T.V. Kalyansundara Menon as editor. He was succeeded by V.V.S. Iyer, a colleague of the Savarkar brothers. These two editors were scholars with a natural, highly readable but polished style of writing.

The freedom movement and the advent of Gandhi also impacted Tamil journalism. Navasakthi, a Tamil periodical edited by Tamil scholar and freedom fighter V. Kalyanasundaram. C.Rajagopalachari began Vimochanam, a Tamil journal devoted to propagating prohibition at the Gandhi Ashram in Tiruchengode in Salem district.

In 1926, P. Varadarajulu Naidu, who was conducting a Tamil news-cum-views weekly 'Tamil Nadu' started a daily with the same name. Its forceful and colloquial style gained it a wide readership but after the paper failed to take sides with the 1930 Civil Disobedience Movement, the Congress Party decided to bring out a new Tamil daily – India, edited by renowned poet Subramania Bharati. India showed great promise but could not establish itself financially, and folded up soon after Bharati was exiled to Pondicherry. All these papers were published from Madras.

In 1933, the first Tamil tabloid – the 8 page Jayabharati began at a price of $1/4$ anna. It closed in 1940 as the price could not sustain even its postage.

In September 1934, S. Sadanand (who was running The Free Press Journal) started the Tamil daily Dinamani with T.S. Chockalingam as editor. It was priced at 6 pies, contained bright features and was fearlessly critical. It was highly successful and its circulation eclipsed the total circulation of all other Tamil dailies. Soon 'India' was incorporated into Dinamani. Dinamani made a studied and conscious effort to make the contents of a newspaper intelligible even to the newly literate. In 1935, Viduthalai was begun, but it was more of a views-paper than a newspaper. The Non-Brahman Movement also gave an impetus to Tamil journalism. Newspapers like the *Bharat Devi* were strong supporters of this movement.

Many magazines began in Tamil Nadu during the 1920s and '30s. The humour magazine Ananda Vikatan started by S.S. Vasan in 1929 was to help create some of the greatest Tamil novelists. It is still running successfully after 80 years and the Vikatan group today also publishes Chutti Vikatan, Junior Vikatan, Motor Vikatan and other special interest magazines. R. Krishnamurthy serialised his short stories and novels in Ananda Vikatan and eventually started his own weekly Kalki. The name Kalki denotes the impending tenth Avatar of Lord Vishnu in the Hindu religion, who it is said, will bring to an end the Kali Yuga and reinstate Dharma or righteousness among the worldly beings. He used the name because he wanted to bring about liberation of India.

In 1942, Dina Thanthi (*Daily Telegraph*) was started in Madurai with simultaneous editions in Madras, Salem and Tiruchirappalli. It was founded by S.P. Adithanar, a lawyer trained in Britain. He modeled Thanthi on the style of an English tabloid- The Daily Mirror. He aimed to bring out a newspaper that ordinary people would read, and which would encourage a reading habit even among the newly literate. In the past, the daily newspaper which was printed in Madras reached the southern Tamil region after at least one day. Thanthi used the public bus system to distribute the paper throughout the south Tamil region and capitalized on the hunger for war news that arose after Singapore fell to the Japanese. Due to financial constraints, its Salem and Tiruchirappalli editions had to be closed down for a while. Thanthi emphasized local news, especially crime and the courts. It used photographs extensively and brought banner headlines to Tamil journalism. It could fit one story on an entire broadsheet page, mainly filled with large easy-to-read headlines. One of its biggest scoops was the murder of the editor of a scandalous film magazine by two actors. Thanthi covered the trial in Madras in detail, and its reporters phoned the daily account to the printing centre in Madurai. Thanthi was the first Tamil paper to understand the people's fascination with crime and film stars. The paper was popular and it was said that Tamils learned to read in order to read the newspaper.

Dina Thanthi became one of the largest Tamil language dailies by circulation within a few years; it has been a leading Tamil daily since the 1960s. It has today 14 editions. It is the highest circulated Tamil daily in Bangalore and Pondicherry. It issues a book called 10th, +2 Vina Vidai Book, on every Wednesday during the second part of the year. The model question papers of all the subjects of Standard 10 and 12 are provided with answers along with the question papers of board exams that are conducted previous year.

Popular fiction

Crime and detective fiction has enjoyed wide popularity in Tamil Nadu since the 1930s. Popular authors in the years before independence included Kurumbur Kuppusami and Vaduvur Duraisami Iyengar. In the 1950s and '60s, Tamilvanan's detective hero Shankarlal carried readers to a variety of foreign locales, while using a pure Tamil with very few Hindi or English loan words. These writers are often extremely prolific, with hundreds or even thousands of short novels to their credit, and one or more short novel published in a monthly periodical. Indra Soundar Rajan, another popular modern author, writes supernatural crime thrillers usually based around Hindu mythology.

In the 1940s and 1950s Kalki Krishnamurthy was notable for his historical and social fiction.

In the 1950s and 60s, Chandilyan wrote a number of very popular historical romance novels set in medieval India or on medieval trade routes with Malaysia, Indonesia and Europe.

From the 1950s, spanning six decades, Jayakanthan authored around 40 novels, 200 short stories, apart from two autobiographies. Outside literature, he made two films. In addition, four of his other novels were adapted into films by others. His works revolve around the lives of underclass people like rickshaw-pullers, prostitutes and rag-pickers.

Arunaa Nandhini is one of recent Tamil novelists who has entered the hearts of many Tamil readers, and her story covers family subject, romance, reality, with some humor added for the readers to enjoy their leisure.

Modern romance novels are represented by the current bestselling author in the Tamil language, Ramanichandran.

Though sales of Tamil pulp fiction have declined since the hey-day of the mid-1990s, and many writers have turned to the more lucrative television serial market, there remains a thriving scene.

New media

The rise of the Internet has triggered a dramatic growth in the number of Tamil blogs and specialist portals catering to political and social issues.[798] Tamil literature is even available in the form of e-books.

References

<templatestyles src="Refbegin/styles.css" />

- Hart, George L. (1975). *The poems of ancient Tamil : their milieu and their Sanskrit counterparts*. Berkeley: University of California Press. ISBN 0-520-02672-1.<templatestyles src="Module:Citation/CS1/styles.css"></templatestyles>
- Majumdar, R.C. (1987). *Ancient India*. India: Motilal Banarsidass Publications. ISBN 81-208-0436-8.<templatestyles src="Module:Citation/CS1/styles.css"></templatestyles>
- Nilakanta Sastri, K.A. (2000). *A History of South India*. New Delhi: Oxford University Press. ISBN 0-19-560686-8.<templatestyles src="Module:Citation/CS1/styles.css"></templatestyles>
- Nilakanta Sastri, K.A.; Srinivasachari (2000). *Advanced History of India*. New Delhi: Allied Publishers Ltd.<templatestyles src="Module:Citation/CS1/styles.css"></templatestyles>
- Zvelebil, Kamil V. (1973). *The smile of Murugan: on Tamil literature of South India*. Leiden: Brill. ISBN 90-04-03591-5.<templatestyles src="Module:Citation/CS1/styles.css"></templatestyles>
- "The beginning of Tamil journalism"[799]. *S. Muthiah*, The Hindu, *Jul 23, 2003*. Retrieved 2006-05-23.<templatestyles src="Module:Citation/CS1/styles.css"></templatestyles>
- "Portrait of a novelist as a social reformer"[800]. *S. Viswanathan*, Frontline, *Volume 22 – Issue 17, Aug 13–26, 2005*. Retrieved 2006-05-23.<templatestyles src="Module:Citation/CS1/styles.css"></templatestyles>

External links

 Wikimedia Commons has media related to *Tamil literature*.

- தமிழ் இலக்கியம் – A repository of Tamil Literature[801]
- Largest Collections of Tamil Literature Articles[802]
- Tamil Literature Collection – தமிழ் மொழி ஆர்வலர்களுக்காக[803]

Telugu literature

Telugu literature

Part of a series on the
Culture of Andhra Pradesh

History
• History of Andhra Pradesh • Economy of Andhra Pradesh • Culture of Andhra Pradesh • Politics of Andhra Pradesh
People and culture
• Telugu people • Telugu language • Telugu cuisine • Music of Andhra Pradesh • Shadow puppets of Andhra Pradesh • Telugu literature • Tourism in Andhra Pradesh • Telugu cinema •   Andhra Pradesh portal

- v
- t
- e[804]

Part of a series on the
Telangana Culture

Telangana portal

- v
- t
- e[805]

Telugu literature or **Telugu Pandityam** (Telugu: తెలుగు పాండిత్యము) is the body of works written in the Telugu language. It consists of poems, novels, short stories, dramas and puranas. Telugu literature can be traced back to the early 10th century period (*Prabandha Ratnavali*(1918) talk about the existence of Jain Telugu literature during 850-1000AD) followed by 11th century period when Mahabharata was first translated to Telugu from Sanskrit by Nannaya. It flourished under the rule of the Vijayanagara Empire, where Telugu was one of the empire's official languages.

Telugu split from Proto-Dravidian between 1500-1000 BC. Telugu became a distinct language by the time any literary activity began to appear in the Tamil land, along with Parji, Kolami, Nayaki and Gadaba languages.[806]

Telugu is a Dravidian Language native to India.

Sources

There are various sources available for information on early Telugu writers. Among these are the prologues to their poems, which followed the Sanskrit model by customarily giving a brief description of the writer, a history of the king to whom the book is dedicated, and a chronological list of the books he published. In addition, historical information is available from inscriptions that can be co-related with the poems; there are several grammars, treatises and anthologies that provide illustrative stanzas; and there is also information available from the lives of the poets and the traditions that they followed.

History of literature <templatestyles src="Nobold/-styles.css"/>by region or country
General topics
• Basic topics • Literary terms • Criticism • Theory
Types
• Epic • Novel • Poetry • Prose • Romance
Lists
• Books • Authors
Middle Eastern
• Ancient
• Sumerian
• Babylonian
• Egyptian   • Ancient Egyptian
• Hebrew
• Pahlavi
• Persian
• Arabic
• Israeli
European

- Greek
- Latin
- Early Medieval
  - Matter of Rome
  - Matter of France
  - Matter of Britain
- Medieval
- Renaissance

Modern

- Structuralism
- Poststructuralism
- Deconstruction
- Modernism
- Postmodernism
- Post-colonialism
- Hypertexts

North and South American

- American
- Canadian
- Mexican
- Jamaican

Latin American

- Argentine
- Brazilian
- Colombian
- Cuban
- Peruvian

Australasian

- Australian
- New Zealand

Asian

East / Southeast

- Chinese
- Japanese
- Korean
- Vietnamese
- Thai

South

- Sanskrit
- Indian
- Pakistani
- Assamese
- Bengali
- Gujurati
- Hindi
- Kannada
- Kashmiri
- Malayalam
- Marathi
- Nepali
- Rajasthani
- Sindhi
- Tamil
- Telugu
- Urdu
- Indian writing in English

African

• Moroccan • Nigerian • South African • Swahili
Related topics
• History of science fiction • List of years in literature • Literature by country • History of theatre • History of ideas • Intellectual history
📖 **Literature portal**
• v • t • e[807]

Subject matter

Early Telugu literature is predominantly religious in subject matter. Poets and scholars drew most of their material from, and spent most of their time translating epics, such as the *Ramayana*, the *Mahabharata*, the *Bhagavata* and the *Puranas*, all of which are considered to be storehouses of Indian culture.

From the sixteenth-century onwards, rarely known episodes from the *Puranas* would form the basis for the tradition of Telugu-language *kavya*. Literary works drawn from episodes of the *Puranas* under the name *Akhyana* or *Khanda* became popular along with depictions of the fortune of a single hero under the title of Charitra, Vijaya, Vilasa and Abhyudaya. Such titles are examples of what would become the most common subject matter of poetry.

In the eighteenth-century, marriages of heroes under the title Parinaya, Kalyana and Vivāha became popular.

Religious literature consisted of biographies of the founders of religion, their teachings (*Sara*) as well as commentaries (*bhashya*).

Traditional Hindu knowledge systems such as astrology, law, grammar, ballets, moral aphorisms, and devotional psalms to deities within the Hindu pantheon are characteristics of more popular works of Telugu literature.

Forms

The various forms of literature found in Telugu are:

- *Prabandham*: Stories in verse form with a tight metrical structure and they have three forms mentioned below.
  - *Prakhyātam*: Famous story.
  - *Utpadyam*: Purely fictional story.
  - *Mishramam*: Mixed story.
- *Champu*: Mixture of prose and poetry.
- *Kāvyam*: Poem which usually begin with a short prayer called a Prarthana, containing initial auspicious letter "Shri" which invokes the blessings of the god. The occasion and circumstances under which the work is undertaken is next stated.
- *Padya kāvyam*: Metrical poetry.
- *Gadya kāvyam*: prose poetry.
- *Khanda kāvyam*: Short poems
- *Kavita*: Poetry
- *Śatakam* (anthology): Shatakam is a literary piece of art. The name derives from Shata, which means a hundred in Sanskrit. Shatakam comprises a hundred poems. Hence, a Shatakam is a volume (book) of hundred poems. Shatakams are usually devotional, philosophical or convey morals.
- *Daśaka* (anthology): Dasakam or Dashakam comprises ten poems.
- *Avadhānam*: Avadhanam involves the partial improvisation of poems using specific themes, metres, forms, or words.[808]
- *Navala*: Navala is a written, fictional, prose narrative normally longer than a short story.
- *Katha* : Style of religious storytelling.
- *Nātakam*: Drama.
- *Naneelu*:Epigrams.

Ashtadiggajas have written in all three of the *Prabandham* genres during the *Prabandha yugam*.

Telugu literature uses a unique expression in verse called Champu, which mixes prose and poetry. Although it is the dominant literary form, there are exceptions: for example, Tikkana composed *Uttara Ramayana* entirely in verse.

As Champu Kavyas and Prabandhas were beyond the comprehension of masses, new devices for the dissemination of knowledge among the people were developed in the form of the Dvipada and Shataka styles. Dvipada means two feet (couplet) and Shataka means hundred (a cento of verses). (Popular shatakas: Sarveshvara shataka, Kalahastishvara shataka, Dasarathi Shataka)

There are some Shatakas which are divided into ten groups of ten verses called Dasaka which is adopted from Prakrit.

Avadhanam is a literary performance popular from the very ancient days in Sanskrit and more so in Telugu and Kannada languages. It requires a good memory and tests a person's capability of performing multiple tasks simultaneously. All the tasks are memory intensive and demand an in-depth knowledge of literature, and prosody. The number of Prucchakas can be 8 (ashtavadhanam) or 100 (shataavadhaanam) or even 1000 (sahasravadhanam). A person who has successfully performed Ashtavadhanam is called as Ashtavadhani, a shatavadhanam is called a Shatavadhani and sahasraavadhaanam is called Sahasravadhani.

Author's craft

Praudha Prabandha or **Maha Kavya** is considered as highest form of verse. The essentials of such a composition according to the Telugu poetic theory are

- *Śaili (Style)*: The words chosen neither soft nor very musical but dignified (Gambhira), Sweetness (Madhurya), Grace and Delicacy (Sukumara), Fragrance (Saurabhya) and Symphony. In choice of vocabulary, Vulgar language (Gramya) is avoided.
- *Pāka (Mould)*: Refers to the embodiment of ideas in language, and the nature and texture of the language employed. There are three types of pakas namely
  - *Drāksha (wine or grape)*: Draksha is a crystal clear style where everything is seen through a transparent medium. Mostly Nannaiyah uses this mould.
  - *Kadali (Plantain)*: Kadali is complex paka because the soft skin has to peeled to reach the core of the subject. Mostly Tikkana uses this mould.
  - *Narikela (coconut)*: Narikela is the most difficult mould to employ because one has to break the rind to understand the idea. Vishnu Chittiyam or Krishnadevaraya are cast in this paka.
- *Rasa (Sentiment)*: Rasa is the heart and soul of any Telugu poetry which follows rule or (Sutram) *"Vākyam Rasātmakam Kāvyam"* which means that the soul of a sentence is Rasa. There are nine Rasas, known as the Nava Rasas. A perfect kavyam uses all nine of these, namely:
  - Śṛṅgāra (love)
  - Hāsya (Comic)
  - Karuṇā (Sympathy)
  - Raudram (Horror)
  - Bhayānaka (Fear)
  - Bībhatsa (Disgust)

- Vīra (Heroic)
- Adbhuta (wonder)
- Shantam (Peace)

- *Alamkāra (Ornamentation)*: There are Śabdhalamkāras (ornaments of sound) and Arthalamkāras (ornaments of thoughts). Slesha (double entendre) and Yamaka (alliteration) are Śabdhalamkāras. Upamāna (simile) Utpreksha (hyperbole) are Arthalamkāras. We find usage of Alamkaras in description of events, places and proceedings etc.Wikipedia:Citation needed

History

Early writers

The Pre-Nannayya Period (before 1020 AD)

In the earliest period, Telugu literature existed in the form of inscriptions, precisely from 575 AD on-wards.Wikipedia:Citation needed

The 6th or 7th century Sanskrit text *Jānāśrayī Chandoviciti* (or *Janāśrayachandas*) deals with the metres used in Telugu, including some metres that are not found in Sanskrit prosody. This indicates that Telugu poetry existed during or around the 6th century.

The Jain Literature Phase(850-1000 AD)

Historically, Vemulawada was a Jain knowledge hub and played a significant role in patronizing Jain literature and poets.1980s excavations around Vemulawada revealed and affirmed the existence of Telugu Jain literature between 850-1000 AD.Wikipedia:Citation needed

Malliya Rechana-First Telugu Author (940AD) -

Malliya Rechana has composed the first Telugu poetic prosody book Kavijanasrayam(Pre-Nannayya chandassu) around 940 AD. This was a popular one and referred by many poets. There seems to be even an earlier prosody book by Rechana's guru Vaadindra Chudamani which is not available.

Veturi Prabhakara Sastry in 1900s mentioned about existence of *Pre-Nannayya Chandassu* in Raja Raja Narendra Pattabhisekha Sanchika. Accurate dating of this piece of literature happened after the 1980s discoveries in Karimnagar.

Prabandha Ratnavali(1918) also talks about a verse from Telugu *Jinendra Puranam* by Jain Padma Kavi(Pampa), a couple of verses from Telugu *Adi*

Puranam by Sarvadeva and *Kavijanasrayam*'s affiliation to Jainism were discussed.P.V.P Sastry also points out that many Jain works could have been destroyed. Historical rivalry among Hinduism, Jainism and Buddhism is well known

The Age of the Puranas (1020-1400AD)

This is the period of Kavi Trayam or Trinity of Poets. Nannayya, Tikkana and Yerrapragada (or Errana) are known as the Kavi Trayam.

Nannaya Bhattarakudu or Adi Kavi (1022–1063 AD)

Nannaya Bhattarakudu's (Telugu: నన్నయ) *Andhra mahabharatam*, who lived around the 11th century, is commonly referred to as the first Telugu literary composition (*aadi kaavyam*).Wikipedia:Citation needed Although there is evidence of Telugu literature before Nannaya, he is given the epithet *Aadi Kavi* ("the first poet"). Nannaya was the first to establish a formal grammar of written Telugu. This grammar followed the patterns which existed in grammatical treatises like Aṣṭādhyāyī and Vālmīkivyākaranam but unlike Pāṇini, Nannayya divided his work into five chapters, covering samjnā, sandhi, ajanta, halanta and kriya. Nannaya completed the first two chapters and a part of the third chapter of the *Mahabharata* epic, which is rendered in the Champu style.Wikipedia:Citation needed

Tikanna Somayaji (1205–1288 AD)

Nannaya's *Andhra Mahabharatam* was almost completed by Tikanna Somayaji (Telugu: తిక్కన సోమయాజి) (1205–1288) who wrote chapters 4 to 18.Wikipedia:Citation needed

Errapragada

Errapragada, (Telugu: ఎర్రాప్రగడ) who lived in the 14th century, finished the epic by completing the third chapter.Wikipedia:Citation needed He mimics Nannaya's style in the beginning, slowly changes tempo and finishes the chapter in the writing style of Tikkana.Wikipedia:Citation needed These three writers – Nannaya, Tikkana and Yerrapragada – are known as the *Kavitraya* ("three great poets") of Telugu. Other such translations like Marana's *Markandeya Puranam*, Ketana's *Dasakumara Charita*, Yerrapragada's *Harivamsam* followed. Many scientificWikipedia:Writing better articles#Stay on topic works, like *Ganitasarasangrahamu* by Pavuluri Mallana and *Prakirnaganitamu* by Eluganti Peddana, were written in the 12th century.Wikipedia:Citing sources#What information to include

Baddena Bhupala (1220-1280AD)

Sumati Shatakam, which is a *neeti* ("moral"), is one of the most famous Telugu Shatakams.Wikipedia:Citation needed Shatakam is composed of more than a 100 *padyalu* (poems). According to many literary criticsWikipedia:Manual of Style/Words to watch#Unsupported attributions *Sumati Shatakam* was composed by Baddena Bhupaludu (Telugu: బద్దెన భూపాల) (CE 1220–1280). He was also known as Bhadra Bhupala. He was a Chola prince and a vassal under the Kakatiya empress Rani Rudrama Devi, and a pupil of Tikkana.Wikipedia:Citation needed If we assume that the *Sumati Shatakam* was indeed written by Baddena, it would rank as one of the earliest Shatakams in Telugu along with the *Vrushadhipa Satakam* of Palkuriki Somanatha and the *Sarveswara Satakam* of Yathavakkula Annamayya.Wikipedia:No original research The *Sumatee Shatakam* is also one of the earliest Telugu works to be translated into a European language, as C. P. Brown rendered it in English in the 1840s.Wikipedia:Citation needed

The Age of Srinatha and the Prabandhas (1400–1600 AD)

Srinatha

Srinatha (Telugu: శ్రీనాథుడు) (1365–1441) popularised the *Prabandha* style of composition. He was a minister in the court of Pedakomati Vemareddy of KondaveeduWikipedia:Citation needed and wrote *Salivahana Saptasati, Shivaratri Mahatyam, Harivilasa, Bhimakanda, Kashi khandam, Shringara Naishadham, Palanati Veera charitra, Dhananjaya Vijayam, Sringara Dipika.* These works were concerned with history and mythology.Wikipedia:Citation needed Srinatha's *Srungara Naishadhamu* is a well-known example of the form. Srinatha was widely regarded as the *Kavi Sarvabhowma* ("the emperor among poets").Wikipedia:Citation needed

Vemana

Kumaragiri Vema Reddy (Telugu: వేమన), popularly known as Yogi Vemana, was a 14th-century Telugu poet. His poems were written in the popular vernacular of Telugu, and are known for their use of simple language and native idioms.Wikipedia:Citation needed His poems discuss the subjects of Yoga, wisdom and morality.Wikipedia:Citation needed There is no consensus among scholars about the period in which Vemana lived. C.P. Brown, known for his research on Vemana, estimates the year of birth to be the year 1352 based on some of his verses.Wikipedia:Citation needed His poems are four lines in length. The fourth line is, in majority of the cases, the chorus *Vishwadhabhirama Vinura Vema* – he thus conveyed his message with three small lines written in a simple vernacular.Wikipedia:Citation needed He travelled widely across south India, acquiring popularity as a poet and Yogi.Wikipedia:Citation needed So high was the regard for Vemana that a popular Telugu saying goes 'Vemana's word is the word of the Vedas'.Wikipedia:Citation needed He is celebrated for his style of *Chaatu padyam*, a poem with a hidden meaning.Wikipedia:Citation needed Many lines of Vemana's poems are now colloquial phrases of the Telugu language.Wikipedia:Citation needed They end with the signature line *Vishwadhaabhi Raama, Vinura Vema*, literally *Beloved of Vishwadha, listen Vema*. There are many interpretations of what the last line signifies.Wikipedia:Citation needed

Bammera Potanaamatya

Bammera Potanaamatya (Telugu: బమ్మెర పోతన) (1450–1510) is best known for his translation of the *Bhagavata Purana* from Sanskrit to Telugu.Wikipedia:Citation needed His work, *Andhra Maha Bhagavatamu*. He was born into a Brahmin family and was considered to be a *sahaja Kavi* ("natural poet") who needed no teacher. He wrote *Bhogini Dandakam* a poem praising king Singa Bhoopala's consort danseuse, Bhogini, while young. This is the earliest available Telugu *Dandaka* (a rhapsody which uses the same gana or foot throughout).Wikipedia:Citing sources#What information to include His second work was *Virabhadra Vijayamu* which describes the adventures of Virabhadra, son of Shiva.Wikipedia:Citation needed As a young man, he was a devotee of Shiva and also Rama and was more interested in salvation, from which came the inspiration to translate the *Bhagavata Purana*.Wikipedia:Citation needed

Annamacharya

Tallapaka Annamacharya (or Annamayya) (Telugu: శ్రీ తాళ్ళపాక అన్నమాచార్య) (9 May 1408 – 23 February 1503) is known as the *Pada-kavita Pitaamaha* of the Telugu language.[809] He was born to a Vaidiki Brahmin family and his works are considered to have dominated and influenced the structure of Carnatic music compositions.Wikipedia:Citation needed Annamacharya is said to have composed as many as 32,000 sankeertanas (songs) on Bhagwaan Govinda Venkateswara, of which only about 12,000 are available today. His keertana compositions are based on the Vishishtadvaita school of thought.Wikipedia:Citation needed Annamayya was educated in this system of Ramanuja by Sri Satagopa Yateendra of the Ahobila matham.Wikipedia:Citation needed

Tallapaka Tirumalamma

Tallapaka Tirumalamma (Telugu: తాళ్ళపాక తిరుమలమ్మ) (Annamacharya's wife) wrote *Subhadra Kalyanam*, and is considered the first female poet in Telugu literature.Wikipedia:Manual of Style/Words to watch#Unsupported attributions Her main work, *Subhadra Kalyanam*, which consists of 1170 poems, is about the marriage of Arjuna and Subhadra, who are characters that appear in the *Mahabharata*. She presented the Telugu nativity and culture in the story taken from Sanskrit epic.Wikipedia:Citation needed

Allasani Peddana

Allasani Peddana (Telugu: అల్లసాని పెద్దన) (15th and 16th centuries) was ranked as the foremost of the *Ashtadiggajalu* the title for the group of eight poets in the court of Krishnadevaraya, a ruler of the Vijayanagara Empire.Wikipedia:Citation needed Peddana was a native of Somandepalli near Anantapur.Wikipedia:Citation needed Allasani Peddana wrote the first major *Prabandha* and for this reason he is revered as *Andhra Kavita Pitamaha* ("the grand father of Telugu poetry").Wikipedia:Citation needed It is believedWikipedia:Manual of Style/Words to watch#Unsupported attributions that he was also a minister in the king's court and is hence sometimes referred as *Peddanaamaatya* (*Peddana* + *Amaatya* = Peddana, the minister).Wikipedia:Citation needed He wrote *Swaarochisha Manu Sambhavam* (also known as *Manu Charitra*), which is a development of an episode in the Markandeya Purana relating to the birth of Svarochishamanu, who is one of the fourteen Manus. Pravarakhya is a pious Brahmin youth who goes to the Himalayas for Tapasya. In the Himalayas Varudhini, a Gandharva girl, falls in love with him, but Pravarakyudu rejects her love. Knowing this a Gandharva youth who was earlier rejected by Varudhini assumes the form of Pravarakhya and succeeds to win her love. To them is born Svarochisha, the father of Svarochishamanu.Wikipedia:Citing sources#What information to include The theme for his *Manu Charitra* is a short story from Markandeya Purana. It is about second *Manu* of fourteen manus (fathers of mankind societies according to Hindu mythology), translated into Telugu from Sanskrit by Marana (1291–1323),Wikipedia:Citation needed disciple of Tikkana. The original story was around 150 poems and Peddana extended into six chapters with 600 poems by adding fiction and descriptions.

His work was treated as one of the *Pancha Kavyas*, the five best works in Telugu. Some of his other famous works such as *Harikathaasaaramu* are untraceable now.Wikipedia:Citation needed

Middle age writers

Dhurjati

Dhurjati or Dhoorjati (Telugu: ధూర్జటి) (15th and 16th centuries) was a poet in the court of Krishnadevaraya and was one of the 'Ashtadiggajalu'.Wikipedia:Citation needed He was born to Singamma and Narayana in Sri Kalahasti and was the grandson of Jakkayya.Wikipedia:Citation needed. His works include *Sri Kalahasteeshwara Mahatyam* (The grace/miracles of lord Shiva) and *Sri Kalahasteeshwara Shatakam* (100+ poems in the praise of lord Shiva). Dhurjati took themes from Puranas and added local stories and myths in his work.Wikipedia:Citation needed Unlike contemporaries such as Peddana and Mallana, who chose the stories of kings, he chose devotion as his theme.Wikipedia:Citation needed. Krishnadevaraya praised Dhurjati, saying *"Stuti mati yaina Andhrakavi Dhurjati palkulakelagalgeno yetulita madhuri mahima...."* (How is Dhurjati's poetry so immeasurably beautiful)^{810} On a personal note, he was known as *Pedda Dhurjati* ("elder Dhurjati") as there were four other people from the same family line who went by the name of Dhurjati during the same period and after him.Wikipedia:Citation needed. His grandson Venkataraya Dhurjati, wrote *Indumati Parinayam* ("marriage of Indumati"), a story from Kalidasa's Raghuvamsam.

Krishnadevaraya

Krishnadevaraya (Telugu: శ్రీ కృష్ణదేవరాయ) was an emperor of Vijayanagara Kingdom. Literary activities flourished during the rule of the Vijayanagara dynasty,Wikipedia:Citation needed and the period of Krishnadevaraya's rule in the sixteenth century is consideredWikipedia:Manual of Style/Words to watch#Unsupported attributions to be the golden age of Telugu literature.Wikipedia:Citation needed Krishnadevaraya, a poet himself, introduced the *Prabandha* to Telugu literature.Wikipedia:Citation needed *Amukta Malyada*. Krishna Deva Raya wrote the book *Amuktamalyada* in Telugu, describing the pangs of separation suffered by Andal (an incarnation of the goddess Mahalakshmi. He describes Andal's physical beauty in thirty verses; using descriptions of the spring and the monsoon as metaphors.Wikipedia:Citation needed As elsewhere in Indian poetry, the sensual pleasure of union extends beyond the physical level and becomes a path to, and a metaphor for, spirituality and ultimate union with the divine.Wikipedia:Citation needed His court had the *Ashtadiggajas* ("eight elephants"), who were considered to be the greatest of poets of that time.Wikipedia:Citation needed Some criticsWikipedia:Manual of Style/Words to watch#Unsupported attributions dismiss the following period, dominated by *prabandhas*, as a decadent age.Wikipedia:Citation needed Of the dozens of works of the eighteenth- to mid-nineteenth century, Kankanti

Paparaju's *Uttara Ramayana* in *campu* style, and the play *Vishnumayavilasa* stand out.Wikipedia:Citation needed Other genres bloomed at the same time.Wikipedia:Avoid weasel words Yakshaganas, indigenous dramas of song and prose, were also produced.Wikipedia:Citation needed

Tenali Ramakrishna

Garlapati Tenali Ramakrishna (Telugu: గార్లపాటి తెనాలి రామకృష్ణ), popularly known as Tenali Rama and Vikata Kavi, was another sixteenth-century court poet of the Vijayanagara empire and also one of the *Ashtadiggajas*. His family had originally hailed from Tenali in Guntur District, he was born in a Telugu Niyogi Brahmin family. His famous work *Panduranga Mahatyamu* is one among the Pancha Kavyas.Wikipedia:Citation needed He dedicated that to Viruri Vedadri. This book is about the Pundarika Kshetram on the banks of river Bhaimi and its legend. He also composed *Udbhataradhya Charitram* on the story of Udbhata, a monk, as well as *Ghatikachala Mahatyam* about Ghatikachalam, a place of worship for God Narasimha near Vellore. He followed the Prabandha style. He took the theme for *Panduranga Mahatyam* from the Skanda Purana and enhanced it with many stories about the devotees of God Vitthala (Panduranga). He is noted for brilliance and wit and for mocking other poets and great personalities. He created a celebrated character called *Nigama Sarma akka* (sister of Nigama Sarma) and a story about her without giving her a name. He also had written many *Chatuvu* (extempore poems).

Kshetrayya

Kshetrayya or Kshetragna (Telugu: క్షేత్రయ్య) (c. 1600–1680 CE) was a prolific poet and composer of Carnatic music. He lived in the area of Andhra Pradesh. He composed a number of *padams* and *keertanas*, the prevalent formats of his time. He is credited with more than 4000 compositions, although only a handful have survived. He composed his songs on his favourite deity Krishna (Gopala) in Telugu. He perfected the *padam* format that is still being used today. His *padams* are sung in dance (Bharatanatyam and Kuchipudi) and music recitals. A unique feature of his padams is the practice of singing the *anupallavi* first then the *pallavi* (second verse followed by first verse). Most of the padams are of the theme of longing for the coming of the lord Krishna. He wrote with Sringara as a main theme in expressing *madhurabhakti* (devotion to the supreme). Sringara is a motif where the mundane sexual relationship between a Nayaki (woman) and a Nayaka (man) is used as a metaphor, denoting the yearning of jeeva (usually depicted as the Nayaki) to unite with the divine (usually depicted as the man). In most of his compositions, Kshetrayya has used the *mudra* (signature) "Muvva Gopala" as a reference to himself, which is also a name for the Lord Krishna in Kshetrayya's village Muvva, now called as Movva. Kshetrayya's work has played a major role in influencing poetry, dance, music of the South Indian tradition. Kshetrayya was intimately connected with the devadasi women of the temples of south India, who were the subject of many of his compositions. The devadasis were traditionally in possession of the musical/poetic interpretations of his work for a long period of time till the devadasi system was abolished and the compositions became more accepted in the musical community as valuable works of art. The musical community also owes a lot to Veena Dhanammal and T. Brinda, who popularised Kshetrayya's songs with their beautiful musical interpretation. Kshetrayya's padams now form an integral part of the dance and musical traditions of South India, where his songs are rendered purely as musical works or as accompaniments to dance.

Kancherla Gopanna

Kancherla Gopanna (Telugu: కంచెర్ల గోపన్న) (c 1620–1680 CE), popularly known as Bhadradri Ramadasu or Bhadrachala Ramadasu (Telugu: భద్రాచల రామదాసు), was a 17th-century Indian devotee of Rama and a composer of Carnatic music. He is one among the famous vaggeyakaras (same person being the writer and composer of a song) in the Telugu language. His devotional lyrics to Rama are famous in South Indian classical music as *Ramadaasu Keertanalu*. Even the doyen of South Indian classical music Saint Thyagaraja learned and later improved the style now considered standard krithi form of music composition. He also written Dasarathi Shatakamu a collection of nearly 100 poems dedicated to the son of Dasaratha (Lord Rama).

Venkamamba

Tarikonda Venkamamba (Telugu:తారికొండ వెంకమాంబ ; alternate spelling: Vengamamba, born 1730) was a poet and staunch devotee of Lord Venkateswara in the 18th century. She wrote numerous poems and songs.

Tyagaraja

Tyagaraja or Tyagabrahmam (Telugu: కాకర్ల త్యాగబ్రహ్మం) (1767–1847) of Tanjore composed devotional songs in Telugu, which form a big part of the repertoire of Carnatic music. In addition to nearly 600 compositions (kritis), Tyagaraja composed two musical plays in Telugu, the *Prahalada Bhakti Vijayam* and the *Nauka Charitam*. *Prahlada Bhakti Vijayam* is in five acts with 45 *kritis* set in 28 ragas and 138 verses, in different metres in Telugu. *Nauka Charitam* is a shorter play in one act with 21 *kritis* set in 13 *ragas* and 43 verses. The latter is the most popular of Tyagaraja's operas, and is a creation of the composer's own imagination and has no basis in the *Bhagavata Purana*. Often overlooked is the fact that Tyagaraja's works are some of the best and most beautiful literary expressions in Telugu language.Wikipedia:Citation needed

Valmiki composed the Ramayana, the story of Rama, with 24,000 verses and also composed 24,000 kritis in praise of the lord.Wikipedia:Citation needed

Paravastu Chinnayasuri

Paravastu Chinnayasuri (Telugu: పరవస్తు చిన్నయ సూరి) (1807–1861) wrote *Baala Vyaakaranamu* in a new style after doing extensive research on *Andhra Grammar*Wikipedia:Please clarify which is his greatest gift Wikipedia:Manual of Style/Words to watch#Puffery to Telugu people. Other notable works of Chinnayasuri include *Neeti Chandrika*, *Sootandhra Vyaakaranamu*, *Andhra Dhatumoola* and *Neeti Sangrahamu*. Chinnayasuri translated Mitra Labham and Mitra Bhedam from the Sanskrit Panchatantra as *Neeti Chandrika*. Kandukuri Veeresalingam and Kokkonda Venkata Ratnam Pantulu followed his style of prose writing and wrote *Vigrahamu* and *Sandhi* in a different pattern.Wikipedia:Please clarify

Modern or Adhunika Sahityam

Modern Asian literature
• Arabic literature
• Bengali literature
• Chinese literature
• Indian literature
• Japanese literature
• Korean literature
• Nepalese literature
• Pakistani literature
• Sindhi literature
• Vietnamese literature
• v • t • e[811]

Kandukuri Veeresalingam

Kandukuri Veereshalingam (Telugu: కందుకూరి వీరేశలింగం) (also known as Kandukuri Veeresalingam Pantulu (Telugu: కందుకూరి వీరేశలింగం పంతులు), (16 April 1848 – 27 May 1919) was a social reformer of Andhra Pradesh. He was born in an orthodox Andhra Brahmin family. He is widely considered as the man who first brought about a renaissance in Telugu people and Telugu literature. He was influenced by the ideals of Brahmo Samaj particularly those of Keshub Chunder Sen. Veereshalingam panthulu is popularly called *Gadya Tikkana*.Wikipedia:Citation needed He wrote about 100 books between 1869 and 1919 and introduced the essay, biography, autobiography and the novel into Telugu literature[812] His *Satyavati Charitam* was the first social novel in Telugu.Wikipedia:Citation needed He wrote *Rajashekhara Charitamu* inspired by Oliver Goldsmith's *The Vicar of Wakefied*. To him literature was an instrument to fight social evils.Wikipedia:Citation needed

Mangalampalli Balamurali Krishna

Mangalampalli Balamurali Krishna (Telugu: మంగళంపల్లి బాలముర‌ళీకృష్ణ) ◄ pronunciation Wikipedia:Media helpFile:Pronunciation of 'Mangalampalli Balamuralikrishna'.ogg (born 6 July 1930) is a Carnatic vocalist, multi-instrumentalist and a playback singer. He is also acclaimed as a poet, composer and respected for his knowledge of Carnatic Music. Balamuralikrishna was born in Sankaraguptam, East Godavari District, Andhra Pradesh state.[813] Dr Balamuralikrishna has composed over 400 compositions in various languages like Telugu and Sanskrit. His compositions ranges from Devotional to Varnams, Kirthis, Javalis and Thillans. His greatest achievement are the compositions in all the fundamental 72 melakarta ragas.

Aatreya

Aacharya Aatreya (Telugu: ఆచార్య ఆత్రేయ) or *Kilambi Venkata Narasimhacharyulu* ◄ pronunciation Wikipedia:Media helpFile:aathreya.ogg (7 May 1921 – 13 September 1989) was a playwright, lyrics and story writer of the Telugu film industry. He was born as Kilambi Venkata Narasimhacharyulu on 7 May 1921 in the Mangalampadu village of Sullurpeta Mandalam in the Nellore district of Andhra Pradesh. His pen name is based on their family Gotra. Known for his poetry on the human soul and heart, he was given the title 'Manasu Kavi'(Poet of Heart), which can be rewritten as 'Mana Su Kavi'(Our Good Poet). His poetry is philosophical and intellectually satisfying.Wikipedia:Citation needed

Tripuraneni Ramaswamy

Tripuranēni Rāmasvāmi (January 15, 1887 – January 16, 1943) was a lawyer, famous poet, playwright and reformer active among the Telugu-speaking people. Popularly known as Kaviraju, he is considered the first poet to introduce rationalism and humanism into Telugu poetry and literature. Ramaswamy chose literary writing as the vehicle for expressing his rationalist thoughts. His famous work 'Sutaparanam' in four cantos was a fierce attack on the ancient Puranas, he has attained the state of excellence in poetic&literary criticism. His poetic work "Kuppuswamy Satakam" reveals the theme of social revolution and talks about social evils, blind faith and indignity to man. He was against Congress and its fight against independence. In his other works such as "Sambhukavadha", "Suthashrama geethaalu', 'Dhoortha maanava', 'Khooni', 'Bhagavadgita', 'Rana Pratap' and 'Kondaveeti pathanam', he made a rational analysis of dogmas prescribed by ancient classics and the injustice these dogmas did to people belonging to the lower social orders. Moreover, he attacked discriminatory practices and fought against the idea of untouchability. Sambhuka Vadha created lot of controversy. Sambhuka was a character who did tapas to go heaven with live body before death. That was considered as adharma and was killed by Lord Rama. This story was interpreted that Brahmins do not like doing tapas by non-Brahmins, which is why Sabhuka was killed.

Popular authors and works

- Arudra (ఆరుద్ర) – *Samagraandhra Saahityamu* (సమగ్రాంధ్ర సాహిత్యము) (The Complete Telugu Literature)
- Adavi Baapiraju – *Gona Gannareddy, Naarayanarao, Tuphaanu (The storm), Amshumati*
- Addepalli Ramamohana Rao – *Poga choorina Aakasam*
- Ajanta – Penumarti Viswanatha Sastry (born 1922)
- Allasani Peddana – *Manu Charitra* (The History of Swarochisha Manu)
- Aatreya – *NGO, Kappalu*
- Avasarala Ramakrishna Rao (1931–2011) – *Sampengalu-Sannajajulu*
- Atukuri Molla – *Molla Ramayanam*
- Bammera Potana – *Bhagavata Purana*
- Buchchibabu – *Chivaraku Migiledi* (What is Left at the End)
- Balivada Kanta Rao (1927–2000) – *Balivada Kanta Rao Kathalu* (Winner of the Kendriya Sahitya Academy Award Awarded in 1998 by the Government of India)
- Boyi Bhimanna – *Gudiselu Kaalipotunnaayi*
- C. Narayanareddy – *Vishwambhara* (Won the Jnanpith Award for this novel in the year 1988)
- Cha So (1915–1993)
- Chalam – *Chitraangi, Maidhaanam, Saavitri, Janaki, Ameena, Brahmaneekam, Musings*
- Chilakamarti Lakshmi Narasimham – *Gayopaakhyaanam, Prahasanamulu*
- Daasarathi Krishnamacharyulu – *Timiramuto samaramu* (Fighting against the darkness)
- Devarakonda Balagangadhara Tilak – *Tilak Kathalu, Amrutam Kurisina Raatri*
- Dhurjati – *Srikaalahasteesvara Satakam*
- Duvvoori Ramireddy – *Paanasaala, Krusheevaludu*

- Devulapalli Krishnasastri – *Krishna pakshamu* (The Brightening Fortnight)
- Garikapati Narasimha Rao – *Saagara Ghosha* (Boisterousness of Ocean)
- Gona Budda Reddy- *Ranganatha Ramayanam*
- Gurajada Apparao – *Kanyaasulkamu*
- Gurram Jashuva – *Gabbilamu* (The Bat), *Firadausi*
- Kaloji- *Naa Godava, Idee Naa Godava* (Autobiography)
- Kandukuri Veeresalingam – *Andhrakavula Charitra* (The History of Andhra Poets), *Raajasekhara Charitra* (The History of Rajasekhara),
- Kanety Krishna Menon - *KRATUVU*
- Jandhyala Papayya Sastry - *UdayaSri, VijayaSri, KarunaSri, Amarkhyam, Telugubala*
- Kasula Purushottama Kavi – *Andhranayaka Satakamu*
- Kavitrayam (Nannayya, Tikkana, Yerrapragada) – *Andhra Mahaabhaaratamu* (The Great Mahabharata in Telugu)
- Kethu Viswanathareddy – *Kethu Viswanathareddy Kathalu*
- Ko Ku – *Chaduvu*
- Madhurantakam Rajaram – *Halikulu Kushalama*
- Malladi Venkata Krishna Murthy – *Written 153 novels, over 3000 Short Stories and 8 Travelogues covering 33 countries*
- Mokkapati Narasimha Sastry – *Barrister Parvateesam*
- Muddupalani – *Radhika Santvanamu*
- Mullapudi Venkata Ramana – *Budugu, Girisam malli puttadu*
- Muppala Ranganayakamma – *Raamayana vishavr̥ksham, Krishnaveni, sweet home, Janaki Vimukti, Ammaki Adivaram Leda*
- Nandoori Subbarao – *Yenki paatalu*
- Nanne Choadudu – *Kumaara Sambhavamu*
- Nayani Krishnakumari – *Telugu geya vanjmayamu, Agniputri, Kashmira deepakalika*
- Palagummi Padmaraju – *Batikina collegee*
- Panchagnula Adinarayana Sastry - Arya Bharathi Granthamala.
- Panuganti Lakshminarasimha RaoPanuganti Lakshminarasimham - *Narmada purukitsiyamu* (1902), *Sarangadhara* (1904), *Vijaya raghavamu* (1909), *Raathi sthambhamu* (1930), *Ramaraju* (1948)
- Paravasthu Chinnayasuri – *Baalavyaakaranamu, Neeti chandrika*
- Rallapalli Ananta Krishna Sharma- *Meerabai* (1913), *Taradevi* (1911) (both Khanda Kavya's), *Natakopanyasamulu, Vemana* (1928–29), *Saraswatalokamu* (1954) (critical review articles), *Shalivahana Gathasaptashati Saramu* (translation of the Prakrit work into Telugu) (1932), *Chayapa Senaniya, Nrita Ratnavali* (Translation into Telugu, 1969), *Arya* (Translation of Sundara Pandya's Sanskrit work in Telugu, 1970).
- Ravuri Bharadwaja – *Paakudu Raallu* [received the Jnanpith Award 2012

- Sankaramanchi Satyam – *Amaravati Kathalu* (The Stories from Amaravati)
- Sri Krishna Deva Raya – *Aamukta Maalyada*
- Sri Sri – *Maha Prasthanam*
- Sri K Sabha – *Vishwarupa Sandarsanam, Vedabhumi, Mogili, Patala Ganga*
- Srinatha – *Haravilaasamu, Kaasikhandamu, Bhimakhandamu, Palnaati veeracharitra, Sŕngaara naishadhamu*
- Suravaram Pratapareddy – *Aandhrula Saanghika Charitra*
- Tallapaka Annamacharya (1424?-1503) – *Annamacharya kirtanas*
- Tapi dharma Rao 'Vidhi Vilasam', 'Devala paina bootu bommalu, Pelli-Dani Puttupurvottaralu, and film script Rojulu marayi
- Tallapaka Timmakka – *Subhadrakalyanam*
- Tarigonda Venkamamba – *Venkatachala Mahatmyamu, Vasista Ramamyanamu, Rajayogasaramu, Bhagavatamu, Krishnamanjari*
- Tenali Ramakrishna – *Paanduranga maahaatmyamu*
- Tenneti Hemalata - *Raktapankhamu, Mohanavamsi, Omar Khayyam*
- Tikkana – *Nirvachanottara Raamayanamu* -
- Tirupati Venkata Kavulu – *Paandavodyoga vijayamulu, Devi bhaagavatamu*
- Tirumalamba – *Varadambika parinayamu*
- Thiruvarangam Sudhakar - *Sudhakara kavitha jyotsna*
- Tripuraneni Ramaswamy Choudhury – *Sutapuranamu, Karempudi kathanamu, Kurukshetra sangramamu, Kuppuswamy satakamu, Sambhukavadha, Sutashrama geetalu', Dhoorta manava, Khooni, Bhagavadgita, Rana Pratap, Kondaveeti patanam*
- Tripuraneni Maharadhi - *Samagraha Praanam*
- Ushasri – *Sundarakanda*
- Viswanatha Satyanarayana – *Cheliyalikatta, Kalpavrukshamu, Kinnerasaani Paatalu, Srimadraamaayana kalpavŕkshamu Swargaaniki Nichchenalu, Veyipadagalu, Ekaveera, naa ramudu, nepala rajavamsa kathalu* (In Telugu he is the first writer to receive Jnanpith Award for the novel Ramayana Kalpavrukshamu (A resourceful tree:Ramayana) in the year 1970)
- Vemana – *Vemana Satakam*
- Vempalli Gangadhar - *Molakala Punnami*
- Yenugu Lakshmana Kavi – *Bhartruhari Subhashitamulu*
- Yerrapragada – *Harivansamu, Nrusimhapuranamu, half of the Aranya Parva of Maha Bharata*

Modern platforms

Growing Internet users in India led to the birth of online platforms that bring Telugu writers closer to more readers. Pratilipi, SuKatha[814] and Kahaniya[815] are prominent among the new platforms.

External links

- Press Academy of Andhra Pradesh Archives (Telugu)[816]
- Telugu Sahityam, a blog about Telugu literature[817]
- Telugu Literary & Cultural Association[818]

Tulu literature

Tulu language

Tulu	
ತುಳು	
ತುಳು	
Native to	India
Region	Tulu Nadu region (Udupi district and Dakshina Kannada of Karnataka and Kasaragod district of Kerala).
Native speakers	1.85 million (2011 census)

Language family	Dravidian
	• Southern Dravidian
	  • Tulu languages
	    • **Tulu**

Writing system	Kannada script (Contemporary) Tigalari script (Historical-rarely used)
Official status	
Recognised minority language in	India State of Karnataka and Kerala
Regulated by	Karnataka Tulu Sahitya Academy Kerala Tulu Academy
Language codes	
ISO 639-3	tcy
Glottolog	tulu1258[819][820]

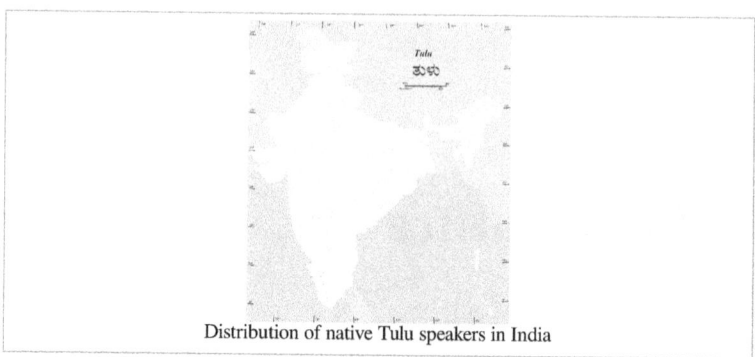
Distribution of native Tulu speakers in India

Tulu (Tulu: ತುಳು ಬಾಸೆ *Tulu bāse* ['t̪ulu 'bɒːsæ])[821] is a Dravidian language spoken mainly in the south west part of the Indian state of Karnataka and also in the Kasaragod district of Kerala. The Tulu speaking region is often referred to as Tulu Nadu. The native speakers of Tulu are referred to as *Tuluva* or Tulu people.

The Indian census report of 2011 reported a total of 1,846,427 native Tulu speakers in India. The 2001 census had reported a total of 1,722,768 native speakers, According to one estimate reported in 2009, Tulu is currently spoken by 3 to 5 million speakers in the world. There is some difficulty in counting Tulu speakers who have migrated from their native region as they often get counted as Kannada speakers in Indian Census reports

Separated early from Proto-South Dravidian,[822] Tulu has several features not found in Tamil–Kannada. For example, it has the pluperfect and the future perfect, like French or Spanish, but formed without an auxiliary verb.

Robert Caldwell, in his pioneering work *A Comparative Grammar of the Dravidian or South-Indian family of languages*, called this language "peculiar and very interesting". According to him, "Tulu is one of the most highly developed languages of the Dravidian family. It looks as if it had been cultivated for its own sake."[823]

Tulu is the primary spoken language in Tulu Nadu, a region comprising the districts of Udupi and Dakshina Kannada in the west of the state of Karnataka and the Kasaragod taluk. Non-native speakers of Tulu include those who speak the Beary language, Havyaka and Gowda dialects of Kannada as also Konkani, Koraga and Malayalam speakers resident in the Tulu Nadu region. Apart from Tulu Nadu, a significant emigrant population of Tulu speaking people is found in Maharashtra, Bangalore, Chennai, the English-speaking world, and the Gulf countries.

The various medieval inscriptions of Tulu from the 15th century are in the Tigalari or Tulu script. Two Tulu epics named *Sri Bhagavato* and *Kaveri* from the 17th century were also written in the same script. However, in modern times the Tulu language is mostly written using the Kannada script. The Tulu language is known for its oral literature in the form of epic poems called *Paddana*. The Epic of Siri and the legend of Koti and Chennayya belong to this category of Tulu literature.

Classification

Tulu belongs to the southern branch of the family of Dravidian languages. It descends directly from Proto-Southern Dravidian, which in turn descends directly from Proto-Dravidian, the hypothesised mother language from which all Dravidian languages descend. The Tulu language originates in the southern part of India.

Etymology

Linguists Purushottama Bilimale (ಪುರುಷೋತ್ತಮ ಬಿಳಿಮಲೆ) have suggested that the word "Tulu" means "that which is connected with water", based on words from Kannada and Tamil. "Tulave" (jack fruit) means "watery" in Tulu; and, other water-related words in Tulu include "talipu", "teli", "teLi", "teLpu", "tuLipu", "tulavu", and "tamel". In Kannada, there are words such as tuLuku means "that which has characteristics of water" and toLeWikipedia:Citation needed In Tamil, thuli means drop of water;Wikipedia:Citation needed and, thulli means the same in Malayalam.

Official status

Tulu is not currently an official language of India or any other country. Efforts are being made to include Tulu to the 8th Schedule of the Constitution. In August 2017, an online campaign was organized to include Tulu to 8th schedule of constitution and in October 2017, when the prime minister, Narendra Modi visited Dharmasthala Temple same demand was presented in front of him.

History

The oldest available inscriptions in Tulu are from the period between 14th to 15th century AD. These inscriptions are in the Tigalari script and are found in areas in and around Barkur which was the capital of Tulu Nadu during the Vijayanagar period. Another group of inscriptions are found in the *Ullur Subrahmanya* Temple near Kundapura. Many linguists like S.U. Panniyadi and L. V. Ramaswami Iyer as well as P.S. Subrahmanya suggested that Tulu is among the oldest languages in the Dravidian family which branched independently from its Proto-Dravidian roots nearly 500 years ago. This assertion is based on the fact that Tulu still preserves many aspects of the Proto-Dravidian language.

This dating of Tulu is also based on the fact that the region where Tulu is natively spoken was known to the ancient Tamils as Tulu Nadu. Also, the Tamil poet Mamular who belongs to the Sangam Age (200 AD) describes Tulu Nadu and its dancing beauties in one of his poems. In the Halmidi inscriptions one finds mention of the Tulu country as the kingdom of the Alupas. The region was also known to the Greeks of the 2nd century as *Tolokoyra*. The history of Tulu would not be complete without the mention of the Charition mime, a Greek play belonging to 2nd century BC. The play's plot centres around the coastal Karnataka, where Tulu is mainly spoken. The play is mostly in Greek, but the Indian characters in the play are seen speaking a language different from Greek.

There is considerable ambiguity regarding the Indian language in the play, though all scholars agree the Indian language is Dravidian, but there is considerable dispute over which one. Noted German Indologist Dr. E. Hultzsch was the first to suggest that the language was Dravidian.Wikipedia:Please clarify The dispute regarding the language in the play is yet to be settled, but scholars agree that the dispute arises from the fact that Old Kannada, Old Tamil and Tulu during the time when the play was written were perhaps dialectical variations of the same proto-language, and that over the years they evolved into their present forms as separate languages.Wikipedia:Citation needed Tulu is widely considered one of the most rich and well organized for many reasons. Found largely in Karnataka, it is spoken primarily within the Indian state. Dating back several hundred years, the language has developed numerous defining qualities. The Tulu people follow a saying which promotes leaving negative situations and finding newer, more positive ones. The language, however, is not as popular as others which means it could become endangered and extinct very soon. The influence of other mainstream languages is present danger for the Tulu people. With the right degree of awareness, we can help promote Tulu to more people who may appreciate it and its uniqueness. [1][824] Today, it is spoken by nearly 5 million people around the globe. Large parts of the language are altered and changed constantly because it is commonly passed down through oral tradition. Oral traditions within Tulu have meant that certain phrases have not always maintained the same meaning or importance.

that Tulu may have been before others in the Dravidian family. The Kannada script has become the contemporary script for the Tulu language gradually. All contemporary works and literature are done in the Kannada script.

Dialects

Tulu language has four dialects, which are broadly similar, with slight variations.

The four dialects are:

1. **Common Tulu**: Spoken by the majority includes the Mogaveera, Bunts, Billava, Kulala Devadiga, Jogi communities and others. This is the dialect of commerce, trade and entertainment and is mainly used for inter-community communication. It is further subdivided into seven groups:
   1. Central Tulu: Spoken in Mangalore.
   2. Northwest Tulu: Spoken in Udupi.
   3. Northeast Tulu: Spoken in Karkala and Belthangady.
   4. Southwest Tulu: Spoken in Manjeshwar and Kasaragod, known as Kasaragod Tulu influencing Malayalam.
   5. Southcentral Tulu: Spoken in Bantwal,.
   6. Southeast Tulu: Spoken in Puttur Sullia.
   7. Southern Tulu: Spoken in South of Kasaragod and Payaswini (Chandragiri) river influencing Malayalam known as Thenkaayi Tulu.
2. **Brahmin Tulu**: Spoken by the Tulu Brahmins who are subdivided into Shivalli Brahmins, Sthanika Brahmins and Tuluva Hebbars. It is slightly influenced by Sanskrit.
3. **Jain Dialect**: Spoken by the Tulu Jains. It is a dialect where the initial letters 'T' and 'S' have been replaced by the letter 'H'. For example, the word *Tare* is pronounced as *Hare*, *Saadi* is pronounced as *Haadi*.
4. **Girijan Dialect**: Spoken by the Koraga, Mansa, other Girijans and Tribal classes.
5. There are numerous variations and dialects of the Tulu language. There's no official script for the language which allows for substantial room in variation and personalizing. Malayalam was the script that was used to help write the Tulu language. However, recent studies show that this script may have been designed based off an original Tulu script that's yet to be found. Of the five Dravidian languages, Tulu is considered one of the oldest as more pieces from its history are being discovered. The different dialects can be based off the location within northern and southern parts of Karnataka. [1]

Spoken characteristics

Phonology

Five short and five long vowels (*a, ā, e, ē, u, ū, i, ī, o, ō*) are common in Dravidian languages. Like Kodava Takk (and also like Konkani and Sinhala), Tulu also has an [ɛ]- or [æ]-like vowel, generally occurring word-finally. Kannada script does not have a symbol to specifically represent this vowel, which is often written as a normal *e*.[827] For example, the first person singular form and the third person singular masculine form of a verb are spelled identically in all tenses, both. ending in *e*, but are pronounced differently: the terminating *e* in the former sounds nearly like 'a' in the English word 'man' (ಮಲ್ಪುವೆ *malpuve* / malpuvæ/, "I make"), while that in the latter like 'e' in 'men' (ಮಲ್ಪುವೆ *malpuve* /malpuve/, "he makes"). Paniyadi in his 1932 grammar used a special vowel sign to denote Tulu /ɛ/ in the Kannada script: according to Bhat, he used two *telakaṭṭu*s for this purpose (usually, a *telakaṭṭu* means the crest that a Kannada character like ಠ, ಥ, ನ has), and the same convention was adopted by Upadhyaya in his 1988 Tulu Lexicon. The long counterpart of this vowel occurs in some words.[828] In all dialects, the pair /e/ and /ɛ/ contrasts.

Additionally, like Kodava Takk and Toda, and like Malayalam *saṁvr̥tōkāram*, Tulu has an [ɯ]-like vowel (or schwa /ə/) as a phoneme, which is romanized as *ŭ* (ISO), *ɯ*, or *ṷ*. Both J. Brigel and A. Männer say that it is pronounced like *e* in the French *je*. Bhat describes this phoneme as /ɯ/. However, if it is like Malayalam "half-u", [ə] or [ɨ] may be a better description. In the Kannada script, Brigel and Männer used a virama (halant), ಼, to denote this vowel. Bhat says a *telakaṭṭu* is used for this purpose, but apparently he too means a virama.[829]

Vowels

	Front		Back			
			Rounded		Unrounded	
	Short	Long	Short	Long	Short	Long
Close	i	iː	u	uː	ɯ (ə)	
Mid	e	eː	o	oː		
Open	ɛ (æ)	ɛː (æː)	ɒ	ɒː		

The following are consonant phonemes in Tulu:

Tulu language

Consonants

		Labial	Dental	Retroflex	Palatal	Velar
Plosive	Voiceless	p	t	ṭ	c (tʃ)	k
	Voiced	b	d	ḍ	ɟ (dʒ)	g
Nasal		m	n	ɳ	ɲ	ŋ
Approximant		ʋ			j	
Lateral			l	(ɭ)		
Tap			ɾ			
Fricative			s		ç (ʃ)	

The contrast between /l/ and /ɭ/ is preserved in the South Common dialect and in the Brahmin dialect, but is lost in several dialects. Additionally, the Brahmin dialect has /ʂ/ and /h/. Aspirated consonants are sometimes used in the Brahmin dialect, but are not phonemic. In the Koraga and Holeya dialects, s /s/ and ś /ʃ/ merge with c /tʃ/ (the Koraga dialect of the Tulu language is different from the Koraga language). Word-initial consonant clusters are rare and occur mainly in Sanskrit loanwords. As noted in 'Dialects/Varieties', the Tulu alphabet resembles the Malayalam script in many ways. It is also similar to many characters found in the Tigalari alphabet. This is from the same region in the state of Karnataka. The Tigilari and Kannada alhpabets include a stress on vowels with "a" and "o" sounds. [1][830] Other vowels include sounds such as "au" "am" and "ah". Numerous consonants have their own origin from the Dravidian languages like "kha" "gha" "dha" and "jha". These are derived from the Tigalari alphabet.

Morphology

Tulu has five parts of speech: nouns (substantives and adjectives), pronouns, numerals, verbs, and particles.[831]

Substantives have three grammatical genders (masculine, feminine, and neuter), two numbers (singular and plural), and eight cases (nominative, genitive, dative, accusative, locative, ablative or instrumental, communicative, and vocative). According to Bhat, Tulu has two distinct locative cases. The communicative case is used with verbs like "tell", "speak", "ask", "beseech", "inquire", and denotes *at whom* a message, an inquiry, or a request is aimed, as in "I told *him*." or "I speak *to them*." It is also used to denote *relationship with whom* it is about, in a context like "I am on good terms *with him*." or "I have nothing *against him*."[832] Bhat calls it the sociative case. It is somewhat similar to the comitative case, but different in that it denotes communication or relationship, not physical companionship. The plural suffix is -rŭ, -ḷu, -kuḷu, or -āḍḷu; as, mēji ("table"), mējiḷu ("tables").[833] The nominative case is unmarked, while the remaining cases are expressed by different suffixes.

The following table shows the declension of a noun, based on Brigel and Bhat (ŭ used by Brigel and ɯ used by Bhat are both shown as ŭ for clarity): when two forms are given, the one in parentheses is by Bhat, and the other is by Brigel.[834,835] Some of these differences may be dialectal variations.

Declension of substantives: example *mara* ("a tree")

Case	Singular	Meaning	Plural	Meaning
Nominative	*mara*	a tree	*marokuḷu* (marakulu)	trees
Genitive	*marata*	of a tree	*marokuḷe* (marakulena)	of trees
Dative	*maroku* (marakŭ)	to a tree	*marokuḷegŭ* (marakulegŭ)	to trees
Accusative	*maronu* (maranŭ)	a tree (object)	*marokuḷenŭ* (marakulenŭ)	trees (object)
Locative	*maroṭu* (maraṭŭ)	in a tree	*marokuḷeḍŭ* (marakuleḍŭ)	in trees
Locative 2	— (maraṭɛ)	at or through a tree	— (marakuleḍɛ)	at or through trees
Ablative	*maroḍŭdu* (maraḍḍŭ)	from, by, or through a tree	*marokuḷeḍŭdŭ* (marakuleḍḍŭ)	from, by, or through trees
Communicative	*maraṭa*	to a tree	*marokuḷeḍa* (marakuleḍa)	to trees
Vocative	*marā*	O tree!	*marokuḷē* (marakulɛ̄)	O trees!

The personal pronouns are irregularly inflected: *yānŭ* "I" becomes *yen-* in oblique cases.[836] Tulu makes the distinction between the inclusive and exclusive "we" (See *Clusivity: Dravidian languages*): *nama* "we (including you)" as opposed to *yenkuḷu* "we (not including you)".[837] For verbs, this distinction does not exist. The personal pronouns of the second person are *ī* (oblique: *nin-*) "you (singular)" and *nikuḷu* "you (plural)". Three genders are distinguished in the third person, as well as proximate and remote forms. For example, *imbe* "he (proximate)", *āye* "he (remote)". The suffix -rŭ makes a polite form of personal pronouns, as in *īrŭ* "you (respectfully)", *ārŭ* "he (remote; respectfully)". Postpositions are used usually with a noun in the genitive case, as in *guḍḍe-da mittŭ* "on the hill".

Tulu verbs have three forms: active, causative, and reflexive (or middle voice).[838] They conjugate for person, number, gender, tense (present, past, pluperfect, future, and future perfect), mood (indicative, imperative, conditional, infinitive, potential, and subjunctive), and polarity (positive and negative).[839]

Syntax

Each sentence is composed of a subject and a predicate and every sentence is a full speech or thought in words. There is both singular and plural while being expressed in first through third person. There are several exceptions to each of these depending on the instance. For example: the verb has to be in a plural style if there are numerous nominatives within a sentence or of different genders that agree with the previous sentence. The verb may also be omitted in some sentences. Present tense and past tense may change and their perception.[840]

Written literature

The written literature of Tulu is not as large as the literature of other literary Dravidian languages such as Tamil. Nevertheless, Tulu is one of only five literary Dravidian languages, the other four being Tamil, Telugu, Kannada and Malayalam. The earliest available Tulu literature that survives to this date is the Tulu translation of the great Sanskrit epic of Mahabharata called **Mahabharato** (ಮಹಾಭಾರತೊ). It was written by *Arunabja* (1657 AD), a poet who lived in Kodavur near Udupi around late 14th to early 15th century AD. Other important literary works in Tulu are:

- Devi Mahatmyam's (ಶ್ರೀ ದೇವಿ ಮಹಾತ್ಮ್ಯ) 1200 AD - Tulu translation
- Sri Bhagavata (ಶ್ರೀ ಭಾಗವತೊ) 1626 AD - written by Vishnu Tunga
- Kaveri (1391 AD)

This script was mainly used to write religious and literary works in Sanskrit.[841,842] Even today the official script of the eight Tulu monasteries (Ashta Mathas of Udupi) founded by Madhvacharya in Udupi is Tulu. The pontiffs of the monasteries write their names using this script when they are appointed.

Modern-day Tulu literature is written using the Kannada script. *Mandara Ramayana* is the most notable piece of modern Tulu literature. Written by Mandara Keshava Bhatt, it received the Sahitya Academy award for best poetry. *Madipu, Mogaveera, Saphala* and *Samparka* are popular Tulu periodicals published from Mangalore. The Tulu Sahitya Academy, established by the state government of Karnataka in 1994, as also the Kerala Tulu Academy established by the Indian State Government of Kerala in Manjeshwaram in 2007, are important governmental organisations that promote Tulu literature. Nevertheless, there are numerous organisations spread all over the world with significant Tulu-migrated populations that contribute to Tulu literature. Some notable contributors of Tulu literature are Kayyar Kinhanna Rai, M. K. Seetharam Kulal, Amruta Someshwara, B. A. Viveka Rai, Kedambadi Jattappa Rai, Venkataraja Puninchattaya, Paltadi Ramakrishna Achar, Dr. Sunitha M. Shetty, Dr. Vamana Nandavara, Sri. Balakrishna Shetty Polali.

Oral traditions

The oral traditions of Tulu are one of the major traditions that greatly show the finer aspects of the language. The following are various forms of Tulu oral tradition and literature.

- Paddanas: A form of oral epic poem sung in a highly stylised manner during the Hindu rituals of Bhuta Kola and Nagaradhane, which are peculiar to the Tulu people. These Paddanas are mostly legends about gods or historical personalities among the people. The longest of them being **Siri Paddana**, which is about a woman called Siri who shows strength and integrity during adverse times and in turn attains divinity. The Paddana greatly depicts the independent nature of the Tulu womenfolk. The entire Paddana was written down by Finnish scholar Lauri Honko of the University of Turku and it falls four lines short of Homer's Iliad.
- Riddles: They are another important aspect of Tulu oral traditions. These riddles are largely tongue twisting and mostly deal with kinship and agriculture.
- Bhajans: Bhajans sung in numerous temples across the Tulu region are varied and are dedicated to various gods and goddesses. Most of these are of the Hindu tradition, others being Jain. They are sung in both the Carnatic style as well a style similar to what is used in Yakshagana.
- Kabitol: Songs sung during the cultivation of crops, the traditional occupation of the people. **O Bele** is considered the finest among them.

Theatre

Theatre in the form of the traditional Yakshagana, prevalent in coastal Karnataka and northern Kerala has greatly preserved the finer aspects of the Tulu language. Yakshagana which is conducted in Tulu is very popular among the Tuluva people. It can also be seen as a form of temple art, as there are many Yakshagana groups that are attached to temples, for example that of Kateel Durga Parameshwari Temple as also the Udupi Krishna Temple.

Presently, eight professional Yakshagana troupes perform Tulu-language YakshaganaWikipedia:Citation needed not only during the Yakshagana season

Figure 98: *A Yakshagana Artist*

but also during the off-season in various places in Karnataka and outside.Wikipedia:Citation needed In Mumbai, Tulu Yakshagana is very popular among the Tulu audiences. More than 2,000 Yakshagana artistes take part in the performance in various places in Mumbai annually.Wikipedia:Citation needed Notable performers include Kalladi Koraga Shetty, Pundur Venkatraja Puninchathaya, Guru Bannanje Sanjiva Suvarna and Pathala Venkatramana Bhat.

Tulu plays are among the major entertainment for admirers of art and culture in the Tulu Nadu. Tulu plays, generally centered on the comic genre, are very popular in Mumbai and Bangalore outside Tulu Nadu.

Tulu cinema

The Tulu cinema industry is fairly small; it produces around five films annually. The first film, *Enna Thangadi*, was released in 1971. Usually these films are released in theatres across the Tulu Nadu region and on DVD. The critically acclaimed film *Suddha* won the award for Best Indian Film at the Osian's Cinefan Festival of Asian and Arab Cinema in New Delhi in 2006. As of 2015, *Oriyardori Asal* (2011) has been the most commercially successful Tulu film. Chaali Polilu is the longest-running film in Tulu film history, as well as the highest-grossing film in the Tulu film industry. It has successfully completed

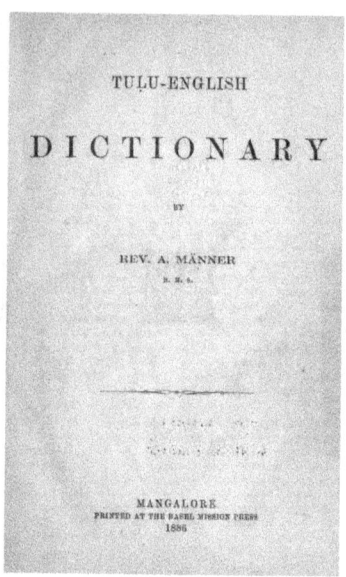

Figure 99: *The front cover of the Tulu dictionary published by Männer in 1886.*

470 days at PVR Cinemas in Mangalore. The 2014 film *Madime* was reported to be remade in Marathi, thereby becoming the first Tulu film to be remade in another language. *Shutterdulai* was the first remake in Tulu cinema. *Eregla Panodchi* is the second remake in Tulu cinemas. A suit for damages of Rs. 25 lakhs was filed against the makers of the Telugu film *Brahmotsavam* for copying the first 36 seconds of the song *A...lele...yereg madme* by Dr. Vamana Nandaavara found in the *Deepanalike* CD composed for the Siri channel. The song was used in the movie in a sequence involving the lead actor who, while accompanying his family on a tour, dances to the tune of the hit Tulu song.

Centres of Tulu study and research

Tulu as a language continues to thrive in coastal Karnataka and Kasaragod in Kerala. **Tulu Sahitya Academy**, an institute established by the state government of Karnataka, has introduced Tulu as a language in schools around coastal Karnataka, including Alva's High School, Moodbidri; Dattanjaneya High School, Odiyoor; Ramakunjeshwara English-medium High School, Ramakunja; and Vani Composite Pre-University College, Belthangady. Initially started in 16 schools, the language is now taught in over 33 schools, of which 30 are in Dakshina Kannada district. More than 1500 students have opted this language.

Tulu is also taught as a language at the post graduate level in **Mangalore University**, and there is a dedicated department for **Tulu studies, Translation and Research** at **Dravidian University** in Kuppam Andhra Pradesh.**The Government Degree College** at Kasaragod in Kerala has also introduced a certificate course in Tulu for the academic year 2009-2010. It has also introduced Tulu as an optional subject in its Kannada post-graduation course. It has adopted syllabi from the books published by the Tulu Sahitya Academy.

German missionaries Revs. Kammerer and Männer were the first people to conduct research on the language. Rev. Krammer collected about 3,000 words and their meanings until he died. Later his work was carried on by Rev. Männer, who completed the research and published the first dictionary of the Tulu language in 1886 with the help of the then Madras government. The effort was incomplete, as it did not cover all aspects of the language. The Govinda Pai Research Centre at MGM College, Udupi started an 18-year Tulu lexicon project in the year 1979.

Different dialects, special vocabularies used for different occupational activities, rituals, and folk literature in the forms of Paād-danāas were included in this project. The Centre has also released a six-volume, trilingual, modestly priced Tulu-Kannada-English lexicon. The Tulu lexicon was awarded the Gundert Award for the best dictionary in the country in 1996. In September 2011, the Academic Council of Mangalore University accepted a proposal, to allow the university and the colleges affiliated to it to offer certificates, diplomas and postgraduate diploma courses in Tulu, both in regular and correspondence modes

References

- Caldwell, R., *A Comparative Grammar of the Dravidian or South-Indian family of languages*, London: Harrison, 1856.; Reprinted London, K. Paul, Trench, Trubner & co., ltd., 1913; rev. ed. by J. L. Wyatt and T. Ramakrishna Pillai, Madras, University of Madras, 1961, reprint Asian Educational Services, 1998. <templatestyles src="Module:Citation/CS1/styles.css" />ISBN 81-206-0117-3
- Danielou, Alain (1985), *Histoire de l'Inde*, Fayard, Paris. <templatestyles src="Module:Citation/CS1/styles.css" />ISBN 2-213-01254-7
- Hall, Edith (2002), "The singing actors of antiquity" in Pat Easterling & Edith Hall, ed., *Greek and Roman Actors: Aspects of an Ancient Profession*, Cambridge University Press, Cambridge. <templatestyles src="Module:Citation/CS1/styles.css" />ISBN 0-521-65140-9
- Thesis of Viveka Rai[843]

- Lauri Honko, *Textualisation of Oral Epics.* <templatestyles src="Module:Citation/CS1/styles.css" />ISBN 3-11-016928-2
- William Pais, *Land Called South Canara.* <templatestyles src="Module:Citation/CS1/styles.css" />ISBN 81-7525-148-4
- Bhat, S.L. *A Grammar of Tulu: a Dravidian language.* <templatestyles src="Module:Citation/CS1/styles.css" />ISBN 81-85691-12-6
- Männer, A. *Tuḷu-English dictionary*, Mangalore 1886
- Männer, A. *English-Tuḷu dictionary*, Mangalore 1888 | *English-Tuḷu Dictionary.* <templatestyles src="Module:Citation/CS1/styles.css" />ISBN 81-206-0263-3 [a reprint?]
- Briegel, J. *A Grammar of the Tulu language*, Char and Roman. <templatestyles src="Module:Citation/CS1/styles.css" />ISBN 81-206-0070-3
- Bhat, D. N. S. (1998), "Tulu", in Steever, Sanford B., *The Dravidian Languages*, Routledge, pp. 158–177, ISBN 0-415-10023-2<templatestyles src="Module:Citation/CS1/styles.css"></templatestyles>
- Vinson, Julien (1878), *Le verbe dans les langues dravidiennes : tamoul, canara, télinga, malayâla, tulu, etc.*, Maisonneuve et cie., Paris
- Burnell, Arthur Coke (1874), *Elements of South-Indian Palæography from the Fourth to the Seventeenth Century A.D.*, Trübner & Co.
- Krishnamurti, Bhadriraju (2003), *The Dravidian Languages*, Cambridge University Press. <templatestyles src="Module:Citation/CS1/styles.css" />ISBN 0-521-77111-0
- G., L. R. (2013). Elements of comparative philology. Place of publication not identified: Hardpress Ltd.
- Maenner, A. (1886). Tulu-English dictionary: By Rev. A. Männer. Mangalore: Printed at the Basel Mission.
- C. (1875). A comparative grammar of the dravidian or south-Indian family of languages. London: Trübner and Co., Ludgate Hill.
- Bhatt, S. L. (2005). A grammar of Tulu: a Dravidian language. Thiruvananthapuram: Dravidian linguistics association.
- Goddard, C. (2009). The languages of East and Southeast Asia: an introduction. Oxford: Oxford Univ. Press.
- Padmanabha, Kekunnaya. K. (1994). A comparative study of Tulu dialects. Udupi.
- Narayana, S. B. (1967). Descriptive analysis of Tulu. Poona: Deccan College Postgraduate and Research Institute.
- Upadhyaya, U. P. (n.d.). Tulu Lexicon: Tulu-Kannada-English Dictionary. Udupi.
- Brigel, J. (2010). Grammar of the tulu language. Place of publication not identified: Nabu Press.
- Aiyar, L. R. (1936). Materials for a sketch of Tulu phonology. Lahore.

- G., L. R. (2013). Elements of comparative philology. Place of publication not identified: Hardpress Ltd.
- Maenner, A. (1886). Tulu-English dictionary: By Rev. A. Männer. Mangalore: Printed at the Basel Mission.
- C. (1875). A comparative grammar of the dravidian or south-Indian family of languages. London: Trübner and Co., Ludgate Hill.
- Bhatt, S. L. (2005). A grammar of Tulu: a Dravidian language. Thiruvananthapuram: Dravidian linguistics association.
- Goddard, C. (2009). The languages of East and Southeast Asia: an introduction. Oxford: Oxford Univ. Press.
- Padmanabha, Kekunnaya, K. (1994). A comparative study of Tulu dialects. Udupi.
- Bhat D. N. S. (1967). Descriptive analysis of Tulu. Poona: Deccan College Postgraduate and Research Institute.
- Upadhyaya, U. P. (n.d.). Tulu Lexicon: Tulu-Kannada-English Dictionary. Udupi.
- Brigel, J. (2010). Grammar of the tulu language. Place of publication not identified: Nabu Press.
- Aiyar, L. R. (1936). Materials for a sketch of Tulu phonology. Lahore.
- *Full Text of "Elements of Comparative Philology"*. N.p., n.d. Web. 2 May 2017.
- "Tulu (ತುಳು ಬಾಸೆ)." *Tulu Language and Alphabets*. N.p., n.d. Web. 2 May 2017.

External links

 Wikimedia Commons has media related to *Tulu language*.

 Tulu edition of Wikipedia, the free encyclopedia

- Official Website of Karnataka Government's Tulu Academy[844]
- Tulu Wikipedia[845]
- Online Tulu Dictionary[846]
- Tuluver.com[847]
- Tulu Language: Its Script and Dialects[848] Boloji.com
- Common Kannada, Tulu and Konkani phrases[849] Mangalore.com
- Tulu Literature[850]

Urdu literature

Urdu literature

Part of a series on
Islamic culture

Architecture

- Azerbaijani
- Indo-Islamic
- Moorish
- Moroccan
- Mughal
- Ottoman
- Pakistani
- Tatar
- Persian
- Somali
- Sudano-Sahelian

Art

- Calligraphy
- Miniature
- Oriental rug
- Arab carpet

- Persian carpet
- Turkish carpet

Dress

- Abaya
- Agal
- Boubou
- Burqa
- Chador
- Jellabiya
- Niqāb
- Salwar kameez
- Songkok (Peci)
- Taqiya
- Keffiyeh (Kufiya)
- Thawb
- Jilbab
- Hijab

Holidays

- Ashura
- Arba'een
- al-Ghadeer
- Chaand Raat
- al-Fitr
- al-Adha
- Imamat Day
- New Year
- Isra and Mi'raj
- al-Qadr
- Mawlid
- Ramadan
- Mid-Sha'ban

Literature

- Arabic
- Azerbaijani
- Bengali
- Indonesian
- Javanese
- Kashmiri
- Kurdish
- Malay
- Pashto
- Persian

Urdu literature

- Punjabi
- Sindhi
- Somali
- South Asian
- Turkish
- Urdu

Music

- Dastgah
- Ghazal
- Madih nabawi
- Maqam
- Mugam
- Nasheed
- Qawwali
- Sufi

Theatre

- Bangsawan
- Jem
- Karagöz and Hacivat
- Sama
- Ta'zieh

- Islam portal

- v
- t
- e[851]

Urdu literature (Urdu: ادبیات اردو, *"Adbiyāt-i Urdū"*) is literature in the Urdu language. has a history that is inextricably tied to the development of Urdu, the register of the Hindustani language written in the Perso-Arabic script. While it tends to be dominated by poetry, especially the verse forms of the *ghazal* and *nazm*, it has expanded into other styles of writing, including that of the short story, or *afsana*.

Urdu literature is mostly popular in Pakistan, where Urdu is the national language and India, where it is an official language. It is also widely understood in Afghanistan.Wikipedia:Citation needed

Origin

Indian literature
• Assamese
• Bengali
• Bhojpuri
• English
• Gujarati
• Hindi
• Kannada
• Kashmiri
• Konkani
• Malayalam
• Meitei
• Marathi
• Mizo
• Nepali
• Odia
• Punjabi
• Rajasthani
• Sanskrit
• Sindhi
• Tamil
• Telugu
• Urdu
• v • t • e[852]

Urdu Developed in Malegaon. Urdu literature originated some time around the 14th century in present-day North India among the sophisticated gentry of the courts. The continuing traditions of Islam and patronisations of foreign culture centuries earlier by Muslim rulers, usually of Turkic or Afghan descent, marked their influence on the Urdu language given that both cultural heritages were strongly present throughout Urdu territory. The Urdu language, with a vocabulary almost evenly split between Sanskrit-derived Prakrit and Arabo-Persian words, was a reflection of this cultural amalgamation.

Special contributors

Amir Khusro exercised great influence on the initial growth of not only Urdu literature, but the language itself (which only truly took shape as distinguished from both Persian and proto-Hindi around the 14th century). He is credited with the systematization of northern Indian classical music, including Hindustani music, and he wrote works both in Persian and Hindavi. While the couplets that come down from him are representative of a latter-Prakrit Hindi bereft of Arabo-Persian Vocabulary, his influence on court viziers and writers must have been transcendental, for a century after his death Quli Qutub Shah was speaking a language that might be considered to be Urdu. Sultan Muhammed Quli Qutb Shah was a scholar in Persian and Arabic. He also wrote poetry in Telugu language, Persian language and Urdu language. His poetry has been compiled into Dewan or volume entitled "Kulliyat-e-Quli Qutub Shah." Muhammed Quli Qutub Shah had the distinction of being the first Saheb-e-dewan Urdu poet and is credited with introducing a new sensibility into prevailing genres of Persian/Urdu poetry. It is said that the Urdu language acquired the status of a literary language due to his contributions. He died in the year 1611.

Sayyid Shamsullah Qadri is considered as the first researcher of Deccaniyat. some of the works of Allama Hakeem Sayyid Shamsullah Qadri are Salateen e Muabber 1929, Urdu-i-qadim 1930, Tareekh E Maleebaar, Mowarrikheen E Hind, Tahfat al Mujahidin 1931, Imadiya, Nizam Ut Tawareekh, Tareekh Zuban Urdu-Urdu-E-Qadeem, Tareekh Zuban Urdu Al Musamma Ba Urdu-E-Qadeem, Tareekh Zuban Urdu Yaani Urdu-E-Qadeem, Tarikh Vol III, Asaarul Karaam, Tarikh Shijrah Asifiya, Ahleyaar, Pracina malabar

Dastaangoi (epics)

Urdu literature was generally composed more of poetry than of prose. The prose component of Urdu literature was mainly restricted to the ancient form of epic stories called Dastan (داستان). These long stories have complicated plots that deal with magical and otherwise fantastic creatures and events.

The genre originated in the Middle East and was disseminated by folk storytellers. It was assimilated by individual authors. Dastan's plots are based both on folklore and classical literary subjects. Dastan was particularly popular in Urdu literature, typologically close to other narrative genres in Eastern literatures, such as Persian masnawi, Punjabi qissa, Sindhi waqayati bait, etc., and also reminiscent of the European novel. The oldest known Urdu dastans are *Dastan-i-Amir Hamza*, recorded in the early seventeenth century, and the on longer extant*Bustan-iKhayal* (*The Garden of Imagination* or *The Garden of Khayal*) by Mir Taqi Khayal (d. 1760). Most of the narrative dastans were recorded in the early nineteenth century, representing the inclusion of 'wandering' motifs borrowed from the folklore of the Middle East, central Asia and northern India. These include *Bagh-oBahar* (*The Garden and Spring*) by Mir Amman, *Mazhab-i-Ishq* (*The Religion of Love*) by Nihalchand Lahori, *Araish-i-Mahfil* (*The Adornment of the Assembly*) by Hyderbakhsh Hyderi, and *Gulzar-i-Chin* (*The Flower Bed of Chin*) by Khalil Ali Khan Ashq. Other famous Urdu dastans include *Nau tarz-i murassa'* by Husain 'Atā Khān Tahsīn, *Nau ā'īn-i hindī* (*Qissa-i Malik Mahmūd Gīti-Afroz*) by Mihr Chand Khatrī, *Jazb-i 'ishq* by Shāh Husain Haqīqat, *Nau tarz-i murassa'* by Muhammad Hādī (a.k.a. Mirzā Mughal Ghāfil), and *Talism Hoshruba* by Muhammad Husain Azad.

Tazkiras

Tazkiras, are compilations of literary memoirs that include verses and maxims of the great poets along with biographical information and commentaries on their styles. They are often a collection of names with a line or two of information about each poet, followed by specifics about his composition. Some of this Tazkiras give biographical details, and a little idea of the style or poetical power is transmitted. Even the large anthologies do not systematically review an author's work. Most of them have the names in alphabetical order, but one or two are ordered by historical chronology. The majority quote only lyrics, and the quotations are usually chosen randomly.

Poetry

Urdu poetry reached its peak in the 19th century. The most well-developed form of poetry is the ghazal, known for its quality and quantity within the Urdu tradition.

Sonnets

Urdu poets influenced by English and other European-language poetry began writing sonnets in Urdu in the early 20th century.[853] Azmatullah Khan (1887-1923) is believed to have introduced this format to Urdu poetry.[854] Other renowned Urdu poets who wrote sonnets are Akhtar Junagarhi, Akhtar Sheerani, Noon Meem Rashid, Mehr Lal Soni Zia Fatehabadi, Salaam Machhalishahari and Wazir Agha.

Novels

Initially, Urdu novels focused on urban social life, eventually widening in scope to include rural social life. They also covered the changing times under the progressive writing movement inspired by Sajjad Zaheer. He was not novlist but a short story writer. However, the independence of Pakistan in 1947 greatly affected the novel, bringing up questions of identity and migration as can be seen in the major works of Intezar Hussain and Quratulain Haider. Towards the end of the last century the novel took a serious turn towards the contemporary life and realities of the young generations of India. The most significant novels of the current generation of Indian novelists in Urdu, which demonstrate a new confidence in contemporary life, are *Makaan* by Paigham Afaqui, *Do Gaz Zameen* by Abdus Samad, and *Pani* by Ghazanfer. These works, especially *Makaan*, brought the Urdu novel out of the prevailing themes of the independence of Pakistan in 1947 and identity issues and took it into the realm of modern-day realities and issues of life in India. *Makaan* influenced many English writers such as Vikram Seth, who turned to novel writing. These Urdu novels further affected significant works such as *Andhere Pag* by Sarwat Khan, *Numberdar Ka Neela* by S M Ashraf and *Fire Area* by Ilyas Ahmed Gaddi. Paigham Afaqui's second major novel, *Paleeta*, was published in 2011 and depicts the tension of the political sickening of a common Indian citizen in the six decades after India's independence. Bewildered by the disappointing state of democracy and the transformation of Indian society into a mental desert the central character dies after leaving behind his writings which catch fire.

Famous novels

- *Mirat-al-Urus* (*The Bride's Mirror*; 1868–1869) by Deputy Nazeer Ahmed is regarded as the first novel in Urdu. Within twenty years of publication over 100,000 copies had been printed; and was also translated into Bengali, Braj, Kashmiri, Punjabi, and Gujarati. It has never been out of print in Urdu. In 1903 an English translation was published in London by G. E. Ward.
- *Umrao-Jaan* by Mirza Hadi Ruswa is also considered the first Urdu novel by many critics.Wikipedia:Citation needed
- *Bina-tul-Nash-* (*The Daughters of the Bier*, a name for the constellation Ursa Major) is another novel by Deputy Nazeer Ahmed. It was his 2nd novel after *Mirat-tul-uroos*. Like *Mira-tul-Uroos*, this novel is also on the education of women and their character building.
- *Zindagi* (*Everything Happens in Life*; 1933–1934) by Chaudhry Afzal Haq describes the ups and downs of life for developing moral values and

guidance of young people. His entire work is full of the teaching of moral values.
- *Taubat-un-Nasuh* (*Repentance of Nasuh*; 1873-1874) by Deputy Nazeer Ahmed also focused on moral lessons for youth.
- *Fasaana-e-Mubtalaa* (1885) was another novel for developing moral values and guidance for youth.
- "Aag Ka Darya" by Quratulain Haider
- "Udas Naslain" by Abdullah Hussain
- "Jangloos" by Shaukat Siddiqui
- "Pir e kamil" by Umera Ahmad
- "Khuda Ke Saaye Mein Ankh Micholi " by Rahman Abbas
- "Ek Mamnua Muhabbat Ki Kahani" by Rahman Abbas
- "Rohzin" By Rahman Abbas

In the first decade of twenty first century Rahman Abbas has emerged as most influential Urdu fiction writer. 'The Hindu', writes about work of Rahman Abbas that With his uncanny ability to subvert what people believe, Rehman Abbas raises the art of story-telling to a new level.

Short stories (afsanah nigari)

Urdu literature has included the short story form for slightly more than one hundred years. During this period it has passed through some major phases including the early romantic period, progressive writings, modernist writings, and the current phase. Although a number of male and female writers wrote short stories during the first phase G(including bMJHoth romantic stories and social criticisms), the short story crystallized as a regular part of Urdu literature in the growth of the writings of Munshi Premchand. His notable short stories include "Kafan" and "Poos Ki Raat". The Urdu short story gained momentum with the phenomenal publication of *Angare*, a collection of many writers towards the end of the life of Premchand. Writers like Ghulam Abbas, Manto, Rajinder Singh Bedi, Krishan Chander and Ismat Chughtai, to name but a few, turned the short story into a major genre of Urdu literature.

The next generation of Urdu short story writers included Qurratulain Hyder, Qazi Abdul Sattar and Joginder Paul. The short story tradition continues with younger generation writers like Zahida Hina, Paigham Afaqui, Syed Mohd Ashraf, Salam Bin Razzaq, Naeem Baig, Akhlaq Ahmed Khan and Moinuddin Jinabade.

Urdu short stories have dealt with a wide range of the dimensions of life, but the most famous stories concern the trauma of the independence of Pakistan in 1947 and the violence generated out of it. Towards the end of the last century, short stories became grounded in the complexity of daily life which can be seen in the unique collection of short stories in Paigham Afaqui's *Mafia*. An entirely different approach is seen in the collection of short stories *T'abir* by Moinuddin Jinabade and *Taus Chaman Ka Maina* by Nayyer Masood.

Drama

Urdu drama evolved from the prevailing dramatic traditions of North India raas as practiced by exponents like Nawab Wajid Ali Shah of Awadh. His dramatic experiments led to the famous Inder Sabha of Amanat and later this tradition took the shape of Parsi Theatre. Agha Hashr Kashmiri is the culmination of this tradition.

Urdu theatre traditions have greatly influenced modern Indian theatre. Among all the languages, Urdu (which was called Hindi by early writers), along with Gujrati, Marathi, and Bengali theatres have remained popular. Many Urdu dramas have also been made into films.

Classic playwrights include Prof Hasan, Ghulam Jeelani, J. N. Kaushal, Shameem Hanfi and Jameel Shaidayi. Danish Iqbal, Sayeed Alam, Shahid Anwar, Iqbal Niyazi and Anwar are a few of the post-modern playwrights actively contributing to Urdu drama.

Sayeed Alam is known for his wit and humour in plays like *Ghalib in New Delhi*, *Maulana Azad* and *Big B*.

Danish Iqbal's *Dara Shikoh*, directed by M S Sathyu, is considered a modern classic for its use of newer theatre techniques and a contemporary perspective. His other plays are *Sahir*, on the famous lyricist and revolutionary poet; *Kuchh Ishq kiya Kuchh Kaam*, a Celebration of the Faiz's poetry, featuring events from the early part of his life, particularly the events and incidents of pre-independence days which shaped his life and ideals; and *Chand Roz Aur Meri Jaan*, another play inspired from Faiz's letters written from various jails during the Rawalpindi Conspiracy days. He has written 14 other plays including *Dilli Jo Ek Shehr Thaa* and *Main Gaya Waqt Nahin hoon*.

Shahid's *Three B* is also a significant play. He has been associated with many groups including 'Natwa'. Zaheer Anwar has kept the flag of Urdu Theatre flying in Kolkata. Unlike the writers of the previous generation, Sayeed, Shahid, Iqbal, and Zaheer do not write bookish plays but rather their work is a product of a vigorous performing tradition. Iqbal Niyazi of Mumbai has written several plays in Urdu. His play *Aur Kitne Jalyanwala Baugh??* won several awards. Hence this is the only generation after Amanat and Agha Hashr who actually write for the stage and not for libraries.

Literary movements

Progressive Writers Movement

According to The Dawn, the Progressive Writers Movement in Urdu literature was the strongest movement after Sir Syed's education movement.Wikipedia:Citation needed

Modernism

The modernist movement started in Urdu literature around 1960. This movement laid more stress on symbolic and other indirect expressions as opposed to direct and clear expressions. The most well-known names in this movement included Shamsur Rehman Farooqui and Gopichand Narang and the poets Noon Meem Rashid and Meeraji. Apart from them, a number of other poets like Zafer Iqbal, Nasir Kazmi, Bashir Bader and Shahryar are related to this movement.

Halqa e Arbab e Zauq

Halqa e Arbab e Zauq was a literary movement begun in Lahore, British Raj, India in 1936. Early members included poets Noon Meem Rashid, Zia Jallandhari, Muhtar Siddiqui, Hafeez Hoshiarpuri and Meeraji, brought to the meeting by his friend, Qayyum Nazar, an active member of the group. The Halqa was the second modern literary movement in Urdu poetry in the 20th century, founded just a couple of years after the leftist Progressive Writers' Movement, and is considered to be the most influential group on modern poetry in the Urdu Language.

Post-modernism

Post-modernism was introduced to Urdu literature by Gopi Chand Narang. Many other critics in Urdu literature are also attached to this approach to criticism. Post-modernism does not claim to be a movement and does not demand any writer to adopt a particular style of writing. It generally concentrates on a method of understanding contemporary literature in the light of its content—mostly examining features like feminism, dalit, regional and other types of literature as opposed to seeking uniformity in the global literature on the basis of internationally established trends.

Independent writers

By the end of the 1980s the atmosphere in Urdu literature became very depressing. The progressive movement was almost dead and the modernist movement had started running out of ideas. But this was also the time for an upsurge of new creative forces rooted in the new life that was metamorphosing the socio-economic and political climate in the sub-continent. It was under this climate that a new era of fiction started with the publication of Paigham Afaqui's novel *Makaan*. Afaqui and other writers refused to be identified by any movement and displayed complete independence in using personally developed styles and techniques for writing novels and explored their own philosophy and vision of life. It was a serious departure from the theme of independence which dominated writers like Qurratulain Hyder and Abdullah Hussain and the theme of existentialism which was the benchmark of modernism. Writers like Ghazanfer and Musharraf Alam Zauqi have further widened the horizons of new themes and concerns.

Theatre of the Absurd

Theatre of the Absurd is a new and somewhat rare genre in the history of Urdu Literature[855]. The first play of the genre was written and published by the Pakistan research-writer, poet, lawyer and columnist Mujtaba Haider Zaidi in December 2008 under the title *Mazaron Ke Phool*[856] (i.e. *Graveyard Flowers*).

Further reading

- Muhammad Husain Azad: *Ab-e hayat* (Lahore: Naval Kishor Gais Printing Wrks) 1907 [in Urdu]; (Delhi: Oxford University Press) 2001 [In English translation]
- Shamsur Rahman Faruqi: *Early Urdu Literary Culture and History* (Delhi: Oxford University Press) 2001
- M.A.R. Habib: *An Anthology of Modern Urdu Poetry* in English translation with Urdu text. Modern Language Association (2003). <templatestyles src="Module:Citation/CS1/styles.css" />ISBN 0-87352-797-6
- Alamgir Hashmi, *The Worlds of Muslim Imagination* (1986) <templatestyles src="Module:Citation/CS1/styles.css" />ISBN 0-00-500407-1.
- Muhammad Sadiq, *A History of Urdu Literature* (1984).
- Alamgir Hashmi, ed. Rafey Habib, Faruq Hassan, and David Matthews, tr., *Your Essence, Martyr: Pakistani Elegies* Plainview (2011). <templatestyles src="Module:Citation/CS1/styles.css" />ISBN 9789699670008
- *The Annual of Urdu Studies*, 1981-.

- "Urdu Afsana : Soorat o Ma'na" (Urdu) by M. Hameed Shahid National Book Foundation Islamabad Pakistan 2006-1.an eminent poet of moder age akhlaque bandvi.
- Noorul Hasnain- 'Naya Afsana-Naye Naam.<templatestyles src="Module:Citation/CS1/styles.css" />ISBN 978-93-81029-29-9. Published by Arshia publication Delhi 110095. Edition 2012 (Article o n EK Mamnua Muhabbat Ki Kahani page 316 to 321)
- EK Mamnua Muhabbat Ki Kahani-by Rahman Abbas, Published by Educational Publishing House, Delhi-6 <templatestyles src="Module:Citation/CS1/styles.css" />ISBN 978-81-8223-491-8

External links

Wikibooks has a book on the topic of: *Urdu*

Wikisourcehas the text of the 1911 *Encyclopædia Britannica*article **Hindōstānī Literature**.

- Columbia University: Urdu Language Sources[857]
- Maḫzan al-asrār. Niżāmī raqm-i Muḥammad. Dessinateur 1538 AD[858]
- Best Urdu Quotes[859]
- Hindustani Language and Literature[860]

Appendix

References

[1] //en.wikipedia.org/w/index.php?title=Template:Hindu_scriptures&action=edit
[2] "Veda" http://www.dictionary.com/browse/veda. *Random House Webster's Unabridged Dictionary*.
[3] see e.g. ; Witzel, Michael, "Vedas and ", in: ; ; *Sanskrit literature* (2003) in Philip's Encyclopedia. Accessed 2007-08-09
[4] Sanujit Ghose (2011). " Religious Developments in Ancient India http://www.ancient.eu.com/article/230/" in *Ancient History Encyclopedia*.
[5] Vaman Shivaram Apte, *The Practical Sanskrit-English Dictionary* http://www.aa.tufs.ac.jp/~tjun/sktdic/, see apauruṣeya
[6] D Sharma, Classical Indian Philosophy: A Reader, Columbia University Press, ISBN , pages 196-197
[7] Jan Westerhoff (2009), Nagarjuna's Madhyamaka: A Philosophical Introduction, Oxford University Press, , page 290
[8] Warren Lee Todd (2013), The Ethics of Śaṅkara and Śāntideva: A Selfless Response to an Illusory World, , page 128
[9] Sheldon Pollock (2011), Boundaries, Dynamics and Construction of Traditions in South Asia (Editor: Federico Squarcini), Anthem, , pages 41-58
[10] Hartmut Scharfe (2002), Handbook of Oriental Studies, BRILL Academic, , pages 13-14
[11] Seer of the Fifth Veda: Kṛṣṇa Dvaipāyana Vyāsa in the Mahābhārata https//books.google.com Bruce M. Sullivan, Motilal Banarsidass, pages 85-86
[12] "As a skilled craftsman makes a car, a singer I, Mighty One! this hymn for thee have fashioned.If thou, O Agni, God, accept it gladly, may we obtain thereby the heavenly Waters". – *Rigveda 5.2.11*, Translated by Ralph T.H. Griffith<ref>
[13] Bloomfield, M. The Atharvaveda and the Gopatha-Brahmana, (Grundriss der Indo-Arischen Philologie und Altertumskunde II.1.b.) Strassburg 1899; Gonda, J. A history of Indian literature: I.1 Vedic literature (Samhitas and Brahmanas); I.2 The Ritual Sutras. Wiesbaden 1975, 1977
[14]
[15] A Bhattacharya (2006), Hindu Dharma: Introduction to Scriptures and Theology, , pages 8-14; George M. Williams (2003), Handbook of Hindu Mythology, Oxford University Press, , page 285
[16] Jan Gonda (1975), Vedic Literature: (Saṃhitās and Brāhmaṇas), Otto Harrassowitz Verlag,
[17] A Bhattacharya (2006), Hindu Dharma: Introduction to Scriptures and Theology, , pages 8-14
[18] Barbara A. Holdrege (1995), Veda and Torah: Transcending the Textuality of Scripture, State University of New York Press, , pages 351-357
[19] Elisa Freschi (2012): The Vedas are not deontic authorities in absolute sense and may be disobeyed, but are recognized as an deontological epistemic authority by a Hindu orthodox school;<ref>Elisa Freschi (2012), Duty, Language and Exegesis in Prabhakara Mimamsa, BRILL, , page 62
[20] "astika" http://www.britannica.com/topic/astika and "nastika" http://www.britannica.com/topic/nastika. *Encyclopædia Britannica Online*, 20 Apr. 2016
[21] see e.g. Pokorny's 1959 *Indogermanisches etymologisches Wörterbuch* s.v. '²; *Rix' Lexikon der indogermanischen Verben*, '.
[22] , page 1015 http://www.ibiblio.org/sripedia/ebooks/mw/1000/mw__1048.html
[23] , page 1017 (2nd Column) http://www.ibiblio.org/sripedia/ebooks/mw/1000/mw__1050.html
[24] , page 1017 (3rd Column) http://www.ibiblio.org/sripedia/ebooks/mw/1000/mw__1050.html
[25] Sanskrit: य: समिधा य आहुती यो वेदेन ददाश मर्तो अग्रये । यो नमसा स्वध्वर: ।॥५ ॥, ऋग्वेद: सूक्तं ८.१९ http://sa.wikisource.org/wiki/ऋग्वेद:_सूक्तं_८.१९, Wikisource
[26] K.F. Geldner, Der Rig-Veda, Harvard Oriental Series 33-37, Cambridge 1951

[27] HH Wilson, Rig-veda Sanhita https://archive.org/stream/rigvedasanhitc04wils#page/290/mode/2up Sixth Ashtaka, First Adhayaya, Sukta VII (8.19.5), page 291, Trubner London
[28] Vasudha Narayanan (1994), The Vernacular Veda: Revelation, Recitation, and Ritual, University of South Carolina Press, , pages 194
[29] John Carman (1989), The Tamil Veda: Pillan's Interpretation of the Tiruvaymoli, University of Chicago Press, , pages 259-261
[30] Vasudha Narayanan (1994), The Vernacular Veda: Revelation, Recitation, and Ritual, University of South Carolina Press, , pages 43, 117-119
[31] Gavin Flood sums up mainstream estimates, according to which the Rigveda was compiled from as early as 1500 BCE over a period of several centuries.
[32] Witzel, Michael, "Vedas and ", in:
[33] The early Buddhist texts are also generally believed to be of oral tradition, with the first Pali Canon written many centuries after the death of the Buddha. UNIQ-ref-0-a33abbaafb66ca9c-QINU
[34] Witzel, Michael, "Vedas and ", in: ; For oral composition and oral transmission for "many hundreds of years" before being written down, see: .
[35] Buswell, Robert E.; Lopez, Jr., Donald S. (2013). *The Princeton dictionary of Buddhism.* Princeton: Princeton University Press. Entry on "Nālandā".
[36] Sukumar Dutt (1988) [First published in 1962]. *Buddhist Monks And Monasteries of India: Their History And Contribution To Indian Culture.* George Allen and Unwin Ltd, London. pg. 332-333
[37] according to ISKCON, Hindu Sacred Texts http://hinduism.iskcon.com/tradition/1105.htm, "Hindus themselves often use the term to describe anything connected to the Vedas and their corollaries (e.g. Vedic culture)".
[38] 37,575 are Rigvedic. Of the remaining, 34,857 appear in the other three Samhitas, and 16,405 are known only from Brahmanas, Upanishads or Sutras
[39] Klaus Klostermaier (1994), A Survey of Hinduism, Second Edition, State University of New York Press, , pages 67-69
[40] Witzel, Michael, "Vedas and ", in: .
[41] For a table of all Vedic texts see Witzel, Michael, "Vedas and ", in: .
[42] The Vedic Sanskrit corpus is incorporated in *A Vedic Word Concordance* (') **prepared from 1930 under Vishva Bandhu, and published in five volumes in 1935-1965. Its scope extends to about 400 texts, including the entire Vedic Sanskrit corpus besides some "sub-Vedic" texts. Volume I: Samhitas, Volume II: Brahmanas and Aranyakas, Volume III: Upanishads, Volume IV: Vedangas; A revised edition, extending to about 1800 pages, was published in 1973-1976.**
[43] Edward Roer (Translator), to *Brihad Aranyaka Upanishad* at pages 1-5; Quote - "The Vedas are divided in two parts, the first is the karma-kanda, the ceremonial part, also (called) purva-kanda, and treats on ceremonies; the second part is the jnana kanda, the part which contains knowledge, also named uttara-kanda or posterior part, and unfolds the knowledge of Brahma or the universal soul."
[44] Wiman Dissanayake (1993), Self as Body in Asian Theory and Practice (Editors: Thomas P. Kasulis et al.), State University of New York Press, , page 39; **Quote**: "The Upanishads form the foundations of Hindu philosophical thought and the central theme of the Upanishads is the identity of Atman and Brahman, or the inner self and the cosmic self.";
[45] Michael McDowell and Nathan Brown (2009), World Religions, Penguin, , pages 208-210
[46] Patrick Olivelle (2014), The Early Upanisads, Oxford University Press, , page 3; **Quote**: "Even though theoretically the whole of vedic corpus is accepted as revealed truth [shruti], in reality it is the Upanishads that have continued to influence the life and thought of the various religious traditions that we have come to call Hindu. Upanishads are the scriptures par excellence of Hinduism".
[47] Jamison and Witzel (1992), Vedic Hinduism http://www.people.fas.harvard.edu/~witzel/vedica.pdf, Harvard University, page 6
[48] J. Muir (1868), , 2nd Edition, page 12

[49] Albert Friedrich Weber, , Volume 10, pp 1-9 with footnotes (in German); For a translation, , page 14
[50] For an example, see Sarvānukramaṇī Vivaraṇa http://hdl.library.upenn.edu/1017/d/medren/3178027 Univ of Pennsylvania rare texts collection
[51] Ṛgveda-sarvānukramaṇī Śaunakakṛtā'nuvākānukramaṇī ca, Maharṣi-Kātyāyāna-viracitā,
[52] Michael Witzel, "Vedas and ", in: , Quote: "... almost all printed editions depend on the late manuscripts that are hardly older than 500 years"
[53] //en.wikipedia.org/w/index.php?title=Template:Vedas_and_Shakhas&action=edit
[54] ; Witzel, Michael, "Vedas and ", in:
[55] Witzel, M., " The Development of the Vedic Canon and its Schools : The Social and Political Milieu http://www.people.fas.harvard.edu/~witzel/canon.pdf" in
[56] Jamison and Witzel (1992), Vedic Hinduism http://www.people.fas.harvard.edu/~witzel/vedica.pdf, Harvard University, page 21
[57] Witzel, M., " The Development of the Vedic Canon and its Schools : The Social and Political Milieu http://www.people.fas.harvard.edu/~witzel/canon.pdf" in
[58] • Original Sanskrit: Rigveda 10.129 https://sa.wikisource.org/wiki/ऋग्वेद:_सूक्तं_१०.१२९ Wikisource; • Translation 1: • Translation 2: • Translation 3:
[59] see e.g.
[60] For 1,028 hymns and 10,600 verses and division into ten mandalas, see: .
[61] For characterization of content and mentions of deities including Agni, Indra, Varuna, Soma, Surya, etc. see: .
[62] see e.g. Max Müller gave 1700–1100 BCE, Michael Witzel gives 1450-1350 BCE as *terminus ad quem*.
[63]
[64] Original text translated in English: The Rig Veda, Mandala 10, Hymn 117, Ralph T. H. Griffith (Translator);
C Chatterjee (1995), Values in the Indian Ethos: An Overview http://jhv.sagepub.com/content/1/1/3.short, Journal of Human Values, Vol 1, No 1, pages 3-12
[65] For example,
Hymn 1.164.34, "What is the ultimate limit of the earth?", "What is the center of the universe?", "What is the semen of the cosmic horse?", "What is the ultimate source of human speech?"
Hymn 1.164.34, "Who gave blood, soul, spirit to the earth?", "How could the unstructured universe give origin to this structured world?"
Hymn 1.164.5, "Where does the sun hide in the night?", "Where do gods live?"
Hymn 1.164.6, "What, where is the unborn support for the born universe?";
Hymn 1.164.20 (a hymn that is widely cited in the Upanishads as the parable of the Body and the Soul): "Two birds with fair wings, inseparable companions; Have found refuge in the same sheltering tree. One incessantly eats from the fig tree; the other, not eating, just looks on.";
Sources: (a) Antonio de Nicholas (2003), Meditations Through the Rig Veda: Four-Dimensional Man, , pages 64-69;
Jan Gonda, A History of Indian Literature: Veda and Upanishads, Volume 1, Part 1, Otto Harrassowitz Verlag, , pages 134-135;
Rigveda Book 1, Hymn 164 Wikisource
[66] Michael Witzel, The Rigvedic religious system and its central Asian and Hindukush antecedents http://www.ling.upenn.edu/~rnoyer/courses/51/Witzel2002.pdf, in The Vedas - Texts, Language and Ritual, Editors: Griffiths and Houben (2004), Brill Academic, , pages 581-627
[67] (from """, the term for a melody applied to a metrical hymn or a song of praise, .
[68] Witzel, M., " The Development of the Vedic Canon and its Schools : The Social and Political Milieu http://www.people.fas.harvard.edu/~witzel/canon.pdf" in
[69] M Bloomfield, , pages 402-464
[70] For 1875 total verses, see the numbering given in Ralph T. H. Griffith. Griffith's introduction mentions the recension history for his text. Repetitions may be found by consulting the cross-index in Griffith pp. 491-99.
[71] Annette Wilke and Oliver Moebus (2011), Sound and Communication: An Aesthetic Cultural History of Sanskrit Hinduism, Walter de Gruyter, , page 381

[72] Michael Witzel (2003), "Vedas and Upaniṣads", in The Blackwell Companion to Hinduism (Editor: Gavin Flood), Blackwell, , pages 76-77
[73] Antonio de Nicholas (2003), Meditations Through the Rig Veda: Four-Dimensional Man, , pages 273-274
[74] Witzel, M., " The Development of the Vedic Canon and its Schools : The Social and Political Milieu http://www.people.fas.harvard.edu/~witzel/canon.pdf" in
[75] Witzel, M., " The Development of the Vedic Canon and its Schools : The Social and Political Milieu http://www.people.fas.harvard.edu/~witzel/canon.pdf" in
[76] Paul Deussen, Sixty Upanishads of the Veda, Volume 1, Motilal Banarsidass, , pages 217-219
[77] CL Prabhakar (1972), The Recensions of the Sukla Yajurveda, Archív Orientální, Volume 40, Issue 1, pages 347-353
[78] Paul Deussen, The Philosophy of the Upanishads https://archive.org/stream/philosophyofupan00deus#page/22/mode/2up, Motilal Banarsidass (2011 Edition), , page 23
[79] Patrick Olivelle (1998), Upaniṣhads, Oxford University Press, , pages 1-17
[80] Frits Staal (2009), Discovering the Vedas: Origins, Mantras, Rituals, Insights, Penguin, , pages 136-137
[81] Frits Staal (2009), Discovering the Vedas: Origins, Mantras, Rituals, Insights, Penguin, , page 135
[82] Alex Wayman (1997), Untying the Knots in Buddhism, Motilal Banarsidass, , pages 52-53
[83] "The latest of the four Vedas, the Atharva-Veda, is, as we have seen, largely composed of magical texts and charms, but here and there we find cosmological hymns which anticipate the Upanishads, – hymns to Skambha, the 'Support', who is seen as the first principle which is both the material and efficient cause of the universe, to Prāna, the 'Breath of Life', to Vāc, the 'Word', and so on." .
[84] Laurie Patton (2004), Veda and Upanishad, in *The Hindu World* (Editors: Sushil Mittal and Gene Thursby), Routledge, , page 38
[85] Jan Gonda (1975), Vedic Literature: Saṃhitās and Brāhmaṇas, Vol 1, Fasc. 1, Otto Harrassowitz Verlag, , pages 277-280, Quote: "It would be incorrect to describe the Atharvaveda Samhita as a collection of magical formulas".
[86] Kenneth Zysk (2012), Understanding Mantras (Editor: Harvey Alper), Motilal Banarsidass, , pages 123-129
[87] On magic spells and charms, such as those to gain better health: Atharva Veda 2.32 Bhaishagykni, Charm to secure perfect health http://www.sacred-texts.com/hin/sbe42/av064.htm Maurice Bloomfield (Translator), Sacred Books of the East, Vol. 42, Oxford University Press; see also chapters 3.11, 3.31, 4.10, 5.30, 19.26;
On finding a good husband: Atharva Veda 4.2.36 Strijaratani http://www.sacred-texts.com/hin/sbe42/av102.htm Maurice Bloomfield (Translator), Sacred Books of the East, Vol. 42, Oxford University Press; Atharvaveda dedicates over 30 chapters to love relationships, sexuality and for conceiving a child, see e.g. chapters 1.14, 2.30, 3.25, 6.60, 6.78, 6.82, 6.130-6.132; On peaceful social and family relationships: Atharva Veda 6.3.30 http://www.sacred-texts.com/hin/sbe42/av153.htm Maurice Bloomfield (Translator), Sacred Books of the East, Vol. 42, Oxford University Press;
[88] Kenneth Zysk (1993), Religious Medicine: The History and Evolution of Indian Medicine, Routledge, , pages x-xii
[89] Witzel, M., " The Development of the Vedic Canon and its Schools : The Social and Political Milieu http://www.people.fas.harvard.edu/~witzel/canon.pdf" in
[90]
[91]
[92] Moriz Winternitz (2010), A History of Indian Literature, Volume 1, Motilal Banarsidass, , pages 175-176
[93] Michael Witzel, "Tracing the Vedic dialects" in *Dialectes dans les litteratures Indo-Aryennes* ed. Caillat, Paris, 1989, 97–265.
[94] Biswas et al (1989), Cosmic Perspectives, Cambridge University Press, , pages 42-43
[95] Klaus Klostermaier (1994), A Survey of Hinduism, Second Edition, State University of New York Press, , page 67
[96] Paul Deussen, Sixty Upanishads of the Veda, Volume 1, Motilal Banarsidass, , page 63

[97]
[98], The Calcutta Review, Volume 60, page 27
[99] Jan Gonda (1975), Vedic Literature: (Saṃhitās and Brāhmaṇas), Otto Harrassowitz Verlag, , pages 319-322, 368-383 with footnotes
[100]
[101] AB Keith (2007), The Religion and Philosophy of the Veda and Upanishads, Motilal Banarsidass, , pages 489-490
[102] Max Müller, The Upanishads https://archive.org/stream/upanishads01ml#page/n93/mode/2up, Part 1, Oxford University Press, page LXXXVI footnote 1
[103] Mahadevan 1956, p. 59.
[104] PT Raju (1985), Structural Depths of Indian Thought, State University of New York Press, , pages 35-36
[105] WD Strappini, , The Month and Catholic Review, Vol. 23, Issue 42
[106] Wiman Dissanayake (1993), Self as Body in Asian Theory and Practice (Editors: Thomas P. Kasulis et al), State University of New York Press, , page 39; **Quote:** "The Upanishads form the foundations of Hindu philosophical thought and the central theme of the Upanishads is the identity of Atman and Brahman, or the inner self and the cosmic self.";
Michael McDowell and Nathan Brown (2009), World Religions, Penguin, , pages 208-210
[107] Patrick Olivelle (2014), The Early Upanisads, Oxford University Press, , page 3; **Quote:** "Even though theoretically the whole of vedic corpus is accepted as revealed truth [shruti], in reality it is the Upanishads that have continued to influence the life and thought of the various religious traditions that we have come to call Hindu. Upanishads are the scriptures par excellence of Hinduism".
[108] See to *Brihad Aranyaka Upanishad* at pages 1-5; Quote - "The Vedas are divided in two parts, the first is the karma-kanda, the ceremonial part, also (called) purva-kanda, and treats on ceremonies; the second part is the jnana kanda, the part which contains knowledge, also named uttara-kanda or posterior part, and unfolds the knowledge of Brahma or the universal soul." (Translator: Edward Roer)
[109] Stephen Knapp (2005), The Heart of Hinduism: The Eastern Path to Freedom, Empowerment and Illumination, , pages 10-11
[110] Patrick Olivelle 1999, pp. xxiii.
[111] James Lochtefeld (2002), "Vedanga" in The Illustrated Encyclopedia of Hinduism, Vol. 1: A-M, Rosen Publishing, , pages 744-745
[112] Annette Wilke & Oliver Moebus 2011, pp. 391-394 with footnotes, 416-419.
[113] Harold G. Coward 1990, pp. 105-110.
[114] Annette Wilke & Oliver Moebus 2011, pp. 472-532.
[115] Harold G. Coward 1990, p. 18.
[116] BR Modak, The Ancillary Literature of the Atharva-Veda, New Delhi, Rashtriya Veda Vidya Pratishthan, 1993,
[117]. http://www.ibiblio.org/sripedia/ebooks/mw/0200/mw__0240.html Accessed 5 April 2007.
[118] Paul Kuritz (1988), The Making of Theatre History, Prentice Hall, , page 68
[119] Sanskrit original: Chandogya Upanishad http://sa.wikisource.org/wiki/छान्दोग्योपनिषद्_४, Wikisource;
English translation: Chandogya Upanishad 7.1.2 https://archive.org/stream/Shankara.Bhashya-Chandogya.Upanishad-Ganganath.Jha.1942.English#page/n383/mode/2up, G Jha (Translator), Oriental Book Agency, page 368
[120] Greg Bailey (2001), Encyclopedia of Asian Philosophy (Editor: Oliver Leaman), Routledge, , pages 437-439
[121] Ludo Rocher (1986), The Puranas, Otto Harrassowitz Verlag, , pages 1-5, 12-21
[122] Ludo Rocher (1986), The Puranas, Otto Harrassowitz Verlag, , pages 12-13, 134-156, 203-210
[123] Greg Bailey (2001), Encyclopedia of Asian Philosophy (Editor: Oliver Leaman), Routledge, , pages 442-443
[124] Dominic Goodall (1996), Hindu Scriptures, University of California Press, , page xxxix
[125] Dominic Goodall (1996), Hindu Scriptures, University of California Press, , page xli
[126] BN Krishnamurti Sharma (2008), A History of the Dvaita School of Vedānta and Its Literature, Motilal Banarsidass, , pages 128-131

[127] Müller, Friedrich Max (author) & Stone, Jon R. (author, editor) (2002). *The essential Max Müller: on language, mythology, and religion.* Illustrated edition. Palgrave Macmillan. Source: https://books.google.com/books?id=Q96EsUCVILsC&printsec=frontcover&dq=Max+M%C3%BCller&ei=SRjkS6LcI4TuIQSj6InGCQ&cd=3#v=onepage&q&f=false (accessed: Friday May 7, 2010), p.44

[128] "A Critical Study of the Contribution of the Arya Samaj to Indian Education", p. 68. by Pandit, Saraswati S

[129] "Lectures on the science of language, delivered at the Royal institution of Great Britain in 1861 [and 1863], Volume 1", by Max Müller, p. 148

[130] https://books.google.com/books?id=2CEj6wRqeRAC

[131] http://www.springerlink.com/content/x0000788497q4858/

[132] //www.worldcat.org/oclc/713426994

[133] http://catalog.hathitrust.org/Record/009657393

[134] //www.worldcat.org/oclc/929704391

[135] http://www.sanskrit-lexicon.uni-koeln.de/scans/MWEScan/2013/web/index.php

[136] //www.worldcat.org/oclc/5333096

[137] https://books.google.com/?id=_VCXTBk-PtoC

[138] https://books.google.com/?id=J8Zo_rtoWAEC

[139] https://books.google.com/books?id=gnVxqvPg9aOC

[140] //doi.org/10.2307%2F1062753

[141] //doi.org/10.1093%2Fjaarel%2FLXII.2.377

[142] https://books.google.com/books?id=KZCMe67IGPkC

[143] https://www.jstor.org/stable/592303

[144] http://www.people.fas.harvard.edu/~witzel/Veda.in.Nepal.pdf

[145] http://www.sub.uni-goettingen.de/ebene_1/fiindolo/gretil.htm#Veda

[146] https://archive.org/stream/vedicconcordance00bloouoft#page/n7/mode/2up

[147] http://www.people.fas.harvard.edu/~witzel/VedicConcordance/ReadmeEng.html

[148] http://www.sacred-texts.com/hin/index.htm#vedas

[149] //en.wikipedia.org/w/index.php?title=Template:Hindu_scriptures&action=edit

[150] Atharva Veda 11.7.24, 15.6.4

[151] Chāndogya Upaniṣad 7.1.2,4

[152] Datta 2004, p. 720

[153] * Book:Lalita Ke Ansoo on worldcat http://www.worldcat.org/title/lalita-ke-amsu-sri-lalabahadura-sastri-ke-jivana-para-adharita-eka-karuna-kavya-krti/oclc/60419441&referer=brief_results

[154] *Hindustan* (Hindi daily) New Delhi 12 January 1978 (ललिता के आँसू का विमोचन)

[155] Panchjanya (newspaper) A literary review 24 February 1980

[156] //en.wikipedia.org/w/index.php?title=Template:Hinduism&action=edit

[157] "Mahabharata" http://dictionary.reference.com/browse/Mahabharata. *Random House Webster's Unabridged Dictionary*,

[158] "Mahabharata" http://www.oxforddictionaries.com/definition/english/Mahabharata. *Oxford Dictionaries Online*.

[159] Brockington (1998, p. 26)

[160] Van Buitenen; *The Mahabharata* – 1; The Book of the Beginning. Introduction (Authorship and Date)

[161] *bhārata* means the progeny of *Bharata*, the legendary Jain king who is claimed to have founded the Bhāratavarsha kingdom.

[162] Spodek, Howard. Richard Mason. The World's History. Pearson Education: 2006, New Jersey. 224, 0-13-177318-6

[163] Amartya Sen, *The Argumentative Indian. Writings on Indian Culture, History and Identity,* London: Penguin Books, 2005.

[164] Hermann Oldenberg, *Das Mahabharata: seine Entstehung, sein Inhalt, seine Form*, Göttingen, 1922.

[165] "The Mahabharata" http://www.harekrsna.com/sun/features/07-06/features360.htm at *The Sampradaya Sun*

[166] *A History of Indian Literature* https//books.google.com, Volume 1 by Maurice Winternitz

[167] Buitenen (1973) pp. xxiv–xxv
[168] Sukthankar (1933) "Prolegomena" p. lxxxvi. Emphasis is original.
[169] Gupta & Ramachandran (1976), citing *Mahabharata*, Critical Edition, I, 56, 33
[170] SP Gupta and KS Ramachandran (1976), p.3-4, citing Vaidya (1967), p.11
[171] 18 books, 18 chapters of the *Bhagavadgita* and the Narayaniya each, corresponding to the 18 days of the battle and the 18 armies (Mbh. 5.152.23)
[172] The Spitzer Manuscript (Beitrage zur Kultur- und Geistesgeschichte Asiens), Austrian Academy of Sciences, 2004. It is one of the oldest Sanskrit manuscripts found on the Silk Road and part of the estate of Dr. Moritz Spitzer.
[173] J.A.B. van Buitenen, *Mahābhārata, Volume 1*, p.445, citing W. Caland, *The Pañcaviṃśa Brāhmaṇa*, p.640-2
[174] Dio Chrysostom, 53. 6 http://penelope.uchicago.edu/Thayer/E/Roman/Texts/Dio_Chrysostom/Discourses/53*.html#6-7, trans. H. Lamar Crosby, Loeb Classical Library, 1946, vol. 4, p. 363.
[175] Christian Lassen, in his *Indische Alterthumskunde*, supposed that the reference is ultimately to Dhritarashtra's sorrows, the laments of Gandhari and Draupadi, and the valor of Arjuna and Suyodhana or Karna (cited approvingly in Max Duncker, *The History of Antiquity* (trans. Evelyn Abbott, London 1880), vol. 4, p. 81 https://books.google.com/books?id=gIkBAAAAQAAJ&pg=PA81). This interpretation is endorsed in such standard references as Albrecht Weber's *History of Indian Literature* but has sometimes been repeated as fact instead of as interpretation.
[176] The *Ashvamedhika-parva* is also preserved in a separate version, the *Jaimini-Bharata* (*Jaiminiya-Ashvamedha*) where the frame dialogue is replaced, the narration being attributed to Jaimini, another disciple of Vyasa. This version contains far more devotional material (related to Krishna) than the standard epic and probably dates to the 12th century. It has some regional versions, the most popular being the Kannada one by Devapurada Annama Lakshmisha (16th century). The Mahabharata http://www.harekrsna.com/sun/features/07-06/features360.htm
[177] In discussing the dating question, historian A. L. Basham says: "According to the most popular later tradition the Mahabharata War took place in 3102 BCE, which in the light of all evidence, is quite impossible. A more reasonable is another tradition, placing it in the 15th century BCE, but this is also several centuries too early in the light of our archaeological knowledge. Probably the war took place around the beginning of the 9th century BCE; such a date seems to fit well with the scanty archaeological remains of the period, and there is some evidence in the Brahmana literature itself to show that it cannot have been much earlier." Basham, p. 40, citing HC Raychaudhuri, *Political History of Ancient India*, pp.27ff.
[178] M Witzel, *Early Sanskritization: Origin and Development of the Kuru state*, EJVS vol.1 no.4 (1995); also in B. Kölver (ed.), *Recht, Staat und Verwaltung im klassischen Indien. The state, the Law, and Administration in Classical India*, München, R. Oldenbourg, 1997, p.27-52
[179] A.D. Pusalker, *History and Culture of the Indian People*, Vol I, Chapter XIV, p.273
[180] FE Pargiter, *Ancient Indian Historical Tradition*, p.180. He shows estimates of the average as 47, 50, 31 and 35 for various versions of the lists.
[181] Pargiter, *op.cit.* p.180-182
[182] B. B. Lal, *Mahabharata and Archaeology* in Gupta and Ramachandran (1976), p.57-58
[183] Gupta and Ramachandran (1976), p.246, who summarize as follows: "Astronomical calculations favor 15th century BCE as the date of the war while the Puranic data place it in the 10th/9th century BCE. Archaeological evidence points towards the latter." (p.254)
[184] Gupta and Ramachandran (1976), p.55; AD Pusalker, HCIP, Vol I, p.272
[185] AD Pusalker, *op.cit.* p.272
[186] Bhandarkar Institute, Pune http://www.virtualpune.com/html/channel/edu/institutes/html/bhandark.shtml—Virtual Pune
[187] Several editions of the Kisari Mohan Ganguli translation of the *Mahabharata* incorrectly cite the publisher, Pratap Chandra Roy, as the translator and this error has been propagated into secondary citations. See the publishers preface to the current Munshiram Manoharlal edition for an explanation.
[188] The Mahabharata of Krishna-Dwaipayana Vyasa translated by Kisari Mohan Ganguli http://www.sacred-texts.com/hin/maha/index.htm at the Internet Sacred Text Archive

[189] The *Mahabharata of Krishna*-Dwaipayana Vyasa translated by Romesh Chunder Dutt http://www.gutenberg.org/ebooks/19630 at the Online Library of Liberty.
[190] http://www.penguinbooksindia.com/category/Non_Fiction/The_Mahabharata_9780143100133.aspx
[191] The Mahabharata as Theatre http://www.boloji.com/hinduism/084.htm by Pradip Bhattacharya, June 13, 2004.
[192] (1920 film)
[193] (1988–1990 TV series)
[194] (1989 mini-series).
[195] p. 351-52
[196] vol 1 pp. 14–15
[197] p. 377
[198] p.305
[199] p. 351
[200] refer story of Neminatha
[201] Maharishi Mahesh Yogi; On The Bhagavad Gita; A New Translation and Commentary With Sanskrit Text Chapters 1 to 6, Preface p.9
[202] Stevenson, Robert W., "Tilak and the Bhagavadgita's Doctrine of Karmayoga", in: Minor, p. 44.
[203] Jordens, J. T. F., "Gandhi and the Bhagavadgita", in: Minor, p. 88.
[204] https://books.google.com/books?id=gwUF11NRyT4C
[205] https://books.google.com/books?id=HR-_LK5kl18C
[206] https://books.google.com/books?id=wFtXBGNn0aUC
[207] https://books.google.com/books?id=hC1d-xN6nzoC
[208] https://books.google.com/books?id=Tarbo7OzEO8C
[209] https://books.google.com/books?id=-0tcQr3WzqsC
[210] http://www.wilbourhall.org/pdfs/chandravasu/book4.pdf
[211] https://books.google.com/books?id=rFyUHC-ORp4C
[212] https://web.archive.org/web/20101107222102/http://www.sub.uni-goettingen.de/ebene_1/fiindolo/gretil/1_sanskr/2_epic/mbh/sas/mahabharata.htm
[213] http://www.holybooks.com/mahabharata-all-volumes-in-12-pdf-files/
[214] http://www.Brown.edu/Departments/Sanskrit_in_Classics_at_Brown/Mahabharata/MBh2Biblio.html#Poona
[215] //en.wikipedia.org/w/index.php?title=Template:Hinduism&action=edit
[216] "Ramayana" http://dictionary.reference.com/browse/ramayana. *Random House Webster's Unabridged Dictionary*.
[217] Ramayana By William Buck https//books.google.co.in
[218] Rajarajan, R.K.K. (2001) *Sītāpaharaṇam*: Changing thematic Idioms in Sanskrit and Tamil. In Dirk W. Lonne ed. *Tofha-e-Dil: Festschrift Helmut Nespital*, Reinbeck, 2 vols., pp. 783-97. ". https://www.academia.edu/2514821/S%C4%ABt%C4%81pahara%E1%B9%89am_Changing_thematic_Idioms_in_Sanskrit_and_Tamil
[219] Rajarajan, R.K.K. (2014) Reflections on "Rāma-Setu" in South Asian Tradition. *The Quarterly Journal of the Mythic Society*, Vol. 105.3: 1–14, . https://www.academia.edu/8779702/Reflections_on_R%C4%81ma-Setu_in_South_Asian_Tradition
[220] Joefe B. Santarita (2013), Revisiting Swarnabhumi/dvipa: Indian Influences in Ancient Southeast Asia
[221] https://books.google.com/?id=2UszWGeqkZcC
[222] https://books.google.com/?id=qSfneQ0YYY8C&pg=PA116
[223] https://books.google.com/?id=4Wzg6wFJ5xwC&printsec=frontcover
[224] https://books.google.com/?id=RPKav7K9eNUC
[225] https://books.google.com/?id=MDf8N9nMlugC
[226] http://www.claysanskritlibrary.org/volume-v-78.html
[227] https://books.google.com/?id=3XIatVGyjmQC
[228] https://books.google.com/?id=DWX43jnbOngC&printsec=frontcover
[229] https://books.google.com/?id=BJMWT0ZJYHAC&printsec=frontcover
[230] https://books.google.com/?id=sFmsrEszbxgC&printsec=frontcover
[231] https://books.google.com/books?id=vYBwPgAACAAJ

[232] http://www.gutenberg.org/dirs/etext05/8ntle10.txt
[233] https://web.archive.org/web/20120808182601/http://www.ejvs.laurasianacademy.com/ejvs1006/ejvs1006article.pdf
[234] //www.worldcat.org/issn/1084-7561
[235] http://www.ejvs.laurasianacademy.com/ejvs1006/ejvs1006article.pdf
[236] https://books.google.com/?id=zupDCwE73O0C&printsec=frontcover
[237] https://books.google.com/books?id=xgzhAAAAMAAJ
[238] https://books.google.com/?id=em3XAAAAMAAJ
[239] https://books.google.com/?id=xPYp7_kMBK4C&pg=PA106
[240] https://web.archive.org/web/20101027001647/http://www.hinduonnet.com/thehindu/fr/2005/08/12/stories/2005081201210200.htm
[241] http://www.hinduonnet.com/thehindu/fr/2005/08/12/stories/2005081201210200.htm
[242] http://www.ramayanabook.com/
[243] http://bombay.indology.info/ramayana/statement.html
[244] http://gretil.sub.uni-goettingen.de/gret_utf.htm#Ram
[245] https://www.wisdomlib.org/jainism/book/trishashti-shalaka-purusha-caritra/d/doc213981.html
[246] http://valmikiramayan.net
[247] https://vedicfeed.com/the-ramayana-summary-the-deeds-of-rama
[248] http://www.sacred-texts.com/hin/rama/index.htm
[249] http://www.sacred-texts.com/hin/dutt/rama01.htm
[250] https://archive.org/details/RamayanaTheEpicOfRamaPrinceOfIndiaCondensedIntoEnglishVerseBy
[251] https://archive.org/details/ramayanablaknda00vlgoog
[252] https://archive.org/details/ramayana01duttgoog
[253] https://archive.org/details/ramayanaranyakn00vlgoog
[254] https://archive.org/details/TheRamayanaKishkindhaKandam
[255] https://archive.org/details/ramayana03vlgoog
[256] https://archive.org/details/TheRamayanaUttaraKandam
[257] https://books.google.com/books?id=nAzNbPus9TcC
[258] http://oll.libertyfund.org/index.php?option=com_staticxt&staticfile=show.php%3Ftitle=1778&Itemid=28
[259] https://web.archive.org/web/20130501055540/http://orias.berkeley.edu/hero/ramayana/index.html
[260] //en.wikipedia.org/w/index.php?title=Template:History_of_literature_by_era&action=edit
[261] //en.wikipedia.org/w/index.php?title=Template:Vedas_and_Shakhas&action=edit
[262] Frazier, Jessica (2011), The Continuum companion to Hindu studies, London: Continuum, , pages 1–15
[263]
[264] Klaus Klostermaier (2007), A Survey of Hinduism: Third Edition, State University of New York Press, , pages 46–52, 76–77
[265] RC Zaehner (1992), Hindu Scriptures, Penguin Random House, , pages 1–11 and Preface
[266] Wendy Doniger O'Flaherty (1988), Textual Sources for the Study of Hinduism, Manchester University Press, , pages 2–3
[267] James Lochtefeld (2002), "Smrti", The Illustrated Encyclopedia of Hinduism, Vol. 2: N–Z, Rosen Publishing, , page 656–657
[268] Purushottama Bilimoria (2011), The idea of Hindu law, Journal of Oriental Society of Australia, Vol. 43, pages 103–130
[269] Roy Perrett (1998), Hindu Ethics: A Philosophical Study, University of Hawaii Press, , pages 16–18
[270] Michael Witzel, "Vedas and Upaniṣads", in: Flood, Gavin, ed. (2003), The Blackwell Companion to Hinduism, Blackwell Publishing Ltd., , pages 68–71
[271]
[272] Vijay K. Jain 2011, p. vi.
[273] Jaini 1998, p. 82.
[274] https://books.google.com/books?id=zLmx9bvtglkC

[275] https://books.google.co.in/books?id=wE6v6ahxHi8C
[276] http://www.sanskrit.nic.in/DigitalBook/M/Mswk.pdf
[277] http://www.sub.uni-goettingen.de/ebene_1/fiindolo/gretil.htm
[278] http://sa.wikibooks.org/wiki/Main_Page
[279] http://titus.uni-frankfurt.de/indexe.htm?/texte/texte2.htm#ind
[280] https://web.archive.org/web/20060111075741/http://vedabase.net/
[281] http://www.claysanskritlibrary.org
[282] http://sanskritdocuments.org
[283] //en.wikipedia.org/w/index.php?title=Template:Theravada_Buddhism&action=edit
[284] //en.wikipedia.org/w/index.php?title=Template:Buddhism&action=edit
[285] //en.wikipedia.org/w/index.php?title=Template:PaliCanon&action=edit
[286] Gombrich 2006, p. 3.
[287] Harvey 1990, p. 3.
[288] Maguire 2001, p. 69–.
[289] If the language of the Pāli canon is north Indian in origin, and without substantial Sinhalese additions, it is likely that the canon was composed somewhere in north India before its introduction to Sri Lanka.<ref name="FOOTNOTEWynne2003">Wynne 2003.
[290] , Quote: "As of the Pali Canon of Sri Lanka, it was extensively redacted in the fifth or sixth century A.D. (Bechert 1978; Collins 1990; Trainor 1997)".
[291] Stargardt, Janice. *Tracing Thoughts Through Things: The Oldest Pali Texts and the Early Buddhist Archaeology of India and Burma.*, Royal Netherlands Academy of Arts and Sciences, 2000, page 25.
[292] Gombrich 2006, p. 4.
[293] Encyclopædia Britannica 2008.
[294] Gombrich 2006, p. 20.
[295] Gombrich 2006, p. 153-4.
[296] Morgan 1956, p. 71.
[297] McDaniel 2006, p. 302.
[298] Mendelson 1975, p. 266.
[299] Brown 2006.
[300] Manné 1990, p. 103f.
[301] Gethin 1998, p. 43.
[302] *Book of the Discipline*, volume VI, page 123
[303] Norman 2005, p. 75-76.
[304] Harvey 1995, p. 9.
[305] Wynne 2007, p. 4.
[306] "I am saying that there was a person called the Buddha, that the preachings probably go back to him individually... that we can learn more about what he meant, and that he was saying some very precise things."<ref name="FOOTNOTEGombrich (b)">Gombrich (b).
[307] Gombrich 2006, p. 20f.
[308] Peter Harvey https://web.archive.org/web/20130415212658/http://buddhistethics.net/index.php/network-members/itemlist/user/89-peterharvey
[309] "While parts of the Pali Canon clearly originated after the time of the Buddha, much must derive from his teaching."<ref name="FOOTNOTEHarvey19903">Harvey 1990, p. 3.
[310] "there is no evidence to suggest that it was formulated by anyone else than the Buddha and his immediate followers." <ref name="FOOTNOTEWarder1999inside flap">Warder 1999, p. inside flap.
[311] De Jong 1993, p. 25.
[312] "If some of the material is so old, it might be possible to establish what texts go back to the very beginning of Buddhism, texts which perhaps include the substance of the Buddha's teaching, and in some cases, maybe even his words", <ref name="FOOTNOTEWynne2003">Wynne 2003.
[313] Nakamura 1999, p. 57.
[314] Davidson 2003, p. 147.
[315] Ronald Davidson states, "most scholars agree that there was a rough body of sacred literature (disputed) that a relatively early community (disputed) maintained and transmitted."<ref name="FOOTNOTEDavidson2003147">Davidson 2003, p. 147.

[316] Buswell 2004, p. 10.
[317] Ronald Davidson, academic profile http://www.fairfield.edu/academic/profile.html?id=50
[318] about Geoffrey Samuel http://www.cardiff.ac.uk/share/contactsandpeople/academicstaff/P-T/samuel-geoffrey-dr-overview_new.html
[319] Samuel 2012, p. 48.
[320] Schopen 1997, p. 24.
[321] Wynne 2003.
[322] Warder 1963, p. viii.
[323] Cousins 1984, p. 56.
[324] Bechert 1984, p. 78.
[325] Gethin 1992, p. 42f.
[326] Gethin 1992.
[327] Nakamura 1999, p. 27.
[328] "as the Buddha taught for 45 years, some signs of development in teachings may only reflect changes during this period."<ref name="FOOTNOTEHarvey19903">Harvey 1990, p. 3.
[329] Ñāṇamoli 1982, p. xxix.
[330] Cousins & 1982/3.
[331] Harvey, page 83
[332] Gethin 1992, p. 48.
[333] Wynne 2004.
[334] Ñāṇamoli 1982, p. xxxixf.
[335] Gethin 1992, p. 8.
[336] Harvey, page 3
[337] von Hinüber 2000, pp. 4–5.
[338] Grönbold 1984, p. 12 (as noted there and elsewhere, the 1893 Siamese edition was incomplete).
[339] Allon 1997, pp. 109–29.
[340] Warder 1963, pp. 382.
[341] Hamm 1973.
[342] Tipiṭaka Studies https://web.archive.org/web/20090305071619/http://tipitakastudies.net/
[343] Sri Lanka Tripitaka Project https://web.archive.org/web/20100615203958/http://buddhistethics.org/palicanon.html
[344] Cone 2001.
[345] Norman 1996, pp. 80.
[346] Gombrich (b).
[347] *Journal of the Pali Text Society*, Volume XXIX, page 102
[348] Griffiths 1981, pp. 17-32.
[349] https://suttacentral.net
[350] Norman 1983.
[351] von Hinüber 2000, pp. 24-26.
[352] Harvey, 1990 & appendix.
[353] Manné 1990, pp. 29-88.
[354] Harvey 1990, p. 83.
[355] Gethin 1998, p. 44.
[356] Cousins 1982, p. 7.
[357] Most notably, a version of the Atanatiya Sutta (from the Digha Nikaya) is included in the tantra (Mikkyo, rgyud) divisions of the Taisho and of the Cone, Derge, Lhasa, Lithang, Narthang and Peking (Qianlong) editions of the Kangyur.<ref name="FOOTNOTESkilling199784n, 553ff, 617ff.">Skilling 1997, p. 84n, 553ff, 617ff..
[358] http://fo.ifeng.com/special/beiyejing/
[359] http://www.budsir.org/program/
[360] https://web.archive.org/web/20160124085341/http://www.ordinarymind.net/Interviews/interview_jan2003.htm
[361] http://www.purifymind.com/RichardGombrich.htm
[362] http://journals.ub.uni-heidelberg.de/index.php/jiabs/article/view/8546/2453
[363] https://books.google.com/books?id=62KQpPX1oVkC&pg=PA69

[364] https://web.archive.org/web/20140901075241/http://www.palitext.com/JPTS_scans/JPTS_1990_XV.pdf
[365] http://www.palitext.com/JPTS_scans/JPTS_1990_XV.pdf
[366] http://journals.ub.uni-heidelberg.de/index.php/jiabs/article/view/8965/2858
[367] https://books.google.com/books?id=qYyRAgAAQBAJ&pg=PA76
[368] http://www.bodhgayanews.net/pali.htm
[369] http://www.sri-lankan-pali-texts.net/
[370] http://www.tipitaka.org/
[371] http://www.vridhamma.org/Home.aspx
[372] https://books.google.com/books?id=8jPYUCy-GxQC&pg=PA4
[373] https://web.archive.org/web/20150309051940/http://www.ocbs.org/images/documents/Wynne.pdf
[374] http://www.ocbs.org/images/documents/Wynne.pdf
[375] http://journals.ub.uni-heidelberg.de/index.php/jiabs/article/view/8945/2838
[376] https://archive.org/details/historyofpalilit035453mbp
[377] http://www.bps.lk/olib/wh/wh217-u.html
[378] https://web.archive.org/web/20080724041344/http://web.ukonline.co.uk/buddhism/tipintro.htm
[379] http://www.aimwell.org/Books/Suttas/Paritta/BioMingun/biomingun.html
[380] http://pathpress.wordpress.com/bodhesako/beginnings-the-pali-suttas/
[381] https://web.archive.org/web/20030601154657/http://www.accesstoinsight.org/canon/index.html
[382] http://www.nibbana.com/tipitaka/tipilist.htm
[383] http://www.wisdompubs.org/book/middle-length-discourses-buddha/selections
[384] http://www.wisdompubs.org/book/numerical-discourses-buddha/selections
[385] https://suttacentral.net/
[386] http://www.84000.org/
[387] http://www.aathaapi.org/Thripitaka.php
[388] http://dsal.uchicago.edu/dictionaries/pali/
[389] //en.wikipedia.org/w/index.php?title=Template:Indian_literature&action=edit
[390] //en.wikipedia.org/w/index.php?title=Template:Culture_of_Assam&action=edit
[391] //en.wikipedia.org/w/index.php?title=Template:Assamese/Asamiya_literature&action=edit
[392] //en.wikipedia.org/w/index.php?title=Template:History_of_literature_by_region_or_country&action=edit
[393] example of language:
age yena manusye laware kharatari
chaga buli baghar galata ache dhari
manusye erante galara nere baghe
"if a man runs fast
and catches hold of the neck of a tiger thinking it is only a goat
and then tries to leave it, the tiger would not let him go"
[394] References to *camua* (verse 176), *cor* (verse 57), and *phura* (verse 70) indicated that Vipra was either acquainted with the Ahom Kingdom, or even belonged there.
[395] The text indicates change overs from time to time (*madhava bolanta aita acho ehimana*, let me leave this here) and that the poet directed the course of the narration as the courtiers desired .
[396] *purvakavi apramadi madhav kandali adi
pade virachila rama katha
hastira dekhiya lada sasa yena phure marga
mora bhaila tenhaya avastha.*
[397] Brown, Nathan (1848). Grammatical Notices of the Assamese Language. American Baptist Missionary Press, Sibsagor, Assam
[398] Mills, A.G. Moffat (1853). Report of A.G. Moffat Mills, Judge, Sudder Court, Mymensingh dated 24th July 1853, on the province of Assam
[399] https://books.google.com/books?id=zB4n3MVozbUC&lpg=PP1&pg=PA1692
[400] https://books.google.com/books?id=KYLpvaKJIMEC&lpg=PP1&pg=PA3
[401] https://books.google.com/books?id=fo6VpP78pJcC

[402] http://www.atributetosankaradeva.org/movement_lit_prose.htm
[403] https://archive.org/details/someassamesepro01gurdgoog
[404] Goswami, Golockchandra (1982), *Structure of Assamese*, Page 11, Western Assamese dialect, the sole medium of all ancient Assamese literature including the buranjis written in the Ahom court
[405] Goswami 2007, p. 436.
[406] Hartmann 2011, p. 228.
[407] Sarkar, J. N. (1992) *The Buranjis: Ahom and Assamese* in The Comprehensive History of Assam Vol II (ed H K Barpujari), Publication Board, Assam
[408] Goswami & Tamuli 2007, p. 436.
[409] Saikia 2004, p. 6.
[410] https://archive.org/details/in.ernet.dli.2015.97610
[411] https://books.google.com/books?id=jPR2OlbTbdkC
[412] https://books.google.co.in/books?id=WfSmsuO6QugC
[413] //doi.org/10.1017%2FS002246340001554X
[414] //doi.org/10.1177%2F001946460804500401
[415] Akademi, p. 62
[416] https://books.google.com/?id=m1R2Pa3f7r0C&pg=PA65&dq=Nilmani+Phookan&cd=5#v=onepage&q=Nilmani%20Phookan&f=false
[417] //en.wikipedia.org/w/index.php?title=Template:Bengali_literature&action=edit
[418] //en.wikipedia.org/w/index.php?title=Template:Medieval_and_Renaissance_literature&action=edit
[419] //en.wikipedia.org/w/index.php?title=Template:Bengalis&action=edit
[420]
[421] *Songs of Kobisena* by Steve Leblanc in *Version 90*, PMS Cafe Press, Alston, MS, USA.
[422] https://www.loc.gov/acq/ovop/delhi/salrp/bengali.html
[423] http://www.barnamala.org
[424] http://baudelaireetbengale.blogspot.com
[425] http://www.bangla-literature.ueuo.com
[426] Dr. Viveki Rai, *Bhojpuri Katha Sahity ke vikaas*
[427] भोजपुरी साहित्य के संत-रामनाथ पांडेय http//hindi.webdunia.com Webduniya.
[428] Dr. Viveki Rai, "Introduction of sundar kaka"
[429]
[430] https://books.google.com/books?id=9FZgWwjXEZoC&lpg=PT87&dq=bhojpuri%20upanyaas&pg=PT87#v=onepage&q=bhojpuri%20upanyaas&f=falseUntouchable
[431] //en.wikipedia.org/w/index.php?title=Template:History_of_modern_literature&action=edit
[432] https//www.amazon.com https//www.amazon.com
[433] *Songs of Kobisena* by Steve Leblanc in *Version 90*, PMS Cafe Press, Alston, MS, USA.
[434] http://menanddreamsinthedhauladhar.com
[435] http://menanddreamsinthedhauladhar.com/indian-writers-in-english-literature-and-their-works.php
[436] https://www.amazon.in/dp/8172736029
[437] https://www.amazon.in/dp/9352072499
[438] //en.wikipedia.org/w/index.php?title=Template:Indian_literature&action=edit
[439] Hindi literature http://languages.iloveindia.com/hindi.html
[440] Hindi in Constitution http://www.abhivyakti-hindi.org/snibandh/hindi_diwas/samvidhan_me_hindi.htm
[441] //en.wikipedia.org/w/index.php?title=Template:History_of_literature_by_region_or_country&action=edit
[442] Introduction to Hindi http://charm.cs.uiuc.edu/~bhatele/hindi/hindi_intro.htm University of Illinois at Urbana-Champaign
[443] Mystic poet Kabir http://www.crl.edu/focus/Spr05litGems.asp?issID=3
[444] http//wapedia.mobi
[445] Lucy (aka "Ludmila") Rosenstein, editor, translator, author of the "Introduction" https://books.google.com/books?id=yt2ROIhYfC4C&printsec=frontcover#PPA1,M1, *New Poetry in Hindi: Nayi Kavita: An Introduction*, Anthem Press, 2004,

[446] Indian Poets Writing In Hindi https://web.archive.org/web/20091026144551/http://geocities.com/indian_poets/hindi.html
[447] http://kavitakosh.org
[448] http://www.geeta-kavita.com
[449] https://www.youtube.com/user/wowHindiKavita
[450] http://blogs.navbharattimes.indiatimes.com/manishgupta/dont-cry-for-hindi/
[451] http://www.amarujala.com/news/samachar/reflections/vyang/satire-on-election/
[452] Dimitrova, p. 15
[453] Datta, p. 1075
[454] Nagendra, p. 661
[455] http://www.panchjanya.com/8-4-2001/18c.html
[456] https//books.google.com
[457] https://books.google.com/books?id=FA9qAKpUtTIC&printsec=frontcover&dq=Hindi+theatre#v=onepage&q&f=false
[458] https//books.google.com
[459] http://www.cs.colostate.edu/~malaiya/hindiint.html
[460] //en.wikipedia.org/w/index.php?title=Template:History_of_literature_by_era&action=edit
[461] Krishnamurti (2003), p. 78; Steever (1998), p. 129, 131.
[462] Ramanujan, A. K. (1973), *Speaking of Śiva* Harmondsworth: Penguin, p. 11,
[463] R.S. Mugali (2006), *The Heritage of Karnataka*, pp. 173–175
[464] Kannada literature http://original.britannica.com/eb/article-9044579. (2008). Encyclopædia Britannica: "The earliest records in Kannada are full length inscriptions dating from the 5th century AD onward. The earliest literary work is the Kavirajamarga (c. AD 850), a treatise on poetics based on a Sanskrit model."
[465] David Crystal's *Dictionary of Language*, , "... with inscriptions dating from the late 6th century AD, ...
[466] Other scholars have dated the earliest Kannada inscription to 450 A.D., 500 A.D. , and "about 500" . Epigraphist G. S. Gai has dated it to the "end of the fifth century A. D. or the beginning of the 6th century A.D." ; epigraphist, D. C. Sircar to "about the end of the 6th century," ()
[467] Zvelebil (2008), p.2
[468] Steever, S.B. (1998), p. 129; Krishnamurti (2003), p. 23; Pollock (2007), p. 81; Sahitya Akademi, *Encyclopaedia of Indian Literature, vol.* 2 (1988), p. 1717
[469] Kittel in Rice E.P. (1921), p. 14
[470] Sastri 1955, pp. 355–365
[471] Narasimhacharya (1934), pp. 17, 61
[472] Narasimhacharya (1934), pp. 61–65
[473] Rice E. P, (1921), p. 16
[474] Narasimhacharya (1934), pp. 1, 65; Sastri (1955), pp. 355–366
[475] Rice E.P. (1921), p. 17; Kamath (1980), pp. 49–50, 67, 88–90, 114–115, 132–134
[476] Dalby (1998), p. 300; Masica (1993), pp. 45–46; Kamath (1980), pp. 143–144
[477] Sahitya Akademi (1988), pp. 1474–1475; Sastri (1955), p. 355; Steever (1998), p. 4
[478] N.S. Lakshminarayan Bhatta in Kavirajamarga, Encyclopaedia of Indian Literature, Volume 3, 1994, pp. 2033–2034; Mugali (1975), p. 13
[479] Seshagiri Rao (1994), pp. 2278–2283; B.L.Rice (1897), pp. 496–497; Narasimhacharya (1934), p. 2; E.P.Rice: (1921), p. 25
[480] Murthy (1997), p. 190
[481] See Discovery and dating of the Halmidi inscription.
[482]
[483] Shiva Prakash (1997) p. 163
[484] Shiva Prakash (1997), pp. 167, 202
[485] Sahitya Akademi (1987), p. 248
[486] Shiva Prakash (1997), p. 210
[487]
[488] Shiva Prakash in Ayyappapanicker (1997), p. 203
[489] Narasimhacharya (1934), p. 27
[490] Sahitya Akademi (1996), pp. 4002–4003

[491]
[492]
[493] Karmarkar (1947), p. 124
[494] Shipley (2007), p. 528
[495] Sahitya Akademi (1988), p. 1717
[496] Sahitya Akademi (1996), p. 4392
[497] Kamath (1980), p. 83
[498] Sahitya Akademi (1988), p. 1150
[499] Sahtiya Akademi (1987), pp. 183–184
[500] Murthy (1997), p. 167
[501] Kamath (2001), pp. 277–278
[502] Murthy (1997), pp. 189–190
[503] Kamath (1980), p. 89
[504] Sahitya Akademi (1988), p. 1699
[505] Rice B.L. (1897), p. 326
[506] Sahitya Akademi (1988), pp. 1474–1475
[507] Rice E.P., (1921), pp. 25, 28
[508] Narasimhacharya (1934), p. 18
[509] Sahitya Akademi (1988), pp. 1474, 1699
[510] Sastri (1955), p. 356
[511] Sahitya Akademi (1988), p. 1253
[512] Bhat (1993), p. 105
[513] Sahitya Akademi (1988), p. 1180
[514] Rice E.P. (1921), p. 31
[515] Narasimhacharya 1934, p. 18
[516] Kamath (1980), p. 90
[517] Rice, E.P. (1921), pp. 31–32
[518] Kamath (1980), pp. 114, 132–134, 143–144
[519]
[520]
[521] Rice E.P. (1921), p. 32
[522] Sahitya Akademi (1988), p. 1149
[523] Sahitya Akademi (1988), p. 1024
[524] Narasimhacharya (1934), pp. 64–65,
[525] Rice E.P. (1921), p. 34
[526] Sastri 1955, p. 358
[527] Sahitya Akademi (1988), p. 1475
[528] Derret and Coelho in Kamath (1980), pp. 124–126
[529] Narasimhacharya (1934), pp. 19–21
[530] Kamath (1980), pp. 50–52, 54–56
[531] Nagaraj in Pollock (2003), p. 366
[532] Rice E.P. (1921), pp. 45–46
[533] Narasimhacharya (1934), p. 66
[534] Sastri (1955), pp. 361–362
[535] Rice E.P. (1921), p. 60
[536] Sastri (1955), p. 362
[537]
[538] Sastri (1955), p. 364
[539] Sastri (1955), pp. 358–359
[540] Rice E.P. (1921), pp. 43–44
[541]
[542] Kamath (1980), p. 157
[543] Sastri (1955), p. 363
[544] Sinopoli (2003) pp. 130–131
[545]
[546]

[547] Srinatha called himself "Karnatadesakataka" (Narasimhacharya 1934, pp. 27–28)
[548]
[549] Kamath (1980), p. 108
[550] Rice E.P. (1921), p. 42
[551] Sahitya Akademi (1988), p. 1324
[552] Sahitya Akademi (1987), p. 191
[553] Rice B.L. in Sastri 1955, p. 361
[554] Shiva Prakash 1997, pp. 167–168, 178, 181
[555] Nagaraj, 2003, p. 348
[556]
[557] Sahitya Akademi (1988), p. 1165
[558]
[559]
[560]
[561] Moorthy (2001), p. 67
[562] Iyer (2006), p. 93
[563] Shiva Prakash (1997), pp. 196–197
[564] Rice E.P. (1921), p. 80
[565] Shiva Prakash (1997), pp. 198–200
[566] Shiva Prakash (1997), pp. 200–201
[567] Sahitya Akademi (1988), p. 1551
[568] Nagaraj (2003) p. 377
[569] Nagaraj (2003), p. 378
[570] Pranesh (2003), preface chapter p. i–iii
[571] Kamath (2001), pp. 229–230
[572] Narasimhacharya (1934), pp. 23–26
[573] Kamath (1980), p. 281
[574] Pranesh (2003), p. 20
[575]
[576] Narasimhacharya (1934), p. 24
[577] Prasad (1987), p. 16
[578] Prasad (1987), pp. 9–10
[579] Shiva Prakash (1997), p. 191
[580] Prasad (1987), pp. 5–6
[581] Narasimhacharya (1988), p. 59
[582] Sahitya Akademi (1988), p. 1182
[583] Sahitya Akademi (1988), p. 1077
[584] Pranesh (2003), p. 37–38
[585] Pranesh (2003), p. 37
[586] Pranesh (2003), p. 53
[587] Narasimhacharya (1934), p. 26
[588] Murthy in George K.M(1992), p. 167
[589] Kamath (1980), p. 279
[590]
[591] Murthy (1992), pp. 168–169
[592] Sahitya Akademi (1988), pp. 1077–78
[593] Murthy (1992), pp. 170–171
[594] Murthy (1992), p. 172
[595] Murthy (1992), p. 173–175
[596] Sahitya Akademi (1987), p. 413
[597] Murthy (1992), p. 173
[598] Das (1995), p. 148
[599] Murthy (1992), p. 174
[600] Punekar in Sahity Akademi (1992), pp. 4159–4160
[601] Sahitya Akademi (1988), p. 1057
[602]

[603] Murthy (1992), p. 176
[604] Murthy (1992), p. 177
[605] Murthy (1992), p. 178
[606] Murthy (1992), p. 178–179
[607] Murthy (1992), p. 179
[608] Murthy (1992), p. 183
[609] The Growth of the Novel in India 1950–1980, P. K. Rajan, p. 112, 1989,
[610] Sahitya Akademi (1992), p. 4185
[611] Murthy (1992), pp. 179–180
[612] Murthy (1992), p. 180
[613] Murthy (1992) p. 181
[614] Sahitya Akademi (1987), p. 689
[615] Sahitya Akademi (1987), p. 429
[616] Murthy (1992), p. 182
[617] Sahitya Akademi (1987), p. 430
[618] Sahitya Akademi (1992), p. 4049
[619] Handbook of Twentieth-Century Literatures of India, Nalini Natarajan, Emmanuel Sampath Nelson, p. 170, 1996,
[620] Murthy (1992), p. 184
[621] Sahitya Akademi (1992), p. 4031
[622] Murthy (1992), p. 665
[623]
[624] Sahitya Akademi (1992), p. 4403
[625] Murthy (1992), p. 187
[626] Sahitya Akademi (1987), p. 165
[627] Sahitya Akademi (1992), p 4308
[628] Sahitya Akademi (1992), p 4309
[629] Murthy (1992), p 189
[630] https://books.google.com/books?id=3GU5FWs1pBEC
[631] https://books.google.com/books?id=nOMbAAAAIAAJ&dq=
[632] //lccn.loc.gov/80905179
[633] //www.worldcat.org/oclc/7796041
[634] //www.worldcat.org/oclc/8221605
[635] https://books.google.com/books?id=T7Wv4ncys88C&printsec=frontcover&dq=dravidian+languages
[636] //doi.org/10.1017%2Fs0041977x00072487
[637] //www.worldcat.org/oclc/2492406
[638] https://books.google.com/books?id=KrICwjXaC3gC
[639] https://books.google.com/books?id=xowUxYhv0QgC&pg=PA323&dq=critical+tensions+in+history+kannada+literary+culture
[640] https://books.google.com/books?id=yhXRDSgBuL0C
[641] https://books.google.com/books?id=nOTmIt3wumwC
[642] //doi.org/10.2307%2F2659022
[643] //www.jstor.org/stable/2659022
[644] https://books.google.com/books?id=0UCh7r2TjQIC&dq
[645] http://www.columbia.edu/cu/mealac/faculty/pollock/mss_cult.pdf
[646] https://books.google.com/books?id=sxpCAAAAIAAJ&pg=RA1-PA501&dq=Gazetteer+of+Mysore++Kannada+literature
[647] https://books.google.com/books?id=-5irrXX0apQC&pg=PA345&dq=romilla+thapar+kannada+literature
[648] http://www.britannica.com/eb/article-74974/Dravidian-languages
[649] Neab International Kashmiri Magazine http://www.neabinternational.org
[650] Debiprasad Chattopadhyaya, *History of Science and Technology in Ancient India*, Firma K.L Mukhopadhyaya (1986), pp. 486-494
[651] Satya Prakash, *Founders of Sciences in Ancient India* (part II), Vijay Kumar (1989), p.471
[652] B.S. Yadav & Man Mohan, *Ancient Indian Leaps into Mathematics*, Birkhäuser (2011), p. 78

[653] M. I. Mikhailov & N. S. Mikhailov, *Key to the Vedas*, Minsk-Vilnius (2005), p. 105
[654] Sures Chandra Banerji, *A Companion to Sanskrit Literature*, Motilal Banarsidass (1989), p. 59
[655] Helaine Selin, *Encyclopaedia of the History of Science, Technology, and Medicine in Non-Western Cultures*, Kluwer Academic Publishers (1997), p. 977
[656] Martin Levey, *Early Arabic Pharmacology: An Introduction Based on Ancient and Medieval Sources*, Brill Archive (1973), p. 10
[657] P. N. K. Bamzai, *Culture and Political History of Kashmir* - Volume 1, M D Publications (1994), p.268
[658] S.K. Sopory, *Glimpses Of Kashmir*, APH Publishing Corporation (2004), p. 62
[659] Krishan Lal Kalla, *The Literary Heritage of Kashmir*, Mittal Publications (1985), p.65
[660] Guang Xing, *The Concept of the Buddha*, RoutledgeCurzon (2005), p. 26
[661] Phyllis G. Jestice, *Holy People of the World: A Cross-cultural Encyclopedia*, ABC-CLIO Ltd (2004), p. 621
[662] *Encyclopaedia of Indian Medicine: Historical perspective*, Popular Prakashan (1985), p. 100
[663] Ramachandra S.K. Rao, Encyclopaedia of Indian medicine : volume 1, Popular Prakashan (2005), p. 63
[664] Ram Gopal, *Kālidāsa: His Art and Culture*, Concept Publishing Company (1984), p.3
[665] P. N. K. Bamzai, *Culture and Political History of Kashmir* - Volume 1, M D Publications (1994), p.261-262
[666] M. K. Kaw, *Kashmir and It's People: Studies in the Evolution of Kashmiri Society*, APH Publishing Corporation (2004), p.388
[667] Claus Vogel, *Vāgbhaṭa Aṣṭāṅgahṛdayasaṃhitā. The First Five Chapters of Its Tibetan Version*, Franz Steiner (1965), p.13
[668] Anna Akasoy & co., *Islam and Tibet: Interactions Along the Musk Routes*, Ashgate Publishing Limited (2011), p.76
[669] Richard Pischel, *A Grammar of the Prakrit Languages*, Motilal Banarsidass (1999), p. 43
[670] Satya Ranjan Banerjee, *The Eastern School of Prakrit Grammarians: A Linguistic Study*, Vidyasagar Pustak Mandir (1977), p. 31
[671] Kamaleswar Bhattacharya, *India & Beyond*, Routledge (2009), p. 2
[672] John E. Cort, *Open Boundaries: Jain Communities and Cultures in Indian History*, State University of New York Press (1998), p.57
[673] Kolar Sesha Iyer Nagarajan, *Contribution of Kashmir to Sanskrit literature*, V.B. Soobbiah (1970), p. 426
[674] R.N. Rai, *Karanasara Of Vatesvara*, Indian National Science Academy (1970), vol. 6, n. I, p. 34 http://www.new1.dli.ernet.in/data1/upload/insa/INSA_1/20005b63_27.pdf
[675] Vaṭeśvara, *Vaṭeśvara-siddhānta and Gola of Vaṭeśvara: English translation and commentary*, National Commission for the Compilation of History of Sciences in India (1985), p. xxvii
[676] P. N. K. Bamzai, *Culture and Political History of Kashmir* - Volume 1, M D Publications (1994), p.269
[677] Sheldon Pollock, *Literary Cultures in History: Reconstructions from South Asia*, University of California Press (2003), p. 112
[678] Bina Chatterjee (introduction by), *The Khandakhadyaka of Brahmagupta*, Motilal Banarsidass (1970), p. 13
[679] Lallanji Gopal, *History of Agriculture in India, Up to C. 1200 A.D.*, Concept Publishing Company (2008), p. 603
[680] Kosla Vepa, *Astronomical Dating of Events & Select Vignettes from Indian History*, Indic Studies Foundation (2008), p. 372
[681] Dwijendra Narayan Jha (edited by), *The feudal order: state, society, and ideology in early medieval India*, Manohar Publishers & Distributors (2000), p. 276
[682] P. N. K. Bamzai, *Culture and Political History of Kashmir* - Volume 1, M D Publications (1994), p.269
[683] Collective, *The Cambridge History of Iran*, Volume 6, p. 980
[684] Anna Zelkina, *In Quest for God and Freedom: The Sufi Response to the Russian Advance in the North Caucasus*, C. Hurst & Co. Publishers (200), p. 88
[685] Irshad Alam, *Faith Practice and Piety: An Excerpt from the Maktūbāt*, Sufi Peace Mission (2006), p. 20

[686] Shri Ram Bakshi, *Kashmir: Valley and Its Culture*, Sarun & Son (1997), p. 165
[687] Hamid Afaq Qureshi, *The Mughals, the English & the rulers of Awadh, from 1722 A.D. to 1856 A.D.*, New Royal Book Co (2003), p.79
[688] Amaresh Misra, *Lucknow, fire of grace: the story of its revolution, renaissance and the aftermath*, HarperCollins Publishers India (1998), p. 57
[689] Purnendu Basu, *Oudh and the East India Company, 1785-1801*, Maxwell Company (1943), p. 22
[690] Simon Schaffer, *The Brokered World: Go-Betweens and Global Intelligence, 1770-1820*, Science History Publications (2009), p. 53
[691] Surendra Mohan, *Awadh Under the Nawabs: Politics, Culture, and Communal Relations, 1722-1856*, Manohar Publishers & Distributors (1997), p.80
[692] Edited by Bernard Lightman, *The Circulation of Knowledge Between Britain, India and China*, BRILL (2013), p.67
[693] Abida Samiuddin, *Encyclopaedic Dictionary of Urdu Literature*, Global Vision Publishing House (2008), p. 94
[694] Mirza Asadullah Khan Ghalib, *Persian poetry of Mirza Ghalib*, Pen Productions (2000), p. 7
[695] K.C. Kanda, *Masterpieces of Urdu Ghazal from the 17th to the 20th Century*, Sterling (1992), p. 182
[696] K.C. Kanda, *Masterpieces of Urdu Ghazal from the 17th to the 20th Century*, Sterling (1992), p. 182
[697] Ali Jawad Zaidi, *A History of Urdu literature*, Sahitya Akademi (1993), p. 181
[698] D.J. Matthews, *Urdu Literature*, South Asia Books (1985), p. 86
[699] A website on Dr Khalifa Abdul Hakim maintained by a relative and with a lot of bibliographical resources http://khalifaabdulhakim.com/
[700] Punjab's Kashmir connection http://www.kashmirlife.net/punjabs-kashmir-connection/
[701] A Scholar-Intellectual http://www.greaterkashmir.com/news/opinion/story/193515.html
[702] //en.wikipedia.org/w/index.php?title=Template:Indian_literature&action=edit
[703] Dr. K. Ayyappa Paniker (1977). *A Short History of Malayalam Literature*.
[704] Ke Rāmacandṛan Nāyar (1971). *Early Manipravalam: a study*. Anjali. Foreign Language Study. pp.78
[705] Ancy Bay 2015. Translating Modernity: Conversion and Caste in Early South Indian Novel – The Slayer Slain and Saraswathi Vijayam. Calicut: Olive Publishers.
[706] Varughese, Shiju Sam. 2015. "Colonial Intellectuals, Public Sphere and the Promises of Modernity: Reading Parangodeeparinayam". In Bose, Satheese Chandra and Varughese, Shiju Sam (eds.). Kerala Modernity: Ideas, Spaces and Practices in Transition. Hyderabad: Orient Blackswan, pp. 41–58.
[707] https://web.archive.org/web/20030217152754/http://www.prd.kerala.gov.in/prd2/mala/liter.htm
[708] https://www.youtube.com/watch?v=kXPc4KogBtQ
[709] https://web.archive.org/web/20030205030545/http://www.malayalamresourcecentre.org/Mrc/literature/history.html
[710] //en.wikipedia.org/w/index.php?title=Template:Indian_literature&action=edit
[711] Wakoklon Heelel Thilel Salai Amai Eelon Pukok PuYa (□□□□□□□ □□□□□ □□□□□ □□□□□ □□□□ □□□□ □□□□□ □□□□)
[712] Naorem Sanajaoba, Manipur Treaties and Documents-Vol I,1993, New Delhi. Book I: "Twelfth Century Meetei Constitution To Pemberton Report".
[713] Chanam Hemchandra, *Numit Kappa*, translated and rendered into modern Meeteilon, 2008, Imphal, Manipur.
[714] T.C. Hodson, *The Meitheis*, 1908, London. Appendix II, page 180.
[715] Ningthoujongjam Khelchandra, *History of Ancient Manipuri Literature*, Pub-Manipuri Sahitya Parishad, 1969.
[716] //en.wikipedia.org/w/index.php?title=Template:Indian_literature&action=edit
[717] Christian Lee Novetzke 2016, p. 54.
[718] Christian Lee Novetzke 2016, p. 74,86.
[719] Christian Lee Novetzke 2016, p. x.
[720] Christian Lee Novetzke 2016, p. 53.

[721] Christian Lee Novetzke 2016, p. 74.
[722] Christian Lee Novetzke 2016, p. 88.
[723] Chavan, Dilip. (2013). "Language Politics: Translation of Coercion into Consent", Language Politics under Colonialism: Caste, Class and Language Pedagogy in Western India, Cambridge Scholars, 71-135
[724] According to Hartmut Scharfe, Professor Emeritus of Sanskrit, University of California, Los Angeles, USA vide his book "A History of Indian Literature - Grammatical Literature", the author of the first Marathi Grammar was Venkata Madhava, who was a lecturer in Fort St. George College, Madras (now Chennai). Venkata Madhava's three works on Marathi (as was spoken by the then large Maratha colony of Tanjore) exist only in the autographs of the author or his assistant Bhima Pandita. His Marathi Grammar book "महाराष्ट्र प्रयोग चंद्रिका" was written cir. 1827. It has 227 sutras in Samskrt and is accompanied by a Samskrt commentary, a Marathi commentary and Marathi illustrations. The Samskrt section is written in Devnagari script and the Marathi in Modi script. The grammar which generally follows the Siddhanta Kaumudi in its design, was probably meant to introduce Marathi to the neighbouring Tamil speakers.
[725] Issues of Language and Representation:Babu Rao Bagul https://books.google.com/books?id= 1lTnv6o-d_oC&pg=PA368&dq=Baburao+Bagul&lr= Handbook of twentieth-century literatures of India, Editors: Nalini Natarajan, Emmanuel Sampath Nelson. Greenwood Publishing Group, 1996. Page 368.
[726] Mother 1970 http//books.google.com Indian short stories, 1900–2000, by E.V. Ramakrishnan, I. V. Ramakrishnana. Sahitya Akademi. Page 217, Page 409 (Biography).
[727] Jevha Mi Jat Chorali Hoti (1963) https://books.google.com/books?id=zB4n3MVozbUC&pg= PA1823&dq=Baburao+Bagul&lr=. Encyclopaedia of Indian literature vol. 2. Editors Amaresh Datta. Sahitya Akademi, 1988. Page 1823.
[728] https://books.google.com/books?id=z9kbDQAAQBAJ&pg=PA54
[729] https://archive.org/stream/apg4681.0001.001.umich.edu#page/n3/mode/2up
[730] https://archive.org/details/apg4681.0001.001.umich.edu
[731] http://www.museindia.com/focuscontent.asp?issid=59&id=5420
[732] http://india.poetryinternationalweb.org/piw_cms/cms/cms_module/index.php?obj_id=2682
[733] https://web.archive.org/web/20151208065121/http://www.museindia.com/viewarticle.asp?myr=2005&issid=3&id=69
[734] http://www.prophet666.com/2010/10/aartis-marathi-english.html
[735] https://web.archive.org/web/20110218214220/http://yabaluri.org/TRIVENI/CDWEB/ModernMarathiPoetryARemarkableDecadeJul31.htm
[736] http://www.marathimati.com/Maharashtra/Literature/Literature.asp
[737] https://www.loc.gov/acq/ovop/delhi/salrp/marathi.html
[738] http://sachinketkar.blogspot.in/2011/02/inventing-third-nation-brief-history-of.html
[739] //en.wikipedia.org/w/index.php?title=Template:Indian_literature&action=edit
[740] Lalthangliana, B., UNIQ-nowiki-0-a33abbaafb66ca9c-QINU Mizo tihin ṭawng a nei lo UNIQ-nowiki-1-a33abbaafb66ca9c-QINU tih kha http://www.vanglaini.org/index.php?option=com_content&view=article&id=12917:mizo-tihin-tawng-a-nei-lo-tih-kha&catid=105:articles&Itemid=466/
[741] Chawngthu, Tluanga, Mizo thuhlaril hmasawn dan part -I http://www.misual.com/2011/09/17/mizo-thuhlaril-hmasawn-dan-part-i/
[742] Khiangte, Laltluangliana, Thuhlaril, 2nd Edition, 1997.
[743] Lalthangliana, B., Mizo literature. Second edition, copyright 2004, MC Lalrinthanga.
[744] Chawngthu, Tluanga, Mizo thuhlaril hmasawn dan - Part 2 http://www.misual.com/2011/09/26/mizo-thuhlaril-hmasawn-dan-part-2/
[745] Chawngthu, Tluanga, Mizo thuhlaril hmasawn dan - Part 4 http://www.misual.com/2011/09/27/mizo-thuhlaril-hmasawn-dan-part-4/
[746] Vanglaini, April 24, 2012 http://commons.wikimedia.org/wiki/File:BOOK_of_the_year_chuanna.pdf
[747] Vanglaini, 22 April, 2014. http://www.vanglaini.org/tualchhung/18015,
[748] https://web.archive.org/web/20140415093344/http://www.rubypressco.in/
[749] //en.wikipedia.org/w/index.php?title=Template:State_of_Odisha&action=edit
[750] //en.wikipedia.org/w/index.php?title=Template:Indian_literature&action=edit

[751] Mukherjee, Prabhat. *The History of medieval Vaishnavism in Odisha.* Chapter: *The Sidhacharyas in Odisha* Page 55.
[752] http://odisha.gov.in/e-magazine/Orissareview/2014/mar/engpdf/26-29.pdf
[753] http://oaob.nitrkl.ac.in/58/1/Prachina_Odia_Kabita.pdf
[754] http://odisha.gov.in/e-magazine/Orissareview/2014/July/engpdf/69-73.pdf
[755] http://odisha.gov.in/e-magazine/Orissareview/may-2007/engpdf/Page46-48.pdf
[756] http://odisha.gov.in/e-magazine/Orissareview/june_july-2007/engpdf/Pages25-26.pdf
[757] http://odisha.gov.in/e-magazine/Orissareview/jul2005/engpdf/BKP_SBCD_monobodha_chautisa.pdf
[758] Istahar-92, (26th Volume, 2nd Issue),
[759] https://web.archive.org/web/20071117111717/http://india_resource.tripod.com/orissa.html
[760] https://web.archive.org/web/20071122143104/http://www.iit.edu/~laksvij/language/oriya.html
[761] https://web.archive.org/web/20071212024352/http://tlt.its.psu.edu/suggestions/international/bylanguage/oriyachart.html
[762] https://web.archive.org/web/20071214035207/http://oriya.sarovar.org/
[763] //en.wikipedia.org/w/index.php?title=Template:Punjabis&action=edit
[764] (citation: *Encyclopaedia of Indian Literature*)
[765] *Encyclopaedia of Indian Literature* (Vol. 2), Sahitya Akademi, p. 1263
[766] http://www.apnaorg.com/poetry/bullahn/
[767] Gill, Tejwant Singh, "Reading Modern Punjabi Poetry: From Bhai Vir Singh to Surjit Patar" in *Journal of Punjab Studies* (Spring-Fall 2006, Volume 13, No. 1 &2).
[768] http://www.panjabdigilib.org
[769] http://www.shellybuall.com
[770] //en.wikipedia.org/w/index.php?title=Template:Indian_literature&action=edit
[771] South Asian arts. (2008). In Encyclopædia Britannica. Retrieved January 31, 2008, from Encyclopædia Britannica Online: http://www.britannica.com/eb/article-65211
[772] http://www.iias.nl/iiasn/21/theme/21T11.html
[773] http://indiansaga.com/languages/rajasthani_lang.html
[774] https://web.archive.org/web/20071118185411/http://www.bastigiri.org/crs/
[775] http://www.ethnologue.com/show_family.asp?subid=90927
[776] http://tdil.mit.gov.in/CoilNet/IGNCA/rj189.htm
[777] //en.wikipedia.org/w/index.php?title=Template:Modern_Asian_literature&action=edit
[778] //en.wikipedia.org/w/index.php?title=Template:Islamic_culture&action=edit
[779] //en.wikipedia.org/w/index.php?title=Template:Indian_literature&action=edit
[780] http://sindhipedia.org/Aziz_Kingrani
[781] http://www.thesindhtimes.com/entertainment/new-book-of-renowned-critic-mubarak-ali-lashari-published/
[782] http://www.pakistanpressfoundation.org/news-archives/8694/editor-passesaway/
[783] http://www.sindhiadabiboard.org/Catalogue/children_Litrature/Main_Children.HTML
[784] http://www.encyclopediasindhiana.org
[785] http://www.voiceofsindh.net
[786] http://www.sindhiana.com
[787] https://www.webcitation.org/query?url=http://www.geocities.com/thebhittai&date=2009-10-25+22:53:28
[788] http://www.sindhisangat.com
[789] //en.wikipedia.org/w/index.php?title=Template:Sangam_literature&action=edit
[790] See Majumdar, p 193
[791] See Zvelebil, pp. 45–47
[792] The age of Sangam is established through the correlation between the evidence on foreign trade found in the poems and the writings by ancient Greek and Romans such as *Periplus*. See Nilakanta Sastri, K.A., History of South India, p. 106
[793] Witzel, Michael (2005), "Indocentrism", in Bryant, Edwin; Patton, Laurie L., The Indo-Aryan Controversy. Evidence and inference in Indian history, Routledge
[794] Bryant, Edwin (2001), The Quest for the Origins of Vedic Culture: The Indo-Aryan Migration Debate, Oxford University Press, .

[795] See Majumdar, p 194
[796] See KAN Sastri, A History of South India, p. 338
[797] The Diversity in Indian Islam http://www.international.ucla.edu/southasia/article.asp?parentid=27779
[798] Tamil blogosphere http://www.hindu.com/2007/08/04/stories/2007080450970200.htm
[799] http://www.hinduonnet.com/thehindu/mp/2003/07/23/stories/2003072300090200.htm
[800] http://www.hinduonnet.com/fline/fl2217/stories/20050826000807700.htm
[801] http://ilakkiyam.com
[802] http://www.valaitamil.com/literature
[803] http://thamizhilakkiyam.com/
[804] //en.wikipedia.org/w/index.php?title=Template:Culture_of_Andhra_Pradesh&action=edit
[805] //en.wikipedia.org/w/index.php?title=Template:Culture_of_Telangana&action=edit
[806] Telugu Split from Proto-Dravidian https://lists.hcs.harvard.edu/mailman/listinfo/proto-dravidian
[807] //en.wikipedia.org/w/index.php?title=Template:History_of_literature_by_region_or_country&action=edit
[808] Amaresh Datta, *The Encyclopaedia of Indian Literature*, v. 1, "Avadhanam" https//books.google.com (Sahitya Akademi, 2006;)
[809] Source of his history: http://www.svasa.org/annamacharya1.html
[810] Dhurajti http://www.textbooksonline.tn.nic.in/Books/09/Telugu/Poetry/6%20Cheladi%20Purugu.pdf
[811] //en.wikipedia.org/w/index.php?title=Template:Modern_Asian_literature&action=edit
[812] Natarajan, Nalini and Emmanuel Sampath Nelson, editors, *Handbook of Twentieth-century Literatures of India*, Chapter 11: "Twentieth-Century Telugu Literature" by G. K. Subbarayudu and C. Vijayasree' ', pp. 306–328, retrieved via Google Books, January 4, 20089 https://books.google.com/books?id=1lTnv6o-d_oC&pg=PA306&lpg=PP9&output=html
[813] Mangalampalli can't wait to come home http://www.hindu.com/thehindu/2003/03/01/stories/2003030108610300.htm
[814] https://www.sukatha.com
[815] https://www.kahaniya.com/
[816] https://web.archive.org/web/20130620090429/http://www.pressacademyarchives.ap.nic.in/Newspaper.asp
[817] http://www.telugusahityam.com/
[818] http://www.tlca.com/new/about.html
[819] http://glottolog.org/resource/languoid/id/tulu1258
[820] Hammarström, Harald; Forkel, Robert; Haspelmath, Martin, eds. (2017). "Tulu" http://glottolog.org/resource/languoid/id/tulu1258. *Glottolog 3.0*. Jena, Germany: Max Planck Institute for the Science of Human History.<templatestyles src="Module:Citation/CS1/styles.css"></templatestyles>
[821] Tulu can be written in three different scripts: *Tulu bāse* is written in Tulu script, in Kannada script . *bhāṣe*, , *bhāśe*, and *bāśe* are alternative spellings for the Tulu word *bāse* in the Kannada script. The correct spelling for the word "language" in Kannada is *bhāṣe*, but that is not necessarily true in Tulu. Männer's *Tulu-English and English-Tulu Dictionary* (1886) says, " **bāsè**, **bāsè**, *see* ." (vol. 1, p. 478), " **bhāšè, bhāshè**, *s*. Speech, language." (vol. 1, p. 508), meaning that the four spellings are more or less acceptable. The word is actually pronounced *bāse* in Tulu. Note that **š** and **sh** in his dictionary correspond to *ś* and *ṣ*, respectively, in ISO 15919.
[822] " Language Family Trees: Dravidian, Southern http://www.ethnologue.com/show_family.asp?subid=1286-16", *Ethnologue* (16th ed.).
[823] Caldwell (1856), p. 35.
[824] https://archive.org/stream/elementsofcompar00lathrich/elementsofcompar00lathrich_djvu.txt
[825] http://www.daijiworld.com/news/newsDisplay.aspx?newsID=138784
[826] http://shivallibrahmins.com/tulu-language/tulu-nadu-the-land-and-its-people/
[827] Bhat (1998), p. 163.
[828] Bhat (1998), p. 161.
[829] Bhat (1998), pp. 162–163.
[830] http://www.omniglot.com/writing/tulu.htm

[831] Brigel (1872), p. 10.
[832] Brigel (1872), p. 122
[833] Brigel (1872), pp. 10–11.
[834] Brigel (1872), pp. 14–15.
[835] Bhat (1998), p. 164.
[836] Brigel (1872), p. 37.
[837] Brigel (1872), p. 33.
[838] Brigel (1872), p. 43.
[839] Brigel (1872), p. 45.
[840] https://archive.org/details/grammaroftululan00briguoft
[841] http://www.censusindia.gov.in/2011Census/Language-2011/Statement-1.pdf
[842] Burnell (1874), p. 35.
[843] http://journal.oraltradition.org/files/articles/11i/15_rai.pdf
[844] http://www.tuluacademy.org/
[845] http://tcy.Wikipedia.org
[846] http://www.tuluworld.org/dictionary
[847] https://web.archive.org/web/20090622104844/http://www.tuluver.com/home/
[848] http://www.boloji.com/places/0020.htm
[849] http://www.mangalore.com/documents/languages.html
[850] http://www.tulu.chilume.com
[851] //en.wikipedia.org/w/index.php?title=Template:Islamic_culture&action=edit
[852] //en.wikipedia.org/w/index.php?title=Template:Indian_literature&action=edit
[853] Encyclopedic dictionary of Urdu literature p.565 https://books.google.com/books?isbn= 8182201918
[854] The Encyclopaedia of Indian Literature (Volume Five) p.4146 https://books.google.com/books?isbn=8126012218
[855] https://www.hamarihub.com/
[856] Ilm-o-Irfan Publishers, Urdu Bazaar, Lahore, Pakistan
[857] http://www.columbia.edu/itc/mealac/pritchett/00urduhindilinks/hu_urdu_learning.html
[858] http://gallica.bnf.fr/ark:/12148/btv1b8432899d/f20.zoom
[859] https://poonder.com/urdu-quotes/
[860] http://www.urdustudies.com/pdf/26/13AbdaliDeTassy.pdf

Article Sources and Contributors

The sources listed for each article provide more detailed licensing information including the copyright status, the copyright owner, and the license conditions.

Vedas *Source:* https://en.wikipedia.org/w/index.php?oldid=865117369 *License:* Creative Commons Attribution-Share Alike 3.0 *Contributors:* 1truthsoul, AbHiSHARMA143, Abecedare, Amitrochates, AndrewN, Anjalipatwal, Ankush 89, Ankushksharma, Ansuva, Anzar, Aoidh, Arch dude, Ashishjain190, Ashishtripat, Ashvawiki, B9 hummingbird hovering, BD2412, Barnwalusa, Begoon, Bender235, Bharathpv 9, Bhawani Gautam, Bhuvann, Bladesmulti, Borris83, Brijeshkrishnan, BullRangifer, C.R.Selvakumar, Capankajsmilyo, Capitals00, Carlossuarez46, Chandra Kishore R, Citation bot 1, Citizen Canine, Cjhareen, Clean Copy, CommonsDelinker, Compfreak7, Curb Chain, DMahalko, DRAGON BOOSTER, DadaNeem, DanielRigal, Dbachmann, DeirdreAnne, Doug Weller, Dr.Siju, Editswikifornepali, Ekabhishek, Engineering Guy, Faolin42, Fazla Rabbi, Fiddlersmouth, Florian Blaschke, FolkTraditionalist, Foreverknowledge, Giraffedata, Gobbleswoggler, Guptasuneet, Harsimaja, Hiplibrarianship, IamNotU, InMooseWeTrust, Ira Leviton, Ism schism, Iulius, Iztwoz, J 1982, Jadzia2341, JamesBWatson, Jdcullum, Jedrysikqs, Jeff G., John of Reading, Jonesey95, Jroberson108, Juneright, JustAMuggle, Kamenev, Kautilya3, Kkm010, Krakkos, LeadSongDog, Lele giannoni, Loopy30, LordSuryaofShropshire, Lucent474, MKar, Magioladitis, Mandruss, Manpoudar, Mark Arsten, Mark Ironie, Martarius, Materialscientist, MatrixMechanics13, Mayankjohri, Mcc1789, Mild Bill Hiccup, Mogism, Mohammedadhil16, Ms Sarah Welch, Myedits2, Naveen Sankar, Nayansatya, NeOFreedom, NeilN, Nidafatimashahi, Nihiltres, North Atlanticist Usonian, Nyttend, Omnipaedista, Onel5969, Ontoraul, Parsa, Parulsingh1478, Pasuhi, Peru Serv, Peter James, Piperh, Poipoise, Qualities108, Rajkumar 1 02, Randy Kryn, Red Daredevil, Rich Farmbrough, Rockin It Loud, Rudrasharman, SQGibbon, Sainath468, Sardanaphalus, Sathya venkat, Sbblr0803, SchreiberBike, Semitransgenic, Shii, Sindhu kb, Sligocki, Solomon7968, Someone65, Soni Ruchi, Soumit ban, SpacemanSpiff, Stamptrader, Stogerov, Sun Creator, Thamis, Thanatos666, The Rahul Jain, The wub, Thomas Paine1776, ThreePointsShort, Titodutta, Tommy2010, Uanfala, Unjpmaiya, Vakatiseshu, Vedicweb, Vibiesh, VictoriaGrayson, Vishvas vasuki, Vkbmenon, Voice of Clam, Wavelength, Wiki-uk, Wikiuser13, Will Beback, Wjhonson, Woohookitty, WookieInHeat, Xyzspaniel, Yoddhānāth, Yoonadue, Zuggernaut, 41 anonymous edits 3

Indian epic poetry *Source:* https://en.wikipedia.org/w/index.php?oldid=862499407 *License:* Creative Commons Attribution-Share Alike 3.0 *Contributors:* A Musing, Aayush18, Abecedare, Awadhesh.Pandey, BSI, Bender235, Boojam, BostonMA, BreakfastJr, Caltas, Canyouhearmenow, Captain panda, ClueBot NG, Dangerous-Boy, Dazedbythebell, Dbachmann, Debresser, Discospinster, Doc245, Doug Weller, Dragonzz, Ekabhishek, Elaqueate, Elgin222, Florian Blaschke, GeeJo, Generalboss3, Ghushe, Gnanapiti, Goethean, Goustien, Grafen, Harsimaja, Imc, Ivan Štambuk, Jagged 85, Jcbarr, Jorge Stolfi, Jwy, Kajasudhakarababu, Kkm010, Kkrystian, Lady Mondegreen, Lalu Hrishikesh, Linuxbeak, Lususromulus, Materialscientist, Mattisse, Mjs1991, Mrt3366, Mykhal, NewEnglandYankee, Nick Number, Nodab, Ogress, Oldag07, Omnipaedista, Opfallon, Orenburg1, Orso della campagna, PM Poon, Phil wink, PlyrStar93, Rajarajan90, Redheylin, Redtigerxyz, Robin klein, Rudrasharman, Sam Bailey~enwiki, Savithru, Scriber~enwiki, Shaan1616, ShelfSkewed, Shibingeorge, Shreevatsa, Shyamsunder, Sk A Hakim19521971, SlaveToTheWage, Stormie, Townblight, Uanfala, Uttam7186, Uwo222, Venu62, Vinay.iyer1, WereSpielChequers, फ़िलप्रो, 67 anonymous edits 22

Mahabharata *Source:* https://en.wikipedia.org/w/index.php?oldid=861149727 *License:* Creative Commons Attribution-Share Alike 3.0 *Contributors:* 11 Arlington, A. Parrot, ABTHEBOSS, Abecedare, Abhi.Wiki.Account, Abstruce, Accesscrawl, Adellefrank, Akash.kad, Anjali das gupta, Apoorv020, Arasan.rl, Arayan9641, Aristophanes68, Arlene47, Ashvath16, Avlokeshkumar1203, BD2412, Babagi anadi, Baddu676, Bender235, Berek, Bladesmulti, Boleyn, Bongan, BrightStarSky, Capankajsmilyo, Carlossuarez46, CensoredScribe, Chaipau, Charbak Dipta, Coinmanj, Conradjagan, Contentlagh, Cpt.a.haddock, Daniash007, DarkAudit, Dbachmann, Dewritech, Dharmadhyaksha, Dharmil007, Diet Coke Diego, Dixitsandeep, Doug Weller, Download, Droigheann, Duhshala, Earthwit, Ekabhishek, Engineering Guy, FireflySixtySeven, GeoffCapp, Getallica, Goethean, GoldCoastPrior, Gotitbro, Graphium, Gunkarta, HamadaFanFFSM, Hamiltondaniel, Harsimaja, Hawa-Ave, Hebrides, Here2help, Hinduresci, Hmains, Hridith Sudev Nambiar, Human10.0, Humboldt, Huon, I dream of horses, Imc, India142, Iridescent, Itsyouranmol, Iztwoz, JamesMLane, Jhala shivrajsinh, JimRenge, Jonathansammy, Joshua Jonathan, Josve05a, Julietdeltalima, Kajan lakhan, Kamleshp798, Karna fans, Kashmiri, Khazar2, Kingcircle, Kkm010, Koodfaand, Koresdcine, Kvng, Lankandude2017, Lo Ximiendo, Lotje, MKS Harsha, MKar, MagicatthemovieS, Magioladitis, Makyen, Mandruss, MaoGo, Marcocapelle, Martarius, Mas Rodin, Materialscientist, Mikalra, Missvain, Mital2003, Mogism, Ms Sarah Welch, Myasuda, Naniwako, Napoleon 100, Narayansg, Narky Blert, Naveen Sankar, Nemo Kartikeyan, Nightpotato, Nizil Shah, Ogress, Ohnoitsjamie, Omnipaedista, Onel5969, Orisingsun, Packer1028, Panchalidraupadi, Parabolooidal, Parik92, PhnomPencil, Piggy58, Poipoise, Polmandc, Prabhu Prasad Tripathy, Prof.Dr.A.Yeshuratnam, Prohairesius, Prymshbmg, Rahul Ramamoorthy, Raimundo, Rajaram Sarangapani, RajeshUnuppally, Rajkumar 1 02, Ramkumaran7, Randy Kryn, Rao Ravindra, Rashkeqamar, Rattans, Rayman60, Redtigerxyz, RightBKC, Risssa, Rivertorch, Ronakshah1990, Rpyle731, SY23454, Sai santhosh00, Sanjoydey33, SchreiberBike, SergeWoodzing, Shadowowl, Shrawanroy, Shreevatsa, SimonDeDanser, Sitush, SkrapMason, SpacemanSpiff, Spicemix, Srich32977, Srikanth Aviator, Srisanjana venkatesan, Srkris, Stevenmitchell, Summichum, Swamiblue, TAnthony, Tamil 120, The Blade of the Northern Lights, The Herald, Therash09, Tigercompanion25, Titodutta, Trappist the monk, Ubiquity, Uj1202, User000name, Utcursch, Vanished user qwqwijr8hwrkjdnvkanfoh4, Verbum Veritas, VictoriaGrayson, Vivek Ray, Vreswiki, Vssun, Wareh, Wiae, Wiki-uk, Willard84, WolfgangRieger, Writeecrit, Yb2 26

Ramayana *Source:* https://en.wikipedia.org/w/index.php?oldid=864656507 *License:* Creative Commons Attribution-Share Alike 3.0 *Contributors:* AWG97, Abecedare, Allforrous, Alternativity, Aman Kumar Tiwari, Amitsingh.aug08, Ammarpad, Ashish hindu, Aspening, Avantiputra7, BD2412, Barek, Bingobro, Braincricket, CAPTAIN RAJU, CLCStudent, Capankajsmilyo, Capitals00, Chanrasmey Miech, Chetnnya, ClueBot NG, CommonsDelinker, Crawford88, D4iNa4, Dharmasansthapana, Dollydubey, Doug Weller, Drarvindr1984, Enbeeone3, Finngall, Gilo1969, GorgeCustersSabre, GorillaWarfare, Greyjoy, Gunkarta, Heihsj, Home Lander, Hyacinth, Iridescent, JMS Old Al, Jakichandan, January3, Jasper0070, Jessicapierce, Jim1138, Johnweslys, Jprg1966, King Prithviraj II, Kirbanzo, Kvalia2018, Lakshya94, Last edited by:, Lyndonbaines, Maczkopeti, Madrenergic, Mark the train, Marvellous Spider-Man, Mohanbhan, Mortee, Mykhal, N0n3up, Narky Blert, Omnipaedista, Onel5969, Oshwah, Parashurama007, Pikamander2, PohranicniStraze, Prabhat Kumar Tiwari, Prabhu Prasad Tripathy, Prince.foreigner, Rattans, Redtigerxyz, Rkrish67, Rodw, Roshanmotwani, Sagarlakhani.752, Sally Mires, Santhapriya, Serols, Shamanthbka, ShotgunMavericks, Shreevatsa, Skyrim9, SolicitAdi, SpacemanSpiff, Syedfazal, Tailor jigyasu 12345, Tuany Cavichon, Usernamekiran, Vermont, Vesuvius Dogg, Vin09, WilliamThweatt, Xoloitzcuintle, Yug4panchaL, 180 anonymous edits 55

Sanskrit literature *Source:* https://en.wikipedia.org/w/index.php?oldid=861021657 *License:* Creative Commons Attribution-Share Alike 3.0 *Contributors:* -revi, Aadal, Aaron Booth, AbdulAliAbdullah, Abecedare, Adellefrank, AgnosticPreachersKid, Amitrochates, Andres rojas22, Andrew Dalby, Aniljava, Ansumang, Aoidh, Aristophanes68, Asherek, B9 hummingbird hovering, Bender235, Bennó, Bharu12, Bkrish68, Bodha2, Brandmeister, Bsskchaitanya, Buddhipriya, Colfer2, Coolgama, Correctionwriter, Cowlibob, CsDix, Dbachmann, Devanampriya, Devendra.philo, Dimadick, Discospinster, Doug Weller, Dr.p.k.mishra, Dream of Nyx, Ecelan, Ekabhishek, El C, Elaqueate, Encyclopedian Clerk, Epicgenius, Equilibrial, Faizan, Flammingo, Florian Blaschke, Galygal, Generalboss3, Gryffindor, Hmains, Hrihr, Indopug, Innuo, Interlingua, Ism schism, Ivan Štambuk, JHunterJ, Jagged 85, Jaggi81, Jaichetr, Javierfv1212, Jonoikobangali, Joy1963, Juneright, Katyayani Mohapatra, Kaveri, Khamgatam, Khazar2, Ksuriv, Kwamikagami, Lightmouse, Madhero88, Magioladitis, Materialscientist, Mattisse, Merbabu, Mereda, Mhockey, Mikhail Ryazanov, Ms Sarah Welch, Myedits2, Nagarjuna198, Nagesh.adiga, NaserBanaqeeb, Opfallon, Phil wink, Philip Trueman, Ponydepression, RainbowOfLight, Rayfield, Redtigerxyz, Rgimvl, Richard Kielbasa, Robevans123, Rocketrod1960, Rramphal, SDas, SUSHRUTA, Sadads, Sammod, Sandan222, Sarbeswar.meher, ShelfSkewed, Shreevatsa, Shyamsunder, Sindhutvavadin, Skinsmoke, Smurali49, Solomon7968, Soni Ruchi, SpacemanSpiff, Sreekanthv, Srisharmaa, StasMalyga, Sun Creator, Superguin17, Sydney Ambrose, Task all, Timawesomeness, Topbanana, Townblight, Tuncrypt, Tychon Davydov, Uanfala, Ujjwol, Vegetarianchad3, Verbum Veritas, Victuallers, VoABot II, Wareh, Wiki-uk, Wiki.authoring, Wikidas, Wordboy121, WrobjexWiki, Xoloitzcuintle, Yaditiva, Zaven2, Zerokitsune, Zloyvolsheb, 105 anonymous edits 90

Pāli Canon *Source:* https://en.wikipedia.org/w/index.php?oldid=864123542 *License:* Creative Commons Attribution-Share Alike 3.0 *Contributors:* 2know4power, AkilaMK, Alfonso Márquez, Anandajoti, Andycjp, Ankuaayu, Aoidh, Aristophanes68, AssociateLong, Babbage, Bhikkhu Sujato, Boedawgyi, Bunnyhop11, Cadsuane Melaidhrin, Cailil, Chris the speller, ClamDip, ClueBot NG, Cminard, Cnwilliams, Craig Pemberton, CsDix, DadaNeem, Dakinijones, DeXXus, Deeptii, Derek R Bullamore, Dharmalion76, Dimadick, Dinakarr, DiogenesTCP, DivineAlpha, Docu, Donfbreed, DrakeUnlimited, Dream of Nyx, Echalon, Efficiencyc62, Ekrpat, ErikvanB, Esteban.barahona, Fountain Posters, Frappyjohn, Fyrael, Gherkinmad, Gilberta09, Gmm1990, Gorthian, Graham87, GünniX, Hanbud, Happyseeu, HarvardKing, Helpsome, Iamnotapoohead, Ianjm, IdealistCynic, J D, Jarble, Javierfv1212, Jennica, Jijnasu Yakru, JimRenge, Joefromrandb, JohnGH, Johnbod, Johnpacklambert, JorisvS, Joshua Jonathan, Kaldari, Kanonkas, Knife-in-the-drawer, LWG, Lambiam, Larry Rosenfeld, Lotje, LuisGomez111, Magioladitis, Majora4, Makeswell, Matthew Proctor, Menchi, Menduri, Mitsube, Mr.choppers, Ms Sarah Welch, Mzilikazi1939, Naraht, Ninly, Ocdnctx, Omnipaedista, Otr500, Paine Ellsworth, Peter jackson, Peter1c, Ph0kin, Phreakazoas, Rich Farmbrough, Richard Arthur Norton (1958-), Ricjs, Ricky81682, Rjwilmsi, Robertinventor, Rossen4, SWR2.9, Sacca, Sadhu44, Sam Sailor, Samuel de mazarin, Santhapriya, Seba5618, Sethian, Sizeofint, Spacepotato, Spasemunki, Srnec, Stiphan1, Sujato, Sweepy, Sylvain1972, Sevinti fav, Tengu800, Termininja, Thanissaro, Thisara.d.m, Timrollpickering, Tommy2010, Uncle Milty, Using entropy84, Utcursch, Vegetarianiwow9, Verbum Veritas, VictoriaGrayson, Vinegarymass911, VoABot II, Wingspeed, Woohookitty, Yaditiva, Zenwhat, प्रसाद साळवे, 000, 0, 배우는사람, 79 anonymous edits 96

Assamese literature *Source:* https://en.wikipedia.org/w/index.php?oldid=858835901 *License:* Creative Commons Attribution-Share Alike 3.0 *Contributors:* Abhijit borah, AnjanBorah, Anshuman.jrt, Arch dude, Athanasius1, Betacommand, Bikram98, Bineswar Baro12, Bishnu Saikia, Buljit, Chaipau, ChildofMidnight, ClueBot NG, CommonsDelinker, Dl2000, Ekabhishek, ExplodingPoPUps, Footage, Generalboss3, George Sharma, Gilliam, Gitanjali9, HangingCurve, Hemanta91, Hmains, Hmainsbot1, Hullaballoo Wolfowitz, JASDVI, Jagged 85, Jim1138, John of Reading, Jown dutta, Khazar2, Lilac Soul, Me, Myself, and I are Here, Msasag, Nandadulal69, Nborkakoty, Nvkashraf~enwiki, Ohnoitsjamie, Parikhit phukan, Pete unseth, Priyankoo~enwiki,

R'n'B, Ragib, Redheylin, Sayakbannerghata, Sewali Dutta, Shadowjams, Shyamsunder, Simplexity22, Slowmover, Slowmoverz, StAnselm, Svabhiman, Tachs, Tinucherian, Trappist the monk, Utcursch, WereSpielChequers, Xeteli, Zvn, 77 anonymous edits 115

Buranji *Source:* https://en.wikipedia.org/w/index.php?oldid=825321858 *License:* Creative Commons Attribution-Share Alike 3.0 *Contributors:* A2Kafir, Arjayay, B13775, Benzband, Bhaskarbhagawati, Bishnu Saikia, Brookie, Celestianpower, Chaipau, Chris the speller, Cpt.a.haddock, DalQ95, Dkonwar, Fadesga, Footage, Godric on Leave, Hongooi, Mais oui!, Nzd, Ogine, Pegship, Ponyo, Qwertywander1, Shekhar Jyoti Das, SpacemanSpiff, Stormie, Utcursch, 20 anonymous edits 124

Assamese poetry *Source:* https://en.wikipedia.org/w/index.php?oldid=858835741 *License:* Creative Commons Attribution-Share Alike 3.0 *Contributors:* Aeonx, Another Believer, Boing! said Zebedee, Bonadea, Ekabhishek, Fabrictramp, Favonian, FoCuSandLeArN, GoingBatty, Maadad, Malcolma, Me, Myself, and I are Here, Q48dado, SMasters, Slowmoverz, StAnselm, 2 anonymous edits 126

Bengali literature *Source:* https://en.wikipedia.org/w/index.php?oldid=864271676 *License:* Creative Commons Attribution-Share Alike 3.0 *Contributors:* AFBorchert, Abid Ahmed, Adam9030, Allbloom, Amarkolkata, Amartya.talukdar, AmenaKhatun, Anandmoorti, Anendlessgrid, Arr4, Asma Zenzali, Ayomoy, BD2412, Bengaliarit, Bob1960evens, Bodhisattwa, Bongwarrior, Camboxer, Chandan Guha, Chip123456, Chitraved, Chris the speller, ClueBot NG, ColonelHenry, CommonsDelinker, Courcelles, DVdm, Daiyusha, DemocraticLuntz, Dialectric, Diannaa, Djembayz, DocWatson42, Doug Weller, Download, Durgapurbiman, Edward321, Ekips39, Farhana2012, Finnusertop, Freebook4us, Gaurh, GoingBatty, Guddumitra, Gumnam rahi, GünniX, Haridaspal, Irani goswami, Jame Uddin, Jaytarapublisher, Jcb, Jeff G., Jonoikobangali, K6ka, Kalikkhyapa, Kkm010, Kontrola, Kushalmani59, Kwamikagami, M-le-mot-dit, Matthiaspaul, Mediavalia, Msnicki, Muktijoddha, Munira Mustasri, Nafsadh, Narky Blert, Nasima Akhter, NeilN, Nillohit, Nilsanka, Nusaiba Tasnim, Obangmoy, Onel5969, Orko9696, PKT, Pinakpani, Pranabbasuray, R'n'B, Ragib, Revent, Rich Farmbrough, Roland zh, SamuelTheGhost, Sayakbannerghata, SchreiberBike, Seewolf, Shamikbangla, Shish M, Shish Mohammad Zakaria, Smmmaniruzzaman, Srsjnr, Sudiptamunsi, TRBP, Tabletop, Tassedethe, Titodutta, Utcursch, Vanished user kjn lsr35kjhwertsek4, Wavelength, WereSpielChequers, Wiki-uk, Woohookitty, Worldbruce, Yamaguchi先生 , Ymblanter, Zafor2010, Zenuin, Zundark, বিজয় চক্রবর্তী, শুভ্রজি৹ বড়ুয়া, 135 anonymous edits 129

Bhojpuri literature *Source:* https://en.wikipedia.org/w/index.php?oldid=831475706 *License:* Creative Commons Attribution-Share Alike 3.0 *Contributors:* Chandan.kaushik, DragonflySixtyseven, Drdelvik, Fayenatic london, Hempal31, SM7, Shyamsunder, Solarra, Wilhelmina Will, Worldbruce, 2 anonymous edits 147

Indian English literature *Source:* https://en.wikipedia.org/w/index.php?oldid=860529586 *License:* Creative Commons Attribution-Share Alike 3.0 *Contributors:* 2tuntony, A. B., Alexanderraju, Allbloom, American Hindu, Amnawale, Anilm411, Annedeplume, Aretaic, Aristophanes68, Ashwinimk, Atlantic306, Atul Bhattacharyya, BD2412, Bellerophon5685, Bellus Delphina, Bijender Singh Soora, Bijumonjacob, Binksternet, Bluedudemi, Bobo192, Boing! said Zebedee, Brandy99, Chakrashok, Chanchal Srivastava, ChrisGualtieri, Clinton999, ClueBot NG, Crtew, CsDix, Czar, DPRoberts534, Darrenmong, Davidcannon, Dewritech, Dhartilal, Dialectric, Doug Weller, Editorsfrance, Ekabhishek, Ekkavi, Empeejay9, Evaders99, Faizhaider, Fatbong, Foobaz, Frenweh, Galo1969X, George Sharma, GoingBatty, Grafen, Gwernol, Hendrick 99, IceCreamAntisocial, J04n, JaconaFrere, Jim1138, Johnyossarrian, Kalhause, Kevinalewis, Khazar2, Kumar108, Kushan Lahiri, Liberal Humanist, LilHelpa, Magioladitis, Makeishura, Malcolmxl5, Mallip, Mang55, Marvelchanp, Materialscientist, Me, Myself, and I are Here, MegaMan1988, Menkashivdasani, Misarxist, Mitarani, Mogism, Mohitthepoet, Mortense, MrOllie, Mutt Lunker, NawlinWiki, NeilN, Noctibus, Omnipaedista, PMDrive1061, Padmar53, Patiala19, Patoldanga'r Tenida, Pawankahuja, Poetry Watch, Pre097, Prinshukr, Prodego, Pyfan, Qworty, RandomAct, Reconsideration, Relata refero, Rjwilmsi, Robbinsroad, Romanczyk, SHRIPADVAIDYA, Sadads, Scott, Secleinteer, Seewolf, Shatrunjaymall, Shivam.s88, Shreejanarani, Shreevatsa, Shristi dbr, SimonP, Sirajahmeds, Sjblake, Skomorokh, Skr15081997, Soham, Sourjya roy, Spicemix, Subratakdas, Sumitkumar kataria, Tassedethe, TheMidnighters, Tolly4bolly, Tom harrison, Townblight, Ugog Nizdast, Utcursch, VirtualPoetix, Vjhaone, Wisdom89, Woohookitty, Wywax, 216 anonymous edits 149

Hindi literature *Source:* https://en.wikipedia.org/w/index.php?oldid=864960841 *License:* Creative Commons Attribution-Share Alike 3.0 *Contributors:* Aayaam, Abandeali, Adeliine, Adhar Sinha, AmiVam, Amitabh216, AnakngAraw, Ankush 89, Anonymous Dissident, Anoop8725, Apparition11, Aristophanes68, Auric, AvicAWB, Baltshazzar, Bamyers99, Ben Ben, Bens2008, Bernhardt5, Bharat Bhasha, Bhardwas.tarun, Biplab Anand, Bob Burkhardt, Bonadea, Broodwaif raj, CAPTAIN RAJU, Canton japan, Chanan Dhillon, Chris the speller, Ckatz, ClueBot NG, CommonsDelinker, Conradjagan, CsDix, CutOffTies, Cwmhiraeth, Diffeomorphicvoodoo, Dixitsandeep, Dsilentassasin, EdBever, Ekabhishek, El C, EngHindiDOTCom, Erolos, Faradayplank, Fayenatic london, Ferdous, Figureofnine, Flooded with them hundreds, Foreverknowledge, Fraggle81, Gaius Cornelius, Generalboss3, Glorious Beauty, Gocharyaji, Graham87, GrahamHardy, Hanumantkishor, Hu12, Hulo, IceCreamAntisocial, Infinite intimation, Info.abhishek, Itsciinema, J.delanoy, J04n, JaGa, Jac16888, Jim1138, John of Reading, Karanpandey1710, KateWishing, Kautilya3, Kavikamleshgautam, Kavikamleshsanjida, Kdimension000, Krishnakoli, Kwamikagami, LRBurdak, Lalit Kumar, LindsayH, Logical1004, Macsets, Magioladitis, Manishsts5, MarginalCost, Materialscientist, Maximillion Pegasus, Me, Myself, and I are Here, MelbourneStar, Mridul bharti, Mrt3366, Msamiula, Myarticlewikipedia, NadirAli, Northamerica1000, Ohconfucius, Onel5969, Pb14011978, Pepper Black, Photonique, Piandcompany, R'n'B, RajKumar25477, Ranjithsiji, Ravinandan Singh, Reactor, Reconsideration, Rjwilmsi, Rkxingh, Salih, Seemavibhaji, Serols, Shailen, Shellwood, Skippinder, Soni Ruchi, Sophus Bie, SpacemanSpiff, Spjayswal67, T@nn, Tachs, Terbayang, The Thing That Should Not Be, TheSandDoctor, Theo777, Thomas.W, Tigercompanion25, Titodutta, Utcursch, Veritas77777, Vibhachaswal, Victor8949, Vilcxjo, Vishvagyan, Vrenator, Wandering essence, Wasbeer, Wikidas, Wikiuser13, محمد شعيب, फ़िलप्रो, हिंदुस्थान वासी, 185 anonymous edits 161

Kannada literature *Source:* https://en.wikipedia.org/w/index.php?oldid=858835951 *License:* Creative Commons Attribution-Share Alike 3.0 *Contributors:* Abhishekitmbm, Alastair Haines, Amortias, Andycjp, Aristophanes68, Bgwhite, Brenont, Calliopejen1, CaroleHenson, Ceranthor, Chugalah, Citation bot 1, Closedmouth, ClueBot NG, CommonsDelinker, Cpt.a.haddock, DebonairGuru, Dineshkannambadi, Doldrums, Dthomsen8, E2eamon, Edderso, Editor5454, Ekabhishek, Ellisun, EoGuy, Eumolpo, Fowler&fowler, Fratrep, Frietjes, GSS, Giraffedata, GorgeCustersSabre, Grafen, Haldodderi, Hammersoft, Happysailor, Haris04, Hmains, Holenarasipura, Imc, Iridescent, John of Reading, Jonesey95, Jrsanthosh, KNM, KanLit, Kanatonian, Koavf, Kpbolumbu, Lakswp1, Magioladitis, Mandarax, Mandya Venus, Marcus Cyron, Mathighat, Mattisse, Mayasandra, Me, Myself, and I are Here, Michael Devore, MikeLynch, Mr Stephen, Mst minchu, Mynameisnikhil, Nascar1996, Neelix, Ogress, Onel5969, Penbat, Pied Hornbill, Pulakeshi2nd, Rakeshonsou, Redtigerxyz, Rich Farmbrough, Rivertorch, Rjwilmsi, Roland zh, Rpeh, Sardanaphalus, Sarvagnya, ShelfSkewed, Signalhead, Sindhurocks93, Tamilyomen, Tassedethe, TexasAndroid, Trappist the monk, Utcursch, Vhsatheeshkumar, Vivvt, Woohookitty, YellowMonkey, امين اكبر, 99 anonymous edits 177

Literature of Kashmir *Source:* https://en.wikipedia.org/w/index.php?oldid=857538757 *License:* Creative Commons Attribution-Share Alike 3.0 *Contributors:* A.j.roberts, A.n.a.o.l, Afghana～enwiki, Aimaadi, Anu lonya, Anupam, Ardegloo, Aristophanes68, Arslan-San, Atulsnischal, BD2412, Bamyers99, Bender235, Bgwhite, Cerabot～enwiki, Changetrl, ChauriCh, Chris the speller, Chris troutman, ChrisGualtieri, Coffee, Colonies Chris, Crystallina, Daniel Robert Sum, Dbachmann, DoctorZargar, Ekabhishek, Gazal world, Generalboss3, Gismkutre, Hmains, Ifnord, Instantnood, Iridescent, John of Reading, Joyous!, KH-1, Kashmiri, Kbdank71, Kohlrabi Pickle, Las Joo, LilHelpa, LordSimonofShropshire, LouisAragon, Mam Neelima, Man vyi, Mar4d, Meatsgains, Mrt3366, Mukerjee, Munaji999, Onkoul, Pacifist94, Pegship, Pjoef, Rachitrali, Reza Sheikh, Rjwilmsi, Rkathome, Robina Fox, Safiya khursheed, Scopecreep, Shahmukhi, Shivi511, Shyamsunder, SoWhy, Stemonitis, Sunsandrains, Sverdrup, Tashmead, Townblight, Updatehelper, Utcursch, Vanished user wdjklasdjskla, Voceditenore, Waseem1034, Wavelength, فرح ديسائي, 149 anonymous edits 209

Malayalam literature *Source:* https://en.wikipedia.org/w/index.php?oldid=856680660 *License:* Creative Commons Attribution-Share Alike 3.0 *Contributors:* Acatgain, Amire80, Amithajith, Anoopan, Anoopkn, Apparition11, Aravindmshankar, Aristophanes68, Arjayay, Arjuna lal, Arjunkmohan, Atlantic306, BD2412, Bentogoa, BrownHairedGirl, Buckleyt, CAN, Caliburn, Capitalismojo, Catlemur, Chris the speller, ClueBot NG, CommonsDelinker, Crknair, Crystallizedcarbon, Cwmhiraeth, Cyfal, David Haslam, DevipriyaC, DhiluSen, DocWatson42, EmanWilm, Flyer22 Reborn, Frze, Generalboss3, Giraffedata, Habinafi, HadrianTheMystic, Harithvh, Hbr123, Hu12, Icarusgeek, Indian poet dr.k.g.balakrishnan, Jalakam, Jfmantis, John of Reading, Kalidasa Vijaya Q, Keith D, Kjbinukj, Kkutty, Leovizza, LilHelpa, Magioladitis, Malayala Sahityam, Materialscientist, Mccapra, Mercurywoodrose, Mydreamsparrow, Naduvattom, Nairunni64, Niceguyedc, Nmkuttiady, O.Koslowski, Ohconfucius, Omni Flames, Onel5969, Ramannair r, Randy Kryn, Rodw, Roland zh, Sadads, SafeerTirur, Salih, Sangeetha Chenampulli, Shebaly, Shijusam, Shinemonmk, Signalhead, Sitush, Stickee, Sureshkuzhuppulli, Tabletop, Tachs, Tassedethe, Terrek, TheRedPenOfDoom, Thirdright, Trakesht, Unnikqu, Utcursch, Vaageeswari1, Vanished user qwqwijr8hwrkjdnvkanfoh4, Venugopal.tp, Vinodag, Vkbmenon, Vksrihari, Vs.subash, Vssun, Wavelength, WereSpielChequers, Widr, Wikipelli, Ἀλέξανδρος ὁ Μέγας, 176 anonymous edits 217

Meitei literature *Source:* https://en.wikipedia.org/w/index.php?oldid=853052287 *License:* Creative Commons Attribution-Share Alike 3.0 *Contributors:* Alvin Seville, AvicAWB, Avicennasis, Awangba Mangang, Bearcat, Betathita, Bmusician, Chris the speller, Ekabhishek, Fundamental metric tensor, George Sharma, Hmains, Ingudum, Ish ishwar, John of Reading, Katharineamy, Kithira, Kwamikagami, LilHelpa, Magioladitis, Malcolma, MichealH, Ms Sarah Welch, Ninfo mn, Nongdamba, Ohconfucius, OlEnglish, Pablomartinez, R'n'B, Rojiousham, Sfan00 IMG, Shyamsunder, Simongraham, Solomon7968, Tachs, Tigercompanion25, Titodutta, Vrenator, Wikid77, Ykhwong, 22 anonymous edits 235

Marathi literature *Source:* https://en.wikipedia.org/w/index.php?oldid=863225597 *License:* Creative Commons Attribution-Share Alike 3.0 *Contributors:* Alren, Ananda Rao Vasishta, Ankush 89, Ashokshubhada, AvinashDawari, Belasd, Ben Ben, Bgwhite, Bobrayner, Buddhipriya, Chirag, Chris the speller, Cmdrjameson, Commander, Deepak D'Souza, Dharmadhyaksha, Download, Drbreznjev, Ekabhishek, Electronz, EsdnePyaJ, Fconaway, Fraggle81, Gaius Cornelius, Garzo, Generalboss3, Gilliam, Giraffedata, Greatgavini, Hariwiki123, Harshadkhandare, Hmains, Instantnood, Itenthu, John of Reading, Jonathansammy, Joy1963, Jumping cheese, LITERATURELOVER007, LogX, Lotje, MER-C, Magioladitis, Marathikavita, Marshmir, Matthew-Vanitas, Mereda, Mike.lifeguard, Milowent, Mmavkvba, Mogism, MrOllie, Mskadu, Mu Mind, MuffledThud, Mushroom, NawlinWiki, Ojus.narawane, PhilKnight, Piano non troppo, Piyushthorat19, Poetrywala, Pradeep.khot, Quadrius, Quinton Feldberg, Raanoo, Redtigerxyz, Riana, Rich Farmbrough, Rupeshkhandekar, Rvktkd, Sachinketkar, Sajjangad, SalilSBudhe, Sameer swapna, Sd280391, Shantanu1985, Shivashree, Shyamsunder, Signalhead, Sitush, Sleepingwithmymuse, Srujan tilve, Stateofart, Storms991, Toohool, Uanfala, Utcursch, Vasant valanju, Vin09, Vinitagangurde, Vishalkhapre, Vishu123, Wayland, WikHead, Willking1979, Woohookitty, YH1975, Yash10ingale, 161 anonymous edits 239

Mizo literature *Source:* https://en.wikipedia.org/w/index.php?oldid=858848339 *License:* Creative Commons Attribution-Share Alike 3.0 *Contributors:* Chhandama, Chris the speller, Coolcolney, CouchSurfer222, DBigXray, Ekabhishek, Hmains, Jesse V., John of Reading, Mabdul, Me, Myself, and I are Here, Mizofa, Nocowardsoulismine, Onel5969, RMizo, Rubbish computer, Sun Creator, Tachs, TutterMouse, Utcursch, WilliamThweatt, ZŏràmTán, 14 anonymous edits 249

Odia literature *Source:* https://en.wikipedia.org/w/index.php?oldid=863152837 *License:* Creative Commons Attribution-Share Alike 3.0 *Contributors:* 7Sidz, Abecedare, Ace Cronof, AddisWang, Akkida, Amartyabag, Anshuman2111, Aparida1295, Ashwin147, Avoryfaucette, BD2412, Balloonguy, Basanta25, Basua, Bgwhite, Bishupriyaparam, Biswa bisruta, Biswabiscuit, Bmusician, ChinmayHota, Chinu9732, Claireney, Cpt.a.haddock, D6, Davewho2, Dawn Bard, Debee2810, Donner60, Drmies, Dsp13, Ekabhishek, EoGuy, Feanor0, Felunayak, Fixer88, Freedomji, Generalboss3, GoingBatty, Gopalray999, Harsimaja, Himansu Sekhar Fatesingh, Himansu36, Hmains, Hu12, I dream of horses, Indian explorerpro, Indu, JaGa, Jitendra.muduli, John of Reading, Jusdafax, Kalkimunee108, Kanu786, Kap82, Keith D, Kenfyre, Kishore Panigrahi, Kwamikagami, LilHelpa, Luxure, MKar, MZMcBride, MasterOfHisOwnDomain, Materialscientist, Me, Myself, and I are Here, Meetdevin, Mild Bill Hiccup, Mogism, Mohantysr, Munishlin, Mx. Granger, Myasuda, Natg 19, Neelix, OdiaSam, Odiamagazine, Ogress, OlEnglish, Omnipaedista, Orlady, Padmacharan123, Pais, PatiMadhusudan1958, Pearll's sun, PohranicniStraze, Prabhu Prasad Tripathy, Pradeepkpanda, Psubhashish, Ranjan dr Dash, RegentsPark, Routout 132, Rubbish computer, Sachinketkar, Salil.kar, Samarendranath Mahapatra, Sanbiwiki, SchreiberBike, Sitansusekhar07, Sjsingh kld, SpacemanSpiff, Sphilbrick, Ssrout, Subhransupanda, TanmayaPanda, Tarun Kanti Mishra, Thingg, Tigercompanion28, Trappist the monk, Tripathy pratyush, Utcursch, Victuallers, We hope, Welsh, WereSpielChequers, Wik-Head, 186 anonymous edits 257
Punjabi literature *Source:* https://en.wikipedia.org/w/index.php?oldid=864974558 *License:* Creative Commons Attribution-Share Alike 3.0 *Contributors:* 3swordz, A.amitkumar, Ali-Rana-77, Amirsaeed77, Apparition11, Apuldram, Ar 77, BD2412, Beetstra, Bhagwant Sangrur, Bhatti BP Singh, Bodhisattwa, CAPTAIN RAJU, Chanan Dhillon, Chris the speller, ClueBot NG, Colonies Chris, CommonsDelinker, Dusti, Dusty777, Ekabhishek, Excirial, Fabrictramp, Generalboss3, Guglani, Hardevgrewal, Joaquin008, Khalid Mahmood, King john7, Kintetsubufalo, Kwamikagami, Leolaursen, LilHelpa, LittleWink, Mar4d, Mogism, Muhammadali 1970, Mukerjee, Niceguyedc, Nirvana888, Pajjar, Pakwaseb, Peeta Singh, R1l2c3k4, Rk.radhekrishan, Robina Fox, Roger Markham, RoysmithSpiff, Sphilbrick, Ssrout, Subhransupanda, TanmayaPanda, Umar farooq miana, Woohookitty, Wrelwser43, عربى, ਗੁਰਮੀਤ ਸਿੰਘ, 254 anonymous edits 279
Rajasthani literature *Source:* https://en.wikipedia.org/w/index.php?oldid=852273420 *License:* Creative Commons Attribution-Share Alike 3.0 *Contributors:* Ajaykumarsoni875, Allens, Anubhab91, Aristophanes68, Chris the speller, ChrisGualtieri, Ekabhishek, ImmortalSpartans, JamesBWatson, Koala34, Kosher Fan, Lalit82in, Leolaursen, Little green rosetta, OlEnglish, Onef9day, Pruthvi.Vallabh, Rajah, SchreiberBike, Shyamsunder, Sitush, Sushant jain, Townblight, Welsh, Woohookitty, 37 anonymous edits 285
Sindhi literature *Source:* https://en.wikipedia.org/w/index.php?oldid=843947058 *License:* Creative Commons Attribution-Share Alike 3.0 *Contributors:* Abelmoschus Esculentus, Abrorulles, Afghana~enwiki, AhmadLX, Alixafar, Anupam, Anwerroshan, Arsenalkidgooner, Arslan-San, Art wart1234, Ata Fida Aziz, AtticusX, Ayazrb, Azadsanwal, BD2412, Bakasuprman, Barticus88, Bazonka, Ben Ben, Bgwhite, Bobblehead, Brendon, Carlossuarez46, ClueBot NG, Colombiansar, Desertphoenix7, Ekabhishek, Farhanshaikh01, Generalboss3, Gherkinmad, Gyrofrog, Hide&Reason, Hmains, Hongooi, Ibraheembhatti, Indusian1236, Ismet Saif, Izharsoomro, J04n, JaGa, Jeff3000, Jeraphine Gryphon, JogiAsad, John "Hannibal" Smith, Joseph Biddulph, Jublums, Khalid Mahmood, Khalidkhoso, Latisharma, McGeddon, Mehran Mangrio, Miloom, Mojo Hand, MrOllie, Niceguyedc, Nick Number, Nomanwaheed, Noorulwahabi555, Nscheffey, Orenburg1, Pacifist94, Pax:Vobiscum, PeterCanthropus, Pgdodeja, Poonta, Primefac, Prolog, Riana, Rich257, Rjwilmsi, RoySmith, S (usurped also), Sadads, Serols, Shah Inat, SiobhanHansa, SoWhy, Soman, Soni Ruchi, SteinbD, Stevemarlett, Storkk, Szhaider, Thinkali, Thomas.W, Townblight, Utcursch, Vanisaac, Wasell, Wavelength, Welsh, Zahoor2000, Zvar, سرمست ديسانى فقيل فرح كاشف, 65 anonymous edits 289
Tamil literature *Source:* https://en.wikipedia.org/w/index.php?oldid=860263084 *License:* Creative Commons Attribution-Share Alike 3.0 *Contributors:* 2know4power, ARUNKUMAR P.R, Aadal, Aayush18, Aegon Mediservice, Allforrous, Alvestrand, Amithshs, Anand v21, Anwar saadat, Aristophanes68, Arjayay, Avedeus, BD2412, Bhagya sri113, Brenont, CALR, CAPTAIN RAJU, CaroleHenson, Closedmouth, ClueBot NG, Cribananda, Cryptic, CultureDrone, David Kernow, Deli nk, Dineshkannambadi, Discospinster, Download, Dskumar.science, Eshwar.om, Euchiasmus, Faizhaider, Fixer88, Flooble9191, Gadget850, Gerda Arendt, Geronimogold, Grafen, Green Giant, I dream of horses, J04n, Jambolik, Japjams, Jataayu1, John of Reading, Jonesey95, Joshua Jonathan, Justinrejimone, K.chandraseharan, Kanatonian, Karthicknanmaran, KazakhPol, Kbdank71, Keyan20, Khazar, KiloSierraCharlie, L293D, Lalu Hrishikesh, Librarykannan1, LilHelpa, LogX, MER-C, Maayan pandithevan, Madhava 1947, Magioladitis, Marudubshinki, Materialscientist, Me, Myself, and I are Here, Mereda, MikeEagling, Mital2003, Mjs1991, Murtasa, Mx. Granger, Nahomi, Netking, Nmadhubala, Nposs, Nsugavanam, Onel5969, Parthizplus, Penpositive, Qmwne235, Rajarajancheetak2010, Rajkumarth, Ram thigiri, Ranee Narendranath, Rasnaboy, RedUser, Redheylin, Redtigerxyz, Rojypala, Roland zh, Rossen4, Rubbish computer, S3000, Sadads, Sai2sundar, Sangam senthil, Saravanan070776, Sarvagnya, Schreiber-Bike, Serols, Sharanks, Sitush, Snraj, Sodabottle, SpacemanSpiff, Srini au eee, Sriram mayon, Srkpriv, Sriram mr, Stemonitis, SteveM123, Subhadhyan-raj, Sundar, Swetha Sa, Tamilmankind, Tamilselvi98, Thamizhpparithi, Tigercompanion25, Tonythiru, Townblight, Trappist the monk, Umashankar81, Utcursch, Vadakkan, Varathatheboss, Veerdev, Venu62, Wasell, Wavelength, Weaponsgrade, WereSpielChequers, Whygreen44, Widr, WikiJedits, Wikiuser111, Wise111, YellowMonkey, Yogesh Khandke, Yom, Yrum, 170 anonymous edits 299
Telugu literature *Source:* https://en.wikipedia.org/w/index.php?oldid=859037268 *License:* Creative Commons Attribution-Share Alike 3.0 *Contributors:* Abrahmad111, Adits90, Aggi007, Ahmed Nisar, Alarichall, Anwesh Pokkuluri, Aristophanes68, Arunspeed, Avsrk67, BD2412, Beheshtihosein, Bgwhite, Bhaskar kusar, Chris the speller, ChrisGualtieri, ClubOranje, ClueBot NG, Coolabahapple, Criticpanther, Crown Prince, Crow, CsxDix, David.moreno72, Debresser, Dhharma, Dumbpotato5, Flyer22 Reborn, Gangadhar. vempalli, Gongshow, Harshavd, Hitectcity, Ihcoyc, Ijon, Jajundhar RG, Jim1138, JorisvS, Jpawan33, K.Venkataramana, Khazar2, Krishna2142, Kumar560, Laodah, Largoplazo, Madhav165, Mccapra, Mean as custard, Moviehub, Murralli, Nagarjuna198, Nandiwada, Narayan, Nick Number, Nsk3vk, Obonfucius, Ohnoitsjamie, Oop, Oshwah, Pdeverak, PhnomPencil, Poglkpri, Pratyya Ghosh, R'n'B, RTPking, RamuluReddy, Readanything1729, Rohinimahesh, Ritatavarty, SJ Defender, Sadads, Sai santhosh00, Salvio giuliano, SchreiberBike, ShadedO, ShadowRatchet6, Sitush, Skyerise, SpacemanSpiff, Sree Vasista, Srikanth Aviator, Starpchack, StasMalyga, Subhashinilyer, Svabhiman, Svpnikhil, Tassedethe, Telugujoshi, Titodutta, Tony johnsong, Topbanana, Train2104, Trmwikifa, Utcursch, Vamshi kanety, Vempalligangadhar, Vin09, Vipranarayana, Visdaviva, Wavelength, Woohookitty, Yprasannas, अजन्मा सिंह, ఐఅంబెట్లు, తెలుగు, 108 anonymous edits 321
Tulu language *Source:* https://en.wikipedia.org/w/index.php?oldid=863334348 *License:* Creative Commons Attribution-Share Alike 3.0 *Contributors:* 42Q7, Abrahamic Faiths, Anishviswa, Arjayay, Ayazmaqbool, Aykumar77, Aymatth2, BD2412, BHARATHESHA ALASANDEMAJALU, Batternut, Bender235, Bigerck, BrightStarSky, Buni56, CIMM, ChidanandaKampa, ClueBot NG, Codename. Cyberbot II, Cyphoidbomb, Daspd, Deep-akpadukone20, Derek R Bullamore, Dewritech, Dl2000, Dongar Kathorekar, Dr.Sherly, EagerToddler39, Errantlinguist, Evano1van, Florian Blaschke, Gherkinmad, Gsmanu007, Gyopi, GünniX, I dream of horses, Iamyashwin, IceKarma, Iseult, J.smith, Jayanna, Jaywardhan009, Jim1138, John of Reading, JorisvS, Julien Baley, K6ka, Karthik shankar bhat, Karthiksabaasha, Kishorechan, Koryakov Yuri, Kwamikagami, KylieTastic, Largoplazo, Last edited by:, LeoFrank, Lfdder, Liahey, LilHelpa, Linguisticgeek, Madhuri Upadhya, Magioladitis, Mahagaja, Maproom, Marekr69, Mediran, Melcous, Mogism, Naveen Sankar, Nesara Kadanakuppe, Niceguyedc, NinthBhargava2016, Omnipaedista, PWilkinson, PageImp, Pavanaja, Paxsiminus, Peterbruce01, Plantdrew, Plastikspork, Prahlad balaji, Pranav pk, Prashpro, Prithviamin, Psubhashish, Purodha, QuartierLatin1968, Quintucket, R'n'B, Ravichandar84, Rayabhari, Redpy71, Roland zh, Rossen4, Sabeenashetty, SilverFox183, Smaran alva, Spindocter123, Seasermr, Sunnya343, Supreeths12, Surajt88, Swastik Naik Talangare, Tbhotch, The Immortal Excalibur, The Mighty Glen, The Rahul Jain, Thomas.W, Tigercompanion25, Titsfortats, Topbanana, Trappist the monk, தமிழ்க்குரிசில், தா, 190 anonymous edits 343
Urdu literature *Source:* https://en.wikipedia.org/w/index.php?oldid=863356982 *License:* Creative Commons Attribution-Share Alike 3.0 *Contributors:* Abdulrauf2, Alvin Seville, Amartyabag, Ammaramin123, Andrewman327, Anypodetos, Aparker7651, Apparition11, Aqsahaheenn, Aristophanes68, Arjayay, Arshadmiraj, AtticusX, Bandvi, Beetstra, Bejnar, Bender235, Bismillahnews, Bob Burkhardt, Boxman88, Certes, Chris the speller, ClueBot NG, Comradesaad, Delljvc, Dewritech, Doug Weller, Dr aquil ziad, Ecelan, Ekabhishek, Faisal Hussain mohammed, Fayenatic london, Fictionacademy, Foaq Alig, Frietjes, GermanJoe, GünniX, Gidonb, Gnangarra, GoingBatty, Goodboy991, Green Giant, GünniX, Hadescurve, Hajatvrc, Hayjamalo, Hinahanif90, Hu12, Husainzaheer, Iqbal niyazi, Iqbalhl, Jabberjaw, Jim1138, John of Reading, Jonesey95, JustAGal, Justice007, Khawarmirza, Legobot, LouisAragon, Loupiotte, MER-C, Magioladitis, Malik mati, Mark Arsten, Materialscientist, Mausman0102, Mean as custard, Miacek, Mirzaailloveyou, Msbchulhul, Muhaneds, Mumbabooks, NadirAli, Nestwiki, Noorulwahabi555, Nrolande, OMHalick, Omer123hussain, Pahari Sahib, Penster92, Qasimyad, Reperspark, Riders2013, Rubywine, Schfronscarlett, Sajid khan jadoon, Saleemshahab, SamuelTheGhost, Sardarkhan, ShedSkewed, Sj234, Solarra, Soni Ruchi, Sun Creator, Tarun marwaha, Tdslk, TheUserWiki, Thomas.W, Trappist the monk, UF Ali Rizvi, Urdureader, Vice regent, WLU, Wamiq, Waqas4566, Wavelength, WikiDan61, Woohookitty, Writer201300, Yintan, Zaamsyed, Zananiri, Zunaira jamil, فرح سام, 195 anonymous edits 361

Image Sources, Licenses and Contributors

The sources listed for each image provide more detailed licensing information including the copyright status, the copyright owner, and the license conditions.

Image *Source:* https://en.wikipedia.org/w/index.php?title=File:Padlock-silver.svg *Contributors:* AzaToth, BotMultichill, BotMultichillT, Gurch, Jarekt, Kallerna, Multichill, Perhelion, Rd232, Riana, Sarang, Siebrand, Steinsplitter, 4 anonymous edits 3

Image *Source:* https://en.wikipedia.org/w/index.php?title=File:Om_symbol.svg *Contributors:* AnonMoos, Ashkan P., BD2412, BRUTE, Bdk, BotMultichill, Cathy Richards, Davin7, Dbachmann, Editor at Large, Exact~commonswiki, Gregory Orme, Herbythyme, Hyacinth, Jafeluv, Jcb, JurgenNL, Kashmiri, MGA73bot2, Marshie, Michaeldsuarez, Ms Sarah Welch, Mystical Sadhu, Nilfanion, Nishkid64, Om.sukanta, Rugby471, Sahaguru, Stewi101015, Tangopaso, The Evil IP address, Toyboy84, Túrelio, Wutsje, Xhienne, अभय अग्रवाल, 71 anonymous edits 3

Figure 1 *Source:* https://en.wikipedia.org/w/index.php?title=File:Atharva-Veda_samhita_page_471_illustration.png *License:* Public Domain *Contributors:* Ms Sarah Welch, Prosody 4

Figure 2 *Source:* https://en.wikipedia.org/w/index.php?title=File:Rigveda_MS2097.jpg *License:* Public Domain *Contributors:* Abhishekjoshi, Auntof6, BernardM, David.Monniaux, Imz, Ranveig, Senator2029, Un1c0s bot~commonswiki, Wieralee, Yann, 1 anonymous edits 7

Image *Source:* https://en.wikipedia.org/w/index.php?title=File:Om2.svg *Contributors:* Hyacinth, Kashmiri, Ms Sarah Welch, Sarang 10

Figure 3 *Source:* https://en.wikipedia.org/w/index.php?title=File:Taittiriya_Samhita_Vedas,_Devanagari_script,_Sanskrit_pliv.jpg *Contributors:* User:Ms Sarah Welch 12

Image *Source:* https://en.wikipedia.org/w/index.php?title=File:Vedas_palm_leaf_manuscript,_Tamil_Grantha_Script,_Sanskrit,_Tamil_Nadu.jpg *Contributors:* User:Ms Sarah Welch 14

Image *Source:* https://en.wikipedia.org/w/index.php?title=File:16th_century_Vedas_palm_leaf_manuscript,_Malayalam_Script,_Sanskrit,_Kerala.jpg *Contributors:* User:Ms Sarah Welch 14

Image *Source:* https://en.wikipedia.org/w/index.php?title=File:Commons-logo.svg *License:* logo *Contributors:* Anomie, Callanecc, CambridgeBayWeather, Jo-Jo Eumerus, RHaworth 21

Image *Source:* https://en.wikipedia.org/w/index.php?title=File:Wiktionary-logo-en-v2.svg *Contributors:* User:Dan Polansky, User:Smurrayinchester 21

Image *Source:* https://en.wikipedia.org/w/index.php?title=File:Wikiquote-logo.svg *License:* Public Domain *Contributors:* Rei-artur 21

Image *Source:* https://en.wikipedia.org/w/index.php?title=File:Kurukshetra.jpg *License:* Public Domain *Contributors:* Dbachmann, Jarekt, Man vyi, Mentifisto, Ranveig, Redtigerxyz, Roland zh, Titodutta, Vadakkan, 11 anonymous edits 26

Image *Source:* https://en.wikipedia.org/w/index.php?title=File:Aum_Om_red.svg *Contributors:* Cathy Richards, Hyacinth, Kashmiri, Ms Sarah Welch, Sarang 26

Figure 4 *Source:* https://en.wikipedia.org/w/index.php?title=File:Krishna_and_Arjun_on_the_chariot,_Mahabharata,_18th-19th_century,_India.jpg *License:* Public Domain *Contributors:* Aavindraa, Abhishekjoshi, Ekabhishek, KTo288, Redtigerxyz, Roland zh, 2 anonymous edits 28

Figure 5 *Source:* https://en.wikipedia.org/w/index.php?title=File:Karwar_Pictures_-_Yogesa_19.JPG *License:* Creative Commons Attribution-Sharealike 3.0 *Contributors:* User:Yogesa 28

Figure 6 *Source:* https://en.wikipedia.org/w/index.php?title=File:Sauti_recites_the_slokas_of_the_Mahabharata.jpg *Contributors:* Aschroet, Jhala shivrajsinh, LX 29

Figure 7 *Source:* https://en.wikipedia.org/w/index.php?title=File:Snakesacrifice.jpg *License:* Public Domain *Contributors:* Aavindraa, Fallschirmjäger, PawełMM, Redtigerxyz 31

Figure 8 *Source:* https://en.wikipedia.org/w/index.php?title=File:Painted_Grey_Ware_Culture_(1200-600_BCE).png *License:* Creative Commons Attribution-Sharealike 3.0 *Contributors:* User:Avantiputra7 35

Figure 9 *Source:* https://en.wikipedia.org/w/index.php?title=File:Ganesha_write_Mahabharata.jpg *License:* Creative Commons Zero *Contributors:* Baddu676, Redtigerxyz 36

Figure 10 *Source:* https://en.wikipedia.org/w/index.php?title=File:Ravi_Varma-Shantanu_and_Satyavati.jpg *License:* Public Domain *Contributors:* BotMultichill, Finavon, Ies, Ingolfson, Kashyap Chetan Kotak, Mtt, Praveenp, Ranveig, Redtigerxyz, Renamed user ixgysjijel, Roland zh, Tetraktys, Utcursch, WikiMan88, 1 anonymous edits 37

Figure 11 *Source:* https://en.wikipedia.org/w/index.php?title=File:Draupadi_and_Pandavas.jpg *License:* Public Domain *Contributors:* Printed by Ravi Varma Press 38

Figure 12 *Source:* https://en.wikipedia.org/w/index.php?title=File:Swayamvara_Draupadi_Arjuna_Archery.jpg *License:* Creative Commons Attribution-Sharealike 2.0 *Contributors:* Charles Haynes 40

Figure 13 *Source:* https://en.wikipedia.org/w/index.php?title=File:Disrobing_of_Draupadi.jpg *License:* Public Domain *Contributors:* Nainsukh 41

Figure 14 *Source:* https://en.wikipedia.org/w/index.php?title=File:The_center_of_battle_of_Kurukshetra.jpg *License:* Creative Commons Attribution 2.0 *Contributors:* Divya and Deepak 42

Figure 15 *Source:* https://en.wikipedia.org/w/index.php?title=File:Totheforest.jpg *License:* Public Domain *Contributors:* Great farmer, Jhala shivrajsinh, Redtigerxyz, Revent, Romaine, Salomis, Sridhar1000 43

Figure 16 *Source:* https://en.wikipedia.org/w/index.php?title=File:Wayang_Wong_Bharata_Pandawa.jpg *License:* Creative Commons Attribution-Sharealike 3.0 *Contributors:* Gunawan Kartapranata 45

Figure 17 *Source:* https://en.wikipedia.org/w/index.php?title=File:Razmnama_Bhishma.jpg *License:* Public Domain *Contributors:* Aavindraa, Amandajm, Calame, Ekabhishek, Gryffindor, Johnbod, Kairios, Mani1~commonswiki, Ranveig, Redtigerxyz, Romaine, Siebrand, 1 anonymous edits 47

Figure 18 *Source:* https://en.wikipedia.org/w/index.php?title=File:FullPagadeYakshagana.jpg *License:* GNU Free Documentation License *Contributors:* BotMultichillT, Elcobbola, Mattes, Ppntori, Ranveig, Wst 49

Figure 19 *Source:* https://en.wikipedia.org/w/index.php?title=File:Neminath_Wedding.JPG *License:* Public Domain *Contributors:* Anishshah19 50

Image *Source:* https://en.wikipedia.org/w/index.php?title=File:Wikisource-logo.svg *License:* Creative Commons Attribution-Sharealike 3.0 *Contributors:* ChrisiPK, Guillom, INeverCry, Jarekt, JuTa, Leyo, Lokal Profil, MichaelMaggs, NielsF, Rei-artur, Rocket000, Romaine, Steinsplitter 54

Image *Source:* https://en.wikipedia.org/w/index.php?title=File:Indischer_Maler_von_1780_001.jpg *License:* Public Domain *Contributors:* Durga, Ekabhishek, Emijrp, File Upload Bot (Eloquence), Redtigerxyz, Roland zh, Thnidu 55

Figure 20 *Source:* https://en.wikipedia.org/w/index.php?title=File:Valmiki_Ramayana.jpg *License:* Public Domain *Contributors:* Aschroet, Baddu676, Billinghurst, Chaoborus, Copydays, Intelligent 1000, Jcb, Mu, Redtigerxyz, Renebeto, Sitush 57

Figure 21 *Source:* https://en.wikipedia.org/w/index.php?title=File:Avatars.jpg *License:* Public Domain *Contributors:* the Victoria and Albert Museum 59

Figure 22 *Source:* https://en.wikipedia.org/w/index.php?title=File:Hanuman_before_Rama.jpg *Contributors:* Aavindraa, File Upload Bot (Magnus Manske), IngerAlHaosului, Objectivesea, OgreBot 2, Redtigerxyz, Roland zh 60

Figure 23 *Source:* https://en.wikipedia.org/w/index.php?title=File:Rama_and_monkey_chiefs.jpg *License:* Public Domain *Contributors:* Intelligent 1000, Redtigerxyz 60

Figure 24 *Source:* https//en.wikipedia.org *Contributors:* BotMultichill, BotMultichillT, Docu, GerardM, Redtigerxyz 62

Figure 25 *Source:* https://en.wikipedia.org/w/index.php?title=File:Ramayana_-_Marriage_of_Rama_Bharata_Lakshmana_and_Shatrughna.jpg *License:* Public Domain *Contributors:* Ekabhishek, Nmisra, Redtigerxyz, Roland zh 64

Figure 26 *Source:* https://en.wikipedia.org/w/index.php?title=File:Rama_leaving_for_fourteen_years_of_exile_from_Ayodhya.jpg *License:* Public Domain *Contributors:* Cpt.a.haddock, Dharmadhyaksha, Ekabhishek, Moe Epsilon, Sridhar1000 65

Figure 27 *Source:* https://en.wikipedia.org/w/index.php?title=File:Ravi_Varma-Ravana_Sita_Jathayu.jpg *License:* Public Domain *Contributors:* Aavindraa, Badbuu1000, BotMultichill, Butko, CommonsDelinker, Filo cz, Mattes, Praveenp, Ranveig, Redtigerxyz, Roland zh, Utcursch, 月下薄氷, 1 anonymous edits 66

Figure 28 *Source:* https://en.wikipedia.org/w/index.php?title=File:Stone_bas_relief_at_Banteay_Srei_in_Cambodia.jpg *License:* GNU Free Documentation License *Contributors:* DoktorMax, Fritzpoll, Quadell 68

Figure 29 *Source:* https://en.wikipedia.org/w/index.php?title=File:Sita_at_ashokavana.jpg *License:* Public Domain *Contributors:* Editor at Large, Ekabhishek, Redtigerxyz, Roland zh, TheMandarin, 1 anonymous edits 68

Figure 30 *Source:* https://en.wikipedia.org/w/index.php?title=File:Battle_at_Lanka,_Ramayana,_Udaipur,_1649-53.jpg *License:* Public Domain *Contributors:* Abhishekjoshi, Editor at Large, Ekabhishek, Hekerui, Homonihilis, Julia W, Labattblueboy, M0tty, Redtigerxyz, Roland zh, Shakko, TheMandarin, Yann, İncelemeelemani, Иван Дулин, 1 anonymous edits 70

Figure 31 *Source:* https://en.wikipedia.org/w/index.php?title=File:Hermitage_of_Valmiki,_Folio_from_the_"Nadaun"_Ramayana_(Adventures_of_Rama)_LACMA_AC1999.127.45.jpg *Contributors:* Fæ, Redtigerxyz 71

Figure 32 *Source:* https://en.wikipedia.org/w/index.php?title=File:Wat_phra_keaw_ramayana_fresco.jpg *License:* Public Domain *Contributors:* unknown, photo by "Thaths" 72

Figure 33 *Source:* https//en.wikipedia.org *Contributors:* BotMultichill, BotMultichillT, Docu, GerardM, Redtigerxyz 72
Figure 34 *Source:* https://en.wikipedia.org/w/index.php?title=File:Sita_Ravana_Cambodia.jpg *License:* Public Domain *Contributors:* Decoly, Francis Alexandre 76
Figure 35 *Source:* https://en.wikipedia.org/w/index.php?title=File:Ramayana_Java.jpg *License:* Creative Commons Attribution-Sharealike 3.0 *Contributors:* Gunawan Kartapranata 77
Figure 36 *Source:* https://en.wikipedia.org/w/index.php?title=File:Burmese_Ramayana_dance.jpg *License:* Creative Commons Attribution-Sharealike 2.0 *Contributors:* Nguyen Thanh Long from Sai Gon, Viet Nam 79
Figure 37 *Source:* https://en.wikipedia.org/w/index.php?title=File:Khon_Dance_Frankfurt_Germany_2006.jpg *License:* Public Domain *Contributors:* Günter Trageser 80
Figure 38 *Source:* https://en.wikipedia.org/w/index.php?title=File:An_Ramlila_Actor_In_The_Role_of_Ravana.jpg *License:* Creative Commons Attribution-Sharealike 3.0 *Contributors:* Neeraj ChawlaNeerajhardik 81
Figure 39 *Source:* https://en.wikipedia.org/w/index.php?title=File:Balinese_Ramayan- Sita_and_Hanuman.jpg *License:* Creative Commons Attribution 2.0 *Contributors:* Ekabhishek, Gunkarta, Humboldt, Midori, Opponent, Ranveig, Redtigerxyz 82
Figure 40 *Source:* https://en.wikipedia.org/w/index.php?title=File:Srisita_ram_laxman_hanuman_manor.JPG *License:* GNU Free Documentation License *Contributors:* BotMultichill, Dedda71, Ekabhishek, File Upload Bot (Magnus Manske), MGA73bot2, OgreBot 2, Pandeyasish, Ranveig, Redtigerxyz, Roland zh, Vivek Sarje, Wiki-uk, 1 anonymous edits 83
Figure 41 *Source:* https://en.wikipedia.org/w/index.php?title=File:Devimahatmya_Sanskrit_MS_Nepal_11c.jpg *License:* Public Domain *Contributors:* Abhishekjoshi, CFynn, Ecelan, KTo288, Olaf Studt, Till.niermann, Un1c0s bot∼commonswiki, Yann, 1 anonymous edits 90
Image *Source:* https://en.wikipedia.org/w/index.php?title=File:Books-aj.svg_aj_ashton_01.svg *License:* Public Domain *Contributors:* Anselmi-Juan, Cathy Richards, Einstein2, Jarekt, Liftarn, Phoenix-forgotten∼commonswiki, Rocket000, Skyllfully, Tropicalkitty, VIGNERON, Verdy p, CCCP, 4 anonymous edits 91
Image *Source:* https://en.wikipedia.org/w/index.php?title=File:PD-icon.svg *License:* Public Domain *Contributors:* Alex.muller, Anomie, Anonymous Dissident, CBM, Jo-Jo Eumerus, MBisanz, PBS, Quadell, Rocket000, Strangerer, Timotheus Canens, 1 anonymous edits 94
Image *Source:* https://en.wikipedia.org/w/index.php?title=File:Wikipedia-logo-v2.svg *License:* Creative Commons Attribution-Sharealike 3.0 *Contributors:* Anomie, Jo-Jo Eumerus, Mr. Stradivarius 95
Image *Source:* https://en.wikipedia.org/w/index.php?title=File:Wikibooks-logo-en-noslogan.svg *License:* Creative Commons Attribution-Sharealike 3.0 *Contributors:* User:Bastique, User:Ramac et al. 95
Figure 42 *Source:* https://en.wikipedia.org/w/index.php?title=File:Tipitaka1.jpg *License:* Creative Commons Attribution-Sharealike 2.5 *Contributors:* Bohème, DhJ∼commonswiki, Takeaway, 1 anonymous edits 97
Image *Source:* https://en.wikipedia.org/w/index.php?title=File:Buddhism_dham_jak.png *License:* Public Domain *Contributors:* Beao, Fred the Oyster, Kintetsubuffalo, Teetaweepo, Zscy, 1 anonymous edits 96
Image *Source:* https://en.wikipedia.org/w/index.php?title=File:Dharma_Wheel.svg *License:* Creative Commons Attribution-ShareAlike 3.0 Unported *Contributors:* Anime Addict AA, Asauchi, BabelStone, Bdk, BotMultichill, BrokenSphere, Elvenmuse, Esteban.barahona, Green Mostaza, Madden, Nico-ei, Pinkheartsleeminhook, Roomba, Sarang, Shazz, Wst, 18 anonymous edits 96
Figure 43 *Source:* https://en.wikipedia.org/w/index.php?title=File:Tipitaka_scripture.jpg *License:* Creative Commons Attribution-Sharealike 2.5 *Contributors:* Bohème, DhJ∼commonswiki, Takeaway 99
Figure 44 *Source:* https://en.wikipedia.org/w/index.php?title=File:Burmese-Pali_Manuscript._Wellcome_L0026547.jpg *Contributors:* Dr Lotus Black, Fæ, Jean11, Mladifilozof, Takeaway 104
Image *Source:* https://en.wikipedia.org/w/index.php?title=File:Montage_of_Asamiya_Cultural_Symbols.png *Contributors:* User:Rex86 116
Image *Source:* https://en.wikipedia.org/w/index.php?title=File:Seal_of_Assam.png *License:* Public Domain *Contributors:* OgreBot 2, Roland zh, Shubhamkanodia, Urdangaray 116
Image *Source:* https://en.wikipedia.org/w/index.php?title=File:Bhasha.JPG *License:* Creative Commons Attribution-Sharealike 3.0 *Contributors:* User:JASDVI 122
Image *Source:* https://en.wikipedia.org/w/index.php?title=File:Charyapada.jpg *License:* Public Domain *Contributors:* Bodhisattwa, Cpt.a.haddock, Nasirkhan, Ragib, Roland zh, Vaza12, Wieralee, 2 anonymous edits 129
Image *Source:* https://en.wikipedia.org/w/index.php?title=File:Tagorenazrul.png *License:* Public Domain *Contributors:* ArmanJ, Hindustanilanguage, Roland zh 129
Image *Source:* https://en.wikipedia.org/w/index.php?title=File:Montage_of_Bengal.jpg *Contributors:* User:Ayomoy 130
Figure 45 *Source:* https://en.wikipedia.org/w/index.php?title=File:Charyapada.jpg *License:* Public Domain *Contributors:* Bodhisattwa, Cpt.a.haddock, Nasirkhan, Ragib, Roland zh, Vaza12, Wieralee, 2 anonymous edits 131
Figure 46 *Source:* https://en.wikipedia.org/w/index.php?title=File:Nabanarikunjara_at_Madan_Mohan_Temple_Arnab_Dutta_2011.JPG *License:* Creative Commons Attribution-Sharealike 3.0 *Contributors:* Jonoikobangali 132
Figure 47 *Source:* https://en.wikipedia.org/w/index.php?title=File:Krittibas_Memorial_ver1.jpg *License:* Public Domain *Contributors:* Mukherjiavijit, 1 anonymous edits 133
Figure 48 *Source:* https://en.wikipedia.org/w/index.php?title=File:Manasa_Mangal.jpg *License:* Creative Commons Attribution 2.0 *Contributors:* Jean-Pierre Dalbéra 134
Figure 49 *Source:* https://en.wikipedia.org/w/index.php?title=File:Tomb_of_Michael_Madhusudhan_Dutta.jpg *License:* Creative Commons Attribution 3.0 *Contributors:* Jayantanth 136
Figure 50 *Source:* https://en.wikipedia.org/w/index.php?title=File:Bankim_chandra_chatterjee.jpg *License:* Public Domain *Contributors:* AdamBMorgan, Hedwig in Washington, Kaganer, Magog the Ogre, Moheen, Roland zh, SarkarS, Yann, Zhuyifei1999, 1 anonymous edits 137
Figure 51 *Source:* https://en.wikipedia.org/w/index.php?title=File:Rabindranath_Tagore_in_1909.jpg *Contributors:* Achim55, Adece033090, Ansumang, Arr4, Badmachine, BigJolly9, Bodhisattwa, Caulfield, Jdx, Kal2930, Mar11, Materialscientist, Nagy, Otterathome, Ragib, Roland zh, Sarang, Saravask, Türelio, Veera.sj, Yann, আব্দুল্লাহ, 12 anonymous edits 139
Figure 52 *Source:* https://en.wikipedia.org/w/index.php?title=File:Nazrul.jpg *License:* Public Domain *Contributors:* Arr4, Belasd, BotMultichill, Durga, Jayantanth, Man vyi, Moheen, NahidSultan, Ragib, Shakibul Alam Risvy, Wst, Ö, আব্দুল্লাহ 140
Figure 53 *Source:* https://en.wikipedia.org/w/index.php?title=File:A_poetry_seminar_nandan_kolkata_sujit_sarkar.jpg *License:* Creative Commons Attribution-Sharealike 3.0 *Contributors:* BotAdventures, Cavarrone, Miniapolis, OgreBot 2 141
Figure 54 *Source:* https://en.wikipedia.org/w/index.php?title=File:394_baul-singers-sml.jpg *License:* GNU Free Documentation License *Contributors:* en:User:Mukerjee 143
Figure 55 *Source:* https://en.wikipedia.org/w/index.php?title=File:Shaheed_Minar.JPG *License:* Creative Commons Attribution 2.0 *Contributors:* Mostaque Ahammed 144
Figure 56 *Source:* https://en.wikipedia.org/w/index.php?title=File:Bhasha_Smritistambha_Arnab_Dutta_2011.jpg *License:* Creative Commons Attribution-Sharealike 3.0 *Contributors:* User:Jonoikobangali 145
Figure 57 *Source:* https://en.wikipedia.org/w/index.php?title=File:Arunbhati_Roy_W.jpg *License:* Creative Commons Attribution-Sharealike 3.0 *Contributors:* User:Bellus Delphina 153
Figure 58 *Source:* https://en.wikipedia.org/w/index.php?title=File:Salman-Rushdie-1.jpg *License:* Creative Commons Attribution-Sharealike 3.0 *Contributors:* Ken Conley aka kwc 154
Figure 59 *Source:* https://en.wikipedia.org/w/index.php?title=File:Surya_chariot.jpg *License:* Public Domain *Contributors:* Pandita Vamadhara 167
Figure 60 *Source:* https://en.wikipedia.org/w/index.php?title=File:Devaki_Nandan_Khatri.JPG *License:* Public Domain *Contributors:* Sushil Bhatnagar 171
Figure 61 *Source:* https://en.wikipedia.org/w/index.php?title=File:Camille_Bulcke_(1909-1982).jpg *License:* Public Domain *Contributors:* Grentidez 171
Figure 62 *Source:* https://en.wikipedia.org/w/index.php?title=File:6th_century_Kannada_inscription_in_cave_temple_number_3_at_Badami.jpg *License:* Creative Commons Attribution-Sharealike 3.0 *Contributors:* Dineshkannambadi (talk) 22:48, 30 July 2008 (UTC) 179
Figure 63 *Source:* https://en.wikipedia.org/w/index.php?title=File:Halmidi_OldKannada_inscription.JPG *License:* GNU Free Documentation License *Contributors:* en:User:Dineshkannambadi 180
Figure 64 *Source:* https://en.wikipedia.org/w/index.php?title=File:Kappe_Arabhatta_inscription_at_Badami.JPG *License:* Creative Commons Attribution-Sharealike 3.0 *Contributors:* Dineshkannambadi (talk) 23:32, 30 July 2008 (UTC) 182
Figure 65 *Source:* https://en.wikipedia.org/w/index.php?title=File:Kavi_file2.jpg *License:* Creative Commons Attribution-Sharealike 3.0 *Contributors:* Jrsanthosh (talk) 184
Figure 66 *Source:* https://en.wikipedia.org/w/index.php?title=File:Handwriting_(10th_century)_of_Kannada_poet_Ranna_at_Shravanabelagola.jpg *License:* GNU Free Documentation License *Contributors:* en:User:Dineshkannambadi. Cropped by Ali'i on 14:39, 16 June 2008 (UTC) 185
Figure 67 *Source:* https://en.wikipedia.org/w/index.php?title=File:Hero_Stone_with_old-Kannada_inscription_at_Arasikere.jpg *License:* Creative Commons Attribution-Sharealike 3.0 *Contributors:* Dineshkannambadi (talk) 18:20, 24 May 2008 (UTC) 187
Figure 68 *Source:* https://en.wikipedia.org/w/index.php?title=File:Vijayanagara.jpg *License:* Public Domain *Contributors:* Elcobbola, Linguisticgeek, OgreBot 2, Redtigerxyz, Roland zh 188
Figure 69 *Source:* https://en.wikipedia.org/w/index.php?title=File:Plam_leaf_of_11th_and_12th_Century_with_Vachanas.jpg *License:* Creative Commons Attribution-Sharealike 3.0 *Contributors:* User:Omshivaprakash 190

400

Figure 70 *Source:* https://en.wikipedia.org/w/index.php?title=File:Akkamahadevi_Udathadi1.JPG *License:* Creative Commons Attribution-Share Alike *Contributors:* Amarrg 190
Figure 71 *Source:* https://en.wikipedia.org/w/index.php?title=File:Bronze_bust_of_Basaveswara_on_Albert_Embankment_in_London,_facing_Parliament.JPG *License:* Creative Commons Zero *Contributors:* User:Curran2 191
Figure 72 *Source:* https://en.wikipedia.org/w/index.php?title=File:Kanakadasa_art.jpg *License:* Free Art License *Contributors:* Creator unknown 192
Figure 73 *Source:* https://en.wikipedia.org/w/index.php?title=File:Chikkadevaraja.jpg *License:* Public Domain *Contributors:* Artist unknown, photographer unknown, author: C. Hyavadana Rao 194
Figure 74 *Source:* https://en.wikipedia.org/w/index.php?title=File:Jcrw1.jpg *License:* Public Domain *Contributors:* Badzil, Dr.Kay, FSII, File Upload Bot (Magnus Manske), Linguisticgeek, Morio, OgreBot 2, Papa November, Roland zh 196
Figure 75 *Source:* https://en.wikipedia.org/w/index.php?title=File:Kittel,_Ferdinand_(1832-1903).jpg *License:* Public Domain *Contributors:* BotMultichill, Ephraim33, Frank C. Müller, Man vyi, Martin H., Mu, Roland zh 197
Figure 76 *Source:* https://en.wikipedia.org/w/index.php?title=File:BugleRock_DVG6.JPG *License:* Creative Commons Attribution 2.5 *Contributors:* User:Sarvagnya 198
Figure 77 *Source:* https://en.wikipedia.org/w/index.php?title=File:Stalwarts.jpg *License:* Public Domain *Contributors:* T. S. Nagarajan 202
Figure 78 *Source:* https://en.wikipedia.org/w/index.php?title=File:Portrait_of_Thunchaththu_Ramanujan_Ezhuthachan,_the_father_of_the_Malayalam_language.jpg *License:* GNU Free Documentation License *Contributors:* Abilngeorge 222
Figure 79 *Source:* https://en.wikipedia.org/w/index.php?title=File:Kathakali_BNC.jpg *License:* Public Domain *Contributors:* Ravi Varma, Prakhar.Dwivedi, Wouterhagens 224
Figure 80 *Source:* https://en.wikipedia.org/w/index.php?title=File:Gundert,_Hermann_(1814-1893).jpg *License:* Public Domain *Contributors:* BotMultichill, Ephraim33, Sebastian Wallroth 226
Figure 81 *Source:* https://en.wikipedia.org/w/index.php?title=File:Kerala_Varma_Valiya_Koil_Thampuran_Changanassery_Lakshmipuram_Palace.jpg *License:* Public Domain *Contributors:* BotMultichill, RajeshUnuppally, Roland zh 227
Figure 82 *Source:* https://en.wikipedia.org/w/index.php?title=File:Jnandev.jpg *License:* Creative Commons Attribution-Sharealike 3.0 *Contributors:* Ravi Varma Press 241
Figure 83 *Source:* https://en.wikipedia.org/w/index.php?title=File:Tukaram_by_Raja_Ravi_Varma.jpg *License:* Public Domain *Contributors:* Donaldduck100, INeverCry, Redtigerxyz 242
Figure 84 *Source:* https://en.wikipedia.org/w/index.php?title=File:Sarvajanik_Satya_Dharma_Pustak.jpg *License:* Public Domain *Contributors:* Roland zh, Sankalpdravid, Shivashree 243
Figure 85 *Source:* https://en.wikipedia.org/w/index.php?title=File:Kesari_Editorial.jpg *License:* Public Domain *Contributors:* Padalkar.kshitij, Roland zh, Sankalpdravid 245
Image Source: https://en.wikipedia.org/w/index.php?title=File:Seal_of_Odisha.png *Contributors:* User:Amreshm 257
Image Source: https://en.wikipedia.org/w/index.php?title=File:Punjabi_example.svg *License:* Creative Commons Attribution-Sharealike 3.0 *Contributors:* User:Syed Wamiq Ahmed Hashmi 279
Figure 86 *Source:* https://en.wikipedia.org/w/index.php?title=File:Amrita_Pritam_(1919_-_2005)_._in_1948.jpg *License:* Public Domain *Contributors:* Amarjit Chandan Collection 281
Figure 87 *Source:* https://en.wikipedia.org/w/index.php?title=File:Surjit_Patar.jpg *License:* Creative Commons Attribution-Sharealike 3.0 *Contributors:* User:Journojp 283
Figure 88 *Source:* https://en.wikipedia.org/w/index.php?title=File:Sindhi_Literature.JPG *License:* Creative Commons Attribution-Sharealike 3.0 *Contributors:* User:Khalid Mahmood 290
Image Source: https://en.wikipedia.org/w/index.php?title=File:TajMahalbyAmalMongia.jpg *License:* Creative Commons Attribution-Sharealike 2.0 *Contributors:* amaldla from san francisco 290
Image Source: https://en.wikipedia.org/w/index.php?title=File:Allah-green.svg *License:* Public Domain *Contributors:* User:AnonMoos, User:Darvinek, User:Guanaco, User:Mattes, User:Ttog 292
Figure 89 *Source:* https://en.wikipedia.org/w/index.php?title=File:Thiruvalluvar_Statue_of_kanyakumari.jpg *License:* Creative Commons Attribution-Sharealike 3.0 *Contributors:* User:Arunankapilan 300
Figure 90 *Source:* https://en.wikipedia.org/w/index.php?title=File:Ilango_Adigal_statue_at_Marina_Beach_closeup.jpg *License:* Creative Commons Attribution-Sharealike 3.0 *Contributors:* User:Rakesh.5suthar 302
Figure 91 *Source:* https://en.wikipedia.org/w/index.php?title=File:Thiruvalluvar_Statue_of_kanyakumari.jpg *Contributors:* User:Shivamsp182 302
Image Source: https://en.wikipedia.org/w/index.php?title=File:Hinduism_symbol.png *License:* GNU Free Documentation License *Contributors:* AnonMoos, Durga, Hyacinth, Jcb, MGA73bot2, Nyo~commonswiki, Pierpao, Tacsipacsi, 2 anonymous edits 305
Figure 92 *Source:* https://en.wikipedia.org/w/index.php?title=File:Statue_of_Avvaiyar_(cropped).jpg *License:* Creative Commons Attribution 2.0 *Contributors:* Balamurugan Srinivasan 307
Figure 93 *Source:* https://en.wikipedia.org/w/index.php?title=File:MarinaBeach_Kambar_cropped.jpg *License:* Creative Commons Attribution-Sharealike 3.0 *Contributors:* User:Rasnaboy 308
Figure 94 *Source:* https://en.wikipedia.org/w/index.php?title=File:ஆதி_அற்குர் ஈசுவரன்_(cropped).JPG *License:* Creative Commons Attribution-Sharealike 3.0 *Contributors:* User:Sankar.s 311
Figure 95 *Source:* https://en.wikipedia.org/w/index.php?title=File:Bharathidasan_(cropped).jpg *License:* Public Domain *Contributors:* 2know4power, Dyolf77 312
Image Source: https://en.wikipedia.org/w/index.php?title=File:Lepakshi...jpg *License:* Creative Commons Attribution-Sharealike 3.0 *Contributors:* User:Vinay332211 321
Image Source: https://en.wikipedia.org/w/index.php?title=File:Archbridgegodavari.JPG *License:* Creative Commons Attribution-Sharealike 3.0 *Contributors:* Tatiraju.rishabh 321
Image Source: https://en.wikipedia.org/w/index.php?title=File:Warangal_fort.jpg *License:* Public domain *Contributors:* Andy Dingley, Hydrargyrum, Kajasudhakarababu~commonswiki, Lomita, Materialscientist, O (bot), OgreBot 2, Roland zh, 1 anonymous edits 322
Image Source: https://en.wikipedia.org/w/index.php?title=File:Loudspeaker.svg *License:* Public domain *Contributors:* User:Dbenbenn, User:Optimager, User:Tsca, User:Dbenbenn, User:Optimager, User:Dbenbenn, User:Optimager, User:Tsca 343
Image Source: https://en.wikipedia.org/w/index.php?title=File:Tulu_in_Kedage_font.png *License:* Public Domain *Contributors:* User:Sunnya343 343
Image Source: https://en.wikipedia.org/w/index.php?title=File:Flag_of_India.svg *License:* Public Domain *Contributors:* Anomie, Jo-Jo Eumerus, Mifter 343
Image Source: https://en.wikipedia.org/w/index.php?title=File:Tuluspeakers.PNG *License:* Creative Commons Attribution-Sharealike 3.0 *Contributors:* linguisticgeek 344
Figure 96 *Source:* https://en.wikipedia.org/w/index.php?title=File:Alvakheda_map.jpg *License:* Creative Commons Attribution-Sharealike 3.0 *Contributors:* Gyopi (Gyopi (talk)) 348
Figure 97 *Source:* https://en.wikipedia.org/w/index.php?title=File:Tulubaase4.png *License:* Public Domain *Contributors:* Gyopi (Gyopi (talk)) 348
Figure 98 *Source:* https://en.wikipedia.org/w/index.php?title=File:Kondadakuli.jpg *License:* GNU Free Documentation License *Contributors:* BotMultichill, File Upload Bot (Magnus Manske), MGA73bot2, NeverDoING, OgreBot 2, Redtigerxyz, Tine 355
Figure 99 *Source:* https://en.wikipedia.org/w/index.php?title=File:Tuluenglishdictionary.jpg *License:* Creative Commons Attribution-Sharealike 3.0 *Contributors:* Princeofdark07 356

License

Creative Commons Attribution-Share Alike 3.0
//creativecommons.org/licenses/by-sa/3.0/

Index

'Abd al-Qadir Badauni, 46

Aali Pulavar, 309
Aathichoodi, 307
Aatreya (playwright), 338
Aattakatha (performance), 223
Abaya, 291, 362
Abbas Uddin, 142
Abdul Ahad Azad, 209
Abdul Ghafoor Ansari, 296
Abdul Hakim (poet), 131, 142
Abdul Jabbar, 144
Abdullah-Al-Muti, 141
Abdul Mannan Syed, 142
Abdul Rahim Khan-I-Khana, 166
Abdur Rashid Bhat, 215
Abhang, 242
Abhay K, 157
Abhidhamma Pitaka, 97, 98, 106, 107
Abhidharma Pitaka, 107
Abhijñānaśākuntalam, 32, 226, 230
Abhimanyu Samanta Simhar, 267
Abhimanyu Samanta Simhara, 267
Abhinavagupta, 209, 211
Abhiraj Rajendra Mishra, 94
Abid Azad, 144
Abid Hassan Minto, 214
Ablative case, 352
Abojho, 295
Abubakar Siddique, 143
Abul Hasan (1947-1975), 143
Abul Hasan (poet), 142
Abu Zafar Obaidullah, 143
Academic, 58

Ācārakkōvai, 301

Accusative case, 352
Acharya Bhadrabahu, 74
Achintya Kumar Sengupta, 145
A Comparative Grammar of the Dravidian or
    South-Indian family of languages, 357
Acyutananda, 264, 265
AD, 293

Adams Bridge, 62, 69
Adavi Baapiraju, 338
Adbhuta, 328
Adbhuta Ramayana, 73
Addepalli Ramamohana Rao, 338
Adhyathmaramayanam, 58, 73, 220, 222
Adi Granth, 280
Adi Kaal, 165
Adikavi Pampa, 185, 328
Adil Abbasi, 296
Adi Parva, 32
Adipurana, 185

Ādi purāṇa, 23

Adi Sankaracharya, 165
Adi Shankara, 8, 191
Adivasi, 260
Adjective, 351
Advaita, 17, 241, 310
Advaita Vedanta, 165, 310
Advaitha, 191
Aesthetics, 210
Affinities with Assamese, 119
Afghanistan, 363
A Fine Balance, 154
A Flight of Pigeons, 153
African literature, 118, 150, 163, 324
Agal (accessory), 291, 362
Agama (Buddhism), 98

Āgama (Hinduism), 92

Agastya, 300
Agattiyam, 300
Agglutination, 344
Agha Hashar Kashmiri, 213
Agha Saleem, 296
Agha Shahid Ali, 151, 157, 215
Agha Shorish Kashmiri, 214
Agni, 70
Agnihotra, 108
Agnosticism, 101
Ahiravan, 73

405

Ahmad Salim, 282
Ahmad Sirhindi, 212
Ahom Buranji, 125
Ahom Dynasty, 124
Ahom Kingdom, 120, 121, 124
Ahom language, 124
Ahsan Habib, 143
Aihole inscriptions, 34
Ain-i-Akbari, 166
Aiṅkurunūṟu, 300
Aintiṉai Aimpatu, 301
Aintinai Eḻupatu, 301
Aitareya Upanishad, 8
Ajaib Kamal, 284
Ajita Tirthankara Purana, 23
Ajitha purana, 186
Ajivika, 5
Ajmer, 164
Ajmer Rode, 284
Ak, 385
Akananuru, 304
Akanāṉūṟu, 300
Akaval, 304
Akbar, 47, 166
Akber Jiskani, 297
Akhil Mohan Patnaik, 274
Akhlaq Ahmed Khan, 368
Akhtar Mohiuddin (writer), 210
Akhtar Sheerani, 366
Akhtaruzzaman Ilias, 141, 143
Akhteruzzaman Elias, 141
Akilan, 314
Akkadian literature, 90, 177
Akka Mahadevi, 191
Akkhoykumar Boral, 138
A. K. Ramanujan, 157
A. K. Warder, 207
A.K. Warder, 102
Alain Danielou, 357
Alamkara, 328
Alaol, 131
Albrecht Weber, 379
Alf Hiltebeitel, 52
Al Ghazali, 215
Ali Baba, 296
Ali Muhammad Rashidi, 295
A Little Princess, 84
AllahDad Bohyo, 295
Allama I. I. Kazi, 295
Allama Mustafa Hussain Ansari, 214
Allama Prabhu, 189, 191
Allasani Peddana, 332, 338
Allegory, 56
Alliteration, 328
Al Mahmud, 142, 143
Altaf Malkani, 296, 297

Alupas, 346, 347
Alu Viharaya, 100
Alvars, 5, 306
Amaravati Kathalu, 340
Amar Chitra Katha, 48
Amar Jaleel, 296
Amarjit Chandan, 284
Amar Mitra (writer), 141, 144
Amar Nath Kak, 214
Amazon Standard Identification Number, 158
Ambalappuzha, 223
Ambalika, 51
Ambika (Mahabharata), 51
Ameen Faheem, 296
American English, 27
American literature, 118, 150, 163, 324
Amin Kamil, 209
Amir Khusro, 170, 365
Amish Tripathi, 83
Amitav Ghosh, 153, 156
Amit Chaudhuri, 155
Amiya Chakrabarty, 145
Ammaki Adivaram Leda, 339
Amoghavarsha, 179
Amoghavarsha I, 184
Amrita Pritam, 281, 282
Amrutanubhav, 241
Amrutvel, 246
Amuktamalyada, 333
Anandamath, 137
Anandavardhana, 209, 210
Ananda Vikatan, 314
Anand Narain Mulla, 213
Anand Neelakantan, 83
Anand (writer), 229
Ananta Charan Sukla, 273, 276
Ananta Das, 264, 265
Anasheed, 292, 363
Ancient, 260
Ancient Egyptian literature, 90, 117, 162, 177, 323
Ancient Greek literature, 90, 177
Ancient India, 92
Ancient literature, 5, 117, 162, 323
Ancient Tamil music, 301
Andal, 306
Andha Yug, 48, 170
Andhra mahabharatam, 329
Andhra Pradesh, 81, 260, 334, 348, 357
Anga, 42
Angada, 62, 63, 67
Angare, 368
Angiras (sage), 13
Angkor Wat, 42, 77
Anglo-Indian, 151
Angul district, 258

406

Anguttara Nikaya, 97, 106, 107, 113
Anil Karanjai, 146
Anime, 84
Anis Ansari, 296
Anita Desai, 153
Añjanā, 61
Anju Makhija, 157
A. N. Krishna Rao, 200
A.N. Krishna Rao, 202
Annabhau Sathe, 247
Annada Shankar Ray, 271
Annadashankar Roy, 145
Annamacharya, 331
Anthology, 213
Anubhava Mantapa, 191
Anukramaṇī, 9
Anupallavi, 334
Anushasana Parva, 33
Anwar Shemza, 214
Apauruṣeya, 4
Ape, 67
Aphorisms, 325
Approximant consonant, 351
Appu Nedungadi, 228, 232
Arab, 293
Arab carpet, 291, 361
Arabic, 131, 213, 280, 294
Arabic language, 364
Arabic literature, 91, 117, 130, 162, 178, 289, 291, 323, 336, 362
Arabic maqam, 292, 363
Arab states of the Persian Gulf, 344
Aranyaka, 7, 8, 16
Aranyakas, 4, 10
Aranya Parva, 340
Arasikere, 187
Arbaeen, 291, 362
Archaeoastronomy, 34
Archery, 16
Architecture of Azerbaijan, 290, 361
Arebhashe dialect, 344
Argentine literature, 118, 150, 163, 324
Arhat, 98
Arjuna, 28, 29, 37–40, 46, 51, 186, 332
Arjuna Das, 263
Arjunawiwaha, 46
Armenian literature, 90, 91, 177, 178
Arnab Jan Deka, 155, 157
Arnimal, 209
Ar: ألف ليلة وليلة, 230
A. R. Raja Raja Varma, 227
Arshia Sattar, 53, 87
Artha, 15
Arthashastra, 325
Arthur Anthony Macdonell, 19, 25, 94
Arthur Coke Burnell, 358

Arthur Schopenhauer, 18
Arts of Odisha, 257
Arudra, 338
Aruṇa, 63
Arunabh Sarkar, 143
Arunagirinathar, 310
Arundhathi Subramaniam, 157
Arundhati Roy, 153, 155
Arun Kamble, 247
Arun Kolatkar, 157, 246
Arunodoi, 122
Arupa Patangia Kalita, 123
Arvind Adiga, 154
Aryabhata, 34
Asaf-ud-Daula, 213
Asaga, 23
Asamar Padya Buranji, 125
Asamiya, 116, 122
Asamiya literature, 117
Asam Sahitya Sabha, 123
Ascetic, 193
Asghar Sindhi, 296
Ashadh Ka Ek Din, 170
Ashoka, 103
Ashok Banker, 83
Ashram, 70
Ashrama (stage), 15
Ashramavasika Parva, 33
Ashtadhyayi, 32
Ashtadiggajalu, 332, 333
Ashtadiggajas, 326
Ashta Mathas of Udupi, 353
Ashutosh Mukhopadhyay, 144
Ashvamedha, 33
Ashvamedhika Parva, 33
Ashvins, 39
Ashwamedha, 71
Ashwathama, 33
Ashwatthama, 43
Asian Art Museum (San Francisco), 85
Asian literature, 118, 163, 324
Asoka, 98, 303
Asom Ratna, 117
Assam, 122, 155, 235
Assam Buranji, 125
Assamese language, 58, 73, 119, 122, 124, 126
Assamese literature, 115, **115**, 116, 118, 126, 161, 163, 218, 235, 239, 250, 259, 285, 292, 324, 364
Assamese poetry, 116, **126**
Assam Sahitya Sabha, 117
Assam Valley Literary Award, 117
Aṣṭādhyāyī, 329

Āstika and nāstika, 5

407

Astrology, 213
Astronomy, 293
A Suitable Boy, 153
Aśvaghoṣa, 23
As You Like It, 230
Atharvan, 13
Atharvaveda, 4, 7, 10, 13, 14, 16
Atharva Veda, 23
Athirajendra Chola, 308
Atibadi Jagannath Das, 264, 265
Atin Bandyopadhyay, 144

Ātman (Hinduism), 8, 15

Atmiya Sabha, 135
Atthakatha, 99
Attimabbe, 186
Atul Chandra Hazarika, 123
Atulprasad Sen, 141
Australian literature, 118, 150, 163, 324
Autobiographical novel, 138
Auvaiyar, 309
Avadhanam, 327
Avadhānam, 326
Avant garde, 157
Avant-garde, 146
Avanti (India), 42
Avasarala Ramakrishna Rao, 338
Avatar, 25, 83
A Vedic Word Concordance, 374
Avesta, 90, 177
Avignon, 49
Avvaiyar, 307
Awadhi, 58, 73, 81
Awadhi language, 162
Awards and Honors, 94
Ayaz Ali Rind, 296
Ayilyam Thirunal, 225
Ayodhya, 56, 59
Ayurveda, 16, 209, 210, 265
Ayutthaya Kingdom, 78
Azerbaijani literature, 291, 362
Azhakathu Padmanabha Kurup, 227
Azhvars, 299
Aziz, 296
Aziz Kingrani, 296

Baba Hari Dass, 84
Baba Nagarjun, 169
Babasaheb Ambedkar, 246
Babubhai Mistry, 84
Babu Gulabrai, 172
Baburao Bagul, 247
Babylonian literature, 117, 162, 323
Back vowel, 350
Bad date, 110

Baddena Bhupaludu, 330
Badri Narain Sinha, 173
Baghdad, 293
Bahlika people, 43
Bahmani, 309
Bahmani Sultanate, 242
Bahuk, 48
Bahuka, 48
Baidehisha Bilasa, 267
Baishe Srabon, 146
Bait (poetry), 296
Bakhar, 243
Baladev Rath, 268
Balai Chand Mukhopadhyay, 141
Bala Kanda, 58
Balangir district, 258
Balarama, 43, 74
Balaram Das, 264
Balasore district, 258
Bal Gangadhar Tilak, 52, 245
Bali, 45, 46, 77, 78, 82, 85
Balinese dance, 78, 82
Balinese people, 78
Balinese temples, 82
Balivada Kanta Rao, 338
Bal Kavita, 169
Ballad, 296
Bal Phondke, 246
Balshastri Jambhekar, 244
Balwant Gargi, 283
Bammera Potana, 331
Banamali, 268
Banasura, 188
Bangalore, 155, 344, 355
Bangladesh, 131, 138, 236
Bangladeshi English literature, 150
Bangladesh Liberation War, 139, 143
Bangsawan, 292, 363
Bani Basu, 144
Bankim Chandra Chattopadhyay, 137, 151
Bankura district, 132, 133
Bantwal, 349
Baptist, 122
Bard, 30
Bardhaman district, 134
Bargarh district, 258
Barkur, 345
Baroque literature, 91, 178
Barrister Parvateesam, 339
Basava, 181
Basavakalyan, 190
Basavanagudi, 198
Basavanna, 190
Basava purana, 24
Basavarajavijaya, 24
Basharat Peer, 215

Basudeb Dasgupta, 141, 146
Battles of Tarain, 164
Baul, 143
B. B. Lal, 34
BCE, 98
Beary language, 344
Bedil, 294
Belthangady, 349, 356
Benares, 53, 74
Bengal, 135, 193
Bengali language, 58, 73, 119, 121, 129–131
Bengali Language Movement, 144
Bengali literature, 91, 115, 118, 120, 129, **129**, 130, 150, 161, 163, 178, 218, 235, 239, 250, 259, 285, 289, 291, 292, 324, 336, 362, 364
Bengali novels, 129
Bengali people, 81, 131, 269
Bengali poetry, 129
Bengalis, 130
Bengali science fiction, 129, 141
Benjamin Bailey (missionary), 225
Benjamin L. Rice, 196, 206
Benudhar Rout, 272
Berhampur Patta (Phoda Kumbha) Saree & Joda, 258
Bewas, 296
Bhabendra Nath Saikia, 123
Bhadant Anand Kausalyayan, 169
Bhadrabahu, 50
Bhadrak district, 258
Bhadriraju Krishnamurti, 205, 358
Bhagabata, 265
Bhagavad Gita, 17, 27, 33, 43, 52, 75, 92, 241
Bhagavata, 181, 325
Bhagavata Purana, 17, 92, 132, 133, 242, 331, 338
Bhagavat Gita, 145
Bhagavati Charan Das, 268
Bhagavat Purana, 127
Bhagyawati, 166
Bhajan, 354
Bhakta, 61
Bhaktacharan Das, 268
Bhakti, 73, 162, 165, 166, 172, 181, 192
Bhakti movement, 17, 127, 179, 217, 220, 222, 243, 299, 325
Bhaktivedanta Manor, 83
Bhalchandra Nemade, 246, 247
Bhamaha, 210
Bhandarkar Oriental Research Institute, 45, 53
Bhanubhakta Acharya, 76
Bhanuji Rao, 272
Bharata (Mahabharata), 378
Bharatanatyam, 334
Bharata (Ramayana), 56, 59, 61, 65

Bhāratas, 32
Bhāratavarsha, 378
Bharat Ek Khoj, 48
Bharatendu Harishchandra, 172, 174
Bharathidasan, 312, 313
Bhāravi, 23
Bhartendu Harishchandra, 170
Bharud, 242
Bhasa, 48
Bhāsa, 32
Bhashaposhini, 226
Bhasha Smritistambha, 145
Bhashya, 325
Bhaṭṭi, 23
Bhaṭṭikāvya, 23
Bhau Padhye, 246
Bhau Panchbhai, 247
Bhavabhuti, 71
Bhavarth Deepika, 241
Bhavarth Ramayan, 58, 242
Bhayānaka, 327
Bherumal, 295
Bhikhari Thakur, 147
Bhikkhu Bodhi, 106, 107, 113
Bhikkhu Nanamoli, 106
Bhima, 38–40, 48, 51, 186
Bhima Bhoi, 268
Bhimrao Ambedkar, 247
Bhisham Sahni, 170
Bhishma, 33, 36, 43, 51
Bhishma Parva, 33
Bhittai, 294
Bhoja, 185
Bhojpuri cinema, 148
Bhojpuri language, 147, 162
Bhojpuri literature, 115, **147**, 161, 218, 235, 239, 250, 259, 285, 292, 364
Bhrigu, 32
Bhupendra nath Kaushikfikr, 173
Bhupinder kaur Sadhaura, 284
Bhuta Kola, 354
Bibek Debroy, 47
Bībhatsa, 327
Bibhu Padhi, 157
Bibhuprasad Mohapatra, 277
Bibhutibhushan Bandopadhyay, 141
Bibhutibhushan Bandyopadhyay, 145
Bibhutibhushan Mukhopadhyay, 145
Bible, 27, 122
Bidagdha Chintamani, 267
Bidhayak Bhattacharya, 145
Bidrohi, 139
Bihar, 9, 90, 133, 147
Biharilal Chakraborty, 138
Bihari (poet), 166, 172
Bijapur Sultanate, 242

Bijjala II, 191
Bijon Bhattacharya, 140
Bilhana, 211
Billava, 349
Bimal Kar, 141, 144
Bimal Mitra, 141
Binoy Majumdar, 146
Birbhum district, 133
Birinchi Kumar Barua, 123
Birkhäuser, 389
Bishnu Dey, 145
Bishnupur, Bankura, 132
Blackwell Publishing, 86
Blank verse, 135
Blog, 318
B. M. Srikantaiah, 197
Bollywood, 141
Bomkai Sari, 258
Booker Prize, 152
Borbarua, 124
Borgeet, 119
Boru Chandidas, 119, 132
Boubou (clothing), 291, 362
Boudh district, 258
Boyi Bhimanna, 338
Brahma, 4, 17, 63
Brahman, 8, 15
Brahmana, 5, 7, 8, 15, 16, 31
Brahmanas, 4, 10
Brahmanda Purana, 224
Brahma Sutras, 17
Brahmin, 198
Brahmins, 313
Brahmi script, 348
Brahmo Samaj, 336
Brahmotsavam (film), 356
Braj, 136, 166
Brajanath Badajena, 268
Braj Bhasha, 162
Brazilian literature, 118, 150, 163, 324
BR Films, 85
Brihadaranyaka Upanishad, 8
Brihat-katha, 307
Brihat-Samhita, 35
Brij Narayan Chakbast, 213
Brill Publishers, 391
British East India Company, 166, 201
British English, 27
British Raj, 243
British rule, 260
Bronze Age India, 5
Bronze Age literature, 90, 177
Bronzes, 81
Brundabati Dasi, 266
Buchchibabu, 338
Buddhadeb Basu, 145

Buddhadeb Guha, 144
Buddhadeva Bose, 48, 141
Buddhaghosa, 99
Buddhavacana, 98
Buddhism, 5, 6, 92, 96, 98, 210, 304
Buddhist, 131, 164, 262, 299, 309
Buddhist Councils, 105
Buddhist Hybrid Sanskrit, 109
Buddhist Publication Society, 113
Bulleh Shah, 280
Bundeli, 162
Bunt (community), 349
Buranji, 116, 121, **124**
Burma, 78, 99
Burmese alphabet, 104
Burqa, 291, 362
Burra katha, 326
Bylina, 91, 178
Byzantine literature, 90, 91, 130, 177, 178

Calcutta, 166
Caliphs, 293
Cambodia, 56, 68, 71
Cambridge University, 213
Camille Bulcke, 171
Canadian literature, 118, 150, 163, 324
Canto, 23
Carnatic music, 193, 312, 331, 337, 354
Carvaka, 5
Caryagiti, 262
Caste, 246
Category:Assam, 116
Category:Assam dramatists and playwrights, 116
Category:Assamese-language poets, 116
Category:Assamese-language writers, 116
Category:Assamese literature, 116
Category:Bengali literary awards, 129
Category:Bengali literary institutions, 129
Category:Bengali literature, 129
Category:Bengali novelists, 129
Category:Bengali poets, 129
Category:Bengali writers, 129
Category:Books from Assam, 116
Category:Buddhism, 96
Category:European literature, 150
Category:Hinduism, 26, 55
Category:Hindu texts, 3, 10, 22, 92
Category:Islam, 290, 361
Category:Literature by country, 119, 151, 164, 325
Category:Odisha, 257
Category:Padal Petra Stalam, 305
Category:Political parties in Odisha, 257
Category:Punjabi culture, 279
Category:Ramayana, 89

Category:Theravada, 96
Causative, 352
Cento, 326
Central Asia, 92
Central India, 185
Central Java, 62, 77
Chaali Polilu, 355
Chaand Raat, 291, 362
Chador, 291, 362
Chaganti Somayajulu, 338
Chaitanya Mahaprabhu, 131, 132, 142, 193, 264
Chakhi Khuntia, 276
Chakkiyar Koothu, 223
Chakra, 262
Chakravartin, 74
Chalukya, 179
Chalukyas, 309
Chamarasa, 189
Champu, 182, 326, 329
Chand Bardai, 164, 170
Chandi, 135
Chandidas, 132
Chandilyan, 317
Chandi Purana, 263
Chandogya Upanishad, 8, 17
Chandragiri river, 347
Chandrakala, 84
Chandrakanta (author), 214
Chandrakanta (novel), 166, 172
Chandrasekhar Rath, 274
Chandrashekhara Kambar, 202
Changrung Phukanar Buranji, 125
Channabasavanna, 191
Channabasavapurana, 24
Chapter 10, 25
Charaka, 210
Charaka Samhita, 209
Charans, 286
Charition mime, 346
Charles Philip Brown, 330
Charu Nivedita, 313
Charyapada, 119, 131, 262
Chatur Binoda, 268
Chaudhry Afzal Haq, 367
Chedi Kingdom, 42
Cheliyalikatta, 340
Chemmeen (novel), 228
Chennai, 344
Chennakesava Temple, 40
Chera dynasty, 303, 307
Cherusseri, 221
Cherusseri Namboothiri, 217, 221
Chess, 213
Chetan Mariwala, 295
Chha Maana Atha Guntha, 269
Chhapra, 148
Chhattisgarh, 260
Chhattisgarhi, 162
Chhayavaad, 168, 172
Chidambaram, 312
Chikka Devaraja, 194
Chikka Virarajendra, 201
Chilakamarti Lakshmi Narasimham, 338
Chinese Buddhist Canon, 108, 109
Chinese language, 121
Chinese literature, 90, 118, 150, 163, 177, 289, 324, 336
Chinu Modi, 48
Chiragh Ali, 214
Chitharon Kumpaba, 236
Chitra Banerjee Divakaruni, 48
Chitradurga, 200
Chitrakoot, Madhya Pradesh, 81
Chitrāngada, 36, 51
Chittagong, 140
Chola, 24, 299, 330
Cholas, 303, 307
Cholera, 269
Christianity, 251
Christian Lassen, 379
Christian Lee Novetzke, 248
Christmas song, 253
Chronological, 213
Chronological items, 47
Chutiya Buranji, 125
Chutiya kingdom, 124
Cilappatikaram, 24, 307, 309, 310, 313
Cinema of India, 48
Cinema of Odisha, 257
Cinema of West Bengal, 141
Circa, 179
Cirupāṇārruppaṭai, 301
Cirupañcamūlam, 301
CITEREFAllon1997, 383
CITEREFAnnette WilkeOliver Moebus2011, 377
CITEREFBechert1984, 383
CITEREFBrown2006, 382
CITEREFBuswell2004, 383
CITEREFChristian Lee Novetzke2016, 391, 392
CITEREFCone2001, 383
CITEREFCousins1982, 383
CITEREFCousins1984, 383
CITEREFDavidson2003, 382
CITEREFDe Jong1993, 382
CITEREFEncyclopædia Britannica2008, 382
CITEREFGethin1992, 383
CITEREFGethin1998, 382, 383
CITEREFGombrich2006, 382
CITEREFGombrich (b), 382, 383

CITEREFGoswami2007, 385
CITEREFGoswamiTamuli2007, 385
CITEREFGriffiths1981, 383
CITEREFGrönbold1984, 383
CITEREFHamm1973, 383
CITEREFHarold G. Coward1990, 377
CITEREFHartmann2011, 385
CITEREFHarvey1990, 382, 383
CITEREFHarvey1990appendix, 383
CITEREFHarvey1995, 382
CITEREFJaini1998, 381
CITEREFMaguire2001, 382
CITEREFMahadevan1956, 377
CITEREFManné1990, 382, 383
CITEREFMcDaniel2006, 382
CITEREFMendelson1975, 382
CITEREFMorgan1956, 382
CITEREFNakamura1999, 382, 383
CITEREFÑāṇamoli1982, 383
CITEREFNorman1983, 383
CITEREFNorman1996, 383
CITEREFNorman2005, 382
CITEREFPatrick Olivelle1999, 377
CITEREFPrajapati2005, 93
CITEREFSaikia2004, 385
CITEREFSamuel2012, 383
CITEREFSchopen1997, 383
CITEREFSkilling1997, 383
CITEREFVijay K. Jain2011, 381
CITEREFvon Hinüber2000, 383
CITEREFWarder1963, 383
CITEREFWarder1999, 382
CITEREFWynne2003, 382, 383
CITEREFWynne2004, 383
CITEREFWynne2007, 382
Civaka Cintamani, 24
Classical language, 90, 177, 260
Classical Sanskrit, 23, 109
Classical Sanskrit literature, 32
Classical tradition, 217
Clay Sanskrit Library, 47, 86, 95
Climate, 104
Close vowel, 350
Clusivity, 352
C. Narayanareddy, 338
C. N. Sreekantan Nair, 85
Colombian literature, 118, 150, 163, 324
Colonization, 151
Comitative case, 351
Commons:Category:Bengali literature, 146
Commons:Category:Kannada language literature, 204
Commons:Category:Mahabharata, 54
Commons:Category:Marathi language literature, 248
Commons:Category:Pali Canon, 113

Commons:Category:Tamil literature, 319
Commons:Category:Tulu language, 359
Commons:Category:Vedas, 21
Commons:Ramayana, 89
Commonwealth Writers Prize, 156
Comparative religion, 212
Consonant, 351
Coorg, 201
Counterculture, 157
Couplet, 305, 326
C. P. Brown, 330
C. Rajagopalachari, 48, 315
Creationism, 254
Cremation, 13
Crime fiction, 317
Critical edition, 80
Cuban literature, 118, 150, 163, 324
Cuisine of Odisha, 257
Cultural heritage, 295
Culture, 295
Culture of Andhra Pradesh, 321
Culture of Assam, 116
Culture of Odisha, 257
Culture of Telangana, 322
Cuttack district, 258
C. V. Raman Pillai, 228, 232

Da, 386
Daana Veera Soora Karna, 48
Daasarathi Krishnamacharyulu, 338
Dabestan-e Mazaheb, 212
Dadasaheb Phalke, 247
Dai people, 105
Daitya, 63
Dakkhini, 164
Dakshina Kannada, 343, 344, 347
Dalhana, 210
Dalit, 203, 247
Dalit literature, 203
Dalit (outcaste), 246
Dalit Panther, 247
Dalpat Sufi, 294
Damayanti, 27
Dāna, 11
Danava (Hinduism), 40
Dance in Thailand, 80
Dandaka Forest, 77
Dandi Ramayana, 73
Darbhanga district, 133
Darchhawna, 173
Dasaka, 327
Dasam Granth, 75
Dasbodh, 243
Dasharatha, 56, 58, 59
Dashavatara, 59, 75
Dastgah, 292, 363

Dative case, 352
David Crystal, 204, 386
David Davidar, 155
Daya Pawar, 247
Dayaram Gidumal, 295
Daya Shankar Kaul Nasim, 212, 213
Day of Ashura, 291, 362
D. C. Sircar, 207, 386
Debiprasad Chattopadhyaya, 389
Debut novel, 153
Deccan Plateau, 164, 185, 309
De:Claus Vogel, 390
Deconstruction, 118, 149, 163, 324
Deenbandhu, 245
Dehli, 213
Delhi, 94, 164, 203, 213
Delhi Sultanate, 164, 309
Dental consonant, 351
Deodhai Asam Buranji, 125
Deogarh district, 258
Deomali (mountain), 257
Deontological ethics, 373
Department store, 84
DePaul University, 46
Deputy Nazeer Ahmed, 368
Detective fiction, 317
Devadasi, 335
Devadiga, 349
Devaki Nandan Khatri, 166, 171, 172
Devanagari, 7, 14, 240
Devanagari script, 162, 166
Devanur Mahadeva, 203
Devarakonda Balagangadhara Tilak, 338
Deva Raya II, 189
Devdas Chhotray, 272
Devdutt Pattanaik, 83, 85
Devi Chaudhurani, 137
Devil on the Cross, 313
Devi Mahatmya, 90
Devi Mahatmyam, 353
Devi Prasad Bagrodia, 123
Devudu Narasimha Shastri, 200
Devulapalli Krishnasastri, 339
Dhaka, 135
Dhalapathar Parda & Fabrics, 258
Dhammakaya Foundation, 105
Dhammapada, 100, 108
Dhammasangani, 97, 108
Dhananjaya Bhanja, 267
Dhan Gopal Mukerji, 151
Dhani Ram Chatrik, 281
Dhanusa district, 61
Dharamvir Bharati, 48, 170, 174
Dharma, 39, 83
Dharmaguptaka, 108
Dharma Raja, 223

Dharmasthala Temple, 345
Dharmasutras, 92
Dharmathakur, 135
Dharmavir Bharati, 173
Dharmawangsa, 45
Dharma-yuddha, 44
Dhatukatha, 97, 108
Dhenkanal district, 258
Dhritarashtra, 37, 51
Dhurjati, 190, 333, 338
Dialect, 357
Dictionary, 357
Didactic, 193
Digambara, 93
Digha Nikaya, 97, 107
Dilip Chitre, 157, 246
Dinabandhu Mitra, 135
Dinakrushna Das, 267
Dinanath Nadim, 209
Dina Thanthi, 316
Dio Chrysostom, 32
Dipak Mishra, 272
Discovery and dating, 386
Disposition, 217
Districts of Odisha, 258
Divisions of Odisha, 258
Divya Prabandha, 17
Divya Prabandham, 5
Diwan Singh, 281
Dm, 386
Dnyaneshwar, 241
Doha (Indian literature), 165
Doha (poetry), 294
Dohira, 296
Dom Moraes, 157
Don Webb (writer), 146, 157
Doordarshan, 48, 85
Double entendre, 328
Dramatist, 85
Draupadi, 32, 33, 38, 46, 48, 51
Draupadī, 39
Dravidian language, 178, 344
Dravidian languages, 217, 343, 345, 350, 352
Dravidian peoples, 237
Dravidian University, 357
D. R. Bendre, 198
Dr. Gurbuxani, 295
Dridhbala, 209
Dr. Moti Prakash, 296
Dr. Nikhilanand Panigrahy, 277
Drona, 33, 43, 199
Drona Parva, 33
Dr.Ramesh Chandra Parida, 277
Drupada, 37
Dukhayal, 296
Durgeshnandini, 137

Duryodhana, 35, 39, 48, 51, 186
Dushasana, 39
Duvvoori Ramireddy, 338
Dvaita, 17
Dvārakā, 42
D. V. Gundappa, 198, 199, 202
Dvipada, 326
Dwijendralal Ray, 138, 141
Dwijendra Narayan Jha, 390

Early Buddhist schools, 98, 102, 109
Early Buddhist Texts, 98
Early Medieval literature, 90, 118, 130, 163, 177, 324
Early Modern literature, 91, 178
East Asia, 92
East Godavari District, 337
East Pakistan, 131
Ebrahim Alkazi, 48
Economics, 295
Economy of Andhra Pradesh, 321
Economy of Odisha, 257
Edicts of Ashoka, 103
Edmund Spenser, 220
Education in Odisha, 257
Edward William Lane, 230
Egyptian literature, 117, 162, 323
Eid al-Adha, 291, 362
Eid al-Fitr, 291, 362
Eid al-Ghadeer, 291, 362
Ekalavya, 199
Ekaveera, 340
Ek Mamnua Muhabbat Ki Kahani, 368
Eknath, 58, 242
Eknathi Bhagwat, 242
Elāti, 301
Elections in Odisha, 257
Elegy, 252
Elizabeth II of the United Kingdom, 196
Elphinstone College, 244
Elsa Kazi, 295
Emancipation, 185
Encyclopædia Britannica, 386
Encyclopædia Britannica Eleventh Edition, 176, 372
Encyclopaedia of the History of Science, Technology, and Medicine in Non-Western Cultures, 390
En:Digital object identifier, 20, 126, 205, 206
English, 3, 27, 56
English language, 5, 151, 313, 357
English-speaking world, 344
En:International Standard Serial Number, 87
En:JSTOR, 206
En:Library of Congress Control Number, 204
En:OCLC, 19, 204, 205

Epic of Siri, 345, 354
Epic poem, 217, 354
Epic poetry, 22, 25, 56, 117, 135, 162, 199, 323
Epigraph (literature), 183
Epistemology, 373
Eregla Panodchi, 356
Er. Mayadhor Swain, 277
Ethics, 304
Ettuthogai, 300
Ettuthokai, 301, 303, 304
Etymology, 303
Eunice De Souza, 157
Europe, 296
European literature, 117, 162, 323
Evelyn Abbott, 379
Existentialism, 275
Ezhava, 217
Ezhuthachan, 217
Ezra Pound, 215

Fable, 294
Faizi, 46
Fakir Mohan Senapati, 269, 273
Falguni Roy, 146
Farid Ganj Shakar, 293
Fariduddin Ganjshakar, 280
Farrukh Ahmed, 143
Fateh Faqir, 294
Fazil Shah, 295
Ferdinand Kittel, 196, 197
Festivals of Odisha, 257
Fifth Veda, 17, 27
File:aathreya.ogg, 337
File:Pronunciation of Mangalampalli Balamuralikrishna.ogg, 337
Finger millet, 193
Finnish people, 354
First Anglo-Sikh War, 280
First Buddhist Council, 98, 100
First Opium War, 154
Flap consonant, 351
Flora and fauna of Odisha, 257
Floruit, 99
Foot (prosody), 7
Fort William College, 135, 166
Foundation for the Preservation of the Mahayana Tradition, 113
Fourth Buddhist Council, 98, 103
Franz Kafka, 313
Fraternal polyandry, 39
Free verse, 190
Fricative consonant, 351
Frithjof Schuon, 214
Frits Staal, 19, 376
Front vowel, 350

Future perfect, 344, 353
F.W. Savidge, 251

Gabriel García Márquez, 152
Gada Yuddha, 23
Gajanan Madhav Muktibodh, 168
Gajapati district, 258
Gajapati Kingdom, 263, 266
Ganadhara, 75
Ganapathi, 189
Gandhara, 43
Gandhari (character), 33, 38, 39, 43, 46
Gandharva, 332
Gandharvaveda, 16
Gandhi, 199
Ganesha, 28, 29
Ganga Das, 172
Gangadhar Meher, 269
Ganga (goddess), 36, 51
Ganges, 260
Gangetic basin, 58
Ganjam district, 258
Ganjam Kewda Flower, 258
Ganjam Kewda Rooh, 258
G. Aravindan, 84
Garikapati Narasimha Rao, 339
Garlapati Tenali Ramakrishna, 334
Garuda, 63
Gaudiya Vaishnava, 134
Gaudiya Vaishnavism, 17, 132
Gauhati University, 124
Gautama Buddha, 5, 74, 78, 98, 101, 199
Gautam Ghose, 146
Gavin Flood, 18, 374
Gayatri mantra, 108
Geethams, 193
Geet (song), 296
Genitive case, 352
Genres, 285
Geographical indication, 258
Geography of Odisha, 257
Geomancy, 213
Geo-politics, 188
Georgian literature, 90, 91, 177, 178
Germany, 225
Ghadar di Gunj, 282
Ghalib, 213
Ghananand Das, 166
Ghatikachala, 334
Ghatotkacha, 48
Ghazal, 280, 292, 363, 366
Ghazals, 139
Ghulam Abbas (writer), 368
Ghulam Ahmad Mahjur, 209
Ghulam Murshid, 143
Ghulam Mustafa Tabassum, 213

Ghulam Nabi Firaq, 209
Ghulam Rabbani Agro, 296
Gieve Patel, 157
Gingee Nayaks, 310
Girish Chandra Ghosh, 138
Girish Karnad, 48, 202
Gita Govinda, 264
Gitanjali, 138
Glossary of Hinduism terms, 26, 56
Glottolog, 343, 394
G. M. Syed, 295
Gobind Malhi, 296
God, 44
Godavari, 66, 260
Gokarna, India, 347
Gokulananda Mohapatra, 277
Gona Budda Reddy, 58, 73, 339
Gopabandhu Das, 269
Gopalakrishna Adiga, 201
Gopalakrishna Bharathi, 312
Gopal Chandra Praharaj, 271
Gopal Ganesh Agarkar, 245
Gopal Krushna Pattanaik, 268
Gopalpur Tussar Fabrics, 258
Gopi Kottoor, 157
Gopi Krishna (yogi), 215
Gopinath Mohanty, 273
Gopinath Raina, 215
Gorakhnath, 165
Gorakshanath, 280
Gotra, 337
Gourishankar Ray, 268
Government of India, 338
Government of Odisha, 257
Governor of Punjab, Pakistan, 213
Govindadasa, 134
Govinda Pai, 199
G.P. Rajarathnam, 202
Graham Greene (writer), 152
Grammar, 301, 303
Grammatical case, 351, 352
Grammatical conjugation, 352
Grammatical gender, 351
Grammatical number, 351, 352
Grammatical particle, 351
Grammatical person, 352
Grammatical polarity, 353
Grammatical tense, 352
Gramya, 327
Grand Mufti, 213
Grantha alphabet, 348
Grantha script, 14
Greek language, 5, 294, 346
Greek literature, 118, 163, 324
Gregory Schopen, 102
GRETIL, 88

Grhya Sutras, 30, 32
Gryhasutras, 8
G. S. Gai, 204, 386
G. S. Shivarudrappa, 202
Guardian Prize, 153
Gudipati Venkatachalam, 338
Gujarat, 73
Gujarati language, 286, 293
Gujarati literature, 115, 118, 150, 161, 163, 218, 235, 239, 250, 259, 285, 292, 324, 364
Guntur District, 334
Gupta Empire, 27, 30, 32
Gurajada Apparao, 339
Gurbani, 280
Gurmukhī, 279
Gurram Jashuva, 339
Guru Bhagat Peer Budhu Shah, 284
Guru Bhakt Singh Bhakt, 172
Guru Gobind Singh, 75, 172, 280
Guru Granth Sahib, 75, 241
Guru Nanak, 165, 280
Guru Nanak Dev University, 283
Guruprasad Mohanty, 272
Gutenberg:24869, 88
Guwahati, 121

Haala, 294
Habaspuri Saree & Fabrics, 258
Habba Khatun, 209
Habib Tanvir, 170
Hadith studies, 212
Hafiz Hamid, 295
Hajime Nakamura, 102
Hakeem Manzoor, 214
Hakim Fateh Mohammad Sewhani, 295
Halanta, 329
Halikulu Kushalama, 339
Halmidi inscription, 180
Hamid Naseem Rafiabadi, 215
Hammal Faqir, 294
Hamzanama, 365
Hana Catherine Mullens, 228, 231, 232
Hanuman, 56, 60, 61, 67, 77, 84, 189
Haraprasad Shastri, 131
Haravali, 267
Haribandhu, 268
Haridasa, 179, 181
Haridasas and Carnatic music, 181
Harihara (poet), 186
Harikatha, 193
Hari Kunzru, 215
Harindranath Chattopadhyay, 156
Harishankar Parsai, 169, 173
Harishchandra, 187
Harivamsa, 34, 49

Harivamsapurana, 49
Harivara Vipra, 120
Harvard Oriental Series, 373
Haryana Punjabi Sahitya Academy, 284
Hasan Azizul Huq, 141, 143
Hasan Hafizur Rahman, 144
Hasan Mansoor, 296
Hashoo Kewal Ramani, 295
Hassam-ud-Din Rashidi, 212, 295
Hastinapura, 35, 36
Hāsya, 169, 327
Hatha yoga, 164
Hatigumpha inscription, 261
Haveri district, 193
Havigannada, 344
Havyaka Brahmin, 348
Hazariprasad Dwivedi, 172
Hazrat Khawaja Muhammad Zaman Luari Sharif, 294
Hebrew literature, 90, 117, 130, 162, 177, 323
Heer Ranjha, 280
Heian literature, 90, 177
Helaine Selin, 390
Helal Hafiz, 144
Help:IPA, 344
Hemacandra, 74
Hemant Divate, 246
Hema Saraswati, 120
Hem Barua, 123
Henry Corbin, 214
Henry Louis Vivian Derozio, 156
Heresy, 203
Herman Gundert, 225, 226
Hermann Gundert, 219
Hermann Mögling, 196
Hermann Oldenberg, 29, 53
Hermitage (religious retreat), 71
Hero, 22
Hero stone, 183, 187
High medieval literature, 91, 178
Hijab, 291, 362
Hikayat Seri Rama, 78
Himalaya, 44
Himalayas, 332
Himansu Sekhar Fatesingh, 277
Hindi, 25, 58, 84, 166, 170, 241, 293, 365, 378
Hindi language, 161
Hindi languages, 161
Hindi literature, 115, 118, 150, 161, **161**, 163, 218, 235, 239, 250, 259, 285, 292, 324, 364
Hindi theatre, 170
Hindōstānī Literature, 176, 372
Hindu, 17, 26, 55, 56, 58, 135, 209, 217, 293, 299, 354
Hindu denominations, 4, 17

Hinduism, 3, 8, 26, 55, 92, 108
Hindu philosophy, 4, 13, 16, 27, 52, 92
Hindu scripture, 22
Hindu scriptures, 10, 92
Hindustani language, 162, 363
Hindustani music, 365
Hindu texts, 3, 22
Hinüber, Oskar von, 113
Hi:रस (काव्य शास्त्र), 169
Historic sites in Odisha, 257
History, 293
History of Andhra Pradesh, 321
History of Assamese literature, 116
History of Bengali literature, 129
History of Hinduism, 26, 55
History of ideas, 119, 151, 164, 325
History of India, 27, 81
History of literature, 90, 117, 162, 177, 323
History of modern literature, 91, 118, 149, 163, 178, 324
History of Odisha, 257
History of science fiction, 119, 150, 164, 325
History of Tamil Nadu, 299
History of theater, 151
History of theatre, 119, 164, 325
History of the Hindi language, 365
Hitopadesha, 166
Hmar language, 250
Holeya, 351
Homa (ritual), 5
Homen Borgohain, 123
Homer, 27, 32, 220, 354
Horace Hayman Wilson, 5
Howard Spodek, 378
Hoysala, 179
Hoysala Empire, 40, 186
Hoysalas, 185, 309
Hrishikesh Sulabh, 173
Hukam, 75
Humayun Ahmed, 141, 144
Hum Sub Umeed Se Hain, 214
Huna (people), 31
Hungry generation, 146
Hyderabad State, 164
Hyder Ali, 201
Hyder Bux Jatoi, 296
Hymn, 11
Hymn 117, 375
Hymn 164, 375
Hyperbole, 221
Hypertext fiction, 118, 149, 163, 324

Ibn Arabi, 214
Ida (goddess), 25
Idea, 5
Idyll, 253

I. Gusti Putu Phalgunadi, 46
Ikshvaku dynasty, 58
I. K. Taimni, 214
Ilango Adigal, 302
Iliad, 27, 32, 354
Imagine TV, 85
Imamat Day, 291, 362
Imdad Hussani, 296
Improvisation, 326
India, 25, 56, 58, 84, 133, 138, 151, 178, 210, 260, 303, 343, 346, 363
Indian classical dance, 16
Indian classical music, 365
Indian culture, 22, 170
Indian English, 152
Indian English literature, 115, **149**, 150, 161, 218, 235, 239, 250, 259, 285, 292, 364
Indian epic poetry, **22**, 27
Indian freedom movement, 281
Indian independence movement, 52
Indian literature, 91, 115, 118, 150, 161, 163, 178, 218, 235, 239, 250, 259, 285, 289, 292, 324, 336, 364
Indian martial arts, 16
Indian rebellion of 1857, 135, 153
Indian religions, 92
Indian state, 147
Indian subcontinent, 3, 11, 22, 81
Indian writing in English, 118, 163, 324
Indira Bai, 196
Indo-Aryan languages, 11, 161, 240
Indo-Aryan Migration, 304
Indo-Aryan superstrate in Mitanni, 6
Indo-European studies, 18
Indogermanisches etymologisches Wörterbuch, 373
Indo-Greek, 210
Indo-Islamic architecture, 290, 361
Indologist, 46
Indology, 29
Indonesia, 45, 56, 62, 71, 72, 78, 82, 84
Indonesian literature, 292, 362
Indonesian philosophy, 26
Indra, 39, 63
Indrajit, 63, 69
Indraprastha, 32, 40
Indra Soundar Rajan, 317
Indulekha (novel), 228, 232
In India, 198
Iniyavai Narpathu, 305
Iṉiyavai Nāṟpatu, 301
Inkulab, 314
Inna Narpathu, 305
Iṉṉā Nāṟpatu, 301
Inner peace, 328
Intellectual history, 119, 151, 164, 325

International Society for Krishna Consciousness, 374
International Standard Book Number, 18–20, 53, 86–88, 94, 105, 110–113, 126, 127, 158, 175, 204–207, 248, 255, 277, 278, 318, 357, 358, 371, 372
Internet, 318
Internet Sacred Text Archive, 379
Intezar Hussain, 367
Introduction, 1
Iqbal Academy Pakistan, 212
Iranian architecture, 290, 361
Irayimman Thampi, 223
Iron Age India, 5, 6, 34
Ishaque Ansari, 296
Ishwar Chandra Gupta, 137
Ishwar Chandra Vidyasagar, 135
Islam, 293, 364
Islam and clothing, 291, 362
Islamic architecture, 290, 361
Islamic art, 291, 361
Islamic calligraphy, 291, 361
Islamic culture, 290, 361
Islamic literature, 291, 362
Islamic music, 292, 363
Islamic mythology, 78
Islamic New Year, 291, 362
Islamic philosophy, 215
Islamic theatre, 292, 363
Ismaili, 293
Ismat Chughtai, 368
ISO 15919, 394
ISO 639-3, 343
ISO639-3:tcy, 343
Isra and Miraj, 291, 362
Israeli literature, 117, 162, 323
Itihasa, 56
Itihāsa, 22
Iyengars, 5

Jabalpur, 183
J. A. B. van Buitenen, 46
Jadumani Mohapatra, 268
Jagadananda Roy, 141
Jagadhekamalla II, 186
Jagadish Chandra Bose, 141
Jagadish Gupta, 141, 145
Jagadish Mohanty, 275
Jagamohana Ramayana, 73
Jagannath, 265, 266
Jagannatha Dasa, 193
Jagatsinghpur district, 258
Jagdish Chandra Mathur, 170
Jahnavi Barua, 155
Jai Hanuman, 85
Jaimini, 379

Jain, 74, 188, 328, 329, 354
Jain agama, 74
Jain cosmology, 49, 50, 74
Jainendra Kumar, 172
Jainism, 5, 23, 26, 49, 92, 164, 179, 181, 329
Jain monasticism, 24, 74
Jain monk, 50
Jain Purana, 74
Jain texts, 49, 74
Jaipur, 59
Jairamdas Daulatram, 295
Jaishankar Prasad, 25, 168, 170, 172
Jajpur district, 258
Jakarta, 84
Jalalela Mohar, 246
Jalaluddin Rumi, 213
Jamaican literature, 118, 150, 163, 324
Jamal Abro, 296
Jambavan, 62
James Herbert Lorrain, 251
James Thomas Molesworth, 244
Janaka, 58, 64
Janamejaya II, 29, 31, 32
Janamsakhis, 280
Jana Natya Manch, 170
Jānāśrayī Chandoviciti, 328
Jandhyala Papayya Sastry, 339
Jane Austen, 153
Jan Gonda, 14, 375, 376
Janna, 186
JAOS, 53
Japanese literature, 118, 150, 163, 289, 324, 336
Jasimuddin, 142
Jasobanta Das, 264
Jaswant Singh Rahi, 282
Jataka tales, 78
Jatayu, 63, 66, 67, 84
Jatindramohan Bagchi, 141
Java, 45, 72, 77, 82
Javanese dance, 77, 78, 82
Javanese literature, 292, 362
Javanese people, 78
Jawaharlal Nehru, 215
Jayachamaraja Wodeyar Bahadur, 196
Jayakanthan, 313, 317
Jayanta Bhatta, 210
Jayanta Mahapatra, 157
Jayant Narlikar, 246
Jayasimha II (Western Chalukya dynasty), 186
Jayatirtha, 193
Jaydev, 264
Jazz-rock, 84
Jeet Thayil, 157
Jellabiya, 291, 362
Jem (Alevism), 292, 363

Jerry Pinto, 157
Jesus Christ, 311
Jeyamohan, 313
Jharkhand, 260
Jharsuguda district, 258
Jhetmal Parsram, 295
Jhumpa Lahiri, 151, 156
Jibanananda Das, 141, 145
Jilbāb, 291, 362
Jiva, 334
Jivaka-chintamani, 309
Jnanappana, 222
Jnanpith, 180, 199, 203
Jnanpith Award, 94, 246, 247, 338–340
Jogi, 349
Joginder Paul, 368
Johann Ernst Hanxleden, 225
John Borthwick Gilchrist, 166
John Bunyan, 229
John D. Smith, 48
John Keay, 34, 53
John M. Bennett, 146, 157
John Milton, 136
John Muir (indologist), 19
Jonaki (magazine), 122
Jothi Ramalinga Swamigal, 312
Journal of the American Academy of Religion, 20
JP Das, 274
Juan R. Francisco, 79
Julien Vinson, 358
Just war theory, 44
J.W. de Jong, 102
Jyotiba Phule, 243, 245, 247
Jyoti Prasad Agarwala, 123
Jyotisha, 16

Kabandha, 67
Kabibar Radhanath Ray, 269
Kabir, 165, 166, 172
Kachari kingdom, 124
Kadamba dynasty, 200
Kafi, 280, 296
Kaikesi, 63
Kaikeyi, 56, 59
Kailas Nath Kaul, 215
Kainnilai, 301
Kakatiya, 187, 330
Kakawin Bhāratayuddha, 45
Kakawin Ramayana, 77, 78
Kakkanadan, 229
Kalabhras, 304
Kalachakra (Jainism), 74
Kalachuris of Kalyani, 185, 190
Kalahandi district, 258
Kalapurusha, 272

Kaḷavaḻi Nārpatu, 301, 305
Kalhana, 35, 211
Kalhora Dynasty, 294
Kali, 73, 139, 142
Kalidasa, 185, 187, 210, 211, 220, 226, 333
Kālidāsa, 23, 32, 230
Kalindi Charan Panigrahi, 271
Kalinga (historical kingdom), 260
Kalinga (historical region), 309
Kalingattuparani, 309
Kalippa, 304
Kaliprasanna Singha, 138
Kalittokai, 300
Kali Yuga, 36
Kalki Krishnamurthy, 314, 317
Kaloji, 339
Kalpanakumari Devi, 274
Kalpa (Vedanga), 16
Kalpavrukshamu, 340
Kalyug (1980 film), 48
Kamala Das, 157
Kamalakanta Jena, 277
Kamala Markandaya, 152
Kamal Kumari National Award, 117
Kamal Kumar Majumdar, 141, 144
Kamarupa, 119
Kamarupa inscriptions, 119
Kamarupi Prakrit, 119
Kamata kingdom, 120
Kamayani, 25
Kambaramayanam, 24, 73, 81, 299, 308
Kambar (poet), 24, 58, 73, 81, 120, 308, 309
Kambojas, 43
Kamil Zvelebil, 207, 386
Kamleshwar, 173
Kanaiyalal Maneklal Munshi, 48
Kanaka Dasa, 193
Kanchana Sita, 84
Kanchana Sita (play), 85
Kanchan Baruah, 123
Kancherla Gopanna, 335
Kandathil Varghese Mappillai, 226
Kandhamal district, 258
Kandukuri Veeresalingam, 336, 339
Kanety Krishna Menon, 339
Kangla, 236
Kangla Uttra, 236
Kangyur, 108
Kanhadade Prabandha, 286
Kankanti Paparaju, 334
Kannada, 73, 81, 184, 353, 357
Kannada alphabet, 343
Kannada grammar, 187
Kannada language, 23, 178, 344, 379, 394

419

Kannada literature, 24, 90, 115, 118, 130, 150,
    161, 163, 177, **177**, 218, 235, 239, 250,
    259, 285, 292, 324, 364
Kannada poetry, 24
Kannada script, 178, 345, 348–350, 394
Kannauj, 164
Kannauji, 162
Kanvas, 6
Kapalkundala, 137
Kapilendradeva, 263
Kappe Arabhatta, 182, 183
Karachi, 296
Karad, 185
Karagöz and Hacivat, 292, 363
Karaikudi, 300
Karbala, 142
Karine Chemla, 18
Karkala, 349
Karma, 184
Karma in Jainism, 50
Karna, 33, 48, 51, 186
Karna Parva, 33
Kār Nāṟpatu, 301
Karnataka, 49, 178, 343, 344, 347, 356
Karnataka Tulu Sahitya Academy, 343
Kartar Singh Duggal, 283
Karuṇā, 327
Karvalo, 203
Kasaragod, 344, 349
Kasaragod district, 343, 347, 349, 356
Kasaragod taluk, 344
Kasaragod Town, 347
Kashmiri language, 209
Kashmiri literature, 115, 118, 150, 161, 163,
    218, 235, 239, 250, 259, 285, 292, 324,
    362, 364
Kashmiri Pandits, 212
Kashmir Shaivism, 209
Kashmir Valley, 213
Kāśī, 36
Kasim (Sindhi poet), 295
Kasula Purushottama Kavi, 339
Kateel, 354
Kate Milner Rabb, 87
Kathakali, 223, 224
Kathasaritsagara, 211
Katha Upanishad, 8
Kathavatthu, 97, 108
Kattaikkuttu, 45
Katyayana, 16
Kaurava, 27, 33, 35, 39, 42, 51
Kauromal Khilnani, 295
Kausalya, 59
Kavijanasrayam, 328, 329
Kavirajamarga, 179, 184
Kavi sammelan, 169

Kavisurya Baladev Rath, 268
Kavita, 169
Kavitrayam, 339
Kavi Trayam, 329
Kavya, 325, 327
Kāvya, 326
Kawi language, 46
Kaykobad, 138
K. Ayyappa Paniker, 222
Kayyar Kinhanna Rai, 354
Kazi Nazrul Islam, 139, 141
K. C. Kesava Pillai, 227
Kecak, 78, 82, 85
Keffiyeh, 291, 362
Kekaya, 42
Keladi Nayaka, 194
Kena Upanishad, 8
Kendrapada district, 259
Keonjhar district, 259
Kerala, 73, 155, 217, 228, 299, 343, 344, 356
Kerala Tulu Academy, 343
Kerala Varma Valiya Koyithampuran, 226, 227
Keralolpathi, 224, 347
Kersy Katrak, 157
Kesari Kumar, 168
Kesari (newspaper), 245
Keshab Chandra Sen, 336
Keshavdas, 172
Keshavsuta, 244
Keshiraja, 186
Ketana, 329
Kethu Viswanathareddy, 339
Kevala Jnana, 75
Khadiboli, 172
Khair Shah, 294
Khaki, 295
Khalifo Gul, 295
Khalifo Nabi Bux, 294
Khalifo Nabi Bux Laghari, 294
Khandagiri, 260
Khandhaka, 97, 107
Khandua, 258
Khara (Ramayana), 66
Kharavel, 261
Kharavela, 261
Khariboli, 162
Khmer classical dance, 77
Khmer language, 76
Khoja, 293
Khondakar Ashraf Hossain, 144
Khordha District, 259
Khuda Ke Saaye Mein Ankh Micholi, 368
Khuddaka Nikaya, 97, 107
Khuwaja, 293
Kilippattu, 222
Killikkurussimangalam, 223

Kindama, 38
Kingdom of Funan, 76
Kingdom of Mysore, 180, 194, 195
Kinnerasaani Paatalu, 340
Kiran Desai, 151, 153
Kirātārjunīya, 23
Kirmeeravadham, 223
Kisari Mohan Ganguli, 33, 46, 151, 379
Kishkindha, 63, 67
Kishore Chandranana Champu, 268
Kishor Shantabai Kale, 247
Kitne Pakistan, 173
Kluwer Academic Publishers, 390
Kn:ಪುರುಷೋತ್ತಮ ಬಿಳಿಮಲೆ, 345
Knowledge, 3
Kodava Takk, 350
Kodavatiganti Kutumbarao, 339
Kodavur, 353
Kodungallur Kovilakam, 225
Kodungallur Kunjikkuttan Thampuran, 225
Kokkonda Venkata Ratnam Pantulu, 336
Kolam Thullal, 223
Kolathunadu, 221
Kolkata, 57, 145, 369
Konangi, 313
Konark Stone Carving, 258
Konbaung Dynasty, 78
Konkani language, 344, 350
Konkani literature, 115, 161, 218, 235, 239, 250, 259, 285, 292, 364
Koodiyattom, 219, 224
Koothambalam, 219
Koothu, 219, 221
Koraga language, 344, 351
Koraput district, 259
Korean literature, 91, 118, 150, 163, 178, 289, 324, 336
Kosala, 59
Kosala Kingdom, 56
Kosli language, 258
Kota Vamsa, 330
Koti and Chennayya, 345
Koti Brahmanda Sundari, 267
Kotpad Handloom fabrics, 258
Kovalam, 220
Kovid Gupta, 151
Kozhikode, 228
Krant M. L. Verma, 25
Kripa, 43
Krishan Chander, 368
Krishna, 28, 33–35, 45, 47, 74, 134, 165–167, 188, 189, 199
Krishnadasa Kaviraja, 134
Krishnadevaraya, 189, 327, 332, 340
Krishna Dharma, 48
Krishna Hutheesing, 215
Krishna III, 183, 185
Krishnaism, 137
Krishna River, 186
Krishna Udayasankar, 48
Krista Purana, 242
Kritavarma, 43
Kriti, 335
Krittibas Ojha, 58, 73, 81, 120, 134
Krittivasi Ramayan, 58, 73, 81, 120
Krittivas Ojha, 132
Kriya, 329
Krounchavadh, 246
Kshatriya, 43
Kshemaraja, 209, 211
Kshemendra, 211
Kshetrayya, 334
K. Shivaram Karanth, 202
K. S. Narasimhaswamy, 199
K. S. Nissar Ahmed, 202
K Srilata, 157
Kuber Nath Rai, 170
Kuchipudi, 334
Kulala, 349
Kulasekhara, 219
Kulothunga Chola I, 308, 309
Kulothunga Chola II, 308, 309
Kulwant Singh Virk, 283
Kumaran Asan, 217
Kumarasambhava, 23
Kumara Valmiki, 189
Kumara Vyasa, 189
Kumargupta, 261
Kumari Kandam, 303
Kumbhakarna, 63, 84
Kumudendu Muni, 24
Kumud Ranjan Mullick, 141
Kunchan Nambiar, 223
Kundalakesi, 24, 307, 309
Kundalatha, 228, 232
Kundapura, 345
Kunti, 38, 51
Kuppam, 357
Kurdish literature, 292, 362
Kuṟiñcippāṭṭu, 301
Kuru (India), 35
Kuru (kingdom), 34, 51
Kuru Kingdom, 32
Kurukshetra, 23, 25, 28, 39, 42
Kurukshetra War, 27, 34, 35
Kurumbur Kuppusami, 317
Kuruntokai, 303, 304, 313
Kuṟuntokai, 300
Kusha (Ramayana), 61, 70
Kusumagraj, 246, 247
Kutchi language, 293
Kuthyas Kawejan, 296

Kuvempu, 73, 199, 202
K. V. Dominic, 157

Laat, 297
Labanyabati, 267
Labial consonant, 351
Lagadha, 210
Lai languages, 250
Lakho lutufullah, 294
Lakshadweep, 73
Lakshmana, 55, 56, 59–62, 65, 74, 77, 84
Lakshmana rekha, 67
Lakshmi, 61
Lakshmi Holmström, 152
Lakshminath Bezbaroa, 123
Lakshmisa, 195
Laksmi Purana, 264
Lal Bahadur Shastri, 25
Lalchand Amardinomal, 295
Lalita Shastri, 25
Lalleshvari, 209
Lallu Lal, 166
Lalsangzuali Sailo, 249, 254
Lalthangfala Sailo, 253
Laltluangliana Khiangte, 254
Lalzuia Colney, 249, 254
Language family, 178, 343
Languages of India, 93, 151, 348
Languages of Pakistan, 296
Lanka, 56, 61, 62, 70, 82
Lankavatara Sutra, 74
Lao language, 78
Laos, 56, 71
Lari, 293
Lateef (musician), 294
Lateral consonant, 351
Latin, 5, 213, 294
Latin American literature, 118, 163, 324
Latin literature, 90, 118, 163, 177, 324
Lauri Honko, 354, 358
Lava Kusa: The Warrior Twins, 84
Lava Kusha, 84
Lava (Ramayana), 61, 70
Laxman Gaikwad, 247
Laxman Londhe, 246
Laxman Mane, 247
Laxmanshastri Balaji Joshi, 247
Laylat al-Qadr, 291, 362
Leela Majumdar, 141
Lexical category, 351
Lexicon, 357
Lexikon der indogermanischen Verben, 373
Liberty Fund, 89
Lilathilakam, 219
Lingayatism, 23, 179, 181
Linguistics, 303

List of Assamese writers with their pen names, 116
List of authors, 117, 162, 323
List of basic literature topics, 117, 162, 323
List of Bengali language authors (alphabetical), 129
List of Bengali language authors (chronological), 129
List of books, 117, 162, 323
List of characters in the Mahabharata, 32
List of Chief Ministers of Odisha, 257
List of governors of Odisha, 257
List of language regulators, 343
List of literary terms, 117, 162, 323
List of Pali Canon anthologies, 106
List of rulers of Odisha, 257
List of Sahitya Akademi Award winners for Kannada, 180, 203
List of Sahitya Akademi Award winners for Marathi, 247
List of Sahitya Akademi Award winners for Sanskrit, 94
List of Sahitya Akademi fellows, 180, 203
List of Scheduled Tribes in Odisha, 258
List of years in literature, 119, 149, 164, 325
Literary criticism, 117, 162, 200, 323
Literary movement, 146, 157
Literary theory, 117, 162, 249, 323
Literature, 165, 250, 292, 299, 309, 362
Literature of Kashmir, **209**
Little magazine, 246
Locative case, 352
Loeb Classical Library, 379
Lohana, 293
Loiyamba Shinyen, 236
Lokanatha Vidyadhara, 267
Lokayata, 5
London, 191
Lucknow, 213
Lushai language, 250
L. V. Ramaswami Iyer, 345
Lyrical poetry, 284
Lyricist, 198

Madan Gopal Gandhi, 157
Madan Mohan Malaviya, 174
Madhava Kandali, 58, 73, 120
Madhavi Dasi, 266
Madhavi Pattanayak, 266
Madhav Julian, 244
Madhurantakam Rajaram, 339
Madhurya, 327
Madhusudan Rao, 269
Madhvacharya, 186, 192, 353
Madhyamavyayoga, 48
Madhya Pradesh, 32

Madih nabawi, 292, 363
Madime, 356
Madra, 42
Madri, 38, 39, 51
Madurai, 300
Madurai Nayaks, 310
Magadha, 42, 59
Magadhi, 164
Magahi language, 162
Māgha, 23
Magic realism, 152
Mahabharat (1988 TV series), 48
Mahabharat (2013 film), 48
Mahabharat (2013 TV series), 49
Mahabharata, 4, 17, 22, 23, **26**, 54, 56, 58, 75, 145, 151, 154, 181, 185, 221, 242, 263, 322, 325, 353
Maha Bharata, 340
Mahābhārata, 329
Mahabharata (comics), 48
Mahabharatam, 310
Mahabhashya, 209
Mahadevi Varma, 168, 172
Mahadevshastri Joshi, 247
Mahajanapadas, 6, 59
Mahakali, 73
Mahākāvya, 22, 93
Mahalakshmi, 333
Mahamati Pirannath, 294
Mahanubhava, 240
Mahapadma Nanda, 34
Maha Prasthanam, 340
Mahaprasthanika Parva, 33
Maharadia Lawana, 79
Maharaja, 32
Maharashtra, 240, 344
Mahasamghika, 108
Mahasweta Devi, 144
Mahatma Gandhi, 52
Mahavamsa, 103
Mahavihara, 99
Mahavira, 23
Mahavir Prasad Dwivedi, 167
Mahayana sutras, 109
Mahendravarman I, 306
Maheswar Neog, 123
Mahipati, 243
Mahisasaka, 108
Mahmud Gami, 209
Mahoba, 164
Mail art, 146
Maithili language, 73, 119, 133
Maithili Sharan Gupt, 167, 172
Majjhima Nikaya, 97, 103, 106–108, 113
Makaan, 367
Makarand Paranjape, 157

Makhdoom Muhammad Zaman Talib-ul-Mola, 296
Makhdoom Nuh, 294
Malabar (Northern Kerala), 232
Maladhar Basu, 132
Malaipaṭukaṭām, 301
Malayalam, 58, 73, 347, 349, 353
Malayalam calendar, 218
Malayalam language, 217, 344, 350
Malayalam literature, 115, 118, 150, 161, 163, **217**, 218, 235, 239, 250, 259, 285, 293, 324, 364
Malayalam script, 14, 348
Malayali, 228, 232
Malay Roy Choudhury, 146
Malaysia, 56, 71, 78
Maldives, 71
Malgudi, 152
Malik Muhammad Jayasi, 165, 172
Malkangiri district, 259
Malladi Venkata Krishna Murthy, 339
Malliya Rechana, 328
Malnad, 186
Malwa, 185
Mamoni Raisom Goswami, 123
Manabodha Chautisha, 268
Manasa, 135
Manasi Pradhan, 272
Man Booker Prize, 153
Mandavi, 61, 65
Mandodari, 73
Mangalampalli Balamurali Krishna, 337
Mangalkavya, 131
Mangal-Kāvya, 135
Mangalore, 347, 349
Mangalore University, 357
Mangalsutra, 198
Mangesh Narayanrao Kale, 246
Manik Bandopadhyay, 141
Manik Bandyopadhyay, 145
Manikkavacakar, 305
Manikkavasagar, 306
Manimegalai, 24
Manimekalai, 307, 309
Manipravala champu, 220, 221
Manipravalam, 217, 219
Manipur, 235
Manipuri alphabet, 236
Mani Rao, 157
Mani Shankar Mukherjee, 141, 144
Manjeshwar, 349
Manjeshwaram, 353
Mankuthimmana Kagga, 199
Manohar Malgonkar, 152
Manohar Oak, 246
Manoj Bhawuk, 148

Manoj Das, 152, 273, 274
Manoranjan Das, 276
Manthara, 65
Manthar Faqir Rajar, 294
Mantra, 7
Manu (Hinduism), 25, 332
Manushyaputhiran, 314
Manusmriti, 211
Manya Joshi, 246
Mappila songs, 73
Maqbool Shah Kralawari, 209
Maraimalai Adigal, 312
Marana, 329
Maranao people, 79
Maratha, 242
Marathi language, 58, 73, 192, 240
Marathi literature, 115, 118, 150, 161, 163, 218, 235, 239, **239**, 250, 259, 285, 293, 324, 364
Marathi Vishwakosh, 247
March 1966 Mizo National Front uprising, 254
Margamkali, 223
Maricha, 61, 66, 72
Maritime history of Odisha, 257
Markandeya, 332
Markandeya Purana, 332
Marriage, 13
Marthanda Varma, 223, 228
Marthanda Varma (film), 228
Marthandavarma (novel), 228, 232
Marwari language, 162
Mary Lamb, 230
Masti Venkatesh Iyengar, 197, 202
Mathematics, 213
Mathura Mangala, 268
Mathura, Uttar Pradesh, 42
Matira Manisha, 271
Matsya, 42
Matter of Britain, 90, 118, 130, 163, 177, 324
Matter of France, 90, 118, 130, 163, 177, 324
Matter of Rome, 90, 118, 130, 163, 177, 324
Maturaikkāñci, 301
Maulana deen Muhammad Wafai, 295
Maulana Din Muhammad Wafai, 295
Maurice Bloomfield, 7
Maurya Empire, 6
Mausala Parva, 33
Mawlid, 291, 362
Maximilian Wolfgang Duncker, 379
Maximum City, 154
Max Müller, 5, 8, 18, 19, 375, 378
Maya Sita, 70
Mayasura, 40
Mayurbhanj district, 259
Mazaron Ke Phool, 371
Mazhar Tirmazi, 284

Medang Kingdom, 77
Medhātithi, 211
Media:aathreya.ogg, 337
Media:Pronunciation of Mangalampalli Balamuralikrishna.ogg, 337
Medicine, 293
Medieval, 260
Medieval Bulgarian literature, 91, 178
Medieval Dutch literature, 91, 178
Medieval French literature, 91, 178
Medieval German literature, 91, 178
Medieval literature, 91, 118, 130, 163, 178, 324
Medieval Serbian literature, 91, 178
Medieval Spanish literature, 91, 178
Medieval Welsh literature, 91, 178
Meena Kandasamy, 157
Meenakshi Sundaram Pillai, 311
Meeraji, 213
Meerut, 167
Meetei Mayek, 236
Meghaduta, 145
Meghadūta, 220
Meghnad, 136
Mehar Chand Advani, 295
Mehr Lal Soni Zia Fatehabadi, 366
Mehrunnisa Parvez, 173
Meidingu Bodhchandra, 236
Meidingu Loiyamba, 236
Meidingu Pamheiba, 236
Meitei language, 235
Meitei literature, 115, 161, 218, 235, **235**, 239, 250, 259, 285, 293, 364
Melpathur Narayana Bhattathiri, 221
Memory of the World Programme, 18
Memory of the World Register – Asia and the Pacific, 18
Menander I, 210
Mendicant, 195
Metaphor, 189
Metaphysics, 213, 214, 217
Meter (poetry), 182, 296
Metre (poetry), 24, 184, 328
Mexican literature, 118, 150, 163, 324
Michael Madhusudan Dutt, 135, 151, 156
Michael Rothenberg, 158
Michael Witzel, 10, 20, 54, 375, 376, 381
Middle Ages, 91, 178
Middle English literature, 91, 178
Middle Persian literature, 90, 177
Midnights Children, 152
Mid-Shaban, 291, 362
Mid vowel, 350
Milinda Panha, 210
Mirabai, 172
Mir Abdul Hussain sangi, 295

Miran Mohammad Shah, 295
Mir Hasan Ali, 295
Mirijiyori, 123
Mir Mosharraf Hossain, 138, 142
Mir Tanha Yousafi, 282
Mirza Kalich Beg, 295
Mirza Qalich Baig, 296
Mirza Sahiba, 280
Misri Shah, 294
Missionaries, 122
Mithila (ancient), 64
Mithila (region), 59, 61, 65
Mizo language, 249, 250, 252
Mizo languages, 250
Mizo literature, 115, 161, 218, 235, 239, **249**, 250, 259, 285, 293, 364
Mizo peoples, 250
M.J. Akbar, 215
M. K. Seetharam Kulal, 354
M. Mukundan, 229
Modernism, 118, 163, 280, 324
Modernist literature, 149
Modern period, 249
Modern Standard Hindi, 162
Mogaveera, 349
Mohammad Hashim, 295
Mohammad Tabish, 215
Mohammad Tughlaq, 203
Mohanatarangini, 193
Mohan Rakesh, 170
Mohan Rana, 173
Mohan Singh (poet), 282
Mohapatra Nilamani Sahoo, 274
Mohism, 217
Moinuddin Jinabade, 368
Mokkapati Narasimha Sastry, 339
Moksa (Jainism), 50, 74
Molla (poet), 81, 338
Momin Khan Momin, 213
Monier Monier-Williams, 19
Monk, 107
Moodbidri, 356
Mood (grammar), 353
Moorish architecture, 290, 361
Moortidevi Award, 48
Morality, 251
Moritz Winternitz, 29
Moriz Winternitz, 94
Moroccan architecture, 290, 361
Moroccan literature, 119, 164, 325
Moropant, 243
Motilal Banarsidass, 18, 46, 94
Moti Lal Kemmu, 210
Moti Nandi, 144
Movva, 335
M. P. Pandit, 214

M. T. Vasudevan Nair, 229
Muddupalani, 339
Mudra (music), 334
Mughal architecture, 290, 361
Mughal Empire, 166
Mughals, 212
Mugham, 292, 363
Muhammad, 311
Muhammad Asim Butt, 214
Muhammad Ibrahim Joyo, 295
Muhammad Iqbal, 212–214
Muhammad Mohsin Bekas, 294
Muhammad of Ghor, 164
Muhammad Younis Butt, 214
Muhammed Amin Andrabi, 214
Muhammed Azam Didamari, 212
Muhammed Zafar Iqbal, 141, 144
Muhyadheen mala, 217
Mukhlis, 295
Mukhya Upanishads, 8
Mukundaraja, 241
Mulk Raj Anand, 151, 152
Mullaippāṭṭu, 301
Mullapudi Venkata Ramana, 339
Mumbai, 202, 247, 348, 355
Mumbai Musical, 85
Mu Metha, 314
Mummadi Krishnaraja Wodeyar, 195
Munir Niazi, 282
Munshi Premchand, 166, 167, 172, 368
Muppala Ranganayakamma, 339
Murudeshwara, 28
Muruga, 310
Murugan, 310
Music, 213, 294
Musical composition, 193
Musician, 294
Music of Andhra Pradesh, 321
Musicologist, 211
Muslim, 73
Muslim holidays, 291, 362
Mutumoḻikkāñci, 301
M. V. Seetharamiah, 202
Myanmar, 56, 78, 98, 236
Mysticism, 293, 294

Na, 386
Naalayira Divyap Prabhandham, 306
Naa ramudu, 340
Nabaneeta Dev Sen, 144
Nabarangpur district, 259
Nadia district, 133, 134
Nadir Shah Di Vaar, 280
Naeem Baig, 368
Nāga, 61
Nagaland, 236

Nagaradhane, 354
Nāgarī script, 166
Nagasena, 210
Nagavarma I, 182, 185
Nagavarma II, 186
Naimisha Forest, 29
Naimisharanya, 32
Naiṣadhacarita, 23
Najm Hosain Syed, 282
Nakula, 38, 39, 51
Nala, 69, 193
Nalacharitham, 223
Nalanda, 6
Nalatiyar, 305
Nālaṭiyār, 301
Nalini Bala Devi, 123
Nalini Priyadarshni, 157
Nalin Vilochan Sharma, 168
Nambiyandar Nambi, 305, 306
Nambudiri, 219
Namdeo Dhasal, 246, 247
Namdev, 241
Namdev Dhasal, 247
Namvar Singh, 148
Nanak Singh, 281
Nanda Kishore Bal, 269
Nandamuri Balakrishna, 85
Nandan (Kolkata), 142
Nandoori Subbarao, 339
Naneelu, 326
Nāṉmaṇikkaṭikai, 301
Nannaiyah, 327
Nannaya, 322
Nannayya, 329
Nanne Choadudu, 339
Narahari, 81
Naraharitirtha, 193
Narain Das Bhambhani, 296
Naraka (Jainism), 74, 75
Narasaraja Wodeyar II, 195
Narasimha, 193, 334
Narasimha I, 187
Narayan Gangopadhyay, 141, 144, 145
Narayaniyam, 221
Narendra Kohli, 173
Narendra Modi, 345
Narendranath Mitra, 141
Naresh Mehta, 168, 173
Narikela, 327
Narrative, 326
Naṟṟiṇai, 300
Nasadiya Sukta, 11
Nasal stop, 351
Nātakam, 326
Nathamuni, 306
Nathan Brown (missionary), 122

National anthem, 138
National Book Trust, 148
National Poet, 139
Natya Shastra, 17
Navakanta Barua, 123
Nava Rasas, 327
Nawab of Oudh, 213
Naxalite, 143, 284
Nayagarh district, 259
Nayakas of Keladi, 180
Nayanars, 305
Nayani Krishnakumari, 339
Nayanmars, 299, 306
Nayantara Sahgal, 215
Nayantara Sehgal, 152
Nayyer Masood, 369
Nazm, 363
Neminatha, 49
Neo-romanticism, 168
Nepal, 6, 9, 56, 58, 90, 104, 131
Nepala rajavamsa kathalu, 340
Nepal Bhasa, 76
Nepal Bhasa literature, 91, 178
Nepal Bhasa renaissance, 76
Nepalese literature, 289, 336
Nepali language, 76
Nepali literature, 115, 118, 161, 163, 218, 235,
    239, 250, 259, 285, 293, 324, 364
Neṭunalvāṭai, 301
Neustadt International Prize for Literature, 154
New Delhi, 355, 378
New York University, 47
New Zealand literature, 118, 150, 163, 324
Ngũgĩ wa Thiongo, 314
Niddesa, 104
Nigerian literature, 119, 150, 164, 325
Nihar Ranjan Gupta, 144
Nijaguna Shivayogi, 191
Nikaya, 107
Nikāya, 106
Nīlakaṇṭha Caturdhara, 47
Nila (Ramayana), 69
Nil Darpan, 135
Niqāb, 291, 362
Nirad C. Chaudhuri, 151
Niranam poets, 220, 221
Nirgun Nirakaar Bramh, 165
Nirmalendu Goon, 143
Nirmal Verma, 168, 173
Nirukta, 16
Nirvana, 167
Nirvana (Buddhism), 99
Nissim Ezekiel, 157
Niyoga, 37, 51
Niyogi, 334
Nizam, 164

Nl:Petrus Abraham Samuel van Limburg Brouwer, 233
Nobel Prize, 138, 139, 156
Nominative case, 352
Nondualism, 17
Non-resident Indian and person of Indian origin, 81, 151
Noon Meem Rashid, 366
Noor-ud-din Sarki, 296
Northern Black Polished Ware, 6
North India, 364
Nouka Charitram, 335
Noun, 351
Novel, 117, 151, 162, 296, 323, 326
Novelist, 296
N. T. Rama Rao, 48, 84
Ntuppuppakkoranendarnnu, 229
Nuapada district, 259
Nuchhungi Renthlei, 253
Numbers, 24
Nun, 107
Nund Rishi, 209
Nurul Momen, 138, 140, 143

Obaidullah Aleem, 214
Object (grammar), 352
Oblique case, 352
O. Chandhu Menon, 228, 232, 233
Octavio Paz, 282
October revolution, 269
Odia alphabet, 258
Odia Hindu wedding, 257
Odia language, 58, 73, 258, 260, 269
Odia literature, 115, 161, 218, 235, 239, 250, **257**, 258, 259, 267, 285, 293, 364
Odia morphology, 258
Odia people, 258
Odisha, 257, 260
Odisha High Court, 257
Odisha Legislative Assembly, 257
Odisha Police, 257
Odissi, 258
Odissi dance, 260
Odissi music, 260
Odra Desha, 260
Odyssey, 27
Old English literature, 91, 178
Old Irish literature, 91, 178
Old Norse literature, 91, 178
Old Turkic, 91, 177
Oliver Fallon, 25
Omkar N. Koul, 214
One Thousand and One Nights, 230
Open vowel, 350
Opera Jawa, 84
Oral literature, 345

Oral tradition, 6, 92, 170, 250
Oriental Institute, 80
Oriental rug, 291, 361
Orissa Ikat, 258
Oriya language, 119
Oriyardori Asal, 355
Or:ଓଡ଼ିଆ ସାହିତ୍ୟ, 260
Orthography, 303
Osians Cinefan Festival of Asian and Arab Cinema, 355
Other (philosophy), 276
Ottan thullal, 223
Ottoman architecture, 290, 361
Ougri Sheireng, 236
Outline of Buddhism, 96
O. V. Vijayan, 229
Oxford Dictionaries Online, 378

Paadal Petra Sthalam, 305
Paād-danāas, 357
Pablo Neruda, 282
Pada (Hindu mythology), 7
Padayani, 223
Paddanas, 354
Padma Bhushan, 173
Padmanabh Jaini, 49, 74, 94
Padmanath Gohain Baruah, 123
Padmapurana, 74
Padma Shri, 173, 253, 254
Padmavat, 172
Padshah Buranji, 125
Pahlavi literature, 117, 162, 323
Paigham Afaqui, 367–369
Painted Grey Ware, 34, 35
Painting, 291, 361
Paintings, 81
Paite language, 250
Pakistan, 32, 210, 212, 363, 367
Pakistani architecture, 290, 361
Pakistani English literature, 150, 215
Pakistani literature, 118, 150, 163, 289, 324, 336
Pakistan Movement, 367, 368
Palagummi Padmaraju, 339
Paḷamoḷi Nāṉūṟu, 301
Palatal consonant, 351
Pali, 260
Pāli, 98, 210
Pali Canon, 108
Pāli Canon, **96**, 97
Pali literature, 90, 177
Pali Text Society, 104
Palkuriki Somanatha, 330
Pallava, 306
Pallavi, 334
Palm-leaf manuscript, 57, 98, 99

Palsanthmalai, 309
Pampa (Jain poet), 23
Pāñcāla, 39
Pañcaratra, 17, 31
Panchagnula Adinarayana Sastry, 339
Pancha Kavyas, 332, 334
Panchala, 42
Panchasakhas, 264
Panchatantra, 210, 336
Panchavati, 66
Panchavimsha Brahmana, 31
Panchjanya (newspaper), 378
Pandalam Kerala Varma, 227
Pandava, 27, 29, 35, 39, 42, 45, 49, 51
Pandavacaritra, 49
Pandavapurana, 49
Pandavas, 35, 38, 47
Pandey Kapil, 147
Pandit Taba Ram Turki, 212
Pandiya, 300
Pandu, 37, 51
Pandya, 299, 306, 309, 310
Pandyan Dynasty, 42
Pandyas, 303, 305
Panegyric, 199
Pāṇini, 5, 30, 32, 53, 209, 227, 329
Panuganti Lakshminarasimham, 339
Panuganti Lakshminarasimha Rao, 339
Parallels, 106
Parama Kambojas, 42
Paramananda, 209
Paravasthu Chinnayasuri, 339
Paravastu Chinnayasuri, 336
Pariksha guru, 166
Parikshit, 34, 44
Parinibbana, 98
Parinirvana, 100
Paripaatal, 304
Paripāṭal, 300
Paritta, 99
Parivara, 97, 107
Parliament of the United Kingdom, 191
Parmanand Mewaram, 295
Parthiban Kanavu, 314
Partition of India, 131, 281
Parva (novel), 201
Parvati, 84, 187, 189
Pash, 282, 284
Pashto literature and poetry, 150, 292, 362
Patanjali, 209
Patañjali, 6
Pathinenkilkanakku, 304
Pathinenmaelkanakku, 301
Pathummayude Aadu, 229
Patimokkha, 107
Patiṉeṇkīlkaṇakku, 301
Patiṉeṇmēlkaṇakku, 300
Patiṟṟuppattu, 300
Patras Bokhari, 213
Patrick Olivelle, 374
Patriotism, 294
Pattachitra, 258
Patthana, 97, 108
Paṭṭiṉappālai, 301
Pattupattu, 301
Pattuppattu, 301
Paul Deussen, 376
Paul J. Griffiths, 106
Pavuluri, 329
Payaswini, 349
Pazhamozhi Nanuru, 305
Peary Chand Mitra, 138
Peel (fruit), 327
Peer Budhu Shah Ji, 284
Penataran, 78
Penguin Books, 154
Penukonda (city), 332
Penumarti Viswanatha Sastry, 338
Periplus, 393
Periyalvar, 306
Periyapuranam, 308, 312
Periya Puranam, 24, 299, 305
Persian carpet, 291, 362
Persian language, 43, 46, 131, 164, 280, 364
Persian literature, 91, 117, 130, 162, 178, 292, 323, 362
Perso-Arabic script, 363
Perumpāṇāṟṟuppaṭai, 301
Peruvian literature, 118, 150, 163, 324
Peshwa, 243
Pessimist, 217
Peter Brook, 49
Petruk, 46
Phanishwar Nath Renu, 173
Philippines, 56, 71, 79
Philosophiæ Naturalis Principia Mathematica, 213
Philosophy, 304
Phoneme, 350
Phonetics, 301
Phra Lak Phra Lam, 78
Phulia, 133
Pilgrimage, 43
Pipili applique work, 258
Pir-e-Kamil, 368
Pir Hadi abdul Mannan, 282
Pir Nooruddin, 293
Pir Sadardin, 293
Pir Sadruddin, 293
Pitaka, 98
P. Kesava Dev, 228
P. Lal, 47, 52, 152, 157

P. Lankesh, 202
Plato, 191, 276
Plosive, 351
Pluperfect, 344, 353
Poet, 252
Poetics, 301
Poetry, 117, 162, 293, 296, 323, 326
Political radicalism, 217
Politics, 295
Politics of Andhra Pradesh, 321
Politics of Odisha, 258
Polyandry, 46
Ponniyin Selvan, 314
Poonthanam, 222
Poonthottam Achhan Nambudiri, 225
Poonthottam Mahan Nambudiri, 225
Poornachandra Tejaswi, 203
Portal:Andhra Pradesh, 321
Portal:Assam, 116, 117
Portal:Bangladesh, 129
Portal:Buddhism, 96
Portal:Hinduism, 10, 26, 56, 92
Portal:Islam, 292, 363
Portal:Literature, 91, 117, 119, 129, 130, 151, 164, 178, 249, 325
Portal:Mizoram, 249
Portal:Odisha, 259
Portal:Punjab, 279
Portal:Telangana, 322
Portal:West Bengal, 129
Poruṇarāṟṟuppaṭai, 301
Post-colonialism, 118, 149, 163, 324
Postcolonial literature, 151
Postcolonial theory, 156
Postmodernism, 118, 149, 163, 324
Poststructuralism, 118, 149, 163, 324
Potana, 338
Prabandha era, 326
Prabhanda, 308
Prabhulingaleele, 24
Pragatishila, 200
Prahlada Bhakti Vijayam, 335
Prahlad Keshav Atre, 244
Prakalpana Movement, 146, 157
Prakash Jha, 48
Prakrit, 98, 109, 164, 262, 364, 365
Prakrit literature, 90, 177
Pramathanath Bishi, 145
Prambanan, 62, 72, 78, 82
Pramod Kumar Tripathy, 276
Prana Krushna Parija, 277
Prarthana, 326
Prathapa Mudaliar Charithram, 313
Pratibha Ray, 48
Pratilipi, 341
Pratishruti, 277

Prativa Satpathy, 272
Prativasudeva, 74
Pravarakhya, 332
Prayudh Payutto, 101
Premendra Mitra, 141, 145
Preposition and postposition, 352
Pre-sectarian Buddhism, 101, 102
Prime Minister, 213
Princely state, 195
Printing press, 122
Prithvi, 71
Prithviraj Chauhan, 164
Prithviraj Raso, 164, 170
Progressive Writers Movement, 370
Progressivism, 203, 295
Project Gutenburg, 87
Pronoun, 351
Prose, 117, 162, 323, 326
Prosody (linguistics), 309
Prosody (poetry), 185
Proto-Dravidian, 345
Proto-Dravidian language, 346
Proto-Indo-European language, 5
Proverb, 305
P. S. Chawngthu, 253
Public domain, 46, 94, 106
Pudhumaipithan, 314
Puffery, 336
Puggalapannatti, 97, 108
Pulikeshi II, 34
Pulitzer prize, 156
Pumsavana, 120
Punakawan, 46
Pune, 45, 244
Punjabi diaspora, 279, 284
Punjabi language, 279, 293
Punjabi literature, 115, 150, 161, 218, 235, 239, 250, 259, **279**, 285, 292, 293, 363, 364
Punjabi people, 279
Punjabi Qissa, 280, 284
Punjabi writer, 283
Punjab region, 11
Punjab (region), 279
Punokawan, 77
Purana, 185, 224
Puṟanāṉūṟu, 300
Puranas, 17, 22, 34, 92, 127, 135, 181, 193, 237, 240, 322
Purandara Dasa, 193
Purani Assam Buranji, 125
Puran Singh, 281
Pure Tamil Movement, 312
Puri district, 259
Puruṣārtha, 57
Purusharthas, 27

Purushottam Das Tandon, 175
Puttur, Karnataka, 349
P. Varadarajulu Naidu, 315
PVR Cinemas, 356
Pyu city-states, 98

Qadaryar, 280
Qawwali, 292, 363
Qazi Abdul Sattar, 368
Qazi Qadan, 294
Q:Ramayan, 89
Quli Qutub Shah, 365
Quran, 27, 293
Quratulain Haider, 367, 368
Qurratulain Hyder, 368

Raajneeti, 48
Raavan (TV series), 86
Rabindranath Tagore, 131, 138, 139, 141, 151
Rabindra Nath Tagore, 286
Rabindra Puraskar, 144
Radha, 166
Radhamohan Gadnayak, 272
Radhavallabh Tripathi, 93
Radhika Santvanamu, 339
Rafiq Azad, 143
Raga, 335
Ragas, 193
Raghavanka, 186
Raghu Arakhsita, 266
Raghunath Pandit, 243
Raghuvamsa, 211
Raghuvamsam, 333
Raghuvamsha, 23
Raghuvir Sahay, 173
Rahman Abbas, 368
Rahman Rahi, 209
Rahul Sankrityayan, 169, 172
Raja Dhale, 247
Rajah Rama Varma, 228
Rajanikanta Sen, 141
Rajaraja Chola I, 308
Raja Raja Chola I, 305
Rajaraja Chola II, 309
Raja Rao, 151
Raja Ravi Varma, 37, 38, 66
Rajasekhara, 339
Rajasthan, 286
Rajasthani language, 286
Rajasthani literature, 115, 118, 161, 163, 218, 235, 239, 250, 259, 285, **285**, 293, 324, 364
Rajasthani people, 285
Rajasuya, 32
Rajatarangini, 35
Rajathi Salma, 314

Rajendra kishore Panda, 272
Rajeswar Singha, 124
Rajgir, 98
Rajinder Singh Bedi, 368
Rajkamal Chaudhary, 173
Rajkumar Santoshi, 49
Rajput, 164, 286
Rajputana, 286
Rajshekhar Basu, 141, 144
Rakshasa, 63, 84
Rakshasi, 66
Rallapalli Ananta Krishna Sharma, 339
Ralph T. H. Griffith, 5, 18, 88
Rama, 25, 55, 56, 58, 59, 62, 63, 74, 81, 165, 331, 335
Ramachandra Pattanayaka, 267
Ramacharitamanas, 25, 70, 81, 165, 172
Ramacharitamanasa, 120
Ramacharitam of Cheeraman, 217
Ramadan, 291, 362
Rama in Jainism, 56
Ramakanta Rath, 272
Ramakien, 78, 80
Ramakrishna, 142
Ramanand, 165
Ramanand Sagar, 85
Ramanattam, 223
Ramanichandran, 317
Ramanuja, 308, 331
Ramanujacharya, 186
Rama Panikkar, 220
Ramapurathu Warrier, 223
Ramavataram, 73, 120, 308
Ramayan (2002), 85
Ramayan (2008 TV series), 85
Ramayan (2012 TV Series), 85
Ramayana, 22, 23, 27, **55**, 89, 133, 136, 145, 181, 189, 223, 325, 336
Ramayana Ballet, 78
Ramayana Series, 83
Ramayana: The Epic, 84
Ramayana: The Legend of Prince Rama, 84
Ramayana War, 69
Ramayan (TV series), 85
Rambhadracharya, 94
Ramcharitamanas, 58
Ramdhari Singh Dinkar, 25, 168, 172
Ramendra Sundar Tribedi, 138
Ramesh Chandra Jha, 147, 148, 173
Ramesh Menon, 48
Ram Ganesh Gadkari, 244
Ramlila, 81
Ram Mohan Roy, 135
Ram Nath Kak, 152, 215
Ram Nath Pandey, 147
Ramprasad Sen, 142

Ram Ratan Bhatnagar, 172
Ramtanu Lahiri, 138
Randidangazhi, 228
Random House Websters Unabridged Dictionary, 373, 378, 380
Ranganatha Ramayanam, 73, 81, 339
Rani Rudrama Devi, 330
Ranjit Hoskote, 157
Ranna, 23, 185, 186
Rasa (aesthetics), 165, 327
Rasheed Amjad, 214
Rashmirathi, 25
Rashtrakuta, 179
Rashtrakuta Dynasty, 184
Rashtriya Sanskrit Sansthan, 94
Rasokallola, 267
Rasool Bux Palijo, 295
Rasselas, 234
Rassundari Devi, 138
Rasul Mir, 209
Ratan Lal Basu, 141, 155
Ratan Nath Dhar Sarshar, 213
Rathore, 164
Ravana, 56, 62, 63, 66, 70, 73, 74, 84, 136, 189
Ravanavadha (Bhattikavya), 78
Ravenshaw College, 270
Ravi Kiran Mandal, 244
Ravuri Bharadwaja, 339
Rayagada district, 259
Razia Butt, 214
Razmnama, 47
Razmnameh, 46
R. C. Majumdar, 53
Reamker, 76
Rebati, 269
Recension, 7
Redaction, 9, 30
Reflexive verb, 352
Register (sociolinguistics), 162
Reincarnation, 184
Relief, 68
Religion, 304
Religion in Assam, 116
Renaissance literature, 91, 118, 130, 163, 178, 324
Retroflex consonant, 351
Rhetoric, 183, 301
Rice, 193
Richard Crasta, 157
Richard Gombrich, 101
Richard Kostelanetz, 146, 157
Richard Pischel, 390
Rich Like Us, 152
Rigveda, 4, 7, 9–12, 14, 16, 58
Rig Veda, 11

Rigvedic deities, 11
Rishabhadeva, 185
Rishi, 4, 32
Rishis, 63
Riti Juga, 266, 267
Ritwik Ghatak, 141
River of Smoke, 154
R. K. Narayan, 48, 151, 152
Robert Caldwell, 344, 357
Robert Charles Zaehner, 20
Robert P. Goldman, 57
Robin Ngangom, 157
Rohal, 294
Rohinton Mistry, 151, 154
Rohzin, 368
Romance (heroic literature), 117, 162, 323
Romanization, 350
Romantic poetry, 244
Romesh Chunder Dutt, 46, 48, 57, 88, 89, 138, 156
Roquia Sakhawat Hussain, 141
Roundedness, 350
Routledge, 358, 390
R. S. Manohar, 85

Ṛṣyasringa, 27

Rudrabhatta, 186
Rudradaman, 261
Rudrata, 210
Rukmini Bhaya Nair, 157
Rupa Bhavani, 209
Rupert Gethin, 100
Rupinderpal Singh Dhillon, 284
Ruskin Bond, 153
Russia, 295

Sa:, 95
Saadat Hasan Manto, 214, 368
S. Abdul Rahman, 314
Sabha Parva, 32
Sabit Ali Shah, 294
Sachal Sarmast, 294
Sachchidananda Hirananda Vatsyayan Ajneya, 168, 169
Sachin Sengupta, 145
Sacred Books of the East, 18
Sadhukaddi, 165
Safdar Hashmi, 170
Sage (philosophy), 4
Saguna, 165
Sahadeva, 38, 39, 51
Sahajanand Saraswati, 172
Sahasrara, 262
Sahibdin, 70
S:A History of Sanskrit Literature, 19, 94

Sahitya Academy Award, 338
Sahitya Akademi, 94, 153, 173, 247, 392
Sahitya Akademi Award, 152, 247
Sahitya lahri, Sur Sarawali, 172
Saint Thomas Christians, 223
Saiva, 306, 308
Saivism, 308
Sake Dean Mahomet, 151
Salaam Machhalishahari, 366
Salabega, 266
Salam Bin Razzaq, 368
Saleel Wagh, 246
Saleh Muhammad Safoori, 280
Salman Rushdie, 151, 154, 215
Salman Taseer, 213
Samarasam, 314
Samaresh Basu, 141, 144
Samar Sen, 145
Samarth Ramdas, 243
Sama (Sufism), 292, 363
Samaveda, 4, 7, 10, 12, 14
Sambalpur district, 259
Sambalpuri saree, 258
Sambandar, 305
Samhita, 4, 10, 12, 13, 15, 16
Samhitas, 5, 8
Sami(poet), 294
Samir Roychoudhury, 141, 146
Samjnā, 329
Samma Dynasty, 293
Sampati, 63, 67
Sampoorna Ramayana, 84
Sampoorna Ramayanam (1958 film), 84
Sampoorna Ramayanamu, 84
Sampurnanand Sanskrit University, 6
Samudragupta, 261
Samuel Johnson, 234
Samuel Vedanayagam Pillai, 313
Samyutta Nikaya, 97, 106–108
Sandesa Kavya, 220, 221
Sandhi, 329
Sandipan Chattopadhyay, 141, 144, 146
Sane Guruji, 244
Sangam landscape, 301, 304
Sangam literature, 22, 90, 177, 299, 300, 347
Sangam period, 24, 304
Sangha, 98
Sangha (Buddhism), 98, 107
Sangita Ratnakara, 211
Sanjay Khan, 85
Sanjay Patel, 85
Sankara Panikkar, 220
Sankardev, 123, 127
Sankatmochan Mahabali Hanuman, 86
Sanskrit, 3, 5, 22, 23, 26, 27, 55, 56, 71, 91–93, 109, 131, 133, 164, 209, 210, 217, 219, 244, 260, 280, 304, 308, 328, 348, 349, 353, 364
Sanskrit Epics, 17
Sanskrit language, 27, 56, 76, 193
Sanskrit literature, 3, 27, 90, **90**, 115, 118, 126, 161, 163, 177, 218, 230, 235, 239, 250, 259, 285, 293, 324, 364
Sanskrit prosody, 16, 328
Santanu Kumar Acharya, 274
Sant (religion), 58
Saptakanda Ramayana, 58, 73, 120
Sapta Sindhu, 11
Saradindu Bandopadhyay, 141
Saraiki language, 293
Sarala Das, 58
Sarala-Das, 263
Sarala Dasa, 73
Sarala Temple, 263
Sarangadeva, 211
Sara (religion), 325
Saraswati (magazine), 167
Sarat Chandra Chattopadhyay, 141
Sarojini Naidu, 156
Sarojini Sahoo, 273, 276
Sarpasattra, 44
Sarvajna, 195
Sarvastivada, 108
Sarvepalli Radhakrishnan, 19
Sarwanand Koul Premi, 210
Sassi Punnun, 280, 294
Satapatha Brahmana, 25
Satasai, 166, 172
Satasari Assam Buranji, 125
Satinath Bhaduri, 141, 145
Sati (practice), 39, 183
Satire, 191
Satna, 32
Satru Bhanja, 261
Satyajit Ray, 49, 141, 144
Satyaki, 43
Satyam Sankaramanchi, 340
Satyashraya, 186
Satyavati, 36, 51
Satyavrat Shastri, 94
Sauptika Parva, 33
Saurabh Kumar Chaliha, 123
Saurabhya, 327
Sayana, 5
Sayyid Shamsullah Qadri, 365
Scholar, 295
Schwa, 350
Scion of Ikshvaku, 83
Scripture, 98
Sea of Poppies, 153
Seerapuranam, 311
Seethakaathi, 311

Sekkizhar, 305
Selina Hossain, 143
Semar, 46, 77
Seuna (Yadava) dynasty, 240
Seuna Yadavas of Devagiri, 185
Sexual relationship, 304
Seyyed Hossein Nasr, 214
Shabari, 67
Shadow Puppets of Andhra Pradesh, 321
Shafqat Tanvir Mirza, 282
Shah Abdul Karim Bulri, 294
Shah Abdul Latif, 294
Shaheed Minar, Dhaka, 144
Shaheed Quaderi, 144
Shah Hussain, 280
Shahid Nadeem, 214
Shahidullah Kaisar, 143
Shahidul Zahir, 141
Shah Inayat Rizvi, 294
Shah Jo Risalo, 294
Shah lutufullah Qadri, 294
Shah Mohammad, 280
Shahmukhi, 279
Shaikh Abdullah, 213
Shaikh Ayaz, 296
Shaivism, 181, 264, 299, 305
Shakha, 5, 9, 10, 14, 16
Shakhas, 10, 92
Shakti, 262
Shakti Chattopadhyay, 144, 146
Shakuni, 38
Shalwar kameez, 291, 362
Shalya, 33
Shalya Parva, 33
Shamsuddin Bulbul, 295
Shamsuddin Sabzwari, 293
Shamsur Rahman (poet), 142
Shantabai Kamble, 247
Shantanu, 36, 51
Shantiniketan, 143
Shanti Parva, 33
Shanti Purana, 23
Shapeshifting, 67
Sharadindu Bandyopadhyay, 145
Sharankumar Limbale, 247
Shareef Kunjahi, 282
Sharon Maas, 48
Shashi Tharoor, 154
Shataka, 326
Shatakam, 330
Shatapatha Brahmana, 13, 14
Shatpadi, 181
Shatrughna, 56, 59, 61, 65
Shaunaka, 16
Shawkat Ali, 143
Shawkat Osman, 141, 143

Sheila Murphy, 146, 157
Sheldon Pollock, 206, 210, 390
Shesha, 61
Shibram Chakrabarti, 141
Shikhandi, 37, 46
Shiksha, 16
Shirshendu Mukhopadhyay, 141, 144
Shiva, 65, 84, 181, 187, 308, 331
Shivaji, 243
Shivakotiacharya, 23, 184
Shivalli Brahmins, 349
Shivaram Karanth, 197
Shiv K. Kumar, 157
Shiv Kumar Batalvi, 282
Shloka, 27, 56
Short stories, 322
Short story, 228
Shrauta Sutras, 8, 23
Shravanabelagola, 185
Shravanabelagola inscription of Nandisena, 183
Shreekrishna Kirtana, 119
Shreekumar Varma, 155
Shridhar Prathak, 167
Shridhar Venkatesh Ketkar, 246
Shringar, 166
Shrutakirti, 61, 65
Shudras, 263
Shunya Samhita, 264
Shutterdulai, 356
Shyamal Gangapadhyay, 141
Shyama Sangeet, 139, 142
Shyam Benegal, 48
Shyamchi Aai, 244
Sialkot, 213
Sibsagar, 122
Siddha, 164
Siddhidas Mahaju, 76
Sikhism, 241
Silappadhikaram, 24
Silappatikaram, 302
Silk Road, 379
Silver Pagoda, 77
Simone de Beauvoir, 276
Simon Schaffer, 391
Sindh, 293, 295, 296
Sindhi Adabi Board, 297
Sindhi Adabi Sangat, 296
Sindhi language, 289, 293–297
Sindhi Language Authority, 297
Sindhi literature, 115, 118, 150, 161, 163, 218, 235, 239, 250, 259, 285, 289, **289**, 292, 293, 324, 336, 363, 364
Sinhala language, 350, 382
Siribhoovalaya, 24
Sir Isaac Newton, 213

Śiśupālavadha, 23

Sita, 55, 56, 61, 74, 84, 189
Sitakant Mahapatra, 272
Sita Sings the Blues, 84
Sivagamiyin Sabadham, 314
Siva prakasar, 310
Sixth Buddhist council, 100
Siya Ke Ram, 86
Skanda Purana, 310, 334
S. K. Pottekkatt, 228
S. L. Bhyrappa, 201
Slesha, 328
Smartha, 188
Smita Agarwal, 157
Smriti, 3, 8, 22
Smṛti, 4
SOAPBOX, 169
Sobhan Babu, 84
Socialist, 295
Social novel, 232, 337
Social progress, 217
Sociative case, 351
Sohni Mahiwal, 280
Somalian literature, 292, 363
Somali architecture, 290, 361
Somananda, 210
Somandepalli, 332
Song dynasty, 109
Songkok, 291, 362
Sonnet, 296, 366
Sonnets, 135
Sony TV, 86
Soubhagya Kumar Mishra, 272
Soul, 337
South African literature, 119, 150, 164, 325
South Asian, 280
South Asian literature, 292, 363
South Canara, 347
Southeast Asia, 92
Southern Dravidian, 343, 344
South India, 188
Sovanna Maccha, 77
Sovira, 42
Spiritual Heritage of India (book), 87
Sports in Odisha, 258

Śraddhā, 25

S.Ramakrishnan, 313

Śramaṇa, 5

Sri Amarajeevi Potti Sri Ramulu Nellore district, 337
Sri Aurobindo, 156, 214

Śrīharṣa, 23

Srijit Mukherji, 146
Sri Kalahasteeshwara Mahatyam, 333
Sri Kalahasteeshwara Shatakam, 333
Sri Kalahasti, 333
Sri K Sabha, 340
Sri Lal Sukla, 169
Sri Lanka, 56, 98, 99, 103, 299
Sri Lankan Tamil people, 299
Srimadraamaayana kalpavŕkshamu, 340
Srinatha, 190, 330, 340
Sringara, 327, 334
Sripadaraya, 193
Sri Ponna, 23, 185
Sri Ram, 84
Sri Ramacharit Manas, 73
Sri Rama Rajyam, 85
Sri Ramayana Darshanam, 73, 199
Srirangam Srinivasarao, 340
Sri Vaishnavism, 306

Śruti, 3, 4, 22

S. Sadanand, 316
S:sa:महाभारतम्, 54
S:sa:रामायणम्, 89
Stark Electric Jesus, 146
Star Plus, 85, 86
State University of New York Press, 390
Stay on topic, 329
Stemma codicum, 30
Sthanika Brahmins, 349
Sthapatyaveda, 16
Stone sculpture, 81
Story within a story, 29
Stri Parva, 33
Structuralism, 118, 149, 163, 324
Stuthi Chintaamani, 268
Stuttgart, 225
Subarnapur district, 259
Subcommentaries, Theravada, 99
Subhadra, 40, 46, 332
Subhash Kak, 215
Subhas Mukhopadhyay (poet), 145
Subimal Basak, 141, 146
Subimal Mishra, 141
Subodh Ghosh, 141, 145
Subramania Bharathi, 299
Subramanya Bharathi, 311, 312
Such a Long Journey (novel), 154
Suchitra Bhattacharya, 144
Sudano-Sahelian architecture, 291, 361
Suddha (film), 355
Sudeep Sen, 157
Sudharak, 245

Sudhindranath Dutta, 145
Sufi, 209, 293
Sufia Kamal, 143
Sufi music, 292, 363
Sugriva, 61–63, 67, 68, 84
Suhas Shirvalkar, 246
Sujata Bhatt, 157
Sukanta Bhattacharya, 145
Sukaphaa, 124
Suketu Mehta, 154
Suktimuktavali, 211
Sukumara, 327
Sukumar Sen (linguist), 145
Sullia, 349
Sullurpeta, 337
Sultan, 73, 202
Sultan Bahu, 280
Suman Pokhrel, 48
Sumerian literature, 90, 117, 162, 177, 323
Sumitra, 59
Sumitranandan Pant, 168, 172
Sundanese people, 78
Sundarar, 305, 306
Sundargarh district, 259
Sundarikalum Sundaranmarum, 229
Sunil Gangopadhyay, 141, 144
Suniti Kumar Chattopadhyay, 145
Sunnar kaka, 147
Surajmal Misrana, 286
Surat Singh, 295
Suravaram Pratapareddy, 340
Surdas, 165, 172
Surendra Mohanty, 273
Surendra Verma, 170
Surjit Kalsi, 284
Surjit Paatar, 284
Surjit Patar, 282, 283
Surpanakha, 61, 63, 66, 84
Sur Sagar, 165
Sur Saravali, 165
Surya, 51, 167
Suryakant Tripathi Nirala, 168, 172
Suryakumar Pandey, 169, 172
Sushruta, 210
Sushruta Samhita, 210
Sutra, 32, 327
Sūtra, 8
Suttanipata, 103
Sutta Pitaka, 97, 98, 101, 106, 107
Suttavibhanga, 97, 107
Svarga, 34, 44
Svargarohana Parva, 34

Śvētāmbara, 93

S V Ranga Rao, 84

Swadesamitran, 313
Swahili literature, 119, 164, 325
Swami and Friends, 152
Swami Vivekananda, 52
Swarajatis, 193
Swaras, 294
Swargaaniki Nichchenalu, 340
Swathi Thirunal, 225
Swayamvara, 36, 39, 46, 189
Sweet home, 339
Switzerland, 225
Syed Ali Ahsan, 143
Syed Mohd Ashraf, 368
Syed Mujtaba Ali, 141
Syed Mustafa Siraj, 144
Syed Shamsul Haque, 141, 143
Syed Sultan, 131
Syed Thajudeen, 82
Syed Waliullah, 141, 143
Syriac literature, 90, 177

Tabish Khair, 157
Tailapa II, 186
Taisho Tripitaka, 108
Taittiriya Shakha, 10
Takakusu Junjiro, 106
Tales from Firozsha Baag, 154
Tales from Shakespeare, 230
Tallapaka Annamacharya, 340
Talpur dynasty, 294
Tamil cinema, 85, 300
Tamil culture, 45
Tamil diaspora, 299
Tamil–Kannada languages, 344
Tamil history from Sangam literature, 301
Tamil Jain, 24, 299, 304, 305, 307, 309
Tamil language, 5, 17, 58, 73, 84, 299, 300, 303–305, 347, 353
Tamil literature, 24, 115, 118, 150, 161, 163, 218, 235, 239, 250, 259, 285, 293, **299**, 324, 364
Tamil movie, 84
Tamil Muslim, 299, 314
Tamil Nadu, 155, 299
Tamil people, 299, 303, 346
Tamils, 81
Tamil Sangams, 301, 303
Tamil Thai, 300
Tamilvanan, 317
Tanbur, 294
Tanjore, 335
Tantra, 264
Tantras, 109
Tapan Kumar Pradhan, 157
Tapasya, 332
Taqiyah (cap), 291, 362

Tara (Ramayana), 67
Tarasankar Bandyopadhyay, 145
Tarashankar Bandopadhyay, 141
Tarigonda Venkamamba, 340
Tarikonda Venkamamba, 335
Taslima Nasrin, 143
Tatar mosque, 290, 361
Tatpuruṣa, 57
Tattvartha Sutra, 93
Taufiq Rafat, 215
Taxila, 6, 29, 32
Tazieh, 292, 363
T. Brinda, 335
T.C. Hodson, 236
Tcy:, 359
Telinga, 42
Telugu cinema, 85, 321
Telugu cuisine, 321
Telugu film, 84
Telugu Language, 48, 58, 73, 81, 84, 310, 321, 322, 329–337, 340, 353
Telugu literature, 91, 115, 118, 130, 150, 161, 163, 178, 182, 218, 235, 239, 250, 259, 285, 293, 321, **321**, 324, 364
Telugu movie, 84
Telugu people, 321, 336
Template:Bengali literature, 129
Template:Bengalis, 130
Template:Buddhism, 96
Template:Culture of Andhra Pradesh, 322
Template:Culture of Assam, 116
Template:Culture of Telangana, 322
Template:Hinduism, 27, 56
Template:Hindu scriptures, 3, 22
Template:History of literature by era, 91, 178
Template:History of literature by region or country, 119, 164, 325
Template:History of modern literature, 151
Template:Indian literature, 115, 161, 218, 235, 239, 250, 260, 285, 293, 364
Template:Islamic culture, 292, 363
Template:Medieval and Renaissance literature, 130
Template:Modern Asian literature, 289, 336
Template:PaliCanon, 97
Template:Punjabis, 279
Template:State of Odisha, 259
Template talk:Bengali literature, 129
Template talk:Bengalis, 130
Template talk:Buddhism, 96
Template talk:Culture of Andhra Pradesh, 322
Template talk:Culture of Assam, 116
Template talk:Culture of Telangana, 322
Template talk:Hinduism, 27, 56
Template talk:Hindu scriptures, 3, 22
Template talk:History of literature by era, 91, 178
Template talk:History of literature by region or country, 119, 164, 325
Template talk:History of modern literature, 151
Template talk:Indian literature, 115, 161, 218, 235, 239, 250, 260, 285, 293, 364
Template talk:Islamic culture, 292, 363
Template talk:Medieval and Renaissance literature, 130
Template talk:Modern Asian literature, 289, 336
Template talk:PaliCanon, 97
Template talk:Punjabis, 279
Template talk:State of Odisha, 259
Template talk:Theravada Buddhism, 96
Template talk:Vedas and Shakhas, 10, 92
Template:Theravada Buddhism, 96
Template:Vedas and Shakhas, 10, 92
Tenali, 334
Tenali Ramakrishna, 340
Tenneti Hemalata, 340
Terminus post quem, 6
Terracottas, 81
Terukkuttu, 45
Tevaram, 305
Text corpus, 178
Thailand, 56, 71, 72, 99
Thai literature, 118, 163, 324
Thakazhi Sivasankara Pillai, 228
Thames & Hudson, 53
Thane, 348
Thangwai Ningthouba, 236
Thanjavur Nayaks, 310
Tharu people, 147
Thawb, 291, 362
Thayumanavar, 310
Theater of ancient Greece, 27
Theatre of Cambodia, 77
Theatre of the Absurd, 371
The Autobiography of an Unknown Indian, 151
The Calcutta Chromosome, 153
The Circle of Reason (novel), 153
The Comedy of Errors, 230
The Dance of the Peacock, 159
The Five Great Epics of Tamil Literature, 22, 301, 302, 309
The Free Press Journal, 316
The Glass Palace, 153, 156
The God of Small Things, 155
The Golden Gate (Vikram Seth novel), 153
The Great Indian Novel, 154
The History and Culture of the Indian People, 53
The Holy War, 229

The Hungry Tide, 153
The Inheritance of Loss, 153
The Jain Literature Phase.28850-1000 AD.29, 322
The Mahabharata (1989 film), 49
Thembavani, 311
The Metamorphosis, 313
The Orissa Official Language Act, 1954, 258
Theosophy (Blavatskian), 13
The Palace of Illusions: A Novel, 48
The Pilgrims Progress, 229
Theravada, 96, 98
The Second Sex, 276
The Shadow Lines, 153
The Spitzer manuscript, 30
The White Tiger, 154
The Winters Tale, 230
Thirugnana Sambanthar, 306
Thirumazhisai Aazhwar, 306
Thirunavukkarasar, 306
Thiruppugazh, 310
Thiruvalluvar, 302
Thiruvananthapuram, 228
Thiruvarangam Sudhakar, 340
Tholan, 219
Thomas Candy, 244
Thomas Hardy, 152
Thomas Hardys Wessex, 152
Thomas Stephens (Jesuit), 242
Thomas the Apostle, 223
Thunchaththu Ezhuthachan, 58, 220, 222
Thunchaththu Ramanujan Ezhuthachan, 73
Tibetan languages, 121
Tigalari alphabet, 344, 348
Tikkana, 327, 329, 340
Timmakka, 340
Tiṉaimalai Nūṟṟu Aimpatu, 301
Tiṉaimoḻi Aimpatu, 301
Tipu sultan, 200
Tirath Wasant, 295
Tirikaṭukam, 301
Tirthankara, 23, 49, 50, 74, 181
Tirukkural, 302, 305, 310
Tirukkuṛaḷ, 301
Tirumalamba, 340
Tirumandhiram, 305
Tirumangai Alvar, 306
Tirumular, 305
Tirumurai, 305
Tirumurukāṟṟuppaṭai, 301
Tirunavukkarasar, 305
Tirupati Venkata Kavulu, 340
Tiruvacakam, 305
Tiruvannamalai, 310
Tiruvasakam, 306
Tiruvisaippa, 305

Toda language, 350
Tolkaappiyam, 301, 312
Tolkappiyam, 303, 310
Tolkāppiyam, 300
Torave Ramayana, 73, 81
Toru Dutt, 156
Tourism in Andhra Pradesh, 321
Tourism in Odisha, 258
T. Padmanabhan, 229
T. P. Kailasam, 198
Traditional animation, 84
Traditionalist School, 214
Transmigration of the soul, 75
Travancore, 220, 228, 232
Travancore Kingdom, 223
Travel literature, 169
Treta Yuga, 57, 58
Tridib Mitra, 146
Trinidad and Tobago, 156
Tripadi, 180, 182
Tripitaka, 98
Tripura, 235
Tripura Buranji, 125
Tripuraneni Maharadhi, 340
Tripuraneni Ramaswamy Choudhury, 340
Trisastisalakapurusa charitra, 74
Trishira, 70
T. R. Subba Rao, 200
T. S. Eliot, 202
Tübingen, 225
Tukaram, 242, 243
Tulsidas, 25, 58, 70, 73, 81, 120, 165, 172
Tulu cinema, 355
Tulu Jains, 349
Tulu language, **343**
Tulu Nadu, 343, 344, 347, 348, 355
Tulu people, 344
Tulu script, 343, 394
Tuluva, 347, 348
Tuluva Hebbars, 349
Tungkhungia Buranji, 125
Turkish carpet, 291, 362
Turkish literature, 91, 178, 292, 363
T. V. Venkatachala Sastry, 183, 207
Twipra Kingdom, 124
Tyagaraja, 335

Ubud, 82
Udayagiri and Khandagiri Caves, 260
Udgatr, 12
Udupi, 347, 349, 353, 357
Udupi cuisine, 348
Udupi district, 343, 344, 347, 348
Udupi Krishna Temple, 354
Udyoga Parva, 33
Ugrasrava Sauti, 29, 30, 32

Ulka, 246
Ulloor S. Parameswara Iyer, 217, 220, 227
Uluwatu Temple, 82
Umar Marvi, 294
Umaru Pulavar, 311
Umera Ahmad, 368
Umer Bin Mohammad Daudpota, 295
Ummachu, 229
UNESCO, 18
Unification of Karnataka, 198
United Kingdom, 122, 295
United States, 156
Universe, 236
University College Thiruvananthapuram, 227
University of California, Berkeley, 80
University of California Press, 390
University Of Chicago, 46
University of Chicago Press, 52
University of Illinois at Urbana-Champaign, 385
University of Michigan, 157
University of the Philippines Manila, 79
University of Turku, 354
Unnayi Variyar, 223
Unnuneeli Sandesam, 220
Unsupported attributions, 152, 263, 330, 332, 333
Upamāna, 328
Upanishad, 15, 92
Upanishads, 4, 8, 10, 193, 306
Upasana, 4, 10
Upendra Bhanja, 267
Upendranath Ashk, 170
U.R.Anantha Murthy, 203
Urbanization, 58
Urdu, 282, 363, 364
Urdu language, 363
Urdu literature, 115, 118, 150, 161, 163, 218, 235, 239, 250, 260, 285, 292, 293, 324, **361**, 363, 364
Urdu poetry, 363
Urmila, 61, 65
Uroob, 229
Urubhanga, 32, 48
Urvashi, 25
Ushasri, 340
Usman Deplai, 296
Ustaad Bukhari, 296
Ustad Daman, 281
Uthram Thirunal Marthanda Varma, 225
Utkala Deepika, 260, 268
Utkala Kingdom, 260
Utkaliya Vaishnavism, 264
Utpala (astronomer), 211
Utpaladeva, 211
Utpreksha, 328

Uttara Kannada, 347
Uttarakhand, 94
Uttararamacarita, 71
Uttara Ramayana, 326
Uttar Pradesh, 147, 237
U.V.Swaminatha Iyer, 312, 313

Vaar, 280
Vachana, 181, 190
Vachana Sahitya, 181, 190
Vaddaradhane, 23, 184
Vadirajatirtha, 193
Vaduvur Duraisami Iyengar, 317
Vaee, 296
Vagbhata, 210
Vaidiki Brahmins, 331
Vaikom Muhammad Basheer, 229
Vaisampayana, 29, 30
Vaishnava, 131, 142, 165, 179, 192, 306, 308
Vaishnava Bhakthi, 264
Vaishnavas, 264
Vaishnavism, 179, 181, 236, 299
Vajrayana, 164, 262
Vajrayāna, 109
Valayapathi, 24, 307, 309
Vali (Ramayana), 62, 63, 67, 68
Vallathol Narayana Menon, 217, 227
Valmiki, 55, 56, 73
Valmiki Ramayana, 73
Vamana Purana, 126
Vaman Pandit, 243
Vanamali, 85
Vana Parva, 32
Vanaprastha, 15
Vanara, 61–63
Vande Mataram, 137
Vanna Parimala Pulavar, 309
Varahamihira, 35
Varanasi, 147
Varjesh Solanki, 246
Varkari, 243
Varudhini, 332
Vasanavikriti, 228
Vasant Abaji Dahake, 246
Vashista, 58
Vashistha, 187
Vassal, 184
Vasudeva, 74
Vasugupta, 209, 210
Vatesvara, 210
Vaṭeśvara-siddhānta, 210
Vattacharja Chandan, 146, 157
Vattagamani Abhaya of Sri Lanka, 103
Vayu, 39
Veda, 92
Vedanga, 92

Vedanga Jyotisha, 210
Vedangas, 6
Vedanta, 8, 142, 181, 240
Vedānta, 15
Vedantic, 52, 211
Vedas, 3, 10, 21, 58, 92, 331, 348
Vedic, 58
Vedic astrology, 325
Vedic Brahmanism, 188
Vedic chant, 6, 9
Vedic India, 34
Vedic period, 5, 6, 11, 30
Vedic Sanskrit, 3, 6, 7, 11, 23, 31
Veena Dhanammal, 335
Veera Ballala II, 188
Veeramamunivar, 311
Veerashaiva, 179
Veerashaivism, 190
Veer Lorik, 147
Velar consonant, 351
Vellore, 334
Velutheri Kesavan Vaidyar, 225
Vemana, 330, 340
Vempalli Gangadhar, 340
Vemulawada, Karimnagar district, 328
Venad, 228
Vengayil Kunhiraman Nayanar, 227
Venkataraya Dhurjati, 333
Venmani Achhan Nambudiripad, 225
Venmani Mahan Nambudiripad, 225
Venpa, 306
Verb, 351
Versailles (city), 136
Verse (poetry), 56
Versions of Ramayana, 56
Veterinarian, 152
Veyipadagalu, 340
Vibhanga, 97, 108
Vibhishan, 84
Vibhishana, 63, 69
Vibhuti Narain Rai, 173
Vichitravirya, 36, 51
Victoria and Albert Museum, 59
Victorian literature, 46
Videha, 9
Vidura, 38, 39, 51
Vidyapati, 132, 165, 172
Vietnam, 71
Vietnamese literature, 118, 150, 163, 289, 324, 336
Vihang A. Naik, 157
Vijaya Dasa, 193
Vijaya Lakshmi Pandit, 215
Vijayanagara, 191
Vijayanagara empire, 179, 188, 322, 345
Vijayanagar empire, 309

Vijay K. Jain, 94
Vijay Tendulkar, 246
Vikalp Printers, 94
Vikarna, 39
Vikrama Chola, 309
Vikramarjuna Vijaya, 23, 185
Vikramashila, 6
Vikram Chandra (novelist), 154
Vikram Chandra (reporter), 154
Vikram Seth, 153, 157, 367
Vilanka Ramayana, 58, 73, 263
Vilas Sarang, 246
Vinaya Patrika, 165
Vinaya Pitaka, 97, 98, 101, 106, 107
Vinay Patrika, 172
Vinda Karandikar, 247
Vīra, 328
Virabhadra, 331
Virama, 350
Virarajendra Chola, 309
Virata, 33, 42
Virata Parva, 33
Vir Gatha Kaal, 165
Viruri Vedadri, 334
Viruttam, 309
Visakham Thirunal, 225
Vishishtadvaita, 331
Vishnu, 25, 58, 59, 63, 64, 83, 306
Vishnu Chittiyam, 327
Vishnu Purana, 188
Vishnu Sakharam Khandekar, 246, 247
Vishnu Sharma, 210
Vishnuvardhana, 186
Vishrava, 63
Vishvamitra, 187
Vishwamitra, 58
Visuddhimagga, 99
Viswanatha Satyanarayana, 340
Vittala, 193
Vitthala, 334
Viveki Rai, 147, 148, 173, 385
V. K. Gokak, 201
Vocative case, 352
Voice (grammar), 352
Voiceless, 351
Voice (phonetics), 351
Voltaire, 18
Vowel, 350
Vowel length, 350
Vriddha-Garga, 35
Vrindavana Dasa Thakura, 134
V. Shantaram, 247
V. S. Khandekar, 48
V. S. Naipaul, 151
Vulture, 63, 67
Vyakarana, 16

439

Vyangya, 169
Vyasa, 26, 27, 30, 37, 51, 189, 310
Vyasatirtha, 193

Walter de Gruyter, 113
Waris Shah, 280
Warkari, 240
Waskaro (Childrens Magazine), 297
Watford, 83
Wat Phra Kaew, 80
Wayang, 45, 78
Wayang kulit, 82
Wayang orang, 82
Wayang wong, 45, 78
Wazir Agha, 366
Wendy Doniger, 46
West Bengal, 131–133, 144, 260
Western Chalukyas, 185
Western Ganga Dynasty, 179, 184
Western literature, 170
Western Odisha, 260
Western world, 48
What information to include, 329, 331, 332
W. H. Auden, 202
Wikibooks:Sanskrit, 95
Wikibooks:Urdu, 372
Wikimedia Commons, 89
Wikipedia, 95, 359
Wikipedia:Avoid weasel words, 334
Wikipedia:Citation needed, 31, 46, 66, 69, 75, 101, 102, 122–124, 146, 236, 243, 246, 247, 276, 286, 312, 314, 328–337, 345, 346, 354, 355, 363, 367, 370
Wikipedia:Media help, 337
Wikipedia:No original research, 330
Wikipedia:Please clarify, 336, 346
Wikisource, 54, 89, 176, 372
Wikisource:The Mahabharat, 54
Wiktionary:canon, 22
Wiktionary:proto-language, 346
Wiktionary:Veda, 21
Wiktionary:Vedic, 21
William Buck, 85
William Buck (translator), 48, 86
William Carey (missionary), 244
William Shakespeare, 27, 230
Wit, 5
Wodeyar, 179
Woodblock printing, 109
World War I, 295
World War II, 296
Writer, 296
Writers Workshop, 47, 152
Writing, 326
Writing system, 161, 343
Written language, 250

Yadavas of Devagiri, 179
Yadu, 33, 42
Yagna, 71
Yajna, 12, 14
Yajnaseni, 48
Yajnaseni (play), 48
Yajnavalkya Smriti, 92
Yajurveda, 4, 7, 10, 12, 14, 16
Yakshagana, 49, 189, 194, 334, 354, 355
Yak: The Giant King, 85
Yamaka, 97, 108, 328
Yama Zatdaw, 79
Yashobanta Das, 265
Yashodhara Mishra, 274
Yashpal, 172
Yasodharā, 74
Yathavakkula Annamayya, 330
Yayati, 48
Yenugu Lakshmana Kavi, 340
Yerrapragada, 329, 340
Yoga, 52, 164, 192, 330
Yogasutra, 209
Yogyakarta, 72, 78, 82
YouTube, 234
Yudhishthira, 32, 33, 35, 38, 39, 46, 51, 58
Yuga, 58
Yuyutsu, 43
Yuyutsu Sharma, 157

Zahida Hina, 368
Zairema, 254
Zauq, 213
Zee TV, 85
Zia (Persian poet), 296
Zinda Kaul, 209

www.ingramcontent.com/pod-product-compliance
Lightning Source LLC
Chambersburg PA
CBHW021138160426
43194CB00007B/623